M^cKEAN'S SUNDAY SCHOOL BOYS GO TO WAR

The Story of the 77th Bemis Heights Battalion in the Great Rebellion

DAVID ALLEN HANDY

Copyright © 2014 David Allen Handy
All rights reserved.

ISBN: 0615958818
ISBN 13: 9780615958811

Library of Congress Control Number: 2014901577
David Handy, Schenectady, NY

To my brother, Larry, who pushed me to write this book, and to my wife, Paula, and children, Joel, Alyssa, and Emily who continue to humor me.

CONTENTS

1 "Come, Boys!" 1

2 "Forest of Bayonets" 37

3 "Get Into your Tents Boys!" 79

4 "Men of the 77th, Now is the Chance to Cover Yourselves in Glory!" 111

5 "The Most Miserable Day in My Life" 159

6 "The Damned Rebels . . ." 183

7 "Oh! What a Cruel Sight" 219

8 Write Your Name on It! 255

9 "We Can Whip them on Our Own Soil" 313

10 "Hurrah for'e Union!" 357

11 "Boys, Don't Run" 401

12 "Attention, Battalions! Forward, Double-quick! Charge!" .. 453

13 "We Are Licking the Rebs Every Time We Meet Them" 501

14	The Three Jims	555
15	"We Have Got Everything, God Damn Them!"	595
16	"My God, General! See 'em Run!"	645
17	"Give to Them, Damn them; They Are Cowards, and I Know It!"	663
18	"Make the Fur Fly!"	717
	Appendix	753
	Died in Confederate Prisons	757
	Photographic Gallery	759
	Bibliography	773
	Miscellaneous	787
	Notes	789

1

"COME, BOYS!"

At 4:30 in the morning on April 12, 1861, Edmund Ruffin, a fire-eating secessionist and rabid champion of slavery, gave the signal to Confederate Captain George S. James. As soon as it was received, James fired a ten-inch mortar from James Island, beginning the bombardment of the beleaguered Federal garrison in Fort Sumter in the harbor at Charleston, South Carolina. The shell exploded above the fort, its fragments showering the deserted parade ground. Immediately, 30 guns and 17 mortars sent their iron missiles blasting against the Union fort.

Thus began the bloody epic of the American Civil War which spilled the blood of the nation in numbers never before or after incurred in *all* wars the nation fought. Upwards of 750,000 men were killed in battle, or died of wounds or from disease. In addition, more than 400,000 were wounded, many of whom bore the effects of catastrophic injuries for the rest of their lives in the form of amputated arms and legs.[1]

Four months later, after personally witnessing the sweeping rout of the Yankee army at Bull Run, 40-year-old Congressman James B. McKean of Saratoga Springs, New York, issued a circular to his constituents from his home calling for the formation of a battalion he called the Bemus Heights Battalion:

> FELLOW CITIZENS OF THE FIFTEENTH CONGRESSIONAL DISTRICT, -- Traitors in arms seek to overthrow our constitution and to seize our capital. Let us go and help defend them. Who will despond because we lost the battle of Bull Run? Our fathers lost the battle of Bunker Hill, but it taught them how to gain victory at Bemus Heights.
>
> Let us learn wisdom from disaster, and send overwhelming numbers into the field. Let farmers, mechanics, merchants, and all classes – for the liberties of all are at stake – aid in organizing companies.
>
> I will cheerfully assist in procuring necessary papers. Do not misunderstand me. I am not asking for office at your hands. If you who have most at stake will go, I will willingly go with you as a private soldier.
>
> Let us organize a Bemus Heights Battalion, and vie with each other in serving our country, thus showing we are inspired by the holy memories of the Revolutionary battle-fields upon which we are serving.[2]

James Bedell McKean was born in Hoosic, New York on August 5, 1821. He was one of two sons born to Rev. Andrew McKean, a strict Methodist minister, and his wife, Catherine Bedell. His father's family originated from Glencoe, Scotland, and immigrated to Cecil County, Maryland, in the mid-18th century. His grandfather, James McKean, was the cousin of Thomas McKean, one of the signers of the Declaration of Independence. McKean's mother descended from French Huguenots who settled in New York in the late 17th century. Well aware of his heritage, McKean said that it was his duty to raise a regiment. After all, the site where he was born was on the Revolutionary War battlefield of Bennington.

Soon after he was born, McKean's family moved to the town of Saratoga. In his youth, McKean taught in district schools, and for a time was one of the professors at Jonesville Academy in Jonesville, New York. At 21-years-old, McKean was elected colonel of the 144th Regiment of New York State Militia commissioned by Governor Silas Wright, which he commanded for several years.

In June 1847, McKean joined the law office of Bullard & Cramer. His career as an attorney flourished, and he soon decided to open his own office in Saratoga Springs. In 1850 he married Katherine Hay, the daughter of Judge William Hay. McKean's skill as a lawyer prompted county officials to nominate him for county judge, and he was easily elected to office. His reputation and political stature grew and McKean was nominated and elected in 1858 to the 15th Congressional district, representing Essex, Fulton, and Saratoga counties. He was re-elected in 1860. Upon leaving for Washington in February 1861, McKean said to a friend, "I expect to return soon to raise a regiment of volunteers from this."[3]

In support of the congressman, the Saratoga *Republican* published McKean's circular and remarked:

> We hope he [McKean] may succeed, as he must, if those Wide Awakes in this Congressional district who stuck by him so close last Fall, will stand by him and come forward at his call, as we really hope they may, The judge we know would make a good military officer, and hope to see him lead the 'Bemus Heights Battalion' to 'victory or death.'

But seriously, we hope the judge may meet with all the success which his patriotism in the present crisis deserves.[4]

McKean's call for volunteers reverberated beyond the bounds of his Congressional district with sincere approbation. The *Troy Times* wrote that ". . . [McKean] has issued a circular letter to the people, full of patriotic exhortation, and with the ring of true metal in its composition." The Schuylerville *American* added, "That's the kind of talk we like to hear; we go in for a regiment, and for the judge as Colonel, which position his former military experience renders him abundantly competent to fill." Even the anti-Republican *Troy Whig* weighed in with its approval: "When Republican members of congress volunteer to go to war as privates, we think better of them and of their cause, and hope for the Country rises."[5]

While McKean's call for volunteers garnered the support of newspapers outside of his district, his circular created a firestorm of patriotism in Saratoga Springs and surrounding communities. Summoning forth the fathers of the Revolution, Bunker Hill, and the liberty they fought and sacrificed for, McKean touched the hearts of every man. To be sure, Americans of the Civil War generation revered their Revolutionary forebears. Both Northerners and Southerners believed themselves to be custodians of the legacy of 1776. Men flocking to the Confederate army came to fight for liberty and independence from a tyrannical government. In the North, volunteers entered military service to preserve the nation conceived in liberty from dismemberment and destruction. But for the inhabitants of Saratoga County the identification with their Revolutionary forebears was exceptionally deep – within the heart of the county lies the battlefield of Saratoga, the definitive turning point of the war for independence.

Early in 1777, Britain began to prepare for operations to cut off New England – the "head" of the Revolution – from the rest of the colonies by seizing New York's Hudson Valley. General John Burgoyne was to come down from Canada in the spring along the Champlain-Hudson route to Albany, where he would join Lieutenant Colonel Barry St. Leger. St. Leger would travel east from Fort Ontario through the Mohawk Valley. At the same time, General William Howe would meet Burgoyne and St. Leger, coming from the south up the Hudson River. None of the Englishmen would be successful, however. After defeating the patriots at Oriskany, St. Leger was turned back at Fort Stanwix. Instead of heading north, Howe moved against Philadelphia. Burgoyne steadily pushed southward, only to be defeated at Bemis Heights and surrender his army.

The first of the two engagements on Bemis Heights, representing the Battles of Saratoga, took place on September 19, 1777, when an advance party ahead of Burgoyne's column ran into the riflemen of Daniel Morgan at Freeman's Farm. Morgan had been ordered by the commander of the American Army, General Horatio Gates, to reconnoiter in response to reports of Burgoyne's advance party down the Albany Road. Morgan's riflemen cut down most of the advance party with one well-aimed volley. The skirmish quickly grew into a major engagement as both Burgoyne and Gates funneled more men into the fray. The results were indecisive, with both armies fortifying their positions.

On October 7 Burgoyne sent out an armed reconnaissance to probe the American left, and again touched off a major battle. At a critical point in the contest, Benedict Arnold, who had not been given another command after the battle at Freeman's Farm, leaped on his horse and galloped into the fight. Arnold threw himself into the struggle, assuming command of the troops on the field and leading the assault against the British center. Despite stubborn resistance, the British forces were pried from the Breymann Redoubt on their right flank. With the redoubt in their possession, the Americans now held the high ground and could sweep the Redcoat's main force that manned the Balcarres Redoubt with artillery, hence forcing Burgoyne to retreat. Soon thereafter, on October 17, Burgoyne surrendered his army. Thus, not only were the battles fought at Bemis Heights the turning point of the American Revolution, but they also represented the supremacy of the American ideal of liberty.

After McKean's issuance of his circular calling for volunteers, Benjamin F. Judson immediately began recruiting a company for the battalion in Saratoga Springs by opening an office at the *Saratogian* newspaper of which he was the co-owner. "Come Boys!" he wrote, "Join the 'Bemus Heights Battalion' to protect the Union, and to compel the rebels to acknowledge the good old 'Star Spangled Banner!' . . . Let the sons of Saratoga rally to serve their country." In an effort to "stimulate" the men of Saratoga to "noble sacrifice of selfish affection to the altar of sacrifice," the *Saratogian* published a letter from a patriotic mother to her son, who was contemplating enlisting in the battalion:

> I mistrust you are going to war soon; if so, you need not fear to tell us when. When a babe I gave you to the Lord to go wherever he might send you, and now shall I say 'no' to such a call? I believe this is god's work; but if not, this one thing I know, that our government is in danger, and must be protected and preserved. Many a mother to-day mourns over a son lost on the battle-field, and though hard, it is no worse for me than others. Come and see us before you go, if possible. If you cannot, send me a lock of your hair.[6]

New recruits were received daily at the office of the *Saratogian*, and by mid-September 60 had joined. Yet 40 more were needed, and Judson again wrote "Now is the time! The Saratoga Company enlisting for the Bemus Heights Battalion . . . has on its rills of 60 good men. But there is room for more, and I call on the patriotic young men of the county to come forward and fill up the ranks." Judson appealed to their stout hearts and strong arms to defend "your country, Constitution, and flag."[7]

One anonymous volunteer of the Saratoga Company added that the war was "the contest between a wicked rebellion on the one side, and Constitutional liberty on the other." In a letter published by the *Saratogian*, the volunteer adeptly argued what many people in the North deeply felt about the war:

> . . . Never before had men so just a cause to fight for, as we have this 'war for the Union.' Never before had men such interests at stake. The government founded by Washington is threatened with overthrow, and by ingrates and traitors who have fattened upon this bounty. They would pull down this fabric of constitutional freedom upon our heads, and destroy the hopes of mankind forever. All we love and venerate in the past – all we enjoy in the present – all we hope to leave for posterity in the future is in peril . . . Stay not at home to gather in the crops; let the gray-haired father see to that – let your sisters, if necessary, aid him – and let all, as night casts her pall over the earth, send up petitions to the Heavenly Father for the protection of the soldier who has gone to fight for the Union . . . Now is the time, therefore, to fill up the ranks, and extinguish the rebellion this coming winter. Come Boys, Rally . . .[8]

The village of Ballston Spa, just south of Saratoga Springs, responded with great rapidity to McKean's call to arms. The next day after McKean's circular was issued, Clement C. Hill, a prominent lawyer in the village "believing that this locality ought to be represented in the regiment being raised" invited "all persons who desire to unite in forming a company for a said regiment to give me their names without delay." To sweeten the pot and induce eligible men to enlist, Hill broadcasted that "the pay of the soldier is now $13 a month, with board. Clothing, and medical attendance added, and no loss of time on account of sickness."[9]

Hill's bid to form a Ballston Spa Company was met with much enthusiasm. The following Friday evening a meeting was held at Waverly Hall, which congressman McKean attended. Hill briefly addressed the assembly stating:

> We are in the midst of war – war waged by traitors against the best government in the world . . . The door is closed against compromise. The rebels will accept none that does not recognize independence. Shall we do it? Are any willing? For one, I say never . . . This Government costs too much. It has cost a great deal of blood and treasure, and is worth much more . . . The long and the short of it is the south will conquer us, or we must crush the rebellion. We must fight! I am here beating up for volunteers, and as I never ask anyone to go where I will not go myself, I will say I am ready to go, and have here a paper of the names of men who will go with their lives in their hands, and march up to the cannon's mouth if ordered. I ask first, men without families, but men with families are likewise called upon, for the country has even higher claims than family.[10]

Inside Waverly Hall the crowd responded with deafening applause, and only quieted when McKean stood to speak. "I like Mr. Hill's speech," McKean said. "'I ask no man to go where I will not go myself.' I say the same. Though you were pleased to make me your representative to Congress, I can be spared from the House and will go with you into the battle field." McKean warned that, "Some men must leave wife and children," and that, "It is a great sacrifice, but liberty and rights . . . cost our forefathers much blood and treasure." Then pausing and surveying the patriotically-charged crowd, McKean, his voice rising against the din of the gathering, fairly shouted, "Come let us crush this serpent rebellion, and put down secession forever!" By night's end, 34 men enlisted.[11]

The following Tuesday, a public meeting was held at the Armory in the village to continue the receiving of enlistments into the Ballston Spa Company. Once again, Clement C. Hill called the meeting to order: "We are here to receive names for enlistment in the Ballston Spa Company . . . We commenced only last Saturday night, and now have 34 names . . . It is believed that no company in the state has been gathered in so short a time. In a few days, a week at furthest, we expect to have a hundred men." Several men quickly came forward to join the ranks. Stephen S. Horton, soon to be elected second lieutenant of the now forming company, was called upon to speak. Horton reluctantly stood up and began to address those assembled:

> I cannot make a speech. We are engaged in a glorious cause. I address you as soldiers, for I have enlisted with you. We go to the battlefield, and there are no hardship's falling to a soldier's lot that we are not willing to share. We go as the defenders of our country and our flag, -- not to subjugate, but to preserve our country, and the blessings and privileges bought by the blood of our patriot ancestors. We follow the flag first unfurled on our soil, and for our country we will live, for our country we will die. My life is my country's, and here I pledge it on the altar of my country.[12]

By the end of the evening, the total enrolled in the company was fifty-four. One week later, eighty men from Ballston Spa and the towns of Ballston and Milton enlisted in the company. It was directed to start at Camp Schuyler, the designated depot for newly forming regiments in Saratoga Springs. On September 23, the night before the company was to leave, another public meeting was held at Waverly Hall. The object of the meeting was to bid the company farewell, and to raise funds to provide for the new volunteers' families. There, the company was assembled and villagers filled the hall. Speaking directly to the enlisted men, James M. Cook – a banker, manufacturer, state politician, and vehement opponent of secession – promised to "make arrangements to provide for the proper care of your families." William T. Odell, popularly known as "Colonel" because of many years involved in the state Militia, then addressed the recruits:

> It is no time to ask what brought on this national trouble? This is the question for us – what can we do to sustain the Government and support the constitution of our country. When the rebellion is put down, then we may settle the question as to who originated this war. As volunteers, you occupy a proud position, as the defenders of your country, and we are proud of you as representatives of our town. We expect much of you, and you will not disappoint us. Remember Saratoga, and let the remembrance nerve your arms to deeds of valor and renown.

Judge Scott, of Ballston Spa, a past assemblyman and state senator, was called on and spoke:

> I came to hear others, not to make a speech. This is an occasion that occurs but seldom. A few years ago several of our citizens went to the Mexican War. They returned and their reception was honorable. You go forth, not against a foreign foe, but to put down a domestic enemy. You go against a most gigantic rebellion warring upon the most

beneficent Government in the world. You go forth, I trust, not to a long war. I hope it will soon be ended. I trust the day is not distant when this rebellion will be crushed – when the deluded men of the South will return to their allegiance, and you will come back to us with honor.[13]

The next morning, at 8 o'clock a.m., the newly enlisted men gathered at the armory and formed a marching line. They passed down Milton Street into Front Street and then into Bath Street to the Depot, where they were met by a throng of well-wishers. Full of patriotic pride, the loud crowd cheered their departure. The *Ballston Spa Journal* proudly noted the event:

> Their fine appearance elicited a very general remark, and it is not too much to say that our stay-at-homes were elated with pride as they gazed upon those who have the honor of representing Old Ballston in the tented field. It was a proud day when we sent a noble band to our army in Mexico against a foreign foe; but a far prouder day was Tuesday, when our company of volunteers for the war departed for camp drill at the County Fair Grounds, preparatory to sharing the toils, privations, sacrifices, losses, and above all successes and glories which must fall to the lot of the panoplied hosts who go forth to rescue the Government of their country from the clutches of an infamous rebellion. To aid in preventing the subversion of a blood-bought Constitution, which embodies the undying principles of freedom; to share in the mighty struggles necessary to defend principles of freedom; to share in the mighty struggles necessary to defend our nationality and our national institutions; and to march with the hosts whose right arm is to dethrone the malicious power of Davisdom; this is a grand privilege which every loyal heart might covet.[14]

A few days later, the company numbered more than 90 men. Clement C. Hill was elected as captain; Noble P. Hammond, as first lieutenant; and Stephen S. Horton, as second lieutenant. While officially designated Company B in the forming regiment at Camp Schuyler, the new recruits named their company the "James M. Cook National guard" in gratitude for Cook's efforts to provide for the families the volunteers were leaving behind.

Recruiting fever was also raging in the area of Wilton, ten miles north of Saratoga Springs. Like Ballston Spa, Wilton responded to McKean's call to arms in a matter of days. A war meeting was held at the old school house in Wilton. Winsor B. French arrived from Saratoga Springs to address the meeting. Upon arriving he found John Carr and twelve others already enrolled. Before the end of the meeting, French became so excited that when a former pupil of his said that "if Winsor will put his name down for enrollment we will follow," he accepted and became a member of the forming company. Not long after, on September 14, another war meeting was held for the "friends of freedom" at the Loudon Church in South Wilton for the "purpose of aiding and encouraging the formation of a Company of volunteers for the war." Winsor French again spoke, resulting in 39 new recruits.[15]

Winsor Brown French, who would eventually succeed McKean in command of the regiment, was born in Proctorsville, Vermont, on July 28, 1832. His parents were Luther and Lydia Brown French. Luther was a member of an old Massachusetts family, and a grandson of Joseph French, a lieutenant in the Revolutionary War. Lydia was a descendent of Chad Brown of Providence, Rhode Island, and also Roger Williams.

When Winsor was four years of age, his father moved the family from Proctosville to the town of Wilton and began farming. The young French attended district school in the town, and later Clinton Liberal Institute in Clinton, New York. Showing considerable promise as a student, he enrolled in Woodstock Academy, Vermont, and in the fall of 1855, entered Tufts College in Massachusetts. French's father was unable to furnish the necessary means at Tufts, and Winsor was obliged to work in addition to his studies. He taught school in the winters, and assisted his father on the farm in the summers. French graduated with honors and was a student orator at commencement.

After graduation, French returned home and began the study of law in Saratoga Springs, first with McKean, and later with Pond & Lester, then the most prominent lawyers in the county. After two years of study, he was admitted to the bar in May of 1861. After barely four months of the practice of law, French was a soldier.

While Wilton was fast forming a company of volunteers for the Bemus Heights Battalion, Albert F. Beach, of Charlton Village, began to organize for the recruitment of a company and set up headquarters at Barnard's Hotel. Inviting McKean and Clement C. Hill to speak, a union meeting was held. The Charlton Band applauded McKean and Hill as they eloquently invited Charlton's men, young and old, to defend the government their forebears had struggled to establish in the face of Britain's opposition. As recruitment efforts in Charlton continued, weekly Wednesday night meetings were held at Barnard's Hotel to enlist new recruits.

By the end of September, the Charlton Company left for Camp Schuyler. Passing through Ballston Spa "they numbered 73, drawn by 21 teams, eight of them 4-horse." They were escorted by the Ballston Spa Washington Zouaves, a company of boys "whose appearance in full dress, with fife and drum, and a martial mien, were admirable." The procession was very imposing as it passed along, with stirring music from the Charlton Band. On an elegant banner were the words, "Charlton Union Guard," and the stars and stripes floated from two flagstaffs. As the column moved on it was greeted by the cheers of men and women who "complimented" them "by the waving of handkerchiefs in their fair hands." The scene was inspiring to every patriotic heart. The *Ballston Spa Journal* commended the Charlton Union guard, saying that, "WE always expect great things from Charlton, and are never disappointed... and the noble company... may challenge comparison with any Township in the County."[16]

In the southern tip of Saratoga County, Jesse White opened a recruiting station at the law office of E. F. Bullard at Waterford three days after McKean's appeal for men to form a regiment. Judson B. Andrews, associate principal of Mechanicsville Academy, joined White in recruiting for the Battalion. The *Waterford Sentinel* encouraged the men of Waterford and surrounding villages to "swell the ranks of the Bemus Heights Battalion," while promising that "the company and the Regiment will be officered by the best military gentlemen that can be secured." By September 21, the company was fast filling up, and the *Waterford Sentinel* continued to urge all able-minded men to enlist to put down the wicked rebellion and to restore the nation's honor:

> If there ever was a time when every nerve ought to be strained to put down the enemies of the Government, when every able-bodied man who has a spark of patriotism in his bosom, should enroll himself in the ranks of his country's defenders, that time is *now*. We speak more particularly of the young men – of whom there are scores in this place and its vicinity who should be standing side by side with the noble patriots of the North who compose the army of the Republic. If this struggle is to be brought to a speedy settlement it must be done by such demonstration of force,

and such determination on the part of the North as shall unmistakably prove the inability of prolonged resistance.

Therefore, young men in the flower of health and strength without a moment's delay connect themselves with the army and lend their might toward suppressing this wicked rebellion. We urge them to fly to arms and share the honors and blessings which await the noble brave who have buckled on the armor and resolved to retrieve the nation's honor and uphold its precious ensign.

Fall into the ranks young men, and fill up Col. McKean's Regiment forthwith. Your country needs you, and you will never have a better opportunity to do her service.

Later invoking the visage of their Revolutionary forebears, the *Sentinel* encouraged potential recruits by reminding them that, "Those who come after us will regard this struggle to uphold the government as important as that by which our independence was achieved, and those who take part in this conflict will be pointed out hereafter as patriots who are to be ranked side by side with those who took part in the Revolution."[17]

Neil Gilmour, of Ballston Spa, focused his efforts in the heavily wooded northwestern corner of Saratoga County in the Sacandaga Valley and adjacent sections. Purposing to raise a company of "Sacandage Braves," Gilmour convened a mass meeting at Fish House with McKean in attendance. Calling for, "Hardy, intelligent, enthusiastic 'six-footers' and less, of the mountains and valleys of Providence, North Hampton, Edinburg, and Day," Gilmour proclaimed, "now is your time . . . Let the hunters, trappers, woodmen, lumbermen, and others be on hand to enlist a company . . . and form a part of the Bemus Heights Regiment, which, for officers, equipments, and character, will have few if any superiors in the volunteer service." A second mass meeting to enlist recruits and stimulate support for the war was convened and "although the weather was unfavorable . . . people kept pouring in from the surrounding country." The assembled crowd proceeded – accompanied by bands from neighboring villages – to the Presbyterian Church. The choir sang "America," followed with prayer by Reverend Burham. Winsor French was then introduced and made a stirring speech proclaiming "war to the knife" as his motto. McKean followed and "held for over an hour a breathless audience." Moving far beyond "the expectations of every individual," McKean's discussion of, "Liberty and sarcasm against 'Secesh' was received with tremendous applause." Then Gilmour rose and delivered yet another powerful speech "greatly encouraging patriots and handling 'Secesh' without gloves." After singing the "Star Spangled Banner," the crowd, much buoyed with patriotic ardor, dispersed, with some remaining to sign on to the Bemus Heights Battalion.[18]

All in all, Saratoga County furnished men enough to form seven companies within the regiment. Rounding out recruitment efforts in the county were Lewis Wood of Greenfield, Judson B. Andrews of Mechanicsville, and Calvin Rice of Northumberland. Yet another company numbering 76 men and 15 commissioned and noncommissioned officers would be recruited in August 1862 to replenish the regiment's decimated ranks due to illness on the Virginia Peninsula.

Westport, nestled in the Adirondack Mountains in Essex County, was alive with martial spirit well before McKean called for a regiment to fight to put down the rebellion. Westport had earlier provided men for Company K of the 38th New York, and now again rallied to the flag to form a company for the Bemus Heights Battalion. The center of Main Street was used daily for the drilling of squads of eager young men, and the air was full of war talk and military terms. Living in the village was William Harris, who had been in the United States Dragoons under General Harney on the Western Plains. Too old now for military service himself, Harris threw himself into the work of drilling men from all walks of life who aspired to become soldiers. A recruiting office was opened in the village by Renel Arnold.

By mid-September, Arnold had enlisted 50 young recruits, mostly in their twenties, from Westport and Elizabethtown. On September 15 they were ordered to proceed to Camp Schuyler to rendezvous with the other companies of the battalion. The company of enlisted volunteers was formed on Main Street and presented "a splendid national ensign by the ladies of Westport," and then moved to Richard's Hotel where they enjoyed a "rich and magnificent supper furnished by the citizens of Westport." At 11:30 that night the company embarked for Whitehall, at the southern end of Lake Champlain, on the steamer *America*. At Whitehall, the Adirondack Company took the train to Saratoga Springs, arriving at 6:30 a.m. Enjoying a night's accommodation at White's Hotel, they later marched to Camp Schuyler. [19]

Farther north in Keeseville, Wendell Lansing, a staunch Methodist, energetically recruited for the regiment. Lansing was born in Perryville, Madison County, New York, on September 18, 1807. He went to common schools and then to Cazenovia Seminary. At 21-years-old, he entered a printing office in Greenwich, New York, as an apprentice. Excelling and thriving in his trade, eight months later Lansing became proprietor of a newspaper. In 1839 he moved to Keeseville to start the *Essex County Republican*, which became quite successful. After seven years, Lansing's health failed him, and he left the newspaper business to engage in farming. With the birth of the Republican Party, Lansing returned to Keeseville, and published the *Northern Standard*, a strident mouthpiece for the Party. Drawing men primarily from Keeseville and Black Brook, he provided a second company from Essex County for the Bemus Heights Battalion.

As the companies began filtering into Camp Schuyler, a brief controversy arose concerning the correct spelling of "Bemus." In the circulars and letters relating to the battalion, the name had been spelled "Bemus" and "Bemis" indiscriminately. The family that occupied the Heights in the time of Burgoyne's defeat was called "Behmus." The Post Office designation was "Bemus," but popular usage, and the practice of the family's descendants sided with "Bemis." After some discussion, it was decided that "the spelling" was "to be 'Bemis'." [20]

By mid-October, all ten companies of the Bemis Heights Battalion had made their rendezvous at Saratoga Springs, the branch depot for Albany designated by Governor Edwin D. Morgan's Special Order No. 326. They then entered Camp Schuyler, so named after Major General Philip Schuyler who served in the Continental Army under George Washington, and whose vast estate included land and a house in Old Saratoga, now known as Schuylerville. Located on the fairgrounds of the Saratoga Agricultural Society southeast of the city and down Nelson Street, the new recruits entered the camp astir with the hammering and sawing of carpenters fitting the "Agricultural Hall with 'bunks' for the accommodation of the troops." Other buildings on the fairgrounds likewise were fast transforming to meet military needs. Floral Hall provided more bunks for the men, while the Eating Hall also received extensive additions to accommodate the incoming volunteers. Soon to be filled with the sick, a hospital was built on the west side of the fairgrounds. Robert H. Skinner (Co. D) mustered in as corporal, but was promoted to sergeant that same day. He wrote to his former professor at Fort Edward Institute, Adam Clark Works, offering a cryptic yet vivid account of his first few days in camp:

> I guess I am smuggled into Uncle Sam's School . . . The quarters and fare are good enough. Have made no

associates . . . Not in a hurry about it . . . Not much drunkenness . . . Great deal of vulgarity . . . Eating and sleeping are great institutions . . . Supped at the Barracks, found some fat pork, clinched it with my fingers and teeth . . . Desperate struggle ensued. Knife and fork came to the rescue. Have butter for tea & breakfast. This morning I emptied the contents of a tea cup partly within and partly on my clothes, lost my temper & remainder of my breakfast. Drill six hours per day, every phase of human nature and otherwise. Bed – one bag of straw & one blanket, bedfellow T.[Private Thomas] Fowler [Company D], in particular & all the soldiers in general, about bunk time I imagine we present the appearance of a frog pond – water & filth, some singing, some croaking, some swearing, some telling yarns, & some asleep.[21]

Numerous groups of spectators visited the camp daily to watch the new soldiers in drill or on parade. Delighted to see so many earnest men preparing for war, their hearts were filled with a grand pride. The *Saratogian* crowed that, "Military men, who have visited the camp, are profuse in their praises of the excellent material of which the regiment is composed, the ability of the officers, and the perfection of drill already acquired." Speaking for those from surrounding communities who witnessed camp activities, the *Saratogian* continued, "The regiment is made up of excellent material throughout . . . if it be its fortune to meet the foe, her sons will emulate the deeds performed on Bemis Heights in 1777, and add lusture (sic) to the fame of her Revolutionary annals."[22]

For the most part, the many visitors perceived the men as entirely contented, very much enjoying camp life. Yet disease would bring suffering almost as soon as the battalion's companies arrived. Most newly formed regiments suffered outbreaks of the contagious childhood diseases in their initial camp assembly. The main offenders were measles and mumps. It was frequently noted that new troops could be distinguished from old at night by the amount of coughing. Diphtheria also sporadically ravished the health of new recruits. While some of the old army expressed surprise and puzzlement at the epidemics that swept the camps in a way never experienced in the prewar army, the explanation was rather straightforward: "The old army had been small and its units were widely dispersed; recruitment had been continual but on a small scale, and large numbers of susceptibles had not been brought together as in 1862."[23]

Measles surpassed all other early contagious diseases in importance from the viewpoint of numbers, serious complications, and easy communicability. Recruits who contracted measles frequently developed acute and chronic bronchitis and pneumonia, sometimes resulting in death, and it was measles that quickly took hold of the battalion. Witnessing the new soldiers drill in November, the *Waterford Sentinel* became alarmed by "the men coughing in echoes." Passing through the barracks, the *Sentinel* advised "that more care should be used in ventilation." The air, it noted, "is very close, with a number of men sleeping there, and in addition some have boarded up their bunks into tight boxes, and then there were two large stoves kept very hot in the same building." Fearful of the potential long-term consequences to the soldiers, the *Sentinel* opined that the "great heat of the buildings and the lack of ventilation will result in some permanent damage . . . to some whose lungs would stand the ordinary exposures of Camp Life." Sergeant Skinner lamented that "a great number of soldiers are sick with measles. Our Company which seemed so prosperous and vigorous is almost stricken down. This morning we paid the last honors to the corpse of one of our numbers, Wm. Jenkins."[24]

Measles were not the only cause of death in camp. Private Henry Breut (Co. H), a volunteer from Charlton, succumbed to diphtheria. His remains were taken home, accompanied by a military escort and band, and buried with military honors. Another soldier from Union Village, named Morris, was suddenly stricken with a catastrophic stroke while the battalion was drilling. Stumbling from the line, he died almost instantly. Patrick Rudy (Private, Co. B), suffering from advanced alcoholism, died in the wretched throes of delirium tremens.

Very soon after entering Camp Schuyler, the enlisted men were outfitted with uniforms. While many had poor luck in obtaining proper fits, they were issued a dark blue New York Volunteer short jacket with light-blue piping; light-blue pants; a woolen shirt; cotton flannel underclothes; socks, black shoes derisively nicknamed "Ferry-boats," and "Pontoons"; and a blue cap with black visor. Sergeant Skinner was not the least impressed with his new garb: "Look something as I did when my mama first put trowsers on me – Rather Boyish." [25]

As for all regiments in camps of instruction, both north and south, the primary experience at Camp Schuyler was to drill, "six hours a day, every day, every phase of human & otherwise." Drill was essential in order to generate a disciplined and effective combat machine. Amid the sound, fury, and bloody carnage of battle, the instant reaction to orders often made the difference between success and failure; life and death.[26]

Based on 19th-century close order drill, the men of the battalion marched four-abreast in column. They had to learn to shift quickly and seamlessly from columns of four to two closely aligned ranks, the usual line of battle during the war. Broken down into squads of eight, the recruits in camp learned an intricate, often frustratingly complex, set of movements. Even the act of loading and firing a rifled musket required rigidly proscribed motions. The soldier drew from his cartridge box a cartridge which consisted of a ball and a charge of powder wrapped together in paper. Opening the cartridge with his teeth, he emptied the powder down the barrel of the musket and inserted the bullet point up. Following the insertion of the bullet, the soldier pulled the ramrod from beneath the barrel and tamped down the bullet and powder, and then replaced the ramrod. Then he half-cocked the hammer and affixed a firing cap on a small protrusion at the back of the barrel. Finally after taking position, the soldier fully cocked back the hammer, aimed, and pulled the trigger. It was a process so cumbersome and time-consuming that a seasoned veteran could manage no more than two or three shots per minute!

In order to drill the green recruits, the officers had much to learn. Many officers in new regiments were just as unfamiliar with military life and discipline as the soldiers they drilled. Housed within the confines of Congress Hall, the officers of the battalion burned the midnight oil studying Winfield Scott's *Infantry Tactics*, William J. Hardee's *Rifle and Infantry Tactics*, and army regulations. Excluding McKean, so green were the officers that they often first learned of particular drill maneuvers the night before they were to teach the same to their men.

Evenings at Camp Schuyler brought a most welcome break in the drill regimen. While the men readied themselves for inspection, crowds gathered each evening for dress parade and to witness the sunset cannon ceremony. These evenings were pleasant with the spectators' obvious pride boosting the self-esteem of the battalion. One Sunday evening, however, the crowd witnessed a horrifying sight. Private Thomas Joyce (Co. F), who had enlisted only a few days before, was tragically killed by the discharge of the sunset cannon. He "was standing near the gun when the match was applied, and when the gun appeared to hang fire, he deliberately stepped before the muzzle, a few feet off, just in time to receive the discharge." The "back part of his head was blown completely off, killing him instantly." [27]

Sundays, the men were largely free to spend the day resting. Robert Skinner wrote that, "we are allowed to attend church on the Sabbath by going" into Saratoga Springs "in squads under the eye of a sergeant." Skinner and many others of the battalion also attended "bible class on the Sabbath afternoon." Those whose homes or family were close by, would go home to visit and to put their affairs in order before going to the front. Visiting families and friends was a joyful, if not bittersweet, moment, but for Thomas Fowler (Private Co. D), the visit home to Cohoes was filled with profound sadness. His sister had suddenly drawn ill and died, and now his brother too lay upon his deathbed. [28]

As each company of the battalion filled up, their respective officers were elected. Most of the elections of company officers were uneventful while confirming the foregone conclusion that the persons most responsible for recruiting companies and the regiment would become its officers. This was largely the case for the Bemis Heights Battalion, except for Wendell Lansing, the primary force in bringing to Camp Schuyler one of the companies from Essex County. For reasons unexplained, Lansing mustered in as a private, but was promoted to Commissary Sergeant. Bristling at this unexpected slight, the *Elizabethtown Post* remarked, "The smallest favors thankfully received." Referring to the integrity of Lansing, the *Post* sarcastically asked, "O Lord, what could an honest Essex County man do with Saratogians?" Nevertheless, the paper continued, "Essex County boys" would "do their duty, and their whole duty, bravely, let who will be field officers." [29]

While the regiment's company officers were elected by the enlisted men, the colonel received his commission from the governor of the state in which the regiment was raised. The commissioning of the colonel of the regiment was more often than not a mere formality, the appointment going to the primary organizer and force behind its recruitment. James B. McKean was the obvious choice for the colonelcy, but his appointment was not without opposition. Colonel C. T. Peek of the 29th New York State Militia, and military Inspector and Commandant of Camp Schuyler, vigorously challenged McKean's right to be commissioned colonel of the Bemis Heights Battalion.

In January 1861, Colonel Peek made a request to the Adjutant General's Office that the 29th be "recruited up to the full standard, to be in readiness to take the field when called for...." His request went unheeded, but Peek was undeterred. Desiring a "movement which would give those citizens of Saratoga patriotically inclined, an opportunity to organize, and tender themselves to the government," Colonel Peek secured during the first week of August 1861 a public recommendation from a number of prominent residents of Saratoga Springs:

> We the undersigned, most respectfully ask the Commander in Chief of the militia of the State of New York to commission Col. C. T. Peek with authority to raise a regiment of soldiers to enter the service of the Government, and that said regiment, while forming, and until ordered into service, rendezvous at Saratoga Springs. Said regiment to be formed in compliance with general order No. 78, issued from the Adjutant General's Office July 30, 1861 . . .

Presented to Governor Morgan, the recommendation elicited an approving reply:

General Head Quarters, State of N. Y.
ADJUTANT GENERAL'S OFFICE
Col. C. T. Peek, 29th Reg't, N. Y. S. M.
Ballston Spa

Sir:

I am directed by Gov. Morgan to acknowledge the receipt of your letter of the 6th inst., and state that your offer was accepted, subject to the conditions respecting the same, prescribed in General Orders No. 78, a copy of which is herewith enclosed.

I am respectfully

Your obdt. Servant,
D. Campbell, Asst. Ajt. Genl. [30]

Peek was sick in bed when he received a copy of the Adjutant General's reply. Eight days later, he was astounded to read McKean's circular calling for the formation the "Bemus Heights Battalion." One week later, Colonel Peek was sufficiently recovered to leave his bed and sought out McKean. Finding the congressman "in the streets of Saratoga Springs," Peek, "offered to co-operate with him in getting up the battalion," but was rebuffed by McKean "who hurried away down the street." Later, armed with the appointment of Military Inspector for recruits arriving at Camp Schuyler, Peek approached McKean "in the matter of recruits to be gathered here . . . but I could never obtain much opportunity, because he always professed in too great a hurry, whenever I met him, to converse on the subject." [31]

Determined to take charge of the recruits for the battalion arriving in camp, Peek appeared at the railroad depot at Saratoga Springs to take charge of Renel Arnold's company of men from Essex County. Soon McKean approached to collect Arnold's men, and a heated argument erupted. As Colonel Peek remembered, McKean professed that he alone was "authorized by the Governor and Adjutant General to make all arrangements and contracts here, saying that he had done everything toward getting up the regiment and depot here, and if he could not have control of the matter, he would blow it all up, and send circulars to the men that they need not come." Arnold and his recruits were dumbstruck witnessing the angry display before them. McKean demanded that Arnold put himself in charge of his friend, J. T. Butler, but Arnold refused and submitted to Peek's authority. [32]

Furious, McKean traveled to the Adjutant General demanding clarification of the situation. Quartermaster General Van Vechten and Brigadier General John F. Rathbone, commander of the Albany Depot of Volunteers, were present when the congressman angrily attacked Colonel Peek for usurping his authority to receive recruits for the battalion. Endorsing McKean, General Rathbone then telegraphed Peek and requested him to "relieve them of this annoyance and to do nothing to discourage enlistments, or to break up the regiment, for the Government wanted more troops."[33]

C. T. Peek could not bring himself to allow McKean to command the new recruits and attacked him in the pages of the *Ballston Spa Journal* and the *Saratogian*, causing McKean's lengthy retort:

Some months ago, while I was in Washington, Mr. G. S. Batchellor wrote me that Col. Peek desired to reorganize the 29th Regiment, an old Militia Regiment, and get it into service, and wished me to see Secretary Cameron upon the subject. Being willing then, as I am now, to aid in reorganizing that regiment . . . I wrote Col. Peek . . . that I would try and accommodate him . . .

Several other gentlemen, residing in this and adjoining counties, wrote me while I was in Washington in reference, not to a Militia, but a Volunteer Regiment, and urged me to issue a call for one. I was assured that Col. Peek had done nothing and could do nothing whatever towards reviving his old Militia Regiment, much less towards raising a Volunteer force to be collected from several counties . . . almost all the competent men in this county, who are willing to raise companies and take Captains' and Lieutenants' commissions, protested that he must have nothing to do with the enterprise. I issued a call to the people of the 15th Congressional district to organize a BEMIS HEIGHTS BATTALION, and obtained an order from the Governor and Adjutant General, establishing a branch military depot at this place . . . I did not send my circular to Col. Peek for the simple reason I did not wish him to have anything to do with the enterprise, being satisfied that his connection would defeat it. I conferred, corresponded and traveled extensively, addressed meetings, and commenced the organization of companies . . . And then Col. P. who did not (I will not say could not) raise a squad of men, appeared here, claiming to have been authorized by Brig. Gen. Rathbone to inspect the troops, to contract for their subsistence, and to command the depot. During the parts of two days that he stood in that relation to the regiment, some of the gentlemen who were recruiting and expected to be Captains and Lieutenants, tendered me their muster rolls, saying they would do nothing more; others sent messages to the effect that they could get no more recruits, and could not hold what they had, unless Col. Peek was removed. I saw the BEMIS HEIGHTS BATTALION was going to destruction faster than any regiment was ever mowed down on the field of battle.

I applied to the government at Albany to rescue the regiment before it was too late. Gen. Rathbone informed me that Col. Peek had called on him and asked for certain orders in reference to the BEMIS HEIGHTS BATTALION; that he told Col. Peek he must first obtain my consent; that the Colonel afterwards came to him again and told him that he had spoken to me upon the subject; that I consented to his having the authority he asked for, and that by arrangement with me he had come to get it. Gen. Rathbone then appointed him commandant of the depot, &c, &c. I must say here that I never consented that Col. Peek should have any authority in reference to the depot here, or the regiment that we were organizing; he never asked me for such consent, and never intimated to me that he intended to apply for such authority. *After* he obtained it, I learned of his movements for the first time. His statements to Gen. Rathbone were utterly false. When the facts were before the Government, Gen. Rathbone decided to remove Col. Peek...[34]

Aware of Peek's maneuvering for command, the elected officers of the battalion petitioned Governor Morgan. "The...officers would respectfully urge the appointment of Hon. Jas. B. McKean as Colonel of the Bemis Heights Regiment, and would also represent that it is the unanimous choice of the non-commissioned officers and privates of our respective companies that he be so appointed."

Realizing that he had no support in the regiment and that General Rathbone was to remove him from duty, Colonel Peek resigned his command, and McKean was commissioned Colonel at the regiment's request on November 23, 1861.[35]

If the duty of the men at Camp Schuyler was to prepare for war, to honor the legacy of their Revolutionary fathers, and to defend the Constitution, then the patriotic duty of the women of Saratoga Springs and neighboring communities was to meet the material needs of the men in service. Addressing the ladies of Saratoga on "Home Matters," the *Saratogian* offered that, "Your patriotic brothers are enlisting in the Bemis Heights Battalion to sustain the government which we all cherish. They will be exposed to danger and sickness, and every comfort which the wounded and sick can possibly have, under the circumstances, should be theirs." Following closely the recommendations of the Sanitary Commission, the *Saratogian* asked women to provide numerous items for the soldier's comfort:

> Blankets for single beds;
> Quilts of cheap material, about seven feet long by fifty inches wide;
> Knit woolen socks; -- three or four sizes.
> Woolen or Caston Flannel Bed Gowns, Wrappers, Undershirts and Drawers;
> Small Hair and Feather Pillows and Cushions for wounded limbs;
> Slippers;
> Delicacies for the sick – such as farina, arrow root, corn starch, cocoa, condensed milk, and nicely dried fruit. Also aromatic spirits and waters; light easy chairs for convalescents; nicely made splints for wounded limbs; checker and backgammon boards, and like articles for the amusement

of wounded men; books for desultory reading, magazines, especially if illustrated, will be useful.

The *Saratogian* further urged that "the effort be universal that every patriotic woman in the county may feel that she has done something for the comfort of those willing to brave danger and death in our defense." [36]

The solicited items rapidly began arriving in camp. Several churches gathered a variety of books and periodicals for the men along with "1,000 testaments" ordered by the Executive Committee of the County Bible Society. Among the recruits in camp, Sergeant Skinner was especially "glad to read any reading matter." The ladies of Galway busied themselves by knitting stockings and mittens and the women of Stillwater sent to Captain [Judson B.] Andrews' (Co. F) men "a lot of quilts, comforters, towels, housewifes, fine tooth combs, stockings... (and)...shirts for hospital use." Not to be outdone, the good women of Saratoga Springs raised a substantial sum with which they purchased materials and manufactured "mattresses . . . for the sick of the regiment." Proud of the women's accomplishments, the *Saratogian* wrote that "the patriotic ladies of this village have done their whole duty in providing for the comfort of the Volunteers." [37]

Much attention was focused on providing the new soldiers with "Water Proof Blankets – either India Rubber, or blankets made of strong sheeting and covered with a composition prepared for the purpose." Some blankets were purchased. Many were also made. Ballston Spa held a concert at Waverly Hall to raise the necessary funds to purchase Indian rubber blankets for Company B, and noted that "were it not for the kindness of the ladies, many a poor soldier would be deprived of many an article necessary for his comfort." In Saratoga Springs, the kind-spirited women raised $140 to purchase blankets for Captain Benjamin F. Judson's Company C. The women folk of Wilton gathered at Emerson Church with their sewing machines to sew water proof blankets for Company D.[38]

Finally on November 23, 1861, the Bemis Heights Battalion was mustered into Federal service by Major L. Sitgreaves as a regiment of the New York State Volunteers. The ceremony was an impressive one in which the regiment was formed in line by companies. Major Sitgreaves inspected the men and officers individually and collectively. The volunteers then took off their hats, "raised their right hands, and bowed in assent" to the oath of allegiance. After avowing their undying loyalty to the United States government, the articles of war were read. At the conclusion of the muster, the "boys gave three cheers for the Union." [39]

Colonel James B. McKean (Wikipedia)

McKEAN'S SUNDAY SCHOOL BOYS GO TO WAR

Although the application to raise a Saratoga regiment was numerically 44, the regiment successfully petitioned Governor Morgan to designate it as the 77th in honor of the county in which the battles of Saratoga were fought in 1777. Thus designated, the 77th New York State Volunteer Infantry, the newly sworn in officers were:

Colonel, Kames B. McKean
Lieutenant Colonel, Joseph C. Henderson
Major Seldon Hetzel
Surgeon, John L. Perry
Assistant Surgeon, George T. Stevens
Chaplain, David Tully
Adjutant and Lieutenant, Winsor B. French
Second Lieutenant and Quarter Master, Lucius E. Shurtleff

Company A. Captain, Renel W. Arnold; First Lieutenant, William Douglas; Second Lieutenant, James H. Farnsworth

Company B. Captain, Clement C. Hill; First Lieutenant, Noble P. Hammond; Second Lieutenant, Stephen S. Horton

Company C. Captain, Benjamin F. Judson; First Lieutenant, Luther M. Wheeler; Second Lieutenant, John Patterson.

Company D. Captain, John Carr; Adjutant and First Lieutenant, Winsor B. French; Second Lieutenant, Chester H. Fodow

Company E. Captain, Lewis Wood; First Lieutenant, William B. Carpenter; Second Lieutenant, Halsey Bowe

Company F. Captain, Judson B. Andrews; First Lieutenant, Jesse White; Second Lieutenant, John J. Cameron

Company G. Captain, Calvin Rice; First Lieutenant, George S. Orr; Second Lieutenant and Quarter Master, Lucius E. Shurtleff.

Company H. Captain, Albert F. Beach; First Lieutenant, N. Hollister Brown; Second Lieutenant, George D. Storey

Company I. Captain, Franklin Norton; First Lieutenant, Jacob F. Hayward; Second Lieutenant, Martin Lennon

Company K. Captain, Nathan S. Babcock; First Lieutenant, John W. McGregor; Second Lieutenant, Philander A. Cobb

Eagerly awaiting orders to proceed to the seat of war, many of the officers received gifts from their respective communities. Captain Judson Andrews was presented the unusual gift of a "MacIntosh Overcoat" from Rev. J. P. Newman, formerly of Mechanicsville, and now living in New York City. In a letter presenting the handsome coat to Andrews, Rev. Newman wrote:

> Learning of your enlistment in the ranks of the brave army of the north, and that as Captain you are soon to lead your noble band from the upper valley of the Hudson to crush a *shameful rebellion*, and defend the rights of Constitutional law, and maintain the supremacy of our National Government, I present to you a 'MacIntosh Coat' to protect you from the inclemency of the weather incident to *camp life* – and may no rebel sabre or bullet penetrate it . . . I have worn it in all my journey's to the 'Old World.' It has been on the grand battle fields of Europe, at Waterloo, Marengo, Magenta and Solferino, and has smelt powder at Capua where the heroic Garibaldi fought for Italian Independence . . . May it be of service to you, protecting you from the dews of the night and the winter rains. [40]

Most of the officers were presented swords. Captain Lewis Wood was given both a sword and a revolver at "The Soldier's Festival and Sword Presentation" at Jamesville. Captain Wood's company was transported to the festival in wagons furnished by area townsmen to witness the presentation. Taking place at a church, a large crowd was in attendance. J. S. L'Ammoreaux gave a speech and presented the sword and revolver to Wood who graciously accepted the gifts. Then followed a "feast of all good things that farmer's wives know so well how to provide, and overflowing in abundance. The soldiers complimented the fare in the most practical way by making the most of their opportunity, and spent the day in uninterrupted enjoyment." [41]

The most impressive of all presentations took place at Tweddle Hall in Albany, presided by Captain Ira Ainsworth. There, friends presented Lieutenant Colonel Joseph Henderson with a sword, sash, belt, saddle, trunk, and $200 in gold. Facing Henderson, John G. Saxe began to speak:

> In the name and behalf of your neighbors and friends in Albany, I have honor to present you – the second officer of the 77th (Bemis Heights) Regiment of the New York State Volunteers – the complete military equipment appropriate to you rank, consisting in part, of this beautiful sword and those other martial accoutrements, and further represented by the well-filled purse of gold.

Saxe turned his attention to the conflict at hand:

> Of the War in which you are soon actively to enter, I would say a few words. A war for the defense of the best and most benign Government the world has yet seen, and pregnant with the fate of free institutions in all time to come. History, it seems to me, affords no example of a struggle

so momentous, or so worthy of the benediction of the God of Grace, and the omnipotent aid of the God of Battles. It is a war waged on our part, not for lust or wealth, not for the unhallowed glory of conquest; nor for the abolition of any constitutional right of the weakest state in the great Republic, but for the abolition of treason and the subjugation of traitors. And may we not hope that those brilliant achievements of the Federal arms which have so lately thrilled the hearts of loyal men, are but the incipient wave of a swelling tide of victory which shall overwhelm the cohorts of treason and sweep away forever the standards of revolt. May God mercifully grant it, and may you, having borne some noble part in a war nobly conducted and honorably ended – return in health and safety . . . [42]

With the muster of the 77th New York State Volunteer Infantry, orders were received to proceed to Washington, the departure date set for November 28. War awaited the volunteers, and they felt pleased to finally do their share in defending the Constitution. Speaking for the soldiers of the new regiment, Sergeant Skinner wrote, "I submit willingly to every duty . . . I feel proud to know that I can enter these duties without a murmur." [43]

2

"FOREST OF BAYONETS"

On the morning of November 27, 1861, the sun rose to the sights and sounds of the men of the 77th hurriedly attending to the last minute details of breaking camp for the move to the seat of war in Washington. Now ready, new soldiers formed into column and departed Camp Schuyler, preceded by the regimental band playing, "Leaving the Girl Behind Us." In unison, they began their march to the train at the Rensselaer and Saratoga Railroad station. On the way they halted and were drawn up before a large crowd at the Temple Grove Seminary to receive the regiment's national flag. Made by the young women of the Seminary, the flag was "of fine silk, handsomely embroidered, and lettered in gilt, '77th REG'T N. Y. S. V.'" [1]

For this most solemn occasion, the men put on their best appearance and manners as relatives, friends, dignitaries, and well-wishers gathered for the presentation. The flag presentation was much more than pomp and circumstance; it was a defining moment, a moment when their mission was articulated by the entire community. More so, the presentation solidified the bond between community and soldier that began with recruitment and was to continue throughout the bloody years of war to follow.

Rev. Dr. L. F. Beecher, proprietor of the Temple Grove Seminary, issued the primary address. Declaring solidarity of cause, and linking the men of the Bemis Heights Regiment to their patriotic fathers who triumphed at Saratoga, Beecher began:

> In behalf of the Teachers and Pupils of the Institution of learning under my care I present to you this NATIONAL BANNER, as a testimonial of their interest in the cause which you go to defend, and there is not one, who does not unite with enthusiasm in the presentation. It was at their option to present either this, or the regimental banner, but they preferred to give you this NATIONAL banner, this flag of the whole country. Here for the first time, as many believe, was the symbol of our nationality unfurled in the presence of any considerable number of our troops, and that too in the presence of those men, flushed with victory, which was the turning point, in our great struggle for freedom, in the year 1777.
>
> In commemoration of this important event, and doubtless, with the hope, that the same spirit and courage may be found in which was found in our Patriotic Sires, your regiment has been named the 77th.
>
> This number you will bear with you emblazoned upon your banner, a reason in addition to others, why you should defend its integrity with your lives . . .

The men of the 77th, Beecher asserted, were compelled to engage in a holy mission to defend the flag that heralded freedom around the world. It was their mission to restore the most beneficent government, now threatened by traitors, of which it symbolized:

> Four more than eighty years, has this flag floated without dishonor, over a nation of freemen, and the heroic deeds which have been achieved under it, constitute no unimportant part of the history of the last hundred years. It pioneered us through our Revolutionary struggles, and the proud cross of St. George was more than once lowered to the Stars and Stripes. It has been carried around the world, at the peak of our national vessels, a herald of freedom, to the downtrodden, victorious always, when opposed by an equal force, and often victorious when matched against fearful odds, and its proud escutcheon was never stained till it was torn down from the public buildings at Charleston, and traitor hands, in defiance of authority it represents, trailed in the dirt. The challenge thus rudely thrown down, we have accepted. You have taken the field that you may once more lift up this banner, over the places whence it has been rudely torn down. You have taken up arms, with the determination not to lay them down, till every stain is wiped from its fair escutcheon, and it again floats on every good rood of our country from the lakes to the gulf – from rippling waters of the Eastern Sea, to the mouth of the Columbia.
>
> You have not taken up arms in Fratricidal warfare against your brethren, but traitors among your brethren, who, for wicked and ambitious ends, have combined to overthrow the most liberal government upon the earth. You have taken up arms to restore a government over the whole country, bequeathed to us by our patriotic sires; and which they did not think was too dearly purchased by their

blood – to open a free channel for all our great rivers to the ocean, -- to secure to every man the right to labor, and to enjoy undisturbed the results of his own industry and skill, the right to think, and speak, and print, and vote, on every question of National polity, accountable only for its abuse. Without these we have neither freedom or prosperity at home, nor security or respect abroad. You go forth therefore on a holy mission, and we invoke upon your arms the blessing of him alone who giveth success. Take then this proud banner. It is no longer ours, but our country's. Bear it into the thickest of the fight, and remember that there is nothing you should dread so much as the dishonor of your flag. When we hear the battle is joined, many an eager eye will look for tidings from the 77th and in the midst of danger and din of battle let this thought thrill you, like a trumpet's call.

Beneath these silken folds may you find protection in the midst of conflict, and may the God of battles give you victory.[2]

Following Rev. Beecher's presentation, Mary Carlton Beecher bid the soldiers of the 77th adieu with poetic flourish:

The Stars and Stripes, wrought by fair hands and true,
The flag of our Union we tender you;
Let its silken folds wave as you march to the strife,
And part with it never, except with your life.
If the battle grow fierce and your courage should lag,
Look up to the Stars on your beautiful flag;
That bright constellation, set in Heaven's own blue,
One unbroken cluster is entrusted to you,
The Star Spangled Banner, how proud we shall be,
When triumphant it floats o'er the land and the sea.

M^CKEAN'S SUNDAY SCHOOL BOYS GO TO WAR

Then on, ye brave soldiers, right on to the fight,
Wield the good sword of freedom with your power and might;
Set your face to the foe, and never turn back,
While the traitor is left to lurk in your track.
Bring again this proud Banner all serrated with shot,
Stained with powder and gore where the battle was hot.
Once more we shall see it, victorious we trust,
But never by traitor hands trailed in the dust.
The Star Spangled Banner, how proud we shall be,
When triumphant it floats o'er the land and the sea.

But sadness may sometimes your spirits appall,
As you think of the cherished ones dearer than all,
The home of the mother, the babes and the wife,
And all those sweet ties which entwine round your life.
And start from those eyes unaccustomed to weep;
But dash them away and your spirits regain,
When thought cheers your heart that their rights you maintain,
The Star Spangled Banner, how proud we shall be,
When it floats o'er the land and the sea.

And loud cheers for our flag shall ascent to the skies.
The Star Spangled Banner, how proud we shall be,
When triumphant it floats, o'er the land and the sea.[3]

Colonel McKean responded in "appropriate and eloquent terms, his remarks being warmly applauded." Cheers were given by the regiment for the flag, for the young women of the Temple Grove Seminary, and for Rev. Beecher, and the young poetess, Mary Beecher. The march was then resumed toward the railroad station on Division Street, where once again the regiment met a large crowd gathered to offer their heartfelt farewell. Observing the power of the moment, the *Saratogian* later reported, "The moist eyes, the tears which bedewed many cheeks, the reluctant parting word, and the hearty 'Good bye, God bless you,' all told with what varied and deep emotion and separation was regarded." All knew that many would never return, but with passion for country they "looked confidently forward to see the regiment perform deeds worthy the name they bear, and the people whom they represent." [4]

Filling eighteen passenger cars, the 77th's train slowly pulled away from the station. Simultaneously, the inhabitants of Ballston Spa gathered at the village's train station, the next in line south of Saratoga, to bid the soldiers Godspeed and to "offer them such little delicacies as had been prepared by their friends for their comfort." However, to their consternation, the train did not stop, but carried on toward Albany. Nevertheless, the men of the regiment were in fine spirits, and the *Ballston Spa Journal* was confident that "should they ever be called into action they will do their whole duty, and will sustain the honor and glory so dearly won by their forefathers at the memorable battle of Bemis Heights." Speaking for the entire village, the *Journal* looked forward to when "Jeff Davis & Co. are thoroughly crushed" and the "country restored to peace" and the men of the 77th "all return safe and sound to their friends, never more to be called to defend our glorious flag from traitors at home and abroad." [5]

Three hours later, the 77th arrived in Albany. Leaving the cars at the foot of Lumber Street, the men marched down Broadway to the steamboat landing, crowds lining the way and cheering them onward. From there, the men boarded the steamer *Knickerbocker*, "an old dismantled craft, unfit for any purpose but the transportation of soldiers; whose deck was covered in mud an inch depth, and whose doors having been thrown overboard, a free circulation of the rough November air was allowed in every part." Several hours passed while the *Knickerbocker* took on stores and baggage before its moorings were cast off and the vessel swung out into the Hudson River southward to New York City.[6]

The overnight was most uncomfortable. To Waldo Potter, co-editor of the *Saratogian* traveling with the regiment, the "want of sufficient space on the boat for nearly 900 men, soon became palpably evident. After filling the cabin below, and the saloon and staterooms above, there remained two whole companies utterly destitute of any place to lie down, except the wet and muddy deck, and who had no protection from the damp and chilly air except their blankets." Some of the soldiers fortified themselves with whiskey smuggled aboard in canteens and "succeeded in making night somewhat hideous with their boisterous mirth." [7]

The next morning was gray with fog and a steady rain fell as the 77th reached New York City. Through the rain, the regiment debarked at the foot of Fourteenth Street, entered Broadway, and marched to the barracks in Battery Park. There they stood, drawn up in line, to receive their Enfield rifles. But for unexplained reasons, the guns did not come. In the meantime, the committee of the Sons of Saratoga residing in the City arrived with a splendid band, and escorted the rain-soaked soldiers to dry quarters. The volunteers were provided with their first substantial meal since leaving Saratoga Springs. After dinner, the Enfields finally arrived with sabre bayonets, and the men once again formed ranks, standing in line to receive the rifles by companies. Writing to his brother Frank, Lieutenant Luther Wheeler (Co. C) remarked that, "The boys were very much pleased with their Enfield rifles, they were part of 5,000 stands captured in a British vessel on the southern coast trying to run the blockade." [8]

Once the regiment was equipped with their new rifles, they formed in front of City Hall to receive a regimental flag presented by the Sons of Saratoga. The flag was made of heavy, deep blue silk, bordered with a thick fringe of yellow silk cord. Painted on both sides, the flag was "an exquisite piece of work... On one side was represented the engagement in which American soldiers, led by Washington, were fighting under the old flag – thirteen stripes and the union jack. On the reverse was a picture of the surrender of Burgoyne, at Saratoga, under a new flag – the stars and stripes – first unfurled in the goodly city of Albany, and first baptized in the blood at the decisive battle of Bemis Heights, which resulted in the surrender of Burgoyne and the virtual success of the Revolution." Underneath, in gilt letters, were the words "BEMIS HEIGHTS REGT. 77TH N. Y. S. V." The flagstaff was mounted by a pike head, or esponton, taken from the battle at Saratoga on Bemis Heights.[9]

Handing the regimental banner to Colonel McKean, Hiram Ketchum "spoke of the pride felt by the Sons of Saratoga and the satisfaction" that he and his associates felt in welcoming "so noble a regiment... on its way in putting down a great and wicked rebellion." Ketchum, and those in attendance, "felt that the honor of Saratoga was committed in good hands" and that if in conflict "Any should fall," the Sons of Saratoga would be among the first "to bedew the graves of the fallen heroes with their tears." Trusting that their New York friends would never be ashamed of the Bemis Heights Battalion, the devout McKean said that he should not make any promises, for he felt, in the words of Holy Writ, "Let not him boast who putteth on his armor, but him who putteth it off." [10]

Shortly thereafter, the 77th once again formed, and marched down Broadway to the pier near the Battery, where they boarded a ferry and crossed into New Jersey at Amboy. There, a train waited to take the New Yorkers over the Camden and Amboy Railroad to Philadelphia. The condition of the cars was appalling, and the officers and men at first refused to board, protesting that "these vehicles were unfit for transportation." But with no other visible alternative, the regiment concluded to go on. Last used to transport livestock, the men of the regiment were made as comfortable as possible while "crowded into a number of shaky old cars, reeking with filth, and redolent of the most noisome odors." [11]

After suffering through the cold night ride, the 77th's early morning reception at Philadelphia "was like finding a living spring in a sandy desert." Mounting a barrel, a kind old gentleman welcomed the regiment to Philadelphia, and invited the men to breakfast at one of the two saloons providing refreshments for hungry volunteers passing through the city on their way to war. While the main part of the regiment took their places at the well-spread tables of the saloon, Assistant Surgeon George T. Stevens was burdened with the care of the sick. [12]

The young George Thomas Stevens was born on July 25, 1832 in the small village of Jay, Essex County, New York. He was the son of Congregational minister Chauncey Coe and Lucinda Hoadley Stevens. Stevens received his early education in the schools of the county and also studied with his scholarly father. After receiving his medical degree at Castleton Medical College in Vermont, Stevens returned to New York to practice medicine in Wadhams Mills, Essex County. There he met Harriet Weeks Wadhams. Falling deeply in love, the pair married on April 17, 1861. Five months later, Stevens was persuaded to leave his new wife to enlist as assistant surgeon to the 77th. He was soon promoted to the rank of surgeon and served in the Army of the Potomac as operating surgeon for the Second Division, Sixth Corps, and for a brief time was Medical Inspector. Following the war, Stevens chronicled his experience in *Three Years in the Sixth Corps*.

Remembering that morning in Philadelphia, Stevens wrote, "Many of our men were sick when we left Saratoga, and the unaccustomed hardships, with cold and rain thus far on the route, had greatly prostrated them. Many others had also been seized with violent illness, so that our single medical officer had been taxed beyond his strength in looking after the wants of the sick, while the little cases of medicine with which we started from Saratoga were exhausted." Soon the assistant surgeon was approached by the same kind gentleman who conducted the regiment to breakfast. "If you will get your sick together, we will conduct them to comfortable quarters, and see that they are well cared for." The sick were then quickly gathered together and brought to the Soldier's Retreat to receive medical attention. Thus relieved, Stevens then joined in the repartee of the regiment and their obliging hosts at the breakfast table. As the meal ended, Colonel McKean called upon the volunteers for three cheers for the hospitality of the Philadelphians. [13]

Following the splendid breakfast, the 77th left Philadelphia for Baltimore by rail. The train moved at a glacial pace because of the decrepit condition of the cars. As Potter complained, "We left Philadelphia at 7 o'clock on Saturday . . . a distance of about 100 miles, which we accomplished in *twelve hours!*" Reaching Baltimore on Sunday, the regiment was required to transfer to another train. In a postwar anamnesis Corporal David Weatherwax (Co. G) drew an animated picture of that night:

> Here we received our first orders, i.e., to fix bayonets and in marching through the city to keep our ranks well closed, as the regiment previous to ours had been fired into by the mob. Lieutenant [Noble] Hammond of Company B led, his being the first company upon our right, and he did lead us too as he went on a double quick most of the way. It being in the night the consequence was we stretched out like a piece of India Rubber, causing people to make many remarks such as: 'That is the largest

regiment I ever saw – is there no end to it – I hope you will all be killed you d-d yanks.' However we were fortunate enough to get through without any accident. [114]

They then boarded yet another train, and if Potter thought the trip from Philadelphia was agonizingly slow, one can imagine his ire that it took seven hours to travel less than forty miles during "an uncomfortable as such a trip could be made," for "most of the cars were made for freight, with no seats except for boards without backs, no means of getting out or in while in motion, and no lights or fires." [15]

After three days of the most arduous and grueling travel, the 77th finally arrived at Washington on Sunday morning, December 1, just before the sun appeared over the horizon. Though the sky was still dark, the city had come alive with the frenetic activity of an army organizing for war. George Stevens observed uniformed men mounted on lathered horses galloping in every direction delivering urgent orders, and long trains of army wagons clattering down the streets with squads of soldiers quick stepping to destinations known only to them. While the exhausted New Yorkers were assigned temporary quarters near the railroad station, Stevens and Quarter Master Lucius E. Shurtleff rode to Meridian Hill to select a site for the regiment's camp. This was quickly accomplished, and the soldiers then marched the final two miles to their newly appointed place of rest. They began pitching their tents in the raw, cold air of the night. Many flopped down in exhaustion and slept on the ground, but Robert Skinner was exhilarated in his newfound environment, and challenged "the company for a foot race . . . Volunteers to stand sentinel around our camp were called for. I stepped up and thereby lost my sleep, for the most of the night." [16]

Meridian Hill, once the estate of Commodore David Porter, renowned commander of the *U.S.S. Essex* during the War of 1812, father of Admiral David Dixon Porter, adoptive father of David Farragut, provided an excellent panoramic view of Washington. Dotted with groves of oak and chestnut, the grounds were also trimmed with boxwood and juniper. With an avid, life-long interest in botany, Assistant Surgeon Stevens declared "the country in rear of the encampment was charming. Fine groves, traversed by streams of pure, sweet water, and fields surrounded by hedges, stretched far to the northward. The dark green leaves of the magnolia were to be seen here and there among the trees of larger growth, and the shining, ever-green laurel forming a dense undergrowth, gave the woods a lively, spring-like appearance." While agreeing that, "We now occupy the most beautiful place," Sergeant Skinner wrote, "We are completely surrounded by camps. The vicinity presents a grand sight . . . . The fields about us are covered with Regiments, Brigades, and Battalions. The neighborhood looks like a forest of Bayonets when they are on drill." [17]

MCKEAN'S SUNDAY SCHOOL BOYS GO TO WAR

Louis N. Rosenthal Lithographs, The historical Society of Pennsylvania

Designated "Camp Hillhouse", the 77th spent the next several days settling into their new quarters and receiving visitors. Correspondents from the *Ballston Spa Journal* commented on the festive spirit found in camp:

> Yesterday we had the privilege of roughing it with the soldiers in their camp, where life is anything but dull. All sorts of amusements are extemporized as occasion offers, wit is allowed free scope, and jokes are free as air. We took supper in the tent of Capt. Beach, of the Charlton company, with a select number of guests. The fare was excellent, and well seasoned with cheerful conversation and pleasant repartee. Capt. Beach dilated upon the woes of Camp Life in a mirthful strain, kept up long enough to almost split the sides of the company. At 9 P. M. we stretched ourselves out on straw beds, and slept comfortably, although the night was very cold.[18]

The Washington correspondent for the *Saratogian* also visited Camp Hillhouse and vividly described what he saw for interested readers back home:

> I found the camp all laid out in streets, the tents in line, and the ground all graded out in fine order. The first street we entered was Milton. Here we found Capt. Hill's company enjoying themselves in a variety of ways. Passing on to Broadway we found the tents of the officers. Facing this street and leading from it, we saw the familiar names of others, as Bemis Heights, Charlton, Ausable, &c., along which on each side are arranged the tents of several companies . . . Everything necessary for the comfort of the man is provided, and the various departments of Quarter-Master, Commissary, Sutler, Post Office, &c. are now in fine working order.[19]

For Robert Skinner, however, the idyllic atmosphere of camp soon deteriorated along with the weather. "Thus far the weather has been fine," the young sergeant wrote to his former professor at Fort Edward Institute, "but last evening the rain descended and the winds blew . . . and this is not a very agreeable day. It rains and snows and blows, and the smoke and the mud flies, and we slip and stumble wherever we got. Our tents being so small and quite well fitted afford us a magnificently poor retreat." Standing by the cook's fire, Skinner "looked upon our little tents which are to afford us shelter during the coming night . . . I declare I could not refrain from laughing right out at the very idea. I think we might crave the hospitality of a chicken coop if it would afford a dry bed." With "everything decently mudded over," Skinner observed that some of the men "have the blues and some a lack of patience." There was little to do in such miserable weather. "In our tent we are beguiling the hours, each in his own way. Fowler smokes his pipe. [Private David] McNeal [Co D] likewise. [Corporal] Sid King [Co. D] is singing. [Private Frederick] Perkins [Co. D] is on guard. Skinner is trying to write and cannot do it for cold fingers." [20]

In time, the soldiers made improvements in their living arrangements and fixed up their tents to resemble home. Rather proud of the embellishments to their quarters, Sergeant Skinner offered Professor Works a detailed tour of his tent:

> You asked me some questions concerning our tent and furniture . . . Well, we live now four in a tent, whose dimensions a 8 ft. by 7 ft. and 7 ft. high in the middle . . . But we have made ours larger by putting a plank wall under it of about 18 inches height . . . First on the list of furniture is our improved bed made on the principle of the 'Shanghai,' made by ourselves. We have on each bunk 2 bags of straw, and two blankets . . . Next is our little Army stove made of

sheet iron, in volume about one and a half cubic ft. . . . Our library consists of a piece of plank with books piled there and our cupboard is a cartridge box. I mean a wooden box for packing cartridges. Our silver cups are made of tin. Our plates are made of the same metal. An inventory would run like this – One bed – 1 stove – 1 cupboard – 4 tin cups – 4 knives – 4 forks – 4 spoons, 4 rifles, 4 knapsacks, 4 haversacks, 4 canteens, 4 belts, 4 cartridge boxes, 4 cap boxes, 1 axe, 1 pick-axe, 1 stew pan, 1 wash dish, 1 lot of books, 2 plank seats – 1 sword . . . Thus you see, our house is well filled. Perhaps better filled than furnished . . . I think we can brave the fury of a Lapland winter. [21]

In the same letter, Skinner turned his attention to the company cook who "I suppose . . . belongs to the race of white men, but having discarded his indelicateness to nature he assumes a color of his own notion which is about the same as that of his camp kettles and full as greasy." Perhaps revealing his lack of culinary skills, the cook "adopted the plan of boiling as the mode of cooking." In the same vein, Skinner provided a comical description of the day's typical menu:

Our bread is good. It is baked in the basement of the capitol where most of the army bread is baked. We have coffee twice a day and sometimes tea. Our meat is generally good for the stomach. Sometimes beef and something they give us what they call pork. Perhaps you have heard of it. It is of the genus hog and of Biblical notoriety. With this pork they sometimes give us what they call beans. This strange dish is I believe of unknown origin, but as I understand they were known to and used by the New England states as early as the Seventeenth Century and I doubt not that ere this they have found their way into the State of N. Y. We have another article of food called potato. This I believe is of the genus root, and a production of S. America, carried through a refining process in Ireland and imported thence to the U. States for the use of <u>Soldiers</u> and <u>Students</u>. We have rice several times a week. Molasses and sugar likewise . . . Our food is good when not spoiled in cooking. [22]

In the early days at Camp Hillhouse, whiskey readily made its appearance among the men. Remarking that, "Some of the men in camp are occasionally attacked with a peculiar fever, called 'Canteen fever,'" the *Ballston Spa Journal* humorously described the symptoms as a "fiery excitement throughout the whole system, pulse beating rapidly, mind confused and sometimes frenzied, breath offensive, tongue thick and garrulous, upper extremities feeling after supports, lower extremities weak and oscillating, and tumble-down tendencies." Colonel McKean, the ever-strict Methodist teetotaler, however, saw no such humor in drunkenness and had in fact forbidden the drinking of liquor except for bona fide medicinal purposes. It was soon apparent that whiskey was being smuggled into camp by women selling candies and apples to the soldiers. When the women's' supplier was identified, McKean sent a squad of men under Captain Nathan Babcock (Co. K) and Lieutenant Stephen S. Horton (Co. B) "to a brick house quite near the city. Over one door was 'Citizen's Provision Store,' inside was soldier's poison by the barrel." The proprietor barred the entrance, but "melted and opened the door" when "the officers presented loaded pistols, the boys loaded guns, and bayonets charged." Barrel after barrel was rolled out along with great quantities of white wine. Colonel McKean came along and after watching a while, said, "Roll it out boys, roll it out." After the liquor had been spilled into the street, the owner was locked in the Central Guard House. [23]

Day to day routine at the camp varied little. Reveille sounded at 6:30 in the morning "when every one must be out and answer to his

53

own name at first roll call," followed by the surgeon's call at seven o'clock. The men washed and then ate breakfast. After breakfast the call for Brigade Guard was sounded. The Guard assembled on the parade ground and, as one soldier of the 77th observed, "To see two hundred men in line, all inspecting arms at once, the band playing, officers in full uniform, and men fully equipped, seems quite like actual war besides being a very dressy and imposing scene." By 9 o'clock a.m., company drill commenced and the drill grounds echoed with "the sharp commands of the company officers to 'Order arms!'; 'Shoulder arms!' as the men exercised in squads." At 12:30 in the afternoon came the call to dinner which resulted in "a general scramble – a kind of Bull Run quickstep," those "nearest the head of the line generally faring best." At two o'clock the companies assembled for battalion drill lead by Colonel McKean, which usually culminated with dress parade at four or five o'clock in the afternoon. The volunteers would eat supper and relax around the evening fire until 8:30 p.m., when Tattoo was sounded. Soon after, Taps called them to their tents and lights were extinguished. [24]

Chaplain David Tully (United States Army Military History Institue)

MᶜKEAN'S SUNDAY SCHOOL BOYS GO TO WAR

Each Sunday morning at 11 a.m., the entire regiment assembled for divine worship led by Chaplain David Tully, by order of the strictly devout Colonel McKean. "All officers, non-commissioned officers, musicians and privates of the Regiment who are not excused for sufficient cause, shall . . . attend Divine Service," he ordered. The men were drawn up in companies while Chaplain Tully offered a sermon from the piazza of Commodore Porter's mansion. Owing to this unwavering observance of the Sabbath, the 77th soon became known as "McKean's Sunday School Boys." Not all of the men of the regiment, however, shared the colonel's devotion to the Christian faith. One afternoon Chaplain Tully went around to all the tents, and handed out religious tracts and other readings for the New Yorkers. Some read them, some listened to the chaplain's words of faith, but "some *naughty ones*, when the chaplain passed, lit their pipes with the tracts and puffed their religious reading out in the way of tobacco smoke." [25]

When there was free time or regiment business warranted it, the 77th's soldiers would go into Washington. Musician James A. Barnes (Co. A) Was "at a loss how to begin to speak of affairs in and around Washington, for everywhere you go and almost everything you see here has a warlike aspect. The streets in the city are thronged from morning until night, with officers and soldiers; long trains of army wagons are moving all the while, in every direction." Barnes counted over ninety wagons in one train and was awed by the number of regiments that constantly flowed through the city. Writing anonymously, one well-read member of the 77th held the city in low regard:

> . . . oh such muddy places, I have never before beheld . . . Washington is literally all *pudding* in the streets, it would not equal a western country town; and the inhabitants too, I think may be correctly compared to

> Pickwick's description of Stroud, Rochester, &c., where he says 'the principle productions are soldiers, sailors, Jews, chalk, shrimps, officers, and dock-yard men, the streets presenting a lively and animate appearance, occasioned chiefly by the conviviality of the military. It is truly delightful to see these gallant men stagger along under the influence of an overflow, both of animal and ardent spirits.' The comparison is perhaps severe, but in the main true . . .

Yet while he had "no particular affection for the city," he had a "deep and lasting one for the Capital as the *Capital of our government*" and vowed that "no cowardly and villainous rebel ever be allowed to desecrate it with his presence." [26]

While at Camp Hillhouse, the 77th experienced their first Christmas and New Year away from home. Their tents were "trimmed with ever-greens, and carried out Merry Christmas as far as *show* could do it." Many that Christmas dined on turkey "and the soldier's heart was made glad." Many others "had something good from home and the express office was visited more than once . . . not without effect." For one soldier, however, Christmas and New Year in the southern clime was a far cry from those enjoyed back home:

> We who have been accustomed to northern winters and institutions, could hardly be made to believe that Christmas and New Years could come without a good big snow storm, sleigh rides, balls, parties, oyster-suppers, donations, visits, etc., etc., and yet it did come without either for us. Both Christmas and New Years were as warm and pleasant as October; the boys sat outside their tents in the sun, as they would a pleasant day in March. On New Years

the boys has had a moonlit dance and our tents were comfortable enough without a fire. [27]

New Year's Day brought temporary disappointment for the regiment. The 77th had been apprized by several letters from home that Robert McMichael, one of the proprietors of Congress Hall in Saratoga, had sent "600 cooked turkeys and chickens for their New Year's dinner." Assured that the teams would bring up the feast, the New Yorkers eagerly awaited the holiday meal. Yet it did not come and the men were "obliged to put up with usual rations – beef, pork, beans, bread, sugar, &c." The volunteers grumbled aloud as they remembered McMichael's less than edible provisions offered them while at Cap Schuyler. But the grumbling changed to accolades the *next* day when dinner finally arrived:

> Every company had over 30 lbs. of turkey and chicken, quite enough to give every soldier a good dinner if put in with his sugar, rice, wheat bread, coffee, &c. Didn't every soldier thank McMichael for this feast! And could you have heard the *cheers* – three times three from every company – all that was ever said against McMichael while in Saratoga was taken back, and they sincerely desired that they might sit again at his table, and no word of complaint should ever escape their lips. [28]

One observant volunteer, identifying himself only as *One of the 77th*, in correspondence to the *Saratogian*, visited Washington and the White House on New Year's Day. Viewing the military display of army officers at the White House, he wondered at "the vanity of military men" and offered a wonderful account of his experience:

The President received calls from 11 1-2 to 2 o'clock; from 11 1-2 to 12 1-2, army officers; from that time till 2 the public officers, in full uniform, with epaulets, sword, belt, sash, pistols, &c.; and officers in undress uniform. Generals, Colonels, Majors, Captains and Lieutenants, regardless of rank, rushed in to see 'Old Abe' and his short wife, to shake his hand and smile at his family; and your correspondent among the rest went to the *show*. The Navy band of thirty pieces, all dressed in their red coats and military hats with black feathers, were playing most beautifully.

We passed through the halls and into the green room – shook the President's hand – what a shake – looked upon his short wife, passed through the celebrated 'East Room,' of which we have read, and so out again, taking in all I could at a hasty glance. I left with strange feelings. All I had read about Oriental magnificence, and the splendor of monarchial palaces came to mind, and I said to myself, is this the capital of our free country – the house of the President of the United States? [29]

While many from the 77th wrote home glowing accounts of camp life, not all was well, for Meridian Hill proved to be an unhealthy environment. The unhygienic surroundings of the encampment were described by a medical inspector in January 1862 because of complaints lodged by the regiment. "...the atmosphere is impregnated with a malarial odor, arising from the decomposition of animal matter just below an open field, where a large number of dead horses are deposited upon the surface and allowed to remain and decompose. This, with the rather poor policing of the camp, has given rise to typhoid fever, from which, I regret to say, we have lost ten or twelve men already." [30]

The stench of the decaying horses was overpowering, but the cause of the rise of typhoid fever within the New Yorkers camp was most likely contaminated drinking water. Nevertheless, typhoid made deadly inroads into the regiment. Yet typhoid was not the only concern as Private Shallum West (Co. G) revealed in writing back home to Mr. Bacus in Bacon Hill. "It is very sickly now. The small Pox is all around us." Writing to his mother, Lieutenant Luther Wheeler noted, "The new recruits are dieing off very fast, one dies most every day. None have died from my Co and more are very sick. Mr. Hayes [Private Clark Hayes, Co. I] died last night and has taken up his claim of 'sacred soil' as the boys say when a man dies and is buried. He was buried this afternoon. Many of the new men who come down were unfit for soldier life so the weakest ones die." Unlike the new recruits, Wheeler asserted, "The old veterans are never sick, no fatigue affect them, they are proof against any thing except secsh bullets. The weak ones among them have long since died or been discharged." Before the end of January, however, veteran Privates Otis Holbrook and Dudley See from Company B, Sergeant Smith Herrick and Private William Monroe from Company D, and privates Charles Higgins and Nelson Hopkins, Company E, were dead. So too was Private James O. Green (Co. E). Herrick's death in particular greatly affected his comrades, and Adjutant Winsor B. French wrote that, "He was a noble boy, and had already been promoted; and had he lived would still have advanced. His unbounded integrity and manly bearing made him a subject for promotion and esteem. We all loved him, and his death makes us sick and sad." [31]

Battling disease instead of Rebels, the 77th continued to receive recruits at Camp Hillhouse to replace those who died or became too ill to remain in service. Toward the end of January, Captain Calvin A. Rice (Co. G) and Lieutenant N. Hollister Brown (Co. H), along with Sergeants Seymour Burch (Co. G), Edgar W. Dennison (Co.

K), David A. Thompson (Co. F), and Henry R. Wilcox (Co. I) were detailed to return to New York in order to recruit for the regiment. Captain Rice and Lieutenant Brown set up a recruiting office in a white cottage north of the fairgrounds in Saratoga Springs where recruits assembled before leaving for Camp Hillhouse.

Back in Washington, thirteen-year-old John E. Evans, the youngest to enlist in the 77th, was added to the muster roll. Evans had earlier enlisted in the 52nd New York at New York City, but his mother intervened, and he was discharged from the regiment. Asking why the young teen had enlisted, Evans said to his mother, "Grandmother and you have often told me that Grandfather and Great-uncle served eight years in the war of the Revolution. That an uncle had served in the Mexican War; so I thought I would represent the family in this war." Evans then told his mother in no uncertain terms that, "If you will not let me go I will go to another state and enlist; and will not let you know where I am." Reluctantly accepting her son's stubborn determination to enlist, Evans' mother gave her consent for John to go with his uncle in the 87th New York which was brigaded with the 77th at Washington. Never later explaining why, Evans instead enlisted in the 77th and served first as a musician and then later as a private until January 1865 when he received his discharge from service. Speaking of his enlistment many years after the war, Evans, during a reunion of his comrades, remarked, "I have no regret, as they were a splendid lot of fellows." [32]

By mid-January, the soldiers of the 77th had yet to receive any pay from Uncle Sam, causing one noncommissioned officer to write to the *Saratogian* that he hoped "the good people at home" would "not fail to look after the families of those who had gone to war." How some of the families would "get along between their payments from the government" he did not know, but he thought it was "hard, after enduring the privations of camp life . . . to be harassed by thoughts of a suffering family at home." But payday finally did come on Friday, January 17, with the arrival of "Mr. Cash." Paymaster Major H. P. Andrews was greeted with enthusiasm as he opened his trunk. Companies A, B, and C came at the "double quick" and received their pay. One member of Company C later wrote, "O blessed day, when my eyes first beheld – treasury notes, gold, silver, new pennies – Oh! Oh!" Company D was next in line and Robert Skinner exclaimed in a letter to Professor Works, "I wish you could see some of the fellows today. How brave! How patriotic! Shouts and cheers!" Yet Skinner knew all too well that a "soldier's money goes more rapidly than it comes" and feared that "many will soon be penniless again." By the time Company E was paid, it was dark and Major Andrews left camp with the promise to return the next morning, but after having arrived home "in getting out of the carriage, he fell and broke his leg square off, close to his body." Unfortunately, the rest of the New Yorkers had to wait until the following Monday before they received their pay. [33]

Once paid, it was time to settle debts with the camp sutler. Writing once more to his professor at Fort Edward Institute, Sergeant Skinner remarked that, "It was laughable when our sutler opened his stand a few weeks ago. The boys had no money and he sold them out on trust. For some days he was overwhelmed. His stand was surrounded," and "some climbed trees and looked longingly on the scene." But now, Skinner observed, "they are beginning to curse the sutler." [34]

Now organized with the 85th and 87th New York Regiments, and forming the Third Brigade of the division of Major General Silas Casey, the daily routine had become dull and monotonous as the novelty of camp life began to wear thin among the soldiers of the 77th. But a great commotion swirled about Camp Hillhouse with the sudden arrest of Captain Albert Beach of Company H. The cause of his arrest and concomitant consternation in camp was a private, but libelous letter Beach wrote to his cousin, L. M. Crane, who lived in Milton, just north of Saratoga Springs. In the letter, Captain Beach accused Colonel McKean of "receiving from the Quarter Master [Lucius Shurtleff] a bonus of $25 per month, in addition to a percentage on the profits of his office." While the 77th was at Camp Schuyler, Crane had sought from Colonel McKean the appointment of quarter master, but his request was denied. Still smoldering in anger over McKean's rejection, Crane added additional accusations, and published Captain Beach's letter in the Saratoga *Republican and Sentinel*.[35]

Upon his arrest, Captain Beach was flooded with remorse and wrote McKean a tortured letter of apology from the guard house:

> A day or two since I read the article in the Saratoga Republican and Sentinel which was very abusive and insulting to you and the Quarter Master of the Regiment and which was wholly false. It was purported to be written by a commissioned officer of this Regiment. That officer was no other than myself and knowing what is due you from me as a superior officer and a gentleman whom every officer in the Regiment has reason to cherish the highest respect and esteem, I take this method of doing all in my power to repair the deep injury I have done you in the first place. What I did write was wholly false and it was published with great additions to it which made it very odious. It was a private letter to L. M. Crane of Milton Saratoga Co. N. Y. and written merely for his gratification and he in his treachery to me has had it published with a great deal added to it, and the whole thing is false from beginning to end and I am very glad to do all in my power to show things up to the public in their true light. The above statement I make freely and to be used in any way you may see proper. It is done as

no more than due from me to yourself and Quartermaster Shurtleff...[36]

Colonel McKean responded with Special Order No. 1:

> Captain Albert F. Smith, of Company H, having been placed under arrest for conduct unbecoming an officer and gentleman, in this, that he wrote a false and libelous article against the Colonel of this Regiment, which was printed in the Saratoga Republican and Sentinel newspaper of January 17th of January inst., and the said Captain having confessed that he wrote part of said article, and that the article was wholly false, and having humbly asked pardon for his offense, the Colonel being convinced that malicious men in civil life are greater offenders than the offending Captain, hereby orders that said Captain Albert F. Beach be released from his arrest and permitted to wear his sword...

Released from the guard house, but not his shame, Captain Beach met privately with Colonel McKean, resigned his commission, and returned home.[37]

Not only did the 77th struggle with the boredom of daily routine at Camp Hillhouse, but anxiety began to surface that the war would end without their contribution in battle. At the beginning of the war, both sides felt that the fighting would be brief, perhaps one or two battles deciding the outcome. This notion was badly shaken by the first battle at Bull Run, but most still believed that the war would be short. Robert Skinner wrote in his ongoing correspondence with Professor Works at Fort Edward: "The story of this rebellion will soon be told. My fear is that I shall not be allowed to participate in glorious works. I shall be unwilling to return home until I have shouted amid the crashing ring of that miserable fabric of boasted Southern rights." Another comrade exclaimed, "We are all anxious to move . . . Are we going to lie here always? Can we not have a chance to fight? How can we of the 77th remain quiet while such splendid victories are being won by our western brothers? Mill Spring, Fort Henry, Roanoke, and last of all, Donnelson, haunt us in our sleep, and we feel we must move." One can imagine, then, the New Yorkers excitement when on Sunday evening, February 16, 1862, during dress parade, "the Adjutant [French] rode up, himself and his horse all covered in mud, and announced the 77th was ordered to join Smith's division in Virginia; that the transport teams were ordered, and that every man must be ready to march tomorrow morning at three o'clock, with two days rations." Cheers roared through the camp and "every man seemed anxious to out do his neighbors in shouts of joy." [38]

Upon hearing the news, the 85th New York, with whom the 77th had been brigaded since they arrived in Washington, expressed their regret at the 77th being called away and their good feeling for the regiment "by a beautiful serenade from their band." Major A. J. Wellman of the 85th made a parting speech to which Colonel McKean warmly responded. The band then marched through the street of every company, followed by the commissioned officers of the 85th. Stopping in front of McKean's tent, they played "Home, Sweet Home." Writing a letter home as the band played, *One of the 77th* noted that it was "peculiarly affecting, just at this time. While we are surrounded by all the excitement and danger of war, we don't forget our homes. We are not enervated by thinking and hearing of home; tears may fill our eyes as we think of those who we love, but they are not tears of regret that we are soldiers, or that we have left behind us our friends. No, we are made stronger and more determined to strike a blow that will tell against this most accursed rebellion."[39]

M^CKEAN'S SUNDAY SCHOOL BOYS GO TO WAR

With excitement running high, the remainder of the evening was a scene marked by noise and confusion. Assistant Surgeon Stevens remembered that "the pounding and tearing of boards, the shouting of men and the braying of mules, combined in a grand uproar. Bonfires blazed from every part of camp, and the whole night was spent in tearing down quarters and loading the stuff into army wagons as they presented themselves in great numbers." For the doctor, it was a rare sight as he looked upon "a hundred fires, and the men and teams moving about them like spectres." [40]

Monday morning came and brought with it a tremendous storm of rain and sleet, and the volunteers began their march through mud nearly up to their knees. Traveling slowly because of the mud, the men and over 106 mule team wagons carrying the regiment's baggage, tents, and supplies formed a line down Fourteenth Street from their camp extending all the way to the White House. Coming to the Chain Bridge, the wet and muddy men "climbed the ladder to get upon the tow-path, and having crossed . . . struck the Langley Turnpike and traveled for the 3d Brigade, which we found at about 2 p.m." Colonel McKean sent out Adjutant French and Quarter Master Shurtleff in advance of the regiment to pick out a camping ground. To the New Yorkers, the chosen site seemed hardly habitable. Where once stood a thicket of scrub pines, were now only stumps and brush. For George Stevens, the prospect of camping amid the stumps and brush was rather forbidding. Describing the scene as he surveyed the camp ground for those back home, one volunteer wrote, "Think once of being set down one of those pine plane lots around Saratoga, where the wood has been cut off, and the stumps from three to four feet high stand as thick as hay stubble, brush all over the ground." By now the rain and sleet had turned to snow and the ground was blanketed with several inches of wet slush, yet the men, "tired and wet, cold and hungry," pitched their tents, cooked their suppers, and turned in for the night. The next morning rain deepened the mud while the volunteers put their camp in order." [41]

The division to which the 77th was assigned was commanded by Brigadier General William Farrar "Baldy" Smith. Born in St. Alban's, Vermont, on February 17, 1824, Smith graduated fourth in his class at West Point in 1845. Prior to the outbreak of the Civil War, Smith served as an engineer officer and instructor at West Point. At the beginning of the war, he was commissioned Colonel of the 3rd Vermont, and was promoted to Brigadier General of Volunteers and assigned command of the Second Division of the Army of the Potomac.

The 77th joined the 33rd New York, 49th New York, and the 7th Maine to form the Third Brigade, commanded by Brigadier General John Wynn Davidson. Now 38-years-old, General Davidson was born in Fairfax County, Virginia. His grandfather had been an officer in the Continental Army during the Revolution, and his father graduated from West Point in 1815. A classmate of "Baldy" Smith at West Point, he subsequently was assigned frontier duty in Kansas and Wisconsin, and took part in the Mexican War, fighting mainly in California with the Army of the West. Davidson was promoted in 1855 to Captain of the 1st Dragoons, and fought Indians in New Mexico and California where he received a wound in a skirmish with Jicarilla Apaches. At the beginning of the Civil War, Davidson was stationed at Fort Tejon, near Los Angeles, and was called back to the Washington defenses. He was commissioned Brigadier General of Volunteers in February of 1862, when he took command of the Third Brigade.

The 77th's new camp was christened Camp Griffin, and the New Yorkers quickly settled into army routine. One volunteer complained, "Details, details every day; 1st Central Grand guard, then Division Guard, then fatigue duty, then picket." For Sergeant Skinner, however, Camp Griffin offered the novelty of target shooting. Organized practice with live ammunition was quite rare during the war. It was mostly informal with soldiers going out in small groups on their own, sometimes with a few of their officers, trying out their muskets on ready targets such as trees, fence posts or small games. But General Davidson, a steady if not remarkable officer, ordered "two companies of the best marksmen in each Regiment" of the brigade to be "drilled in Target practice.[42]

Those not detailed for target practice and instructions as skirmishers took their turn on the picket line. Picket duty, while taxing, was not dangerous as no Rebels had been seen along the line of the Third Brigade for months. For one volunteer, the view looking out across "Secessia" was "nothing but woods, woods, woods, large oak and chestnut." Yet he offered the readers of the *Saratogian* a graphic account of his experience on the line:

> ... Yesterday I went on the picket lines, and saw one farm that looked really like living. There is an old-fashioned, one story, white-washed, front-on-the-back-side farmhouse, gambrel-roofed barn, and comfortable outbuildings, and what I have not seen before, the real Virginia rail fence, laid up in good shape. As we approached the house, a kind looking old man saluted us and seemed pleased to answer all our questions. An old lady was carrying in some firewood, and two young ladies showed themselves in the door, looking as if they would say, 'come in, we are in favor of union,' but we did not get to go in, thinking perhaps it would be better to call again. We shant forget the Virginia girls ... We also went to Lewinsville – what a ville! The principle house a little brown cottage – doors and windows all knocked out, and the inside badly damaged.

A church, once painted white, stands out alone, and looks God-forsaken indeed; the other houses are made up of one little negro hut, one tenant house, blacksmith shop, *minus* blacksmith, corn barn minus corn, and one or two little buildings too mean to mention. Near by a beautiful peach orchard, the only redeeming feature of the place – that's Lewinsville. [43]

On Sunday evening, February 23, Colonel McKean received a command to take the 77th on a thorough reconnaissance towards Vienna – their first expedition into the enemy's country! His orders were to "march at 2 a.m. on Monday . . . to the point where the Lewinsville and Freedom Hill Road crosses the turnpike leading to Leesburgh." The news of the movement spread through the regiment like a summer brushfire as the camp was ablaze with excited anticipation. Looking upon the scene with considerable amusement, Assistant Surgeon Stevens observed that, "Some who had been on the sick list, and were excused from camp duty, sought . . . permission to accompany the expedition, while a few who had been, up to this time, well, were earnest in their application to be excused from the march." [44]

The regiment formed at "ten o'clock Sunday night in the thick darkness, darkness of the blackest and most intense degree." Stevens remembered that, "One could scarcely see his neighbor whose shoulder touched his own." A guide from brigade headquarters appeared to lead them to their destination. Passing through a number of regiments, the 77th observed strict silence and marched into the night. The roads were in a frightful condition and knee deep in mud. Many of the volunteers lost both their shoes and stockings in the mud. Some of the sick who could not be kept from falling in the ranks now fell out and returned to camp. Although only a distance of six miles, the regiment did not reach their destination until 4 o'clock in the morning. Finding "bough houses which had been used by rebel cavalry," Colonel McKean deployed two companies as skirmishers with the remaining companies formed in detachments in support. After remaining concealed in the woods for several hours, and after "seeing nothing of interest or importance occurring," the 77th returned to Camp Griffin. Except for a few "babies," the New Yorkers returned in good order without stragglers. [45]

While the 77th and the rest of the Army of the Potomac remained static, pressure in Washington mounted for a general movement against the Confederate forces commanded by Brigadier General Joseph Johnston, ensconced behind their fortifications at Manassas, a mere 25 miles from the Union capital. Much of that pressure was focused upon George "Little Mac" Briton McClellan. Fresh from victory in western Virginia, McClellan came to Washington to assume command of the Army of the Potomac in July 1861. The youngest major general in the United States Army at 35, McClellan was a man of overwhelming charm who appeared well-cast as the triumphant young Napoleon come to save the Union: "short and broad-shouldered, with a quick eye and jaunty confidence, he never displayed anything less than a commanding presence." His men quickly came to idolize him, and years after the war, McClellan's name still stirred feelings of deep affection and regard among many veterans. [46]

By November, Little Mac assumed command of all Federal forces. Under McClellan's leadership, the Army of the Potomac had undergone a profound transformation from a defeated and demoralized collection of men broken down by the rout at Bull Run to an efficient, well-oiled military machine of nearly 150,000 men, the largest army ever before brought together on North American soil. Yet McClellan did nothing about the Confederate army only 25 miles away threatening Washington. Nor did he move against the Confederate batteries across the Potomac River that effectively prevented vital commercial shipping from ascending the river. This inactivity caused many in Washington to openly cast doubt upon McClellan's allegiance to the Union. The Northern press, Congress, and members of Lincoln's cabinet who had once hailed him as the Union's savior, now condemned McClellan as a cowardly procrastinator at best, a treacherous traitor to the Union at worst.

The reason for McClellan's refusal to move against Joseph Johnston's Rebel army at Manassas was a persistent, peculiar, continual hallucination that marked his military career: he was vastly outnumbered by a well-equipped, well-disciplined, entrenched enemy horde. Adding fuel to this remarkable delusion was a trusted private detective, Allan Pinkerton, whom McClellan brought to Washington. Pinkerton had a particular talent for estimating enemy troops at two or three times their actual numbers. It was this private detective who supplied McClellan with the incredible estimate that Joe Johnston's command at Manassas was at least 100,000 men. In fact, there were no more than about 50,000 soldiers under Johnston's command. Nevertheless, believing without question Pinkerton's intelligence reports, McClellan petitioned President Lincoln for an army of 273,000 men, including 250 regiments of infantry, 100 batteries of 600 guns, 20 regiments of cavalry, five engineering regiments, and a strong supporting naval force. Without this army of leviathan proportions, McClellan asserted he could not move against Manassas.

Despite Lincoln's repeated attempts to persuade McClellan to move against Manassas, "Little Mac" held firm to his obsession and continued to argue for more men before an advance could be made. By February 1862, an exasperated Lincoln ordered a general advance of all Union forces to take place on George Washington's birthday. February 22 arrived, however, and the Army of the Potomac stayed put in their camps, idle except for the firing of salutes in honor of Washington. At Camp Griffin, the 77th formed in line and "Washington's Farewell Address was read to the regiment at 11 o'clock, and at dress parade we had a flag raising, and a capital speech from the Colonel." [47]

Three days prior, Johnston was in Richmond meeting with Jefferson Davis and his cabinet discussing the fate of his army. All knew that in its present position at Manassas, Johnston's army was overextended and badly outnumbered, and that it must withdraw to better defensive ground to strongly protect Richmond, as the Federals would surely soon advance. Their only fear was that Johnston would not be able to retreat soon as rains had made the Virginia roads around Manassas virtually impassable rivers of mud.

While the Confederates waited for the roads to dry up, McClellan was formulating his own plan. Firmly fixed in his mind that a direct assault on Manassas was suicide, McClellan turned to a new plan of campaign. He would outflank Johnston by an amphibious landing at Urbanna on the Rappahannock River due east of Richmond. This would maneuver Johnston out of his entrenchments at Manassas by requiring him to shift his forces southeast to defend Richmond and give battle on McClellan's terms. The result would be the complete control of Virginia and the death knell of secession. Lincoln reluctantly accepted the Urbanna plan, but in so doing, he ordered the Army of the Potomac reorganized into army corps and named the officers who were to command the corps. Erasmus D. Keyes took command of the Fourth Corps to which the 77th's Third Brigade was assigned. Furthermore, Lincoln ordered that the Army of the Potomac must begin its move no later than March 18.

No sooner had this taken place than the Urbanna plan was made useless, as Johnston began to evacuate his troops from their entrenchments all through the weekend of March 8 and 9. By having them take up a new position behind the Rappahannock, Johnston had to abandon a number of batteries of heavy guns on the Potomac. At Manassas, the soldiers marched to the supply depots where they were turned loose to help themselves. In no time at all they filled their haversacks with large quantities of food and their canteens with whiskey. The cavalry rear guard torched the depots and a huge meat curing plant, and the soldiers gazed upon an eerie glow of yellow and blue flames which spread the smell of fried bacon for twenty miles around.

News of the retreat broke in Washington on Sunday evening, March 9, Little Mac was in conference with President Lincoln and Secretary of War Stanton when word came of the retreat, and he quickly hurried off to headquarters and began issuing orders for an advance against Manassas. At midnight, the 77th was awakened to unexpected orders to be ready to "march with five days rations at 4 a.m." The order to march was read and "the whole camp was instantly alive with busy men. Some were cooking, some singing, and . . . all were packing for a speedy march." George Stevens remembered that, "Little rest we got that night; the hammer and axe were plied vigorously in tearing down quarters and packing stores." Company C sang patriotic songs as they formed into line, and the 77th was ready at the appointed hour. The movement of the whole army was for Stevens a sublime spectacle, "an immense line of troops pouring along hour after hour, stretched over the hills as far as the eye could reach; a hundred and twenty thousand troops on the move! Just beyond and above them, in the gray sky of the morning, hung a beautiful rainbow." Soon it began to rain and continued to do so throughout the day. [48]

The night before, Sergeant Skinner was out on picket with four companies of the regiment, and at daybreak began to march to Lewinsville to rendezvous with the rest of the 77th. "Not being allowed to return to our camp, we were deprived of many of our little necessaries. We had neither slept nor rested during the night. It began to rain at sunrise, and rained throughout our march as usual and we pickets had neither breakfast or dinner." Yet, "we all felt stimulated at the thought of an advance. We felt sure we were looking for someone to fight. And altogether we had a jolly time." Along the march, a slave inquired of Colonel McKean if it was true that runaways were shut up in jail. McKean answered that that was not so, to which the slave exclaimed, "Then this chile goes," and began walking northward. [49]

By 5 o'clock in the afternoon the 77th arrived tired, drenched, and dirty at Flint Hill near Fairfax Court House. Doctor Stevens was awed by the panorama before him: "Great numbers of troops had already occupied the fields and the whole country seemed alive with men and horses, artillery and wagons." The men devoted their time to making themselves as comfortable as possible under their shelter tents, and as evening came, the hills were illuminated with countless campfires. Few in the 77th slept that night, partly from the continued excitement of the movement, and partly because they were unaccustomed to sleeping upon a wet ground with only a single blanket wrapped around them. Most stood in groups "about the camp fires, talking in low tones and wondering what was to happen in the morning." With the early morning sun shining forth upon the "hills dotted with tents and stacked muskets came the disappointing news that Manassas was deserted." [50]

With McClellan pondering his next move, Stevens took a pleasant ride to Fairfax Court House:

> The village was pleasantly located on high ground, surrounded by fine groves. It contained some pretty residences which were occupied by officers at head-quarters: their

horses, in some instances, being picketed on the porticos, and in others in the kitchen. The village was nearly deserted by its own people, not more than fifty of the original inhabitants being left, though the population of the town before the war was nearly six-hundred. Houses which were deserted were generally stripped of everything. The court house was a solid brick building of very limited dimensions, with a little bell swinging in a comical looking steeple. The court house was by no means an exception to the general rule of destruction; the seats were torn out, and the judge's bench had been split into pieces, and nearly all carried by the pocket full, as relics. At one of the houses where the family remained, a party reined up and made some inquiries of the *pater familias*, a hang-dog looking specimen, with an old slouched hat covered to the crown with rusty crape, a mark of second-hand gentility in these parts. He said that 'this yer war' had caused such a famine among the people, that nearly all of them have been obliged to leave; some had gone to Washington and some to Richmond, 'a right smart lot of them had gone to Richmond.' He had 'reckoned onct or twict' that he would have to go too, but he 'had succeeded in hanging on so long.'

Others traveled to Centreville and Manassas. One soldier writing under the nom deplume of *DIXIE*, described what he saw to the folks back home in Ballston Spa:

> Centreville is a miserable looking place of some fifteen old houses and a small Episcopal Church. The fortifications of the Rebels there scarcely deserve the name. A single division with three batteries of artillery could have taken the place in twenty minutes. There was no preparation made to defend either flanks of the position. The idea

of making a stand at Centreville never could have been seriously entertained by the Rebels. Their encampment of log huts show that they have had a large force during the winter at Centreville and Manassas. They had a graveyard inside of their fortifications. I counted 26 graves recently filled and one open. They seem to be abundantly supplied with everything. In their huts I found biscuit, flour, hams, salt, fresh beef, and even dough on the tables. Their quarters were far more comfortable than our troops had around Washington. Their encampments are continuous from Centreville to Manassas. They had corduroyed the road between the two villages and covered it with clay. [51]

Later *DIXIE* crossed the Bull Run at Blackburn's Ford where the battle of July 18 was fought. On the old battlefield lay the bleached bones of both horses and men killed in the struggle. Portions of human skeletons protruded from shallow graves hastily covered over by their comrades. Strewn about the ground as far as the eye could see were shell fragments, solid shot, and broken muskets. "Quaker Guns," old chestnut logs with blackened ends, were mounted in some of the embrasures, indicating to DIXIE that "the enemy has apparently no artillery, either at Centreville or Manassas this winter." [52]

McClellan now gave up his Urbana plan, and proposed instead to move against Richmond from a point seventy-five miles southeast of the Confederate capital at the Federal-held Fortress Monroe. On March 13, Lincoln approved the new plan after stipulating that both Manassas and Washington must be secure by sufficient troops to protect against a future Rebel attack. Jubilant, Little Mac issued a proclamation to the Yankee camps: "I have held you back that you might give the death-blow to the rebellion that has distracted our once happy country . . . The moment for action has arrived, and I know you wish to be, -- on the decisive battlefield." The coming campaign up the Peninsula would require "great, heroic exertions, rapid and long marches, desperate combats, privations," but McClellan assured the soldiers of the Army of the Potomac of victory in a righteous cause." [53]

On March 15, the 77th began the march toward Alexandria at daybreak to board their transports to the Peninsula. The morning was overcast and a drizzling rain began to fall upon the men. The rain became a heavy, drenching, down pour, making marching very unpleasant. Filing down the Little River Turnpike, the New Yorkers were afforded "a view of the mighty column for miles to the front, and at other times we could see it pouring onward an endless stream of cavalry, infantry, artillery, and wagons, far from the rear." Making no halt for dinner, the 77th turned off into a piece of woods at Clouds Mill. Colonel McKean shouted against the rain, "Boys, make yourselves as comfortable as possible," and the men set up camp. Now the rain came down in sheets. "We were thoroughly wet," wrote Robert Skinner, "even the clothes in our knapsacks." The ground soon became so flooded that sleeping upon the ground became untenable. For the sergeant, it was a miserable night:

> Though tired, we had to keep stirring both for want of a place to rest and also to prevent being chilled. We built good fires – the only comfort we could enjoy. During the night the rain ceased. Felt like sleeping, but my clothes being wet I feared to lie down. Commenced to dry them piece by piece, stockings first – pulled them off and stood barefooted in the mud. While holding them over the fire I grew quite sleepy, nodded, and reeled – staggered, tumbled, gathered up, awoke with my foot in the midst of the fire. Caught up my stockings, wrung the water out of them and began to sing. *The conquer we must.* Having partially dried my clothes I threw myself upon some pine boughs and slept.

Corporal William H. Wright (Co. K) thought better of rain and mud and quietly "took a French leave for Alexandria, where I got a good, hot supper." [54]

The next morning brought more misery to Skinner and trouble for Corporal Wright. "Morning came, but brought us Hunger without bread," Skinner complained. "The rain had so swollen the creek so as to cut off communication with the city. The use of firearms forbidden I took five smooth stones and went rabbit hunting. We went three times during the day without success." Skinner and his comrades concluded that "foraging was a humbug and returned to camp." At night, fortunately, provisions arrived and Skinner "feasted on raw bacon and Boston crackers." When Wright returned to camp that morning, he learned that he had been reported by his sergeant as missing and "was called before Lieutenant Colonel Henderson, who said as he ordered me to go to my quarters, 'I will see if a ball and chain will keep you.'" [55]

The 77th named their most disagreeable stay near Cloud's Mill "Camp Misery." There they remained for several days, waiting to embark for Fortress Monroe. On the Virginia Peninsula, the volunteers would pass the test of battle, yet few would die from shot, shell, or musket fire. Instead scores would be felled by typhoid fever and malaria. They entered the campaign filled with optimism, but would leave with the burden and humiliation of defeat.

3

"GET INTO YOUR TENTS BOYS!"

On the evening of March 22, the order to march for the transports at Alexandria was read during dress parade. Hearing the good news, and glad to be leaving Camp Misery, the "77th gave three hearty cheers." The next morning they marched with the Second Division, and in Alexandria joined the other divisions of Keyes' corps, as well as troops from Samuel Heintzelman's corps. *DIXIE* surveyed the scene and was struck by all that befell his eyes. "East and North river steamboats and barges lay in the harbor at Alexandria and Washington in great numbers." Great numbers indeed! In order to transport the Army of the Potomac, McClellan had amassed the greatest flotilla ever before seen in North America, consisting of 389 vessels. Assistant Secretary of War, John Tucker, chartered every available steamboat on the east coast. One-hundred-thirteen Hudson River excursion boats, trans-Atlantic packets, Long Island side-wheelers, and Philadelphia ferry boats were chartered at a cost of $23,400 per day. Rounding out the flotilla were 276 schooners, barges, and canal boats outfitted to transport animals, artillery, and necessary war material. [1]

The 77th embarked at Alexandria on three different vessels. As it took the better part of the day to load the regiment, they "dropped down the river six miles and anchored for the night." At an early hour the next morning, the boats transporting the New Yorkers, along with twenty other vessels, weighed anchor and steamed down the Potomac. For *DIXIE* "the fleet presented a grand sight as it glided quietly down that grand old stream" for "the Potomac is one of the most beautiful rivers on the continent." Assistant Surgeon Stevens was equally affected by the view: "How different was all this from our Hudson! The country bordering the river is beautiful; nature has made everything for it." As they passed Mount Vernon, "every eye was turned toward the spot made sacred by the ashes of our great and glorious Washington . . . the bells of the fleet tolling." Looking at Washington's tomb in the midst of a clump of firs near the house, *DIXIE* thought "through all time may the star-spangled banner wave over the Mount so dear to every American heart." [2]

Around noon, the 77th passed Matthias Point, "where the blackened chimneys of the notorious thief and rebel Floyd stand as a fitting monument of his folly and his crime." Past the Point, the vessels carrying the 77th joined with the main fleet of transports, and "several times during the day we counted seventy vessels within sight at the same time." Toward evening squalls blew through the fleet and the men were ordered below to render the boats steady. In one of the vessels, Sergeant Skinner, already suffering from a cold that left him with "a stubborn hoarseness," spent a miserable night:

> I foresaw a scramble for sleeping places and therefore secured one by sprawling myself on the floor. Thought myself well-fixed but soon a heavy pane of glass

fell edgewise from a beam above and nicely sawed my underlip to the teeth. How lucky it did not fall on the floor and break! The blood started and so did I! On reaching the outer deck, I was assailed on all sides with, 'What ails you?' 'What's the matter?' etc., etc. Being horse I whispered to one and told him to proclaim it to everyone that asked, and thus I was relieved from answering foolish questions. After a while I stopped the blood, washed and dressed the wound, patched it with adhesive plaster, went back and found two fellows disputing over my bed. I decided the question according to the best of my judgment. Concluded that the plaster was not the proper thing. Got up, tore it off, put on a tobacco leaf, and retired for the night. [3]

By morning, the 77th awoke lying anchor under the guns of Fortress Monroe. The *U. S. S. Monitor* was nearby "with its steam up watching for her former antagonist [*C. S. S. Merrimack*] to make an appearance from Norfolk." Gazing upon the Monitor, Sergeant Skinner thought, "She is the most contemptible looking thing I ever saw in the shape of a boat. In fact she looks like a short piece of plank afloat, on each end of which is a piece of brickbrat and in the middle is an old fashioned round snuff box." Pulling up anchor, the 77th sailed to Hampton. There they landed, and stepped onto the banks of the James River. On shore, George Stevens noted the noise and chaos of the Army of the Potomac landing: "The whole army was pouring out upon this shore, and at Fortress Monroe. Dense masses of infantry, long trains of artillery and thousands of cavalry, with unnumbered army wagons and mules, were mingled in grand confusion along the shore; the neighing of horses, the braying of mules, the rattle of wagons and artillery, and the sound of many voices, mingled in one grand inharmonious concert." [4]

Once ashore, the 77th waited for its baggage. During the wait several soldiers explored Hampton, which now lay in ruins. The previous fall John Magruder, commander of the Army of the Peninsula, burned the village to the ground after reading a newspaper story, which proved to be no more than rumor that the Yankees intended to create a settlement for runaway slaves at Hampton. *DIXIE* recorded for Saratogians back home his observations and actions as the regiment awaited the order to march:

> Here we were delighted to find the peach and apricot trees in blossom. And in the gardens we gathered flowers enough to make a beautiful and fragrant bouquet. Not a dwelling on the west side of the inlet escaped the torch of the rebel vandals, except one solitary hut owned by an aged negroe. The churches of the living God were not even spared. The Episcopal Church, built in the form of a cross, was the oldest church in the Dominion. This edifice, rendered sacred by the hallowed association of two hundred years, was not consumed by the flames, but its blackened walls battered with hammers to reach the contents of its corner stone. Monuments and tombstones which for centuries have marked the places of the sleeping dead were designedly broken into pieces . . . On the east side of the inlet stands the summer residence of the late President Tyler, and near by it that of Mallory. The former we visited with three friends and found it crowded with contrabands from the cellar to the attic. They were learning to read. Suitable books have been furnished by the Boston Tract Society. Mrs. Tyler's fine bedstead and wardrobe are now used by a family of contrabands. [5]

That night, the New Yorkers marched half way between Hampton and Newport News, and bivouacked on the ground of a fine plantation on the shore of Hampton Roads. "The encampment was handsomely located and the weather as pleasant as your finest days in May or June." While there, Corporal David Weatherwax was shaken by "a very sad scene. Two men had been found sleeping at their posts while doing guard duty, and the Colonel ordered the regiment out to witness their punishment. The guards came forward with the prisoners in charge. Colonel McKean told them the penalty of such a crime is death; 'but,' said he. 'I will take the responsibility of pardoning you, but the next man who is convicted of a similar offense, DIES.'" If the New Yorkers had not yet divined the serious nature of military duty in war, McKean's threat no doubt provided a vivid illustration. [6]

Impressed by what he witnessed, Private Charles A. Blanchard (Co. A) vowed to remain alert and not to sleep during his turn at picket duty. Perhaps too alert for his own good:

> ... The right and left company were detailed for picket and telegraph line. It was my turn to be number one near the reserve. After the picket was established it was the duty of number one to form a line back to camp so as to give the alarm if pickets were attacked. I was particularly ordered not to fire unless attacked. It was a dark and rainy night. It was almost time for me to be relieved when I heard what sounded like a company of men coming from towards the enemy's line. In a trembling, whispering voice, I said Halt! All was quiet for a short time, then I heard the noise as before. Listening, very attentively, the tramp sounded nearer, when in my excitement I drew up my rifle and fired in the direction of the tramping, when I heard a terrible scampering. About the same time number two fired and then number three and so on down the camp, before the report of the last gun ceased to be

heard and the . . . corps was ready for action. To quiet the line the sergeant of the guard and I walked up to number two, gave the countersign and 'all is well,' and so on down the line to camp. In the morning some of the boys relived from picket brought in some of the dead, of which I ate for breakfast in the shape of pork chops. But it was a long while ere I heard the last of the episode. [7]

There the 77th remained but for a few days when an order came at midnight for the army to march the next morning. At daybreak, George Stevens and several other officers mounted their horses and rode to Fortress Monroe to procure much needed medical stores and quarter master material which was also in short supply. Along the road they passed men cooking their breakfast and artillery batteries rushing toward Newport News. After passing through countless sentinels and exchanging signs and countersigns, they reached the fortress. At the door of the citadel, Stevens wrote "we were halted by a sentinel, and each examined for the countersign. The sentinel called the corporal of the guard; who after satisfying him that we were Union officers shouted to the sergeant. The great iron door ground upon its massive hinges as it swung open just enough to permit the sergeant to squeeze through, and again it was closed, and the heavy bolts rung as they flew back." Returning with the officer of the guard, the heavy door opened slowly, and Stevens and company were admitted to the fort. After obtaining the needed supplies, they returned to the regiment. [8]

Returning to camp, Stevens discovered Baldy Smith's division in column and on the road. With Smith's soldiers in the lead on the James River Road, the 77th marched as far as Deep Creek. Porter's division had already reached Great Bethel on the right, and the New Yorkers "could see huge columns of smoke rising in that direction, and hear the roar of artillery." An aide to General Davidson rode up with news that the Rebels were up ahead in line of battle. The 77th, hearts pounding expecting to face the enemy for the first time, swung into battle line and advanced through patches of woods and cleared fields, but no more than a few Confederate cavalry pickets were seen. The Southern troopers were fired upon by a Parrott gun, which sent them galloping toward Yorktown. [9]

The New York regiment followed the retreating Rebels and entered "into their camp just deserted – fires not out yet, and the beds of the varments not cold." The column "marched no farther, but halted and slept in the open field." Robert Skinner rose from slumber the next morning expecting to advance, "But . . . we were disappointed . . . we were brought into line faced about and marched back about 4 miles." Skinner was not alone as "bitter indignation pervaded our ranks! Many were the Horrid curses heard upon the perfidious heads of the cowardly Rebels! But such is war, and we must yield to the powers that be!" [10]

On the march back to a new encampment, two miles shy of Newport News, the 77th passed through a piece of woods, and came within sight of what appeared to be a Confederate battery. Advancing toward the battery, Corporal Weatherwax was "expecting every moment to see the infernal thing belch forth a shower of leaden hail, but none came." Closing in on the battery, the New Yorkers "found an old ox cart minus the box, a large wooden mortar '10 inch bore' with a hogshead in its mouth." "There is the first Quaker gun we have seen on the Peninsula," one officer remarked. Colonel McKean told the officer, "You must sketch it," which the officer did. [11]

Camped on the bank of the James River, men could daily be seen bathing and harvesting the rich supply of oysters. One day as several hundred men had gathered in the river, Lieutenant William Douglas (Co. A), who was on the picket line, spotted a gunboat steaming down the river. It was the *C. S. S. Teaser*, a wooden tug that dated to about 1855, now outfitted with two 32-pounder guns assigned to the James River Squadron to lay mines in the James to prevent Federal vessels navigation upriver. Douglas called to the major in command of the picket line and pointed out the gunboat. The major reined up his horse, and after examining the boat through his field glass, said, "she must be up to some mischief as she has her steam up." At the same moment, Assistant Surgeon Stevens was enjoying a quiet walk back from visiting the sick in the hospital wards. Holding wild flowers he had picked along the way, the doctor saw the *Teaser* rapidly steaming toward the men dredging for oysters, and assumed it was a Union gunboat. But a puff of smoke from the Rebel gunboat, and the shriek of a shell overhead quickly disabused Stevens from that notion. The shell burst a few yards from the Yankees in the river. Pandemonium erupted as the startled men rushed from the water. As the *Teaser* threw a couple more shells at the Yankees, Captain Renel Arnold (Co. A) called out to those in camp, "Get into your tents, boys! Get into your tents!" Simultaneously, Captain Arnold ran as fast as he could to his own tent, fell to the ground, and "pressed nose as close as he could into the sand." Following Arnold's call to the tents, a soldier in Company B rushed into his tent and called out to his comrade, "Come into the tent, John, you'll get hit standing out there." [12]

C. S. S. Teaser (Library of Congress)

Not all panicked, however. A squad of cavalry came charging up to the riverbank and fired at the gunboat. Captain Benjamin Judson (Co. C) was also at the riverbank with Lieutenant Luther Wheeler (Co. C). When the first shell burst exploded, he ordered up a section of the brigade battery, but before it could get into position to fire "the gunboat changed front and disappeared, throwing shells as it went, over and in our camp vicinity, which, because of the elevation of our position, spent their fury in the woods beyond our camp." Stevens later remembered, "from that day on soldiering lost its attraction for a good number of men and the ranks of the regiment began to thin out." The first casualty was Captain Arnold, who quietly resigned his commission the next day and returned home." [13]

While McClellan positioned the Federal army to advance up the Peninsula, fifty-two-year-old Confederate Major General John Bankhead Magruder was busy preparing to meet him. Speaking with a lisp, and uniformed in dramatic elegance, the Rebel commander was tall and handsome with a full head of hair, bushy sideburns, and a superbly manicured mustache. Known in the prewar army as "Prince John," he possessed considerable theatrical flair. To relieve boredom of peacetime garrison duty, Magruder reveled in singing in a clear tenor songs of his own composition, and staging concerts and amateur theatricals in which he always played a leading role.

Finding himself critically short of war material, Magruder could hardly muster more than 10,000 soldiers for combat. He constructed an advance line of infantry outposts and artillery redoubts across the Peninsula about twelve miles from Fortress Monroe. Never intending to hold this line, it was primarily meant to block Little Mac from viewing the main defensive line Magruder was hurriedly constructing several miles up the Peninsula. Known as the Yorktown line, the defenses ran from Mulberry Island on the James River to Yorktown on the York River, including the fortifications on Gloucester Point on the north bank of the river. The strongest parts of the line were its flanks with heavy guns at Yorktown and Gloucester Point – preventing any passage on the York – and batteries on Mulberry Island guarding the James. Between the James and York Rivers flanks, Magruder constructed a string of rifle pits, redoubts, and fortifications behind the Warwick River. A sluggish stream 20 to 30 feet wide, and bordered by marshes, the Warrick originated a bit west of Yorktown and crossed the Peninsula, flowing into the tidal marshes of the James at Mulberry Island. On the Warwick were two gristmill dams at Lee's Mill and Wynn's Mill. Magruder enlarged the millponds by building three more dams, thus turning the Warwick into a powerful military obstacle. The line was studded with artillery, but woefully short on manpower. Magruder would have to be at his theatrical best if he was to stall McClellan along the Yorktown line, while waiting for reinforcements from Richmond.

On April 4 at 6 a.m., the Army of the Potomac was formed into column to begin its march to Richmond. Backed by a reserve infantry division, a brigade of Regulars, and the reserve artillery, the Federal advance would be two-pronged. On the right was Samuel

Heintzelman's corps, ordered to proceed on the direct road to Yorktown. On the Lee's Mills Road on the left, was Earasmus Keyes' corps, the 77th's Third Brigade, Smith's division, in the vanguard of the column. Riding with the Third Brigade was a New York Times correspondent who recorded the inaugural moment, stating, "The day was all that could be wished; officers and men were filled with enthusiasm, and never did stouter hearts move to more willing tread. 'On to Richmond' had been the soldier's dream and anticipation, and it was about to be realized. The General's [Davidson] eye, at a glance, took in the *status* of his brigade, and a brave heart and head gave the word 'Forward,' and the column moved." [14]

The day was warm and clear. Carrying 50 to 60 pounds on their backs and 60 rounds of ammunition, Sergeant Orrin P. Rugg (Co. G) soon observed that "the boys began to throw their things away having more than they thought they could carry. All extra clothing, under clothing, and in fact overcoats, blankets, rubber blankets and every such thing strewed the road from this point." Unlike these soldiers divesting themselves of anything deemed unnecessary, Rugg "was bound to stick by my blanket and things for well I knew I should need them as we have no tents with us and we were obliged to lie down at night with nothing but the heavens over us." As George Stevens recalled, the "roads which were at first dry and firm, were badly cut up, and great difficulty was experienced in getting the trains along." [15]

After crossing Watt's Creek, the column's skirmisher's encountered Rebel pickets. Keyes ordered the column closed up, but the pickets retreated from the Third Brigade's 7th Maine's skirmishers. The column, the Third Brigade still in the lead, then continued on about two miles before the country opened up and Confederate fortifications at Young's Mill became visible about 1,000 yards in advance of some woods. Smith immediately deployed three regiments from his Second Brigade and moved onward toward the Rebel works. A few shots were fired, wounding one private of the 5th Vermont before the butternuts hastily evacuated their fortifications.

Upon entering the well-constructed works, the 77th found fires burning with rations half-cooked. With "five large barracs capable of holding 4 or 5 thousand troops," Sergeant Rugg found Young's Mill "not a very interesting place." Still, Rugg was happy that the enemy "had cut and run and left us the fort," for "it was on a hill and to reach it we would have to cross a ravine deep and almost impossible except by a narrow road and if they stayed there, they might have given us some trouble." Halting for the night, pickets were sent out and the men bedded down, Rugg no doubt pleased that he kept his blanket. [16]

At dawn on April 5, the Third Brigade again advanced with the 7th Maine thrown out as skirmishers. Rain fell early and continued in torrents, rendering the roads nearly impassable for army wagons and artillery. As Assistant Surgeon Stevens looked on, each "piece of artillery made the road worse, until the axles dragged in a river of mud." Soon the 77th came upon Warwick Court House, "a little southern city of about 6 or 8 houses, a court house and a jail, and a little small coop capable of holding 10 or 15 prisoners." The column continued on and about 11 a.m., skirmishing began between the 7th Maine and Rebel cavalry. Suddenly, Stevens remembered, "a terrific thunderstorm burst upon us . . . Seldom, if, ever, have we of the northern states witnessed such an exhibition of the sublimity and terrific magnificence of the workings of the elements. The vivid lightning and terrific peals of thunder seemed to presage work to come." Slowly the Confederates fell back through some woods, the Third Brigade in line of battle in close pursuit. The 77th emerged from the marshy woods scratched and bleeding from the tangle of briars into a clearing in which stood the home of a Southern officer. A couple of female slaves in bright red turbans and long woolen gowns were brought to General Keyes. They freely volunteered that just beyond a small hill ahead of the line were Rebel batteries and a large number of infantry. Pointing to the troops of Smith's division, they exclaimed, "but laws a massa, nothing like all dese yer." [17]

Under the fire of a shell thrown from the Confederate batteries beyond the woods, the clearing was cautiously crossed; the 77th and 33rd New York in line of battle. The 49th New York in reserve also marched in close column, followed by Wheeler's battery. Entering the woods, the ground proved to be wet and marshy, and Wheeler's battery advanced along a road through the muck. At around 2 p.m., an open space was reached, in which two enemy regiments stood in line. General Davidson advanced the Third Brigade and the Rebels, recognizing they were outnumbered, quickly retreated into yet another marshy stand of trees. Passing through these woods in the same order, shell, grape, and canister fell thick on all sides.

Coming to yet another field, the 77th was sent to the right of the road. Wheeler's guns were brought up into position at the end of the road, the 33rd New York at its left and the 49th New York further yet to the left, while the 7th Maine still advanced as skirmishers. At this point the brigade found itself opposite two Confederate forts at Lee's Mill on the opposite side of the Warrick River fronted by swampy ground covered with trees and underbrush. General Davidson, Lieutenant Albert Allberger, and Captain Martin Ayres "road boldly down to the front, under a shower of bullets to reconnoiter the Rebel position. It was discovered that the opposite bank was lined with rebel rifle pits." Davidson and his companions "returned safely to the admiration of the troops." [18]

Upon returning, Davidson sent the 49th New York further down to the left within 300 yards of the Rebel rifle pits. The New Yorkers took shelter behind trees and stumps, and at once opened fire along with the rest of the brigade. Davidson's aide-de-camp, Lieutenant William Long of the 33rd New York, then climbed a tree for observation upon the left of the line and spied two Confederate infantry regiments, two to three-thousand strong, heading toward the brigade's left flank. General Davidson acted quickly and pulled back the 49th at an obtuse angle to meet the expected attack, but the graycoats never came. What in fact Lieutenant Long saw, were the grandest theatrics of Prince John's military career. With a cast of thousands, Magruder dramatically put on a brave front to McClellan's army. Throughout the day of skirmishing, Prince John had a number of regiments march in circles, letting Federal outposts see his apparently endless line of soldiers. Players in the ruse, the 14th Louisiana marched from Yorktown to the James and back six times. Among the actors, Magruder's artillery also took part in the production, shifting from one point to another along his line, and constantly firing upon anything that moved.

Surgeon George T. Stevens (New York State Division of Military and Naval Affairs)

All, however, was not mere illusion. As George Stevens recalled, the "enemy was not slow to acknowledge our presence, and as a token of greeting sent some twelve-pound shells crashing in among us." The firing quickly escalated and raged well into the afternoon. At one point the 77th was ordered to lie down as the Union batteries returned the Confederate fire. "It being the first time our regiment was under fire," Corporal Weatherwax wrote, "there were many pale faces, you can bet. I for one, wished to bury myself in the mud out of sight, but like Hamlet's ghost I would not go down." Colonel McKean soon saw that the 77th's colors were still in their black enameled case and shouted to the color bearer, "Unfurl those colors, it does not look well to have your colors draped in mourning in the first time we meet the enemy!" Just then two staff officers passed in the rear of the New Yorkers and dropped down behind a large oak tree. While looking through their field glasses "a percussion shell struck the butt of the tree and exploded, causing each man to make a rotary movement from the centre at the double-quick. Brushing the mud and chips from their eyes, they struck a bee line to the left and passed out of sight," apparently unhurt. Not so for Private Frank Jeffords (Co. C) whose leg was nearly torn off at the knee by an exploding shell, and Private Charles Hodges (Co. C) who was accidently wounded by another nervous soldier in Company E, making the pair the first in the regiment to be wounded in action. Amid the shriek of shell and the rattle of grape and musket fire, Captain Ayres sighted a gun in his battery upon the flagstaff of the smaller of the two forts that brought it toppling down to the ground, causing the 77th to send up a cheer. The firing died down at night, but the occasional shell and sporadic report of a musket "showed that watchfulness was the way of the night." [19]

The New Yorkers bedded down in a swamp without tents, many without blankets, and many more without food. Some of the more industrious officers and men built platforms of logs and bark to keep out the water. Sharing blankets, Colonel McKean and Assistant Surgeon Stevens found a dry spot just to the left of the regiment. As he recalled some years after the war,

> There was a big pine stump which we selected as a good place, and, perhaps, incidentally, a good protection against the shells of the rebs. I gathered some pieces of bark and built a fort of bolster for our heads and then spreading one blanket beneath us and drawing one over us we laid down for a night's rest. We had just settled into a quiet state of repose with our stump between us and the rebel guns when a full charge of shrapnel crashed into our defense, raising a tremendous racket and scattering fragments of our stump in all directions. The Colonel and I arose without ceremony and turning toward each other in the darkness the Colonel remarked, 'Well, Doctor, had we best look for a more quiet place?' 'Colonel,' I replied, 'I have not seen two shells strike in the same spot today. Let us stay where we are. We immediately spread our blankets again and rested undisturbed the remainder of the night." [20]

At daybreak the fight was renewed and the firing was continuous from both sides with showers of canister and grape in the 77th's camp. Fortunately, the Rebel fire was high and much of the fire snapped off tree tops and branches in the swamps at the New Yorkers' rear. During the cannonade, however, a percussion shell passed through the corner of a limber in Wheeler's battery between the 77th and 33rd New York, exploding its contents and setting fire to another box of ammunition. Artificer James Hickcock and Sergeant David Smith of the gun crew acted quickly, throwing a bucket of water on the remaining shells. Private William Kershner rushed up and pulled out the remaining ammunition, thus preventing a tragic explosion of shot and shell which could have maimed or killed the gun crew and supporting infantry.

While the 77th and the rest of the Third Brigade weathered the storm of cannon fire, Baldy Smith, an aggressive commander, ordered Brigadier General Winfield Scott Hancock to take the 5th Wisconsin and 6th Maine on a reconnaissance of the Confederate lines above Lee's mills "and if he could find a place where we could force the line, to hold it and send word to me and I would at once march to his aide with the other brigades in the division." As Hancock led away his regiments, Smith rode to General Keyes' headquarters to "in a conversational way" inform of Hancock's movement. While talking to Keyes, an orderly came up and handed Keyes a communication. After reading the communique, Keyes silently turned and handed it to Smith. It was an order from McClellan "to the Army not to undertake any offensive operations until the line had been thoroughly examined by the engineers." "Very much chagrined," Smith hurriedly rode off to recall Hancock. Upon finding him, Hancock reported to Smith that he had found a weak point in the Rebel line, and that it could easily be taken. Having no alternative, he ordered Hancock back to the main line. For the remainder of his life, Old Baldy maintained that had it not been for McClellan's order, the fateful siege of Yorktown would never have taken place. [21]

McClellan was spooked. His military intelligence was all wrong. Army maps wrongly labeled the Warwick River little more than an inconsequential stream of no military importance. Instead, Little Mac was confronted with fortifications along a damned Warwick stretching from the James across the Peninsula to the York. Finalizing his disillusionment, Winfield Hancock brought back four prisoners from the 14th Alabama. Quite probably sent over by Prince John Magruder as bit players in his drama, the four willingly volunteered to one of Pinkerton's detectives that the Confederate line along the Warwick held 40,000 soldiers; Joe Johnston was on his way with 60,000 more. To assault an entrenched army 100,000 strong was military suicide. McClellan's best laid plans for turning the Confederates at Yorktown no longer mattered. Nothing was left to do but to lay siege and blast them out of their stronghold.

That evening the 77th relieved the 49th New York from its position, and while their brigade fell back about three-quarters of a mile, a line of pickets was advanced. Corporal David Weatherwax was one of the pickets that first day. Many years after the war, he recounted his experience for the *Daily Saratogian*:

> After dark we marched through the woods, coming upon our skirmishers. Every man had taken possession of the biggest tree he could find within reach of his post. They were exchanging shots with the enemy as lively as you please. As we stood and viewed the flashes along the line it reminded me of fire-flies after a shower of rain. When the boys knew they were to be relieved they ceased firing and we took possession of the trees; the order being to hold the line at all hazards. As daylight approached I hugged my tree very close I can assure you. I found we lay upon the bank of the Warwick River, which is about five rods in width, with the 'Jonnies' on the opposite bank. We lay and fired at everyone we saw moving and more times at random. One man at my right, by the name of Tate Venderwerker [Private, Co. G], said, 'Dave, come here, there is a reb over there who has fired several times at me and I cannot stop him. You come over here and try a shot.' I crept to the tree and lay upon the ground, while Vanderwerker pointed out the spot whence the shots had been fired. I shot, coming within six inches of the spot, but it came very near being my last, as a bullet struck the ground too close to me to be comfortable. I rolled over on my back behind the tree and wiped the dirt from my face an eyes. Loading my gun again and raising the sights to three hundred yards, I fired again. This time the shot was not returned. I then crawled back to my own tree. It commenced to rain in the afternoon. You all know what a Virginia rain is. Night approaches

and we are not relieved. At dark there came an order to Lieut. Rugg to send a Corporal and two men down the riverbank some forty yards in advance of his picket line. He ordered a detail. Then Corporal Harris T. Vandenburgh and J. Vanderburgh [both from Company G] were drawn for this duty. When the Corporal reported to Lieut., Rugg for instructions, he looked more like a corpse than a living man, and I thought he had an attack of the ague the way he shook. The Lieutenant said: 'Corporal Weatherwax, you will take charge of this detail.' Ah, then it was my turn to shake . . . I took my men and went very cautiously down through the woods until I came to the bank of the river. Here we found a stick of timber hewn out for the knee of a vessel. There we sat though the long weary hours of night listening to the rain and watching one solitary light on the enemy's fort, just up the river. A little before daylight, we reported to our command, when our company were relieved and went into camp, some half mile to the rear. [22]

Picket duty was equally harrowing for Lieutenant Luther Wheeler (Co. C). "If a man showed himself outside his tree he was sure to get a rifle shot very near his head . . . Many rifle shots came near me as I exposed myself to get a shot at them. I got behind a log and shot twice at a 'sesch,' don't know whether I hit him or not but I know that he ran as fast as his legs would carry him out of danger behind a tree. I had to crawl away on my belly like a snake back into the woods again from my log as they knew I was behind it and watching it. They saw me and gave me a shot when I got up and ran as fast as I could for a tree." If Wheeler was not dodging bullets, he had to contend with "showers of grape and canister . . . cutting off [tree] limbs in every direction." Yet, Lieutenant Martin Lennon (Co. I) found that such duty suited him quite well. "It was no boys play: for they sent a bullet mighty close to my head whenever they got a chance. I got the better of them, however, for they did not hit me, and I either killed or wounded one of them. He dropped when I fired . . . I never thought I would like to shoot at a man, but I like to shoot a sesch." [23]

For the next two days, the 77th's pickets were within speaking distance of the enemy. In the midst of whistling bullets, both Yankee and Rebel traded taunts and insults. George Stevens remembered that "a good deal of hard talk passed between one of our pickets and one of the 'Jonnies.'" Suddenly the opposing picket "thrust his hand beyond his tree holding a bottle, and shaking it, challenged the Yankee to come and take it."

The Yankee quickly squeezed off a round, but missed the tormentor.

"Ha, ha! Why don't you take it? What do you think of Bull Run?" the Southerner taunted. While the two traded barbs, "Yankee number two crept round behind a log, and drawing on the Southerner, blazed away at him."

The saucy Rebel grasped his shoulder and fled howling to the rear. "There you fool," shouted Yankee number one, "I told you that a blind man would be shooting you soon." [24]

Marked by steady firing from both sides, picket duty was dangerous. Frequent forays by the enemy at night made the men on duty skittish. The slightest rustle of brush or leaves would ignite a roll of musket fire up and down the line. More often than not, as Corporal Albert H. Kingsley (Co. H) soon discovered, a false alarm could bring embarrassing results:

> One day . . . Companies A., H., and F. of our regiment and one company of the seventh Maine were detailed to

go on picket. Company A was left at a deserted building; the other companies advanced as a picket line, after Major Hyde of the seventh Maine, who was in charge, told us that no fires could be made, that we should be alert. That if we were attacked, as we might be, we must hold our position until reinforced. Two mounted orderlies, [Privates, Co. H] Charles Severence, Pat Bolyn, [James] Willis, and I were stationed on the left. If attacked, the orderlies were to immediately ride to brigade headquarters and inform General Davidson. Though the day had been hot, the night was dark and so cold we got very chilly. About an hour after we had gone to post, Severence, declaring he was sleepy, went into a dilapidated shed near by and from the snoring was soon soundly sleeping. H company disregarded orders and started fires. About midnight Pat Bolyn said: 'Listen I hear something.' 'In what direction asked I' 'I do hear something,' he repeated. The two orderlies agreed with him. Pat was so sure and begged so hard to be allowed to fire that I ordered him to fire. The two orderlies also fired their revolvers at the foe. Willis and I fired as Charles Severence came rushing out of the shed. The pickets ran in and as the foe was perfectly quiet some one volunteered to go out; about one hundred paces in the front he soon found out on the ground two dead – calves. Major Hyde came rushing up on his horse and asked, 'what is the matter boys; what does the firing mean?' After hearing our explanation he ordered us back to our positions where we remained the rest of the night without visitation from the enemy. [25]

Kingsley's and a multitude of other evening false alarms often resulted in the entire Third Brigade being called out into line, much to the consternation of General Davidson. "This is not a war of pickets," he scolded, "All firing by outposts is strictly forbidden except in defense against the enemy. Once more all firing within the lines is forbidden." Davidson then ordered that any "Regiment in which this offense is repeated will be made . . . to stand with its Colonel at its Head for twelve hours under arms." Corps commander Keyes shared Davidson's dismay, and in also forbidding outposts from firing unless actually attacked, warned the Fourth Corps that an "Army which can be easily stampeded will soon be worn out and beaten." For Corporal Weatherwax, however, one false alarm led to a promotion:

> While encamped around Lee's Mills, General Davidson issued strict orders to allow no soldier to fire his gun without permission from his superior officers. The enemy would do everything to annoy and break us of our rest all night by firing at our pickets at all hours of the night, when the order would be, '77th fall in!' and we had to go out and support our pickets. One dark and rainy night, as all the boys were reposing on our flowery beds of ease, oh no, I mean pine boughs, we were aroused by the rattle of musketry and that well known 'boys fall in on the color line,' of our Colonel. As every man came up he had to put his hand out and feel for his next comrade because of the pitchy darkness. It was the only way we could tell whether we were in line or not. One man in the confusion asked Captain [Jesse] White [Co. F] who had command . . . if he could fire off his gun, and the Captain misunderstanding him said yes, when bang went his gun just as my hand touched his shoulder and the voice of Colonel McKean was heard asking who fired that gun . . . Under the circumstances and excitement, I 'froze' to the man when he said, 'D-m you, let go of me,' and tried to get, but I was like that old Virginia plaster you read about – the more you try to pull it off, the tighter sticks the plaster . . . I said to the Colonel, 'Hold your lantern this way and we will see who he is,' when General Davidson came

and saw who the man was and who held him. The General said, 'Send this man to my headquarters under escort.' He was a rebel spy in our camp and had fired his gun to let the rebels know where to direct their fire. When we mustered for pay your humble servant was promoted to fifth Sergeant. [26]

Day after day, the skirmishing was continuous and the 77th's soldiers became so accustomed to the constant fire that they carried on, unconcerned, the business of throwing up breastworks and building roads. Ignoring mine balls and artillery, curiosity prompted George Stevens to pass from one end of the Third Brigade to the other. Along the way, he found Baldy Smith "with his shoulders braced against a tree which interposed its broad trunk between him and the enemy, and a few steps further on met four soldiers walking and chatting." As Stevens came opposite them, "a rebel shell landed at their feet, exploded and sent them sprawling to the ground." He "rushed to them and found that one of them was fatally hurt, and the two others badly shaken up." After caring for the wounded men and having the most severely wounded removed on a stretcher, the curious doctor went on his way. [27]

When not on the picket line, the 77th joined countless others in the Army of the Potomac in the herculean labor of constructing siege works along the Yorktown line, made all the more difficult by Confederate fire and near constant rain. "No rest was allowed," Stevens wrote. *DIXIE* complained that the New Yorkers were "*all the time performing the most exhausting labor, building bridges, throwing up earthworks . . . and doing the other necessary duties of a soldier.*" [28]

As McClellan's army was digging in and building fortifications, so too was Prince John's outnumbered command. More importantly, Magruder's army was growing in number as reinforcements began trickling into the Confederate entrenchments. Previously hesitant to reinforce Magruder until McClellan's intentions were revealed, Robert E. Lee, at that time military advisor to Jefferson Davis, telegraphed Joe Johnston, who held his command behind the line of the Rappahannock and Rapidan Rivers, and ordered him to send troops to the Peninsula without delay. Shortly after, realizing that Magruder's situation was critical, Richmond ordered Johnston's army to the Peninsula. The Army of the Peninsula was incorporated into Johnston's command. Now known as the Army of Northern Virginia, the Confederate forces comprised approximately 55,000 soldiers.

On April 16, McClellan ordered the 77th's Second Division to stop the Rebels from strengthening their defenses near Lee's Mill behind the Warwick River at Dam No. 1 where scouts had discovered that the river could be forded. Ironically, this was the very same spot Hancock had wanted to attack on April 6. On the Federal side of the Warwick was a large clearing in which stood the Garrow farm. Burned by the Confederates, all that remained were three chimneys. The Yankees dubbed the clearing "Burnt Chimneys." Prominent opposite Burnt Chimneys were three Rebel earthworks in which 24 and 12-pound howitzers were placed.

At McClellan's instruction, General Smith planned the operation. An artillery barrage would silence the Southern howitzers. Once silenced, a regiment would then wade across and conduct a reconnaissance-in-force on the enemy's earthworks. If the results of the reconnaissance were favorable, Smith would send across a larger column to establish a fixed position. Little Mac gave the plan his nod, and Smith coordinated the details. Revealing McClellan's abiding distrust of the Fourth Corps commander's military prowess, Keyes was never consulted.

McKEAN'S SUNDAY SCHOOL BOYS GO TO WAR

That morning, word passed through the 77th's division that an assault was to be made. Orders came to move, and the division descended upon the Garrow farm at Burnt Chimneys. The Second Brigade occupied the first line, supported by the First and Third Brigades. As the 77th moved to take its position in line, Assistant Surgeon Stevens looked up to the sky at "an American eagle" that "whirled above our heads in elegant circles and at length floated toward the south, the boys swinging their hats and cheering the bird with loud huzzahs." [29]

At 6:30 a.m., Companies E, F, D, and K of the 3rd Vermont began the work as skirmishers. Mott's, Kennedy's, and Wheeler's batteries opened an eighteen-gun cannonade which lasted nearly all morning before silencing the Rebel guns on the north bank of the Warwick. The 3rd Vermont skirmishers retired for dinner and thoroughly rested themselves. At about 3 p.m. they were called up, formed into line, and told by their colonel in a brief speech that the work expected of them was to charge across the Warwick and take the enemy's entrenchments. Under the covering fire of Yankee batteries, the Green Mountain Boys marched steadily at the double quick to the edge of the river, and plunged in on the run. The water unexpectedly deepened. The men were soon wading in up to their chests, their cartridge boxes slung over their shoulders and their Springfield rifles held over their heads. The moment the Vermonters entered the water, the Rebels swarmed on the edge of their rifle pit, and rained a deadly fire of bullets on the advancing Northerners. The Vermonters loaded and fired as they waded. Their killed and wounded began to fall from the instant of entering the water. Many of the wounded were carried across and laid down on the opposite bank. As soon as they emerged, the 3rd Vermont received the order to charge, and drove the enemy from the rifle pits. The Confederate response was immediate, and the Green Mountain Boys found themselves hard pressed as gray-uniformed reinforcements arrived at the scene. An urgent request for reinforcements was sent back to Baldy Smith, but none came, perhaps because Smith had been victimized by an unruly horse which threw him twice, leaving him stunned and unaware of the advantage gained. For 40 minutes the 3rd Vermont hung on, but with their ammunition exhausted, they were forced to draw back across the river. Half of the regiment was left behind.

Undeterred, Smith ordered a second attempt to take the enemy's rifle pits. Again the Union batteries sent their deadly missiles into the Rebel position. At approximately 5 p.m. the 6th Vermont waded across while the 4th Vermont crossed on the top of Dam No. 1. As it was with the 3rd Vermont, the attack was quickly repulsed, and the Vermonters again fell back across the Warwick to the Garrow farm at Burnt Chimneys. Total casualties for the day were 165 killed, wounded, or captured. One of those killed was Private William Scott of the 3rd Vermont who had earlier been pardoned from a death sentence for sleeping at his post on the picket line. His pardon was received while he stood before the firing squad. Hearing the news, Scott blurted out, "I will show President Lincoln that I am not afraid to die for my country." [30]

The 77th stood in reserve during both assaults biting at the bit, desperate to be called to support the Green Mountain regiments. Horrified by the sight of the Vermonter's "covering themselves behind trees, and fighting as they went" the New Yorkers stood helplessly by as the New Englanders "recrossed the stream, carrying with them all the wounded . . . Many were now shot in the water, and drowned beyond all possibility of help." Later, George Stevens bitterly complained that the "Battle at Lee's Mill" was "fought in which two hundred men gallantly captured an important work of the enemy, and thousands of their companions burning with desire to share in their glory stood by and saw them abandon it." Though thousands were eager to celebrate the Vermonter's success, McClellan wanted no general engagement. His orders were simply to force the enemy to discontinue work on its fortifications at Lee's Mill. Observing the operation, Little Mac offered no advice, and left satisfied that the object of disrupting work on the Confederate works had been accomplished. [31]

That night, the 77th dug in and threw up breastworks in the small clearing opposite Dam No. 1. "In the morning," *DIXIE* wrote home, "the rebels woke to find every gun on their side controlled by 2 of our batteries, 2 howitzers, and a company of Andrews' sharpshooters." It soon became risky for the Rebel gunners to man their guns as the sharpshooters' bullets unerringly hit home. Watching from a safe distance, *DIXIE* noted with satisfaction that "When it became perilous to load the guns, they sent out negroes, and when they found that our sharpshooters paid no respect to color, they abandoned the use of the their guns altogether." One sharpshooter was reported to have killed eighteen of the enemy.[32]

Yankees and Rebels faced each other for several days while the dead of the Vermont regiments lay where they fell, bloating and blackening in the hot weather. Finally the Confederates "sent out a flag of truce, asking us to come and bury our dead of the 2d brigade that fell on their side of the creek." Availing himself to the opportunity to personally examine the positions of both sides, *DIXIE* tagged along with the men detailed to collect their dead comrades. "They sent our dead, 20 in numbers, by negroes, across the dam, and our men met them there." Ominously signaling more death to come, "Hancock's brigade was pounding them a little farther up the stream." [32]

As the siege wore on, the scourge of disease began to decimate the ranks. As early as April 7, Medical Director Charles S. Tripler openly worried that the swamps in and around the Federal camps would soon become "prolific of malarial poison." His anxiety was not that exaggerated for malarial and typhoid fevers became epidemic. By May 4, the 77th's Fourth Corps collected 1,200 of their sick and moved them to hospitals behind the lines. Day after day, Assistant Surgeon Stevens lamented "men who worked at the breastworks one day would be found in the hospitals on the next, burning with fever, tormented with insatiable thirst, racked with pains, or wild with delirium; their parched lips, and teeth blackened with sordes, the hot breath and sunken eyes, the sallow skin and trembling pulse, all telling of the violent workings of these diseases." [33]

Compounding the suffering was the near complete lack of necessary medical supplies. The small supply of medicine each regimental surgeon brought with them to the Peninsula was exhausted in a matter of days. Surgeons spent considerable time going from one regiment to another begging for any amount of quinine and opium for their sick. Desperate to obtain medicine for the regiment's sick, George Stevens rode to Young's Mill where a hospital had been established in the old Confederate barracks. "When I arrived at the hospital and told the surgeon in charge of my sore need, the big and rather hard faced man looked at me with tears in his eyes. He silently took me by the hand and led me to the dispensary. He showed me a row of big bottles with spirits of turpentine and another row filled with castor oil. For two days he had no medicines and new typhoid cases constantly arriving." [34]

Returning empty handed, Stevens reported to Colonel McKean who fired off a passionate letter of protest to Medical Inspector Joseph Brown:

> For some days . . . the Regiment has performed the most exhausting duties on picket and fatigue duties in the

trenches – much of the time under fire and often, very often, standing to arms in the night time. During all this time they have had the medical care of the Assistant Surgeon only who has no hospital tent, and much of the time no medicines or none that were suitable. You will not fail to see at a glance why so many men are now in the Hospital. No wonder I am oppressed with the most intense anxiety . . . Could my men receive the medical treatment that ought to have in camp few comparatively would have to be sent to the rear . . . and the Regiment would not be so rapidly diminishing . . . I have had the power to raise a Regiment – would that I could save it from disease. [35]

Soon the large temporary hospitals organized by Tripler on the Peninsula were overcrowded with sick men. To free up much needed space for the continual flow of patients, Tripler arranged for transportation to take the sick to hospitals in Washington, Georgetown, Alexandria, Annapolis, Baltimore, Philadelphia, New York, and Boston. Many of the 77th's ill soldiers were transported to these northern hospitals, but not so Robert Skinner who was prostrated with typhoid fever: "the surgeon, my comrades and captain urged me to go to some hospital But I positively refused, thinking it better to live or die in camp rather than in an Army hospital, alias prison." A plethora of men in the ranks shared Skinner's sentiment, for the odds of regaining health in the hospital were not in the soldier's favor. Medicines were as limited as medical knowledge, while food was often tainted with salmonella and other toxins. Worse, filth and overcrowding in the hospitals were the norm leading to outbreaks of gangrene, osteomyelitis, erysipelas, and other deadly diseases. [36]

Daily, scores of men who had left home months earlier to defend the Union succumbed from their illness. "At times," Assistant Surgeon Stevens sadly observed, "one might sit in the door of his tent and see as many as six or seven funeral parties bearing comrades to their humble resting places." Embalmers set up their tent and enjoyed a steady and profitable business of preparing the dead for shipment back home, and "everywhere north . . . express cars groaned with the weight of coffins containing the remains of youths who . . . had now yielded, not to bullets of the enemy, but to the grim spirit" of disease. Writing to the *Daily Saratogian*, one soldier bemoaned that "the names of those smitten by that dreaded swamp fever are too numerous to mention. The weeping families at home can tell a sad story, that they lost a soldier, brother, husband or friend at Yorktown; but how he came to die they will never know only that it was caused by fever. Yet it's a soldier's death, and just as noble as thought suffered on the battle field." [37]

While thousands fell to malaria and typhoid, McClellan confidently brought up his enormous siege train of heavy guns. By the end of April, fifteen batteries for the Union siege guns were dug and fortified. Six-hundred wagon loads of powder and shot and shell were needed to supply 70 heavy rifled pieces of 20-pounder and 30-pounder Parrots, two 200-pounder and twelve 100-pounder Parrots, 4-inch Rodman rifles, ten 13-inch seacoast mortars firing 220-pound shells, and 25 10-inch mortars. Now, with the siege guns in place, McClellan was ready to pound the Rebels into submission. It didn't matter one bit, of course, since Joseph Johnston was planning to abandon the line along the Warwick as soon as possible.[38]

The Southern general never met a defensive line he liked, and as early as April 14, Johnston reported to Jefferson Davis that the Yorktown and Warwick River defenses were poorly engineered and far too weak to withstand McClellan's superior artillery. He proposed to withdraw all the forces on the Peninsula and to concentrate them in the Richmond defenses. During an all-night conference with President Davis, Secretary of War George W. Randolph, and

Robert E. Lee, Johnston's plan was rejected. Reinforced by the divisions of Gustavus W. Smith and James B. Longstreet, Johnston continued to fret that the Yorktown line was too weak to defend. On April 29, he informed Richmond that his army would abandon the Peninsula as soon as the condition of the roads would permit such a huge undertaking.

On Saturday evening, May 3, the Confederate withdrawal began. To provide cover, Rebel artillery fire pounded the Yankee line. The "roar of artillery exceeded anything that had been heard before," George Stevens asserted. "From one end to the other the shells and shot poured into our camps, and the arches of fire that marked the courses of the shells, with the flames spouting from the mouths of the guns, created a magnificent pyrotechnic display." [39]

At daylight the next morning, General Hancock rode up to Old Baldy Smith's division headquarters with two contrabands in tow, who informed him that the works in front of the division had been evacuated. After Lieutenant George Custer and Captain Read scouted the deserted works, Smith's division was ordered to take possession of the Confederate fortifications near Lee's Mill. The 77th led the Third Brigade over Dam No. 1 and entered the Rebel works. Suddenly "there was an explosion like a pistol shot" at the feet of Privates Franklin H. Jucket and John Harris, both of Company E, blowing leaves and dirt into their faces. Colonel McKean came back down the column, and lifting up with the tip of his sword a piece of old cloth lying on the ground, uncovered the nipple of a torpedo. Filled with powder, torpedoes were Columbiad shells of eight or ten-inch mortar shells buried a few inches in the ground fitted with either a fulminated mercury detonator or an ordinary artillery friction primer. Stepping on the detonator or primer caused the torpedo to explode, killing or maiming those in close proximity to the buried shell. Luckily for Privates Jucket and Harris, only the primer exploded. Speaking for the 77th, *DIXIE* was indignant and furiously proclaimed that "these infernal machines were placed there by incarnate demons who . . . resort to such barbarous practices against the living." [40]

These "infernal machines" were fashioned by Confederate Brigadier General Gabriel J. Rains, whose brigade had manned the main redoubt at Yorktown. His goal was to slow the pursuing Federal columns. However, some of the men in his command became overly zealous and hid torpedoes inside houses and around wells, and even in flour barrels. When this came to the attention of Major General Longstreet he was soundly disturbed, and promptly ordered Brigadier Gains to cease what he considered to be an uncivilized act of war.

Temporarily halted in the earthworks around Lee's Mill, *DIXIE* found the Confederate works formidable. "The rifle pits were very extensive. Every camp was entrenched for miles in rear of the line of works." His observations turned to indignant anger toward the enemy "who exhibits their fiendish hate by the most brutal and shameful treatment of the bodies of our honored dead. Some are found stripped of their clothes and bayoneted after death. Other with their throats cut from ear to ear." By afternoon, the 77th was ordered to send their sick to the rear and marched after Joe Johnston's retreating army. Once again, the call was "Forward to Richmond." [41]

4

"MEN OF THE 77TH, NOW IS THE CHANCE TO COVER YOURSELVES IN GLORY!"

By evacuating the Yorktown defenses, Joe Johnston hoped to rapidly retreat to the close vicinity of Richmond itself. Once in front of Richmond, Johnston concluded he would no longer be bothered by the risk of being outmaneuvered by McClellan's command of the York and James Rivers around the lower Peninsula.

The Confederate army traveled toward Richmond along two narrow roads – the Yorktown Road and Lee's Mill Road that ran parallel to the James River. For Johnston's men, it was a grueling night march. The darkness allowed little visibility and the soldiers were knee deep in mud. Artillery pieces and supply wagon wheels sunk so much that the retreat would halt until they could be dragged free. This constant stop and go continued throughout the night and the Rebel column did not reach Williamsburg until mid-morning on Sunday, a distance of only 12 miles. The Confederates immediately began building, along with slaves, a defensive line that stretched a little more than four miles from Tutter's Neck Pond on the army's right, to Jones Pond and Cub Dam Creek on the left. It included 13 flanking redoubts and a large bastion, Fort Magruder, in the center. This fort had a parapet 6 feet high. In front was a ditch, 9 feet in depth and 9 feet wide. To enlarge their field of fire and to hamper an attacking force, a broad swath of trees was felled to form a tangled maze of abatis along the face of the woods fronting the line.

The Union army "made little delay among the Rebel intrenchments; only long enough to glance over the formidable works, where the enemy had abandoned seventy-two pieces of artillery, mostly of the heavy caliber, with immense numbers of shovels, picks, wheelbarrels and other paraphilia of an army." The sick of the 77th were sent to the rear to field hospitals organized at Young's Mill and Fortress Monroe, many of them "so attached to the regiment... that they "wept upon parting with their men." [1]

McClellan's infantry and artillery marched along the same two roads to Williamsburg that the Confederates had traveled the evening before. Their progress was painfully slow as the previous passage of the enemy's infantry, artillery, and supply wagons left the water-saturated roads in worse condition than they were before. They were in such bad shape that a rumor swept through the ranks that a mule sunk up to his ears in mud. Despite the hard march, Assistant Surgeon Stevens, ever the botanist, recounted the scenery as charming beyond description:

Magnificent forests of oak and pine, interspersed with clearings, the residences of farmers, with fine fields, covered with green blades of the newly springing wheat, met the view along the road; while the woods were adorned with innumerable flowers. The tall dogwood, with its clusters of large flowers like swarms of white butterflies, mingled with the Judas tree, whose leafless boughs were densely covered with racemes of purple blossoms. The azalea and the honeysuckle beneath formed a delightful contrast with the gorgeous floral display above. [2]

By nightfall General Joseph Hooker's Division, followed by Baldy Smith's, halted short of the entrenched Confederates before Williamsburg now under the command of General James Longstreet. *One of the 77th* wrote back home that "we slept before Williamsburg under a rail fence close to the enemy. During the night we were awakened by the rain pattering down on our uncovered faces." As the rain turned into a downpour Lieutenant Wheeler found sleep impossible while "expecting to have a terrible fight" in the morning "as the enemy's strongest works were still in their possession." Captain Calvin Rice (Co. G) and Private George Tucker (Co. G) made their "beds in the mud and rain and laid down, with rubber blankets under and over us" when Orderly Sergeant George Ross (Co. G) "called George up to go with him and others into the timbers to put up shelter tents and build fires for the line officers." [3]

On May 5, at 7 o'clock in the morning and in the midst of a hard rain, General Hooker and his chief of artillery, Major Wainwright, walked up the road to the edge of the trees to reconnoiter and to find a position for his division's artillery. The only open space they could find was the road itself and a small cornfield on their right. The position faced the junction of the Lee's Mill and Yorktown Roads and beyond that Fort Magruder. Consequently Wainwright ordered up Battery H, 1st U.S. Artillery. As the artillerists slogged forward in the mud and rain and unlimbered their guns, Rebel gunners in Fort Magruder and the adjoining redoubts opened fire on them. Hence, the Battle of Williamsburg began.

Hooker immediately called up his infantry and ordered his men into the woods and abatis west of the Lee's Mill Road. In concert with Hooker's infantry forming into battle lines, Major Wainwright called upon more artillery until he had ten cannons positioned in the road and the cornfield to the right and began throwing shot and shell into Fort Magruder. Here the 77th was positioned supporting the battery. Private Silvanus Morse (Co. A) stood in line, his senses assaulted by "a continual roar of musketry and the canon" sent forth like "messengers of death." Colonel McKean thought "a cannon ball flying through the air sounded like a tornado, concentrated to the diameter of a few inches, moving with the rapidity of a comet, and sounding like the defiant scream of an infernal spirit on its mission of evil." [4]

Initially Hooker quickly pushed back the defending Rebels from their forward rifle pits but halted, expecting troops of Smith's Division to advance on his right. But no advance was forthcoming. This allowed Longstreet to bring up three of his brigades in addition to two already manning the Fort Magruder line. A fourth was held in close reserve. By midday the fight became more intense along Hooker's front. Soon the Confederates, having the advantage of numbers, began to push back Hooker's men and gravely threatened to turn his flank.

As the fighting intensified Joe Hooker called for reinforcements, but they did not come. Earlier that morning, a lone contraband entered the Yankee line offering battle-changing intelligence. To the right of the Union line was a woodland trail that led to a dam on Cub Creek, a branch of Queen's Creek, and continued beyond the right flank of the Rebel defenses.

Hooker went on to relate that the enemy had a redoubt covering the dam, but that there was no one manning it. An officer was sent to confirm the fugitive slave's story and came back affirming that he was telling the truth. The entire Confederate left flank was unguarded, hanging in the air.

General Winfield Scott Hancock's brigade, along with the 7th Maine and 33rd New York of the 77th's brigade, were ordered to take the unmanned redoubt in an attempt to flank the Rebels and roll up their line. As they set off on a winding two-mile march through the woods toward the dam on their right, to the west the sounds of battle became ever more intense as the Confederate reinforcements closed in on Hooker's soldiers.

Joe Hooker's left flank west of Lee's Mill Road was soon overlapped and bent while steadily being pushed back toward the road. The onrushing Rebels soon broke through the road and Wainwright's battery had to be abandoned, the gunners escaping into the thickets and woods to the east. Fortunately, they carried off four of their cannons while the other six were mired in the mud and could not be dragged out. A half mile to the rear, Major Wainwright placed his remaining artillery pieces across the road in a small clearing. He ordered canister and when the charging enemy was 150 yards away he blasted the Rebels, obliterating the head of the column. Those who survived fled for cover in the woods.

In the midst of the bloody chaos of the Confederate advance, Hooker's corps commander, General Heintzelman, rode up. Upon seeing some regimental bands standing by looking bewildered and shaken, he asked them to rally the troops with music. Over the din of battle wafted "Yankee Doodle" and "Three Cheers for the Red, White, and Blue." The music inspired the fleeing troops and stemmed the tide of skulkers to the rear. But the arrival of General Philip Kearny's division of the First Corps saved the day on Hooker's left flank. Kearny had forcefully driven his men through the deep mud toward the sound of musketry and pushed the stragglers abandoning the battle line. His command beat the Confederates back to the Lee's Mill Road and into the woods and abatis, but they stubbornly held on there. In the late hours of the afternoon, bloody firefights continued in the stand of trees and thickets. [5]

Meanwhile on the right flank General Hancock had expertly maneuvered his troops so that they faced the Rebel's left flank. He had brought his column through the woods and across the Cub Creek dam and advanced past the empty redoubt the contraband had reported, and on to a second empty redoubt. The two Confederate redoubts were unguarded because they went unnoticed in the rain and mist that made them impossible to see. About a mile from Fort Magruder, Hancock's column filed into line. He arranged his batteries and men on a slight rise overlooking a wheat field. Soon Confederates under General Jubal Early were sent to counter Hancock's advance. Rather rashly, Early sent in his brigade without first reconnoitering the Federal position but was savagely repulsed. As this part of the battle was unfolding, the 77th was sent to reinforce Hancock. The day after the battle Private Silvanus Morse (Co. A) wrote "we were ordered forward to help him on the double quick and we went through mud up to our knees, but we cared not for the mud, but when we came in sight of the fort the Stars and Stripes floated proudly over them as the day was won." [6]

Private Franklin Jucket (Co. E) entirely missed the call of the regiment to support Hancock. Tired of standing in the mud and rain, Jucket discovered, "There was a hoe-cake shanty not far from our line and I, being somewhat of a reconnoiterer, got consent of Orderly Sergeant Henry Rowland (Co. E) to go to the shanty for a supply. While waiting my turn I thought that possibly the regiment might move, so I concluded to return. On getting outside I found that the regiment had gone on. Grape and canister were singing their usual song, accompanied by bullets dropping to the ground. I finally reached the regiment in line. The battle was shortly over, the victory ours." [7]

As evening approached the battle wound down to sporadic skirmishes and the firing of pickets. Colonel McKean solemnly surveyed "the ground strewn with their dead and wounded." In this field of human wreckage the 77th "slept . . . in line of battle, expecting in the night or the next morning the fight would be resumed, not supposing that the rebels were not yet sufficiently beaten." But the battle was not renewed as once again the Confederate army had slipped away. [8]

One of the 77th the next morning entered Williamsburg – once the capitol of the colony of Virginia – describing it as "an old Ante-Revolutionary town," scarcely a house in it that was not built in "good old colony times." "William's and Mary's College, and Insane Asylum," he continued, "are about the only decent buildings, and even these are not gotten up with much taste. William's and Mary's College is a small two story building with two wings, and were then filled with rebel wounded. Poor fellows! As I approached them with a kind word, they would say, 'this is a bad job.'" Including the Insane Asylum, outside of the College, "Every available place was filled with the wounded." Turning his attention to the fairer sex, he wrote, "Many of the ladies of the town – so homely, that were I wounded I should say, 'a rough soldier's face is more congenial to me than their sour countenances,' waited upon them, and gave them delicacies."

The soldier was acutely aware that, "No white residents were to be seen; they had locked their homes and taken refuge in their cellars and garrets." Perhaps unconsciously revealing a racist view, "The only pleasant faces" he wrote "were the *grinning negroes*, who showed their ivory to an amazing extent." Continuing on through the city, the soldier "saw an old darkey marching along, with a black slouched hat, cane in his hand, and a bundle slung on a stick across his shoulder." He asked, "Hey, Uncle Tom, where are you going?" Stopping to answer, "The old negro opened his mouth, rolled up his eyes, grinning, and said, 'Going, heh! Dis nigger ben slave 500 year, don't tink I's gwain free now, eh?' The reply was so earnest, and Uncle Tom so joyful I could but note it." [9]

Later that day, twenty-year-old Private Francis N. Perkins (Co. D) and Sergeant Skinner set out to place the Stars and Stripes on the home of one Colonel Wise. Leading a squad of men taking care of some sick and wounded, Skinner turned to Perkins and said, perhaps jokingly, "As you are the cook, it is your duty to get something for the boys to eat." At a reunion of the 77th many years later, Private Perkins recalled his surprising encounter while carrying out his mission:

> With haversack and gun I started for 'market.' Returning from my successful marketing, about three blocks from the academy, I reached a house that looked as if it was occupied. In response to my knock, a fine looking old man opened the door and asked, 'What do you want here Yank?' I replied, 'Dinner for six, or you folks may cook this stuff I have here, so that we can eat.' He said that he would, and called 'mother.' He told her what we wanted. After looking at it, she said she could cook the hulled barely if I could wait. As she took it and went in, the old man invited me to come in. I told him that I better stand

guard while the lady was cooking. He asked me what state and regiment I was from. I told him the Seventy-Seventh New York State Volunteers. Said he, 'come in young man, if you are from New York State you are no robber or thief.' He said he had heard that all the northern states had pardoned their prisoners to enlist to take up arms against the south. I told him I had never heard that and that it was a lie. He said did you say the state of New York has 77,000 men in the field? Said, more than that number for I know of the One Hundred and Twentieth New York Volunteers. He asked what part of New York State are you from? I told him Saratoga County. Said he, I used to go to Saratoga Springs to board in the summer. Who is your Colonel? Said I, James B. McKean. With an expression of surprise, he said, "I knew Mr. McKean well. Mother if such persons as he are here we are all right." Said I, perhaps if you have been a visitor to Saratoga Springs you may have met my uncle, Henry Garrison. Said he, I knew Garrison and his little girl, black-eyed Mollie. Said I, that little girl is my sister, mother being dead she is living with my father's sister, Mrs. Garrison. That little girl's name is Mollie Perkins, my sister. I then showed him her picture. He stepped to his door and called his daughter. When she came in, pale and timidly, her father showed her the picture and told her who I was and where from. As she shook hands with me she cried. She went to a closet, returning with a rebel officer's coat, saying as she showed it to me, 'that was the coat of my husband who was killed yesterday, and maybe you are the one who shot him.' Said I, if so it was to prevent him from shooting me first, and there is no knowing how many he and his men may have killed. She forgave our armies, saying they must be in the right or they could not have taken Fort Magruder. The old man told her to get that little Fourth of July flag and a hatchet and nails, saying to put it up somewhere. As she handed it to her father he said I know what it is to be a soldier, young man. I was a colonel in the Mexican war. As I stepped to the door I saw Sergeant Skinner. He came up, and said he was looking for me; we nailed the flag to the jam of the door. They gave us our barley in two tin buckets, well cooked, and bade us good-by and a safe and early return to Saratoga Springs. [10]

While McClellan's army and the 77th maintained their position at Williamsburg, Johnston's Confederates continued their retreat toward Richmond. Except for a heavy skirmish at Eltham's Landing, the Rebel army did not stop until setting up a defensive line behind the Chickahominy River and directly in front of Richmond. Parts of the line were nearly in the city, a mere three miles away. Panic set in as worn out Confederates began to trickle into Richmond. Wagonloads of furniture and family belongings coursed through the streets at all hours of the day. Those who fled flocked to railroad depots and boarded steamers on the James River Canal. While many hurriedly traveled to safer ground, the city received an influx of refugees from the Peninsula to escape the advancing Yankees.

On May 9 – a bright and pleasant day – the Federal army began its ponderous pursuit of Johnston. All along the road "there were the evidences of the haste of the retreating rebels, broken wagons, caissons, dead horses, broken vehicles . . . piled in confusion . . ." The 77th passed by wounded cavalry men in the neighboring farm houses, and the day's march ended as the 77th camped at New Kent Courthouse. [11]

Four days later, the 77th resumed the march winding along the banks of the tortuous course of the Pamunkey River. Assistant Surgeon Stevens was "enchanted by the lovely scenery" which was punctuated by "the profusion of flowers in the forests, the bright green meadows, and the broad fields of newly springing wheat." At every house "the alarmed white people threw out the white flag in token of submission, as though their protection from injury depended upon this symbol of peace." Flocking to the roadside to welcome the Union army were newly freed slaves. They gathered in crowds and shook hands with the marching soldiers. Stevens spied a "gray-haired old patriarch, surrounded be a numerous group of younger chattels . . . exclaiming in a loud voice 'Bress de Lord! I'se been praying for yous all to come all dis time; and now I'se glad yous got so fur; and I pray de Lord dat yous may keep on, and conquer def and hell and de grabe!" That night the 77th camped at Cumberland Landing where the Army of the Potomac stood with "thousands of troops, parks of artillery, squadrons of cavalry, divisions of infantry; some already in camp, others moving about in order, but seeming, from the distance, to be intermingled in the most perfect confusion." [12]

The next morning came the cry, "Fall in!" and the Federals took up a short march to White House Landing on the Pamunkey where the Richmond and the York Railroad crossed, the 77th settling in on the grounds of White House plantation. The sprawling property was now owned by William H. F. "Rooney" Lee, the son of Robert E. Lee. One-hundred years earlier it had been the site of George Washington's courtship of the widow Martha Custis. General Lee's wife was also a Custis, and had been staying at White House until a few days before the Union soldiers came. Their advance guard found a note from her tacked to the front door: "Northern soldiers who profess to reverence Washington, forbear to desecrate the home of his first married life, -- the property of his wife, now owned by her descendants. It was signed, "A Grand-daughter of Mrs. Washington." McClellan immediately placed a guard on the house and forbid its use by the army. Instead, he set up a headquarters and the supply depot for the soldiers. Lieutenant Wheeler (Co. C) surveyed "more than a thousand acres entirely covered with men, their tents being so closely together that you can hardly walk between them." He was awed by the presence of "fifty or sixty thousand men in this single camp and many more at the camp at Cumberland, besides many thousand at New Kent Courthouse." The river was "crowded with craft of every description." To Wheeler, White House was "just my idea of a southern plantation, large fine house and out buildings, and in the rear a long street of negro huts on the river bank, still occupied by . . . slaves . . . the negroes now earn a great deal of money washing for our soldiers and selling fish." Out of 150 slaves, *DIXIE* noted that White House "is the only plantation on this peninsula where I have found a slave that has been taught to read." [13]

On May 18, Old Baldy's division was detached from the Fourth Corps and placed under the command of Brigadier General William B. Franklin's newly formed Sixth Corps, the 77th's brigade now serving with two other brigades of regiments from Maine, New Jersey, New York, and Pennsylvania. The next day the 77th marched another six miles toward Richmond, and by the 21st of May they were a mere eleven miles from the city limits of Richmond.

On the 23rd about noon, the Third Brigade, led by the 77th, marched on, screened by General Stoneman's cavalry. They pushed on the direct road to Richmond toward the small village of Mechanicsville, about eight miles northeast of Richmond. About 4:00 p.m., before the bridge over a small tributary called Brandy Run, Stoneman ran into Col. B. H. Robertson's 4th Virginia Cavalry and the 8th and 9th Georgia Regiments. Dismounting, the Federal troopers opened fire on the enemy cavalry which was posted on an opposite hill. Stoneman's accompanying battery of six pieces quickly returned fire and engaged in an artillery duel with the Confederates positioned before Mechanicsville. The shelling continued for half an hour before silencing the Rebel batteries which were driven back about a quarter of a mile.

Led by the 77th, the Third Brigade soon came up followed by Captain Charles Wheeler's Battery E, 1st New York Light Artillery. The brigade formed into line of battle and General Davidson deployed the 77th as skirmishers along the edge of a deep swampy ravine about a mile to the right of the Brandy Run Bridge. They then were ordered to advance across the ravine. Leading the skirmishers, Col. Mckean was slowed as he "sank deep in the mud and water." Major Winsor B. French "took charge of the left wing . . . I got my horse into the mire so I was obliged to dismount to give her time to get out. She was not much hurt but somewhat strained." On ascending the opposite side of marshy ravine, the 77th moved to the left toward the bridge to reconnect with their brigade. With the Union advance the Rebels withdrew to Mechanicsville forming in and around the sleepy hamlet. As night approached the 77th "slept on their arms . . . in a field of wheat, wet to the middle, and cold." [14]

General Davidson commanded Colonel Mckean to send out pickets toward Mechanicsville. Lt. Wheeler's Co. C and A set out and spent a miserable night "posted very near the enemy. They shot at us a number of times during the night which was not passed in a very comfortable manner, as we were wet to the body after wading through the swamps we had passed, besides the night was cold and our overcoats and blankets were left behind." [15]

At the crack of dawn the next morning, the 77th awoke to a steady pouring rain as General Davidson prepared the Third Brigade to advance on Mechanicsville. The 77th anchored the right flank with three companies of skirmishers of the 33rd New York followed by the 49th New York Regiment with the 7th Maine supporting Wheeler's battery on the left flank. As French recounted, the 77th "filed off into a wheat field in line of battle, and under the crest of a knoll, advanced... when *bang* came a solid shot, just over our heads." The 77th briefly halted there until "ordered up the hill, but as we swung up on the hill, bang, bang came a dose of canister and grape into our ranks, scattering dust and dirt into our eyes." Colonel Mckean dismounted from his horse and commanded, "Down, men! Down!" [16]

Lieutenant Colonel Winsor B. French (L. Tom Perry Special Collections, Harold B. Lee Library, Brigham Young University)

Major French also "dismounted and squatted in the wheat, and the men lay flat on their faces." French remembered, "Bang, bang, she came again, killing one private of Co. I, and slightly wounding five others in the regiment. It threw dirt and gravel against my horse so she jumped away from me and ran, but the Dr. [Stevens] caught here . . . We lay close to the ground for some time." [17]

Sergeant Skinner (Co. D) listened as the shot and shell "passed with terrific whizzing over our 'defenseless heads'" and immediately realized, "If we had stood up we should probably have been cut down in twenty minutes." Private George Russell (Co. K) laid in agony as an exploding shell left him "with three wounds, one in my right hip, one in my shin, and one in my hand." [18]

Wheeler's guns could not silence the hidden Rebel battery or the infantry firing upon the Third Brigade "from the houses, barns, trees and hedges." Davidson called to Stoneman to send up a section of horse artillery. Lieutenant Alexander Pennington's 2nd U. S. Artillery promptly appeared on the battlefield, its gun crews tearing up an old fence, and entered the same wheat field held by the 77th. After unlimbering, Pennington "opened a well-directed and deliberate fire of canister upon the buildings." After firing a few rounds of canister, Pennington's battery received shot and shell from the Rebels who had taken cover in the village, some of which came uncomfortably close to the cannons. Captain Pennington then directed one of his guns where the well-hidden guns were situated and fired off three shells which silenced the Confederate battery.[19]

As soon as General Davidson saw that their pieces had been silenced, he ordered the 77th to "charge upon, seize, and hold the village," and promised the regiment that if they took the village, they should have "Mechanicsville" on their banners. Colonel Mckean "broke the regiment into columns by companies." Then Corporal

William Caw (Co. H) heard Mckean shout, "'Men of the 77th, now is the chance to cover yourselves in glory! Charge!' and on the double quick we charged the village." [20]

As French recalled the next day, "Such a yell you never heard – The Colonel led – I acted as Lieut. Col. – and cheered the boys on." Seeing the 77th advance, the 33rd New York come up on their left and joined the charge. Assistant Surgeon Stevens looked on as the "Seventh and Eighth Georgia Regiments, startled by the shouts, seized their muskets and ran; firing but one parting salute. Their battery also limbered up and beat a hasty retreat; and as our men reached the village they were lashing their horses into a run; and in a moment they disappeared altogether down the road." Two companies of the 77th along with some of the 33rd New York deployed as skirmishers and followed the fleeing Rebels through a field and an adjoining wood, continuing the pursuit down the Dispatch Road to Richmond where they held up at the bridge over the Chickahominy. [21]

77th Charge at Mechanicsville (Saratoga Springs Historical Society)

The danger now gone, Major French strolled through the village, its buildings now riddled with shell and canister, and saw that the Georgia soldiers had left behind "their haversacks, canteens, blankets . . ." and "two or three dead horses." Colonel Mckean was presented with the 4th Virginia Cavalry flag depicting "the Stars and Bars" bearing the motto, "Victory or Death." Lieutenant Wheeler "picked up a fine haversack left on the ground." Finding that many of the houses were also deserted, Wheeler "went into one and found all the sugar and eggs we wanted. My orderly found four dollars in gold on the mantle piece they had forgotten to take in their hurry to leave." Private Allen McLain and three others went into a deserted house and "found a hot breakfast in the fireplace and preserves in the pantry awaiting to be cared for; and we could not be so cruel as to desert them." [19]

The next day, French wrote home to some dear friends:

> I'm sitting in a little house owned by a well-to-do farmer, within five miles of Richmond. The man's name is Grubb, he removed his family, but remained behind with most of his household goods, some packed, some unpacked – *all* in confusion. We (the field and staff) occupy a portion of his domicile, namely the front room and chamber, which affords a good substitute for our tents, which were left behind. A nice fire burns upon the hearth, which felt better last night when we were wet and cold, than to-day in the clear sunshine in May. A few sweet potatoes, pillaged from the fields lately planted, are boiling over the fire, and when done, accompanied by a few dry crackers, will constitute our dinner. [22]

To his disappointment, French was not able to stay long for before the day was out, the 77th along with the rest of the Third Brigade moved down the north bank of the Chickahominy River about five miles and, along with the rest of the Sixth Corps, encamped on the grand farm of Dr. William G. Gaines. He was an ardent supporter of the rebellion and Dr. Gaines was the area's largest landowner and his plantation the most imposing. Not surprisingly, Assistant Surgeon Stevens found:

> Few more charming places than Gaines' Farm. The broad wheat fields, alternating with wooded hills, afforded a scene of enchantment to the weary soldiers. A single wheat field contained four hundred and fifty acres, and a delightful grove in rear of the superb old mansion, furnished a cool retreat during the intense heat of the day. The extensive gardens were filled with rare exotics and most beautiful native plants and trees, and birds of varied and brilliant plumage sported among the flowering shrubs and charmed the air with their lively notes. [23]

Some of the men, however, were less interested in the flora and fauna and headed near the river where they found "a large barn well filled with tobacco, from which the boys of the corps did not hesitate to lay in a full supply." *One of the 77th* remarked "so everybody smoked and nobody complained for the want of 'chew.' We have several Cigar Makers in our regiment. So smoking is not only *fashionable* but *common*; of course we are happy." But perhaps even more so because "Dr. Campbell gives us Whiskey when we *need* it, or when he thinks we need it but we *don't always* approve of his judgment in that matter, so we are happy and ready to 'fight' when it becomes necessary." [24]

Nearby, in the rear of the Sixth Corps, stood Liberty Hall, the birthplace of the defiant revolutionary, Patrick Henry. Its grounds were now littered with hundreds of soldiers, some who were worn out by the fatigue of marching and fighting in the intense Virginia heat, others burning with the fevers of typhoid and malaria. The house itself was turned into a hospital and filled with the sick.

By May 27, the Army of the Potomac was divided as it inched ever so close to Richmond up the north and south banks of the Chickahominy. The Fourth Corps under the command of General Keyes had crossed to the south bank a few days before and had moved several miles to the village of Seven Pines. Heintzelman's Third Corps lay behind and to the left of the Fourth Corps facing White Oak Swamp with its right flank resting on the Richmond & York River Railroad. The north bank of the Chickahominy was anchored on the right by Porter's Fifth Corps and on the left by Sumner's Second Corps. Holding the middle was the 77th's Sixth Corps commanded by General Franklin.

The Chickahominy River rises into the highlands to the north of Richmond, wraps around the city on the north and east sides, then empties into the James River several miles south. The bottom banks between the highlands and White Oak Swamp are only slightly elevated, which means that if the river rises by only a few feet, the area overflows making the groundswell spongy and not practical for cavalry and artillery to commence operations. During the night of May 30 a violent storm raged. A chaplain of the Second Corps vividly recalled, "There were constant rains, and on Friday night . . . the windows of the clouds were wide open, and torrents of water poured out. Lightnings, like zigzag arrows of fire, darted to the earth, followed by long rolls of thunder. The superstitious might have supposed that there was a war in heaven." The Chickahominy now became a raging torrent, rising three to four feet above normal. The swampy bottom lands became completely impassable. Corduroyed roads disappeared in the mud. Bridges became dangerous for infantry and suicidal for artillery as the torrid river ripped and tore at the foundations, threatening to wash them away. Although safely removed from the violent current of the swollen river, the 77th was inundated by the surrounding flood waters. Lieutenant Wheeler was made most uncomfortable that night as "the water came under my tent so that my bed was about six inches under the water. I had to lay upon boards to keep dry." [25]

Recognizing that the two Union corps on the south side of the Chickahominy could only be reinforced over one lone bridge, the rickety Grapevine Bridge, Johnston saw the opportunity and pounced. His plan was to first envelop the Fourth Corps at Seven Pines (Fair Oaks) and then, once it had been shattered, attack and roll up the Third Corps. His plan, however, ran into trouble from the start. Johnston could not effectively coordinate his command. At that time the Confederate Army was not organized into separate corps, so he had to divide his army into ad hoc "wings." This unwieldy command structure, coupled with the complicated plan to move along three different thoroughfares – Nine Mile Road, Williamsburg Road, and Charles City Road – spelled trouble as the wings of his command bottled up on the wet and muddy roads. Originally planned to open battle at eight o'clock in the morning, the resulting traffic jam delayed action until early that afternoon.

About 1 o'clock in the afternoon, D. H. Hill launched the attack with his division, despite the fact that he had no idea whether any of the other Confederate elements had reached their assigned positions. Silas Casey, division commander of the Fourth Corps, had failed to inform his men that he suspected a Confederate attack was imminent, and thus Hill's men shattered the first line of Casey's division within a few minutes. The Union forces fell back to a line of rifle pits, but by 3 o'clock the onrushing Confederates had broken that position as well. Exhausted by the fighting, Hill's division was played out. Just then, Union soldiers from the Third

Corps under General Philip Kearny began to arrive on the field, and bolstered the Union line.

In Richmond the sound of guns became increasingly loud as the day wore on. Church belfries and city rooftops were crowded with worried spectators listening to the guns and watching clouds of battle smoke rising in the distance. Skulkers and walking wounded fleeing from the battlefield were stopped by Richmond citizens demanding news of the fight. Numerous rumors of disaster swept through the city. Edmund Ruffin wrote in his journal, "I again went among the excited crowds in the streets & in the halls of the hotels, & also went to the War Office, to gather the latest rumor of battle. They were too many, & too variant, to be noted." The men of the 77th were equally eager for news as they stood in line of battle where they "could see the smoke of battle and hear the roar of artillery and musketry." But as Assistant Surgeon Stevens later lamented, they "were not able to go to the assistance of their fellows." [26]

Meanwhile, General Edwin V. Sumner of the Second Corps, under orders to remain in readiness, pushed his divisions south across the Chickahominy. Despite fears that it might fail, the Grapevine Bridge held as Union soldiers marched across. After receiving word from Hill that his attack had run out of steam, General G. W. Smith advanced his wing of the Confederate army. W. H. C. Whiting's division proceeded along the Nine Mile Road and encountered Darius Couch's division of the Union Second Corps, and swung into battle at Fair Oaks Station at 4 o'clock that afternoon. General John Sedgwick's division of Sumner's Second Corps had reached Couch and they too aligned for battle. Jefferson Davis, Robert E. Lee, Postmaster General John Reagan, and Joseph Johnston supervised Smith's and Whiting's advance. The fighting raged on, but the Confederates could gain no solid advantage despite the fact that

Whiting kept feeding more troops into action. As fighting petered out around nightfall, the Federal line at Fair Oaks now extended its flanks to rest on the Chickahominy River, protecting the Grapevine Bridge and thus ending the isolation of the Fourth Corps.

Near nightfall, while riding behind Confederate lines near Fair Oaks, Johnston personally inspected the lines. Warned by a staff officer that he was dangerously close to the front lines, Johnston replied, "Colonel, there is no use dodging; when you hear them they have passed." Almost immediately thereafter, a spent bullet hit him in the shoulder. Moments after that, one of the last Union artillery shells fired during the battle burst in the air, throwing fragments into Johnston's chest and thigh. Gravely injured, Johnston relinquished command. Next in line stood G. W. Smith, who while in ill health, temporarily assumed command. [27]

The next morning, June 1, Hill's division renewed attacks in its sector. But failing to make much headway, the division soon ended the effort. Equally exhausted and disorganized by the fighting, the Union troops also settled into their positions. The battle of Seven Pines-Fair Oaks had ended. While the battle itself was indecisive, the casualties were heavy on both sides. The Confederates lost about 6,000 in killed, wounded, and missing; the Federals about 5,000.

At 1:30 p.m., Jefferson Davis rode up to the house of a man named Hughs on the Nine Mile Road, which G. W. Smith had taken as his headquarters. There he told Smith he was giving command of the army to someone else. At 2 o'clock a lone figure rode up to the house. Without ceremony, Smith turned over command of the Army of Northern Virginia to Robert E. Lee.

If Joe Johnston never met a retreat he did not like, then George McClellan never saw a siege he did not like. Not surprisingly, then,

McClellan began a nearly month long siege of Richmond. To develop the siege, he chose the high ground at a crossroads known as Old Tavern on the Nine Mile Road above Fair Oaks Station. From this vantage point, McClellan expected to dominate enough of the surrounding countryside to emplace his heavy artillery that would force the Confederates from their advance fortifications. By repeating this process of "regular advances" McClellan hoped to move step by step to within a couple of miles of Richmond, where his siege guns could bombard the Confederate capital. "Then," he wrote, "I shall shell the city and take it by assault." [28]

Accordingly, on Thursday morning, June 5, the 77th and the Sixth Corps "received an order to be ready 'to march' at 3 a.m. precisely' – that's military – so we bounded out of our tents, and were ready in quick time to march." *One of the 77th* complained, "our march that day was a long one; we were obliged to go down the Chickahominy 9 miles to the rail road bridge" at Dispatch Station "before we could cross; then we passed over the swollen and muddy stream, seemingly a mile wide, and marched up opposite where we were in the morning . . . It was a hard march, the soil of Va. about here is as *treacherous* as her Sons – so miry that after a long rain neither man nor beast can travel . . .." [29]

The 77th's march ended where they joined the Sixth Corps at Camp Lincoln near Golding's Farm "close to the enemy, just in the edge of woods, so that our tents are shaded from the hot sun, as we live so cool and comfortable that we hardly appreciate that we have a large army before us." But that night the 77th's mood was clouded "by a real thunderstorm – and a sublime one, too." One soldier was awed by the sights and sounds of the storm. "I have never heard such thunder, or saw such vivid lightning, as we here. It commences at *any time* and keeps roaring as though it would shake the earth in pieces, and tear the trees and rocks from their places, for hours and hours." [30]

The 77th now lay close to the Confederate lines, separated by "a little wooded ravine and wheat field." With the regiment no more than 200 yards from the enemy "the picket line was but a short distance from the camp." Lieutenant Wheeler wrote to his brother "that there was a great deal of firing on the line and our men had to keep very close behind trees or they would get a hole through them . . . I got shot at as I was passing along the line by one of the rascals and came near being stuck . . . ." That morning "at daylight they opened on our camps and picket line from a battery of artillery and made us hug the ground pretty close to keep out of the way of the shells which burst over and around us, making the bark and dead limbs of the trees fly in every direction . . . One man over in the camps beyond was cut in two by a solid canon shot." Wheeler was more than relieved that "soon after two companies of Berdan's sharpshooters came on the line and picked off eight or ten of the rebel gunners with their Sharps rifles. That silenced their fire." [31]

Soon, however, to Sergeant Skinner's pleasure, "by mutual agreement, picket firing was stopped." One soldier in Luther Wheeler's company met a Rebel half way between the picket lines and swapped coats. "After a long talk, the rebel said they would never shoot on our pickets if we did not on theirs, that they did not consider it any better than murder to shoot a man on picket." With the cease fire agreed upon by the opposing pickets, they began "meeting half way and swapping canteens, coats, buttons . . . and exchanging New York papers for Richmond papers." [32]

Day and night, the men of McClellan's army, when not on picket, worked to build eleven bridges over the Chickahominy River and corduroyed the approaches to them – often while standing in water up to their waists. By June 19, the Federal army also had constructed 11 strong redoubts connected by rifle pits, containing seventy pieces of heavy siege artillery, including 4 ½-inch Rodmans and 8-inch mortars, on a five mile line from White Oak Swamp on the south to the vicinity of Mechanicsville north of the Chickahominy. It did not come without cost. As Assistant Surgeon Stevens later recalled, the soldiers worked "under constant fire of the enemy; no day without its skirmish . . . soldiers were daily brought to the hospitals with wounds, even in the most quiet times." [33]

Shot, shell and minie ball where not the only source of danger for the men of the 77th and the Union army. While laying out the lines, the army's engineers gave little thought to hygiene. The 77th and its brethren were forced to drink contaminated surface water. Where no wells or natural springs were to be found, the predominant method of obtaining water was to dig a hole two or three feet deep, insert in it an empty commissary barrel or hardtack box with the bottom cut out, and wait for often contaminated subsurface water to well up and fill it. Consequently typhoid fever swept through the ranks. Sergeant Skinner became desperately ill, but like so many soldiers, the hospital was seen as no more than a sentence to death: "For my Sergeon (sic), my comrades and captain urged me to go to the hospital But I positively refused, thinking it better to live or die in camp rather than die in an Army hospital, alias prison." Typhoid also struck down Colonel McKean, separating him from the regiment, never to return. [34]

Before the month wore down, malaria became more and more deadly. The hospitals daily became increasingly full and even the strongest were constantly failing. Assistant Surgeon Stevens vividly recalled that along with typhoid and malaria, "Diarrhea . . . and other miasmatic maladies, became almost universal. Men who worked at the breastworks one day would be found in the hospitals on the next, burning with fever, tormented with insatiable thirst, racked with pains, or wild with delirium; their parched lips, and teeth blackened with sordes, the hot breath and sunken eyes, the sallow skin and trembling pulse, all telling of the violent working of disease." Stevens mournfully went on:

> Day after day, scores of brave men, who had left their northern homes to aid in the hour of their country's need, were borne to lowly graves along the banks of that fatal river . . . Hospital steamers plied constantly from White House to Washington, Alexandria and Philadelphia, bearing thousands of these victims of disease; and many, with stoic indifference, lay down in their shelter tents and gave themselves over to death, without even applying to comrades or surgeons for assistance . . . Everywhere at the north, men were seen on cars and steamers, on the streets and in the houses, whose sallow countenances, emaciated appearances, and tottering steps, marked them as victims of 'Chickahominy fever.' Express cars groaned with the weight of coffins containing the remains of youths who but a few months before had gone to war in the pride of their strength, and had now yielded, not to the bullets of the enemy, but to the grim spirit which hovered over their death.

By June 14, the 77th which had embarked upon the Peninsula 1,000 strong was now down to "about 275 effective men – and about 12 company officers who are well." Yet Lieutenant Wheeler was able to write home to his mother, "I am tough as ever and am growing fat." [35]

While McClellan dithered just miles before Richmond, Robert E. Lee meant to attack and drive the Federals from the Peninsula. But first he began refitting the Confederate army and preparing it again for battle. Lee ordered earthen fortifications around Richmond strengthened so they might be made secure by fewer men, freeing more troops for offensive operations. He called forces from around the Confederacy to move to Richmond in preparation for the offensive. What Lee hoped for most was time; that McClellan would not attack him before he launched his offensive. McClellan gave him that time.

The Virginian believed he would be able to maneuver a large force around the Fifth Corps, McClellan's exposed flank on the north side of the Chickahominy near Mechanicsville. If he succeeded, Lee believed, the resultant threat to the Union supply line would cause McClellan to retreat away from Richmond and buy the Confederacy much needed time. But before he could launch his attack, Lee needed information. He called for his chief of cavalry, General James Ewell Brown (JEB) Stuart and ordered him to scout the exposed Federal flank. Lee needed to know the exact position of the Union line as well as its strength. Sometimes a reckless adventurer, Stuart did more than reconnoiter McClellan's flank; he rode completely around the Army of the Potomac. June 15, Stuart reported the Union right flank was still vulnerable. The next day, Lee ordered General Thomas "Stonewall" Jackson to move his troops out of the Shenandoah Valley in the west toward Richmond in preparation for the movement on the exposed flank near Mechanicsville.

On the afternoon of June 23, Lee met with his generals, Jackson, his brother-in-law D. H. Hill, James Longstreet, and A. P. Hill at the house of Mary Dabs on the Nine Mile Road east of Richmond. He informed his commanders that they were to attack McClellan within days. At the meeting it was resolved to begin the offensive on the morning of June 26.

Uncharacteristically, McClellan was also planning an attack, the first and only one of his Peninsula campaign. Near Oak Grove was a thick patch of thickets and low pines filled with swamps and ponds in no-man's-land between the Union and Confederate lines. McClellan wanted control of the woods so he would know what the Rebels were up to on the far side. Accordingly, on June 25, Third Corps commander Heintzelman sent Hooker's division forward to capture the woods and quickly met stiff resistance from the Confederates. As the battle raged, the 77th could only anxiously stand by ready to be called into the fight while the "woods rang with the sharp sounds of musketry and the deep tones of the artillery, as the clouds of smoke obscured the scene from view." Stevens watched as "ambulances were emerging from the woods bearing the wounded; and bloody forms on stretchers, and the less seriously wounded leaning on the shoulders of comrades, made up a melancholy procession." [36]

The battle waxed and waned until dark. Indecisive, indeed a tactical draw, the Federals gained a mere six-hundred yards. The cost, however, was severe as together both armies lost more than 1,100 men. Union losses equaled one casualty per yard. Neither side knew that the Battle of Oak Grove was merely the first in a week of unimagined bloodshed that would become known as the Seven Day's Battle.

On the morning of the 26th, Porter's Fifth Corps occupied the high ground around Mechanicsville overlooking the swampy valley of the Chickahominy. Lee's battle plan called for a decisive maneuver by Stonewall Jackson's force to effect a turning movement, getting above and behind the Union army, threatening its supply line. Jackson's presence would force the Federal soldiers out of Mechanicsville, and it would clear the way for Lee to move his army to the northern side of the river. This, in turn, would create a numerical advantage that would allow Lee to launch a crippling attack.

Although Jackson and his men covered 18 miles of difficult marching that day, they did not arrive north of Mechanicsville at the appointed time. Impatient, fiery A. P. Hill prematurely sent his division across the Chickahominy at Meadows Bridge. Hill's men swept into Mechanicsville, driving off the "Pennsylvania Reserves" division of George A. McCall. The Pennsylvanians abandoned the village in favor of a strong defensive position on the eastern side of Beaver Dam Creek, about one mile from Mechanicsville.

Directly opposite the battlefield, on the south side of the Chickahominy, Lieutenant Wheeler listened as the "cannonading fairly made the ground tremble in our camp." Stevens recalled "we could watch columns of smoke as they rolled up from the scene of carnage, and see the flashes of bursting shells, like sheets of lightening in the dark thunder clouds." [37]

The Union soldiers had retired to a line behind trees they had felled earlier in June as obstructions. In some places they had built an earthen parapet to shelter both infantrymen and artillery. The position also enjoyed a broad field of fire, making any direct approach exceedingly dangerous for attackers. Soon five or six brigades under A. P. Hill, nearly 11,000 men altogether, pushed to the edge of the creek and entered the Federal field of fire. At this moment, the 77th could view the battle from their vantage point. And again they stood by, and "as the rebels charged (they) could watch the movements of both armies." What they saw was the carnage of the advancing Confederates mauled by deadly artillery and musket fire. As darkness fell upon the battlefield, the battle ended. [38]

Believing that the Rebels had been soundly defeated, Major French described the scene: "...our hearts throbbed with joy as away behind us we heard the cheers of our soldiers. The General commanded that the regiment be formed and that it be announced that we had beaten the enemy at every point . . .Oh, how we did cheer! Three times three went up from our joyful throats, and yet we were not satisfied. Again we were called out, and a second time informed of the glorious success of McCall, under Porter. Again we cheered, shook hands, thanked God, and said we will soon end this accursed rebellion. The bands of the whole Division played the liveliest and loveliest music; every drum corps beat Yankee Doodle, and every throat that could sing, made the air ring with 'Hail Columbia,' 'The Star Spangled Banner," and 'America.' So we rejoiced till late at night, when we went to our tents happy with the reflection that we should soon be at home, and the rebellion put down." The next day, however, the 77th would be sorely disabused of the notion of a final victory as Lee's army once again attacked the Fifth Corps. [39]

McClellan and Fitz John Porter spent the night discussing the situation of the army, and Porter understood that he was to be entrusted with fulfilling a crucial assignment. McClellan, still deluded into believing the Rebel army vastly outnumbered him, had decided the time had come to let go of his supply line – the Richmond & York Railroad – and move toward the James River to establish a new base at Harrison's Landing. This would be a dangerous operation in the presence of a large and aggressive enemy, but faced with the choice of standing and fighting or changing base, McClellan opted for a retrograde movement. He needed time to move the army, its 3,000 wagons, the heavy guns of the artillery, the sick and wounded, the 2,000 head of cattle, and countless tons of supplies. Porter and his men would buy that time.

Reinforced to a strength of 35,000 men, Porter formed his defense on high ground east of Gaines Mill and behind Boatswain Creek. Like the previous line at Beaver Dam Creek, this naturally strong position rose to wooded heights that dominated a boggy creek bottom, but Porter's men made it even stronger by felling trees and digging rifle pits on the steep slope and placing batteries along the top of the hill. A. P. Hill's men attacked around 2:30 p.m., testing the Fifth Corps position near Cold Harbor. Porter's men repulsed the Rebel advances throughout the afternoon, and hundreds of men, Union and Confederate, fell on the slopes above the creek bottom. As daylight waned, though A. P. Hill and Longstreet's division had been feeding men into battle all afternoon, they made no substantial progress. Much to Lee's frustration, Longstreet and Hill lacked support from the left of the line. For the second time in two days, Stonewall Jackson was late.

Long into the afternoon, Jackson arrived at Old Cold Harbor and deployed for battle. At 7 p.m., less than an hour before sunset, Lee ordered a general assault and the Rebel infantry advanced along a two-mile front, crossing long open stretches, thick woods, and steep slopes. Hampered by the terrain, formations disintegrated, blunting the momentum of the attack. Union musketry and cannon fire were deafening. Sergeant Skinner wrote "the fight was in plain view on Dr. Gaines' farm . . . It was really a privilege – we were permitted to witness the battle in the open field . . . it was laughable to see them Skedaddle like sheep when our Parrot Guns . . . poured upon their uncovered ranks a storm of shot and shell." Nevertheless, the Southerners pressed the outnumbered Fifth Corps at every point along the line. John Hood's "Texas Brigade" broke through at Boatswain Creek, and on the far eastern end of the line, Jackson's men breached the line near the road to the Chickahominy. Porter's line subsequently began to crumble. In desperation, cavalry commander Philip St. George ordered a cavalry charge intended to thwart the charging Rebels long enough for the Union infantry and artillery to escape. Cooke's charge failed, and Union forces lost 22 cannons and thousands of prisoners in the withdrawal. [40]

At dusk, the 77th was no longer merely an interested observer. Lieutenant Wheeler wrote "they attacked our position first with artillery by opening a crossfire from in front and from the other side of the Chickahominy." Major French, now commanding the regiment in place of Colonel McKean, wrote, "so thick and fast that we were obliged to seek protection in the rifle pits we had thrown up but a few days before. Our tents were riddled with balls; one solid shot struck the Dr. (Stevens) tent and passed quite through." French ordered the 77th's ranks to form in the face of fire and as he "was forming the battalion a solid shot came close by me, and struck Isaac Boice (Private Co. B) and John Seeley (Private Co. E). It was a spent shot which came from Gaines' Mill. I saw it as it came like a fluttering partridge, and gave warning, but not in season to prevent the accident." [41]

The Battle of Gaines Mill was a clear Confederate victory. Porter's Fifth Corps, seriously outnumbered much of the day, had held its own but at a fearful cost – about 6,000 men killed, wounded, missing or captured in seven hours of fighting. Lee had won his first battlefield victory at a steep price of 9,000 men. With nearly 95,000 men engaged, Gaines Mill set a new mark for blood-letting in the eastern theater. Though the two armies that battled at Shiloh several weeks before had almost 25,000 casualties in two days of fighting, Lee and Porter had together lost 15,000 men in a single afternoon.

Before the sun arose on June 28, as the 77th lay guarding the front, General Davidson came with news of retreat: "Mr. French, this is for your ear: take a commissioned officer of each company and go to camp; pack up a few articles of value, such as you can carry on your horse or back, and be ready to march at a moment's notice. We are to change our position and only one wagon will be allowed to a regiment." Entirely shocked, Major French blurted, "My God General, does the Army of the Potomac retreat?" Silencing his protest, Davidson said only, "No questions – go quickly." [42]

That morning the 77th had been on picket and were ordered into camp by company as they were being relieved by the 33rd New York. They were rudely interrupted by Confederates under the command of John Magruder. On Garnett's farm, David R. Jones, one of Magruder's division commanders, became aware of the movement in his front. Suspecting the withdrawal of the Union forces, he sent Robert Tombs to conduct a reconnaissance in force to verify or refute suspicion. Toombs, the Confederacy's first Secretary of State, who held a deep disdain for professional soldiers – he described his superior as "that old ass Magruder" – took it upon himself to turn the reconnaissance in force to an outright assault. The attackers were none other than the 7th and 8th Georgia Regiments that the 77th had faced the previous month at Mechanicsville.

Captain Martin Lennon was posted with a small detachment of the 77th at an advance redoubt or lunette which had been thrown up earlier by men of Hooker's division. Lennon's first intimation of danger "was that a shell passed behind me and struck in a bank beyond me, and nearly at the same instant another struck the ground at my feet and exploded, doing me no injury except nearly knocking me down, and deafening me nearly all day." He quickly got up and realizing he was "in the open field, in direct range of their guns . . . I got out of that into woods as soon as possible and . . . started for camp." Just as he was heading toward the woods, he was passed by the 77th's pickets also fleeing from the onrushing Georgians. All but Private John Ham (Co. D) were brushed aside. Ham, who had earlier vowed never to retreat before the enemy, stood like a veteran at the lunette, firing off ten rounds and killing four rebels before being wounded in the leg and falling to the ground. Even after this misfortune, he was bayonetted three times by the rebels.

Meanwhile, Captain Lennon found himself in a harrowing position:

> I crossed the ravine and came out into the open field in front of our camp. To get to my regiment I had to turn

to the left and go about sixty rods. You may imagine my surprise when I say that the enemy had got through ahead of me, and that fifty of them were between me and camp. They saw me at about the same time I saw them, and some twenty of them turned and fired at me, but fortunately their aim was not very good, for none of the balls hit me, and they were not more than twenty rods distant. I have, probably, to thank secesh whiskey for my life that time, for we afterwards learned that most of them were drunk. You need not puzzle your brain wondering what I did under the circumstances. My regiment had all gone except me, and there but few of the other regiments, and what few there were getting into camp as lively as they possibly could. I could not go to my own camp; that was certain. So I just turned to the right as the rest were doing and went into the camp of another regiment (33rd New York) of our brigade. You may perhaps, think I didn't run. If you do, I beg to inform you that you are terribly mistaken for I did run like a white-head. You never heard of such time as I made. My legs did their duty nobly that time, if they ever did. There was the most lively buzzing around my head that I ever heard, for the enemy kept a perfect shower of balls coming all the time.

Lennon leapt into the rifle pits of the 33rd New York just as they released a volley into the Confederates following close behind him. As the fighting continued, the 7th and 8th Georgia Regiments became entangled by the thick woods and underbrush of the swampy ground. This gave Lennon and the 33rd New York an opening to face about and hurriedly retreat to the breastworks of Fort Davidson, a strong redoubt with a trench in front preceded by a double line of rifle pits. As they reached the breastworks they hunkered down as shell and canister flew over their heads. [43]

Now facing their foe, the 8th Georgia, under the command of Colonel Lucius Lamar, formed a new line of battle. They were followed alongside by the 7th Georgia. They came on with reckless abandon. Major French remembered that the Georgians fought with "a desperation almost unheard of . . . They were so reckless that they would deliberately jump on top of a breastwork, behind which they halted, and expose themselves recklessly to a galling fire." Two of the 7th Georgia color bearers were shot down and the attack soon lost momentum with the Confederates retreating to the other side of the field. But Colonel Lamar reformed the Georgians and once again they charged only to be rebuffed again. Lamar was mortally wounded in the charge and taken prisoner along with Lieutenant Colonel John Towers of the 8th Georgia. Among them were a number of prisoners. One of the prisoners told Martin Lennon "that they always got scorched when they pitched into Old Baldy's division." [44]

After the intense, bloody skirmish Lieutenant Wheeler surveyed the field before him: "two hundred of the enemy were piled on a piece of ground only a few rods square." Sergeant Skinner walked the battlefield and picked up a souvenir that he sent back to his old professor at the Fort Edward Institute, A. C. Works: "'The knife and fork belong together – are very common in the army. I had one similar and lost it . . . I send you these, because they are from 'Secesh' taken from the pocket of a <u>Slain Rebel</u>, after the battle was over . . . I hope you will accept the relic, as such and not accuse <u>me</u> of <u>vandalism</u> for I did not rifle the pockets of the brave dead – It is proper to say that such is a very common practice and is not considered <u>criminal</u>. The 'reb' used them in eating <u>his</u> rations. I have used them eating mine, and you are at liberty to do so if you are not afraid of the <u>Secesh temper</u> of it. You may hand it down to your <u>posterity</u>.'" [45]

Captain Lennon returned from the battlefield to find the 77th prepared to join the Army of the Potomac in the retreat to James

River and Harrison's Landing. The regiment had left the breastworks in and around Fort Davidson and gone into camp. There, Major French looked on as the men of the 77th "picked up our haversacks and brought what we could carry." They had been "ordered to leave all tents standing, that the enemy be deceived." While the 77th left their tents standing, they rendered them useless by cutting large slices in the sides with their sabre bayonets. Guns that were to be left behind were broken up. Indeed, everything that was to be left behind was destroyed. [46]

The Regiment settled down in the shade of a grove of trees until 2 a.m. Along with Smith's division, they marched toward Savage's Station, keeping close to the Chickahominy. The march was a slow one. The roads were crowded with the retreating multitude of the Union army. Along the narrow roads, some no larger than a cow path, moved endless streams of footsore men, army wagons, artillery trains, ambulances, and thousands of beef cattle. The 77th arrived at Savage's Station on the Richmond & York River Railroad where the bulk of McClellan's army was now concentrating at 4 p.m. The men filed into a thick stand of trees and rested while they waited for other divisions to pass by. Surgeon Stevens took in the scene before him at Savage's Station, describing it as one of "wonderful confusion." In what had before been a Federal supply depot, Stevens now saw before him, "Immense heaps of commissary stores, arms and ammunition were waiting destruction lest they should fall into the hands of the enemy, and hundreds of sick and wounded men were taking sad leave of their friends; for it had been determined that these brave unfortunate men must be left to the tender mercies of the rebels." As he watched, Stevens was awestruck by the furious work of destruction before him:

> Boxes of hard bread, hundreds of barrels of flour, rice, sugar, coffee, salt and pork were thrown upon the burning

piles and consigned to the flames. One heap of boxes of hard bread as large as a good sized dwelling made a part of the sacrifice. Boxes of clothing and shoes were opened and every man as he passed helped himself to whatever he thought worth carrying away. . . . Thousands helped themselves, and huge boxes of clothing were cast into the flames.

Two years later, when the Army of the Potomac was once again on the Peninsula, Stevens was surprised that many of the surrounding dwellers "were clothed and shod with articles left by us at Savage's Station on the grand retreat." [47]

Destroying quartermaster and commissary stores was one thing; disposing of the immense stockpile of munitions was quite another. Disposal of kegs of gunpowder, cartridges, shot and shells required much care and ingenuity. As Stevens wrote after the war, a spectacular pyrotechnic display ensued:

These were loaded into cars; a long train was filled with these materials, and then, after setting fire to each car, the train was set in motion down the steep grade. With wildest fury the blazing train rushed; each revolution of the wheels adding new impetus to the flying monster, and new volumes to the flames. On and on the burning train thundered like a frightful meteor. Now, the flames being communicated to the contents of cars, terrific explosions of shells and kegs of powder lent new excitement to the scene. The air was full of shrieking, howling shells, the fragments of which tore through the trees and branches of the forest; and huge fragments of cars were seen whirling in the air. . . At length the train reached the river; and such was its momentum, that notwithstanding the bridge was burned, the engine and the first car leaped over the first pier in the stream, and the cars hung suspended.

With munitions exploding, the 77th and Smith's division once again took up the march and moved beyond Savage's Station toward White Oak Swamp. [48]

The Army of Northern Virginia was in hot pursuit of the retreating Federal army as Lee continued his offensive to drive McClellan off the Peninsula. Once again "Prince John" Magruder found himself in the limelight. Three months had passed since the Virginian had duped McClellan with theatrics at Yorktown. Now he was at the heart of Lee's plan to crush the Union army. Unfortunately, though, Magruder was barely up to the task. He had been ill with acute indigestion and was taking medication laced with opium. He could not relax enough to sleep and seemed to some of his command to be nearing the end of his endurance. Nevertheless, the decisive hour was at hand, and Lee expected Magruder to do his duty. The general's orders were plain: press vigorously toward Savage's Station.

Around 5 p.m., after the 77th had marched several miles toward White Oak Swamp, Stevens saw a "huge cloud in the direction of the camps we had deserted." The cloud signaled the advance of Magruder's approaching column straddling the Richmond & York River Railroad. In the center was a new invention of war, the "Land Merrimac," an armored 32 pounder Brook naval gun pushed slowly by a locomotive in the center. As the Confederates neared Savage's Station, the Merrimac threw a shell into "the Hospital camp thinking it a camp of soldiers, but desisted after a surgeon came out with a white flag and told them it was a hospital." While Magruder was busy forming his forces into line of battle, a severe artillery duel erupted. "Shells screamed from one side to the other, and the bright flashes and sharp reports, as they burst in the air, mingled with the noise and smoke of battle, as battery responded to battery." [49]

At the sound of artillery, word was sent to General Davidson to return the Third Brigade to Savage's Station to reinforce the Federal line. The 77th soon arrived at the scene of battle and was placed in reserve in a large open field. Although the Confederates and Northerners committed only a fraction of their men, the fighting was intense. For a while the Federals stubbornly held their ground, yet near dark the two brigades of Joseph B. Kershaw and Paul J. Semmes threatened to pierce the Union line. The 77th expected to be called up to stem the tide when they saw Union Brigadier General T. H. Brooks' Vermont Brigade storm into the woods to meet the charging Rebels. For a short time, the fight in the darkening woods matched anything Shiloh or Seven Pines or Gaines' Mill could boast in the way of ferocity.

In no time the ground was littered with the bodies of dead and wounded Vermonters. The 5th Vermont lost 206 men, more than half its strength, within twenty minutes. Among the fallen were five Cummings brothers, one of their cousins, and a brother-in-law. Six of the seven men were killed; only the eldest brother, Henry Cummings, survived. The Confederates of Kershaw and Semmes brigades paid an equally steep price. As so often was the case in the Civil War, with darkness the battle ended. A correspondent for the *New York World* reported that the macabre "scene on the field was bloody in extreme. Heaps upon heaps of the dirty, grimy coated traitors lay dead or writhing in agony. In many places they lay in swaths, marking the track of the terrible discharge" of musketry and artillery. [50]

The night held no rest for the 77th and the Army of the Potomac, for the march to the James continued. With Smith's division acting as rear guard, the 77th turned toward White Oak Swamp. Six of the 77th, including Private Edwin Ham (Co. D), and many from other regiments were detailed to stay behind and bury the dead and consequently became prisoners. The thousands of sick and wounded too weak to move were left to fall into the hands of the Rebels following on the heels of the retreating Union army. Houses along the roadside were filled with the wounded. Emanating from the houses, Lieutenant Wheeler "could hear the groans and screams as we marched along." He pitied the many injured soldiers who struggled along trying to keep up with the Northerners. "The poor fellows," he wrote, "could be seen along the roadside, limping along with a look of agony in their faces, with every species of wounds." [51]

Private Edwin Ham (L. Tom Perry Special Collections)

The night's march was long and difficult for the healthy as well for it rained hard throughout the night. The road became so muddy that the soldiers' feet got stuck in the mire. The road to White Oak Swamp was crowded with wagons, ambulances and artillery trains, mingled with horsemen and infantry, all pushing forward to their destination. The men of Smith's division picked their way among the chaos, losing all organization, each bent upon making his way forward regardless of others. Writing to his mother, Wheeler took note that, "There was a good many wagons disabled and left by the roadside, some held whiskey; these wagons were completely surrounded and covered with a straggling mass of soldiers, with cups in their hands trying to get the whiskey." The sight reminded the Lieutenant of "a swarm of bees in a bee hive." Many who imbibed became drunk and went to sleep by the side of the road only to be taken prisoner as the Confederate army passed by. [52]

After the exhausting night march, the 77th finally reached White Oak Swamp before daylight. Hours later, the regiment crossed White Oak Bridge and immediately positioned themselves on a small rise to the left of the road. Major French thought "surely we had crossed the Jordan and were in a place of safety." The 77th then bedded down for much needed sleep. With the sun climbing in the horizon, the men were awakened by the sound of teamsters driving their wagons from a hill behind them. General Davidson ordered the 77th to take a position in a stand of pines, fronting and guarding a road entering the swamp east of the burned White Oak Bridge. [53]

Unbeknownst to the 77th and the rest of Smith's division, Thomas Jackson had marched his pursuing column up to the opposite bank of the swamp at noon, stopped only by the ashes and remaining cinders of the White Oak Bridge. The bridge had been burned by the Federals only two hours earlier. The marshy bottomland of the swamp precluded any crossing of his wagons and artillery. Standing unnoticed at the edge of the stream flowing through White Oak Swamp, Jackson observed several Union batteries, supported by infantry across the stream. Still unseen, Jackson quietly deployed his cannon, screened by thick vegetation and trees.

At 2 p.m., Sergeant Skinner was sitting "with my haversack open, Equipments off and in the act of appropriating a lunch of raw bacon and hard bread" when the air fairly exploded with Jackson's batteries of over thirty artillery pieces. Overestimating the number Lieutenant Wheeler wrote, "You have no idea of the noise made by forty or fifty pieces of artillery revved as they were during this battle, it was a continuous roar." To Wheeler "the air seemed full of the hissing missiles which were bursting over our heads, and scattering their death dealing fragments." Major French noted, "It made the bravest quake and shudder, and leave for shelter." Many of the shot and shells concentrated around a small dwelling house where Generals Smith, Davidson, Brooks and their staff were staying. Three shots passed through the room where Smith was taking a bath. Smith lost everything, even his watch and pistols. Another killed the elderly man who owned the house and two orderlies. Horses were laid dead before the door of the house and aids were running for protection, having had their horses shot from underneath them. Teamsters cut loose their mules and ran for dear life. The 77th fortunately stood in line just out of range of fire supporting Mott's battery which had the misfortune of being the focus of several of the Rebel batteries. Wheeler watched in horror as Mott "lost all of its horses and half its men, and the pieces were all disabled." However, the artillerymen were able to take off all but one gun. [54]

"All was confusion," French wrote, "and what the rebels intended had been accomplished – *a panic.*" The 20th New York, known as Turners Rifles, recently added to the Third Brigade, broke and ran to the rear to escape the deadly missiles. They were led by their commander, Colonel Francis Weiss, who earlier had boasted he would draw blood on the field. The 20th's Private Friedrich Meyer (Co. H) remembered that, "The colonel and most of the officers fled the field without giving any indication of what the men should do. The colonel even abandoned his horse. Most of the regiment, in the wildest disorder, followed their example." The field was littered with their haversacks and Hardee hats as they dodged terrified horses running from the stream that were being watered by teamsters when the bombardment had begun. [55]

Mott was able to wheel his battery back in place and his guns were hotly engaged in a duel with the opposing Confederate batteries. In time Mott silenced the Rebel cannon in his front. The 77th again supported Mott's battery, but, Major French said "it required a good deal of pluck." Suddenly some of Hancock's men who on the left were nearest to the Confederates filed by the 77th on the double quick and left the regiment exposed to fire from three directions. French complained "no orders yet. "As the artillery duel met a desultory end, the 77th was ordered to move by the right flank to a new position away from shot and shell. There the regiment laid "all the rest of the day in the shade, cool and comfortable" now "in a position where we could whip three times our number." [56]

With Jackson stalled at White Oak Swamp two miles west at about 4 p.m., Lee ordered Longstreet to advance against the head of McClellan's retreating army now located at Glendale – the wartime home and property of the R. H. Nelson family. Longstreet attacked with his own and A. P. Hill's men on both sides of the Long Bridge Road. In position to meet the assault were Hill's adversaries from Mechanicsville and Gaines' Mill, the Pennsylvanians of George McCall's division. Hill's and McCall's soldiers had done more fighting in the last four days than any other troops, but fate threw them together on the Long Bridge Road in what would be perhaps the most savage fighting of the Seven Days Battle.

Twenty-four field guns from six batteries held the crest of a shallow rise above a ravine southwest of Glendale. The batteries presented a formidable front, made even more foreboding by McCall's 6,000 men and Phil Kearney's 7,500 infantrymen. But Longstreet's men were undeterred and lunged forward with almost irresistible recklessness. "But a single idea seemed to control the minds of the men," wrote Brigadier General James L. Kemper of his brigade's advance, "which was to reach the enemy's line by the directest route and in the shortest time; and no earthly power could have availed to arrest or restrain the impetuosity with which they rushed toward the foe." [57]

Kemper's Virginians shattered McCall's left flank, then had to withdraw because supports did not come forward quickly enough. But McCall's line had been broken and would never be fully restored in the seesaw fighting that bore on through the rest of the afternoon. The 12 brigades of Longstreet and Hill repeatedly charged against McCall and Kearny but reeled back under the force of counterattacks. At the apex of battle, Alabamians under Brigadier General Cadmus M. Wilcox captured the six-gun battery of Lieutenant Alanson Randol on the Long Bridge Road. Randol and his gunners, with the Pennsylvanians, counterattacked and retook the guns in hand-to-hand fighting only to lose them again to Virginians under Brigadier General Charles W. Field. Yet McCall and Kearny held the line until the Confederates ceased their attack well after 9 p.m.

As soon as darkness came, the 77th once again took up the line of march for the James River. Major French remembered it "as the severest march of all." The men frequently halted on the crowded road and "officers and men would fall asleep, and could not be aroused by the most violent means." Many hundreds of those deep in slumber lined the roadside and fell into the hands of the enemy. Privates Andrew Williamson and Orville Jeffords of Lieutenant Wheeler's C Company were among those who slept and then found themselves in the midst of the pursuing Rebel army. [58]

After nearly 20 miles of hard marching, the 77th "filed out of the woods, just as day was breaking, and saw before us a large plain, which we believed was the shore of the James." The regiment halted "and dropped down to sleep in a clover field, and slept till the sun was at least an hour high." French later wrote that, "Never did poor soldiers wish more ardently for rest and sleep. The children of Israel could not have wished to view the promised land, across the Jordan, more than the poor weary soldiers of Smith's division the banks of the James." [59]

Their rest was soon broken as the 77th was ordered to the front and occupied a wheat field. Major French was awed by and proud of what lay before him: "I never saw Old Baldy's division look as formidable. The bristling bayonets of the three brigades – Brook's, Hancock's, and Davidson's – the open mouths of his beautiful batteries as they lay in position waiting for the enemy; -- two or three times our number would have been annihilated had they dared to approach." Before the division was "three lines of rebels" but they kept "a proper distance." There the 77th stood expecting to be called forward as they intently listened to "the booming of our field pieces and the dull roar of the heavy guns from the gunboats." [60]

The booming of artillery and gunboats signaled Robert E. Lee's last attempt to inflict a fatal blow on the Army of the Potomac, now resting on Malvern Hill. The slopes of the hill had been cleared of timber, providing great visibility. And the open fields of the north side could be swept by deadly fire from eight batteries of field artillery, with 37 guns placed by Colonel Henry J. Hunt, McClellan's chief of artillery. Beyond the cleared space in front of Malvern Hill, the terrain was swampy and thickly wooded.

Rather than flanking the position of the Union army, Lee attacked it directly, hoping that his artillery would clear the way for a successful infantry assault. Unfortunately for Lee, Henry Hunt struck first, launching one of the greatest artillery barrages in the war. The Union gunners had superior equipment and disabled most of the Confederate batteries. Despite the setback, Lee sent his infantry forward at about 3:30 p.m. and Brigadier General Lew Armistead's brigade made some progress through the lines of Union sharpshooters. By 4 p.m. Magruder was ordered forward to support Armistead. Magruder's attack was piecemeal and poorly organized. Meanwhile, D. H. Hill launched his division forward along the Quaker Road, past Willis Methodist Church. Across the entire line of battle, the Confederate troops reached only within 200 yards of the Union center and were repulsed with frightful losses. Thus ended the Seven Days Battles and McClellan's Peninsula Campaign.

5

"THE MOST MISERABLE DAY IN MY LIFE"

After filling their haversacks during the night, the 77th readied once again to march. At 2 a.m. the regiment left the wheat field they had occupied while the Battle of Malvern Hill raged. After only a mile, Smith's division halted as the rest of the Army of the Potomac passed by. Lieutenant Wheeler remembered, "It was a great sight to see this large army. I saw the whole of it pass by. The road was wide so that four Regiments could march abreast, besides a line of artillery. It took more than twelve hours for the infantry to pass, and they walked very fast. I should think that there was more than ten miles of light artillery passed that morning." [1]

By the time the 77th again took up the march, they had been standing in a torrential rain that was to continue throughout the day. From Malvern Hill to Harrison's Landing was eight miles by way of the River Road. Like every road on the Peninsula when it rained, the River Road became almost a fathomless mud. "Oh, how it did rain," Major French complained, "mud, mud, every soldier was wet and muddy from his head to his toes." The tired men could scarcely drag themselves along, many abandoning their rifles, blankets, and haversacks – anything that encumbered them. Entire wagon trains bogged down in the road and the drenched infantrymen paid no attention to the teamsters' cry for help. As they approached the landing, Wheeler saw "cavalrymen sitting at the corners of roads crying out to the thousands of stragglers . . . 'this way to Sedgewick's and Kearny's Divisions' or 'this way to Smith's and Slocum's.'" It reminded the Lieutenant of, "Circus men crying their shows." [2]

On the 77th marched, leading the Third Brigade. Major French looked forward to General Davidson at the head of the column and encouraged the brigade to close up. With pride French recorded, "He complimented the 77th and called us 'his regiment' and indeed showed us that our good conduct in making long marches, with so few lost, was appreciated by him, and should be remembered." [3]

At about 2 p.m., after "hugging the banks of the James as closely as the country along the river would permit" the 77th arrived at their destination. Harrison's Landing, founded in 1618 and also known as Berkeley Plantation, was their stopping point. One year later the first Thanksgiving celebration by English colonists on American soil was held at this location. Benjamin Harrison, a signer of the Declaration of Independence, and William Henry Harrison, the ninth president of the United States, were born in the great, red-brick plantation house that graced the property. And in 1622, an event that was a little closer to the heart of the common Civil War soldier occurred: the first bourbon whiskey was distilled on the grounds of Berkeley. The main house was filled with the best mahogany furniture, gilded sconces, and delicate, hand-carved chairs. Sadly, under Union occupation the furniture soon became firewood for the soldiers and the fine rugs turned stiff and brown with the blood of the wounded from Malvern Hill. [4]

Cresting a small hill overlooking Harrison's Landing, Major French could scarcely believe "the sight that met our eyes. Here was a vast plantation, miles in length and breadth, covered with corn and wheat, trodden in the mud, and the whole Potomac army encamped, horses, wagons, and men, in some confusion, yet distinct – every brigade and division had its place." The whole army indeed; into this vast plantation bounded on the west by Kimmage's Creek and on the east and curving around to the north the swamp and waterway of Herring Creek, crowded over 90,000 men, 288 cannons, 3,000 wagons and ambulances, 2,500 head of cattle, 27,000 horses and mules. [5]

While French surveyed the wide plain where the Union army now laid, Surgeon Stevens looked outward to the James River "full of transports and gunboats, giving it the appearance of the harbor of some commercial metropolis." As he did so, Stevens observed that "many of the men without waiting for their rations to be brought by the commissary, plunged into the stream, swam to the boats and then procured the coveted food." Many more, however, lay "down in the bed of mud and were soon in heavy slumbers." [6]

As Major French recounted to his friends back home at Saratoga, the 77th finally "halted on a beautiful clover plot" where they were ever so thankful that their teams and private wagons met them. While they rested, Robert E. Lee and his generals discovered that McClellan had vacated Malvern Hill. All that was known for certain was that the Union army had marched east along the north bank of the James River. Needing intelligence on the whereabouts of McClellan, Jeb Stuart was directed to head east with his cavalry to locate the Federals. [7]

On July 3, Stuart came upon the Northerners at Harrison's Landing and chased the Union pickets off the ridge line north of Herring's Creek at Evelington Heights. At about ten o'clock that morning, Stuart, commanding only one howitzer, tossed a few shells into the encamped Yankees. His single-minded bravado stirred the Federals into momentary panic. General McClellan himself galloped to the line and personally directed Smith's division to occupy the heights. As the 77th "moved out to take them," French wrote "they moved away." Outnumbered, Stuart and his troopers hastily beat a retreat and the 77th finally "encamped in a large wheat field, and commenced to entrench ourselves." [8]

As the regiment settled into their new camp, Winsor French took time to reflect upon the Confederate soldier:

> At the north the southern soldier has been underrated. They are Americans, and fight with a desperation peculiar to Americans. At the South *every man* is a soldier. No where, throughout the whole Confederacy, will you see white men able to do duty, out of the army. Public feeling is so strong, that it brands every man who is not a *soldier* a *coward*. Their discipline, too, is most perfect. Their officers are, in most every instance, men of wealth and *influence*, who are fighting to maintain what they have been *taught* to believe is the proper government – an Aristocracy. There are no lukewarm officers, who have enlisted to *draw pay*, or to wear epaulets, for the glory of the thing. They fight, as they say, '"to drive the d—'d Yankees from their homes." What stronger argument can they use to an *ignorant soldier*? Their men fight with desperation almost unheard of. At the battle . . . (Mechanicsville) . . . they deliberately halted, pulled their dead and wounded out of the way, that they might move on

with their massed columns. Every soldier's canteen is said to contain whiskey with powder mixed.[9]

The next day, July 4, 112 years after the signing the Declaration of Independence, McClellan moved to boost the morale of the Union army. First he issued an address to the army, which he praised, telling the soldiers that:

> Your achievements of the last ten days have illustrated the valor and endurance of the American soldier. Attacked by superior forces, and without hope of reinforcements, you have succeeded in changing your base of operations by a flank movement, always regarded as the most hazardous of military expedients . . . Upon your march you were assailed, day after day, with desperate fury, by men of the same race and nation, skillfully massed and led. Under every disadvantage of number, and necessarily of position also, you have, in every conflict, beaten back your foes with enormous slaughter. Your conduct ranks you among the celebrated armies of history. No one will now question that each of you may always with pride say, 'I belong to the Army of the Potomac.'

Underscoring the "victory" McClellan ordered a national salute. At the appointed time, the guns boomed and Surgeon Stevens recalled, "The boys listened for a moment, and then, as if inspired with new life, they made the welkin ring with their cheers. The bands, roused from their long inactivity, pealed forth stirring airs." Exhilarated by the martial music, Major French opined, "While we were following and driving the enemy, our Generals seemed to think it impolitic for the bands to play, or even the 'calls' to be 'sounded' lest the enemy should know our position; this I call a mistaken notion. Were I General, I would have music everywhere, even on the field of battle. No enemy would be close to me to deprive me of music, and that of the most cheering kind." [10]

By evening the celebration had ended and the army bedded down for a night of peaceful rest. Sergeant Skinner walked about the camp and was struck by the quietude and wistfully thought of home:

> The air of the summer eve, the camps and all nature seem to be at rest. A thousand lights burn silently, and silence pervades the whole. No, I hear the rapid puffing of some weary steamship on the river – as it seems to near the landing with its freighted gang drawn slowly along. It reminds me of other days – of times when I could sit on the shores of a peaceful nativity and hear the same congenial puff, puff. It is a real pleasure now to hear the steam whistle. For weeks and even months we are sometimes deprived of that pleasure. [11]

The day was not entirely uneventful for the Confederate army either, for July 4th witnessed the participation of the *C.S. Teaser* – the very same gunboat that had earlier lobbed shells at unsuspecting Yankees harvesting oysters and chased now resigned Captain Arnold into his tent. It also marked the demise of the Confederacy's aeronautical corps; attempting to locate the Union army, Porter Alexander had once again filled his balloon at the Richmond gas works, tethered it to the *Teaser*, and steamed down the James to Malvern Hill. Alexander made the early morning ascension to look for the northerners, but the wind unexpectedly came up. In response the balloon was hastily reeled down, deflated, and stored aboard for future use. Then the *Teaser* had the misfortune to run aground on a sandbar. The tide was out and the *Teaser* stuck fast. Awaiting the rising afternoon tide, the Federal gunboat, the *Marantaza*, appeared around the bend from downriver. Severely outgunned, the little armed tug was a sitting duck, and after firing one shot and tying down the boiler's safety valve, captain and crew abandoned ship and waded across the sandbar to shore. The *Maratanza* secured her prize before the *Teaser* blew up and towed it off, Porter's balloon with it.

Six weeks of "dreary, sickly and monotonous" camp life followed as the 77th and the Army of the Potomac languished at Harrison's Landing. The regiment immediately turned its attention to making their camp as comfortable as possible. The men dug wells as the water around the Union army's encampment was so stagnant "that even the fish died." Some in the regiment went beyond the slashing in front of the army, cut down small pines, and brought them back to camp "by which some degree of protection was afforded against the burning sun." [12]

As the 77th's camp was being made hospitable, the Sixth Corps began the work of throwing up strong entrenchments and mounting cannons. The Third Brigade "was burned by almost unendurable heat" and "nearly devoured by the countless myriads of flies and other annoying insects" as they constructed an extensive earthen fort which mounted several 32-pounder cannons. In front of the fort, the trees and thickets were slashed by countless wood-cutters who sweltered under the burning rays of the sun. Sergeant George Brennan of the 33rd New York commented, "It was a fine sight to see a whole forest rapidly disappear before the sturdy blows of a thousand choppers." While one regiment of the brigade slashed the wood before the earthen fort, another would be posted in front to prevent enemy sharpshooters from firing at them. [13]

Not surprisingly, as at the siege of Yorktown "sickness became almost universal." With water contaminated by the offal of countless horses, mules, and cows and the sewage of men, Surgeon Stevens lamented, "It was not strange that hundreds died in camp, and that hundreds more, with the seeds of death implanted in their constitutions, went to their homes in the north to breathe out their lives in the midst of their friends, or languished in the large government hospitals at Washington, and other cities." The 77th was reduced to so few men that by the end of July Major French was ordered back to Saratoga Springs to drum up new recruits for the regiment. [14]

At least hundreds became sick and died during the Federal army's extended stay at Harrison's Landing. Surgeon Jonathan Letterman took over as the medical director of the army on July 4 and found McClellan's army greatly exhausted. The medical officers were greatly fatigued by the rising numbers struck down with typhoid, malaria, and scurvy. Early in July, over 6,000 men had been sent away on transports to hospitals in Washington, Annapolis, Philadelphia, New York city, and as far away as Providence, Rhode Island. Yet nearly 13,000 remained behind. It was estimated that at least 20 percent of the men were sick. As fast as transports became available men were shipped north. By July 15, another 7,000 sick had been sent, but again close to 13,000 sat tight in camp. Because the sick soldiers tended to become homesick in general hospitals where they were among strangers, Letterman kept as many at Harrison's as possible in tent hospitals that had earlier been set up. [14]

On Surgeon Letterman's recommendations, and in the hope of improving the health of the army, McClellan ordered that wells be dug where possible; that fresh vegetables be issued; that the food be prepared by companies rather than squads; that tents be raised daily and struck and moved to new ground weekly; that camps be near but not in woods; and that the men have breakfast before marching. Further, the soldiers should be compelled to bathe once a week; sinks should be used and six inches of dirt filled in daily; similar holes should be dug for kitchen refuse; and all other refuse from stables and dead animals should be burned or deeply buried.

Thus with the army weakened and the 77th unable to count no more than 250 effectives, Major French readied himself for his assignment to recruit new troops at Saratoga Springs. On the eve of leaving to go north, French reflected on the nature of the conflict and called each "young man" in the surrounding towns to join in putting down the rebellion:

> Now the duty of the North is too plain to need any explanation. There is but one question – shall we conquer? We can, and we must; we have men enough, and means enough, to crush this rebellion in three months, and it only needs the *will*. If we do not conquer, good-bye to free institutions! Adieu to a Republican government! This contest is between men of the same blood, to a great extent, as was the Revolutionary struggle . . . It is a contest to see whether . . . the honest yeomanry, or the hot-headed aristocrats of the South . . . will conquer. Indeed it is simply to decide whether we will maintain the institutions which our forefathers established for us, or live quietly under an aristocratic form of government. It should stir the blood of every true patriot, and imbue him with feelings of patriotism strong enough to compel him to use every means in his power to push forward the cause he loves. Let every town raise a company not of boys and broken down old men, but of stout and intelligent young men who fight for the principle and not for *pay*. Let them have a heart in it, and do with a will that is required of them as men. Now is the time for each young man to show his companions that he is a patriot, and appreciates the blessings of free institutions, 'for what is life worth without liberty, or our country without her beautiful government, where every man, though

he be poor, can have a voice in making laws.' ... Surely there are trials ... surely a soldier's life is replete with dangers, but the greater our army the less the danger individually.

Acknowledging the real possibility of European intervention on behalf of the Confederacy, French finished by saying, "If England and France interpose, as they may, we shall need the right arm of every northern man; and if we have them, we may stand up against the *world* and say 'Our walls are impregnable, *we will be free* – the Union 'shall be kept intact.'" [15]

Death due to illness was often inexorably slow, but at Harrison's Landing it could come unexpectedly and quickly. Accidents claim lives in every army, and the Army of the Potomac was no exception. On July 18, Lieutenant Halsey Bowe (Co. E) returned to the 77th after recovering from typhoid fever during the siege of Yorktown. The next morning, while standing with his fellow officers of Company E "he was shot by an accidental discharge of a pistol, the ball going through his stomach." After being informed of Halsey's tragic wounding, his father traveled down from the Halsey's home to the 77th's camp to care for his son. Captain Wheeler thought Lt. Halsey might live, but he died a few days later. Chaplain Tully had Halsey's body embalmed and his bereaved father brought him back to New York for burial. [16]

From time to time those like Private Edwin Ham, who had been left behind and taken prisoner and then sent to Richmond during the retreat, arrived at Harrison's Landing. "One of them," Lieutenant Orrin Rugg recalled, "was from my company and he gives some very interesting accounts of what he saw. He has seen the elephant and is satisfied. He says they were treated very kindly but the Rebs could not give them much to eat because they did not have it. They had bread and meat but no salt to cook it with and the bread was not salted. They had no coffee or tea. Sugar was $1 to $1.50 per pound. Molasses was $3 to $6 per gal. Tea was $6 per pound. Coffee could not be had for any price. Course shoes were $15 per pair. He also says he suffered a great deal being confined in an open lot and must have been very bad as many were sick and wounded. He says that the Rebs acknowledge our retreat to have been a very skillful one . . . But they say we can't take Richmond." [17]

With the Army of the Potomac licking its wounds on the bank of the James River, McClellan demanded substantial reinforcements. He telegraphed Washington that if he were to capture Richmond and put an end the rebellion, he needed 100,000 or more additional men. McClellan's request was nearly delusional and President Lincoln, on July 8, steamed down to Harrison's Landing aboard the *Ariel* to personally appraise the condition of the army and its generals. McClellan came on board and Lincoln wasted no time and got right down to business. Lincoln asked pointed questions about the size of the Army of the Potomac, the health of the soldiers, and the whereabouts of Lee's army. If McClellan decided to do so, Lincoln asked, could the army be safely removed from the Virginia Peninsula? McClellan replied that it would be a most delicate and very difficult matter.

McClellan, for his part, in turn revealed a profound narcissism by handing Lincoln a letter detailing his views on the state of military affairs throughout the country and advising the president as to the proper conduct of the war. Rebellion had become full scale war, he wrote, and at stake was nothing less than the survival of free institutions and self-government. The war must be conducted "upon the highest principles known to Christian civilization . . . Neither confiscation of property . . . or forcible abolition of slavery should be contemplated for a moment. In prosecuting the War, all private property and unarmed persons should be strictly protected

. . . A system of policy thus constitutional and conservative, and pervaded by the influences of Christianity and freedom, would receive the support of almost all truly loyal men, and would deeply impress the rebel masses and all foreign nations." Only if Lincoln was pledged to such a policy, he said, would victory be possible. McClellan warned that, "A declaration of radical views, especially upon slavery, will rapidly disintegrate our present Armies." To not do so would make raising new troops "almost hopeless." Lincoln quietly read the letter and, without comment, tucked it into his pocket. [18]

Before the President left, Lincoln reviewed the Union army. Sergeant Skinner wrote to his friends at the Fort Edward Institute that, "Uncle Abe came to see us . . . and was greeted with many cheers throughout the army." Jealous of the soldiers' cheers, McClellan sourly wrote to his wife that he had ordered the men to cheer the president and that their cheers were lackluster. Nevertheless, Lincoln was encouraged by what he saw of the Army of the Potomac. He told John Nicolay, his secretary, that there were more men with their colors, and they were in better condition, than he had expected. [19]

When Lincoln returned to Washington, he had decided that the counsel he was receiving from McClellan was inadequate. He then summoned google-eyed Major General Henry W. Halleck from the West to be general-in-chief of the Union armies, effective July 11. Two weeks later Halleck went to Harrison's Landing to assess the situation and to try to develop a strategy to get the war effort going again. His visit was a failure as McClellan offered no concrete plan for renewing the offensive, but nevertheless asked for the outlandish number of 300,000 men to attack Richmond. Halleck could do no more than return to Washington empty-handed to ponder the next move.

Toward the end of July, camp life became a monotonous routine with very little to do. Newly promoted to Captain, Luther Wheeler complained that, "It is getting to be quite difficult to pass the time here in camp with nothing to do, nothing to read, and nothing to see. We never felt so when we were active. I watch for the mails every night – hoping I can get a letter from home so that I can have something to do answering them. I go down to the creek most every day swimming, and sleep a good share of the time, so manage to pass the time somehow." [20]

Wheeler's boredom was happily lifted upon the unexpected arrival of the Paymaster. He proudly announced "I have received 262.00/00, rather more than I could earn at home in sixty days." He sent home $225 to his father, but many others were not so responsible. "It would shock a person brought up to frugal habits to see the way in which the soldiers get rid of their money – you would think that they placed no value on it whatever – will throw away a dollar as quick as a cent – most of them gamble – go any where through the camps you will see them playing at games of chance with all their money." Not all were as frivolous, though. Captain Wheeler saw that, "A great many of the boys go to peddleing, they can sell any thing for any price. One of my boys made eighteen dollars one forenoon peddleing." Camp sutlers took notice and could "clear over a thousand dollars in a day." [21]

By mid-summer Lee no longer believed that McClellan and his army were a genuine threat to Richmond, yet he was not finished tormenting the northern general. On July 31, The Army of Northern Virginia's Chief of artillery led by William N. Pendleton, brought forty-seven rifled guns to the south side of the James River. Pendleton chose Coggins Point and the Coles House for positioning his artillery and determined the ranges so that the attack could be conducted at night. At half past midnight on August 1, the guns fired upon the sleeping Yankee army. "The cannonading waked us very suddenly from our slumbers," Captain Wheeler recounted. Surgeon Stevens wrote years later, "Their shells flew among us in disagreeable proximity, and the long lines of fire traced upon the midnight sky lent a certain charm to the dangerous business." At the height of the barraging Confederate shells Wheeler was amused by, "The contrabands near the landing . . . (who) . . . 'skedaddled' in every direction." Wheeler was not the only one who was amused as, "The soldiers have a say about their running – a soldier will get into a crowd and say, 'did you hear about that Brigade running last night' and some one will answer, 'no what Brigade' and the soldier then answers, 'Greeley's Brigade' and then there is a big laugh." [22]

At the end of July, Halleck ordered McClellan to begin evacuating his sick and wounded troops, ostensibly to make the army less encumbered and more able to move in any direction for a new offensive. The work of evacuating no less than 12,000 sick and wounded from Harrison's Landing was an immense task. The wharves along the banks of the James River buzzed with activity night and day at a frenetic pace. Stevens and other attending surgeons were thrust in the midst of "Ambulances crowded along the banks of the river, laden with sick and wounded, while those from the hospitals able to walk, tottered along with trembling steps, their wan faces and sunken eyes telling their story of suffering." These men rapidly filled the transports waiting for them and steamed off to hospitals from Washington, DC, to Rhode Island. [23]

Finally, Lincoln could no longer tolerate the status quo at Harrison's Landing. An army of 90,000 men camped for a month on the banks of the James River, contributing nothing to the Union war effort, could no longer go on. On August 3, General-in-Chief Halleck sent a telegraph to McClellan ordering the Army of the

Potomac to march to Fortress Monroe. From there the army was to redeploy by water to the Washington area and land at Aquia Creek, on the west bank of the Potomac River. McClellan resented Halleck's order and requested that it be rescinded. Halleck's response was immediate and blunt: "The order will not be rescinded and you will be expected to execute it with all necessary promptness." [24]

It was not until August 10 that the 77th received orders to be ready to march at 2 p.m. on the 11th. Not knowing where they were going, the 77th's camp bustled with hurried activity. Haversacks and extra baggage were sent aboard transports at the landing while the regiment's tents were taken down and their wagons were loaded with six days rations. Yet the 77th did not march until six days later. Instead Captain Wheeler and the men stood by as "the army began to move out of the works by our camp and were passing for two days and nights." [25]

The first day's march was an easy one of five miles before the 77th laid down for the night. The next day they marched to the mouth of the Chickahominy River in the heat of the day. Wheeler marveled as the regiment "crossed a splendid pontoon bridge of 96 boats" two-thousand feet long that had been constructed by Major Duane's engineers to accommodate the Union army's retreat. After crossing, the 77th once again camped for the night. [26]

From the Chickahominy, the 77th followed the same route down the Peninsula that two months earlier had brought them to the outskirts of Richmond – to Williamsburg, then Yorktown, to Big Bethel, Hampton Roads, and finally Fortress Monroe. Luther Wheeler wrote to his mother that, "Coming down the Peninsula the soldiers were allowed to plunder anything they could and nothing was left that could be eaten after the army passed." In a detailed account of the retreat, Captain Lennon wrote to his sister that, "By the time we got into the country where we could get green corn and potatoes, peaches, and watermelons . . . No mortal power could restrain the men from foraging." Lennon went on:

> It was amusing to see the men as they passed along the road. A crowd would rush around the house, some into the pig-pen, and some in the hen-coop, and others would take the field. Before the column would get by, there would be mighty little left for the man to live upon who owned the place. As an instance of the audacity with which some of our soldiers plundered is the following: One of the soldiers went into a man's yard, and, while the man was looking on, coolly proceeded to kill a calf. After killing it, he happened to think that he had no way to cook it, and went into the house and asked the man to give him a piece of pork to fry the veal in. If that was not impudent, I don't know what is. [27]

On August 21, the divisions of the Sixth Corps encamped in the vicinity of Hampton Roads waiting to board steamers at Fortress Monroe to transport them to Aquia Creek. The Army of the Potomac was now crowded along the sandy banks of the James River. Except that the Union army was leaving the Virginia Peninsula, the scene was much the same as when it landed at Fortress Monroe months earlier full of expectation for a glorious campaign. Transports filled the bay and lined up along the wharves. Infantry, cavalry, and artillery, along with wagons, ambulances, and livestock crowded the beach as they waited to board transports north. Surgeon Stevens took note of the steamer *Vanderbilt* which "had been, in other days, an old friend, as she ploughed up and down the Hudson." The dazzling saloons now were "dismantled and disfigured. No gorgeous drapery or gilded mirrors adorned them, but desolation and filth prevailed." [28]

The transformation of the *Vanderbilt* mirrored that of the 77th. Those who remained hardly looked like those who had left the defenses of Washington the previous March. The soldiers' faces were now weather beaten and tanned and their uniforms were tattered and soiled. They wore, "Hats and caps of every description: hats of straw and palm leaf, of brown wool, black wool, and what had been white wool . . ." Indeed, as Stevens observed, a stranger would be hard pressed to determine "what was the regular uniform of our troops." [29]

Finally on the 23rd the Sixth Corps set sail for Aquia Creek. From Washington five months earlier, the 77th filled three steamers to the Peninsula. On the 23rd the regiment had been reduced to little more than 250 men, and was easily accommodated on the *Empire City*. The 77th had arrived at Fortress Monroe filled with excited enthusiasm, but now, on the *Empire City*, a gloom hung over the salty air. Captain Lennon wrote, "My step was not as proud as I thought it might be when I left – we did not return with Richmond on our banners . . . we could not put on much airs." [30]

Around sunset, the *Empire City* arrived at Aquia Creek, yet the 77th could not disembark due to the wharves lining the creek being filled with the artillery and stores of the army. In response, McClellan ordered Franklin to move to Alexandria and land the Sixth Corps there. The regiment did not relish spending another night aboard the crowded transport where the air was stale and the smell foul, rendering it difficult to breathe. The next morning, their discomfort was relieved when the 77th finally set foot on land. The regiment marched through the city to a field about a mile outside of Alexandria near Fort Ellsworth where they made camp.

While McClellan's campaign to capture Richmond was rapidly unraveling under Lee's relentless drive to push the Federal Army off the Peninsula, President Lincoln turned his attention to the scattered Union forces in northern Virginia. With General Orders Number 103, Lincoln created the Army of Virginia from three existing departments operating around Virginia: Major John C. Freemont's Mountain Department, Major General Irvin McDowell's Department of the Rappahannock, and Major General Nathan P. Banks Department of the Shenandoah. To command the newly formed army, Lincoln summoned Major General John Pope from the West.

John Pope had served with distinction on the frontier and in the West. He won recognition for his seizure of Island No. 10 on the Mississippi River in April 1862. While he was a personal friend of the president, Pope was well-known for his rather abrasive, brash personality. He alienated his soldiers by revealing low regard for the Eastern Union armies, and while not named, disparaging McClellan himself by saying:

> I have come to you from the West, where we have always seen the backs of our enemies, from an army whose business it has been to seek the adversary and to beat him when he is found. Whose policy has been to attack and not defense. In but one instance has the enemy been able to place our Western armies in a defensive attitude. I presume I have been called here to pursue the same system, and to lead you against the enemy. It is my purpose to do so and speedily. I am sure you long for the opportunity to win the distinction you are capable of achieving. That opportunity I shall endeavor to give you. Meanwhile, I desire you to dismiss from your minds certain phrases I am sorry to find so much in vogue amongst you. I hear constantly of taking strong positions and holding them, of lines of retreat, and bases of supplies. Let us discard such ideas. The strongest

position a soldier should desire to occupy is one from which he can easily advance against the enemy . . . Success and glory are in advance, disaster and shame lurk in the rear . . .[31]

While Pope insulted McClellan and Union soldiers in the east, he issued several general orders that the Confederates found barbarous. The Army of Virginia was ordered to live off the land by requisitioning supplies locally and paying for these supplies with vouchers from the treasury. Further insult to the Confederates was General Order Eleven. General Order Seven levied a series of fines, indemnities, and impressed service upon civilians living within a five mile radius of communications severed by guerilla forces or houses from which Union soldiers were fired upon. This general order allowed Union commanders to deport any male that would not swear an oath of allegiance to the Union. If an individual was deported and returned, he could be hanged for spying. The South thought these laws heinous. Lee responded with great animosity naming Pope a "miscreant" and specifically telling Jackson, "I want Pope suppressed." He now focused his attention from the Army of the Potomac to the destruction of the Army of Virginia.

Receiving word that Pope was concentrating the Army of Virginia at Culpepper, Lee set in motion a plan that would culminate in the second defeat of a Federal army at Bull Run. On August 24, Lee ordered Jackson to make a broad flanking movement around Pope's right in order to strike his supply base at Manassas Station on the Orange & Alexandria Railroad. Three days later Stonewall swept away the few hundred surprised Union troops guarding the massive supply depot to the delight of his soldiers. The capture yielded a treasure trove of food and supplies beyond the Confederates' wildest dreams. Well over 100 boxcars were lined up over a mile of sidings, all loaded with goods. Countless warehouses were filled with everything from flour to such delights as oysters and pies sold by the sutlers. The southerners took what they could and burned the rest.

After pillaging and torching the supply depot at Manassas Station, Jackson marched his divisions north to the First Bull Run battlefield at Manassas where he took a defensive position behind an unfinished railroad cut below Stony Ridge, which afforded ready-made entrenchments. Given the news of Confederates in his rear, Pope had to react. Accordingly the Army of Virginia marched toward Manassas in the hope of crushing Jackson's forces.

On August 28, Jackson attacked part of McDowell's Corps at Brawner's Farm near Groveton. Halleck ordered McClellan to send the Sixth Corps to support Pope. At Fort Ellsworth tents were struck, haversacks packed, rations provided and the 77th stood in line ready to move. The distant boom of artillery could be heard and contrabands and southern refugees streamed by announcing the fighting at Groveton. But by sunset the 77th and the Sixth Corps had not marched, leaving the soldiers to wonder why they did not go to the relief of Pope's army.

The next day the Second Battle of Bull Run unfolded as the Army of Virginia attacked Jackson's men firmly ensconced behind the unfinished railroad cut below Stony Ridge. Although Pope's men greatly outnumbered Jackson's, the advantage was nullified as his attacks were poorly coordinated and he could not deliver a decisive blow. As the battle raged, the morning brought few indications that the Sixth Corps would advance in support of Pope. "Head quarter tents remained standing, artillery horses stood unharnessed, and everything showed of intentional delay." At length, however, the Sixth Corps set out and the 77th left Fort Ellsworth eager to join the battle. When their division reached Annandale, a mere march of six miles, the 77th was met by fugitives streaming from the battle.

Old Baldy Smith informed Franklin that that there was a large force of Confederates at Fairfax Courthouse. Franklin in turn reported the situation to McClellan who then ordered him to hold the Sixth Corps at Annandale, much to the chagrin of the men in the regiment.[32]

Late in the day Longstreet's corps arrived at the battlefield too late to join the fight. During the night, Longstreet quietly positioned his men across the left flank of Pope's army. Convinced that Longstreet was nowhere near, Pope again attacked Jackson early in the morning on August 30. As they were the day before, his attacks were poorly coordinated. Fully believing that he was on the verge of a glorious victory over Stonewall Jackson, Pope slowly weakened his left wing until almost all was engaged on the right. About 4 p.m. Longstreet's corps crashed into the hollow left of the Union army, forcing Pope to hurriedly withdraw his army toward Centreville.

As the second day of battle raged, the Sixth Corps once again marched to Pope's assistance, but it "moved leisurely along, making very frequent halts." To the 77th, "The firing in front indicated a hardly contested battle" and "knowing that Pope must be in need of reinforcements" the men "were anxious to push forward rapidly . . . but every hour the Corps halted for at least twenty minutes." As the 77th passed Fairfax Courthouse, the roar of musketry and artillery grew louder, and as they neared Centreville, the regiment was ordered to proceed to Cub Run. There they beheld what "seemed to be an indiscriminate mass of men, horses, guns, and wagons, all going pell-mell to the rear." Years later Surgeon Stevens presented a small vignette of the scene near the bridge over Cub Run:

> An amusing encounter occurred between one of this class, a coward in captain's uniform, and one of our own officers, Captain Deyoe, as brave a fellow as ever drew a sword. The

demoralized captain, his sword thrown away and its sheath after it, came hurriedly upon the bridge, where Deyoe was sitting, coolly filling his pipe. The fugitive captain turned his face, pale with fright, to the imperturbable Deyoe, and, striking him on the shoulder, said with as much composure as he could muster, "Captain, we have had hard times of it out there, but *don't be afraid, don't be afraid.*" Deyoe, turning his face toward that of the straggler with a look of unruffled coolness and unmitigated contempt, replied, "Well, who the d—*is* afraid? Oh, yes, I see, *you are.* Well, you had better get away from here then!" [33]

Captain Seth W. DeYoe (NYSDMNA)

The first day of the Second Battle of Bull Run, Colonel McKean lay in his bed at Washington convalescing from the ravages of typhoid fever listening to the rumbling of countless cannons. During the second day of the battle, McKean could no longer contain his anxiety over the outcome of the fighting, and raised his weakened body off of his sickbed determined to ride to the scene. After dressing, he went out and, joined by Stevens who also was in Washington recovering from typhoid, commandeered horses at a nearby livery and galloped toward the sound of guns. However, they were stopped by provost guards and their horses were seized. Not to be deterred, McKean and Stevens secured more horses, only to have them also seized. They then reported to the headquarters of General Wadsworth, military governor of the city. A staff officer gave the colonel and surgeon seats in a wagon loaded with bread and they arrived at the bridge at Cub Run soon after the 77th. Having witnessed the frenzied Union retreat after the First Battle at Bull Run, McKean was once again shocked by the flow of retreating soldiers, and he turned to Stevens, and was heard to say, "This is the most miserable day of my life." [34]

At nightfall the Sixth Corps were ordered to return to Centreville. The scene on the next day was one of confusion. "Thousands of stragglers," Stevens wrote, "wandered about without knowing or caring what became of their commands; long columns of shattered regiments and batteries filed past to take up new positions, either within the intrenchments or on the flanks." The regiments were mere shadows of what they were before the battle began, "the worn and weary appearance of the men, their flags, each surrounded by only enough men to constitute a respectable color-guard, all showed that even the hard experiences of the Army of the Potomac had never had so demoralizing effect as this." Adding to this dismal, morale-deadening scene were, "Long trains of ambulances . . . bringing from the battlefield wounded men, who had been . . . exposed to the burning son" while waiting to be treated for their wounds. Nearby, temporary field hospitals were erected, and overworked surgeons worked day and night amputating arms and legs and otherwise tending to the wounded. [35]

A day later at 3 p.m., the Sixth Corps received orders to march back to the camps they had previously occupied at Alexandria. The 77th reached Fort Ellsworth at 10 p.m. the same night, hence making in a single evening a distance that had required two full days and part of another to march when moving to support Pope during the recent battle. Morale was low and the soldiers wondered who was to blame for the second defeat of a Union army at Bull Run. Perhaps Captain Lennon best expressed the mood of the defeated army: "To sum the whole thing up, we find ourselves, after six months hard work, just where we began; and who is to blame for it? Certainly not the troops, for never did troops fight better. There is fault somewhere, that is quite evident . . . You are having some big stories to read about the war and General Pope's masterly policy. In my opinion the second edition of Bull Run is about the same as the first." [36]

6

"THE DAMNED REBELS..."

As it filed into the camps and defenses around Washington, the Army of Virginia was justly described as used up. A deep gloom bore down at the War Office when confirmation arrived of Pope's disastrous defeat at Bull Run. Pope had clearly lost control of his army, and Lincoln felt a very real concern for the safety of the capital. His anxiety for Washington led Lincoln to summon George McClellan on the morning of September 1 and to order him to take command of the capital's defenses.

As Pope's dispatches the next day became ever more desperate, Lincoln could no longer trust him to him to command the now dispirited army. Lincoln first turned to Major General Ambrose E. Burnside, offering him command of the Army of Virginia. However, Burnside turned Lincoln down because of a combination of his loyalty to McClellan and his lack of confidence in his ability to command such a large force as an army. The only way to effectively save the situation pointed to giving McClellan command of both the

Army of Virginia and the Army of the Potomac. Lincoln knew full well that the general could be stubborn, slow, overly cautious, and flirt with insubordination, but he was also a skilled organizer and still inspired the respect and admiration of his men. It was this talent, Lincoln determined, that the North needed most now.

With messianic vigor, McClellan accepted his new duties, and rode out to meet and encourage his exhausted soldiers. Like wild fire, the news of McClellan's return to command spread and there was hardly a soldier in the army who did not know "Little Mac" was again in command. The news was electric and the men forgot their defeats, weariness, and hunger, and erupted into excited hurrahs. Joyful shouts of "General McClellan is here!" spread throughout the entire army during the evening.

McClellan worked a minor miracle in the next few days as he quickly restored the army's morale and organization, and equally significant, its pride and sense of purpose. McClellan knew the soldiers of the Army of the Potomac well, for it was he who had revived the men in like circumstances after Irvin McDowell's defeat at the First Battle at Bull Run the previous summer. His quick success and control of what had been seen as a totally desperate situation lent credence that he was indeed the man of the hour.

With the Union soldiers licking their wounds behind the defenses of Washington, Robert E. Lee turned his attention northward to Maryland. The notion of invading Maryland was particularly attractive to Lee for military, political, and even psychological reasons. Many Southerners had for some time been calling for an invasion of Northern soil that would turn the course of the war and bring relief to the oppressed citizens believed to be in Maryland. The presence of a large Confederate army north of the Potomac might encourage Confederate Marylanders to overthrow the government and establish a pro-South administration, thereby isolating Lincoln's capital in Washington. Further, a military victory in Maryland might enable Lee to capture Washington by moving against its less defended northern side, thus ending the war.

Too, a Confederate victory in Maryland, or even the simple presence of Southern troops north of the Potomac, might be sufficient to affect foreign intervention or even an alliance with the Confederacy that would steer the course of the war to the South's favor. Harkening back to the French Alliance of 1778 which marked the turning point in the War of Independence, Lee and President Davis hoped for the powers of England and France to ally with the South in pressing for an end to the war.

Lee also hoped that a Rebel victory in Maryland would strengthen the vocal anti-war factions in the North. Both Lee and Davis were well aware that many Northerners objected to Lincoln's suppression of civil rights, particularly in Maryland. Any Confederate victories north of the Potomac, Lee believed, would surely have a profound effect on the Fall Congressional elections in the North.

On September 4, most of Lee's army crossed the rocky Potomac River at White's Ford. The river crossing was a monumental event for the Confederate soldiers. Regimental bands spontaneously filled the air with the joyous notes of "Maryland, My Maryland!" The river crossing was also tough going for many of the barefoot soldiers who gingerly walked over the sharp rocks of the river bottom. Some Texans complained that the water was so cold that all the ice houses in Maryland had been emptied into the river.

On September 6th, the Army of Northern Virginia reached Frederick. As the Confederates filed through the little city, Unionists closed up and barred their doors, and stayed in their cellars.

Confederate sympathizers, on the other hand, threw open their doors and windows and welcomed them. Still, both Unionists and Confederate sympathizers were less than impressed by the ragged condition of Lee's soldiers. Most had been marching and fighting ever since they had left Richmond several weeks earlier, and they were dirty, smelly, exhausted, and badly in need of clothes and shoes.

News that Lee had crossed the Potomac and now occupied Frederick was immediate and McClellan set the Army of the Potomac in motion. The 77th quickly struck their tents and packed up their supplies for the march. They left Alexandria at night, passed Fort Albany, crossed the Long Bridge, and entered Washington with "the moon and stars shining with a brilliancy seldom equated." The denizens of Washington crowded the streets in the moonlight eager to get a glimpse of the now hardened veterans of the Union army. They asked where the army was headed, but the 77th could only answer, "We are going to meet the rebels." Passing through Georgetown, the regiment reached Tanleytown and bedded down for the night. At dawn on September 8, they marched little more than six miles and halted after passing through Rockville. [1]

McClellan seemed to be in no hurry to catch Lee as the 77th found itself two days later in the vicinity of Barnesville, a mere 20 miles or so from Washington. The Third Brigade made their camp on the plantation of a noted secessionist who had vacated his home before the approaching army, much to the delight of the New Yorkers. The plantation owner, Surgeon Stevens noted, left behind "a very large orchard, which trees were loaded with delicious fruit, and his poultry yard well stocked with choice fowls." The industrious soldiers "were not slow to appropriate to their own use these luxuries, which, they declared, were great improvements on pork and hardtack." [2]

At sunrise, September 13, the Sixth Corps again took up a leisurely march. Leading the advance, the Third Brigade crossed the Monocacy River east of Buckystown and continued west over a covered railroad bridge above the B & O Railroad. The 77th halted for an hour in the apple and peach orchards near the Monocacy flour mills and then moved into a quiet meadow. Just ahead, Confederates were discovered screening Jefferson Gap at Catoctin Mountain. Finding the 9th New York already engaged, Colonel Irwin, in command of the Third Brigade since General Davidson had been reassigned to command the St. Louis District in Missouri, detached the 33rd and 20th New York to ascend the mountain to support the 9th.

The New York regiments set down their haversacks and scrambled up the rocky mountain. Like the 9th New York before them, they quickly became entangled in the tree branches and undergrowth while the rest of the Third Brigade continued up the pike in close support. Captain R. P. Chew's Virginia Battery, supported by Captain T. H. Holland's 2nd Virginia Calvary, quickly gave way and beat a hasty retreat down the west side of the mountain. Following the 33rd and 20th New York, the 77th was awed by the beauty of the valley before them studded with farm fields and cattle. Hamlets dotted the valley and the spires of Frederick stood tall in the distance. In the afternoon the 77th moved beyond the mountain gap and entered the village of Jefferson. The villagers treated the Yankees as heroes and, "Fair maids plucked up the richest flowers, and . . . placed them in the hands of the brave New Yorkers. Grave matrons, with ruddy daughters, like Angels of Mercy, came to the gates by the road-side with cups of milk and water to refresh the thirsty soldiers." [3]

Colonel Irwin pushed the Third Brigade forward and about one mile west of Jefferson, the brigade happened upon Captain

Holland's detachment from the 2nd Virginia Cavalry holding the Petersville-Jefferson intersection. A trooper of the 6th Pennsylvania, the Third Brigade's cavalry screen, caught sight of a horse soldier of Holland's detachment. The Virginian hurriedly retreated with the Pennsylvanian in pursuit hooting and hollering. With pistol in one hand and carbine in the other, the Yankee closed in on the flying Rebel and fired both. Unharmed, the Confederate at once surrendered. Caught up in the moment, Colonel Irwin spied several more Rebels and galloped past the triumphant Pennsylvanian with pistol in hand and brought in three additional Rebel cavalrymen.

Earlier in the morning, the advantage in the Maryland Campaign swung dramatically to McClellan's side. The General did not have a clear idea of Lee's plans and had only moved the Union army just far enough to prepare for a defensive strike should the Army of Northern Virginia swing around and attack. Leading the Twelfth Corps into Frederick was the 27th Indiana in Brigadier General George H. Gordon's brigade. There they halted and three men plopped down in a meadow to rest. As they struck up a conversation, Corporal Barton W. Mitchell noticed an envelope lying in the grass that held three cigars wrapped in a sheet of paper bearing the heading, "Hd Qrs Army of Northern Va Special Orders 191," signed, "By command of Gen R. E. Lee." The special orders were a detailed outline of Lee's plan for the capture of Harper's Ferry. Jackson's command would pass over South Mountain and ford the Potomac at Shepherdstown, capture the garrison at Martinsburg, and come in on Harper's Ferry from the west. John J. Walker's division would seize Loudoun Heights, and the divisions of Lafayette McLaws and R. H. Anderson would cross South Mountain into Pleasant Valley, and take Maryland Heights, overlooking Harper's Ferry from the north. Longstreet's command, with D. H. Hill's division as rear guard, would follow the National Road across South Mountain and wait two miles beyond at Boonsboro until Harper's Ferry surrendered. The army would then come together at Boonsboro or at Hagerstown, depending on circumstances. [4]

With Special Orders 191 in hand, McClellan triumphantly crowed, "I have the whole Rebel force in front of me . . . I think Lee has made a gross mistake and that he will be severely punished for it." Turning to his old West Point friend John Gibbon, McClellan boasted, "If I cannot whip Bobbie Lee, I will be willing to go home." Yet Little Mac issued no orders until the next day, September 14. Burnside's right wing would cross South Mountain at Turner's Gap. Franklin's left wing would march to the village of Burkittsville, at the foot of South Mountain, and push his way through Crampton's Gap into Pleasant Valley. McClellan cautioned Franklin that if he was opposed at Crampton's Gap, he was not to assault until hearing the sound of guns at Turner's Gap where Burnside was to attack. The Sixth Corps was to destroy McLaw's command and relieve the garrison at Harper's Ferry. He was then to return through Pleasant Valley to support the main concentration of the army. [5]

The Sixth Corps approached Burkittsville at 1 p.m. and massed in a dense woods east of the village and south of the Burkittsville Road while Slocum's positioned itself on the north side of the road. Slocum's men were to pass right through Crampton's Gap, while Old Baldy's had an important supporting role. Smith was to push the Rebels off South Mountain to the left of Crampton's Gap, unhinging the entire Confederate position. Then Slocum's assault would be much easier, as his troops would not be under enfilade fire from the high ground to their left as they moved through the pass.

Smith's brigades formed into three lines of battle; Brook's Vermont Brigade leading, followed by Irwin's in close support, with Hancock's close by held in reserve. No sooner did the 77th emerge from the woods when a white puff of smoke billowed from a high point on the mountain followed by the shrieking of a shell that passed over the men and exploded in a meadow behind them. The Confederate batteries then came alive and George Stevens thought, "The mountains, like huge volcanoes, belched forth fire and smoke. The earth trembled beneath us, and the air was filled with the howling of shells which flew over our heads and ploughed the earth at our feet." At the same time, a line of Rebel soldiers previously concealed by a stone wall rose up and fired a volley into the advancing Northerners. In the face of exploding shells and countless bullets whizzing by, the New Yorkers "pressed forward at double quick, over ploughed ground and through the cornfields," halting briefly in the village. Stevens was almost disbelieving as:

> The citizens, regardless of the shells which were crashing through their houses, welcomed us heartily, bringing water to fill the canteens, and supplying us liberally from the scanty stores left them by the marauding rebels . . . Patriotic ladies cheered the Union Boys and brought them food; and well might they rejoice at the approach of the Union army, after their recent experience with the rebels, who had robbed them of almost everything they possessed in the way of movable property. [6]

At 3 p.m. the advance was once again sounded, and the 77th moved forward beyond Burkittsville. Ahead of the Third Brigade, Brook's Vermonters attacked. Squeezed between a stand of woods and the road, Brooks formed the 4th and 2nd Vermont in column. The 4th rapidly crossed open ground under scattered shellfire while the 2nd followed close behind. At the base of South Mountain, Rebels manning one the many stone fences on the mountain face opened a brisk fire. With bayonets fixed, the 4th Vermont charged, capturing the Confederate position and twenty prisoners. The 2nd Vermont came up on the 4th's right, and the two Green Mountain regiments went up the mountain meeting little resistance. At the summit, the 4th Vermont wheeled left and captured a number of officers and men of the 6th Virginia. The 2nd Vermont reached the crest and poured down the other side as Slocum's troops surged through the pass itself. Seeing the pass already taken, the 3rd, 5th, and 6th Vermont followed Slocum's soldiers through the gap.

Right behind the Green Mountain Boys was Irwin's Third Brigade. The 77th scrambled up the mountain over the rock ledges on the mountain side, taking hold of bushes to help themselves up the steep slope. Surgeon Stevens could barely take in the scene of carnage as the 77th ascended the mountain:

> Their dead strewed our path, and great care was required, as we passed along the road, to avoid treading upon the lifeless remains which lay thickly upon the ground. On every side there the evidences of the fearful conflict multiplied. Trees were literally cut to pieces by shells and bullets; a continual procession of rebel wounded and prisoners lined the roadsides, while knapsacks, guns, canteens and haversacks were scattered in great confusion. [7]

Franklin's Sixth Corps now had an open road to Harper's Ferry. He moved his corps through Crampton's Gap into Pleasant Valley, but made no move to push on to relieve the now besieged garrison. As the battle of South Mountain raged on at Fox's Gap and one mile north at Turner's Gap into the night, the 77th rested on their arms on the west face of the mountain, fully expecting to renew the battle at dawn.

As the fighting petered out late at night on South Mountain, Lee abandoned Fox's and Turner's gaps. His campaign was fast crumbling and the preservation of the Army of Northern Virginia was now paramount. Sharpsburg provided Lee with the quickest escape route. Two excellent roads led from the Boonsboro vicinity, which straddled Antietam Creek. A night retreat would allow Lee's army to slip away without McClellan's detection. The march to the Potomac River would not be overly taxing, but difficult in the darkness. Lee knew his men were exhausted for many of his soldiers had been awake for twenty four hours with little or no food. In Lee's mind, he could return the army to Virginia, as it would surely be safe – because, he believed, McClellan would not aggressively follow him into the land of secession.

Retreat also had the clear advantage in reuniting the Confederate army. Momentum would be lost, but Lee's army, weakened by thousands of stragglers, would be saved. Plenty of fight and morale remained for a future invasion into Yankee territory. Once reunited in Virginia, Lee's Southerners could speedily march back to Williamsport and launch into Maryland again. He also had the option of simply terminating the campaign, resting and reorganizing his army, and planning another drive north of the Potomac at a more opportune time. But during the somber night march, Lee changed his mind. He ordered his wounded army to reunite for another battle on another day. Lee headed for Sharpsburg, settling in on the west side of the meandering Antietam Creek which provided high ground that precluded the need for building trenches and extensive breastworks. With the Army of Virginia thus concentrated, Lee would patiently await the arrival of McClellan and the Army of the Potomac.

The morning of September 15, the 77th awoke to the pristine beauty of Pleasant Valley. From their camp, George Stevens looked "down upon its green fields, where herds of sleek cattle graze, its yellow harvests glowing and ripening in the September sun; its undulating meadows and richly laden orchards; its comfortable farms houses . . . the whole scene is one of surprising beauty, upon which the eye rests with untiring delight." The sound of war, however, intruded as the artillery of Jackson at Harper's Ferry echoed in the valley. With the Sixth Corps, the 77th prepared to march to the rescue of the beleaguered Federal garrison, but before they started, the firing suddenly died away. Franklin correctly concluded that Harper's Ferry had surrendered and countermanded the order to march. Subsequently the Sixth Corps rested in Pleasant Valley all of the 15 and 16.[8]

Lee did not have long to wait for McClellan's next move, for at 3 p.m. Sumner's Second Corps arrived on the field near Sharpsburg. McClellan, his staff, and headquarters escort waded through the massed soldiers of the Second Corps who enthusiastically cheered as he passed them. At Keedysville he met with Sumner and Fitz John Porter. The cavalcade then rode out to inspect the Rebel position from a ridgeline overlooking the Antietam Creek, and a Confederate battery promptly sent some shells screaming across the stream, dispersing the party of officers. McClellan continued his reconnaissance with only Porter by his side. In the meantime, Rebel gunners aggressively fired upon any soldiers in blue who showed themselves.

Characteristically cautious, McClellan remained true to his abided belief to make no movement until preparations were as complete as circumstances permitted, and to never fight a battle without some definite object worth the probable loss. With only two hours of daylight remaining, McClellan determined that any attack would be an improvised affair lacking careful preparation. No doubt Lee had concealed his reserves and was too strong for him to gain a definite object in that time.

By noon September 16, most of the Army of the Potomac now lined the west bank of the Antietam, and McClellan formulated his plan for battle. He would send the First, Second, and Twelfth Corps against the Confederate left flank, while Burnside's Ninth Corps would take on the Rebel right at Rohrbach's Bridge which would be eternally known as Burnside's Bridge. Porter's Fifth Corps would hold the middle and attack Lee's center at the right moment and drive the Confederate army into the Potomac. Seemingly no more than an afterthought, the 77th's Sixth Corps was ordered to come up from Pleasant Valley and the join the rest of the army, but without a stated purpose.

Late in the afternoon, Major General Joseph Hooker led his First Corps across the upper bridge over Antietam Creek to the Hagerstown Pike two miles north of Sharpsburg and bivouacked on the Samuel Poffenberger farm near the North Woods. Mansfield's Twelfth Corps came up at midnight and encamped a mile to the northwest. The Union soldiers had an uneasy rest and slept on their muskets, prepared to rise to battle at a moment's notice. The night was uncomfortably cold and a chilly, steady rain turned into a downpour in the predawn hours, drenching the men of both armies.

Dawn on September 17 was wet and musty, offering a low mist that obscured fences and fields in front of the First Corps. Hooker's plan of attack was straightforward; he would drive south along the Hagerstown Pike to high ground covered by the West Woods; his mile wide front would aim for the small whitewashed Dunker Church barely visible against the greenery of the West Woods.

As soon as the low fog cleared and the enemy positions could be seen, the artillery of both sides belched forth a steady roar later remembered as "artillery hell." And indeed the booming of cannon marked the beginning of the descent into Hell itself on the open fields and farms around Sharpsburg. This day would become the single bloodiest day in American military history. By nightfall, 23,381 dead, dying, and wounded soldiers would litter the battlefield.[9]

Ten miles south, the 77th stood in their camp and heard the sound of "hundreds of cannon . . . sending forth their messengers of death . . . making a noise that shook the ground." At 6 a.m. the Sixth Corps, the Third Brigade leading, set out for Keedysville, two miles from the where the battle now raged. About 9 a.m., the 77th passed through Rohrersville whose inhabitants cheered the regiment on and gave the men apples and water. As the Empire State men continued their march northward, the echo of battle grew exponentially. Captain McNair of the 33rd New York wrote, "The roar of canon and the clatter of musketry was deafening as we wound down into the valley." The cataclysmic sounds of battle reminded Major Thomas Hyde of the 7th Maine of Fair Oaks during the Peninsula Campaign.[10]

Soon the Third Brigade was met by hundreds of skulkers and wounded soldiers fleeing the carnage. And yet "the diapason of the artillery and the rattle of small arms" grew even louder. Perhaps Major Thomas Hyde, in command of the 7th Maine, spoke for all of the men in the brigade: "we all felt we had got to brace ourselves, for the trying moment must soon come." The 7th Maine was so depleted, mustering only about 180 men, that the worried Hyde ordered his drummers and fifers to arm themselves with muskets picked up along the roadside, and to join their companies.[11]

Marching the last few miles at the double quick, the 77th halted in the woods around the Samuel Pry House where McClellan had set up his headquarters. Baldy Smith rode up to headquarters to get instructions for posting his men. The general was most sanguine, telling

Smith that the fighting on the right was going very well and that he expected Burnsides to attack at any minute on the left. McClellan ordered Smith to take his division across Antietam Creek and place it in a wood on the left of the upper stone bridge. Soon the 77th waded across the cold creek, which was swift, and up to their bellies. On the other bank, they encountered a steady stream of desperately wounded men, some dragging themselves to the rear. There, the regiment formed in line and steeled themselves for the terror to come.

The battle had raged back and forth for six hours from the East Woods across Miller's Cornfield, into the West Woods around the Dunker Church, and to the south along the Sunken Road. Yet neither side could gain a firm advantage. At 1 p.m., the Third Brigade was summoned into the fray to drive out the Confederates of Colonel John R. Cooke's 27th North Carolina and Captain John W. Reedy's 3rd Arkansas Razorbacks from Mumma's swale. Rather than properly form the brigade into a cohesive line of battle, Colonel Irwin unwisely committed his regiments piecemeal into the fight. He personally wheeled the 800-man strong 20th New York onto the Smoketown Road.

The German turners of the 20th New York shouted "Bahn frei!" – "Clear the way!," and advanced in close formation over the dead and wounded on the field past the still glowing remains of the burned buildings of Mumma's Farm. Colonel Ernest Von Vegesack, an explosive Swede who replaced Colonel Weiss who in terror abandoned the regiment at White Oak Swamp, pushed the Turner's southwest toward the plateau before Dunker Church. No sooner did they reach the plateau, though, than the 20th New York came under the murderous fire of shrapnel and canister, which cut a swath of death and destruction through their ranks. The regiment momentarily shuddered until Von Vegesack drew his pistol and raced along the rear shooting at any apparent skulkers. The Germans leveled their rifles and pushed on behind the color sergeant urging them on. Heads down, and leaning into an increasingly dreadful artillery barrage, they redeemed themselves from the humiliating route at White Oak Swamp, and did not break and run. [12]

The 77th came upon the field on the heels of Von Vegeseck's Turner's. Irwin immediately sent the regiment northwest toward the Hagerstown Pike as skirmishers. The 77th fanned out and passed through the East Woods and into the field before the pike. Emerging from the woods, newly appointed to Captain Luther Wheeler saw that the "battle was on open fields so that the contending forces could be seen like a panorama from our position." "It was a splendid sight to see," he later wrote, "but I hope I may never see another like it. The ground in every direction was thickly strewn with the dead and dying, some of them terribly mutilated by cannon shot." [13]

The 7th Maine was third in the column. Major Hyde watched as the long line of the 20th moved obliquely to the left when Irwin's aide, Captain Long, ordered him to take his regiment to the left of the Germans before it could catch up to the 77th. It took but an instant to get the 181-man regiment forward into line, and then, half wheeling like a large company the 7th Maine moved into the East Woods. Rushing past a portion of the 10th Maine, Thomas Hyde took a moment to ask about the state of Colonel Beal and Lieutenant Colonel Fillebrown, who had been acquaintances of his in that regiment. He was greatly saddened to hear that both had fallen to Confederate fire not more than three hours before the 7th Maine arrived upon the field.

The small New England regiment pushed through the woods, and broke into Mumma's plowed field north of the family cemetery.

Each rail fence in their path was quickly torn down as they made their way toward the left flank of the 27th North Carolina. Colonel Cooke called his men to fall back. The southerners fired one last volley at the fast approaching 20th New York, then panicked and fled the field. Major Hyde sent his soldiers scrambling southeast to force out Confederates lingering in the surrounding buildings of Roulette's Farm before connecting with Von Vegesack's left flank.

Meanwhile, the 400-man 49th New York swung left and followed on the rear of the 20th New York at about 100 yards. The regiment set off at the double quick through the clover field south of the Smoketown Road with their muskets at the right shoulder shift, and passed around Mumma's smoldering barn and by the 21st New York. One of the men from that regiment called after them, "You will find a hot time of it in there, boys!" [13]

The 33rd New York, with about 150 men, brought up the tail end of the advancing brigade. They fell into line on the left rear, less Lieutenant John Carter's Company B which was cut off from the regiment by Captain Vanneman's Battery B, 1st Maryland Light Artillery as it passed through the line on its way to the Cornfield. Company B waited for the battery to pass as they listened to bullets whizzing by their heads. By the time Vanneman passed, the rest of Irwin's brigade had gone ahead a considerable distance.

The much disorganized Third Brigade plowed through a torrent of exploding shells toward the western most section of the Bloody Lane. About half way through Mumma's swale, at Baldy Smith's direction, Captain Long ordered the 33rd New York away from the left flank of the 49th New York. Lieutenant Colonel Joseph W. Corning faced his regiment by the right flank and ordered them toward the right flank of the 49th New York. In doing so, the regiment crossed the Hagerstown Pike and entered the West Woods immediately south of the Dunker church.

At the same time, the 7th Maine lay down behind a rail fence on the left of Von Vegesack's Turners, who had fallen back to the swale. The 20th New York was bent at right angles where the Dunker Church ridge turned east to north. Confederate artillery raked their position with canister and solid shot. Private Christoph Niederer of that regiment wrote,

> I just got myself pretty comfortable when a bomb burst over me and completely defened me. I felt a blow on my right shoulder and my jacket was covered with white stuff. I felt mechanically whether I still had my arm and thank God it was still whole. At the same time I felt something damp on my face. I wiped it off. It was bloody. Now I first saw that the man next to me, Kessler, lacked the upper part of his head, and almost all his brains had gone into the face of the man next to him, Merkel, so that he could scarcely see. [14]

Hyde's men fell back behind the cover of large boulders which provided a measure of protection. Major Hyde looked to his right to the 20th New York where the front was more open and noticed that every few minutes one of the Germans was struck and went to the rear, while scarcely any of his regiment was injured. Hyde went over to Colonel Von Vegeseck and told him to drop his colors as the Confederates were singling out his regiment. "Let them wave," the hot-blooded Swede shouted, "They are our glory." The Colonel then rode off, revolver in hand, to shoot the skulkers passing to the rear. [15]

Captain Nathan S. Babcok (NYSDMNA)

Upon entering the Hagerstown Pike, Captain Nathan S. Babcock (Co. K), now in command while newly minted Lieutenant Colonel Winsor B. French was recruiting back home in Saratoga Springs, discovered that the 77th's 175 men were dangerously separated from the rest of the Third Brigade. In an instant, Babcock formed the regiment into column, and by turning by the left flank, double-quicked southward to hook up with the right flank of the 33rd New York. At this juncture, General Smith was on his horse riding along the line and spied Brigadier General Robert Ransom's brigade of North Carolinians hugging the inside edge of the West Woods. As the 77th came up alongside Ransom's soldiers, Old Baldy uttered, "There's a regiment gone to Hell," and sent Captain Long to call the regiment back, but the Captain did not reach the 77th in time to warn of the impending slaughter. [16]

Hurrying down the Hagerstown Pike to link up with the 33rd New York's right flank, just north of the Dunker Church, the North Carolina regiments unleashed a devastating volley into the 77th's ranks that instantly killed or wounded over thirty men. Private

Joseph Meurer (Co. E), the color guard, was shot in the head and fell to the ground. "Scarcely was he down," Private Edward Fuller (Co. C) wrote years after the war, "than the colors were taken up by other hands and carried forward." Captain Stephen S. Horton (Co. B) was cut down with a severe flesh wound in his upper right thigh, which caused him to exclaim, "The damned rebels, not satisfied with the steak in my haversack, they have taken a steak off of my round." [17]

The 77th wavered but a moment, and Captain Babcock steadied the men. According to Babcock, so close were they to the Confederates unleashing their fury upon the 77th, "that you could see the whites of their eyes." After releasing two effective volleys into the enemy, Lieutenant John Carter's Company B 33rd New York – that had been separated by Vanneman's battery – suddenly appeared on the right flank of the 77th. Unnoticed by Ransom's brigade busy wreaking havoc in front of the 77th, Carter's men touched off several compact volleys as fast as they could, directly into the Confederate's left flank, which sent them scurrying back deeper into the West Woods. Though greatly outnumbered, Lieutenant Carter then ordered his small company to charge into the enemy's flank with a yell and "such impestuousity" that the Rebels fled in panic. [18]

Finally Captain Long arrived with Smith's order to fall back. In good order the 77th retreated to the cover of a hill marked by large rock outcroppings about 50 yards distant. A Confederate battery not more than 20 yards to the left front of the 77th raked its position with canister and solid shot. The regiment hugged the ground behind the rocky hill. The barrage terminated Lieutenant Skinner's participation in the war:

> A shell burst on the left of us, and it fairly ploughed our ranks about Center – I felt a tremendous punch as if the Steed of Balaam had kicked me with all his feet at once.

Attempted to rise – found my left leg nonplussed. Looked at it – seemed all right – tried again – no use – made an examination. Found a <u>hole</u> in my left thigh, it began to hurt, not the <u>hole</u>, but the place where it goes in began to hurt. Three men bore me from the field, to some Straw Stacks where lay hundreds of wounded. [19]

Skinner lay among the wounded when, "A Reb surgeon dressed my wound, no other doctors being there. Found that my thigh was broken. He applied what I thought to be cotton. I asked him if I must submit to King Cotton now that I was helpless. He said it was lint – All right, -- Had the ball extracted. It had passed directly through and lodged in the groin area under the skin. It proved to be a round ball – (A number of these are encased in a shell and when it explodes they fly a perfect shower) – The ball being round I think my thigh bone was simply severed but not shattered greatly for Surgeons pronounce a broken thigh the most critical of wounds." [20]

The Lieutenant was "finally carried to the rear and placed in a barnyard where I lay for eight days on my face with but little attention. In fact the doctors seemed to think my case hopeless and passed by me. The first night was 'age of agony' long and painful. An old Surgeon came by me. I asked him for something to make me sleep – No it wasn't best for me. Asked to place my leg in a better position – Could do nothing till morning. Finally told me I was to die, and walked away." Skinner would lie on the ground for eight days, ground that "appeared to be covered with wounded soldiers and they died all around me for want of attention." But although permanently disabled, Skinner resolved to live and was later discharged from service. [21]

The entire Third Brigade hunkered down behind the small hill and rock outcroppings opposite and south of the Dunker Church

M^CKEAN'S SUNDAY SCHOOL BOYS GO TO WAR

for nearly three hours. Near the 7th Maine, Captain Wolcott's Battery B Maryland Light Artillery continued to fire upon Lee's batteries posted upon the Boonsboro Pike. Just before 5 p.m., Captain Emory Upton, the First Division artillery chief, and Colonel Irwin rode into the battery to assess the situation. Captain Wolcott pointed to the haystacks around Piper's Farm south of the Bloody Lane, and complained to Irwin that Rebel sharpshooters there were picking off his battery crews. Colonel Irwin at once rode over to Major Hyde whom he found lying below the crest of Mumma's swale. The Colonel ordered Hyde to "take your regiment and drive the enemy away from those trees and buildings." Thomas Hyde could not believe the command as he had earlier observed a considerable number of Confederates in and around Piper's orchard. "Colonel," he said, "I have seen a large force of rebels go in there, I should think two brigades." The enraged Irwin shouted, "Are you afraid to go, sir?" and repeated the order. The Major, rather than to lose face or to risk court martial for insubordination, replied, "Give the order so the regiment can hear it and we are ready, sir." Colonel Irwin again fairly screamed the order for the 7th Maine to move out. [22]

With a deep sorrow, Major Hyde called the 7th Maine to attention. The regiment proceeded south to the Sunken Road and on toward Piper's Farm. The men could not help but see the devastating carnage that had taken place earlier. Many tried not to look down as they stepped over, around, and on the gray, dead faces of the fallen enemy. Others looked on in astonishment at the broken bodies and equipment that carpeted the bloody road. Still others contemplated their end and prayed for deliverance.

The New Englanders tore down a rail fence, formed into battle formation, and charged into Piper's orchard. There they met an overwhelming force of mixed Confederate units, and were nearly annihilated. In a little more than thirty minutes, 12 men were killed, sixty three were wounded, and twenty were missing or captured. The 7th Maine rallied to the colors with only sixty five enlisted men, three officers, and their brave major. Hyde ordered his men back to their original position on the other side of the Sunken Road.

Later, Major Hyde accused Colonel Irwin of being drunk during the battle which, considering his brash and unwise deployment of the Third Brigade, was not a stretch of the imagination. Indeed Irwin, wounded at the battle of Melino del Ray during the Mexican War, was once brought up on charges with being "so intoxicated as to be unable to perform the duties of a commander at the Grand Review at Munson's Hill, Virginia, on 21 November, 1861 and at Camp Griffin, Virginia, on 22 January, 1862." He was subsequently acquitted of drunkenness. Whether Colonel Irwin was drunk or not during the battle, Major Hyde noted that he was relieved of command early the next morning. [23]

That evening as the bloody contest came to an end, Sergeant Carlos Rowe (Co. I), with Corporal Samuel Dodge (Co. I), set out in search for their company comrade, Private George Huntington:

> Many of our men . . . were searching the fields for the wounded and dead. As we walked around a faint voice called us; going in the direction of the call we found two men, lying side by side on the ground – one dead. The other asked us to 'take the blanket off my brother and put it over me, I am so cold.' Which we did and then got him a canteen of water. All day long had they lay there in the hot sun. Continuing our search we found Huntington – a bullet hole in his head showed that he had been instantly killed. Returning to our regiment, we again went out in the morning and got Huntington's body; carried it to the cemetery near the village (Sharpsburg); dug a grave and with

his blanket around him put him in and covered him with the earth.

An exhausted Private Milton F. Sweet (Co. G) laid down and promptly fell asleep. When he awoke the next morning, he was unnerved by the realization, "I had slept between dead men – blue and gray." [24]

Lieutenant Ansel Dennison (L. Tom Perry Special Collections)

The 77th remained at their position into the night until relieved at 12 p.m. the next day, September 18. Neither Lee nor McClellan was disposed to renew the battle. The collection of the wounded began in earnest. Captain Wheeler noted that "parties went to work picking up the wounded, who were crying for water to every one who came near them." In the afternoon "the rebels sent in a flag of truce for leave to pick up their wounded, which was granted." Wheeler thought it surreal "to see parties from either side talking friendly to each other, when the day before each had been intent to slay the other." [25]

The battlefield was a perfect picture of horror for the young Captain: "The slaughter of some parts of the field was terrible. In one place I counted thirty dead rebels in a few rods square, in other places they lay in ranks as they fell not more than two feet apart. There seemed two of their dead to the one of ours . . . across the battlefield the stench was horrible from the thousands of unburied men and horses." Giving a more detailed report of the nightmarish aftermath of Antietam, Surgeon Stevens wrote:

> The scene on the battle-field was past description. The mangled forms of our own comrades lay stretched upon the ground, side by side with those of the rebels. On almost every rod of ground over one hundred acres, the dead and wounded, some clade in Union blue and some in Confederate gray, were lying. A ghastly sight, presenting all the horrible features of death which are to be seen on such a field. At one point in our own front, for more than half a mile, the rebels lay so thickly as almost to touch each other. On the field where Hooker's men had won and lost the field, the dead and dying were scattered thickly among the broken cornstalks, their eyes protruding and their faces blackened by the sun. Wherever the lines of battle had surged to and fro, these vestiges of the terrible work were left. In the edge of the wood, where the rebels had made a stand against Hooker's advancing divisions, the bodies lay in a perfect line, as though they had fallen while on dress parade. Further to the left there was a narrow row, not more than fifteen feet wide, with high fences on either side. Here a regiment of rebels was posted; when our batteries getting an enfilading fire upon them, and the infantry at the same time opening a murderous fire, the regiment was literally destroyed; not more than twenty of their number escaping. Their bodies filled the narrow road. Some were

shot attempting to get over the fence; and their remains hung upon the boards. A more fearful picture than we saw here, could not be conceived . . . Broken caissons, wheels, dismounted guns, thousands of muskets, haversacks and canteens, were scattered thickly over the field; and hundreds of slain horses, bloated and feet turned toward the sky, added to the horror.

Stevens went on:

Here in the rear of the army for miles, was a succession of hospitals. Every house, and barn, and haystack, formed the nucleus of a hospital, where men, shot through the head, through the limbs, through the body; with every conceivable variety of wounds, lay groaning in anguish. Surgeons toiled day and night with never lagging zeal to relieve these sufferings, but all their labor could only afford slight relief. The labors of medical officers after a great battle are immense, and there is no respite from their toils so long as a wounded man remains uncared for. While others find repose from the fatigues of battle sleep, surgeons are still at work; there is no sleep so long as work remains to be done. [26]

Fortunately for the 77th, there would be no renewal of the fight on the 19th either. Lee observed his severely mauled Army of Northern Virginia and realized McClellan was bound to receive substantial reinforcements, so he finally decided to pull his troops across the Potomac on the night of the 18th. The Confederates crossed at Boteler's Ford and moved on to Martinsburg, Virginia, in the Shenandoah Valley. During the retreat, a regimental band struck up "Maryland, My Maryland" to the jeers of their comrades who were bitter over their losses at Antietam. Some soldiers sang instead "Damn My Maryland."

Not surprisingly, McClellan was in no hurry to pursue Lee. What had become a familiar refrain, the General claimed that the Army of the Potomac was too worn out and his supplies were too depleted to make an advance. Thus, most of the Union army sat idle while squads of soldiers went about burying the dead and collecting the wounded that yet remained on the field.

Smith's division, however, moved forward to bivouac between the Potomac River and Sharpsburg. The 77th passed over the deflating scene of carnage on the battlefield where hundreds of the dead still lay unburied. Burial details were on every part of the field throwing the mangled, disfigured bodies into shallow graces. Twisted, bloated corpses of Confederate soldiers lined the roadsides and broken fences and were scattered around where Rebel hospitals had once been.

When the 77th entered Sharpsburg, evidence of the unimaginable conflict was everywhere. Taking in the surroundings, George Stevens wrote, "Houses riddled by shells and bullets; some of them destroyed by fire, and some battered into shapeless masses; the streets filled with disabled wagons; horses galloping without riders; knapsacks, guns, and equipments cast away in the hasty flight; churches filled with rebel wounded; all helped to make the scene of destruction such as been rarely witnessed." Nevertheless, "The people of the village welcomed us as their deliverers, and brought water, and such refreshments as they had been able to conceal from the rebels." [27]

After the 77th passed through the tatters of Sharpsburg, they soon bivouacked for the night, only to retrace their steps, passing again over the battlefield where the stench of decaying men and horses was unendurable. The regiment reached Williamsport where they saw a division of Pennsylvania Militia drawn up in line of battle.

McKEAN'S SUNDAY SCHOOL BOYS GO TO WAR

The soldiers were amazed at the size of the militia regiments which were larger than the brigades of their division. To the 77th, now hardened veterans, they were a motley crowd:

> They were armed with every variety of fire-arms, from light sporting shot-guns to Sharpe's rifles. Their uniforms had quite as little uniformity as their arms. Some were dressed in gray pants and jackets, others in light blue; and still others in the various fashions which constituted the wearing apparel at home. Grave gentlemen in spectacles, studious young men in green glasses, pale young men who were evidently more at home behind the counter than in line of battle, roughs who had not been tamed by the discipline of military life, and boys who, for the first time, had left the paternal mansion, made up the heterogeneous division. [28]

The 77th stayed at Williamsport until September 23 and then marched on the Hagerstown Pike to Bakersville, where they remained for a little more than three weeks getting much needed rest. Food was plentiful in pro-Union Bakersville, and the people were generous with the soldiers, providing soft bread and other luxuries such as "hasty pudding" and Johnny cake. The process of producing these was a makeshift manner of men who were expert at invention. A tin plate perforated by means of a nail or a sharp point of a bayonet, became a grater or mill for grinding the corn. The neighboring cornfields yielded an abundance of rich yellow corn which was rubbed across the grater, yielding a fine meal like that ground at a grist mill. The corn meal was mixed with a large or small quantity of water – as much mush or cake as was desired – and cooked.

During the Maryland Campaign, Lieutenant Colonel Winsor B. French was busy recruiting troops for the regiment. War meetings were held in an around the villages and hamlets surrounding

Saratoga Springs. In one such meeting, an enormous crowd – among whom many were visitors to the famous Spa's springs – gathered at Pavilion Grove in Saratoga. Stirring speeches whipped up the crowd and the ladies in attendance offered their diamond rings, their watches and other valuables to anyone who would come forward to enlist in the 77th. Caught in the enthusiasm that permeated the crowd, more than 50 young men came forward and enrolled their names, and received the jewels that the fair maidens offered them.

Not to be outdone, the town of Milton held a Sunday evening mass meeting at the recruiting tent on Low Street. A platform had been erected for the speakers, and after several had spoken, Rev. William O. Holman from the Baptist Church mounted the rostrum and made an eloquent and intensely patriotic appeal to the assembled multitude. In the crowd on the street was Mr. Eli Settle, the proprietor of the Blue Mill. Too far advanced in years to enlist himself, he urged a young man to enlist in his name. The young man protested, "I would like to go, but I have nothing to leave my family." Settle took a roll of bills from his pocket and replied, "Here are fifty dollars to give to your wife, and I will see that she wants nothing while you are gone." The young man promptly enlisted. To another, Settle repeated the offer, and another name was enrolled. To a third young man, Mr. Settle explained, "I have but ten dollars left, but if you will enlist, you can have that, and here is my watch for security until I can get to the bank in the morning, when you shall have the other forty." To this the young fellow replied, "I don't want your watch, Mr. Settle, your word is good enough for me." And down went his name. [29]

In neighboring Schuylerville, the site of Burgoyne's surrender in 1777, the patriotic fervor for new recruits came alive. John Rockville, the local newspaper publisher, and William Fursman were fishing together on the Hudson River (along which the little village was built), when Rockwell turned to William and suggested that "we raise a company." Fursman agreed, they reeled in their lines, and rowed to shore. Rockwell hired a room and opened a recruiting station. Posters were printed and circulated calling for recruits. The response was immediate and in ten days a company was raised. [30]

At the same time, the 115th New York was being raised and wanted the company to enter it. Rockwell and Fursman would have nothing to do with it, and traveled to Saratoga Springs to present the company to Lieutenant Colonel French for the 77th. As the prospective officers of the 115th protested the company going to the 77th, French, Rockwell, and Fursman took a train to Albany to petition Governor Morgan to allow the company to enroll in the regiment. Together they explained to the Governor that if the boys of the company were not enrolled in the 77th, they would go back to their homes; they would have nothing to do with the 115th New York. Governor Morgan agreed to their petition and they took a train back to Saratoga Springs where the new company joined other recruits to the regiment at old Camp Schuyler.

As the final days of September passed, General McClellan was reliving his experience at Harrison's Landing in July, brooding over his misfortunes and resentful of the perceived incompetence of his superiors, Halleck and Lincoln. He refused to budge from Antietam while he gathered supplies and the reinforcements that he called for to strengthen his army before initiating any attempt to return to Virginia to engage Lee's soldiers. After sending a dispatch to Washington stating, "This Army is not now in condition to undertake another campaign, nor to bring on another battle," Lincoln became so annoyed that he determined to visit the Army of the Potomac, and to press the ever resistant McClellan into action. [31]

The President arrived at the Union army's camps on October 1 and remained there for four days, visiting hospitals and touring the battlefields of South Mountain and Antietam. On October 3, the Sixth Corps was ordered out for review by Lincoln. The corps was formed on a large flat plain, and the booming of cannon announced the approach of the Commander-in-Chief. Along with Lincoln rode Generals McClellan, Franklin, Smith, some notables, and an immense retinue in tow. In deference to the veterans still recovering from fatigue from the late battle, the President simply passed along the corps, acknowledging the salutations that greeted him without requiring the divisions to march in review. Joining the 77th, the soldiers sent up cheer after cheer in their appreciation of the interest taken by Lincoln.

Before the President left for Washington, Lincoln, short of a direct order, urged McClellan to set the Army of the Potomac after Lee to destroy the Confederate army. Yet Little Mac would not budge. Captain Luther Wheeler strongly agreed with McClellan's unwillingness to pursue Lee. Writing to his mother, the Captain said:

> We expect to stay here all winter if the northern people and papers do not force McClellan to take the field again by continually harping about a forward movement that the soldiers are eager to advance and in good condition, that the army of Lee could be defeated in a single week and all such talk – If they wish to defeat our cause the way to do it is to advance this fall with our army of undrilled men and ragged worn out veterans, we should certainly be defeated. But if we wait until spring we shall have an army of a million drilled soldiers and can put down the rebellion in a hurry. [32]

Soon after midnight on October 11th, the 77th's Sixth Corps was ordered to move to Hagerstown. The corps moved out in the midst of a heavy shower and reached Hagerstown by daylight. Here the

Third Brigade received a much needed infusion of troops. The 21st New Jersey, a nine-month regiment, joined the brigade and about the same time Lieutenant Colonel French returned with approximately three hundred new recruits, including Rockwell's company from Schuylerville. Old Company K was merged with Company E and Rockwell's men formed second Company K. The merging of the two companies caused some hard feelings among some of the officers who saw their chance for promotion disappointed. Disillusioned, Captain Jesse White (Co. F) and Lieutenant Jacob Haywood (Co. I) resigned, and went back home to Waterford and Saratoga, New York.

Captain Wheeler was pleased with the influx of new recruits "for they make our Reg't a very large one, and if they're given us time to drill them, will make a fine Reg't." The Captain drilled the green soldiers every day and was pleased that the "recruits were fast becoming soldiers." Too, Wheeler was amused that "quite a number of the recruits think they have had a hard time and say they did not expect to have such hard times – and wish they were at home again." The veterans "consoled them by telling them that they have not seen no hard times yet." [33]

One such recruit was twenty-six year-old Private Alonzo D. Bump in second Company K. Bump worked as a weaver at the Saratoga Manufacturing Company in Victory Mills about twenty-five miles east of Saratoga Springs. He left behind his wife and young daughter, "Little Mattie," to join the war. Writing to his wife in fractured grammar and his unique spelling, Alonzo reported, "Dear I have Bin to the Provost Gard thiss Morning and the Sargent told me that we was all a coming Back again to Day. i hope that we shall for i had rather Bee thair than in the regiment But then some of the Boys Don't want to Go Back. i do for when i ame thair i Git rid of Doing Picket Duty and Drilling and that is something to Bee Looked at in the winter." [34]

Camp at Hagerstown was quite pleasant. With the enemy far removed in Virginia's Shenandoah Valley, picket duty was relaxing. Those on picket had little trouble finding good food. Dropping their almost inedible hardtack, they readily procured such delicacies as soft bread and hoe cakes from area farmers. Indeed, the inhabitants of Hagerstown seemed glad to furnish the men with all the comforts possible. Except for drilling the new recruits, there was little duty in camp and the invalids had time to recover from their exhausted strength. Captain Wheeler wrote, "I am . . . living first rate, besides having a little fun now and then." No doubt he enjoyed having time to become "acquainted with some of the pretty Maryland girls who live near our camp and think there is nothing better like a Union officer." [35]

The encampment allowed some to be furloughed and they eagerly traveled back home to visit friends and family. Captain Stephen Horton, who had been seriously wounded at Antietam, happily went home to Ballston Spa. News that Horton was returning home on furlough greatly excited the inhabitants of the village and they moved to greet the returning hero. A large crowd gathered at the train station to await his arrival. As Captain Horton's train approached, the "old trophy gun" boomed out a welcome and the crowd enthusiastically cheered. The young captain was brought to a carriage south of Bath Street. The horses had been unhitched and a long rope was attached to the carriage. With the crowd still cheering, 50 or more men and boys drew him up the hill to his home on High Street. Yet, not everyone in the village welcomed the return of Horton. A man named Osgood, known as "Beauregard" because of his sympathy with the South, found Captain Horton seated on the piazza of the Village Hotel, with his crutches by his side. Upon seeing Horton, Osgood loudly remarked, "I would like to see Arnold Harris, Doctor Moore, Jim Cook and Jim Horton strung up, and would like to have to hold the rope." No sooner did the words come out of Osgood's mouth before Horton hopped on one crutch and landed a powerful punch at his insulter, sending Osgood sprawling in the gutter. Standing over "Beauregard," Horton proclaimed, "I can trash any man, even on crutches, who makes such a villainous remark." Humiliated before village onlookers, Osgood crawled to his feet and ran down Spring Street and disappeared. [36]

On October 28, the 77th received orders to send their sick, along with those of the Sixth Corps, to hospitals in Hagerstown. Their march took them from Williamsport to Boonsboro and up the winding hillsides of Pleasant Valley. "The forests on the hillsides, glowing with the brilliant colors of autumn, the fine old residences, appearing here and there among the trees, and the plethoric stacks of hay and grain," Surgeon Stevens wrote, "combined, indeed, to make it a 'pleasant valley,' and, as the long lines of troops filed along the roads, the spectacle was beautifully picturesque." But the scene dramatically shifted as the 77th climbed the west side of South Mountain and crossed the Crampton's Gap battlefield. "Every tree bore lasting marks of a terrible fight. For more than a mile, the forest was completely scarred by bullets and shells; not a tree had escaped, and many of them were pierced like the cover of a pepper box." The regiment halted near Berlin, and on the next morning crossed the Potomac River into Virginia over a pontoon bridge, finally settling in at New Baltimore with the rest of the Third Brigade, in the south gap of the Bull Run Mountains. [37]

The movement of the Army of the Potomac from Sharpsburg across the Potomac into Virginia was a ponderous one taking nearly a month to complete. Despite Lincoln's constant urging for McClellan to engage and destroy Lee's army, the General remained true to form and wildly overestimated the strength of the Army of Virginia and called for increasingly larger reinforcements. Finally the President had lost all patience with McClellan and on November

5, he directed Halleck to relieve Little Mac of command and replace him with Ambrose Burnside.

Born on May 23, 1824, Burnside received an appointment to the U. S. Military Academy at West Point. Unlike his future opponent, Lee, he accumulated scores of demerits. Although he narrowly escaped disciplinary dismissal, Burnside managed to graduate 18th in a class of 38 cadets. He served as an artillery officer in the Mexican War and was later assigned to an isolated post in New Mexico. There, he fought boredom by designing a breech-loading carbine for the cavalry which was later popular in the Civil War. In 1853, he resigned his commission to begin manufacturing his carbine. However, the business failed, and by the eve of the Civil War Burnside was working as a cashier for the railroad owned by none other than George B. McClellan.

Shortly after the bombardment of Fort Sumter, Burnside accepted command of the 1st Rhode Island infantry regiment. His leadership of a brigade at the First Battle of Bull Run earned him a quick promotion to brigadier general. Burnside, in January 1862, directed a successful amphibious expedition that captured Roanoke Island of the North Carolina coast. Success against greatly outnumbered Confederates had come when Union victories were scarce, and by March Burnside was promoted to major general. Though he doubted his own ability, Burnside seemed destined for higher command.

On Sunday, November 9, General McClellan began the process of bidding farewell to his army. That evening was spent with the officers of his staff and escort. The side curtains of his tent were raised and the area was lit by a large log fire nearby. As each man entered, he greeted him and ushered him inside. The best champagne was

M^cKEAN'S SUNDAY SCHOOL BOYS GO TO WAR

opened, and McClellan raised his glass to the assembled company and offered a wishful toast: "To the Army of the Potomac, and bless the day when I shall return." [38]

The next day, the corps of the army was assembled for review, and his farewell address was read to them. "In parting from you I cannot express the love and gratitude I bear to you," he wrote. "As an army you have grown up under my care . . . The battles you have fought under my command will proudly live in our Nation's history. The glory you have achieved, our mutual perils and fatigues, the graves of our comrades fallen in battle and disease, the broken forms of those who wounds and sickness have disabled – the strongest associations which can exist among men – unite us still by an indissoluble tie. Farewell!" [39]

Then McClellan, with Burnside at his side, rode past the solid ranks in review. As they did so, batteries fired salutes and bands played "The Star Spangled Banner" and "Hail to the Chief." Captain Wheeler wrote that the General "was tremendously cheered by everyone." Not really *everyone* cheered, however. Private Bump was decidedly in no mood to do so, and stated "the Boys Cheard Genirl Mcllan as he Past By us But i did not feal Like chearing him as how i wish i was home with you to day. i wold give all the money that i could earn in a year or two But i cant come so i must as well Be contented." As McClellan passed by the 77th, Wheeler saw that Little Mac "looked very sad – he looked like he had been crying." Later Wheeler expressed a certain growing anger present among the troops: "a large part of the army would lay down their arms until he was returned . . . out of opposition to 'the people' who seem to be ruling everything now. They had better come down and fight this war or end it in some way – Most the whole north has . . . turned their backs to the soldiers." [40]

Thus ended the great struggle that was the Maryland Campaign. While the battle between Lee and McClellan was militarily a draw, Lincoln managed to salvage a victory out of an inconclusive battle. The President desired to infuse a revolutionary sentiment to reinvigorate the Union war effort, and decided emancipation of slavery was just the element needed. It would undercut the basis of the South's economic and social structure, would give the North a semblance of moral superiority over the advisory by taking up the cause of human freedom, and would force England and France to seriously consider the unpopularity of allying with a "nation" that supported slavery. Lincoln issued the Emancipation Proclamation on September 22, promising to free all slaves in those states still in rebellion against the Union after January 1, 1863. Hence, Antietam served to make emancipation a primary war issue, one on which the Republic would live or die. However, to free the slaves, the South would have to be conquered, and that would take two and a half more years of increasingly bloody warfare and hundreds of thousands of lives.

1

"OH! WHAT A CRUEL SIGHT"

After the brash and reckless, perhaps drunken, mishandling of the Third Brigade at Antietam, Colonel Irwin was replaced by Brigadier General Francis Laurens Vinton. Born at Fort Preble, Maine, on June 1, 1835, Vinton's father and two of his uncles were graduates of West Point. His father was an officer of the Regular Army and was killed at the siege of Vera Cruz in 1847. Vinton graduated from West Point in 1856, but resigned his commission to study mining engineering in Paris and in 1860 became an instructor of mechanical drawing at the Cooper Union in New York. At the outbreak of war, he was reappointed to the Regular Army and commissioned Colonel of the 43rd New York Infantry.

Taking up his command, Ambrose Burnside reorganized the Army of the Potomac. He combined two army corps into a "Grand Division" and then added some cavalry and artillery. The Federal army's six corps were divided into Right, Center, and Left Grand Divisions. The Right Grand Division combined the First and Ninth corps under Major General Edwin V. Sumner. The Third and Fifth Corps comprised the Center Grand Division with Major General Joseph Hooker commanding. The Left Grand Division, composed of the First and Sixth Corps, came under Major General William Buel Franklin, along with Bayard's cavalry. Baldy Smith was promoted to Sixth Corps command, and was replaced as head of the Second Division by Brigadier General Albion P. Howe. Forty-four years old in 1862, Howe, a Maine native and West Point graduate, had been promoted for gallantry during Winfield Scott's advance upon Mexico City in the Mexican War. Between the wars he was a West Point instructor. Albion Howe spent most of his career in the artillery, not the infantry, but he commanded an infantry brigade during the Peninsula Campaign and performed well.

A certain nervousness descended upon the army concerning Burnside's plans. While the soldiers might dream of reaching Richmond, many, like Luther Wheeler, hoped the army would soon go into winter quarters. Yet uncertainty about where the Army of the Potomac might be headed made the men uneasy. Whether or not the army went into winter quarters, Captain Wheeler knew full well that the future held more death and destruction to come:

> We are inactive, but expect to see stirring times soon. The change in commanders stopped the advance of the army – Burnside will soon get the rains in his hands and then look out for hard fighting – we are not at all anxious to see it – but it must come – As you say we do not look forward to spring, or any other time, but make the best of every day as it comes. It will not do for a soldier to think of the morrow, for his part in the future is beset with danger – a lingering death may await him on the battle field, or a terrible wound make him a cripple for life. We seldom think of these things, but are happy in the present. [1]

MᶜKEAN'S SUNDAY SCHOOL BOYS GO TO WAR

Ambrose Burnside did indeed quickly take up the reins of command. On the same day he assumed command, he established a headquarters at the nearly deserted town of Warrenton. Once an industrious village that boasted a respectable hotel, a few businesses and churches, and some impressive private homes, Warrenton had grown shabby under the burden of war. Many stores were closed, and the sick and wounded of both armies crowded the streets. Coffins filled the Presbyterian Church, while the village's women tended to the already sizable Rebel Cemetery.

Before the day was out, Burnside formulated a plan for a rapid march on Richmond and dispatched it to Henry Halleck. He advised Halleck that he would take the most direct route to Richmond by moving from Warrenton to Fredericksburg, crossing the Rappahannock River to Fredericksburg near Falmouth and heading straight for the Confederate capital 50 miles further south. Simultaneous with the advance of the main army, feints would be carried out in the direction of Gordonsville and Culpeper Court House in the hope of confusing Lee as to the real objective of the army. Two days later, Halleck came to Warrenton to further discuss Burnside's proposed plan to march on Richmond, but as usual, he was unwilling to issue the necessary orders for the campaign to commence. Halleck agreed, however, to present Burnside's plan to Lincoln. If the President approved, Burnside would advance the army to Falmouth and cross the Rappahannock River on pontoon bridges. Halleck would then arrange to have the pontoon trains moved to Falmouth.

Lincoln had considerable reservations about the Fredericksburg route, yet the President hesitated to show any lack of confidence in Burnside, and on November 14, he gave his approval. Halleck immediately wired Burnside of Lincoln's decision giving him the go-ahead. Appended to the approval was the cautionary injunction that in the President's view the campaign would only succeed "if you move rapidly; otherwise not." Burnside recognized the necessity of quickly concentrating his forces and marching, but this curt response from Washington irked him. [2]

Burnside acted as soon as the orders arrived. Sumner, Hooker, and Franklin received their marching orders in the afternoon. At 5 a.m. on November 15, Sumner's Right Grand Division began leaving Warrenton. By late morning most of his men were on the direct road to Falmouth. Hooker's and Franklin's Grand Divisions departed the next day, with Hooker following Sumner's route and Franklin taking a more indirect route to Stafford Courthouse.

In a letter to his mother, Captain Wheeler gave a description, albeit sanitized, of the army on the march:

> In the first place the men have three days rations in their haversacks, consisting of hard crackers, raw pork, or boiled suet beef, coffee and sugar in a little bag, and a quart tin cup to cook their coffee in. On the march they eat the crackers and pork raw, for they never halt at noon to let us make coffee or cook pork. Besides their haversacks the men carry forty rounds of cartridges in their boxes, and a knapsack containing under clothes, a rubber, and a woolen blanket, over coat and half of a tent—when we halt at night the first thing that is done is to put up their tents which takes but a few moments, then they cook their supper and it eat, after which they sit around the camp fires, telling stories and smoking until they get sleepy, then turn in, to their beds, made of a rubber blanket spread on the ground, and sleep, as none but a soldier can . . . On the march when a man gives out the Captain of his Co gives him a pass to leave the ranks and fall to the rear, then he comes on as fast as he

can, and it frequently happens that stragglers do not join their Regts until three or four days after they stop." [3]

The reality of the march for the 77th was much less pleasant than Wheeler's prettified version for his mother. It rained most of the way to Stafford Court House. The countryside was mostly forested, with rough, open fields dissected by narrow country lanes whose condition was made worse by the rains that continued during the march. Soon the men were wet and cold, trudging through thick unfathomable Virginia mud. Some lost their shoes in the mud but had no choice but to carry on the march without them. Impeding the march were the thousands of cumbersome wagons and artillery. Poor roads, mud, and broken down animals assured that the wagon trains could not keep up with the infantry. The 77th frequently found itself blocked by the horse drawn trains. For the sick, the march was a nightmare. The lucky ones rode bouncing around in ambulances. The less fortunate, though weak and debilitated, marched alongside the infantry. Many fell out and died by the roadside. Alonzo Bump wrote the following to his wife, Mary: "We saw men Ley Beside the rode that Cold not goe eny farther and we saw one man that was ded Ley Beside the rode and some of the Boys shook him to finde out if he was ded or not." At least two of Captain Wheeler's company fell out and never returned to the regiment. [4]

The 77th marched through the Virginia countryside and found it to be desolate. Luther Wheeler wrote, "The country we marched through . . . was very poor, very few houses and mostly of logs and but few people." Empathy for the Southerners, however, was in short supply. "The soldiers plunder every thing they come to – Kill all the pigs, cattle, sheep and poultry." Wheeler felt justified for, "The people are all 'secesh' and tell us they hope we may never return alive." [5]

Sumner's Right Grand Division reached Falmouth on November 17. His men were greeted by harassing fire from Lewis' Virginia Battery from across the Rappahannock at Fredericksburg. Captain Rufus D. Pettit's Battery B, 1st New York Light Artillery, with its 10-pounder Parrotts, answered Lewis' battery and silenced him within fifteen minutes. Sumner wanted to cross the river and possess Fredericksburg, but Burnside rejected the idea. The Major General was fearful that Sumner's men might become trapped south of the river by rising water. Burnside also reasoned that it would be safer to wait for his pontoon train (which was expected to arrive at any time) to ensure a safe crossing and secure communications north of the river. By nightfall, Federal artillery lined Stafford Heights overlooking Fredericksburg.

While Hooker's Center Grand Division halted at Hartwood Church above United States Ford on the Rappahannock River, Franklin's Left Grand Division reached Stafford Courthouse November 19. The once neat courthouse now stood in shambles. The surrounding picket fence was torn down for Yankee fires the previous spring. The benches and doors too became fuel for camp fires. Its walls were defaced with graffiti and county documents were scattered on the floor. The jail across the way from the Court House was converted into a guard House.

The 77th bivouacked near the Court House, hoping that they were to go into winter quarters. The weather was cold and at night standing water around camp froze solid. The men made themselves comfortable by logging up their tents and building fireplaces in them to provide heat in the late autumn nights. Military daily routine followed and was predictable. Private Bump wrote, "when we Lie in Camp we haft to Drill 5 hours in a day and when we git in then we haft to Git our Grub and eat it and Buy that time we haft to Go to Bed." Getting grub, Bump wrote to his wife, was a challenge for the men. "Mary you would Laugh to see us all a Cooking around the fire and sum of them gits their Coffee tipt over and sum their meat and some their rise and sum their Beans and then you will hear them sware and then they will scrape it up and eat it and call it good and Let it go at that." Nevertheless, he went on, "Mary, we have a good deal of fun hear. some times the Boys Gits a caring on." [6]

As the Federals advanced in two main columns southeast from Warrenton, Lee kept a keen eye on their progress, but did not yet know Burnside's intentions. While the Union army made its way toward Fredericksburg, Lee's Army of Northern Virginia was dangerously divided. Thirty miles to the west of Culpeper Courthouse was James Longstreet's First Corps. In the Shenandoah Valley, 75 miles northwest of Fredericksburg at Winchester, stood Thomas Jackson's Second Corps. JEB Stuart's cavalrymen screened the countryside along the Rappahannock River. In the event that Burnside attacked, Lee would have to quickly unite his forces.

On November 17, Lee was informed about Sumner's initial move toward Fredericksburg. In response, he ordered two of Longstreet's infantry divisions, under Major General Lafayette McLaws and Brigadier General Robert Ransom, Jr., to head for the threatened city. By the 20th, Lee was certain of Burnside's destination and ordered the rest of Longstreet's First Corps units (the infantry of Richard A. Anderson, George E. Pickett, and John B. Hood) to move swiftly to Fredericksburg. By November 23, nearly 40,000 Confederates were concentrated in the city's vicinity while Lee awaited the arrival Jackson's 38,000-strong Second Corps.

Burnside's entire campaign plan hinged on the timely arrival of his pontoon train at Fredericksburg. What he did not know was that the overland train had not yet left Washington. A series of poorly written orders, little initiative or understanding by junior officers of the importance of the boats in the campaign, and lack of needed parts prevented the pontoon train from reaching Falmouth until November 27. The critical delay in the arrival of his pontoons and concern that Jackson could emerge from the Shenandoah Valley and spring upon him from the rear, convinced Burnside not to storm across the river at once.

The arrival of Burnside's pontoons coincided with Thanksgiving Day. Surgeon Stevens reported that the 77th "enjoyed a very pleasant Thanksgiving." That morning throughout the Sixth Corps, there was brigade inspection. "We put on our good clothes and presented ourselves to our generals, looking our best; then as we marched back into our various camps, we found our dinner smoking in many a cook-tent, and the odor of roast meats rising throughout the whole corps like an odor of sweet incense. Fresh sheep pelts hanging here and there in considerable profusion, told of good cheer among all the men." Captain Wheeler, however, seemed not to have partaken in such a sumptuous meal that Stevens remembered for he wrote home to his mother, "I often thought of home Thanksgiving day and wished myself at your table, which differed from mine I guess – I ate some bean soup 'hardtack" and coffee for my dinner and enjoyed it too for we soldiers have good appetites." [7]

At nightfall "the voice of singing was heard from all the camps, and groups were gathered under the shadow of the chestnut trees, where many pairs of government shoes were shuffling to the music of violins." No doubt music loving Lieutenant Colonel French took up his violin and joined the musicians. "Good humor and mirth prevailed," Stevens recounted, and "the sick forgot their pains, and the home sick ones, for a time, looked bright, as they yielded to the general feeling of happiness." [8]

While Burnside and his army dithered on the north bank of the Rappahannock, Lee summoned Jackson to Fredericksburg from the Shenandoah Valley. Starting on November 21, Jackson's famous "foot cavalry" marched nearly 200 miles in 12 days to reach the rest of the army. With the two armies facing each other across the Rappahannock River, Lee was puzzled by Burnside's inaction. Turning to a subordinate, Lee said, "What the design of the enemy is, I do not know." [9]

Pressure on Burnside to restart his campaign before winter set in by the Northern press, politicians, his officers, and most importantly Lincoln himself, prompted Burnside to look to a prominent bend in the river known as Skinker's Neck. A scout confirmed that the ground could handle a large-scale movement, and that the Confederates had neglected to guard it. Consequently Burnside notified his generals that the army would move to cross the river at Skinker's Neck.

Baldy Smith's Sixth Corps received marching orders on December 5 just as cold weather set in. Heading for Belle Plain, the 77th marched into a bracing wind while drenching rain turned to snow. The New Yorker's wool uniforms became stiff with ice and snow. "The ambulances which carried the sick got stuck in the mud," Luther Wheeler wrote, "and the sick soldiers had to be turned out to walk, three or four of them died by the roadside." At nightfall, the regiment halted at the Aquia Creek Railroad. Bedding down in slush of snow and mud, the rank and file endured a cold miserable night, but so too did the officers. The 77th's baggage train was miles to the rear stuck in the mud, forcing "the Col. And all the officers to go without tents." [10]

The next day before Burnside's column reached Skinker's Neck, scouts reported that the Rebels had appeared in force across the river. Alerted to The Union army's advance, Jackson had sent Jubal Early's division to guard Skinker's Neck. Stymied for the second time, Burnside ordered the soldiers back to their former camps. Once again the march was brutal. Arriving back in their camp, the soldiers of the 77th were hungry, for the supply train with rations could not come up due to the poor condition of the roads. It was also uncomfortably cold. Captain Wheeler and his company managed, however, to tame the cold by "keeping large fires in front of our tents and . . . we lay spoon fashion three or four side by side putting all our blankets over us." [11]

Meanwhile, the Rebel army continued preparing defensive positions behind Fredericksburg. Longstreet's corps took positions at Taylor's Farm, opposite Beck's Island in the Rappahannock, and the high ground south of the city. On the Lansdowne Valley Road, Longstreet's lines linked up with Jackson's corps. Jackson stretched his divisions along the Military Road to Hamilton's Crossing. JEB Stuart's cavalry was posted on Jackson's right to guard the flank and keep watch on the road to Port Royal.

Thwarted at Skinker's Neck, Burnside refused to give up. He searched for another crossing, but found a considerable number of Rebels at every bend of the Rappahannock from Port Royal to the Rapidan. Subsequently, Burnside gave up the idea of an extended campaign against Richmond, and instead focused on swiftly defeating Lee. Wrongly assuming the Army of Northern Virginia was stretched too thin to guard over thirty miles of River, the Union commander wanted to strike where Lee was most vulnerable. Thus, he determined to strike Lee in the center at Fredericksburg itself. He then notified Lincoln of his plans and convened a council of war on December 9. Burnside informed his subordinates that Fredericksburg could be taken as Lee would not expect the Northerners to cross there. He planned a quick lunge across the river, which would catch the Confederates divided and unprepared for what Burnside expected to be the most decisive battle of the war. A lightening thrust would cut off the Rebels above Fredericksburg from those below as the city marked the seam between the corps of Longstreet and Jackson.

Burnside turned to his engineers to prepare for the army to cross Rappahannock. Three separate points along a two-mile stretch of the river were selected. A part of the 50th New York Engineers would build two bridges at the northern end of Fredericksburg. Another contingent would erect a third span at the lower end of the city. The 15th New York Engineers would construct a bridge one mile south of the city, and the U. S. Engineers would build a parallel bridge. The engineers estimated the bridges would measure 400 to 440 feet in length.

Sumner's Right Grand Division would cross at the upper bridge, Hooker's Center Grand Division at the middle span, while Franklin's Left Grand Division filed across the lower bridge. Supporting the crossing were 183 cannons under Brigadier General Henry J. Hunt. These guns were placed on the 30 to 50-foot-high bluffs known as Stafford Heights which ran along the Federal side of the river for five miles. The artillery had three missions: drive the entrenched Confederates from the hills west of Fredericksburg, prevent the Rebels from massing on the plains opposite the lower bridge, and suppress enemy opposition to the bridge building and the subsequent movement of the army across the river.

The morning of December 11 saw the temperature stand at a frigid 25 degrees with dense fog hanging over the area. A little before 6 a.m. the upper and middle bridges were more than half completed. Federal engineers laboring on the pontoon boats in the cold water became visible to Confederate riflemen concealed along the riverbank behind fences and breastworks and in cellars, warehouses, and houses along the riverbank on the south side. These were men from Brigadier General William Barksdale's Mississippi Brigade, as well as the detached 8th Florida Regiment. They had been placed in Fredericksburg by Lee to slow down any Federal crossing of the Rappahannock in order to gain time for the Southern army to meet the enemy south of the city.

As the engineers feverishly worked to complete the bridges, Barksdale's men poured their fire into them. At the upper bridge, deadly fire killed a captain and two enlisted men of the 50th New York Engineers. Support from skirmishers of the 7th Michigan and 19th Massachusetts Regiments was ineffective as the Rebels were largely invisible in the fog. The men had to repeatedly abandon their work and seek cover on the north side of the river on account of enemy fire. At the middle bridge, Confederates rose from their hiding place to fire at the hapless engineers, wounding six and piercing the pontoon boats with bullets.

Earlier in the morning, at 4 a.m., Franklin's Left Grand Division began to move toward the lower bridge crossing. The 77th descended from behind Stafford Heights into the Rappahannock plain. Captain Martin Lennon remembered, "We had proceeded but a short distance when the heavy roar of cannon told us the work had already commenced. We were then about four miles from the firing." The distance was quickly passed, "for our recruits were fast to get a look at the animal called 'secession.'" [12]

As the 77th came in sight of the river, they expected to immediately go into the fray, Lennon recounted, "when to our astonishment and pleasure (to me at least), we discovered that the cause was not a 'conflict dire' but simply that our guns were shelling the city of Fredericksburg." The city indeed was enduring a devastating artillery barrage that would total 8,000 rounds from all the batteries posted on Stafford Heights. A frustrated Burnside had ordered the bombardment to clear Barksdale's Mississippians and the 8th Florida from the city's buildings and streets, so that the engineers could finish building the upper and middle bridges. George Stevens was awed as the cannon belched forth shot and shell on the city:

> The roar of the artillery was terrific, and as the winds rolled away the huge columns of smoke, we saw that the city was on fire, the flames leaping to the skies. The spectacle was one of awful grandeur. The bursting bombs, shooting forth their flashing coruscations from the column of smoke, the great tongues of flame from the burning buildings, leaping to the heavens, the clamor of the bursting shells and the shock of the artillery which shook the earth, made up one of the most terrible magnificent of scenes. [13]

In front of the 77th, Franklin's bridges were completed with minimal opposition by 9 a.m. The Left Grand Division's bridges at the lower crossing stood in contrasting quiet, and unused, even though Union troops anxiously awaited orders to move. Franklin fired off a dispatch to Burnside proposing to cross the river with the Sixth Corps. After crossing, the corps would turn north outflanking Barksdale's defenders, thus taking Fredericksburg. Burnside momentarily entertained the thought, but summarily rejected it. He feared that Franklin's flanking movement would get trapped between Deep Run and Hazel Run before it could reach the city. If the Confederates cornered Franklin, he would then be cut off from reinforcements. Burnside ordered Franklin to stay the crossing until the middle and upper bridges were completed for the entire army to cross.

The bombardment of Fredericksburg, which set the stage for the way armies would fight from then on, failed to dislodge Barksdale's soldiers. Hunt proposed to Burnside that infantry be sent across the river to root out the Rebel riflemen. Gaining approval of his plan, Hunt collared Colonel Norman J. Hall, commander of the 3rd Brigade, 2nd Division, Second Corps, and convinced him to take the job. Hall ordered the 7th Michigan to board pontoons and row to the south bank. The Wolverine's attack would be the first amphibious assault under fire in American history.

Once on the far shore, the 7th Michigan formed under the riverbank and rushed into the city down Water Street. In the space of a few minutes, a number of Confederate soldiers were captured and a secure lodgment was enacted. The rest of the 7th Michigan and the 19th Massachusetts crossed the river as well, fanning out to the left and right of the landing site with the 20th Massachusetts providing support. While the Union troops consolidated their position, Federal artillery blasted away, allowing engineers to finish placing the upper bridge. The 42nd and 59th New York Regiments and the 127th Pennsylvania Regiment rushed across the bridge into Fredericksburg's streets, all the while being fired upon by Rebels hiding in adjacent buildings and alleyways. Slowly the Northerners gained ground, and by nightfall the Confederates withdrew from the city, ending the bloody street fighting. Burnside's army now controlled Fredericksburg.

During the street fighting across the Rappahannock, the 77th lay in full view of the Confederates on the south shore. With the upper crossings now secured, Burnside ordered Franklin to cross his Left Grand Division at sunset. Brigadier General Charles Devins' 2nd Brigade, Sixth corps, led by the 2nd Rhode Island Regiment, dashed over the bridges and quickly established a semicircle around the bridgehead, resting both of its flanks on the river. Captain Lennon felt uniquely privileged to witness the scene:

M^CKEAN'S SUNDAY SCHOOL BOYS GO TO WAR

> I think that was one of the most magnificent sights that I ever saw. Our artillery opened with full force, throwing shell on to the opposite side of the river, causing the few scattering rebels who had been watching us to fall back to their own lines. The sun setting as beautifully as ever a sunset – the smoke of our guns covering the ground, for it seemed to sink to the ground and roll to the to the rear – the bright flash of the shells as they burst in front of us, and the blazing of the city on our right – the rebels hurrying away – formed one of the sights that a man can see but once in a lifetime. [14]

Before any more troops could cross the river, Burnside suddenly changed his mind, and called a halt to the movement, both at the upper bridges and at Franklin's crossing. The 77th returned to Stafford Heights and bivouacked for the night. Both armies settled down for the night to await the morrow while the embers of Fredericksburg still burned. The next morning all three Grand Divisions would cross the Rappahannock and deploy west and south of Fredericksburg.

Before dawn on December 12, the 77th again made its way, along with Franklin's Left Grand Division, to the river. The large influx of troops jammed the bridges. "Thousands," Surgeon Stevens wrote, "crowded upon the banks, or hurriedly dashed across the bridge. The rumble of wheels upon the frozen ground, the tramp of thousands of men, the neighing of innumerable horses, mingled with the roar of musketry from skirmishers that had fanned out in front of the army." Stevens noted that, "The sun rose in splendor, and the spires of the city, two miles to our right, shone brightly, for only the lower part of the town had been destroyed by the conflagration of the day before, and tens of thousands of muskets gleamed in the morning light." The broad plain on the south bank of the Rappahannock crawled with blue uniformed soldiers. [15]

After the Sixth Corps crossed, Old Baldy formed Howe's and Brook's Divisions which cautiously shuffled west; Brook north across Deep Run, and Howe covering Bowling Green Road south of the stream. Captain Lennon described the advance: "our line of battle, as we advanced, was two or three miles long, I should think; at all events, it stretched as far on either side as the eye could see." The Confederate batteries made no contest of this movement, which clearly struck the captain: "It seemed strange to see men moving so steadily onward, when at every moment we were expecting to see death hurled among us from the enemy on the hills. All as still as death; we marched on; nothing to be heard but the orders of officers. We could see no reason why the enemy did not fire upon us, for we were within easy range of them; but there they lay as quietly as though friends were coming to see them." The 77th halted under the cover of a sod fence by the side of the road, and remained there. That night the regiment built fires and bedded down in full sight the rebels. [16]

George Stevens stayed behind to prepare a hospital for Howe's division. Situated on the south bank of the river, and a little below the bridge crossing, stood the elegant stone mansion Mannsfield owned by Arthur Bernard. His vast estate stood adjacent to his brother's Alfred's home and was chosen to house the wounded expected from the next day's battle. Bernard, a bit of a curmudgeon, and what Stevens called "an old secesh bachelor, very aristocratic in his notions," was incensed that his home was invaded by the "hireling Yankees." His protest was to no avail and Bernard was quickly arrested and removed from his estate. Unfortunately, Mannsfield was exposed to Rebel fire during battle. Some of the wounded were brought to the hospital only to be killed by flying shrapnel from exploding shells. During the battle, cavalry general George D. Bayard lay beneath a tree when Confederate shells began tearing up the garden around the house. Before Bayard could get up, a shell ricocheted off the ground and crushed his hip at the joint. Soldiers carried the stricken general into the house, where surgeons declared his wound mortal, and he soon died. [17]

On the morning of December 13, once again thick fog lay over the valley of the Rappahannock River. Jackson's final two divisions were moving into place on Lee's right flank. The Confederate lines along the range of hills behind Fredericksburg ran from Taylor's Hill on the north near the dam above Falmouth, to Marye's Heights behind the city, then southwest to Telegraph Hill (Lee's Hill), and finally, to wooded Prospect Hill near Hamilton's Crossing on the south. One glaring weak point lessened the strength of Jackson's position. Division commander, Ambrose P. Hill had left a 600-yard-wide gap between Brigadier General James H. Lane's North Carolinians on the left and Brigadier General James J. Archer's mixed brigade of men from Alabama, Georgia, and Tennessee on the right. This ground – where the woods extended beyond the Richmond, Fredericksburg and Potomac Railroad – was thick with undergrowth and swampy. A. P. Hill felt certain that these features would prevent any Federal attack on that portion of the field. As a precaution, however, Hill posted Brigadier General Maxcy Gregg's South Carolina Brigade a quarter of a mile to the rear. In front of Franklin's Left Grand Division stood 35,000 Rebel soldiers supported by 54 artillery pieces.

Franklin's men would have to advance across open ground while exposed to artillery fire. Although the river plain provided room for maneuvering, its features could impede any offensive thrust. The Richmond Stage Road ran parallel to the river three-quarters of a mile away. Mounded dirt and ditches on both sides of the road along with fences and scattered cedars could slow down any attacking force. Also to Franklin's front lay muddy fields of corn stubble and wheat traversed by drainage ditches. Some 1,000 yards beyond ran the tracks of the Richmond, Fredericksburg, and Potomac Railroad. On the other side of the tracks, the ground rose toward the wooded crest of Prospect Hill.

In the early morning heavy fog, Howe's division remained in place with its right flank at Deep Run, and massed along the Bowling Green Road. Skirmishers from the Third Brigade were sent out to roam the front. As the rattle of musketry between opposing skirmishers heated up, the 77th's brigade commander, Francis Vinton, ventured forward to examine the skirmish line. He was soon seriously wounded and carried to the division's hospital at Mannsfield. There, surgeons discovered that that the ball had passed deep into his abdomen, and cut it out from his back. With Vinton out of action, 36-year-old Brigadier General Thomas H. Neill of the Regular Army assumed command of the Third Brigade.

Franklin did not receive orders for battle until 7:30 a.m. when Brigadier General James A. Hardie of Burnside's staff rode up. The orders were imprecise and contradictory. Despite the inherent confusion, Burnside wanted Franklin to lead the main attack. The Left Grand division was to force Jackson's Confederate forces from their defenses. Once Franklin penetrated the Rebel lines, the rest of the left wing would move to Hamilton's Crossing. The Left Grand Division would then sever Lee's line of communications to Richmond. At the same time, Sumner's Right Grand division would force another lodgment on the Confederate left. Burnside expected that Sumner's attack would prevent Lee from sending Longstreet's reserves to contain Franklin's breakthrough. Trapped between two Union forces, Lee would have to retreat.

William B. Franklin, however, interpreted his orders differently. Agitated, he refused to take the time to ask Burnside to clarify his orders. Rather than launching a fully coordinated assault,

M^cKEAN'S SUNDAY SCHOOL BOYS GO TO WAR

Franklin believed Burnside's orders instructed him only to make a demonstration. Accordingly, the commander chose Major General John Reynolds' First Corps to make the demonstration. He advised Reynolds to send one division and keep it well supported. The general picked Major General George Meade's division to make the attack. Unfortunately, Meade was not sanguine about its success. He argued with Franklin that attacking with a single division would merely repeat the mistakes of Antietam, where piecemeal assault yielded much meaningless carnage. Meade's division could take the heights, he concluded, but could not hold them. Unmoved, Franklin stated that these were Burnside's orders and that they would have to be obeyed.

Immediately after receiving orders, Meade, with Gibbon's division in support, put his troops in motion. His division marched from Smithfield and approached the Richmond Stage Road. As the Union soldiers came closer, they were in clear view of Lee, Longstreet, Jackson, and Stuart on Prospect Hill. Major John Pelham, the popular youthful head of Stuart's horse artillery, found an ideal spot to put a cannon squarely on Meade's flank. He asked for and received permission from Stuart to take a single 12-pounder Napoleon and advance beyond the Confederate line to engage the oncoming enemy's left flank. Pelham chose an unlikely position in the bottom of a shallow basin to mask his gun as unsuspecting Yankees exposed their flank in the rise above him.

At 10 a.m., the gallant Pelham's lone Napoleon fired, its bark resonating down the Rappahannock River Valley, breaking the morning calm. Meade's men recoiled in surprise. Shots from his single cannon cut down dozens of men and nearly dispersed the division's left flank. Pelham was soon joined by a Blakely rifle. In retaliation, five Union batteries zeroed in on the two Rebel guns, the Blakely being silenced after firing only one shot. When Pelham's ammunition ran low one hour later, his crew limbered their Napoleon and fell back to Hamilton's Crossing – but not before halting Meade's division and forcing the entire force of Brigadier General Abner Doubleday to sit out the rest of the battle to protect against any threat to the Union left. Lee, who had watched Pelham's courageous action, remarked with evident emotion, "It is glorious to see such courage in one so young." [18]

With Pelham's threat silenced, Colonel Charles S. Wainwright, chief of the First Corps artillery, trained his batteries on the Confederate line on Prospect Hill. At 11 a.m. a sudden boom echoed across the river plain as the First Corps guns, supported by Union batteries on Stafford Heights, belching forth their deadly missiles. Martin Lennon remarked, "then began a roar that would shame Niagara . . . the cannonading was the most terrific I ever saw." Each cannon fired every three minutes but provoked no response from the Rebels. The Confederate light artillery was no match for the heavier guns of the Yankees. Jackson thus chose to save his batteries for the infantry to come. Unfortunately, the furious cannonade did little more than random damage among the Southerners. [19]

The First Corps batteries roared for an hour. At noon, Charles Wainwright wrongly concluded that his batteries were effective in softening up the Confederate lines, and recommended that Meade advance. Concurring with his artillery chief, Reynolds ordered Meade to rouse his prone division from the sopping mud. Meade's division, supported by Gibbon's, numbered 8,000 infantrymen. As they passed through Wainwright's cannon, the scene was akin to men on dress parade. Captain Wheeler remembered, "It was a splendid sight, long lines of men, with their colors flying, advanced upon the enemy, as though on drill." [20]

An ominous silence fell upon the field as the Northerners advanced across open ground, for the Confederate artillery was instructed not to fire until the Yankees were within 800 yards. As the bluecoats crossed the Richmond, Fredericksburg and Potomac Railroad beds, fifty Rebel artillery pieces abruptly broke the silence, throwing iron missiles of death into the blue ranks. Captain Wheeler looked on as Meade's men "were received with showers of grape and canister, which mowed them down by the dozens." In horror, Captain Martin Lennon cringed exclaiming, "Oh! What a cruel sight it was to see men cut down so rapidly on both sides. Such firing on both sides, I never saw before." [21]

The Union advance stalled with many soldiers either falling dead or wounded, or else running back into the direction they came from. The First and Sixth corps artillery dueled with the Rebel batteries, inflicting heavy casualties on both sides. Luther Wheeler wrote the 77th "was exposed to bursting shells and canon shot . . . we had many narrow escapes, being covered with dirt a number of times from shells and cannon balls plunging into the ground near us." The anxiety of lying motionless face down in the mud during the artillery duel was uniquely intense. Martin Lennon recalled, "We were under artillery fire all day, or most of the time, which, although not injuring a great many men, was liable to knock a man 'galley west.' One could not tell at what instant his life would be taken from him. We did not know but at any moment we would be engaged with the enemy. There was not excitement enough to drive away the thought of battle, so that we had to lay and think it over, occasionally seeing some person killed or wounded, and wondering if it would not be our turn next." Flattening his body close to the ground, Private Edward Fuller (Co. C) remembered, "Balls, shot and shells from the enemy came fast and uncomfortably near. One solid ball, a foot in diameter, passed a few feet over my head, burrowing in the ground some fifteen feet beyond me." [22]

Captain Martin Lennon (NYSDMNA)

When the Confederate batteries slackened their fire, Meade ordered his men to march over the railroad and attack the Rebel infantry line. Captain Lennon watched the Union soldiers advance, steadily driving back Confederate skirmishers until, "They finally gained a point of woods where they were hidden by my sight, but I could see by the smoke that this was the most terrible part of the battle." By chance, Meade's division stumbled into the gap in the Confederate lines. The difficult terrain broke apart Mead's 1st Brigade and prevented coordination between the regiments. Nevertheless, the disorganized Federals pushed through Gregg's South Carolinians, sparking savage hand-to-hand fighting. Soon they were astride the military road and set to cut Lee's army in half, some even reaching the summit of Prospect Hill. [23]

Despite breaching the Confederate lines, Meade's assault was losing steam, and his disorganized regiments were stalled in the withering Confederate musket fire. Fortunately for the Federals, Gibbon's division finally entered the fight. His brigades carried Union troops over the railroad and engaged in close-quarters fighting, the bayonet being freely employed by both sides. However, Gibbon's advance only bought Meade's shattered division time as it was steadily pushed back by reformed mixed Confederate forces.

The tide of battle changed for good when the unflappable Stonewall Jackson committed Major General Jubal Early's division of Georgians, Louisianans, and Virginians. They quickly closed the gap in the Rebel line and relentlessly pushed Meade's soldiers back down Prospect Hill. Meade begged for reinforcements from Brigadier General David Birney's 1st Division, Third Corps, to no avail. Although Birney's division had been sent across the Rappahannock to assist in the attack, it would never enter into the battle. By 4 p.m., all the gains achieved on the Federal left were reversed. The tattered remains of Meade's division withdrew to the shelter of the Richmond Stage Road where the assault had been launched. Captain Lennon sadly commented, "On the portion of the field where I paid the most attention, I saw five colors go into the woods with full regiments around them, and when they came out there was only two colors, and only about a company with each." On this part of the field, the Confederates lost 2,338 men to the Union's 3,340. [24]

During the battle, the wounded poured into the Union hospital at Mannsfield. Surgeon Stevens observed that, "The unfortunate men were stowed in every part of the great house, and in the smaller buildings surrounding it, and tents furnished shelter for those unable to find room in the buildings. The sight of terrible wounds was ghastly. The chaplain of the 33rd New York, Augustus Lung, assisted the surgeons at the stone mansion and quickly became immured by what he witnessed:

> One man with gun in hand, walking a firm step and a cheerful countenance, having been struck by a piece of a shell in the forehead, laying bare the brain so I could see every pulsation. It is really surprising how soon one becomes accustomed to these scenes of suffering, so that broken bones and mangled limbs can be attended to with untrembling nerve. I was busily engaged in the amputating room where feet, legs, arms, and fingers were cut off. [25]

As Captains Lennon and Wheeler watched the disheartening repulse of Meade's and Gibbon's divisions, the sound of cannon and musketry ripped across the river plain to their right. Burnside had initiated the attack on the Confederate left on Marye's Heights. The Union advance had to march over mostly open ground. Unknown to the commander, the Telegraph Road became a sunken road as it wound around the base of Marye's Heights. The four-foot high stone fences along each side of the road made an excellent fortified position for the Rebels. Nearby, the Southerners had placed 37 artillery pieces to cover the approaches to the stone wall on the heights.

Sumner's Right Grand Division's first assault began in the early afternoon. Sadly, this attack set the pattern for a ghastly series of attacks that came, one after another, until nightfall. As soon as the Northerners marched out of Fredericksburg, Longstreet's artillery wreaked havoc on the blue-coated formations. The Union soldiers then encountered a deadly bottleneck at the canal ditch which was spanned by three partially destroyed bridges. Once across the ditch, the attackers formed shallow battle lines under cover of a hill that shielded them from Rebel gunners. Orders then called out for the final advance. The landscape beyond the canal contained a few buildings and fences, but from the military perspective, it provided virtually no protection. Dozens of Rebel guns immediately reopened on the easy targets, and when the Federals came in range of musketry, sheets of flame spewed forth from the sunken road. Their rifle fire mowed down the Union ranks. Survivors found refuge behind a small swale in the ground or fled back to the canal ditch valley.

Until nightfall, brigade after brigade assaulted the terrible stone wall only to melt away in the face of Confederate muskets. From his headquarters on Telegraph Hill, Robert E. Lee watched the devastating destruction of Burnside's divisions. Turning toward Longstreet, Lee admitted, "It is well that war is so terrible. We should grow too fond of it." Of the 12,600 Union soldiers killed, wounded, or missing during the great conflagration that day, over 7,000 fell in front of the stone wall at Marye's Heights. [26]

As Union troops were being cut down like wheat during harvest, the brigade of Brigadier General Evander Law's Alabamans and North Carolinians appeared in front of the Third Brigade which was supporting the Sixth Corps artillery. Captain Lennon nervously looked on as "the enemy advanced on our front with a double line of battle. I then expected that we must take some fire on our side." The young captain wrote, "Our skirmishers held them back, bravely disputing every inch of ground, but as the enemy came on they were forced to fall back. Our guns, numbering eighteen pieces, opened on them, but still they came on; they came nearly up to us, when the force of our artillery became so heavy that they were forced to fall back to their entrenchments." [27]

The next morning, December 14, was frigid but gusty winds made it feel much colder. Except for the occasional popping of muskets and boom of cannon, the armies of Burnside and Lee quietly faced each other. The Confederate commander spent the day strengthening his lines fully expecting Burnside to renew the battle. And attack is exactly what Burnside had in mind. In a meeting with his generals, the distraught Burnside proposed to personally lead his old Ninth Corps against Marye's Heights. His Grand Division commanders strongly counseled against such an attack. Yet Burnside persisted with the idea of another assault until the next morning when he realized that the condition of the Army of the Potomac was in no condition to do so.

Late in the afternoon of the 15th, a flag of truce was sent out to pick up the wounded and to bury the dead. Union ambulances trundled onto the field and squads fanned out across the battlefield collecting the wounded and the dead. Southern details met their counterparts at the picket line. Together the soldiers from North and South opened the ground in preparing graves for the slain. They dug long trenches and buried the bodies en masse. Burial parties, however, had barely collected the bodies before time ran out on the truce. Many corpses lay unattended in heaps at collection points. In a hurry to finish, Rebels crammed bodies into railroad ditches and shoveled a thin layer of dirt on top of them. Union squads rescued their wounded and brought them across the river to Falmouth. From there, waiting trains carried them to Aquia Landing, where transports brought them to hospitals in Washington and Alexandria.

Having given up the notion of renewing battle, Burnside ordered the army to withdraw across the Rappahannock River under the cover of darkness. Captain Lennon was crestfallen when he received orders to ready his company for the move. "We had laid down for the night, when the adjutant (Isaac Clapp) of the regiment came to me, saying, that I must have my men in line ready to move at a moment's notice, and that we must make as little noise as possible. How my heart did sink at the order, for I knew its import. I called my men, and could see that the old soldiers understood as well as I did what we were going to do. I heard it whispered along the ranks – 'Skedaddle! Skedaddle!'" [28]

So as to not alert Lee of the Union retreat, engineers carpeted the bridges with hay and sod. Some of the engineers even removed their shoes to avoid unnecessary noise. The sounds of artillery batteries, wagons, and ambulances were muffled by wrapping their wheels in straw. The 77th was ordered to pack haversacks tightly so that canteens, tin cups, and accoutrements did not rattle and jingle.

Once the Sixth Corps had reached the north bank of the river, a portion of the 77th formed a picket line along the riverbank. In keeping with the need for silence, they were ordered not to fire unless the enemy did, which caused Private Terrance Gray (Co. B) to protest, "A pretty order to wait till a man is killed before he can fire his gun!" In a letter to his sister, Almeda, Martin Lennon recalled that "three companies of the regiment, under my command, were sent back to the river to act as skirmishers, to protect the engineers in taking up the pontoon bridge. By this time all the troops had crossed. I scarcely got my men in position and readiness before the enemy came in sight. First, a line of skirmishers, followed by a line of battle. They did not harm us much, though, for a few well-directed shots from our artillery sent them back. All the fight we had, was with a few sharpshooters, who annoyed us considerably." [29]

For many in the Northern army, the night time retreat was a profound relief. For others it was nothing short of demoralizing, and they lost their confidence in Ambrose Burnside and the certainty of Union victory in the war. One such soldier was Captain Lennon:

> The papers call this movement a 'reconnaissance in force,' but I don't take much stock in that. I just think that this

army was never so badly whipped as it was on the south side of the river. I suppose the papers are filled with tales of the wondrous deeds that the Army of the Potomac has done in this affair. A few more such advances, and then the rebels will keep us in Washington protecting it from invasion . . . Talk about Little Mac being slow, and about his being a poor general. Poor as he may be, he never did get his army into such a place as Burnside did. You have no idea of the dispiriting effect this movement has caused the army. From every one you may hear Burnside cursed, and McClellan called for. For my own part I have made up my mind that we are not going to whip them at all, and we have got to work pretty sharp to keep them from whipping us . . . How much longer this will continue, I should like to know, for I am tired of seeing men playing soldier as Burny and Mac have been doing for the past year. [30]

Others, Like Captain Luther Wheeler, placed blame elsewhere. "Since the defeat the army wants Mc to come back again, they say he never would have made the blunder of crossing the river. I think the fault should be laid to Halleck and Stanton instead of Burnside – I think he done well to get his army off without losing more than he did – The rebels could have shoved us into the river and would if we had staid much longer on that side." Like Lennon, though, Wheeler said, "I have given up all hopes of ever subduing the south – they are too smart and fight too well." Adding insult to injury he added "when the rebel pickets came down to the river they asked if Burnside was going to Richmond now – the boys told him yes – then then said 'you will have two big Hills and one Stonewall to go over, and a Longstreet to go through before you reach there." [31]

As the 77th went into camp at White Oak Church, a nondescript little whitewashed building without a steeple, the men hoped they would remain there for the winter. Many of the soldiers built log huts with chimneys for their stove fireplaces. The Sixth Corps regiments were "crowded closely together on ground too low and wet for good camping ground." The new recruits "having never before erected winter quarters from shelter tents, were not so expert as they became in succeeding winters; so they suffered from inconvenient quarters." The new recruit, Private Bump, wrote to Mary, his wife, "we have not got But our Little shelter tents to sleep in and it is very cold hear." But referring to their ingenuity, Bump went on that "we went at it and Bilt our tent up on some Poles the other Day and banked it up and Bilt us a Little fire Place in it and it is quite comfortable." [32]

Christmas in the camp passed uneventfully and served for many as a time of reflection. Homesickness and frustration marked the occasion for a number of soldiers in the 77th. Captain Wheeler's Christmas dinner was "some potatoes and beef steak, which we consider a big thing after a month's diet on 'hard tack' and pork." Liquid spirits fortified others in the regiment. Wheeler remarked, "The boys had a big ration of whiskey dealt out to them this morning, and the officers laid in a stick yesterday from the Brigade commissaries at 50c per gal. They drank it all up last evening so have none today – Some of them got very drunk . . . They were all drunk at Brigade Head Quarters, Generals, Aids, and all." Even Wheeler's contraband partook of the celebration: "My servant got down in the evening and I had to put him in bed." [33]

January 1, 1863 brought Lincoln's Emancipation Proclamation into effect. The proclamation radically changed the guiding purpose of the Civil War. At the outset of war, the North keenly identified itself with the founding fathers, and was determined to save the Union. The future of slavery was another matter. But with emancipation, the war began to be framed as a war to free the slaves. Evangelical fervor now interpreted the conflict as between good and evil, a judgment of the divided nation. The Almighty was on the side of good, and the good, clearly was the Union. Captain Wheeler took time out to reflect in a letter to his mother on the role of Divine Providence and the Emancipation Proclamation:

> The rebels fight with desperation and are willing to lose their lives for their cause. You say our cause is just that we are fighting for the right and therefore must succeed. We all believe our cause is just, and so do the rebels, both sides pray fervently for their cause, and believe God will answer their prayers, but both sides can not succeed. Now I think God helps those who help themselves, and the party who brings the most men and the heaviest artillery in to the field will gain the victory. The Emancipation Proclamation may do good, but don't amount to much for the slaves can be free only as far as the range of our artillery extends and our prospects are not very good for extending that range, so the proclamation amounts to about as much as the 'Popes bull against the count.' As to the interposition of Divine Providence in our course, if that was all that was needed we might sit down with our million of soldiers, do no more fighting, slaughter no more men, -- and Providence would bring it all out right. – as I said before, Providence will help that party who has the best generals, best fighting men &c without regard to proclamations. [34]

Despite the decided defeat at Fredericksburg, Ambrose Burnside searched for another crossing point in which to launch yet another offensive against Lee's army. He personally scouted the ground north of Falmouth, and decided upon crossing the army upriver from Fredericksburg at Banks and U. S. Fords. Burnside intended Franklin and Hooker to simultaneously spearhead the movement, and Sumner would follow 24 hours later. His Grand Division commanders were ordered to move on January 17. However, a spy reported to Burnside that the Confederates had dispatched an unknown force to U. S. Ford, but nothing to Banks Ford. The general was delighted with the prospect of catching Lee's army divided, and modified his plans. Burnside ordered his army to move on January 20, with Franklin and Hooker converging on Banks Ford.

Prior to the infantry's march upriver, Burnside spirited his engineers and pontoons out of camp, taking care to keep them under cover near Berea Church on the road to the fords. The embarking pontoons, however, did not go unnoticed in the camp of the 77th. Captain Wheeler wrote, "The pontoon train moved yesterday up the river. I think we are to cross above somewhere." The movement troubled the captain, believing "we shall suffer a great deal in the field at this time of the year. It rained all last night, and rains often now, making it very muddy." Nevertheless, tired of war, Wheeler hoped that whatever the outcome, it would put a final end to the bloody conflict. "I hope if we move against the enemy that we shall either destroy their army or that ours will be destroyed. I want this thing to end in some way. I want something decisive." Yet he had little hope of victory. "I am afraid we shall not succeed any better than we did last time." [35]

Blue-clad troops formed on the morning of January 20, ready to march. At noon, Franklin's Left Grand Division started marching to the right with the 77th's Sixth Corps leading the way over dirt lanes heading toward Berea Church. Excellent, unseasonably warm weather made for a pleasant march. The late start guaranteed a short, easy march. The roads too were in excellent condition, which allowed the head of the columns to reach their destination in good time. The 77th was in good spirits as it went into bivouac on the evening of the 20th.

That night, around 7 p.m., raindrops began pattering on the tents of the 77th. The rain continued to fall throughout the night. It grew stronger and more violent, mixing with sleet as temperatures fluctuated. Wind howled through the regiment's camp, blowing away shelter tents and keeping the men wet and miserable. Unbeknownst to the New Yorkers, Burnside's army had walked into an immense storm front that dropped several inches of rain in a two-day period.

The Union army awoke the next morning after a miserable night to discover the countryside had turned to a sea of mud. Roads had become slick, then muddy, and in a short time they were transformed into a literal pool of liquid muck. The geographical strata of Stafford County, Virginia consisted of a hard crust of surface clay. Water penetrated the clay and saturated the sandy loam beneath, which then liquefied, leaving the surface crust unsupported. Wagons, caissons, and ambulances rutted the softened crust until it collapsed. Army wagons sank up to their hubs, and men staggered through mud up to their knees. Twenty-year-old Private William H. DeYoe (Co. E) estimated that "the mud had Got Somewhere less than 5 feet deep." Surgeon Stevens wrote that:

Horses could not haul artillery or pontoons into position. Men took the place of horses. The whole Vermont Brigade was detailed to drag the pontoons and guns to the river. All day long, working and tugging with the mud above their knees; here a hundred men pulling at a pontoon boat, there a party prying a cannon out of the mire with long levers, and still others laying strips of corduroy road. The Vermonteers passed a disagreeable day. [36]

Burnside spent a nervous day, hoping against all logic that his army could march through the morass. He rode along the columns and at one point personally superintended the placing of a battery into position on the riverbank. Burnside exhausted himself as well as his soldiers, tirelessly urging his men on through the mud and slush. As he rode through the Sixth Corps with two of his staff officers, Stevens observed both "Burnside and his horse were completely covered with mud, the rim of his hat turned down to shed the rain, his face careworn with this unexpected disarrangement of his plans." The surgeon reported "we could but think that the soldier on foot, arm oppressed with the weight of knapsack, haversack and gun, bore an easy load compared with that of the commander of the army, who now saw departing his hopes of redeeming the prestige he had lost at Fredericksburg." [37]

The evening of January 21 rained as relentlessly as the night before. The mud deepened every hour. Dead horses and mules lay by the hundreds where they had been stalled or smothered in the mud. Burnside's army sprawled across the drenched countryside. The 77th rested wearily in drenched woods about a mile from the Rappahannock. The rest of the army was strung out all the way to Falmouth.

The next day brought yet more rain and another titanic struggle against the forces of nature. Rations ran out, and regiments issued a gill of whiskey to each soldier. Animals still sank up to their bellies. Teamsters, known for their proficiency in profanity, spouted new combinations invented for the occasion. Men still labored through knee deep mud. The Army of the Potomac simply wallowed in place.

Before the day was over, the Confederate division of Major General George Pickett amassed on the opposite side of the river at Banks Ford. Pickett's artillery shelled the woods on the opposite side of the Rappahannock. The barrage surprised Union soldiers. Blue-clad men scattered for cover. Union guns, being cemented in mud too far to the rear to help, offered no fire in return. Confederate pickets taunted Yankees across the river. Union soldiers quietly endured their taunts, but bristled when some clever Rebels painted a message on a barn roof: "Burnside stuck in the mud." Southerners happily erected another sign with the same message opposite Falmouth. [38]

Lee had checkmated Burnside and the commander decided to abandon his plans. The 77th began the retreat the next morning. Rain diminished to an annoying drizzle, but the army was awash in a sea of sludge. The regiment struggled to backtrack through the morass. The difficulty of marching became even more laborious in retreat. Union soldiers had floundered for the past two days over poor roads, but now they had to retrace their steps over ground they had thoroughly chewed up during the advance. George Stevens wrote of the return march, "All along the road lay a multitude of dead horses and mules, which had fallen in the tremendous but unavailing efforts of the day before. Artillery and wagons still stuck fast in the mud, and artillery crews and teamsters lifted and tugged with rails and with poles to raise the pieces or the wagons from the mire." [39]

The Union troops were exhausted and discouraged. They straggled badly and dingy ranks broke up and men headed for camp any way they could. Stevens remembered, "Regiments were not to be distinguished. The whole column became an unorganized crowd, pressing toward the old camps." Private Edward Fuller (Co. C) remembered, "As we straggled along in the mud we saw a mule standing knee deep by the road side. A soldier as he went towards the mule said he would help that mule out, and then make him carry his knapsack and equipments to camp. Wading through the mud, as he reached the mule, he said 'Whoa Jack, whoa Jennie.' As he put his hand on the mule's head, he found it was a dead mule. It had died standing up, stuck in the mud." Toward evening the exhausted 77th reached its old camp at White Oak Church. But unfortunately there was little comfort in their arrival. Stevens wrote "on leaving the place, little thinking that we were so soon to return," the 77th "had burned everything combustible, and thus a strip of board or a piece of timber could hardly be found." [40]

Before his army had settled down in their old camps, Burnside was on his way to Washington to meet with President Lincoln. He brought with him General Orders No. 8, cashiering wholesale a number of officers in the Army of the Potomac including Hooker and Franklin. He singled out Hooker for promoting distrust with his disparaging criticisms of the General. At the White House, Burnside handed the president his General Orders No. 8 and said that he did not want to embarrass Lincoln, or to stand in opposition to him, but a choice had to be made. Unless the officers named in the order were removed, Burnside informed the President, he would resign his command of the Army of the Potomac.

On January 25, Lincoln removed Burnside from command and appointed Major General Joseph Hooker to command the Army of the Potomac. Joe Hooker, the grandson of a Revolutionary War captain, hailed from Massachusetts and was a member of the class of 1837 at West Point. As a staff officer during the Mexican War, he won the brevets of all the grades - up to and including lieutenant colonel – for gallant and meritorious conduct. On August 1862, Hooker was commissioned a brigadier general of volunteers. From the Peninsula Campaign where he earned the sobriquet "Fighting Joe Hooker," and from his success in leading succeeding battles including Fredericksburg, he exhibited solid qualifications as a combat officer in charge of a division and then the First Corps.

Lincoln knew Joe Hooker to be rash. He talked too much and too indiscreetly. On his climb to high command, he had acted less than honorably toward his fellow generals. It was this awareness of Hooker's character that prompted the Commander-in-Chief to compose a candid letter to his new army commander. The President's letter was direct and to the point: "I think it best for you to know there are some things in regard to which, I am not quite satisfied with you.

I believe you to be a brave and skillful soldier, which, of course, I like. I also believe you do not mix politics with your profession, in which you are right. You have confidence in yourself, which is valuable, if not an indispensable quality. You are ambitious, which, within reasonable bounds, does rather good than harm." However, during General Burnside's reign of command, the President went on, "You have taken counsel of your own ambition, and thwarted him as much as you could, in which you did a great wrong to the country . . . I have heard, in such a way as to believe it, of your recently saying that both the Army and the Government needed a dictator. Of course it was not *for* this, but in spite of it, that I have given you the command. Only those generals who gain successes can set up dictators. What I now ask of you is military success, and I will risk the dictatorship . . . Beware of rashness, but with energy, and sleepless vigilance, go forward, and give us victories." [41]

Major General Joseph Hooker became the third commander of the Army of the Potomac in little more than a year. In a very short time, he vastly improved the health and morale of his troops, but his time of command would be brief, not adding up to four months. Hooker would lead his army to a crushing defeat at the wilderness around the crossroads at Chancellorsville, Virginia, the first week of May, 1863, and the 77th would lose its most cherished officer in a second charge against Confederate soldiers manning Marye's Heights behind Fredericksburg.

8

WRITE YOUR NAME ON IT!

At the time of Major General Hooker's appointment to command, the Army of the Potomac was organized into four grand divisions. Hooker abolished these divisions and arranged the army into seven corps. Old Baldy, a bitter critic of Ambrose Burnside and a close friend of George B. McClellan, was relieved of command and replaced by Major General John Sedgwick. Beloved by his troops, "Uncle John" was born in Connecticut in 1813 and graduated from West Point in 1837 along with Braxton Bragg, Jubal Early, and Joseph Hooker. Sedgwick served under both Zachary Taylor and Winfield Scott in the Mexican War and won the brevets of captain and major. In 1855, he became major of the 1st Cavalry, commanded by Robert E. Lee. At the outbreak of war, John Sedgwick was commissioned brigadier general of volunteers. In addition, he commanded a division in the Peninsula Campaign. Commissioned major general, Sedgwick distinguished himself for gallantry at Antietam, and was wounded three times before being carried unconscious from the field.

George Stevens remembered "Uncle John" as, "Modest and retiring in his ordinary intercourse with his fellows . . . The dignity of his bearing fitted him to command, and he needed not the insignia of rank to command the deference of those about him." Witnessing the farewell reception of Major General Smith, Stevens compared the stately Smith to that of Sedgwick as they stood side by side: "General Smith, tall, well dressed, his regulation coat buttoned closely about him, his easy and graceful manner and conversation; General Sedgwick, of stouter build, wearing a loose blouse and coarse blue pants, such as are furnished the private soldier, strong and manly in his appearance, and somewhat abrupt in his manner." [1]

During Burnside's calamitous attack at Fredericksburg, the Third Brigade's commander, Brigadier General Francis Vinton was seriously wounded surveying the skirmish line and was replaced by Brigadier General Thomas Hewson Neill, affectionately known as "Beau Neill." A native of Philadelphia, Neill graduated from West Point in 1847 and served on the frontier until commissioned colonel of the 23rd Pennsylvania in February 1862, which he led on the Peninsula. His regiment did not participate at Antietam, but Neill was commissioned brigadier general days later.

Major General Joe Hooker inherited a beaten and severely demoralized Army of the Potomac. Reflecting the low morale of the Union army, Alonzo Bump reported to his wife, "i think thiss thing is Coming to an end fast as it can for the Solgars are gitting tiard of it. i have hurd mor then 10 thousan men say for the Last Month that they wold run away . . . the Boys in thiss regiment all say that they wont stay much Longer and the hole army of the Potomick are gitting Demorilised and if they Don't settal it Before Long they wont git much fiting out of thiss army i can assure for the Boys all say that they will run away as soon as they git their Pay." [2]

For some soldiers of the 77th, low morale deepened after receiving tragic news from home. Hospital Steward Alexander Waldron (Co. D) spoke sadly to the 49th New York's Steward at the brigade hospital when he went there to procure medicine for the regiment. Henry wrote in a letter to his wife that day, ". . . Waldron . . . came here after some medicine the other day. Seeing that he looked unusually Sober I asked him if there was anything the matter. He feelingly replied that he left three playful children at home & he had just rec'd word that the last one had died, leaving his wife alone and destitute. All three had died of Diptheria." [3]

To this demoralized army, paroled prisoner of war veterans began to steadily return to their regiments. One such parolee was the 77th's Corporal George Bolton (Co. B). In a letter to his wife and children, Bolton described his journey back to the regiment's camp at White Oak Church.

> We left Camp Parole on Monday evening and marched down to the city of Annapolis to the United States Navy Yard, we embarked about eight o'clock P.M. on the steamboat Belvedier, about one thousand exchanged prisoners, the passage was much pleasanter than the one from Fort Delaware to Annapolis, we arrived at Aquia Creek on Tuesday about eleven A.M. We had not been there many minutes before the men was to be seen in all directions. They did what they could to get transportation for us on the railroad to Falmouth Station which is twelve miles but we was doomed to disappointment, so we marched that 12 miles first rate we only stopped a few minutes on the way to make some coffee. Falmouth Station is opposite the city of Fredericksburgh. We could see the city very plain the Rebels now occupy that place. Both Armies is very near

each other but I have not heard any firing since I came here, after we got to the station we found to our sorrow that our march was not finished for that day, we had to paddle off again another two miles to be reported to Gen'l Franklin's head quarters, and then from there to the Brigadier General [Neill] head quarters which was two miles more easy enough. You can bet that we was tired enough when we got to the Reg't. I never in my life had my hands take such a shaking. I believe I was real welcome. [4]

Sensing that the morale of the army accurately mirrored its physical health, Hooker took concrete steps to attend to the physical condition of his soldiers. Perhaps no single act of the commander was more significant than when Hooker ordered that soft bread be issued to his men four times a week, fresh potatoes and onions twice a week, and desiccated vegetables once a week. Any commissary officer failing to meet these standards had to provide written proof that his supply lacked the necessary stocks. Brigade bakeries were established, and any company lacking a cook was ordered to get one. Private Bump rejoiced, "we Drad Potatoes turnips Beats Bread Pork Coffie Shugar molasses and Carrats and we Live Like Peacocks in the clover now." Captain Wheeler was much more succinct, saying "I do not eat hard tack and pork now but live very well." [5]

Jonathan Letterman, Hooker's medical director, took steps to lessen the frequency of disease in the army through improved sanitation. He ordered the rotation of campsites, improvement of drainage ditches, removal of latrines from living areas and wells, and the regular airing of tents, huts, and bedding. Letterman even convinced Hooker to order every man in the army to wash both their clothes and themselves. Before long, cases of diarrhea and typhoid dramatically plummeted. Scurvy virtually disappeared by April. Between February 1 and March 28 only 800 men left the army due to illness.

Surgeon Stevens proudly wrote that under Letterman's supervision, "The medical department became so thoroughly systematized, that the wounded and sick men were cared for better than they had ever been in any army force." All labor was concretely delineated. "Every officer and nurse knew exactly what to do: each had his own part of the work assigned to him, and there was no conflicting of orders or clashing of opinions." [6]

George Stevens was right to tout the organization of the Ambulance Corps by Letterman. "The ambulances of a division," he wrote, "always went together, behind the division, and on the march were attended by a surgeon, an assistant surgeon, a hospital steward, a cook, and three or more nurses, who were to tend to the wants of the sick in the ambulances, and at night, if they were unable to return to their regiments, to erect tents for them, and supply them with food and bedding." During battle "the stretcher-bearers of each regiment, with the sergeant reported to the assistant surgeon in attendance with the regiment. As soon as a man was wounded, he was brought to the medical officer, put into an ambulance, and taken to the division hospital." [7]

Yet in another move to restore morale, Hooker borrowed from McClellan's favorite device, staging regular reviews. Their pageantry lent to immense pride within the army. One such review was of the 77th's Second Division of the Sixth Corps by Hooker. Surgeon Stevens years later provided a detailed account of that event:

> The troops were formed in line, and the general and staff were escorted to the ground by the Twentieth New York, of Neill's brigade, in splendid style . . . As the regiment and the cavalcade appeared on the field, it was a brilliant pageant; first came our brigade band, one of the finest in the army, then the pioneers of the Twentieth, their axes,

shovels and picks polished so that they glistened in the sunlight like burnished silver; then the Twentieth regiment, in column by company, marching with perfect step as though all were directed by a single will; following the regiment, rode General Hooker on his superb white horse, a head and shoulders above all his cavalcade. The immense suite, consisting of General Hooker's own staff, and a large number of major-generals and their staffs, completed the brilliant column. The division was drawn up in line, stretching a half a mile across the field, straight as the flight of an arrow, with artillery on either flank. The general and his brilliant retinue, rode to the right of the line, and advanced slowly along the front of the whole division, inspecting closely each regiment as he passed, the bands playing 'Hail to the Chief,' the colors dipping, and the bugles pealing notes of welcome. Having passed the entire front of the line, the chief now road at a rapid pace along its rear to the point of the beginning. He then, with his attendants, took a position on a slight elevation of ground at a distance from the line, when the whole division, in column, marching to the place, passed in review before him, and the pageant was ended. [8]

The greatest of the orchestrated pageants took place in early April, when President Lincoln visited the army and spent several days reviewing its corps. Captain Stephen Horton wrote home to the *Ballston Spa Journal*, providing an account of Lincoln's review of the Sixth and two other corps for its readers:

> They numbered in all, probably 60,000 and the eye could take them all in at a glance. It was drawn up by brigades and divisions, and covered about 10 acres in oblong shape. The President rode by each division, accompanied by

> Generals Hooker, Butterfield, Sedgwick, Slocum, Sickles, Brooks, Howe, and many others with the two stars upon their shoulder straps. On the arrival of the President a salute was fired, drums were sounded, and arms presented. There stood the veterans of the Potomac Army, the heroes of many a well fought battle, their forms erect, and their bayonets glistening in the sun. After the President had passed by each division, the Corps was wheeled into column, and marched by the President, who sat surrounded by the leading Generals, and his son and wife.

Horton went on to describe the immediate euphoria of the review and gratitude the soldiers had for Lincoln's welcome attention:

> It does the soldiers good to witness such sights. People may say that it is all foolishness, this reviewing and parading, but they little know, the great moral effect such exhibitions have upon the soldier. Who would think of employing a servant to perform some duty, and never visit him to see how he succeeded, or give some encouragement in his work? The soldiers feel that somebody cares for them, and that their leaders are desirous of witnessing their proficiency in drill and general appearance. [9]

Perhaps the most well-known of Joe Hooker's efforts to increase morale within the army was the institution of corps badges. The idea of a corps badge is attributed to Major General Philip Kearny early in the war, who ordered the soldiers in his division to sew a two-inch square of red cloth on their hats to avoid confusion on the battlefield. Hooker's chief of staff, Major General Daniel Butterfield, designed a distinctive shape for each corps badge. The badges, which became a source of corps and regimental pride, were to be worn by the troops on top of their kepis, the left side of their hats, or over their left breast. The Sixth Corps badge was the Greek Cross. The 77th's Second Division's flag was a white Greek Cross superimposed on a blue background.

As the morale of the Army of the Potomac swiftly rebounded, a strong peace movement emerged in the North. Peace Democrats, so called "Copperheads," called for peace without a restored Union, and pointed to the demoralization of the army. To those in the Union army toiling at the front, domestic unhappiness with the war effort seemed pervasive, and the soldiers felt deeply betrayed by a lack of support for their immense sacrifice. Anti-war agitators in the North were met with contempt. Back home, the pro-Union newspaper, *The Daily Saratogian*, published a letter From Lieutenant Colonel Winsor French refuting the claim of demoralization and the call for peace at all cost, with the preface:

> Lt. Col. French, it will be seen, indignantly denies the Army of the Potomac is 'demoralized.' This story has been set afoot by Northern Copperheads, for the benefit of the rebels. We advise that class of crawling traitors to read what is said on this point by one who has periled his life in this country's cause . . .

French wrote:

Much is said about the 'demoralization of the army.' I wish the *citizens* of the North were as free from it as are her *soldiers*. I deny that the army is 'demoralized.' I have been *through* it, and am in *it*, and I must say that in this portion of it, good feeling exists . . . I can say truthfully I never saw the 77th in better spirits or more ready for any duty, and fight any foe of their country, against whom they may be lead than at this time. No, I know that I speak the sentiments of the Army when I say, that they would sooner suffer death in a deadly struggle for the mastery, than be the humble and willing slaves of our enemies. We know too well there metal, to submit without a death struggle, a 'peace' where? How? What foundations? 'Union' and 'Jeff. Davis' for our president? – The army would *hate* the country that gave it life. Oh no. There is but one way, *war, war,* and peace only on the ground that those who first took up the sword will perish by the sword, or submit to the constitution and the laws – Unite discordant elements North, feed us, and encourage us instead of discouraging us, and we will bring back the Union or perish in the attempt. [10]

With the Army of the Potomac firmly planted for the winter months, the men of the 77th took up the business of making their quarters as homelike as possible. Despite the inconvenience of having to lug wood on their backs a mile and a half, with which to do their cooking and warm their tents, fellow tent mates Sergeant Albert S. Green, Privates Earl Green, Wells Green, and Alonzo Bump (2nd Co. K) procured enough to also fashion a comfortable bed. In a letter to Nicholas Hagaman, William H. DeYoe described with some pride "we have a very beautiful rain Shelter to Stay in. it is a Squair hole dug down in the Ground & a shelter tent put over it that & a little Sqauir place dug outwards in back for a fireplace & then a chimney made of sticks & Vir. Mud that compose the Outside & in side there is three of us with all our equipments & to sleep on, we have a bunk made of round poles & they answer for bed cords fethers & all & I have Got So use to Sleeping in this position that all the Rough Edges of the poles does not disturb the wearied Soldier boy." Nevertheless, winter weather still brought discomfort among the soldiers of the 77th. Private Thomas M. White (Co. C) told of a nasty storm the eve of Washington's Birthday that lasted well into the next afternoon. He described it as follows:

To-day we are experiencing all the discomforts of a Virginia snow storm. It commenced snowing about 10 o'clock last night, and continued unceasingly until 4 o'clock this afternoon, at which time the snow was about 10 inches deep at the level. The small tents occupied by the troops, though nearly covered this morning from view, gave signs of life and comfort within by the curling smoke that arose from their thin wooden chimneys. Since the storm has ceased the wind has been blowing a gales, drifting the snow in every imaginable shape, and driving it through the cracks and crevices of innumerable shanties, as if trying to peer into the domestic affairs of Uncle Sam's 'mudsills.' [11]

The storm, however, barely hindered the army's celebrating the nation's first President's birthday. Private White recounted for the *Daily Saratogian* that, "To day is Washington's birthday, and one battery of each division in the army fired a National salute, at 12 n., notwithstanding the intensity of the storm, and all the troops were ordered to be paraded at the same hour; but this latter part of the celebration was dispensed with, although every soldier would have been proud to ad his mite to the general rejoicing had the weather permitted." [12]

The day after, the 77th would be called away from the comfort of warm shelter to go on picket. Thomas White did not relish the thought as "the foreshadowings of the next three days speak not of comfort, but of the real hardship of a soldier's life; though this will in some degree be lessened by novelty of marching in snow instead of mud, as has been the case all winter." Taking a jab at the folks back North, White went on to say, "When the snow leaves, which will probably be in a few days, if some impatient Northerners could only see the 'Virginia Boot-jack' that will be left in the roads, they would no longer wonder why the Army of the Potomac won't move." [13]

When snow covered the ground, Surgeon Stevens reported "mimic battles with snowballs were a frequent amusement . . . one regiment would challenge another, and a general melee would follow . . . Each party carried flags and was led by officers chosen for the occasion. The capture of a flag, or of a number of prisoners, from an opposite party, caused great glee among the victors." The Third Brigade's 21st New Jersey never let an opportunity pass for indulging in snowballing. One encounter within the Second Division was of particular note:

> A good deal of interest was excited throughout the Second Division by a snowball battle between one of the Vermont regiments and the Twenty-sixth New Jersey. Both regiments formed a line of battle, each officered by its line and field officers, the latter mounted. At the signal, the battle commenced; charges and counter-charges were made, prisoners were taken on either side, the air was filled with the white missiles, and stentorian cheers went up as one party or the other gained an advantage. At length victory rested with the Vermonters, and the Jersey boys surrendered the field, defeated. [14]

Weather permitting, baseball – its invention wrongly attributed to Abner Doubleday who hailed from Ballston Spa – was a favorite game in the Sixth Corps. Stevens noted that the regiments, including the 77th, fielded a number of excellent ballplayers. Regimental teams often held tournaments much like season play today. These games were "watched by great crowds of soldiers with intense interest." [15]

At the 77th's regimental headquarters, officers collected come evening with those of other regiments to trade amusing stories, converse, and sing. George Stevens remembered, "We had a glee book and an old copy of the 'Carmina Sacra,' and then our friend, Colonel, now Major-General Connor, was never at a loss for a song, and Colonel French often displayed his genius with the violin, and our friend, the chaplain, could always tell a good story or perpetrate a good story." [16]

Religion was important to most soldiers of both sides during the Civil War. There did not tend to be many atheists during a battle marching toward a group of soldiers trying to kill you. The armies of the North and South had chaplains that would comfort the men, more often than not in a field hospital after getting wounded. As did most regimental chaplains, newly arrived Chaplain Norman Fox, Jr. "instituted a series of religious meetings on week days, in addition to regular services on the Sabbath, and a good deal of religious interest was awakened among the men." [17]

When Hooker took command of the Army of the Potomac, desertion was prevalent. At the end of January, deserters made up 30 percent of the absentees. To encourage the soldier who quit the army and returned north to his home, President Lincoln issued a proclamation on March 10 granting amnesty to any man absent without leave if he returned by April 1. The 77th had their share of deserters and those who stayed beyond their time of furlough. Consequently, Lieutenant Colonel French directed Adjutant Isaac Clapp to publish in the *Daily Saratogian* a call for their return:

> I am . . . directed to say that there are deserters from this Regiment who have been faithful soldiers, but in their anxiety to get home so far forget their duty as to lay themselves liable to the severest punishment. If they return promptly to duty their names will not be published. . . Those men who are absent on furlough of ten days, and whose time

has expired, are also notified to return immediately as the orders of the Army of the Potomac recognize no authority except the War Department to extend the furloughs for any cause whatever. Soldiers thus absent are reported as deserters and must be tried and punished accordingly. [18]

As the weather warmed, flowers blossomed, and trees dropped their leaves, it was clear that dry roads would lead to the Spring Campaign and renewed fighting. Even though future battle was certain, Private Bump spoke for many when he wrote, "i hope that we shant haft to fight again." But where the army would go was yet unknown and rumors abounded in the regimental camps. Bump informed his wife, "Thair is such talk around hear now that we are a Goin to stay hear thiss summer and hold thiss Place and sum say that we are a Goin to Washington and to night i hurd that thiss regiment was Goin to Goviners iland and that is Just Below New York But i Don't Bleave it yet for i Don't think there is such Good Luck for us But i should Bee sadisfide if i Go to Washington." [19]

The Union army's direction would soon be made clear to Alonzo Bump and the 77th. By mid-April, Joe Hooker had finalized a skillful, but intricate, plan to bag the army of Robert E. Lee. Major General George Stoneman's Union cavalry was instructed to circle deep behind the Army of Northern Virginia and sever Lee's communications with Richmond. Hooker's infantry would feign the main Federal thrust across the Rappahannock River just above Fredericksburg at Bank's Ford and United States Mine Ford. In concert with Union troops at these fords, a large force under Major General Sedgwick would demonstrate below the city to hold Lee's attention. Simultaneously, the Fifth, Eleventh, and Twelfth Corps, under the temporary command of Major General Slocum, were to cross unnoticed farther upriver at Kelly's Ford and outflank Lee's entrenched army.

After crossing the Rappahannock, Hooker's flanking column planned to move southeast, crossing the Rapidan River and continuing down the southern bank of the Rappahannock to uncover United States Mine Ford. This set up would allow the Second Corps to cross and join Hooker's force advancing on Lee's left flank. Following this march, the Federal flanking force would pass through the thick wooded area marked by a dense mass of brambles, thickets, vines, and low-lying vegetation. It was known locally as the "Wilderness," somewhat hostile terrain surrounding Chancellorsville Crossroads and west of Fredericksburg. If Lee moved to check Joe Hooker's flanking force, Slocum was to take a defensive position near Chancellorsville to receive the attack. If not attacked, Slocum was to continue on this line of march, making Lee's entrenchments behind Fredericksburg untenable. The Army of Northern Virginia would then be caught between Slocum's advancing troops and a powerful Federal force under Sedgwick. In effect, Slocum was to be a large swinging sledgehammer and Uncle John Sedgwick an anvil. Lee would be forced either retreat or fight the much larger Army of the Potomac on Hooker's terms.

On April 26, Hooker was ready to move and issued decisive orders to his corps commanders. Before dawn the following day, the Eleventh and Twelfth Corps were put into motion up the Rappahannock River. As these troops wound their way upriver, the Second Corps received orders to move at sunrise the following day. April 28, two of the Second Corps' divisions moved upriver to Banks Ford where its men began corduroying the muddy roads in an effort to give the appearance of a Federal crossing, while one brigade advanced farther upriver to the vicinity of United States Ford.

On April 28th, the First and Sixth Corps also readied to advance. Surgeon Stevens wrote, "We received orders to break camp, and to be ready to march at a moment's warning." The men struck their tents and tightly packed their knapsacks. Along with personal items, each man carried eight day's rations, overcoat, rubber blanket, full canteen, and 60 rounds of ammunition. After months spent in winter quarters, the 77th's 30 to 40-pound leather pacts felt extra heavy. Still, Stevens proudly remembered that the regiment's soldiers "were in highest spirits, ready and ever anxious for an encounter with the enemy." Indeed, "The regiment, since its organization, was never in such capital condition and so willing to fight." The few sick of the regiment were sent back to the division's hospital, and every man who could walk readied to march. [20]

While the 77th struck camp and prepared to march "a storm of rain of some violence commenced." At noon, the order came to "fall in," and "in five minutes the regiment was on its way, with the rest of the division." Dirt roads were made miserable by the rain and slowed the Sixth Corps progress. Leather knapsack straps dug into the men's shoulders as they marched along in their wet, ankle-high peg shoes. George Stevens toiled along with the regiment "through thickets and bogs" for six miles before halting in a stand of woods in the rear of Falmouth, a short distance from the Rappahannock River where they bivouacked for the night made uncomfortable by intermittent showers. "No fires or noise," Captain Orrin Rugg wrote, "which gave us to understand that thus far at least the movement was designed to be a secret one." [21]

With the First and Sixth Corps in motion, Sedgwick dispatched Major Thomas Hyde (now Provost Marshal of the Sixth Corps) four miles upriver to Third Corps headquarters located near Falmouth with orders to march. From his winter encampment, Daniel Sickles started his Third Corps to a support position on Stafford Heights. Third Corps supply trains remained parked near Falmouth. Sickle's orders were to place his corps to the rear of the First and Sixth Corps in order to provide reinforcement where needed.

On April 30th, the 77th was "awakened at 4 o'clock in the morning, by the roar of musketry and artillery." Troops from Brigadier General David A. Russell's 3rd Brigade, of Brook's division, were pushing over the Rappahannock at Franklin's Crossing in pontoon boats. Pickets of the 54th North Carolina were firing into the fog in the direction of the sound of crossing pontoons. Beaching their boats on the cover of the riverbank, Russell's bluecoats scrambled up the steep riverbank, driving the Confederate pickets from their position. Engineers quickly completed a pontoon bridge, and the remaining regiments of Brigadier General William T. H. Brook's First Division crossed. Brook's soldiers took position around Alfred Bernard's home "The Bend." Spreading out downriver, Union troops positioned themselves around the stone ruins of Arthur Bernard's mansion, "Mannsfield," which served as a Federal field hospital where Surgeon Stevens attended to the wounded victims of Burnside's calamitous assault the previous December.

A mile and a half downstream, at Fitzhugh's Crossing, Major General Reynolds First Corps soldiers were attempting to cross under severe fire from the 13th Georgia and 6th Louisiana Regiments. The latter regiments had felled trees and dug rifle pits on the ruins of "Smithfield" plantation. Nevertheless, the 24th Michigan and 6th Wisconsin Regiments of the "Iron Brigade" established a bridgehead. Engineers quickly built a pontoon bridge and Reynolds' corps began crossing.

At daylight, the 77th formed into line and moved off towards the Rappahannock. "Soon," Orrin Rugg wrote, "we struck a well known trail being no less than the one by which we made an advance on Fredericksburg last winter, after going about two miles farther we came out on the same plain and halted on precisely the same ground as before." As the 77th took position on the river plain, George Stevens remembered, "Our horses cropped the green blades which had sprung from the grain scattered on the ground for their food, just four months before." From their position Rugg noted, "Skirmishing was going on constantly between Brooks troops and the Rebs were in plain sight." At night a very heavy rain set in "and as the flat where we lay was soft ground we were soon ankle deep in mud and this we had to lie down as best we could at night." [22]

By midnight, Lee had deduced that Sedgwick's crossing was a mere diversion, and his army moved to meet Hooker's flanking columns converging in the vicinity of Chancellorsville. Left behind was the division of Major General Jubal Early, Sedgwick's former West Point classmate, to defend the Confederate position to the rear of Fredericksburg. The rebel works were much improved upon since the battle the previous December. Major Alexander S. Pendleton of Jackson's staff described the entrenchments in the spring of 1863:

> The greatest destruction and change in appearance of the country, is from the long lines of trenches and redoubts which crown every hillside from ten miles above Fredericksburg to twenty miles below. The world has never seen such a fortified position. The famous lines at Torres Verdras could not compare to them. As I go to Mossbeck I follow the lines, and have to ride the trenches. These are five feet wide and two and a half feet deep, having the earth thrown towards the enemy, making a bank still higher. They follow the contour of the ground and hug the bases of the hills as they wind to and from the river, thus giving natural flanking arrangements; and from the tops of the hills frown the redoubts for the sunken batteries and barbette batteries ad libitum, far exceeding the number of guns; while occasionally, where the trenches take straight across the flats, a readout stands defiantly in the open plain to receive our howitzers, and

deal destruction broadcast to the Yankees, should their curiosity tempt them to investigate. [23]

May 1, the 77th awoke to continued rain from the night before "but about noon it held up and the sun came out bright and warm." Orrin Rugg listened to skirmish fire across the river, but was relieved there was yet no evidence of full scale battle. Under the parting clouds and the warm rays of the sun, the 77th, along with its fellow regiments, were called into line and Joe Hooker's congratulatory order, General Order No. 47, was read to them. "Received with tremendous cheers," Hooker proclaimed:

> It is with heartfelt satisfaction the Commanding General announces to the army that the operations of the last three days have determined that our enemy must ingloriously fly or come out of his entrenchments and give us battle on our own ground, where certain destruction awaits him. The operations of the Fifth, Eleventh, and Twelfth Corps have been a succession of splendid achievements. [24]

With little danger of being called into battle, the 77th enjoyed a relaxing afternoon. Captain Rugg rejoiced that, "We were mustered for pay this afternoon in full sight of the rebs." George Stevens recounted, "Groups might be seen . . . telling yarns, playing cards, singing songs, playing ball and pitching quoits." Their counterparts at Chancellorsville, however, were not so relaxed. Earlier in the day, Hooker's force had established the Union line on slightly higher ground more favorable to Federal artillery and infantry. Unexpectedly, Hooker stopped his army's advance and ordered his advanced troops back to positions around Chancellorsville Crossroads. He ordered his corps commanders to fortify positions around Chancellorsville. Angry, Hooker's corps commanders reluctantly ordered their men to pull back to Chancellorsville Crossroads and entrench. Fifth Corps commander, the easily irritated Major General George Meade, angrily erupted, "My God! If we can't hold the top of the hill, we certainly can't hold the bottom of it!" [25]

Just after 5 p.m., Sedgwick received a dispatch from Hooker instructing him to make a demonstration short of it being an attack. Uncle John immediately issued orders for a display of force. Brooks' division was positioned as if they were readying to advance. Brigadier General Newton's Third Division, along with five regiments of the Light Division, crossed at Franklin's crossing. At sunset, soldiers of the First and Sixth Corps on the north bank of the Rappahannock marched and countermarched. Orrin Rugg wrote "we paraded back and forth so as to make the force look as large as possible." Surgeon Stevens remembered "one of our bands near the enemy playing 'Dixie.' The rebels hearing the strains, set up a great shout, which was returned by our boys in the most tremendous *yells* imaginable. One point was established – we beat them badly at shouting." As darkness descended, the 77th retired to their tents. [26]

At daylight, May 2, Sedgwick received orders to put Reynolds' First Corps in motion towards Chancellorsville Crossroads. Major General Reynolds had his columns on the move by 7 a.m. The 77th watched as Confederate Parrott rifles of Andrews' battalion began shelling Reynolds' blue columns as they marched back across the Rappahannock. Sixth Corps batteries and Federal Reserve artillery on the opposite side of the river came alive in an attempt to silence the Rebel guns. A sharp artillery duel roared for nearly an hour until Confederate fire slackened. Rebel fire proved accurate as one pontoon boat was hit, killing two Yankees and wounding ten. Ten horses were also killed and three Union limbers were destroyed.

Having crossed the river, the First Corps marched up the Rappahannock past the 77th and north toward Falmouth. The New Yorkers were ordered to cover the ground left vacant by the First Corps. Companies G, H, and I, under Captain Rugg's command, were deployed to the riverbank on picket to spend a lazy afternoon. Rugg wrote, "The reb skirmishers here came down to the opposite bank not a hundred yards from us but no shots were fired." The remaining companies of the regiment were "posted a little way from the river in a pleasant field." George Stevens remembered, "Just in front of us was a lovely spot, the residence of Dr. Morson, for fifteen years a Surgeon in the U. S. Navy. The estate," he continued, "was in remarkable order; the gardens in full bloom; the mocking birds building their nests, and the greenlets warbling sweetly." The men "strolled along the banks gathering flowers and glancing at our 'Secesh' friends across the river, only a few yards distant." [27]

About 5:15 p.m., as the 77th relaxed in the shade of their tents enjoying the charms of a lovely May day, the peaceful air was suddenly disturbed by "the terrible din of battle (that) shook the ground beneath us." Unbeknown to the Sixth Corps, the thundering clamor of battle was Stonewall Jackson and six of his brigades smashing into Hooker's left flank at Chancellorsville. Completely caught off guard, Major General Oliver O. Howard's Eleventh Corps was stampeded. Fortunately for the Federals, Jackson's attack was launched late in the day, which prevented the Confederate soldiers from completely routing Hooker's army. The Union artillery, along with hard fighting, enabled Hooker to establish new lines and check the Confederate onslaught. From their position of relative calm, the 77th could only guess the outcome. What was certain, however, was "that ere the sunset, thousands of our brave comrades must be sacrificed." [28]

At dusk, Companies G, H, and I were recalled to the regiment, and made ready to march across the Rappahannock. Ordered to fall in behind the 49th New York, a large number of soldiers in the 20th New York refused to cross. Dissatisfied with their Swedish colonel Von Vegesac after his reckless performance at Antietam, many in the 20th believed the colonel would lead them "against any battery and into the hottest death," and that he was "prepared to sacrifice every man in the regiment to win promotion to general." The regiment's officers were handed a petition by 35 members of Company A and representatives of several other companies. In it, the signers stated that their enlistments had expired, according to the date they were mustered into service by a representative of the state of New York. The Federal government, however, claimed their service started several weeks later when a Federal representative issued the oath of allegiance. Unmoved by threats of arrest or execution, 201 men laid down their arms and refused the order to fall in. The soldiers who refused to cross the river were court-martialed and received a sentence of hard labor without pay or allowance for the remainder of the war. [29]

Before long, the 77th crossed the river, along with the rest of the regiments of Albion Howe's division. The regiment was positioned in front of the Vermont Brigade close to the riverbank under the bluff. Simultaneously, the flash of Confederate artillery on the heights flickered as the Sixth Corps picket line was extended to the rear of Bernard's Mannsfield estate. Rolling into battery on the open plain, Sixth Corps artillery responded to the Confederate shelling. Union reserve batteries on the north bank of the Rappahannock added their weight in countering Confederate artillery fire. George Stevens wrote home to the *Daily Saratogian* that, "We remained in line all night, sometimes throwing ourselves upon the ground to get a few minutes sleep, then roused in the expectancy of an advance." [30]

That night, the Army of Northern Virginia received a wound from which it would never fully recover. After crushing Howard's Eleventh Corps with his surprise flank attack, Stonewall Jackson determined to renew his assault the next morning. Along with half a dozen officers of his staff, Jackson rode out past the skirmish line of Brigadier General James H. Lane's North Carolina brigade to reconnoiter the Federal flank. Jackson's party, riding slowly, reached an unfinished chapel building about 150 yards beyond Lane's skirmishers. Suddenly, a single shot sounded off, then a spatter of shots, and then a fusillade. Bullets tore through Jackson's party, and the scene became one of desperate confusion. At last the firing stopped, but not before three musket balls had struck Jackson. One hit his right hand, a second struck his left forearm, and a third shattered the bone in the upper left arm near the shoulder. Jackson was brought to Wilderness Tavern where his left arm was amputated at the shoulder. He retired to the home of Thomas Coleman Chandler near Guiney's Station to recuperate, but became ill with pneumonia, and fittingly for the devout soldier, died Sunday May 10.

At 4 a.m. on May 3, the 77th advanced. Sedgwick had earlier received orders from Joe Hooker to "at once take up your line of march on the Chancellorsville Road until you connect with us," and to attack any force he may fall in with on the road. Marching out of the low-lying fog that covered the river and its immediate bank, the 77th formed the vanguard of Howe's division. The night sky was clear and the moon was full. Ahead, the Empire State veterans beheld the magnificent scene of long dark columns of troops with the flashing from the bright barrels and bayonets of the guns. Surgeon Stevens wrote, "Straight across the plain we went until we came to the base of the Heights, where lay thousands of the enemy." The regiment filed right, onto the Bowling Green Road, and proceeded toward Fredericksburg. [31]

As the 77th halted at Hazel Run, just south of the city, Newton's Third Division troops slowly crept through the dark, deserted streets advancing toward the rear of Fredericksburg. Confederate batteries opened up on the Federal soldiers. Sixth Corps artillery unlimbered to the rear of the city and responded to the shelling. The plunging fire of the Rebel guns proved accurate, forcing several Federal guns to reposition. George Stevens looked on at the flashes across the river on Stafford Heights of the Union Artillery Reserve's siege rifles and other large rifled cannon "throwing huge shells across the wide valley and stream into the works of the enemy." The artillery barrage continued as Sedgwick's Sixth Corps soldiers continued to deploy in and around Fredericksburg. A member of the 33rd New York positioned to the right of the 77th observed the bombardment:

> One of the shells exploded a rebel caisson at the redoubt near the stone-wall, and killed ten horses. After blowing up the caisson struck two horses directly behind, and hurled eight others down the steep precipice in the rear into a yawning chasm beneath. They presented a hideous spectacle as they lay at the bottom, dead and dying. [32]

While the 77th held its position on the Bowling Green Road and against Hazel Run, the troops of the Second Corps under Brigadier General John Gibbon that had remained at Falmouth began crossing the Rappahannock into Fredericksburg. Sedgwick instructed Gibbon to deploy his two brigades north of the city, and to carry the heights opposite that point. Uncle John's plan was to weaken Confederate troop strength to his immediate front by forcing the Rebel defenders to counter Gibbon's maneuvers. If the Southern defenders failed to react, their fortified position would be vulnerable to a Union turning movement.

At 7 a.m., Gibbon began advancing his 3,400 soldiers toward the northern edge of Fredericksburg. In advance of Gibbon's troops, Chief of Engineers Major General Gouverneur Warren had ridden ahead. From this forward position, Warren spied a large canal carrying water into the city. Retreating Confederates had earlier dismantled the bridge crossing the 30- foot-wide, six-foot-deep canal. The planks covering the bridge had been torn up, leaving only the large wooden supports spanning the canal. Warren galloped back to Gibbons advancing column and directed squads of pioneers to pull planks from nearby barns to lay across the worn bridge.

Confederates on Taylor Hill watched Gibbon's Federals advancing through the early morning fog, and four rifled guns of the Norfolk (Virginia) Battery opened on the Union column. Their accurate fire forced the Northern pioneers to disperse and take cover. As the shot and shell tore up the ground, Gibbon's 3rd Brigade took cover behind a stone wall along a sunken roadbed. Gibbon sent his 1st Brigade further to his right to cross the canal at another bridge, but its regiments too were compelled to seek protection from the intense Rebel shelling in abandoned entrenchments. The canal was impassable, preventing Gibbon's men from closing from the enemy. Any attempt to repair the exposed bridges was suicidal.

The destroyed bridges over the canal thwarted Sedgwick's attempt at a turning movement. Brigadier General Gibbon was furious over the lack of intelligence concerning the condition of the bridges. As he was not a participant in Burnside's disastrous Fredericksburg Campaign due to three wounds incurred at Antietam, Sedgwick seemingly did not know the location or the condition of the bridges spanning the canal.

In the meantime, at his headquarters in the Chancellor house, Major General Hooker remained in a defensive position as he waited to hear of Sedgwick's advance at Fredericksburg. Just after 9 a.m., one of Lieutenant Colonel E. P. Alexander's Confederate gunners sent a solid shot careening into the wooden porch pillar that Hooker was leaning against. Stunned senseless by the concussion, the major general fell to the ground. With the help of his staff, Hooker got up and was moved a mile away near the Bullock house. Despite being knocked out minutes before, Joe Hooker did not relinquish command, but ordered his commanders to reestablish Union lines. The Northerners around Chancellorsville fell back fighting to a new U-shaped defensive position anchored on both ends by the Rappahannock, which secured a line of retreat by way of United States Mine Ford.

With Gibbon unable to advance, any hope of a turning movement to flank the Confederate position on Marye's Heights from the north had evaporated. The early morning fog had dissipated, but the Confederate works still shielded the defenders from the Sixth Corps commander's view. Sedgwick was unaware that most of Jubal Early's division had earlier moved off the heights to unite with Lee at Chancellorsville. Facing the Sixth Corps was the Mississippi brigade of Brigadier General William Barksdale, plus two Louisiana regiments. Despite too few men to adequately hold the elaborate entrenchments covering the heights behind Fredericksburg, the Rebel defenders were confident that the natural strength of Marye's Heights would compensate for their lack of numbers. The 18th Mississippi and three companies of the 21st Mississippi held the sunken road behind the stone wall at the base of Marye's Heights. The remaining seven companies of the 21st Mississippi were positioned between the Marye house and the Orange Plank Road. The 17th and 13th Mississippi regiments occupied the entrenchments running south, between Marye's Heights and Lee's Hill. At Howison's house to the south, the 6th and 9th Louisiana regiments held the right-most flank of Barksdale's line.

Close to 9 a.m., Sedgwick determined to develop the strength of the Confederate forces that dug in on the heights behind the city. Uncle John ordered Brigadier General Newton to advance a force toward Marye's Heights. Newton sent his 3rd Brigade, under Brigadier General Frank Wheaton, to make the reconnaissance in force. Before Wheaton's regiments advanced 200 yards, they were blistered with Rebel musket fire and artillery that sent them scattering for cover. Looking on, Sedgwick angrily barked, "Will some staff officers rally these men!" Nearby, the six ten-pounder Parrott rifles of the 1st Pennsylvania Battery opened fire in response to the Confederate gunners. Repulsed, Wheaton's troops dropped to the ground for protection behind a slight rise. [33]

Having probed the north and center of the entrenched Confederate line, Sedgwick attempted to reconnoiter the southern flank of Marye's Heights. This section was locally known as Willis Hill. Albion Howe's Second Division was positioned in two lines south of Hazel Run, the Third Brigade in front with the 77th ahead in skirmish formation. Brigadier General Neill ordered three companies of the 77th to advance to explore this section of the Rebel terraced entrenchments. Captain Orrin Rugg wrote to his parents that, "Co. A, G & F were ordered to deploy as skirmishers and advance and take a rifle pit and some buildings about halfway between us and the hills then held by the Rebs. We moved up to about one hundred yards when the Rebs opened on us. My company were just in front of the rifle pit and I ordered my men to fire and then move forward which they did and with a yell we made the Rebs leave." [34]

The 77th's skirmishers were quickly checked at the rifle pit. They were met with Confederate fire from the base of Lee's Hill as well as from the entrenchments below Willis Hill. Rugg wrote of his position in the rifle pit, "We then took possession and used them for a few hours as a means of protection to ourselves." Corporal Albert

Snyder was plagued by shots coming from the enemy hidden in some bushes in front of the rifle pit and decided to do something about it. He went into a deserted house near the line and from an upstairs window "got the drop on the Jonnies." The remainder of the Third Brigade and Howe's division remained protected in ditches that lined each side of the Bowling Green Road. [35]

Just past 10 a.m., Sedgwick received orders from Hooker's headquarters: "You will hurry up your column. The enemy flank now rests near the Plank Road at Chancellorsville, all exposed. You will attack at once." Well aware of the bloody carnage suffered by the Army of the Potomac during Burnside's crushing defeat assaulting Marye's Heights the previous December, Sedgwick dreaded the thought of sending forward his troops on a frontal assault against a well-entrenched Confederate force. Following the disastrous Fredericksburg Campaign, many soldiers of the Federal army referred to the open plain in front of the heights as the "slaughter pen." The broad plain itself presented a dark omen as spring rains had washed out a number of shallow graves, exposing the remains of Union dead slain five months earlier. [36]

Skeptical of assaulting Marye's Heights, Sedgwick nevertheless issued orders for the advance. Sixth Corps commanders understood that the best chance to succeed was to cross the no-man's-land of the open plain as quickly as possible, thus minimizing the exposure time to deadly Confederate fire. Much to the chagrin of Sedgwick's infantrymen, orders were issued forbidding the storming parties from capping their loaded muskets. Uncapped muskets would prevent the attacking Union soldiers from stopping to fire while in the open.

After unslinging their knapsacks, the Light Division regiments of the 61st Pennsylvania and the 43rd New York, followed by the 67th New York and the 82nd Pennsylvania of Major General John

Newton's Third Division, formed into assault columns of four along William Street. Two-hundred yards to the left, on the dirt roadway of Hanover Street, the 7th Massachusetts and the 36th New York of Newton's 2nd Brigade formed two columns of four. Further to the left, a short distance behind Newton's assaulting columns, three regiments of Colonel Hiram Burnham's Light Division, joined by the 23rd Pennsylvania of Newton's 1st Brigade, formed in line of battle as they waited further developments. As they stood in line, Colonel Thomas Allen commanding the Light Division's 5th Wisconsin pointed to the heights and announced, "Perhaps you think you cannot take them; I know you can. When the signal forward is given, you will start at the double-quick, you will not fire a gun, and you will not stop until you get the order to halt! You will never get that order!" [37]

As Newton and Burnham's soldiers prepared, Sedgwick notified Albion Howe of the attack to be launched north of his position. Ordered to assist the assault, Howe responded quickly, and ordered his division's artillery forward to shell the heights directly to his front. Surgeon Stevens looked on at "three batteries of Parrott guns, playing finely into the works of the enemy above." With the 77th already deployed as skirmishers, Howe's infantrymen were commanded to drop their knapsacks and pile them alongside the Bowling Green Road as line officers hurried to bring the division's two brigades into line of battle. [38]

Behind Lieutenant Colonel Winsor French's skirmishers, Howe's division formed into three lines of battle, just south of Hazel Run. The front line was held by the 7th Maine, five companies of the 21st New Jersey, and the 33rd New York. The 20th and 49th New York were held in reserve on the Bowling Green Road. The Vermont Brigade, commanded by Colonel Lewis A. Grant, formed directly behind the Third Brigade. Howe's trailing battle line consisted of the 3rd and 4th Vermont and the remaining five companies of the 21st New Jersey. The 5th Vermont was held in support of Andrew Cowan's six three-inch rifles in battery on the Bowling Green Road.

At 10:35 a.m., Chief of Staff Major General Daniel Butterfield telegraphed from Falmouth to Hooker, "Sedgwick at this moment commences his assault." Along the roadways, Union line officers commanded, "Forward! Double-quick march!," and the colors advanced. Their bayonets fixed, Newton's and Burnham's columns charged over wooden planks placed to bridge the millrace flowing to the rear of Fredericksburg. The columns were immediately hit by Confederate gunners on the heights. From his vantage point in the newly claimed rifle pit, Captain Orrin Rugg saw "the troops to the right of us charge the hill. We were laying where we could see it perfectly plain. It was a beautiful sight. There was a brigade in close column going on the double quick yelling and hooting while at the same time a sheet of fire was pouring from both lines and the artillery playing fiercely all the while. I saw the old flag planted on a hill by the city and then such a cheer passed all along the line, I never heard before." [39]

The cheer had hardly subsided when Orrin Rugg heard the order, "Forward those skirmishers." Rugg's Company G, and Companies A and F, rose up from the rifle pit "and went with a will" across the open plain to the front of the heights where they were raked by the artillery fire from Confederate gun crews on the Howison property, Lee's Hill, and Willis Hill. Captain Rugg wrote, "Over the plain we went under a heavy fire of musketry, grape, and canister & shell. I could see them tear the ground all around me and could hear the grape & canister whizzing all around me." The rest of the 77th's skirmishers, urged forward by Lieutenant Colonel French on his white-faced horse riding before them, quickly came up to Captain Rugg's right. [40]

At the base of the range of hills, the 77th dropped down for cover in a ditch of muddy water from "the heavy fire that we were under from right, left, and center, also a good many sharpshooters." Nineteen-year-old Private Erskine B. Branch (Co. D) remembered, "While we were in the ditch I examined my piece and thought it would be hardly safe to enter into a close engagement with it. So I fixed it as well as I could, leveled it against the bank of the ditch and fired it, and to my surprise I was kicked over in the mud and water, my long-legged boots becoming filled therewith." At this moment the order came for the regiment to rise and advance. "So on we went," Branch recalled, "and with much difficulty I reached the heights with my 'boots load' of mud and water." [41]

The Third Brigade's battle line quickly caught up with the 77th's skirmishers. Exploding shells continued to plough up the ground as the majority of the 33rd New York and 7th Maine continued charging toward the Rebel works between Lee's Hill and Willis Hill. In the excitement of battle, elements of Howe's second battle line of Colonel Lewis A. Grant's brigade mixed in with the Third Brigade. The 2nd Vermont and a portion of the 26th New Jersey joined the right of the 77th. "Up the hill we went together," Captain Orrin Rugg remembered, "yelling like mad men and all the time a sharp fire going on, the rebs retreating as we advanced." [42]

The majority of Grant's Vermonters splashed across Hazel Run. The right of Grant's line joined Maine and Wisconsin men of the Light Division, who were hotly engaged at the stone wall along the base of Willis Hill. The Light Division quickly overwhelmed the Confederate defenders behind the wall. The Green Mountain Boys swarmed into adjacent shelter-trenches on their right. Greatly outnumbered, the Rebel defenders fled the sunken roadbed up the heights to escape capture. Pursuit of the outflanked Confederates was delayed as

Union soldiers continued to receive heavy fire from enemy troops entrenched higher on the heights.

The 77th struggled to maintain battle formation as they fought their way through the rough terrain lining the ravine that Hazel Run cut through. Erskine Branch spied Rebel gun crews of the Washington Artillery endeavoring to place two 12-pounder brass pieces in position. Branch called to his Captain, Seth W. Deyoe, to bring it to Lieutenant Colonel French's attention. Just then, a 12-pound shell hit Private Branch exploding and literally tearing the man behind him to pieces. The young private described "my left leg blown off below the knee, and tore open nearly whole length of my thigh. Also wounded in left arm." The shocked Branch found himself on the ground, quickly threw off his knapsack, and endeavored to stand up on his right leg. Another soldier offered his assistance, but Branch waved him on and began hopping and crawling to the rear. He had not gone far when he met Major Nathan Babcock, pistol in hand, who ordered him to halt. Holding his shattered limb out and pointing to it, Branch incredulously asked the major, "Is this not enough to pass a man to the rear?" Realizing the severity of the wound, Babcock said, "Go ahead, my friend and do the best you can." Private Branch then "jumped on one foot and crawled behind a bank just goin' to tare up my shirt and try to tie up my left leg to stop the blood." Coming upon the severely wounded private, Captain Seth Deyoe summoned Private Jeff Hammond (Co. D) and Sergeant Oscar Lockwood (Co. D) to help Branch. Branch wrote, "our First Sargent . . . took his big silk handkerchief off his neck and they tied my leg up while I held the knots." Supported by his comrades Branch hopped down the heights but, "They knew I couldn't ride in a wagon to Fredericksburg 2 miles so they layed me down under some trees and said if I had any word to send my mother to say it for I couldn't live only a few minutes." Just then a shell went over, and Private Erskine Branch "gave three cheers for our flag and commenced singing red white and blue (The Star Spangled Banner)." Branch survived his wound, only dying after a long and fruitful life in 1932. [43]

Alerted by Captain Deyoe of the brass cannons on Lee's Hill spied by Private Branch, Lieutenant Colonel French rallied the men to the colors. The 77th climbed out of the ravine at Hazel Run and charged the cannon on Lee's Hill. Shouting, "Forward, forward boys!" to his company, Captain Luther Wheeler crumpled to the ground with a bullet in his abdomen, mortally wounded. A shell tore the National flag to shreds, killing the color guard. Captain Stephen Horton was knocked senseless by a concussion from the exploding shell, and was carried off the field. Private Edward H. Fuller spun around like a top when a bullet hit him in the back of his head. First Lieutenant William Fursman (Co. K) pushed up to Adjutant Isaac Clapp and excitedly cried out, "Adjutant, we can't go any further!" Clapp shouted above the din of battle, "Can't go any further? We must go further. Forward march!" The men of Company K rushed forward with renewed vigor. Private William Caw (Co. H) and Corporal Charles Thurber (Co. D) "sought the motherly protection of a large stump" when a shell exploded, wounding Thurber and utterly blowing Corporal Benjamin Day (Co. C) to bits. Close by, Captain Martin Lennon, Private Marcellus Bliss (Co. I) and Sergeant William Merrill (Co. J) escaped serious injury when hit by grape shot. "My orderly (Sergeant Merrill) was hit on the head . . . and knocked down, but sprang up on his feet and went into them again," Lennon recalled. Further up Lee's Hill, Lennon proudly remembered, "Two of my sergeants [George McKee and Bill Merrill] stopped firing and shook hands, when we were not more than two hundred yards from the enemy batteries, and a perfect shower of grape-shot and shell raining over us." [44]

Still the 77th continued up Lee's Hill. Lieutenant Colonel French wrote home to the *Daily Saratogian*, "Oh how nobly the boys moved up. I rushed on with them and captured two brass cannon, a pair of horses, caissons, &c., and about 20 prisoners." One of the prisoners was Lieutenant Colonel William H. Luse of the 18th Mississippi. While astride his horse, French placed his foot on one of the cannons when Brigadier General Neill rode up and exclaimed, "Colonel, write your name on it! You won it! It is yours! Take it!" Right behind Neill galloped up Albion Howe who waved his hat, and proclaimed, "Noble boys – the 77th has covered itself with glory." Close by, near a brick schoolhouse, Corporal Michael Lama seized the colors of the 18th Mississippi. Captain Lennon glowed, "I was never so proud in my life as when we got to the top of the hill. I must have been some seven feet tall about that time." To their right, the soldiers of the Light Division erupted in cheers atop Marye's Heights after driving off the Confederate defenders. Among the captured earthworks, Union troops fired off rifles into the air as men rejoiced. [45]

Private Edward H. Fuller (Saratoga Springs Public Library)

While the 77th was celebrating atop Lee's Hill, Private Edward Fuller stumbled into the same field hospital in Fredericksburg where

Captain Wheeler lay unconscious on a bed of straw, the signs of life quickly ebbing from his body. After regaining consciousness from his bullet wound, Fuller reminisced,

> I got up on my feet, looked around in a dazed condition, wondering where I was at, for I could see no one. So steadying myself, for I was rocking as you sometimes see a man who has imbibed too much, I started to go back... Anybody who could have seen me then would have said 'what a jag Fuller has,' for I walked in a zig-zag line, with bowed head, down the right side of which my blood was running to Virginia's sacred soil. I did not feel the wound because from the feeling I imagined my fist would go into the hole. As I kept going I heard, 'Where are you going soldier?' I walked or rather reeled on without heeding the inquiry. 'Are you wounded?' I heard. Turning around so that he could see the blood, he said, 'all right, keep going on ahead.' Further on another horseman rode up, asking me, 'Where are you going soldier?' I answered not, but walked on as fast as I could, for I was growing weaker. As I turned so that he could see that I was, I recognized our Brigadier-General Neill, who said, 'All right, keep on going,' which I did, and a shortly after I was startled from my daze by hearing, 'Look out there, soldier.' As I looked up I saw I was on a line with a cannon of one of our batteries pointing right at me, when I heard, 'We will not fire until you get by.' Hurrying as fast as I could, I heard the boom of the gun as I passed. Going a short way further I met one of my stretcher bearers, who conducted me to our assistant surgeon, William A. Long, who said as I reeled up, 'Hello Fuller, are you wounded?' Before I could reply I fell unconscious. While in that state he extracted this ball from my head.[46]

On top of Lee's Hill, Captain Orrin Rugg wrote, "Here we tried to get our regiment together and give them a little rest as the men were so tired and could go no further." But the enemy did not oblige the tired 77th: "We lay down in line and the rebs began to shell us. They wounded several and killed one. It was here a piece of shell about as big as my hand went through my sleeve but did not otherwise injure me." The shot and shell issued from the gun sections from Confederates Colonel Henry C. Caball's Artillery Battalion and Captain Henry H. Carlton's Troup (Georgia) Battery on the Leach family's property. Formed on each side of the Telegraph Road at the Leach house were remnants of the 18th and 21st Mississippi regiments gathered by Brigadier General Barksdale and Colonel William Monaghan's 6th and 9th Louisiana. [47]

Confederate gun crews, supported by Barksdale and Monaghan's infantrymen, stubbornly stood fast on the Leach property. After exhausting their ammunition, the Louisiana and Mississippi regiments, along with the Rebel guns, withdrew one mile down the Telegraph Road to a new position at the Cox house where Jubal Early had assembled his division bracing for Howe's division's advance. However, Sedgwick received renewed orders from Hooker to press on to Chancellorsville, causing Howe to halt offensive operation. Not having the opportunity to eat since the previous night, the 77th and the men of Howe's division stumbled back down to the Bowling Green Road to gather up their knapsacks. On the road they quickly refreshed themselves with water and hardtack while celebrating their victory.

The Sixth Corps losses totaled 1,500 killed and wounded during the charge up the steep slopes of Marye's Heights. Major Thomas Hyde vividly remembered, "The green slope was dotted all over with still forms in blue, and prisoners streaming down the hill in hundreds." The wounded streamed into Fredericksburg, some by ambulance, some by walking and hobbling as best they could. Surgeon Charles O. Leary, medical director of the Sixth Corps, and Surgeon Charles F. Crehore, the corps medical inspector, commandeered many of the city's homes, barns, and buildings and converted them into field hospitals. "Churches and private dwellings," George Stevens wrote, "swarmed with the unfortunate men, whose mangled forms told of the fearful work of the day." Surgeons "were hard at work ministering relief to the suffering, binding up the wounds or removing the mangled limbs which offered no hope of recovery." Shot through the thigh, Corporal Henry West said, "I guess that old Joe West's son has lost a leg." Suffering in great agony, a wounded soldier next to him lamented that he had come to the war. West proudly responded, "I am not sorry that I came." Private Erskine Branch was carried of the heights and brought in on a stretcher. While the Rebel shell tore off his left leg below the knee, it also opened up a gaping wound nearly the length of his thigh. Branch fought the attending surgeon over how far above his severed limb to amputate: "The doctor was bound to cut my leg off above the knee and all other wounds, but I fought so hard to save the knee joint. Just then our Dr. George Stevens came in with the German Dr. of the 20th N. Y. They cut it off 4 inches below the knee." Private Branch was later placed in an ambulance and taken to a tent hospital about one mile away and put on a bed of hay on the ground. He remained there for two days, and after a good deal of pleading, Branch was sent to Amory Square Hospital in Washington. For six months, he was unable to rise off his bed without being lifted. Nearly a year to the day of his wounding, Branch underwent a second amputation at a Federal hospital in Philadelphia before being discharged for disability. [48]

When Sedgwick's Sixth Corps captured Marye's Heights, Lieutenant A. L. Pitzer of Jubal Early's staff, on his own initiative, rode to General Lee to relay the disturbing news. Lee immediately responded by dividing his force at Chancellorsville and putting his infantry in motion to reinforce Early. Major General Lafayette McLaw's division of the Army of Northern Virginia's First Corps, along with Brigadier General William "Little Billy" Mahone's brigade of Anderson's division, marched to Early's support. With the infantry, Lee dispatched four guns each from Manly's North Carolina Battery and McCarthy's Richmond Howitzers. Added to the Confederate artillery support was a 14-piece artillery battalion from Lee's Artillery Reserve, under the command of Colonel Edward P. Alexander.

Farther up the ridgeline behind Fredericksburg at "Fall Hill" near the Taylor house, Brigadier General Cadmus Wilcox viewed the assault on Marye's Heights. He responded by sending Colonel H. Forney and his 10th Alabama on the double quick toward the fighting. But, when informed that the Federals had taken the heights, Wilcox recalled the Alabama regiment. Instead, he established his Alabama brigade along a crest of hills that ran from the Orange Plank Road toward Stansbury Ridge. Wilcox's battle line formed 500 yards in front of a house on the Orange Plank Road, owned by George Guest. To their front, four rifled guns from Moore and Pennick's batteries began shelling the Northerner's forming on Marye's Heights.

From atop Marye's Heights, Sedgwick, shells bursting above the newly claimed entrenchments, reformed most of Newton's division in column. With a line of skirmishers thrown forward, the Federals began advancing up the Orange Plank Road toward Chancellorsville. Cadmus Wilcox thought better of his position at the Guest house and withdrew toward Salem Church, stopping at the tollgate on the Plank Road. Reaching the Guest house, Sedgwick ordered a halt, and waited for his corps to assemble.

As the 77th sat in the ditches along the Bowling Green Road to refresh themselves, Brigadier General Brook's First Division moved up the Orange Plank Road. Barely had they begun to chew on their hardtack, when the 77th heard the drum rolls calling the Second Division to fall-in. The New Yorkers fell in line and marched through the war-ravaged city of Fredericksburg and up the Orange Plank Road toward Chancellorsville. The day grew hot and oppressively humid, slowing their march, leaving a number of stragglers behind. A number of men struck down by the heat lined the sides of the road as the regiment continued on up the Plank Road.

Shortly after 2 p.m., the head of Brook's division reached Sedgwick's position at the Guest house. Uncle John determined that the First Division would lead the advance up the Orange Plank Road to Chancellorsville. In column formation, Brooks deployed his first and second brigades on either side of the road. Regiments of Brigadier General Bartlett's brigade wheeled into position on the left side of the Plank Road while the First New Jersey Brigade marched over uneven terrain on the right. Four Federal batteries of Brook's First Division remained in column along the roadway.

To the front of Brook's columns, skirmishers crept forward. Skirmishers from Wilcox's battle line at the tollgate were also thrown forward. Moore and Pennick's Confederate batteries sent shot and shell at the advancing blue skirmishers, slowing Sedgwick's advance by compelling Brook's brigades to deploy. Wilcox was acutely aware that his delaying tactics would merely slow Sedgwick's larger force and that it was simply a matter of time before he would be forced to retire. Little did the Confederate general know, however, Major General McLaws was rapidly marching 9,000 Confederate soldiers toward his position.

En route to link up with Jubal Early's troops, Lafayette McLaws paused to rest his tired men near the junction of the Orange Turnpike and Mine Road. Two miles east stood the Salem Church on the south side of the Orange Plank Road. The red brick, two-and-a-half story Baptist church was situated on the edge of an irregular shaped clearing. Beyond the church and on either side of the clearing was Salem Ridge, a ridgeline tangled with thickets and second growth trees.

Wilcox's Alabama regiments maintained brisk skirmish fire with the advancing Yankees until 4 p.m. when Sedgwick's overwhelming numbers forced them to leave their wounded and withdraw at the double quick, up the Orange Plank Road. At Salem Church, Wilcox placed a company in and around the church. Those unable to fit in the church deployed behind a row of bushes hedging the border of the property surrounding the churchyard. The bulk of Wilcox's brigade was positioned directly behind the church on either side of the Orange Plank Road.

Upon Brook's arrival at the tollgate, Parson's New Jersey Light Battery A's six 10-pounder Parrotts unlimbered on the right of the Orange Plank Road, and shelled the woods on Salem Ridge. Knapsacks still on their backs, Union soldiers formed an extended battle line across the road. Brigadier General Joseph J. Bartlett's 2nd Brigade formed on the left of the Plank Road. To the right of Bartlett's troops were the New Jersey regiments of the 1st Brigade. Extending the line further to the right were two detached regiments of Brigadier General David A. Russell's 3rd Brigade. At the same time, McLaw's reinforcements began arriving from Chancellorsville. Brigadier General Joseph B. Kershaw's brigade filed to the right of Wilcox. Semmes's Georgians formed of Wilcox's left, with "Little Billy" Mahone's regiments coming up to the left of Semmes. A short time later, Brigadier General William T. Wofford's brigade arrived and was positioned at Kershaw's left.

Convinced he faced only one Confederate brigade retreating from his front, Brooks hurried troops forward, Bartlett and Brown advancing up either side of the Orange Plank Road. Parson's Parrotts at the tollgate continued firing as Brook's Yankees advanced in common time (a fast walk) shoulder-to-shoulder. Union skirmishers entered the tangled thickets, the main Union battle line closely following. Once in the dense woods, the Federal battle line was slowed by thick brush and its alignment disrupted. Some Union soldiers found themselves in such tangled thickets that they were hardly able to make headway. Suddenly, a tremendous volley exploded to their front, staggering the advancing blue lines. Surgeon Stevens wrote, "The confederates were lying down in a road which traversed the thickets; and, when the Union line was within twenty yards, they suddenly discharged a volley." The firing of muskets grew ever louder as soldiers of the North and South became heavily engaged. Confederates in and around Salem Church thinned the Union line until companies of the 23rd New Jersey rushed forward to the church, capturing the Rebel riflemen inside. [49]

As Confederate skirmishers fell back to Wilcox's battle line, the action intensified while the irregular lines of Union soldiers fought their way through the dense thickets. The battle raged on either side of the Orange Plank Road as smoke from the firing of hundreds of muskets filled the air, decreasing the already diminished visibility among the thick brush. Shot and exploding shells clipped tree branches and tore through the thickets before hitting their targets. In the intensity of battle, more than one Federal soldier forgot to withdraw his ramrod from his musket, firing it with the bullet.

The battle raging, Newton's regiments were busy marching to the flank, extending the Union lines to the right of the Orange Plank Road. The 10th Massachusetts and 2nd Rhode Island ranged far to the right, but were hit hard by two Georgia regiments of

Semmes's brigade. The Union troops were forced to beat a hasty retreat as their position quickly became untenable. Colonel Henry L. Eustis, commanding the 2nd Brigade as Colonel Brown had been wounded, ordered both regiments back across the field littered with the wounded to join Sedgwick's reserve line.

On the other side of the Orange Plank Road, Brigadier General Wilcox suddenly sent his Confederate brigade forward at the charge. The Northern soldiers could not stand the shock of Wilcox's counterattack and gave way, falling back to the rear. The butternuts chased the Federals through the thickets and beyond Salem Church. Advancing with the Rebel yell, the 10th and 51st Georgia regiments, led by Brigadier General Semmes, joined Wilcox's charge. Falling back through the confusion, squads of Union Soldiers sought cover behind the church, but to their surprise and consternation they were quickly made prisoners.

In response to the Yankees maneuvering toward his left flank, Lafayette McLaws ordered two regiments from Brigadier General William T. Wofford's brigade to the left to support Mahone. Union regiments from Brigadier General Frank Wheaton's 3rd Brigade, Newton's division were advancing, marching by the flank from Sedgwick's reserve line. Wheaton's exposed ranks were raked by blasts of buck and ball, fired from the smoothbore muskets of Semmes' charging Georgians. The bluecoats performed a quick, but orderly, withdrawal to the rear.

Along the Orange Plank Road, Wilcox and Semmes' brutal charge swept Brook's soldiers down the slope toward the tollgate. When most of Bartlett and Brown's retreating troops cleared Sedgwick's reserve line, Union artillery opened a devastating fire on the charging Confederates. Sedgwick personally assisted in directing the Union gun crews. When in range, six 12-pounder smoothbores of the 2nd United States, Battery D showered the charging Rebels with double-shot canister, halting their pursuit. The 51st and 10th Georgia regiments came within 100 yards of the Yankee guns on Sedgwick's reserve line, but without support were forced to fall back.

Toward dusk, Wilcox and Semmes pulled back their triumphant Confederates to their original position behind Salem Church. Sedgwick advanced Newton's reserve line forward to the protection of the crest of Salem Ridge, now strewn with Yankee wounded, in preparation for further attack, but daylight was gone and it was deemed unwise to attempt the woods again. Butler, Cowan, and Harn's batteries, which had been in reserve, were brought forward as Williston, Rigby, and Parson's guns were sent to the rear to replenish their limbers.

Throughout the battle at Salem Church, the 77th remained in column along the Orange Plank Road. Sedgwick, not knowing the exact whereabouts of Jubal Early's division, ordered Albion Howe to guard against a possible Confederate flank attack. The New Yorkers' Second division faced left and threw out skirmishers. After briefly probing the front, no Confederates were uncovered, and Howe placed the Second division at rest alongside the roadway.

The 77th spent a restless night as Union ambulance wagons noisily rumbled down the Orange Plank Road loaded with groaning wounded soldiers crying out for water and help. A majority of Sixth Corps wounded were quickly evacuated from Salem Ridge and ferried over the Rappahannock River via the pontoon bridge just below Fredericksburg. Adding to the cacophony of sound were ammunition and regimental commissary wagons. The 77th was happy to receive rations while some turned their attention to cleaning their musket barrels as ammunition was handed out. The regiment attempted to sleep atop their rifles, but, as George Stevens wrote, "there were many misgivings among officers in regard to what tomorrow might bring forth." [50]

At dawn on May 4, from the vicinity of the Cox house, Jubal Early advanced in two lines of battle north up the Telegraph Road toward Lee's Hill. Early's goal was to connect with McLaws' right flank somewhere near Salem Church. From Lee's Hill, Colonel John B. Gordon's brigade moved toward the Orange Plank Road and came upon a large number of Union soldiers resting along the roadside. The two Confederate 20-pounder Parrott rifles of the First Rockbridge (Virginia) Artillery were immediately put into action. Rebel shells fell among Albion Howe's surprised men as Gordon sent forward his butternut skirmishers.

Caught off guard, Howe's bluecoats scampered for protection. Gordon advanced in line of battle, which quickly caught up with his skirmishers in front of Brigadier General Thomas Neill's brigade near Hazel Run. Howe hurriedly deployed forward the 33rd New York as skirmishers. Along with the 77th, the Third Brigade formed on the slope of a hill to receive the Confederate attack. Gordon's soldiers rushed ahead and engaged the 33rd New York, and brisk skirmish fire ensued. Captain James M. McNair, Company F, 33rd New York, wrote, "The Regiment was thrown forward as a forlorn hope, trusting by desperate fighting we might hold the enemy in check . . . The enemy were rapidly flanking us, when we were ordered to fall back on the run." [51]

The broken terrain disrupted the alignment of Gordon's charge. Fire from the Confederate Parrott rifles sent the 77th and the Third Brigade running for cover on the far side of the Orange Plank Road. As Gordon's infantry forged ahead, they came into the thick brush-covered slopes bordering the ravine containing Hazel Run. The bulk of his brigade plunged into the stream's cold water and emerged wet up to their chests, and continued up toward Neill's Third Brigade.

The 77th reformed along the roadbed of the Orange Plank Road, while others fell back to the cover of abandoned Confederate entrenchments. The First Rockbridge Artillery's 20-pounder Parrott rifles continued lobbing shells in the direction of the Third Brigade. As Howe's Second Division fell back, the 31st Georgia captured a number of men of the 33rd New York and a commissary wagon. This brief, but sharp, 30-minute skirmish gave Early possession of Marye's Heights. Atop Lee's Hill, Jubal Early immediately set his sights on the Sixth Corps.

The same morning at Chancellorsville, Major General Richard H. Anderson's three brigades were deployed on the River Road on Lee's right flank to prevent Hooker and Sedgwick from uniting their forces. Around 7 a.m., Lee ordered Anderson to collect his men and march his troops up the Mine Road to reinforce McLaws at Salem Church.

Uncle John Sedgwick was unable to advance his corps due to McLaws entrenched soldiers on his front, and was now cut off from Fredericksburg by Jubal Early's division to the rear. The Sixth Corps was forced to withdraw into a defensive position that took the shape of a horseshoe. Union line officers made expert use of the terrain, positioning their men along the crests of the hills that rolled through the wooded area. Sedgwick's drawing in of the Sixth Corps safeguarded the Union's interior line. Ever so importantly, Sedgwick's only viable escape route, Scott's Ford, remained protected within the new perimeter.

John Sedgwick's battle line placed the 77th, along with Howe's Second Division, facing east toward Fredericksburg. Albion Howe's left rested close to the Rappahannock River, and his troops extended nearly one mile south to the Orange Plank Road. The 77th's Third Brigade was positioned on Howe's left, while Colonel Lewis A. Grant's 1st Vermont Brigade extended to the right toward the Orange Plank Road. Facing south, parallel to the Orange Plank Road, was Brook's division. Newton's Third Division held the tollgate area and brought the Federal line back toward the Rappahannock.

On Marye's Heights, Early was uncertain about the strength of the Federal force to his immediate front, and needed to determine the size and exact position of the Yankee line. Around 11 a.m., Early sent forward Brigadier General William "Extra Billy" Smith's Virginia brigade to develop the enemy's strength. As Smith's skirmishers approached the Union picket line of the Third Brigade, Lieutenant John Carter, Company B, 33rd New York, hurriedly sent back word to Albion Howe who directed Neill's brigade to double quick about one mile to the left where they formed behind Taylor's Hill, about two miles west of Fredericksburg. The Third Brigade held steady waiting for Smith's brigade to come in range when Confederate artillery sent shells into its ranks. Private Franklin Wunderlin, Company C, 33rd New York, was horrified when one soldier of the 33rd was killed near him.

> [T]he enemy... had a battery in position and dropped shells in on us so thick that we got out of there very quick. I saw a shell bury itself and then burst under one of the boys and when the dirt settled all we could see of him was [his] hand sticking above the ground. [52]

In a short time, Neill's pickets were forced to retire upon their main battle line as Smith's Virginians rapidly advanced. Closing in upon the Third Brigade, the Confederate attackers were hit by heavy artillery and the brigade's musketry. Smith's brigade charged, but after spirited fighting, was forced to retire through canister fire from a section of 12-pounder Napoleons of Battery A, 1st United States, under Captain J. H. Rigby. While the 58th Virginia fell back, their colors were seized by Corporal John P. McVeane of the 49th New York after shooting its color bearer. Several companies of the 58th Virginia sought protection from intense shelling from the Federal artillery in an abandoned house. They were quickly surrounded, and the Virginians were taken captive. Two hundred prisoners of war were the result of a brave counterattack by Colonel Daniel D. Bidwell's 49th New York and soldiers of the 7th Maine. Lieutenant Colonel Seldon Connor, commander of the 7th Maine, wrote home, "This little victory was the work of a single company of the 7th Maine and two companies of the 49th New York." 53

From Marye's Heights, Early sent Lieutenant A. L. Pitzer to report his division's situation to McLaws at Salem Church. Early requested that McLaw's move to attack with two of his brigades. Once McLaws made contact with Sedgwick's troops, Early would pitch in with three of his brigades. However, Lafayette McLaws felt the enemy was too strongly posted on his front to initiate the attack with his force. McLaws, the ranking officer on the field, sent back a dispatch stating that he wanted Early to initiate the attack. He felt certain his battle plan would force the Sixth Corps to expose its flank to an attack by his Confederate brigades.

Richard H. Anderson's Confederate division arrived from Chancellorsville at Salem Church around noon and began positioning his troops. Lee arrived at Salem Church shortly after Anderson's division. Anderson continued to deploy his brigades as skirmishers quickly advanced in order to uncover the Sixth Corp's defensive line. Once in position, Lee's combined force totaled 23,000 soldiers. Confronting him were 19,000 men under the banners of the Greek

Cross. Lee desired to attack Sedgwick's troops from two sides with a coordinated general attack. Early's brigades were to attack in coordination with Anderson's division. Once Early and Anderson's assault hit the Union line, McLaw's entrenched soldiers were to advance and connect with Anderson's left in order to sweep the Sixth Corps from the field.

Awaiting orders, the day seemed to creep by slowly. The 77th nervously waited for developments as the blue Virginia sky became gray from a hazy overcast. That afternoon, the regiment's soldiers watched Rebels moving through the woods to their front. Now and then they heard the Rebel yell and it was apparent that the Southerners were forming into battle lines and preparing for attack. Major Mason Tyler of Sedgwick's First Division spoke for the 77th when he observed, "It was one of the most anxious six or seven hours that I ever spent." [54]

The 77th's division commander, Albion Howe, suspected the Confederates would force his left in an attempt to sever his communications with Scott's Ford, the Sixth Corps' only route of escape. Howe carefully inspected the rolling terrain before him, and determined to occupy two positions, one in front of the other, in order to defend any likely Confederate approach. The Second Division commander placed Neill's Third Brigade in front holding a crest of a hill overlooking a ravine. The Third Brigade's line of battle was anchored near the River Road by the 20th New York. Extending right were the 77th, 33rd New York, 7th Maine, 49th New York, and the 21st New Jersey. Along with its sister regiments, the 77th sent out a detachment of skirmishers to its front. The 5th Vermont from Howe's 2nd Brigade extended the line with the Third Brigade, forming in a small gully near the Guest house in support of four guns belonging to Parson's New Jersey Light, Battery A.

Behind the Third Brigade was another ravine followed by a wooded hill cresting slightly higher in elevation to Neill's battle line. Howe placed the regiments of L. A. Grant's Vermont Brigade in the cover of woods just behind the crest. The Green Mountain Boys hastily built entrenchments by cutting down small trees and placing their knapsacks to their front for protection. Just in front of Grant's line, Captain James Rigby rolled the six 10-pounders of his 1st Maryland, Battery A into position. Adding to Rigby's guns was a two-gun section of 10-pounder Parrott rifles belonging to Lieutenant Martin's 5th U. S., Battery F.

Late in the afternoon, Major Thomas Hyde, Sedgwick's provost marshal, set off to check on the 7th Maine, his former regiment. He recalled,

> I was sitting on the ground with Colonel Connor and Channing, talking over the chances of the fight, for we were skirmishing in three directions, and, pulling out my watch, I said, 'It is quarter of five; if they are coming it will be before five o'clock,' when the rebel yell broke from the woods far in front, and the whole hillside was alive with men. It was a gallant sight! They came on in three lines, about 16,000 strong, and were so near that regimental, brigade, and division commanders with their staff could be plainly seen.

Heading straight toward Major Hyde and the Third Brigade were the brigades of Brigadier General Robert F. Hoke and Brigadier General Harry T. Hays' Louisiana Tigers of Early's division. The 77th's skirmishers fired off one volley from the ravine at Early's gray lines, and with the other skirmishers of Neill's brigade, high tailed it back up the wooded hill to their main battle line. Rigby and Martin's Union batteries instantly came alive and opened up on the attacking Rebels, sending shot and shell crashing into the direction of the rapidly moving enemy. [55]

Private William W. Finch (Saratoga Springs Public Library)

Hoke and Hays' brigades quickly became tangled and their formation disjointed as their troops surged forward at the run. As they rushed up from the ravine to the Third Brigade's front, the men of the 77th heard Brigadier General Neill shout the command, "Fire!" and the Third Brigade unleashed a terrific volley that slowed the butternut attackers. Thomas Hyde saw Beau Neill from atop his horse "draw his little sword as deliberately and gracefully as if at West Point on parade" but was astonished when Neill "made the dreadful mistake of giving the order, 'Forward! 3d brigade!'" for the brigade's regiments "were in a beautiful position on the hillside." The 77th charged into the ravine below with a defiant hurrah. Hyde remembered, "The shock was terrible." The 7th Maine's Colonel Seldon Connor was seriously wounded. Waving his men forward, Neill was also injured and helped off the field after his horse was shot and landed on top of him. A large part of the 21st New Jersey broke for the rear as their Colonel, Gilliam Van Houton, was mortally wounded as well. Detested by his regiment, Colonel Von Vegeseck could not contain his 20th New York, which fled to the rear in a panic. Private Alonzo Bump later wrote, "they Broke and run Like Dogs and it maid it harder for our rigiment." Private William Finch (Co. D), only fifteen years old when he enlisted at Northumberland, was seriously wounded and crept into the ravine and hid under some laurel bushes, only crawling back to the 77th in the dark of night. "In less time it takes to tell it," Major Hyde wrote, "the little brigade had smashed itself to pieces against ten times its numbers." Afterwards, Colonel French could only cry, "Oh, it was awful!" [56]

To the rear of the attacking Confederate brigades, General Lee and Jubal Early stood on a knoll watching Hays' Louisiana Tigers. Both were exhilarated with the progress made to their front. Grabbing his hat and throwing it to the ground, Early exclaimed, "Those damned Louisiana fellows may steal as much as they please now!" Early was referring to theft charges leveled earlier against some of Hays' unruly Louisiana Tigers. [57]

After losing nearly one third of its men, the 77th and the Third Brigade regiments retreated. Passing through the Vermont brigade, the 77th crossed a ravine and reformed on another wooded hill. Colonel C. B. Stoughton's 4th Vermont immediately became hotly engaged on the New York veteran's left flank. Just as Howe had earlier suspected, Early was attempting to crush the Sixth Corps' left in order to break its communication with Scott's Ford. Union reserve batteries across the Rappahannock River opened an accurate fire on Colonel John B. Gordon's Georgia brigade, momentarily slowing their advance. Gordon's determined soldiers forced Martin's gunners to limber up and race to the rear.

Beau Neill's rash Federal counterattack cost the Third Brigade nearly 1,000 men before they could break away from their sanguine encounter with the enemy. The retreat of the 77th's brigade dangerously exposed Howe's right flank, but due to the uneven terrain, the impetus of Early's attack swung to the right, down a ravine toward the front of Howe's second line held by Grant's Vermonters. Hoping to send the Yankees running for the Rappahannock, the winded Southerners rushed up from the ravine. From behind their entrenchments, the 2nd, 3rd, and 6th Vermont rose to their feet and fired. The deadly volley slammed into the attackers, littering the ground with Confederate corpses. The Green Mountain Boys continued firing rapidly into the gray ranks at will.

To the left of Early's brigades, Major General Richard H. Anderson's division also advanced to the attack. Anderson's battle line came into view moving through the thickets near a large brick house opposite the Orange Plank Road. Captain McCartney, commanding Battery A, 1st Massachusetts, quickly sighted a gun and then pulled the lanyard. The shell careened into the house and burst, sending red bricks flying. Presently, the remaining five brass 12-pounders of McCartney's battery belched forth and sprayed the Southerners in the woods to their front with canister. A two-piece section of Parson's battery added their weight in pounding the attacking Rebels. The Union batteries stopped Anderson's men before barely making contact with Brook's First Division. As darkness began to descend on the field, it was impossible for Confederate line officers to coordinate any further advance.

Newton's and Burnham's divisions stood ready to fight, but saw only limited skirmishing as Lafayette McLaws never fully advanced his soldiers to attack. The right portion of McLaws' line did tentatively advance, but because of delay and darkness, no serious attack developed in this sector of the Sixth Corps.

Acrid smoke from the firing of cannon and muskets hung low to the ground as darkness enveloped the battlefield. The Vermont brigade formed a new defensive line across the River Road. Their left rested on the Rappahannock River, and the men stood ready to repel another enemy attack. The Third Brigade extended Howe's position toward the Guest house, where it connected with Brook's First Division. The First Division continued to parallel the Orange Plank Road up to the tollgate, where Newton's division continued the sixth Corps line back toward the river.

Having heard nothing from Hooker at Chancellorsville, Sedgwick dispatched orders for the Sixth Corps to prepare to withdraw across the Rappahannock. Under the protection of 36 artillery pieces of the Union's Artillery Reserve, a new defensive line was chosen along the hills close to Scott's ford. "The wounded," Surgeon Stevens wrote, "were taken to an immense field hospital at Potomac Creek, when hospital tents sufficient to accommodate 8,000 wounded men were erected in a locality where cool breezes could play freely among the encampments, and where pure water could be obtained." [58]

At 2 a.m., May 5, the 77th moved toward Scott's Ford to cross the Rappahannock. Already fatigued by two days of marching and fighting, the regiment's march over the hilly terrain made the night withdrawal slow and difficult. The Third Brigade's 49th New York formed Howe's rear guard, and Companies G, I, and K were nearly left behind. Sergeant Sumner A. Smith wrote in his diary:

> After having repulsed the enemy several times, we returned to the line, where darkness found us waiting for the order to move, and wondering why it did not come. We learned afterwards that an order had been given, at the right, to move off quietly, which was repeated along the line, until it reached an interval between companies and those beyond had received no orders. Most of the regiment had gone some distance, when the absence of three companies was discovered and reported to Colonel Bidwell, who

rode back to see for himself. It was too true. Companies G, I, and K were missing. Colonel Bidwell . . . sent one of his aides to bring them in. In a short time he returned and reported that the enemy had advanced and the men could not be found.

Colonel Bidwell then asked, 'Who will go and bring in these men?' His orderly, Robert H. Johnson, familiarly known as 'Tip' Johnson, knowing where they had been before dark, said he would find them . . . He rode far to the left, arriving at some logs, where he dismounted, when he heard the click of a musket, and a voice which he recognized as belonging to Gustavus Vedder of Company I called out, 'Halt, who comes there?' to which 'Tip' gladly responded, 'A friend, don't you know me, Gus?' 'Who are you anyhow?' demanded Vedder. The enemy's pickets were now awake and silence was in order. Johnson soon found his way to his men and whispered instructions. All very gently moved back, carrying their muskets at 'trail,' ready at any moment for action. The Confederate skirmishers were dimly seen in the darkness marching in the same direction as the men of the 49th Regiment, but at a respectful distance. When the men reached the regiment, all were happy to see them again, for it was their belief that they had been captured. [59]

As the 77th approached Scott's Ford, they heard the echoing boom of Confederate artillery, and could follow the arcing enemy shells by their glowing fuses from Alexander and Hardaway's batteries. Major Thomas Hyde, marching with the 7th Maine, vividly recalled, "When we got down near the pontoon bridges, we found the enemy thought they had our range and were dropping shells toward them from several directions. The firing was like so many graceful curves of rockets, but not a bridge, animal, or man was hit." Sixth

Corps artillery returned the Confederate's fire until they were ordered to retire to the ford. [60]

Having crossed the Rappahannock River, the 77th established camp in a light rain, one mile north from Scott's Ford on the Falmouth Road. They awoke the next morning at daylight to a pouring rainstorm. As the men started fires to make their breakfast, the smoke from the camp fires told of their whereabouts, and Confederate batteries sent some shells into their camp from across the river. The regiment scrambled to get out of range, leaving their breakfast for another time.

Hooker had also decided to withdraw the Army of the Potomac from Chancellorsville on May 5. His force, led by the Federal artillery, began an orderly crossing of the Rappahannock at 7:15 a.m. Hooker successfully sent most of his army across the river before Lee knew his army's crossing had begun. Hooker's men completed their retreat just after daylight on May 6. Greatly fatigued, and visibly discouraged, Hooker's troops slowly marched back to their old camp grounds around Falmouth. Thus ended the Chancellorsville campaign.

Hooker's campaign to crush Robert E. Lee's army was bloody, to say the least, incurring 17,304 casualties. Sedgwick's Sixth Corps was hit hardest with 4,611 out of action. Of these, 850 dead, wounded, and missing came from the 77th's Third Brigade. The 21st New Jersey, and the 20th, and 33rd New York regiments amassed the heaviest casualties numbering over 200 each. Although less affected in battle, the 77th crossed the Rappahannock minus 83 dead, wounded, and missing soldiers.

One death profoundly shook the 77th. After being mortally wounded urging his men forward at Lee's Hill, Captain Luther Wheeler was brought to a barn in Fredericksburg filled with injured

Union soldiers. That evening, after hours of agony, Wheeler succumbed to his fatal wound. Colonel Winsor B. French, the captain's good friend, wrote home, "Oh, my good and true Captain Wheeler, he is gone. He was a noble man, and I challenge the service to furnish his *equal*. Sympathies with his family, and tell them I shed tears on the battle field for my companion and friend in arms." The officers of the 77th gathered in French's tent and issued a resolution to be sent to Luther Wheeler's parents in Saratoga Springs, and published in several newspapers in Saratoga, Essex, and Washington counties in New York.

> *Whereas*, It has pleased kind Providence to remove from among us our senior Captain, the brave, manly and much esteemed Capt. Luther M. Wheeler, who fell on the 3d of May last, while leading his command through the enemy works, which crown the heights of Fredericksburg; therefore, be it
>
> *Resolved*, That we deeply deplore and mourn the loss of an officer who never flinched from duty; who commanded the entire respect of every member of the regiment; who was loved and willingly obeyed in a manner seldom equaled and never excelled; and we feel that in losing this officer, we have lost also, a *companion* and a *friend*, whose affability, truthfulness, social qualities and mental attainments are seldom found equaled in one so young, and by which he had so deeply endeared himself to us that his loss is irreparable.
>
> *Resolved*, That inasmuch as he fell while bravely fighting under his country's flag; -- and as the true soldier only wishes to die, -- he has won the proud distinction of adding his name to the patriotic heroes of history; and we feel that though the tears of bitter grief bedew the lustre of his crown, yet there is lustre emanating therefrom reflecting

honor on his regiment, and the army with which he so faithfully served. [61]

Luther Wheeler's demise was equally shattering to those who knew him back in upstate New York. After Captain Wheeler died, Chaplain Norman Fox had his body embalmed and shipped express to Saratoga Springs. Knowing only that captain was severely wounded, a large crowd gathered at the train station to greet Wheeler. Shock rippled through the expectant greeters when Luther Wheeler's coffin was taken from the train. "Few were prepared to hear of his death, and when the intelligence came, it produced as profound a feeling of sorrow as has never been manifested in this community." [62]

Captain Luther M. Wheeler (NYSDMNA)

The next day a public meeting was held to make arrangements for Captain Wheeler's funeral. To accommodate the expected crowd, the site for the funeral was changed from the Methodist to the larger Baptist church. The day of the funeral, the procession, which was nearly a quarter mile long, proceeded to the residence of Luther Wheeler's father, where the remains were taken in charge, and conveyed to the Baptist church. The hearse, drawn by four gray horses, carried Luther Wheeler's coffin down Broadway. "The streets were lined with people on both sides, nearly the whole population of the village, and hundreds from the country, being out." [63]

Wheeler's funeral service lasted nearly two hours. Rev. David Tully, ex-chaplain of the 77th, opened with a moving prayer. Rev. Spalding of the Methodist church offered the sermon that "consisted almost wholly of a feeling and eloquent tribute to the gallant dead." The Methodist preacher "sketched his traits of character – his manliness, his modesty, his kindness of heart, his youth, his patriotism – giving instances of his early life, as illustrative of his qualities as a leader, and his nobility of nature, culminating in the gallant young patriot, who had freely given up his life on his country's altar." [64]

At the close of the services the funeral procession was reformed, and proceeded to Greenridge Cemetery "followed by a great throng of peoples of all ages and both sexes." Wheeler's open grave rested in a declivity, with high ground on all sides, forming a large amphitheater. Along the high ground stood nearly 3,000 mourners "having fulfilled their office by committing to the earth the remains of the honored dead." Colonel James B. McKean, still in ill health stepped forward "and occupied about fifteen minutes in a glowing and elegant tribute to the deceased." McKean ended his tribute by saying, "Captain Wheeler! Captain Wheeler! My heroic young friend, you have not died in vain. The flag of your country is going on to victory. That dear country for which you have paid the price of your precious life shall yet be saved. No, you have not died in vain." That said, the mourners of Captain Luther Wheeler slowly returned to their homes. [65]

Soon after Luther Wheeler's burial, his father, Frank D. Wheeler received an undated letter from Lieutenant Gilbert Tomas (Co. C). Thomas told of Wheeler's apparent presentiment of his coming death. "A short time before the battle in which he fell, he remarked," wrote Lieutenant Thomas, "if we cross the river I shall be wounded or killed." Captain Wheeler told Captain Stephen Horton that "he should be killed in the battle of Fredericksburg." Lieutenant Laurans VanDemark (Co. C) also reported that Wheeler was depressed before the battle. To VanDenmark, he said, "I know I will be killed in the next battle." After several weeks of illness in the care of Captain Wheeler, Lieutenant VanDenmark was about to embark to a field hospital, but turned to Wheeler and said, "Captain, you better go with me for you have not been well for a week & the Dr. says you are unfit for duty." Looking at the concerned lieutenant, Luther Wheeler, in a low voice, responded, "I can go and I do not want my men to go where I do not myself. Good bye, Van . . . You will never see me again. I am glad you are going to the hospital, for I think you would be shot too if you went into the fight." [66]

9

"WE CAN WHIP THEM ON OUR OWN SOIL"

May 8, from near Scott's Ford, the 77th trudged along the Falmouth Road in a pouring rain back to the vicinity of White Oak Church, and encamped about one mile to the rear of its old camp. The regiment was pleased to camp "where the ground had been unoccupied, and where a growth of young pines, and, in places, considerable groves of oak timber, afforded far more attractive surroundings than the old quarters." [1]

On the afternoon of May 8, 26 Union surgeons were ordered to report to Scott's Ford with their instruments. Five wagon loads of medical supplies accompanied the medical doctors. Their instructions were to report to Assistant Surgeon M. F. Asche U. S. A. when they would be sent under a flag of truce across the Rappahannock to take care of the wounded. Over 400 wagons of the Union Ambulance Corps eventually lined the dirt roads leading down to United States

Mine Ford and Scott's ford. Confederate medical supplies were sorely lacking to treat the wounded, and numerous wagons holding beef, brandy, whiskey, and delicacies were forwarded through the lines by the Union army. Sedgwick's wounded on Salem Ridge were brought to Scott's Ford and Fredericksburg.

On the morning of May 10, Surgeon Stevens was ordered to Bank's Ford where he was to receive Union wounded officers forwarded from behind Confederate lines. At the ford, Stevens found a boat and a flag of truce at his disposal. On the south bank of the Rappahannock, the surgeon approached the Southern officer in command, who politely declared he knew nothing of wounded Union officers to be transported back across the river to Federal lines. Not to be deterred, the surgeon addressed a note to Brigadier General Cadmus Wilcox alerting him to his mission of mercy, but Wilcox also claimed ignorance. "There are plenty of federal officers here . . . and we shall be glad to send them across to your lines at any time when General Hooker shall apply to General Lee for them; but I know of no arrangements of the kind now." Certain that arrangements for the transfer of the wounded had been made, but that Wilcox had not yet received them, Stevens decided to remain on the south bank of the river. The surgeon spent the day among the Rebels,

> . . . conversing with their officers, while his boatmen, having with them a canteen of whiskey, soon made themselves very popular with the crowd of rebel soldiers who gathered about, dressed in motley colors, buff, blue, gray, butternut, and colors indescribable. They were all in good humor and lively, and the hours passed pleasantly, as the men from two opposing armies chatted in the shade of some oak trees. [2]

When it became clear that the arrival of wounded officers was not to be, Stevens sought and obtained permission from General

Wilcox to retrieve the remains of Colonel Gilliam VanHoghten of the 21st New Jersey regiment, who was mortally wounded at Salem Church and died the next day. George Stevens, along with Surgeon McNeil of the 21st New Jersey and a party of men, proceeded to where the colonel was buried, and after uncovering the grave, brought his body to Bank's Ford and across the river to the 21st New Jersey's camp. From there, Stevens reported to Hooker's headquarters where he discovered that no agreement to receive wounded Federal officers had been concluded until late in the day. Except for returning VanHoghten's body to his regiment, the surgeon felt he had wasted a day when he could have been treating the wounded in his division's field hospital.

The Sixth Corp's regiments quickly settled into their camps in hopes of remaining there for some time before the inevitable next campaign began. Where there was no shelter from the sun, small pines were transplanted to company streets to provide shade. At Second Division headquarters, Albion Howe oversaw the building of "a most elegant hall" festooned with boughs of red cedar and pine. George Stevens described the structure as "a wonder of architectural beauty as well as exquisite taste and ingenuity. Its alcoves, its vestibules and the arches, were marvels of elegance." The division's hall became the locus of evening entertainment attended by officers and pretty young ladies from the surrounding countryside, "while bands discoursed stirring music." [3]

The 77th's camp was also adorned with arches and bowers formed from pine and cedar boughs. At regimental headquarters, "a palace of green arose among the trees near our tents." Surgeon Stevens and Quartermaster Thomas W. White were busy erecting the building for the reception of their wives who were traveling south from upstate New York for a planned reunion. "For days," Stevens wrote, "mule teams hauled huge loads of cedar boughs, which were woven into massive pillars or elegantly turned arches, and the structure rose like one of those fair bowers we read of in fairy tales." [4]

In the relatively peaceful setting in camp, the soldiers of the Union army took some time assessing the battles at Second Fredericksburg, Salem Church, and Scott's Ford. Burnside's catastrophic defeat the previous December severely demoralized the Army of the Potomac, but Hooker's retreat was viewed by the soldiers of the 77th as little more than difficult setback rather than a crushing defeat. Though their confidence in Hooker was shaken by his poor performance, the Empire State soldiers were not willing to place sole blame on Hooker for their defeat by Lee's men. Captain Martin Lennon took time to express his thoughts about Hooker, the late campaign, and the need and the ability of the Army of the Potomac.

> I think that Hooker's plan, as far as I can learn it, was one of the most splendid ever conceived, and also think that as far as he was concerned, he did his best to have it successful; but that there is fault in some one is evident from the fact that we did not succeed in our undertaking. It is idle to speculate, however. The moral effect is more to be feared at the north than in the army. There is no one in the army but what is satisfied that all was done that could be done.
>
> There are a great many two years regiments going home now, which is weakening the army, and the deficiency must be supplied from the north, and we needed a decisive victory to infuse a little patriotic spirit into the people in order to have them come willingly. Our operations, however, have demonstrated two things: 1st, that the heights of Fredericksburg can be taken; and 2d, that they can be whipped some time or another. [5]

Although the Chancellorsville Campaign ended in defeat for the Army of the Potomac, the reputation of Sedgwick and the Sixth Corps was greatly enhanced for their heroic performance in a most difficult position during Hooker's offensive. The *spirit de corps* of the Sixth Corps rose to new heights as the soldiers of Sedgwick's command bonded through the knowledge that they had held their own in battle with Robert E. Lee's army. Surgeon Stevens spoke not only for the Sixth Corps but also for the battle-tested 77th:

> The corps had passed through a fearful ordeal, and had shown itself to be made of heroic material. No two more brilliant feats had been performed during the war, than the storming of the heights of Fredericksburg, and the splendid resistance when surrounded and attacked by overwhelming forces. The men came out of the fight, not demoralized, but as ready to scale those terrible heights again, if called upon, as they had been on the 3d of May. [6]

Uncle John Sedgwick's performance during battle endeared him to the men of the 77th along with many others of the Sixth Corps. George Stevens wrote glowingly of the general:

> General Sedgwick had manifested during the fights, those masterly qualities which made him one of the greatest soldiers of the age. His conduct on the retreat was cool and unimpassioned. Personally examining every part of the ground in front and rear, riding from one end of the line to the other, now ordering a battery placed at some commanding point, and now looking out a new position to which his troops might fall back in case of necessity, he was everywhere present, full of energy, as determined to save as he had been to win. [7]

The Army of the Potomac was far from broken after the Chancellorsville Campaign. It was now a well-seasoned veteran army determined to slug it out and to put down the rebellion and to restore the republic. However, the Union soldier increasingly felt a disconnect with those back home who, unlike them, had never seen the horror of battle or heard the screams of the wounded and groans of the dying. Captain Orrin Rugg was intensely aware that life back home at the spas in Saratoga Springs was no comparison to the life of a soldier.

> I suppose Saratoga is now putting on her gayday dress & preparing to receive visitors. A person traveling through the north would not know that there was a war going on. So near from anything they could see there, everything moves just the same. The busy crowds still pursue the almighty dollar or the phantom pleasure with the same eagerness as ever. While we are down here suffering all the inconveniences of a soldier's life, to say nothing of the suffering and death incident to war, to which we are so often exposed. [8]

Still, the soldiers of the 77th longed for home, to be reunited with family and friends. Private Alonzo Bump wrote to his wife, Mary, "i was Dreeaming About you all night. I thought that thiss wicked war was over . . . i hope thiss wicked ware will Bee endid Before Long so i can come home to my Little family once more and if it don't end thiss sumar i hope that god will Spare my Life to come home when it Dos end . . . i send you a thousan sweat kisses in thiss Letter and wish i was thair to Press them to your cheeak." [9]

While encamped near White Oak Church, the Third Brigade was assembled at the hour of evening parade, and formed a hollow square. Earlier, a lieutenant from the 21st New Jersey regiment had been tried by a court martial and convicted of cowardice during the assault on Marye's Heights. The convicted lieutenant was marched to the center of the square, his sentence read to him, which was dismissal from the army in disgrace. The adjutant general of the brigade then executed the details of the sentence. George Stevens described the somber scene: "The sword of the cowardly officer was taken from him and broken over his head; his shoulder-straps and buttons were then cut off, and his pistol broken and thrown away." To complete his public humiliation, "The sentence, and the manner of its execution, were ordered to be published in the newspapers of the county where the regiment was raised." [10]

The same evening, an equally depressing scene took place involving the 77th. The regiment was called out and formed in line, and Private Lewis Burke (Co. F) was brought before his fellow soldiers. Where courage in battle was the highest of virtues in the Civil War, his sin was that of cowardice in the regiment's assault of the heights behind Fredericksburg. His sentence was read, as it was with the cowardly lieutenant of the 21st New Jersey; the blue cord on his coat was cut off, and a placard marked "Coward" was hung from his neck. With fixed bayonets pointed at his back, he was marched off in disgrace to the encampment, while the 77th's regimental band playing "The Rogues' March." Private Burke joined the mutineers from the 20th New York at Dry Tortugas. Like some of the others, he was sentenced to hard labor, without pay or allowance to serve out his time. [11]

Stevens reflected later that evening, "As we looked upon the execution of these humiliating sentences, we could not help feeling how much better it would have been to have fallen nobly on the field of battle, honored and lamented, than to live to be thus degrade and despised. It had never been so forcibly impressed upon our minds, how much better it was to die nobly than to live in disgrace." Still reeling from the death of Captain Luther Wheeler, the surgeon went on, "When we thought of the noble Wheeler and his brave companions, who had given their lives for their country on yonder heights, and then turned to the sickening scene before us, we could but exclaim, 'How are the dead to be envied!'" [12]

While the Army of the Potomac licked its wounds in the Union camps in the vicinity of White Oak Church, General Robert E. Lee was not content to remain entrenched along the heights behind Fredericksburg. He had no wish to fight another battle on the Rappahannock line. Rather, the Southern general desired to take the war to the North. Another summer campaign in Virginia, Lee surmised, would prevent the planting and harvesting of much needed crops. Once across the Potomac, Lee's hungry army could feast off of the fertile fields of Maryland and Pennsylvania. Furthermore, a Confederate invasion on northern soil might relieve pressure on besieged Vicksburg in the west, drawing Union troops east to counter Lee. Also, if England and France saw an aggressive and victorious Southern army, either might enter the war on behalf of the beleaguered Confederacy. Finally, a Confederate victory on northern soil would strengthen the northern peace movement raising the possibility of the Union suing for peace on Richmond's terms.

Before Lee could launch a campaign north, matters of high command demanded his attention. Stonewall Jackson's death necessitated a new commander of the Second Corps. Lee had long believed that the two corps of the Army of Virginia, each containing some 30,000 troops, was too large for one general to manage in battle. To remedy this evil, he added a third corps. Lieutenant General Richard Ewell, an eccentric personality who had proven himself in battle and a good manager of troops, was assigned command of the Second Corps. Aggressive, but sometimes careless, Lieutenant General Ambrose Powell Hill was given command of the newly formed Third

Corps. Lee's "Old Warhorse," Lieutenant General James Longstreet retained his command of the First Corps. By the time he was prepared to cross the Potomac, Lee had under his command 80,000 men of all arms – 67,600 infantry and artillery and 12,400 cavalry under the command of Major General J. E. B. Stuart.

While Lee was reorganizing the Army of Northern Virginia, Joseph Hooker's army was in the midst of command turmoil. After the defeat at Chancellorsville, nearly all of his corps commanders regarded him unfit to command the Army of the Potomac. As early as May 7, with the defeated Union army scarcely in its camps around Falmouth and White Oak Church, and with President Lincoln and General-in-Chief Henry Halleck present to appraise the defeat, Hooker's detractors went to work. General Halleck, who despised Joe Hooker, called the corps commanders into council and learned of their great displeasure with his performance at Chancellorsville. Henry Slocum, Twelfth Corps commander, sought but failed to produce a petition to dismiss Hooker and put Fifth Corps Major General Gordon Meade in his place. Despite being deeply disturbed by the dissension and disloyalty in the officer corps, Lincoln could not find a qualified general who actually wanted to command the Union army. Too, the president had earlier gone on record as supporting Hooker; to dismiss him would signal dissension and weakness within his administration. Consequently, Lincoln would wait and watch, hoping to find a replacement for command of the army or that Hooker could unite his corps generals and bring about a defeat of Lee and his southern troops in the field.

In the lull between campaigns, the Army of the Potomac also experienced organizational change. Within a week of the battle, Hooker initiated a sweeping reform of the artillery. Special orders No. 128 removed the batteries from divisions, regrouped them, and attached them to the army corps. Turning to the cavalry corps,

Hooker shuffled off disappointing General George Stoneman to a desk job in Washington and appointed Major General Alfred Pleasanton to command the Union horse soldiers. The Second Corps commander, Major General Darius Couch, refused to serve under Hooker and was replaced with the competent Major General Winfield Scott Hancock. The Light Division, designed to travel light and move fast, was badly mauled assaulting Marye's Heights. Further weakened by the expiration of enlistments, the Light Division was disbanded and its regiments were distributed to fill gaps in the corps. The 61st Pennsylvania and the 43rd New York regiments were reassigned to the 77th's brigade, replacing the 20th and 33rd New York regiments who mustered out shortly after the Chancellorsville Campaign. The remaining three-year men of the 33rd New York went to the 49th New York.

By June, Lee was set to launch what would become known as the Gettysburg Campaign. The Army of Virginia's three corps was to withdraw westward from the Rappahannock defenses, the Wilderness region west of Fredericksburg screening Lee's opening moves. Once beyond the Wilderness, the Confederate corps would reassemble at Culpeper, a court house village on the Orange & Alexandria Railroad.

Early in the morning on June 3, Lafayette McLaws' division of Longstreet's corps moved out of its entrenchments behind Fredericksburg. That afternoon John B. Hood's division, also from Longstreet's corps, filed out from its position to the south of the Rapidan River toward Culpeper. Longstreet's third division, under George Pickett, remained in place at Hanover Junction to guard Richmond. Over the next two days, Richard Ewell's three divisions joined the march to Culpeper. As Lee shifted two-thirds of his army to the northwest, A. P. Hill's nearly 27,000 troops remained entrenched behind Fredericksburg to observe Hooker and fix him in place long enough to allow the rest of the Confederate army to steal several day's marches on the Federals.

Hints of Confederate activity across the Rappahannock fast reached Joe Hooker's headquarters. Sometime during the day, June 4, Colonel George Sharpe of the Bureau of Military Information reported considerable movement of Confederate troops away from their camps. Hooker was quick to react. He ordered a pair of pontoon bridges thrown across the river just below the mouth of Deep Run (Franklin's Crossing), downriver from Fredericksburg, and ordered a division of Sedgwick's Sixth Corps to cross the Rappahannock for a reconnaissance in force "to learn, if possible, what the enemy is about." Sedgwick selected Howe's Second Division to make the crossing. George Stevens recalled that the 77th "left camp on the morning of June 5, one of the loveliest days, and, taking the road we had already trod on two occasions, halted in the valley of the Rappahannock, on the very spot where we had rested at the first and second battles of Fredericksburg, and prepared, for a third time within six months, to cross the river." [13]

Assembling Howe's division for the crossing took a good part of the day as pontoons and artillery batteries formed long lines behind a slight ridge that ran parallel to the river, and infantry regiments marched and countermarched to get into position. The 77th rested behind the ridge while other elements of the Second division maneuvered into place. At about 5 p.m., along with other curious soldiers of the regiment, Surgeon Stevens stood atop the ridge and gazed "across the river, where the enemy had turned the rifle pits thrown up by our first division, to their own use; and, in return, the rebels raised their heads above the breastworks, or ventured to the river side, wondering what could be the intention of the army, so recently driven from these grounds, in making such preparations for another crossing." [14]

Just then, Union engineers began drawing the pontoons to the edge of the river, and the 77th was summoned to assist in their unloading. From their rifle pits on opposite sides of the river, Confederate sharpshooters opened a brisk fire, killing Sergeant Rex Havens (Co. A), shot through the head, and wounding several others. Sixth Corps artillery pieces quickly rolled out upon the river plain and opened up a fierce cannonade, "until the whole plain, on the further side, was a sheet of flame from the bursting of shells, and the huge clouds of dust, plowed up by shrieking missiles, rose so as to obscure the heights." [15]

The heavy artillery fire sent the Confederate pickets and sharpshooters scampering for cover. Albion Howe ordered the 5th Vermont and several companies of the 26th New Jersey to cross the river and establish a foothold. The Yankee soldiers leaped into pontoon boats under the cover of Federal artillery fire and quickly paddled across the river. Some of the 5th Vermont officers' wives were still with the Second Division, and they had the dubious thrill of watching their husbands go into battle. Once on the south bank, the Green Mountain Boys and Jerseymen rushed from the bank and charged the rifle pits, quickly overwhelming the Rebel pickets and sharpshooters and capturing 75. The remaining regiments of the Vermont Brigade crossed in boats to secure the Sixth Corps bridgehead, and Union engineers soon completed the bridge unhindered by Confederate guns. Throughout the remainder of the day, the Green Mountain Boys skirmished with elements of Major General Richard H. Anderson's division until darkness.

The following morning, musket fire intensified as A. P. Hill added skirmishers to his front. In response to this increased pressure, Howe ordered the Third Brigade, now under the temporary command of Colonel Daniel Bidwell, to cross the river. Bidwell had replaced Brigadier General Neill, who was still recovering from a wound he received when his horse was shot from underneath him a month earlier at Scott's Ford. The 1st New Jersey Brigade crossed also and relieved the battle-weary Vermont Brigade. The 77th took position among the ruins of Alfred Bernard's mansion, "Mannsfield," which earlier served as Second Division's field hospital during Burnside's Fredericksburg Campaign. George Stevens observed, "Now nothing but the bare walls and heaps of rubbish marked the place where the beautiful residence had stood." He disapprovingly wrote, "A regiment of Mississippians had occupied the place, and had ruthlessly and willfully burned it." Still, "the fine chestnuts and the broad-spreading oaks afforded" the 77th "as luxurious a shade as in the palmy days when the old bachelor proprietor lounged beneath their shadow." [16]

The Second Division's picket line extended nearly to the Richmond, Fredericksburg & Potomac Railroad, forming a semicircle radiating from the pontoon bridge. A. P. Hill's troops also formed a strong picket, and the two lines of skirmishers were within a few yards of each other. "It was a beautiful Sabbath Day," Stevens recalled, "and all day long the troops lay upon the plain, wondering what was to be done." The 77th marveled that Confederate batteries on the heights remained silent with the entire Second Division arrayed in clear view on the open river plain. Although the day was marked by sporadic skirmish fire, and the occasional shell exploded among some of the houses on the right of Howe's line, A. P. Hill concluded that the Sixth Corps advance across the Rappahannock was merely a reconnaissance, rather than an attack. [17]

Eventually a quasi-truce was observed, and blue and gray slowly began meeting between the lines. Yankee and Johnnie Reb shook hands and inquired about each other's regiments. George Stevens reminisced, "There came at this time, to each company of one regiment, a copy of the *New York Observer, Independent, Christian Examiner,*

Evangelist, and other papers, and Mr. Alvord, the agent of the Tract Society, had just been among the men, distributing copies of the *American Messenger.* These were soon collected and carried over to be exchanged for copies of the *Richmond Enquirer, Sentinel,* and *Examiner.* The trade was not kept wholly within the limits of literary exchange, but sugar and coffee passed into the rebels' hands in return for plugs of tobacco." At length, Albion Howe felt it got too friendly between the lines and ordered the fraternization stopped. Some of the 77th impishly "declared that they were acting the part of colporteurs to the barbarian rebels, and, if they had been allowed to continue the distribution of religious papers among them, they would soon be convinced of the errors of their ways, and desist from further fighting." [18]

After two days, the 77th, with the Second Division, recrossed the Rappahannock River on the night of June 8, to be replaced by the First Division. The New Yorkers withdrew to Stafford Heights and bivouacked for the remainder of the evening. They remained encamped on the heights for several days wondering what Hooker's next move might be. While there, the artillery on the heights on either side the river exchanged shots. Surgeon Stevens watched "The 32-pounders on our hills sending their huge shot across the opposite heights, and the rebel guns replying, sometimes with shells of the most improved pattern, and at other times throwing huge pieces of railroad iron." [19]

As Ewell and Longstreet's corps marched northward, J. E. B. Stuart was called to screen the infantry. June 5, Stuart's cavalry gathered at Brandy Station on the Orange & Alexandria Railroad. The ostentatious Confederate cavalier held a grand review of his mounted legions. Guests, mostly female, were invited from Culpeper and surrounding counties. Special trains carrying the expectant visitors rolled into Brandy Station. As he led a cavalcade of staff officers to the reviewing stand, trumpets heralded his coming and women and girls strewed his path with flowers. The assembled cavalry brigades stretched a mile and a half before the excited spectators. After Stuart and his staff galloped past the line in review, the Southern troopers saluted the reviewing stand in columns of squadrons. In the evening there was an outdoor ball, lit by soft moonlight and the glow of bonfires.

After abandoning plans to take Richmond, Joe Hooker focused on shadowing the Army of Virginia on their march northward. To ascertain the extent of Lee's movements, Hooker ordered a reconnaissance in force consisting of Pleasanton's Cavalry Corps, Brigadier General David Russell's brigade from the First Division Sixth Corps, Brigadier General Albert Ames brigade from First Division Eleventh Corps, and six batteries of artillery. Pleasanton surprised Stuart's Rebel cavalry still encamped at Brandy Station on June 9. The ensuing battle was the biggest cavalry fight of the war. Although Stuart held the field in the end, for the first time Union mounted troopers held their own in battle against Rebel cavalry. More importantly, Hooker now discovered that Lee was maneuvering his army to begin an invasion of the North.

Hooker knew Lee was moving north, but did not have clear intelligence as to the location of the three corps of the Army of Northern Virginia and where they were bound. The answer came from an unexpected source on June 12. Charley Wright, a contraband from Culpeper and a former servant in Lee's army, provided the Bureau of Military Information with specific knowledge of the whereabouts of the Rebel army. Ewell and Longstreet had marched through Culpeper. Ewell had moved off to the Shenandoah Valley, with Longstreet to follow, and A. P. Hill was still at Fredericksburg. This intelligence was good enough for Hooker, and he set the Army of the Potomac in pursuit of Lee. [20]

Joe Hooker would march north from Falmouth, keeping his army between the Army of Northern Virginia and Washington. The Northern general split his army into two major columns. The westernmost column, under the command of Major General John Reynolds, was to initially aim for Manassas Junction to block any sudden advance by Lee on Washington. Hooker's headquarters traveled with the second column, consisting of the Second, Sixth, and Twelfth Corps, and the reserve artillery. The Sixth Corps would act as a rear guard protecting against a sweep around the army's right flank.

On June 13, the Army of the Potomac began its pursuit of Lee's army. At 10 p.m., forming Hooker's rear guard, the Sixth Corps brigades began vacating their camps. As they marched, they were met by a rolling thunderstorm, dampening the soldiers' enthusiasm. Surgeon Stevens remembered the intense darkness. "Our route for a long time lay through a thick woods, where the branches of the trees, meeting over our heads, shut out the little light that might have penetrated the thunder clouds, and the column was shut in perfect darkness." The downpour muddied the road, bogging down artillery batteries and their crews. "Our men," Stevens wrote, "stumbled over stones and fallen trees, often falling beneath the feet of the horses. Men fell over logs and stones, breaking their legs and arms." In time the rain ceased, and the 77th emerged from the woods to an open road. Still, the going was hard. The road was unevenly corduroyed and many of the logs were rotted through. Wet and slippery from the rain, many soldiers stumbled, some tumbling headlong down the steep road embankments. Some of the more fortunate laughed at their less fortunate brethren and called out, "Have you a pass to go down there?" At 3 a.m., the New Yorkers halted at Potomac Creek, and the weary soldiers slept as best they could on the wet ground. [21]

The 77th was awakened at daylight by the sound of creaking wagons and the braying of mules. "All day long," George Stevens wrote, "the trains crowded by, four and five wagons abreast; the drivers shouting and lashing their beasts to their greatest speed." At the same time, the large field hospitals at Potomac Creek were being dismantled. Heaps piled high with bedding, glass and earthenware, instruments and medicines, cooking pots, and other utensils that couldn't be carried away with the moving army were burned. At sundown, amid the sounds of an army on the move, McKean's Sunday School Boys gathered in a pine grove on a nearby knoll at the beckoning of Chaplain Norman Fox. The chaplain led the men in prayer, followed by the singing of familiar hymns. The service ended with a heartfelt prayer of thanksgiving and an earnest plea for protection from the inevitable fury that was to come. [22]

The same day the 77th left their camp and joined the Union army's track northward to counter Lee. Confederate Richard Ewell's column was fast approaching the Federal garrison, commanded by Major General Robert H. Milroy, at Winchester in the Shenandoah Valley. Defending the town were three forts on high ground north and west of Winchester. Jubal Early pointed out to Ewell higher ground further to the west, a ridgeline that dominated the forts. He suggested a flanking march to take the ridge and place artillery batteries there to wreak havoc on the fort. Ewell agreed, and on Sunday, June 14, Early set off on his flanking march with three brigades and seven batteries of artillery. In the meantime, Ewell held Milroy's attention with loud demonstrations south of Winchester.

As the 77th quietly gathered around Chaplain Fox in the pine grove for prayer pleading for protection in future battles, Early's twenty guns were run up the crest of the ridge into firing position and fired in unison. The defenders were completely overwhelmed by the storm of shells. When the cannonade lifted, Harry Hays' Louisiana Tigers charged into the fort, and the Yankees fled in a panic out the back of the fort. Watching through his field glasses, Ewell was ecstatic. "Hurrah for the Louisiana boys!" he shouted. "There's Early! I hope the fellow won't be hurt." Suddenly, Ewell was nearly knocked off his feet by a spent bullet hitting his chest. Receiving a bad bruise, Ewell shook off the blow and continued cheering his soldiers. [23]

Out maneuvered and out gunned, Milroy began evacuating the remaining forts at 1 a.m., June 15. To quietly slip away unnoticed, all wagons, ambulances, and artillery were left behind. Major General Edward "Allegheny" Johnson's division caught up with Milroy's fleeing Federals in the darkness. After a brief but wild fight, Milroy mentally broke and ordered everyone to get away as fast as they could. The Union general was the first to abandon the field. Union men ran off in all directions and hundreds threw down their weapons. Anderson's troops gobbled up more than 4,000 prisoners. With Winchester in Confederate hands, Richard Ewell had cleared Union troops from the Shenandoah Valley, and opened the way to the Potomac River and Maryland.

As Ewell's command in the Valley was driving Union troops out of their forts defending Winchester, the 77th once again took up the march in the van of Hooker's column. The regiment was in high spirits and pressed forward. Earlier in the day, the New Yorkers heard rumors that Lee had already made his way into Maryland and that Pennsylvania, perhaps even New York were threatened. Yet the regiment was undaunted and the men optimistically boasted, "We can whip them on our own soil. There is no man who cannot fight the better when it is for his own home." The march, however, was trying. In the dark, the pattern of march was to halt, stand idle in the ranks, and then to march for some distance before again stopping and standing in the ranks. In time, the regiment passed regimental camps of the Second and Twelfth Corps that had halted for the night. Bonfires of cedar burned in the camps "and the whole heavens were aglow with the flames." [24]

As morning dawned, the march quickly became a test of endurance. The heat and humidity was oppressive on a breezeless day. "The heat of the sun was almost intolerable, and the dust suffocating," Surgeon Stevens recalled, "Not a leaf stirred on the trees. Vegetation drooped under the scorching rays, and the clouds of dust were so dense, that one could not see the length of a regiment." Men began to fall from exhaustion. At first weary men received passes from Stevens who gave them a swig of whiskey and passes to ride in ambulances, but the medical wagons were crowded, and the exhausted soldier was left behind along the roadside. Private Alonzo Bump wrote to his wife, "thair was Lots of men sun struck on the march But we Could not stop to Do eny thing for them and a Grate meny of them dide i suppose. Mary it is hard to see a man Ly Beside the road and dy and no one can stop to help him." George Stevens vividly described the tortured scene in the oppressive heat and humidity:

> In every corner of the rail fences, and under every tree and bush, groups of men, with faces glowing with redness, some with streams of perspiration rolling down their cheeks, others with their red faces dry and feverish, strewed the wayside and lined the hedges. Here the color-bearer of a regiment, his color laying beside him, lay gasping for breath; there a colonel, his horse tied to the fence, strove to fan the air into a little life with his broad-brimmed hat. Under one little clump of cedars might be an exhausted group of line officers, captains and lieutenants, and under the next, a number of enlisted men who could no longer keep the road. The spectacle along the roadside became

appalling. Regiments became like companies, and companies lost their entity; men were dying with sunstroke; and still the march was continued. [25]

After seventeen hours of constant marching, the 77th came within sight of the deserted town of Dumfries. Along with others of the Sixth Corps, the regiment filed into the adjoining fields of the little town. Feet blistered and raw, the bone-weary New Yorkers threw themselves to the ground for much needed rest. In short time the men made coffee and ate pork and hardtack before bedding down to catch some sleep. At 2 p.m. they were unceremoniously awakened to the call, "Fall-in!" but did not march until two hours later. When the 77th reached Occoquan Creek, they crossed at Wolf Run Shoals and rested for several hours. Many soldiers strolled down to the creek and enjoyed an invigorating swim in the cool water.

Greatly refreshed from their swim, the march was renewed, and the 77th "went shouting, singing and laughing, as though marching was but play." Before dark, they reached Fairfax Station. The Sixth Corps bivouacked in the wooded groves beside the turnpike leading to Manassas. Surveying the surrounding countryside, Surgeon Stevens offered a harsh review.

> It's naturally rich fields were grown up to scrub pines, mugworts and wormwood. Its fair valleys desolate of inhabitants, or inhabited by low white trash, as idle as ignorant . . . the fields were waste land, and the oak timber was all that seemed of any value . . . The scrub pines and dwarf oaks growing upon deserted tobacco fields, where the ridges were still plainly visible, showed that before the war indolence prevailed. [26]

M^CKEAN'S SUNDAY SCHOOL BOYS GO TO WAR

At the same time the 77th marched, Longstreet's First Corps was spread along the eastern base of the Blue Ridge Mountains. Richard Ewell's Confederates had pushed farther north and were crossing the Potomac at Shepherdstown and Williamsport. The crossings were marked by celebration. Bands played "The Bonnie Blue Flag," "Dixie" and repeatedly, "Maryland, My Maryland." When Marylander Brigadier General George Steuart reached the north bank, he dismounted from his horse and kissed the ground of his native state.

At 5 a.m. on June 19, the New York veterans were once again on the march, reaching Fairfax Court House before noon. They soon passed through Centreville. The Union defensive works around the war-torn village were formidable, having been much improved since the Second Battle at Bull Run. The village itself bore the depressing marks of war. George Stevens wrote, "The few dilapidated houses still remaining to mark the site of the village, presented a forlorn and pitiful appearance. Deserted by their owners, occupied as stables and storehouses, some of them falling in ruins, and all dirty and dilapidated, they were a mournful commentary on the ruthless destruction which follows in the footsteps of war." The 77th marched beyond Centreville along the Manassas Gap Railroad. The track was mostly torn up and the railroad ties burned. Remnants of entire trains – wheels, axles, iron bands, braces, couplings – showed where they had been burned. Solid shot, bullets, and fragments of shells marked where carloads of ammunition had exploded in the fires. [27]

After a hard day of marching, the Sixth Corps arrived at Bristoe Station on the Alexandria & Orange Railroad. All that remained intact at the rail station was the tower and windmill used for raising water into the large water tank. Except for the burned remains of what had once been a hotel, all other buildings had been destroyed. The

77th occupied a nearby pleasant field and settled into camp where they would stay for the next several days. The stifling heat and humidity broke and the men enjoyed pleasant weather, lounging in the shade of trees. Some walked along the railroad examining the ruins of burned out trains.

The morning after making camp in the vicinity of Bristoe Station, the 77th awoke to the distant booming of cannons. Major General Alfred Pleasanton's Federal cavalry was at Upperville, a village about four miles from Asby's Gap in the Blue Ridge Mountains. After a nearly day-long fight with J. E. B. Stuart's mounted troopers, Pleasanton withdrew his men back to Aldie for rest and refitting. At Upperville, Stuart denied Hooker of verified intelligence of Lee's movements. However, from Confederate deserters, Pleasanton learned that Longstreet's corps had passed through the Blue Mountain gaps into the Shenandoah Valley. Due to information given by some contrabands, A. P. Hill's Third Corps was also moving with Longstreet on the way to Maryland.

June 22, the day after the cavalry contest at Upperville, Lee started Ewell's Second Corps into Pennsylvania. Ewell's primary orders were to gather in supplies for the army. The Second Corps' three divisions were to advance in a fan-wise movement toward the Susquehanna River. They would cross the Pennsylvania line, marching in parallel columns, and enter the Cumberland Valley. Major Generals Rodes and Johnson's divisions would continue north through Greencastle, Chambersburg and Carlise toward the state capital, Harrisburg. If practicable, Ewell was instructed to capture it. Jubal Early's division would move in an easterly direction to Gettysburg and on to York.

Playing the role of commissary for the army, Ewell was most efficient. Greencastle was the first Pennsylvania settlement called upon for tribute. The requisition list included 120 pistols, 100 saddles and bridles, 1,000 pounds of leather, 2,000 pounds of lead, 200 currycombs, 12 boxes of tin, and such foodstuffs as onions, potatoes, radishes, and sauerkraut. The town council threw up its hands at these demands, after which the Confederates simply collected all they found or were offered and marched on. That proved to be the pattern among the main Rebel army units – they seized whatever they could of their tribute demands, but without resort to violence. [28]

Over the course of two weeks in Maryland and Pennsylvania, the Confederate army collected an estimated 6,700 barrels of flour, 7,900 bushels of wheat, 5,200 cattle, 1,000 hogs, 2,400 sheep, and more than 51,000 pounds of cured meat. No count appears to have been made of horses seized, but they were a favorite target and totaled in the thousands. These figures represent only supplies gathered by officially designated foraging parties. Most certainly, a large volume of farm stock and edibles gathered by Rebel soldiers foraging on their own account went untallied. [29]

The entrance of the Army of Northern Virginia into Pennsylvania triggered a panicked tidal wave of refugees fleeing toward the Susquehanna and Harrisburg. Merchants carrying their goods, bankers holding their receipts, farmers driving their stocks, free blacks evading Rebel slave-catchers, families fleeing the imagined horrors of an invading army – all rushed to the capital from southern Pennsylvania.

Panic also swept through Harrisburg. Charles Coffin of the *Boston Journal* reported the city's railroad stations were "crowded with an excited people – men, women, and children – with trunks, boxes, bundles; packages tied up in bed-blankets and quilts; mountains of luggage – tumbling it into cars, rushing here and there in a frantic manner; shouting, screaming, as if the Rebels were about to dash into town and lay it to ashes . . . There was a steady stream of teams thundering across the bridge; farmers from the Cumberland Valley, with their household furniture piled upon the great wagons . . .; bedding, tables, chairs, their wives and children perched on top' kettles and pails dangling underneath . . ." At a second bridge spanning the Susquehanna, a massive traffic jam formed while the bridge keeper insisted on collecting the set toll. [30]

Pleasanton's forays to break Stuart's cavalry screen of the Army of Northern Virginia were fruitless, but on June 24, John Babcock of the Bureau of Military Information telegraphed from Frederick that the main body of Lee's army was crossing the Potomac at Shepherdstown. Ewell's corps had passed that way two days before and was now in Pennsylvania. In a second telegram that day, Babcock reported that Longstreet and A. P. Hill were rapidly crossing. The lack of Rebels near Frederick and the South Mountain gaps pointed to the Confederate army marching northward to Pennsylvania. Old Joe Hooker was elated; now he had the intelligence he needed. That night he issued orders for the Army of the Potomac to begin crossing the Potomac at Edwards Ferry the next day.

On the evening of June 26, the 77th, along with the rest of the Sixth Corps, began the march to Edwards Ferry. A soaking drizzle made the night march most unpleasant. The unwary straggled fell behind only to be snatched up and taken prisoner by Colonel John Singleton Mosby's guerillas that shadowed the flanks and the rear of the Sixth Corps column. Before the sun appeared on the horizon, the 77th halted at Centreville, and "The men threw themselves upon the ground, and slept for two hours, while the rain beat upon them." At 6 a.m., the regiment was roused from where they lay and called to prepare to renew the march. While they tended to the making of coffee and waited for the final order to march, the only remaining building of note in the tattered village burst into flames. George Stevens angrily recalled, "While taking our coffee . . . some villain, belonging to the troops stationed at Centreville, set fire to the little Episcopal chapel that stood not far from us . . . Those vandals who follow an army, bent on nothing but destruction, are among the unavoidable evils of war, and even the most severe discipline is insufficient to effectually arrest all mischief of the kind." [31]

That night, the 77th reached the vicinity of Dranesville in Virginia's Fairfax County. Early in the morning, June 27, the regiment arrived at Edwards Ferry. All but one other corps of the Army of the Potomac had earlier crossed the Potomac and reassembled on the north bank's surrounding hills in preparation to renew the march. Without breaking rank, the New Yorkers stood in line for some hours as the soldiers of another corps crossed the pontoon bridge into Maryland. The 77th, with the Sixth Corps, followed. Chaplain Norman Fox remembered, "General Sedgwick . . . standing in the rain at the foot of that pontoon bridge, yelling at the teamsters to hurry them up, the long trains requiring so much time to cross. He wore that little round hat and a private's blouse. There was nothing in his dress to indicate his rank; but when he shouted at a slow teamster, it was apparent that he was a man to be obeyed." With the crossing of the Sixth Corps, Hooker's army was poised to follow Lee into Pennsylvania. [32]

This day, the festering relationship between Joe Hooker and Henry Halleck came to the breaking point. The count of the Army of the Potomac had been reduced to 90,000 due to the two-year and nine-month regiments returning home. The Bureau of Military Information's latest intelligence overstated Lee's strength by more than 10,000, but in reality the Southern commander could only call upon 80,000 soldiers. Hooker demanded reinforcements, but was initially rebuffed by Halleck. Fighting Joe then determined to gain the 10,000 men stationed at Harper's Ferry. Halleck's reply stung Hooker. The General-in-Chief asserted that he could not approve the abandonment of Harper's Ferry as it was an important garrison where a great deal of labor and expense had been expended on the works there. Hooker was furious and dashed off a telegram to Halleck and stated, "I am unable to comply with this condition with the means of my disposal, and earnestly request that I may at once be relieved from the position I occupy." Informed of Hooker's stance, President Lincoln reacted swiftly. Aware that the army's corps commanders wanted Major General George Meade for the post, Lincoln issued General Orders No. 194 relieving General Hooker as commander of the Army of the Potomac and appointing George Meade in his place. [33]

That night, James Hardie, of the army's adjutant-general's office, boarded a special train that carried him through Maryland to Frederick. On the morning of June 28th, at 3 a.m., Hardie entered the tent of the sleeping General Meade. He awakened Meade at his Fifth Corps headquarters. At first the startled Meade thought Hardie was there to either relieve him of command or to place him under arrest. After reading the orders Hardie had brought, Meade protested he was not desirous of command, but relented and later wrote to his wife, "as a soldier, I had nothing to do but accept and exert my utmost abilities to command success. This, so help me God, I will do . . ." As the sun began to rise, Meade and Hardie rode to Hooker's headquarters. Fighting Joe had learned of Hardie's arrival. Surmising his mission, Hooker was dressed in full uniform to meet them, and surrendered command of the Army of the Potomac to George Gordon Meade. [34]

While the command of the Army of the Potomac was thrust into Meade's hands, the 77th continued to march. From Edwards Ferry, the regiment passed through Poolesville, halting at Barnstown. The men left the road and settled into the quiet of a shaded grove of Chestnut trees with the intention of eating a meal of cooked rations.

The tolling of a church bell suddenly broke the silence, startling the New Yorkers. Training their eyes in the direction from which the sound came, the men spied a church nearly hidden by trees with churchgoers gathering for service. George Stevens years later wrote, "When the first surprise was over, the word passed from one to another, 'It is Sunday!' 'It is Sunday!' and they set up a shout that demonstrated that they had not forgotten to love the institutions of civilization after so long an absence from the civilized country." The Christian tones reminded the soldiers of peaceful days they left behind back home. [35]

Some of the 77th attended the worship service where the rector prayed for President Lincoln and Washington and prayed for peace. Afterwards, they returned to the regiment and continued the march, stopping for the night at Hyattstown, near Sugar Loaf Mountain. While there, they learned that Hooker had been relieved of command and that Major General Meade now commanded the Army of the Potomac. The sudden announcement was unexpected. Surgeon Stevens evinced an air of indignation upon hearing the news. "To deprive the leader of a great army of his command just upon the eve of a great battle . . . without some offense of a grave character, was an act unheard of before in the history of warfare." Nevertheless, they were as ready to fight under Meade as under Hooker, for the "men of the Union army fought for their country and not for their leaders." [36]

At 6 p.m. that Sunday evening, Fighting Joe Hooker made his farewells to the army. Later, Meade received intelligence given to Colonel Sharpe of the Bureau of Military Information from citizen-spies in Hagerstown that the Rebel army passing through Hagerstown totaled over 80,000 men with 275 pieces of artillery. By evening General Meade issued marching orders to his commanders. The next morning, June 29, the Army of Potomac would head northward in a fan-shaped advance toward the Pennsylvania line. The first day's march would span twenty miles, stretching from Emmitsburg on the west through Taneytown to Westminster on the east. That line, Meade ascertained, would effectively block any Rebel advance toward Baltimore or Washington from their reported positions in Pennsylvania.

Sunday, June 28, proved also to be momentous for Lee. At 10 p.m., the provost guard brought a spy to Lee's headquarters. The news was unsettling. The Army of the Potomac was in the vicinity of Frederick and marching north. As a consequence, Lee dispatched orders for the Army of Northern Virginia to reassemble. Earlier in the day, General Lee had ordered a concerted thrust across the Susquehanna and against Harrisburg. Ewell would lead the way, supported by Longstreet's corps. A. P. Hill would follow Jubal Early toward York. Their objective was to capture Harrisburg and to destroy the railroad network supplying Baltimore and Washington and the Union armies. Instead Ewell was ordered to march due south in the direction of Gettysburg.

From Hyattstown, at 5 a.m., the 77th was once again in the ranks and on the march. The Sixth Corps column snaked through Monroeville, New Market, Ridgeville, and Mount Airy Station, halting for the night at Sam's Creek. The trek north continued early in the morning on June 30. As the 77th passed through Westminster, its citizens rejoiced at the sight of the boys in blue. George Stevens remembered, "The people welcomed us with demonstrations of joy, which were all the earnest, as the rebel cavalry had, but two hours before, taken a hasty leave of them." By sundown the Sixth Corps arrived at Manchester, ending a fatiguing four-day, 100-mile march on Maryland roads. During the northward journey, the early summer days had been sultry, and the men, burdened by their guns, knapsacks, haversacks filled with five days rations, and forty rounds of cartridges, wilted under a burning sun. Yet, Stevens wrote, "The men kept up wonderfully during the trying campaign." Later that night, many of the tired marchers became inebriated upon finding the town well-stocked with rye whiskey. [37]

June 30 also found the lead point of the Army of Northern Virginia, Major General Henry Heth's division of A. P. Hill's Third Corps, at Cashtown, eight miles from Gettysburg. At 5 a.m., Wednesday, July 1, General Heth set off along the Chambersburg Pike to Gettysburg to search the town for military supplies; rumor had it that in Gettysburg there was a substantial supply of shoes for the taking, something much needed by his division. Holding the lead of the column was the brigade of Brigadier General James J. Archer, followed in order by the brigades of Joseph R. Davis, Johnston Pettigrew, and John Brockenbrough. Following them in support, came Major General Dorsey Pender's division. The march started out in the midst of scattered rain showers, but the sun soon broke through, heralding the oppressive, sultry heat of a Pennsylvania's summer day. Alongside the advance guard was Pegram's artillery battalion. Expecting to encounter nothing more threatening than skittish militia, Heth believed a few shots with a cannon would send them running.

Heth's column was not destined to brush aside untrained militia this fated day. Instead the advancing Confederate brigades would find before them 2,950 veteran troopers, in two cavalry brigades, commanded by Brigadier General John Buford. The hard fighting Buford had earlier been ordered to cover and protect the Yankee front at Gettysburg, and he was determined not to give up the town without a fight. Buford planned a defense in depth, fighting his troopers dismounted, using a series of ridges west of Gettysburg to delay the Rebel infantry he was certain that would "come booming" down the Chambersburg Pike. This move provided timely, for Federal infantry to come up in support. The night before, to gain early warning, the cavalry general set picket outposts three miles from town in a wide arc from the Hagerstown Road on the southwest to the Harrisburg Road on the northeast. Anticipating the fight that was sure to come, Buford's troopers slept that night on their arms. [38]

Shortly after 7 a.m., the advanced picket post of the 8th Illinois cavalry spotted a dust cloud over the Chambersburg Pike just west of Marsh Creek. Simultaneously, Buford's dismounted troopers were seen by Colonel Birkett D. Fry's 13th Alabama, marching at the head of Heth's column. Colonel Fry ordered the colors uncased and shook out a skirmish line. Lieutenant Marcellus E. Jones, 8th Illinois, after passing back word of the enemy's approach, took matters in his own hands. One of the men in the lieutenant's command described Jones "took Serg't Shafer's carbine, rested it across a rail-fence and fired at the commanding officer as the column of rebel infantry came across the Marsh Creek bridge . . ." Thus the first shot of the three-day Battle of Gettysburg was fired. When the fighting ceased the evening of July 3rd, the cost of human wreckage totaled over 55,000 casualties, including 7,685 dead Federal and Confederate soldiers. [39]

Gettysburg was far too distant for the sound of guns to be heard as far as Meade's headquarters at Taneytown. Meade did not learn of the fighting there until about 11:30 a.m., when Major General John F. Reynolds' aide, Stephen Weld, galloped up to his tent with news of the ever escalating battle. The Army of the Potomac's commander spent a worried afternoon on July 1 at his headquarters awaiting word from Gettysburg. Around 4:30 p.m., Meade received a situation report from his field commander, Winfield Scott Hancock, unequivocally identifying two Confederate corps (Ewell's and Hill's) fighting at Gettysburg. He immediately turned his attention to assembling all his corps for battle. Meade's biggest concern was bringing up John Sedgwick's corps, totaling one-third of his infantry, in time to thwart Lee's attacks. His message to Sedgwick warned a "general battle seems to be impending tomorrow at Gettysburg... it is of the utmost importance that your command be up." The day began with the 77th and the Sixth Corps 35 miles southeast at Manchester, Maryland, and Meade's orders to march to Gettysburg did not reach Sedgwick until 8 p.m. in the evening. [40]

An hour after receiving Meade's summons, Sedgwick had the Sixth Corps on the road, but it was not until 1 p.m. that the 77th began the long march to Gettysburg. More than a few soldiers, too drunk to march or passed out from partaking of farmer's rye whiskey, were left behind. Surgeon Stevens recounted, they "were quietly thrown into the clumps of bushes by the roadside, and left to be gathered up by cavalry squads that were scouring the country for stragglers." Any of the inebriated not collected by the provost guard were gobbled up by Confederate cavalry scouts. 41

The 77th and the Sixth Corps backtracked along the same road that had earlier led them to Manchester so as to take the Baltimore Pike, the most direct route to Gettysburg. The Third Brigade's night march was slowed by supply and ammunition wagons and artillery clogging the road, causing frequent detours of infantry to the roadside. Ahead of the regiment, a band in Horatio Wright's division played "John Brown's Body," inspiring many marching soldiers to sing the choruses of the battle hymn. To the song's lyrical notes, the 77th quickened its step, eager to come to the aid of the Army of the Potomac.

Shortly after daybreak on July 2, the 77th briefly halted for ten minutes, barely enough time to boil coffee or to grab hardtack from their knapsacks. Then came the order to fall in and the march resumed. Thousands of marching feet pulverized the limestone bedded Baltimore Turnpike sending choking clouds of white dust into the air. The scorching sun high in the cloudless blue sky was unmerciful. A Pennsylvania soldier described, "Toward noon the radiating heat could be observed in waves, like colorless clouds, floating from earth and mingling with the fine dust created by the moving column." The New Yorkers suffered for want of water. While each passing farm house had a spring or well, in most instances, they had no time to stop and fill their canteens. When they did have a few moments to stop and get water from a nearby well, it was dry from hundreds of men who had sipped its last drop. Sergeant A. T. Brewer of the Third Brigade's 61st Pennsylvania wrote,

> A long line of ambulances met us filled with wounded going to the rear, interfering with out movement and causing a temporary delay. I saw a chain pump in the front yard of a house and went to it and began vigorously to turn the crank, but no water came. A woman, her arms akimbo, stood near, with solemn expression, and a far-away look, apparently not noticing me. Addressing her I said, 'Can you tell me where to get water?' The woman instantly began to cry as if her heart would break and between sobs she said to me, 'No, I can't even give you a cup of cold water.' My sympathies were touched, and for a time, at least, I forgot all about my thirst. I wonder if the barren fig tree on the side of Olivet would have been spared if it had burst into tears of regret because it had no fruit for the hungry Galilean. [42]

In the village of Littlestown, inhabitants filled buckets of water and placed them on the horse blocks along the road, and the thirsty marchers dipped in their tin cups as they passed. Nearly every house flew the national flag, and the townsfolk raised a cheer. As the 77th was leaving Littlestown, they were met by civilians bringing in the wounded from Gettysburg in their carriages. The wounded that could walk also passed by, heading for the town. The sight of the wounded spurred the 77th on for, "Our friends were waiting for us." The march became ever more urgent as the sound of guns at Gettysburg grew louder. "Soon," George Stevens remembered, "we saw above the valley that lay before us, clouds of smoke and the white puffs of bursting shells . . . those small fleecy clouds which appeared so suddenly, flashing forked lightening, told us of work ahead." [43]

The 77th filed across Rock Creek, just south and east of Gettysburg at 5 p.m. Charles Carlton Coffin, a well-respected war correspondent, described the scene at Meade's headquarters on the Lister farm. The speed of the approaching column was such that it was believed to be cavalry. "I was at Meade's headquarters; the roar of battle was louder and grew nearer. Hill was threatening the center; a cloud of dust could be seen down the Baltimore Pike. Had Stuart suddenly gained our rear? There were anxious countenances around the cottage where the flag of the commander-in-chief was flying. Officers gazed with their field glasses. 'It is not the cavalry, but infantry,' said one, 'there is the flag, it is the Sixth Corps.' Faces which a moment before were grave, became cheerful." Cheers and shouts of joy filled the air as Sedgwick's troops came filing in. [44]

After crossing Rock Creek, the 77th turned aside into a field to rest a little. Chaplain Fox stated, "They had had nothing to eat since their coffee in the morning, and they went to work frying their pork and boiling their coffee in the most unconcerned manner, paying no attention to the fact that there, but a little distance in front, hundreds of canon were thundering, and there were being enacted scenes which would form one of the great turning points of history." "The roar of battle was terrific," Surgeon Stevens wrote, "On our left, where rose a hill [Little Round Top] covered with timber on the top and side, a fearful struggle seemed in progress, and a roll of musketry and the rapid discharge of artillery was almost deafening." Taking leave from the regiment, along with Adjutant William

Fursman, the curious doctor determined to see what was going on behind Little Round Top that shielded the raging battle from their view:

> We remounted our horses and crossing the creek began to ascend the hill, when we encountered a brigade from the Fifth Corps rushing through the woods to reinforce the Third Corps. We passed between the ranks of this brigade and presently found ourselves on the north side of Little round top which the whole panorama of the battle spread out before us. There was the Devil's Den, the slope of the hill, the Wheat field, and the Peach Orchard revealed to our view. There were the lines of Confederate soldiers with their artillery and the infantry, and, at nearer range, the lines in blue of the Union Army, while the roar of artillery and of musketry filled the air with a terrible tumult. Just in front, in the Wheat field, a big barn was on fire, the flames and smoke mounting high into the sky. We could see the waving of the Union and Confederate lines and hear the shouts of men which mingled with the roar of the guns . . . My companion and I rode east, along Cemetery ridge, encountering numerous batteries as we rode. The captain of one of these called us to dismount from our horses as we were drawing the fire of the enemy by being too conspicuous on the hill. There was a considerable park of ambulances and munition wagons just to our right and in a depressed potion of the hill. The shower of shells which came over from the opposing force stampeded these wagons and blocked the way. We reached the vicinity of the turnpike but the narrow cut in the rocks through which the turnpike defiled was so completely blocked by the trains that it was sometime before we could force our way through, which we did, fortunately, just in time to join

our brigade as it was marching out of the open field in the rear of Round Top.⁴⁵

The 77th's rest was but brief, for shortly after arriving on the field, Meade ordered Beau Neill's Third Brigade to Henry Slocum's aid on Culp's Hill. The brigade went at once to Powers Hill, "a height crowned by a battery," which, Neill understood, General Meade had ordered held "at all hazards." At this time, the 77th saw stragglers from Cemetery Ridge and heard the sounds of Major General Edward Johnson's attack on Culp's Hill, but the Federal right seemed to be holding. To the men of the regiment "the scene on the field at this hour (was) terrible." There was a cloud of smoke over some "slight eminence" in their front, perhaps Cemetery Hill, and "upon the black linings of this cloud continually played the flashings of a battery which was thundering at the enemy from the summit of the knoll." While waiting at the hill, Neill received orders from Slocum to go to the support of besieged Union troops of Brigadier General John W. Geary's Twelfth Corps division, and he moved the Third Brigade closer to Culp's Hill. When the fighting ceased, the Third Brigade returned to Powers Hill, where the 77th bedded down for the night anxious to know what the morning heralded.⁴⁶

The following morning, Slocum ordered Neill to take two Third Brigade regiments to the extreme right of the Union army to keep the enemy from turning that flank. The brigadier led the 7th Maine and 43rd New York back to the Baltimore Pike. After crossing Rock Creek, the Federal regiments turned left through the Baker farmyard and climbed the sharp incline behind it. Along with Lieutenant Colonel Seldon Connor of the 7th Maine, Thomas Neill rode to the top of the hill and saw the J. Taney house ahead. Conferring with Connor, Neill suggested they occupy the house. As he spoke, some Rebel skirmishers from within the Taney house fired off a volley in their direction. At this, Neill went back for the rest of the Third

Brigade, after telling Connor to use his own discretion about taking the house. Connor took the 7th Maine and 43rd New York and set off in a rush for a stone wall near the house that was about 100 yards to their front and took position there. Meanwhile, Neill returned with the 49th New York and the 61st Pennsylvania regiments. The four regiments formed a line behind a wall that stretched from the brow of the hill overlooking Rock Creek on the left, east across an open field to some woods about 200 yards away. Four hundred strong, the 77th remained at Powers Hill to guard Slocum's headquarters and to support the batteries there.

There was only skirmish fire in the open fields in front of the Third Brigade regiments posted behind the stone wall. Confronting the Yankee regiments were a portion of the 2nd Virginia and 1st North Carolina regiments. Colonel Nadenbousch of the 2nd Virginia described the Confederate action: "I advance some distance on the left, driving the enemy's skirmishers from and taking possession of the heights at this point, where I remained during the day, skirmishing with and inflicting some injury of the enemy by killing, wounding, and taking some prisoners, and keeping the left flank clear." Of the Third Brigade's part in the battle, Neill reported that it was sent to the right to prevent the enemy "from turning us." He continued that "upon taking position, I felt the enemy strong in sharpshooters, and put my whole brigade [less the 77th] in position there, and stopped them from going any farther." Seldon Connor wrote that the 7th Maine had some "smart skirmishing" but was not significantly engaged. [47]

By noon, there was a lull in the fighting except for the occasional shot from Union artillery sent screaming into Lee's lines. The noonday heat was a sweltering 87 degrees, and the soldiers from both sides waited with ready rifles, sweat streaming down their faces. From his vantage point, George Stevens wrote, "The rebel lines could be seen moving here and there as if preparing for a desperate struggle." Indeed, General Lee was assembling a large Confederate assault force to stage what he believed would be the final attack that would punch through Federal lines and destroy the Army of the Potomac. [48]

After Confederate attacks on both Union flanks failed, Lee determined to strike the Federal center. The Southern general reasoned that the Union center must now be significantly less well defended. With Longstreet continuing to threaten their left and Ewell still threatening their right, the Federals would be unlikely to risk massing against the threat of assault on their center. And as far as Lee could determine, the Yankees had not entrenched themselves along Cemetery Ridge; all that was visible in the way of breastworks was a low stone wall. The aiming point of the assault would be the 500 yard span between woods to the Rebel left known locally as Ziegler's Grove and a small copse of scrub oaks to their right. Three Confederate divisions would make the attack, forever later known as Pickett's Charge. Three fresh brigades, numbering 5,830 men from Major General George E. Pickett's division would combine with the 7,200 soldiers from the divisions of J. Johnston Pettigrew and Isaac R. Trimble – bringing the total count of infantry to over 13,000. The brigades of Cadmus M. Wilcox and James H. Lane, totally another 1,600 infantry, were designated to support Pickett's right.

Preceding the infantry attack, Lee planned a massive artillery bombardment of the Yankee center between Ziegler's Grove and the copse of scrub oaks. The barrage was the critical element of Lee's plan. He intended the massive volume of gunnery to obliterate the defending Union batteries and to overwhelm the defending Yankee infantry. The cannonade, in short, was designed to even the odds, and then what Lee solidly believed was an invincible infantry would breach the center of the Union line. The Confederate artillery chiefs, Porter Alexander and William N. Pendelton, arranged 163 guns, most of them rifled pieces, forming a sweeping irregular arc from the Peach Orchard northward to a point opposite the town. On Little Round Top, Major Thomas Hyde was awed from his vantage point as he counted 100 guns "seemingly directed toward the centre of our line." When Meade, inspecting his lines, arrived at the little mountain, Hyde "dodged back to tell the general that it looked like a cannonade pretty soon." [49]

At 1 p.m., James B. Longstreet ordered, "Let the batteries open." Two minutes later a pair of signal guns from the Washington Artillery shattered the battlefield quiet. At 1:07 p.m., from the Peach Orchard to the Chambersburg Pike, Confederate gun crews took to their pieces and unleashed the largest artillery barrage to date on North American soil. Shaken, George Stevens remembered, "suddenly, as though pandemonium had broken loose, the air was filled with the shrieks, screams, howls and clangor of bursting shells. The sky was filled with smoke, amid which flames darted in every direction, and the valley and hills quaked with the thunder of artillery." Nineteen year old Private Sanford Campbell (Co. K) remembered, "we were standing in battle line supporting one of Gen. Slocum's batteries. As I was in the rear ranks I stepped back and leaned against a small tree. A shell came along taking off the under jaw of a horse, the forelegs from two others, plowed the ground making the stones fly to beat the band as onward it went without injuring me." Smoothbore solid shot and shells could be plainly seen during their downward arc. From his position in the orchard behind the Union center, Major General John Gibbon wrote that the higher velocity rifled shells "came with a rush and a scream and could only be seen in their rapid flight when they 'upset' and went tumbling through the air, creating the uncomfortable impression that, no matter where you were in front of the gun from which they came or not, you were liable to be hit." [50]

MCKEAN'S SUNDAY SCHOOL BOYS GO TO WAR

Sanford E. Campbell (NYSDMNA)

The target of the Confederate gunners was the Union center on Cemetery Ridge between Ziegler's Grove and the copse of scrub oaks. Unfortunately, the Rebel guns shot long. In consequence, the entire reverse slope of Cemetery Ridge was flooded by a hail of shot and shell. Teamsters and ambulance drivers scrambled for safety as their wagons were hit by the flying iron. Field hospitals were speedily evacuated. Meade's headquarters at the Leister house became a spot of danger as shells hit the foundation and the front porch, tore through the garret, and through the front door, one narrowly missing Meade himself. Major Thomas Hyde wisely took cover behind a large boulder and caught sight of "a man with a long beard and spectacles, wearing a long brown linen duster." As he neared the major, a shell shrieked between the two men, and the inebriated civilian looked down at Hyde, put his hand to his ear, and said, "Listen to the mocking bird." Hyde watched in disbelief as the man staggered safely across open ground when it "seemed impossible for any living thing to remain a minute." [51]

The continuing barrage made it plain to all that Lee intended to launch an infantry assault on the Federal center. Eleventh Corps artillery chief, Thomas Osborn, suggested to the army's Chief of Artillery, Brigadier General Henry J. Hunt, that the artillery cease-fire all along the line would lure Lee into thinking his bombardment was successful and thus persuade him to send in his infantry. Hunt agreed as to do so would also save ammunition to meet the expected infantry attack. The order given, Union batteries on the ridge ceased firing, some limbering up and withdrawing behind the crest of Cemetery Ridge. From Seminary Ridge, Confederate First Corps artillerist, Colonel Edward Porter, took the bait and dispatched a note to Pickett: "For God's sake come quick. The . . . guns are gone. Come quick or my ammunition will not let me support you properly." [52]

Just after 3 p.m., Major General George Pickett moved to the front of his men, turned in the saddle to face them and commanded, "Charge the enemy and remember Old Virginia." Facing the Union lines, Pickett barked, "Forward! Guide center! March!" With that, the Southern advance began, battle flags fluttering, and rifles with bayonets fixed. In the late afternoon heat and humidity, the skirmishers stepped out from the woods along Seminary Ridge and started a 16 minute walk that led over 13,000 Confederates forever into history.[53]

On Cemetery Hill, troops of Winfield Scott Hancock's Second Corps, the divisions of John Gibbons and Alexander Hays, and two brigades from Abner Doubleday's division First Corps, watched the eerily silent approaching Confederate battle lines stretching over a mile in width, dressed as if on parade, while crouched behind stone walls thirty inches high that ran underneath split rail fences. The fence line ran from Bryan's farm south, turning in a right angle west, and then going down Cemetery Ridge before continuing south. Six batteries supported the Federal infantry.

The distance between the advancing Rebel soldiers and the Union line was a little over one mile, and was covered by artillery positioned on Little Round Top, Cemetery Hill, and Cemetery Ridge. Advancing Confederate infantry would be subject to enfilading fire from in front and on both flanks. As soon Southern troops started forward from the tree line, Union gun crews began belching forth a hail of shot and shell, cutting huge swaths in the Rebel ranks. When the Confederate soldiers reached the Emmitsburg Road, Union gunners switched to canister. A single shell left a file of thirteen men from the 53rd Virginia "in a perfect mangled mass of flesh and blood indistinguishable one from another." Still, the Confederate ranks surged forward, swarming an angled stretch of wall 1,000 yards below the Bryan farm. This stretch of wall would become famous as the "Bloody Angle." Directly in their path was the 4th U. S. Artillery, Battery A, supported by Brigadier General Alexander Webb's Philadelphia Brigade. The battery fired double canister at point blank range and a portion of the entire Rebel line – including the officer – simply disappeared. A man of the 7th Michigan wrote home, "I never saw such a slaughter. Never saw men mowed so by canister as they was here." [54]

The Confederate breach of Union lines at the Bloody Angle was brief as overwhelming Federal reinforcements stemmed the tide sending Rebel soldiers streaming back to the wood line of Seminary Ridge. The attack had been a complete disaster. Pickett's division left more than half of its men dead, bleeding, or captured, including all but two of its regimental commanders. Pettigrew and Trimble each also lost a little more than half of their command. Of just over 13,000 men who walked across the field from Seminary Ridge, the South lost nearly 6,500 dead, wounded, and captured.

Though the Confederate attack was shattered, Meade hesitated to order a counterattack. Federal casualties were over 1,500 men

– about a quarter of the troops who were at the Bloody Angle. His men had been savaged on all three days of battle, and through shuttling troops from one position to another in the line, many units had become disorganized. His commanders, too, had suffered. Gibbon was wounded and Hancock too. His life had been spared by his belt buckle when a bullet shattered the pommel of his saddle. In the end, Meade discerned that his troops were exhausted, thus making a counterattack virtually impossible.

The retreat of Pickett's and Pettigrew's and Trimble's shattered divisions marked the end of infantry fighting at Gettysburg. As the sun drifted low in the sky, the task at hand was to care for the wounded. Strewn across the battlefield were nearly 27,000 bleeding soldiers from both armies. George Stevens wrote, "Our wounded were collected in great numbers in and about the field hospitals, which were composed chiefly of hospital tents, some farm house with its large barns, serving as a nucleus for each." Stevens continued, "To these, thousands of our brave comrades were brought with mangled limbs, torn bodies or bleeding heads, yet, notwithstanding their terrible wounds, exhibiting accustomed heroism . . . who never uttered a word of complaint, and who, indeed, appeared cheerful, and some even gay." Like his colleagues, Stevens took off his coat and rolled up his sleeves, toiling steadily on through the night closing wounds and amputating shattered limbs. Soon piles of legs, arms, feet, hands, and fingers would mark the progress of the surgeons' work. [55]

Those who were severely gut-shot or soldiers with what looked to be fatal head wounds were set off to the side somewhere in little groups to die as peacefully as they might. "The first sight that met our eyes," wrote a young Quaker woman who came to Gettysburg to help, "was a collection of semi-conscious but still living forms, all of whom had been shot through the head, and were considered hopeless. They were laid there to die and I hoped that they were indeed too near death to have consciousness. Yet many a groan came from them, and their limbs tossed and twitched." When given time, a compassionate surgeon would inspect those thought to be too far gone to be helped to see if a mistake had been made and one or another might be saved. Sadly, in most cases, the original diagnosis was confirmed. [56]

The three-day battle at Gettysburg was at once the high tide and the beginning of the end of the Confederacy. While the dead and wounded of the Army of the Potomac could readily be replaced by the vast manpower of the North, this was not the case for the South. Some 17,250 of Lee's men were deleted from the Confederate rolls as a consequence of Gettysburg. Robert E. Lee's army was broken. Never again would the Southern general command as large an army as he brought north to Pennsylvania. Never again would the Army of Northern Virginia tread on Northern soil.

10

"HURRAH FOR 'E UNION!"

As the tide of Pickett's charge receded, Lee determined he must get his army back to Virginia with dire speed. The first task was the removal of the Confederate wounded. Brigadier General John Imboden, commanding an irregular band of cavalry, was ordered to organize and lead a train of wagons and ambulances to carry the army's wounded to the crossing of the Potomac River at Williamsport. By 4 p.m., July 4, Imboden's column departed in a steady pounding rain. The cavalry general estimated the wagon train stretched for seventeen miles. It carried between 8,000 and 8,500 wounded men, many crying out in agonizing pain as they were continually jolted over rough and rutted roads.

A second special train was brought together that day. Lee was acutely anxious about the enormous reserve quartermaster and subsistence trains parked eight miles to the rear near Fairfield. Those trains held the stores that Ewell's quartermasters and commissaries of subsistence had collected for the army as they marched north through Maryland and Pennsylvania. More than 5,000 cattle and thousands of sheep and hogs were herded alongside the wagons. Lee wanted the supplies and livestock returned to Virginia intact. He ordered Ewell's chief quartermaster, Major Harman, to immediately take the supply wagons and animals onto the road toward the Potomac and to protect them at all costs.

When darkness fell, Lee had Hill's Third Corps head out onto the Fairfield Road, followed by Longstreet's First Corps and Ewell's Second Corps over the same route. Once General Meade fully realized that Lee was retreating, the Northern commander moved with considerable speed. For the pursuit, Meade divided the Army of the Potomac into three commands, under John Sedgwick, Henry Slocum, and Oliver Howard. They would follow parallel routes to a scheduled rendezvous on July 7 at Middletown, on the Old National Road that led westward across South Mountain toward Hagerstown and the Potomac crossing at Williamsport.

On the morning of July 5, the 77th, with the Sixth Corps, began the pursuit of Lee's army. Their route was over the northeasterly slope of Little Round Top near Devil's Den, diagonally across the Wheatfield, leaving the Peach Orchard to the left, then up and over the ground previously occupied by the Confederate center near Lee's headquarters before leaving Gettysburg on the Fairfield Road, the Third Brigade in advance with cavalry. George Stevens remembered, "The battlefield was horrible. Dead men were thickly strewn over the fields with their faces blackened, and eyes starting from their sockets." Sergeant A. T. Brewer, of the Third Brigade's 61st Pennsylvania, described the scene as they passed over the Wheatfield:

> This piece of ground... had been fought over back and forth by infantry, supported by artillery, and presented a most appalling spectacle. The wounded had nearly all been

taken away, but the dead had not been touched. They lay as they fell, in every conceivable position. Sometimes one lay across another as if the top one had stooped to take a dying message and instantly lost his life. The battle wreckage included everything belonging to soldiers afoot or on horseback, such as caps, hats, shoes, coats, guns, cartridge and cap boxes, belts, canteens, haversacks, blankets, tin cups, horses, saddles and swords . . . we saw where a battery had stood in the midst of a terrific struggle. One gun was dismantled, a caisson had exploded and we noticed one place where three out of four horses belonging to a gun had been killed and lay with their harnesses on.[1]

As the 77th continued along the Emmitsburg Road, they passed by the Sherfy farm. Reverend Joseph Sherfy and Mary Sherfy and their six children were pacifist members of the Church of the Brethren. They were ordered away from the farm on the morning of July 2, driving their stock southeast of the Round Tops and to Two Taverns. While they were gone, the farmhouse was hit by a least seven artillery shells and ransacked. By the evening of July 3, their yard was covered with their possessions, which were trampled into the mud and mixed with blood, body parts, and every imaginable kind of filth. During the battle, a large number of wounded of the 114th Pennsylvania filled Sherfy's barn. Sparks from exploding shells set the barn afire, consuming those so severely wounded that they could not escape the flames. Surgeon Stevens was horrified by what he saw. "The crisp and blackened limbs, heads and other portions of bodies lying half consumed among the heaps of ruins and ashes, made up one of the most ghastly pictures ever witnessed, even on the field of battle." [2]

From east of Rock Creek below Culp's Hill, out the Hunterstown Road, north of Gettysburg along the Carlisle Road, northwest on the Mummasburg Road, west of Gettysburg on the Chambersburg Pike and Fairfield Road, and southwest of town along Marsh Creek and Willoughby Run, the buildings of local farmers and townspeople were filled with the sick, wounded, and dying of Lee's army. In all, there were nearly 40 Confederate hospital and ambulance depot sites in or near Gettysburg. At one of the barns where Rebel wounded lay, Surgeon Stevens recalled a heart rendering exchange with one of the wounded. "At one of these barns . . . was a boy apparently not more than sixteen years of age . . . The lad looked more like a delicate girl than a soldier; his hair fell from his fair forehead in long flaxen curls upon his pillow of straw, some of them matted with blood; his cheek was rosy, and his soft white hand told of a youth spent amid more tender scenes than those of camp. A piece of linen laid across his face covered a ghastly wound where a ball had passed through his face, and had torn both his eyes from their sockets." Stevens spoke a kind word to the young soldier, who stretched out his hand, saying, "Come near me, I want to touch you." The surgeon held the young man's hand, and the wounded soldier was surprised by the realization Stevens was a Yankee. "I did not think a federal would speak so kindly to me; your voice sounds like that of a friend, and your hand feels like one; will you not stay with me?" When the doctor replied that he must follow his command, the soldier replied in distress, "Oh! I shall never hear any one speak so kindly to me again; my mother lives in North Carolina, but she will not see me. Can you not stay?" Stevens could only sadly turn away from the wounded boy soldier and rejoin the 77th in pursuit of Lee.[3]

On the morning of July 6, the 77th passed through the village of Fairfield, near the foot of South Mountain. That same day Meade ordered Neill's Third Brigade, reinforced by a brigade of cavalry under Colonel John B. McIntosh and a battery of light artillery, commanded by Brigadier General Neill, to push forward to probe Lee's defenses at Fairfield Gap and Monterey Pass. Leaving Fairfield and ascending the remote, heavily wooded eastside of South Mountain, the 77th passed by a number of roughhewn log houses. Before each, the owner and his family stood in front gawking as hundreds of blue-clad troops marched by. As Neill's column was passing one such humble abode nearly hidden by sunflowers and flowering pole beans, the soldiers at the head of the column erupted into enthusiastic cheering. George Stevens remembered, "In the midst of the noise, sounded a shrill voice; and as we approached, we saw, sitting upon the fence in front of the cottage, a little boy, about four years old, his face flushed with excitement, his flaxen hair flying in the wind, as he was waving his little hat, and with childlike indistinctness shouting in his shrill tones, 'Hurrah for'e Union! Hurrah for'e Union!" [4]

As the New Yorkers crossed the mountain summit at Monterey Pass, they encountered the wreckage of a recent struggle. In the rainy darkness on July 4, Brigadier General Judson Kilpatrick's troopers swooped down on a portion of Ewell's supply train, taking a good number of prisoners and capturing 30 or more wagons, which were subsequently destroyed. Years later, Stevens wrote, "as we marched down the forest road . . . the scene was heightened by the remains of the ruined wagons which lined the wayside, some burned, some with the wheels disabled by cutting the spokes, others tumbled off the steep embankment." The remnants of this portion of Ewell's train continued to litter the landscape for another three miles. [5]

On July 7, Private Stephen R. Frost (Co. K) walked to Hagan's Field, west of Frederick to view the body of Confederate spy George William Richardson who had been hung a day earlier. Richardson was a known businessman in Baltimore, and had two sons in Lee's army. He posed as a sutler in the Federal camps, selling paper for music and writing paper. Suspected as a spy, Richardson was arrested by Provost Guard, and was found to have maps for the Confederate army and letters from Rebel officers vouching for him. When brought to the cavalry general, John Buford, the commander simply said, "Hang him," and he was subsequently executed without a trial. A rope was placed around his neck, one end thrown over a tree limb, and three soldiers drew him up, dangling in the air, fastened the rope and left him. Richardson's body would be left hanging for a little more than three days before being cut down. In a letter to his sister, Frost wrote, "perhaps you se the a count in the paper of the spy that was hung near Fredrick City in Mariland just after the Battle of Gettes Bourgh. I will enclose a pice of the Barck in this letter that I got off on the tree when he was hanging thare." Private Frost was only one of many to view the dead spy. The days before Richardson was cut down and buried beneath the tree were marked by crowds of curious soldiers and teamsters that came to view the bloated, rotting corpse. Souvenir seekers joined Frost by breaking off pieces of bark from the hanging tree while others took strips of clothes until the body hung naked. [6]

By the middle of the afternoon, July 9, the 77th descended into the Cumberland Valley and arrived at Waynesboro and Neill's command received a warm embrace by the town's inhabitants. Musician James Miles Walker, Company A, 61st Pennsylvania vividly recalled, "At Waynesboro the citizens, men, women and children, formed on the sidewalks and handed us bread, sliced and buttered, cooked meats, pies, and almost everything in the eatable line we could take in our hands as we walked by." Once encamped a short distance away from the town, the 77th was greeted by business minded civilians selling flour and bread procured from far away as Chambersburg at cut rate prices. [7]

While at Waynesboro, the New Yorkers were sent out a mile in advance of the Third Brigade on picket duty along the banks of Antietam Creek. Enjoying the pleasant summer weather, the men were warmly greeted by the surrounding country folk, many opening their homes providing home cooked meals and comfortable beds. In turn, the New Yorkers took to the fields and assisted in harvesting the ripe grain. They "laid down their guns, and swung the cradle and the scythe with a zest that showed they worked with a good will." As the soldiers of the 77th worked the fields, country women baked bread for the veterans, and offered milk, poultry, and apple butter, a vast improvement over hardtack and salt pork. [8]

Lieutenant Sidney O. Cromack (NYSDMNA)

Many years later, Lieutenant Sydney Cromack (Co. B) recalled at a regimental reunion an amusing anecdote that took place while the 77th was on picket involving Captains William Carpenter (Co. E) and Frederick Smith (Co. B):

> We halted near a large white house, which Colonel French will remember for he and other officers took dinner there. Under a shed near the barn stood a wagon in which was a few

sacks of land plaster. Captain Carpenter . . . had a man detailed as cook, one of those wide-awake, never-get-tired fellows who always looked for something to eat. I told him it looked like buckwheat flour in the sacks, and that he had better take some along and surprise Capt. Carpenter, as he was fond of buckwheat cakes. When we halted . . . for dinner, Carpenter came over to B company and invited Captain Smith and myself to come over and have some buckwheat cakes with him. As we walked over Captain Carpenter told us that his man was a hustler and a good all 'round fellow: that if there was anything in the line of eatables lying around loose he would be sure to get some. His man put water into a jar, adding salt and soda and then the flour. When the flour struck the water it set as plaster paris will. Captain Smith laughed. Carpenter's face was a study, and the way he talked to his man for a few minutes would have made the hearer conclude that he had changed his mind as to his man's good qualities. [9]

As the 77th basked in the sun and the glow of their happy welcome at Waynesboro, a division numbering more than 4,000 raw militia commanded by their old corps' Major General William "Old Baldy" Smith, was marching south from Harrisburg to rendezvous with Neill's column. During an unusually dark night on July 8, Smith's division struggled along muddy roads. Many became shoeless, as the untrained soldiers trudged up the slope of South Mountain. Private George W. Wingate wrote of the march:

> As a pitchy blackness rendered everything invisible, a lantern was carried at the head of the column to prevent those behind from being lost. Every few minutes we would be plunged into a mountain stream running across the road, and which could be heard falling an indefinite distance down the other side, wading across this, in an instant more

we would find ourselves struggling knee deep in mud of an unequaled tenacity; and the efforts made to extricate ourselves generally resulted in getting tripped up by projecting roots and stumps. As those in the front reached an obstacle, they passed the word down the line, 'Stump!' 'Ford!' 'Mud hole!' Frequently, this latter cry became altered to 'Man in a mud hole!' 'Two men in the mud hole – look out sharp!' [10]

The arrival of Old Baldy's green militia left the 77th less than impressed. The New York veterans snickered at the citizen soldiers in new blue uniforms unaccustomed to the tribulations of the soldier's life. No stranger to long grueling marches, George Stevens sniffed as upon their arrival "they were all complaining bitterly of the terrible marches they endured, and swore they would shoot the general if they ever got into a fight. They had marched . . . at the rate of from eight to fifteen miles a day!" The unhappy militiamen bitterly complained "they had been subjected to great privations; many of them had not tasted any *butter* for more than a week, and nearly all declared they had nothing to eat for several days." The surgeon simply pointed to their supply wagons loaded with boxes of hardtack. Taking offense the greenhorns objected, "What! You don't expect us to eat that hard tack do you?" [11]

Due to the torrential rains that started on July 4, Lee's timetable for returning his army to the safety of Virginia was dangerously delayed. The flood waters of the Potomac River reached such a depth that the Williamsport ford was impassable. Four miles downstream at Falling Waters, Major Shadrock Foley's mixed Federal cavalry - dispatched from Harper's Ferry by Major General William H. French - destroyed Lee's lightly guarded pontoon bridge. With only one small flatboat at Williamsport, the Army of Northern Virginia had its back against the river, forced to defend themselves against Meade's pursuing columns.

Soon after the rear guard of the Confederate army arrived in Hagerstown on the morning of July 7, Lee undertook an inspection of the approaches to the Potomac by way of the Williamsport-Hagerstown Pike. The lay of the land around Williamsport, Falling Waters, Downsville, and Jones' Crossroads provided a good number of defensive positions. By July 11, Lee had selected a line along high ground with the right resting on the river near Downsville and the left about a mile and a half southwest of Hagerstown, covering the road from there to Williamsport. The sizeable Conococheague Creek, emptying into the Potomac from the north at Williamsport, and the open country through which it flowed protected the Rebel position from a surprise attack from the west. The Southerners erected sturdy breastworks with a six- foot-wide parapet on top and frequent gun emplacements designed to provide a perfect crossfire while sweeping the front. The Confederates also built inner defenses at Falling Waters and Williamsport to cover the passage to the river. By the morning of July 12, the fortifications were effectively completed, and the soldiers in gray prepared to meet General Meade's approaching army.

As the Confederate army was positioning before Williamsport and Falling Waters, Meade again set the Army of the Potomac in motion toward Lee. The Second and Twelfth Corps were ordered to march to Bakersville by way of Keedysville; the Fifth Corps was to move along the Williamsport-Boonsboro Road to the stone bridge over Antietam Creek, at the "Devil's Backbone." The Third Corps was to follow the Fifth Corps. The Eleventh corps and the Artillery Reserve were held in position just west and northwest of Boonsboro, while Sedgwick's Sixth Corps, followed by the First, were ordered to set out on the National Road toward Beaver Creek, screened by Buford's cavalry division. Thomas Neill's "light division," with Smith's green troops in tow, was ordered to rejoin the Sixth Corps in the vicinity of Funkstown.

McKEAN'S SUNDAY SCHOOL BOYS GO TO WAR

On July 11, the 77th withdrew from their picket line and rejoined the already assembled Third Brigade, readying to rendezvous with the Sixth Corps. In the dark, the regiment forded the cold waist-high water of Antietam Creek and halted a short while later at Leitersburg. The New Yorkers took advantage of the break in marching and broke rank to boil coffee and chew on hardtack. At daylight, the veterans were again on the march. Soon, the heat of day became oppressive and many soldiers were laid low by heat exhaustion and sunstroke. The regiment halted at Smithville to allow the First Corps to pass, falling in behind as they marched toward Hagerstown. "At 2 o'clock," Surgeon Stevens wrote, "a most terrific thunder-storm arose, such as had never overtaken our army, even in Virginia. Huge black clouds . . . poured down great volumes of water, until the road through which we were marching, and which was bordered by high banks on either side, was filled with a mad torrent which reached to the knees, and in places to the waists of the men." As the skies cleared and the sun set, the regiment reached Funkstown, and their reunion with the Sixth Corps was met with cheers. [12]

The 77th found the Sixth Corps in line of battle just east of Funkstown, and the Green Mountain Boys of the Vermont Brigade boasted of their part in battle there two days earlier. After the Third Brigade split off from the corps for a detached reconnaissance on July 6, Albion Howe's remaining Vermont Brigade lead the Sixth Corps south to Middleton and then toward Hagerstown. Three miles south of Hagerstown was Funkstown, and there on July 10 Buford's cavalry screen ran into Lee's rearguard, and into trouble. Colonel White's Georgia Brigade forced Buford's troopers back south of the town, and they themselves collided with Lewis Grant's Vermonters, the nearest Federal infantry, rushing up to support the hard pressed Federal troopers.

Grant sent the 5th and 6th Vermont into a skirmish line, and formed the 3rd and 4th Vermont in line of battle behind them, keeping the 2nd Vermont in reserve. The brigade held a good defensive position on a wooded crest with its left flank protected by Antietam Creek. The Georgians in pursuit of the Federal horsemen attacked at about 2 p.m. and were soon checked by the Vermont skirmishers. As the fighting escalated, Grant moved the 3rd Vermont up to the center of the skirmish line. The 2nd Vermont shifted left to block a Confederate thrust over Antietam Creek, and the 4th Vermont sent two companies forward to support the 5th Vermont. Soon the whole brigade was deployed as skirmishers except for three companies of the 5th Vermont. There were no other supporting Union units within a comfortable distance. In a matter of minutes, the Vermont skirmish line was nearly two miles long, as Grant kept extending his line to prevent White's brigade from catching his right flank. The Rebels surged forward but were stopped cold by a crippling volley from Vermonters they could barely see amongst the trees on the crest. White's Georgians had no way of knowing they were up against only one brigade. The two-mile long length of the Union line suggested a much larger force, and no one could tell what was behind it.

Still, the Green Mountain Boys' position soon became precarious as their ammunition ran low. Runners scrambled back to supply wagons, and returned carrying stacks of cartridges on stretchers, racing down the line to pass them out where needed, and the intense rate of fire never slackened. A final, feeble Confederate probe was quickly thrown back, and the Confederates hurriedly retreated north through Funkstown after the rest of Lee's army.

On July 12, just as the Confederates had almost finished preparing their fortifications, Meade's army finally arrived to confront them. At 8 p.m. that evening, Meade met with his corps commanders and proposed advancing the army and making a reconnaissance in force which could be converted into an attack if an opportunity developed. Five of the seven, including the two senior officers, Sedgwick and Slocum, were vehemently opposed to an attack. Only Brigadier James S. Wadsworth, attending in place of Major General John Newton who was sick, and Major General O. O. Howard were for it. Though not agreeing with the adverse opinion of the majority of his infantry generals, Meade postponed an assault until he could personally reconnoiter the positions of the Southerners along their defensive works.

As Meade and his Chief of Staff, Brigadier General Andrew A. Humphreys, inspected the front lines on the morning of July 13, warehouses in Williamsport were hastily torn down and Lee's engineers finished the pontoon bridge from the foraged lumber and the Potomac had subsided enough to be forded. A short while later Lee ordered a retreat. The Southern troops started out in a heavy rain on a pitch-dark night, with orders for Longstreet's and Hill's corps together with the artillery to march across the Pontoon bridge at Falling Waters and for Ewell's corps to ford the river at Williamsport. At 11 a.m. on the 14th, except for Heth's and Pender's divisions, the Army of Northern Virginia had safely reached the south bank of the Potomac.

During the night, as Lee's army was evacuating their works, Meade's headquarters issued orders for four of his corps, which included the Sixth Corps, to begin the reconnaissance in force at 7 a.m. George Stevens revealed the temper of the 77th that night when he wrote, "Much as the veterans, who knew too well the risks of battle, usually dreaded a general engagement, this time there seemed a universal desire, on the part of the men, now to strike a blow which should destroy their adversaries before they should be able to cross the river again." Before 7 a.m., however, Major General Horatio G. Wright of the Sixth Corps First Division received word of an enemy withdrawal and ordered skirmishers forward only to discover the Confederates had left their entrenchments and were nowhere in sight. The 77th was "more incensed than surprised" when they heard the news. Stevens wrote, "There was certainly a very general ill-feeling pervading our army at this easy escape of the rebel army, which even the glorious news of Vicksburg . . . failed to pacify." [13]

The chagrin of the 77th was somewhat lessened as the New Yorkers heard brisk firing in the direction of Falling Waters. Buford's cavalry division coming from the east and Judson Kilpatrick's from the north had come up on Henry Heth's division on a ridge about a mile and a half from Falling Waters. Major General William Pender's division lay behind Heth's waiting for its turn to march over the pontoon bridge. Kilpatrick's attack was a complete surprise, and he caught the Confederates, tired out from the night's hard march, resting amidst their stacked and unloaded muskets. However, he attacked with only two small squadrons without any supports to make the initial charge. The Southerners, wielding their guns as clubs and in some cases using fence rails or axes, tumbled most of the troopers from their horses and killed or wounded them. At the same time, Buford struck the Confederates on their right and rear. Before Heth and Pender could get their divisions over the river, they lost upwards of 1,500 officers and men as prisoners.

July 15, the 77th, with the Sixth Corps, marched to Boonsboro. While there, a large number of Confederate prisoners captured at Falling Waters filed by under the guard of Union cavalry. As they marched by the regiment, the men took pity on the rebel soldiers who were clearly hungry and apparently without provisions. The New Yorkers at once offered the prisoners hardtack and coffee. Ever grateful for this unexpected kindness, the Southerners effusively "declared that it was the best meal they had enjoyed in several weeks." [14]

Crossing the South Mountain range, the 77th arrived at Berlin where a large portion of the Army of the Potomac was preparing to cross the Potomac. While waiting there, the wives of several officers, including that of George Stevens, arrived from Washington to visit their husbands. Harriet Stevens came bearing an unexpected gift for the regiment. She presented to the regiment a pair of silk blue guidons with the Second Division's white Greek cross. In the center of the cross was the number "77." The regiment carried these guidons for the rest of the war and on July 4, 1865 presented them to the State of New York along with the national flag. [15]

Alas, the officer's reunion with their wives was brief, and on July 19 the 77th, with the Sixth Corps, crossed to Virginia with the air of regimental bands playing "Carry Me Back to Virginia." Passing through Lovettsville, the New Yorkers were unexpectedly and joyfully greeted with the cheers of the village's women: "the doors and windows of the dwellings were filled with ladies, whose hair and dresses were decked with ribbons of red, white, and blue, and scores of Union flags waved a welcome to our soldiers." A few miles later, the regiment camped near a pleasant creek which was soon filled with bathers. That night, Colonel Winsor French and several officers left for Saratoga Springs to enlist new recruits to bring the regiment up to strength. [16]

July 20, the 77th marched leisurely toward Warrenton. On the way, they gorged on miles of blackberries that crowded the road. On the 25th, the regiment halted at Waterloo, a short distance from Warrenton. The Third Brigade encamped near an old weathered Baptist church which stood beneath a thick canopy of trees. The following day, the 77th and the 5th Vermont were detailed for picket duty on the bank of the Rappahannock River near the gristmill of Mr. Hart. In a pleasant oak grove they made their camp and enjoyed the spectacular sunsets behind the Blue Ridge Mountains. While there,

Chaplain Norman Fox tended to the spiritual needs of his men. Under his direction, a place among the oaks was selected for Sunday services. A pulpit was erected and pews were made out of logs. On other days of the week, regimental meetings in the evening under colored Chinese lanterns hung among the boughs of the oak trees provided a warm atmosphere for entertainment by the regimental band.

On picket the 77th met with a continuous stream of contrabands making their way to the Union line and freedom from servitude. Cavalry patrols often returned with wagons laden with children, their elders walking beside them. Bent with age and leaning on his staff, one gray-haired contraband caught the attention of Surgeon Stevens. Striking up a conversation with him, the elderly man proudly stood on free soil and referring to the prophet Daniel proclaimed, "Our massas tell us dat dey goin to whip de Yankees and dat Jeff Davis will rule de norf. But we kowd it warnt true so cause de Bible don't say so. De Bible says that de souf shall prevail for a time and den de norf shall rise up and obertow dem." [17]

While the 77th picketed the Rappahannock, Colonel Winsor French arrived in Saratoga Springs to enlist new recruits. Leading citizens of the Spa City determined to assist French by holding a Sunday evening patriotic meeting on the Pavilion Spring grounds. Notice of the meeting was given in all of the churches and the members of the congregation were urged to attend. A platform for the speakers was erected and planks placed upon spring boxes provided seating for the audience. Several hundred citizens, and a number of visitors from the city's hotels and boarding houses gathered and the seats were soon filled. Several clergymen and prominent citizens made stirring patriotic speeches. Colonel French then offered an inspiring address and appeal for volunteers to enlist.

MCKEAN'S SUNDAY SCHOOL BOYS GO TO WAR

Following French's appeal, it was announced that the Federal government paid a $300 bounty to men who enlisted, and a few men came forward and signed the enlistment papers. A long silence pressed upon the crowd as no more came forward. After what felt like an eternity, someone in the crowd announced that in addition to the government bounty, he would give $25 at once to anyone who would sign up, and that brought a few more to the platform. When no more came, another man pledged that he would add $50 to the bounty, and that secured still a few more recruits. By now, the excitement among the crowd was palpable, the people cheering as the young men went to the platform to sign. Then $100 was promised and that induced more enlistments. The excitement continued to build, and when no more were persuaded to sign, one well-to-do woman visiting the Spa took off her jewel encrusted earrings and broach, and holding them up, announced that the lot would go to the next enlistment. Then another woman offered a gold watch and chain. Finally an elderly woman, with a young man by her side, arose and said, "I am a widow; I have no money to give; I have no fine jewelry to give, but I want to aid this good cause and I give my only son. John, go up and sign the enlistment papers," she said to her son. The boyish looking young man dutifully went to the platform and signed as she directed. The women in the crowd gathered around her, shook her hand, complimented her loyalty, and praised her for her great sacrifice. With this final altruistic act, the meeting ended a little after midnight. [18]

However, in nearby Ballston Spa, "Copperheadism" (Peace Democrats) erupted in a war of words with the "War Democrats" in the small village. Following the draft riots in New York City, a militant group of Copperheads from Troy, New York, set off for Ballston Spa to burn down the residences of prominent Republicans, and to destroy the office of the *Ballston Spa Journal* which excoriated the peace movement. Before arriving at the village, their plans became known and Captain Stephen Horton, recovering from his wound at Marye's Heights the previous May, immediately organized an armed "company" of furloughed and returned soldiers, together with the Home Guard.

A little after 8 p.m., the rioters entered the village and gathered at the corner of Front and Bath Streets. They began to make loud threats against the "Black Republicans," and the leader of the marauders shouted, "To the Journal office first!" Edward Grose, editor of the newspaper, who was present, shouted back, "You miserable cowards and villains, go right on; you will find the doors of the Journal office open; you can go in, but how many will be able to come out alive I can't tell." Spooked, some of them believed, "he must have an infernal machine up there." Grose said, "You may get out quicker than you get in. I warn you to be out of town quietly before ten o'clock." Stephen Horton's assembled company then drew up, the drums rattled, pistols were fired, and the Copperheads fled the village. [19]

While the 77th held the picket line along the north bank of the Rappahannock in the vicinity of Hart's Mill, Private Alonzo Bump was detailed to the Provost Guard. On one scout twelve miles or so beyond the picket line, Bump and a small squad of soldiers happened upon a house harboring a Confederate trooper recovering from a severe wound. The trooper was suspected of aiding the partisan ranger Major John Singleton Mosby's guerilla fighters. "We arested one man," Bump wrote to his wife, "and Braught him in to head Quarters. he was Lutenant in the Rebel Caverley. he had on Leg off Below the knee. hee was at home with hiss wife and we went in and took him and Shee Begd on us to Leave him But it was of no use for hee had Bin Ading Garrillies around for some time. the way we found it out was a winch told us and shee told us ware hee Lived so we went and took him and we have got hear to head Quarters." What would happen to the wounded Rebel Lieutnant, Bump could only guess, but he was certain about what should be done. "i know what i should Do with him if it was Left to me. i should shoot him for if hee has Bin adding Garillas around he haint eny Better than they are and if they Ketch one of our Solgars out over the Line they will Kill him if they came. their has Bin 3 of our Solgars found within a weeak with thair throats Cut." [20]

Later, Alonzo Bump was assigned the pleasant duty of guarding the cornfield of a local farmer. The private wrote to his wife:

> i ame about 2 miles from camp and the man that ones the feeald is an Old Secceash and i Go to the house after any meals. i have Just come Back to the feeald. i have Just bin to Dinar. i will tell you what i had for Dinnar. Some Potatoes corne Bread Bacone string Beans and some Colde Boiled Bacone and some sweeat milk and i eat Like a hog. Hee is a rich Old farmer and hiss house is furnisht right up to the handal and hee has Got a coupal of Pritty Girles and they are secess to the Back Bone. i tell you they Don't Like our Soalgars very well But then they haft to Like the Gards that Gard their house. thair is to of us hear on the house and i ame in the feeald. But Mary they Dare not talk eny of their secesh to us for if they did we would Give them enough of that talk for we can Bluf them off in a few minits of talking. [21]

August 3, Lee withdrew the Army of Northern Virginia from Culpeper, moving south of the Rapidan River and setting up his headquarters at Orange Court House. Here, aptly supplied by rail, Lee's army spent the succeeding weeks recuperating from its exhaustion from the Gettysburg campaign. The Southern army was spread along the Rapidan and Rappahannock Rivers, from Sulphur Springs, through Orange all the way to Fredericksburg. The region had been nearly stripped of food over the previous two years of war, so the spread of troops helped the supply situation – especially for the horses. There were adequate rations for the present, keeping the army well fed, with supplies of clothing and shoes delivered from the stocks in Richmond.

Near the end of August, Lee traveled to Richmond to meet with Jeff Davis. While there, the situation in the West was discussed, and President Davis decided to send Longstreet with two divisions to Tennessee in support of Braxton Bragg. The hope was that a quick offensive with seasoned troops would change the strategic situation for the better. Accordingly, the first contingents were under way on September 9, departing from Meadow farm, close to Orange Court House, led by elements of McLaw's division, followed by Hood's division and Porter Alexander's twenty-six pieces of artillery.

General Meade learned of Longstreet's departure on September 11, giving him cause to hope that he might be able to successfully attack Lee's weakened army. Lee had surrendered the area between the Rapidan and Rappahannock Rivers, with Culpeper at its center. The town was strategically important to Meade, due to railroad and storage in the town, which would become the key supply point for the army in any move southward. On September 15, Meade issued orders for his infantry corps to move forward from the Rappahannock. The Twelfth went to Stevensburg, the First midway between Stevensburg and Culpeper, the Second from Culpeper to the Rapidan near Raccoon Ford, with the Fifth in their rear at Culpeper. The Third went between Culpeper and Stonehouse Mountain, with the 77th's Sixth to their right at Stonehouse Mountain. The Eleventh Corps was spread out covering the railroad stations of Catlett's and Bristoe, while covering the fords of the Rappahannock.

MCKEAN'S SUNDAY SCHOOL BOYS GO TO WAR

The 77th reached Stone Mountain the next day, and remained there for several weeks while the two opposing armies settled in to watch each other's camps and to prepare for an advance across the Rapidan. Their days were frequently marked with rain and early morning frost as the monotony of camp routine quickly set in. Still, there were pleasant incidents, one of particular note involving Colonel Winsor French. While James B. McKean had not been with the regiment since the Peninsula Campaign, he did not resign his commission as colonel of the 77th until July 1863. With his resignation, command officially devolved to French. The line officers procured an elegant presentation sword, scabbard, sash, and belt. One soldier of the regiment gave an account of the presentation to the *Daily Saratogian*:

> This evening we were all taken by surprise. One hour ago, while we were all busily engaged in our tents, we suddenly discovered our gallant neighbor, the 7th Maine regiment, drawn up in line in front of our head-quarters, each man of the regiment holding a lighted torch in his hand; their band proceeding to discourse some very fine music; after which, Col Mason addressed some congratulatory remarks to our commander upon his new honors and the tokens he had so recently received of the affection of his officers. Col. French responded, alluding to the long and severe campaigns passed through by the two regiments, side by side, and the strong attachments which had always existed between them. The Maine boys then withdrew, the two regiments vying in their lusty cheers for each other. So we have spent the day. And when in future days we shall take up our pocket memorandums, and turn to the entry – "Sept. 30: *Sword Presentation to Col. French,*" the short sentence will bring up one of the most pleasing recollections of our campaign. [22]

The detachment of James Longstreet's corps for service in the western theatre prompted Lincoln, impatient with Meade's caution, to push the Union general to harass the Confederate army by moving "upon Lee at once in the manner of a general attack, leaving it to developments whether he will make it a real attack." Henry Halleck chimed in with his suggestion to Meade that perhaps "something may be done to weaken [Lee] or force him still further back." Meade protested the practicality of a general attack. "Lee," he reported to Halleck on September 18, "occupies the south bank of the Rapidan, with every available point crowned with artillery, and prepared to dispute the passage . . . [A] passage can be forced, but it would, undoubtedly, result in a considerable sacrifice." Instead, Meade suggested that the disadvantage under which the Army of the Potomac currently operated could be avoided through a demonstration on the Peninsula and changing base to the Fredericksburg Railroad. This, Meade argued, would compel Lee to abandon his lines below the Rapidan. Lincoln and Halleck replied immediately. Summoning the ghost of McClellan, Lincoln rejected the notion of creating a more favorable operational situation by shifting his command to Fredericksburg or menacing Lee's rear via the Peninsula. They also suggested that if Meade did not think he could successfully undertake offensive operations against Lee where he was, then perhaps he could fall back closer to Washington and assume the defensive.[23]

While being dismayed by Lincoln's and Halleck's responses, Meade nevertheless was unwilling to accept a stalemate with Lee. On September 21, Meade ordered Brigadier General John Buford to take his cavalry division up the Rapidan to determine the possibility of turning Lee's left flank. Before Buford could complete his reconnaissance, however, Meade was summoned to Washington. Arriving shortly after midnight on September 22, he learned the administration was pondering detaching troops from the Army of the Potomac and sending them to Tennessee to bolster the Army of the

Cumberland, then bottled up in Chattanooga after its calamitous defeat at Chickamauga. Meade strongly protested, and he informed Lincoln and Halleck that if they were of the opinion that, "I was too slow or prudent, then put some one else in my place." Halleck immediately dismissed the suggestion, and Meade left Washington believing that 'the President was satisfied" with his arguments against lessening the strength of the Army of the Potomac. Hence, Meade was surprised when at 3 a.m. on September 24, orders arrived from Halleck directing him to "prepare the Eleventh and Twelfth Corps to be sent to Washington, as soon as cars can be sent to you." Eight hours later Meade issued orders directing Major Generals Howard and Slocum to take their commands to the capital. The first train left at 5 p.m. on September 25. In total, 23,000 troops, with 1,100 horses, nine batteries of artillery plus hundreds of supporting wagons were transferred within seven days. [24]

It did not take long for Lee to discern that he now faced a significantly diminished enemy and to begin looking for a way to exploit the situation. On October 3, Lee met with Ewell, Hill, and Early at Clark's Mountain, south of the Rapidan where he announced his intention to turn Meade's right flank. The Southern commander hoped to repeat his triumphant victory of the previous summer at Second Bull Run. Much like John Pope's army had been Lee understood that Meade's logistical dependence on the Orange and Alexandria Railroad made him vulnerable to a turning movement to the west. To take advantage of this, Lee decided to try to move around the Union right and threaten the Orange and Alexandria. This, he believed, would force Meade's army into the open and set up an opportunity to strike a decisive blow.

Lee set his flanking operation into motion at 7 a.m. on October 8 when A. P. Hill's Third Corps began moving from its position behind the Rapidan, followed by Richard Ewell's Second Corps.

Federal cavalry pickets picked up evidence of the Confederate move almost as soon as it began, and once their reports reached headquarters, Meade quickly surmised Lee's intentions. Unlike Pope, Meade would give the Confederate commander no opening for a decisive stroke. He issued orders for the Federal army to about-face, march north along the Orange and Alexandria Railroad and to cross Bull Run. In addition, he ordered the preparation of strong defenses at Centreville to thwart a Confederate attack. Through forced marches, the 77th and its fellow soldiers of the Union army quickly negated Lee's head start in the race for Bull Run.

As the 77th marched back to the defenses at Centreville on October 14, they shared the road with medley of traffic. George Stevens recalled, "baggage wagons, pontoons, ambulances, artillery and troops, [were] all thrown together in splendid confusion." The air was filled with the diverse sounds of "Drivers cursing, canon rattling, soldiers singing and shouting, horses racing, and all ... sublime confusion." The New Yorkers reached Centreville at 3 p.m. to the sound of battle to their south. "The booming of canon in the rear," Stevens wrote, "the huge clouds of smoke, and the heavy rattle of musketry, told us there was hot work on the ground we had lately passed over." The 77th was ordered to form a line of battle, and the soldiers were heard to say, "Here is the third Bull Run, but this time the run will be on the other side." While it was not the third Bull Run, the soldiers were right that the run would be on the other side. The sounds of battle were that of A. P. Hill's attack of the army's rear guard at Bristoe Station. [25]

By that afternoon, all but Warren's Second Corps had forded Broad Run on the way to the Bull Run crossings. As Hill moved toward the Orange and Alexandria Railroad, the commander of the Confederate Third Corps spotted Major General Sykes' Fifth Corps crossing Broad Run just East of Bristoe Station. The fiery Hill impetuously determined to strike a blow at the seemingly isolated command as it crossed the stream. Hill's advance set up his command for an ambush of Warren's corps as it moved along the railroad embankment. The Rebel corps was shattered, and upon learning that Warren was engaged, Meade ordered the First and Third corps to march back to Bristoe Station to reinforce him. By the time they arrived, however, the fight was over and the bloodied Confederates had pulled back.

At dark that evening the 77th, along with the Sixth Corps, moved to the vicinity of Chantilly. On picket in the afternoon on October 16, a horseman excitedly galloped up in front of the headquarter tents warning that the left of the picket line was attacked. Some of J. E. B. Stuart's roaming troopers were attempting to seize some Union wagons that had strayed outside the 77th's picket line. The New Yorkers quickly formed and easily pushed back the Confederate horsemen. Private Alonzo Bump, shooting at the enemy for the first time since enlisting a year earlier, boasted of the skirmish to his wife:

> Yestarday we had a fight with the Rebs and we Drove them. I Shot 20 rounds at them and it was Nothing But fun after we Got into it. i think they ware nothing But Old mosbeys Garilleys But they Soon found Out that we ware Enough for them and they Left . . . thair was Not one of the Boys hurt Yestarday in the fight and they would holler at the Rebs and tell them to run. They would say run you Suns of Biches and then the Boys would Let them have it. O it was fun to see them run. You Could not see thair ass from the Dust they ran so and after we had Drove them Our hole Brigaid was out to help us But we Did not nead them for we had Drove them out of sight and hearing . . . some of our Boys shot in to a house and the Ball went threw the side of the house in to the Pantry and the Old man in the house

Picked it up and shode it to us But we Did not Care for that the Rebs ware Behind the house and we ware Bound to Git them from Behind and we Did. they ware Glad to Leave for we fiard a hole voley at them. thiss is the first time that i had a chance to shoot at the Rebs and it is nothing But fun to see them run But i hope that i Shant nevar haft to fiar another Shot at them But if they come in my way i shall Let them have it the Best that i no how you can Bet by on that and win. [26]

October 17, Lee sent a report from Bristoe Station to Jefferson Davis in which he detailed his intentions and his reasons for his next move. He did not consider it feasible to attempt to turn or force Meade back from his entrenched position around Centreville, largely due to supply and the state of his infantry that seriously lacked clothing, shoes, blankets, and overcoats. Accordingly, Lee decided to withdraw to his previous position on the Rappahannock River, where his army could be more easily supplied. The retreat to the Rappahannock began early in the morning, around 1 a.m. on October 18 when Major General Richard H. Anderson's division began its march on difficult roads, made muddy and slippery by the disagreeable stormy weather of the previous few days. By the end of the day, October 19, the morning marked by a miserable rain, Lee's army was concentrated south of the Rappahannock. Jubal Early's division, however, remained in the area of the Rappahannock pontoon bridge, with brigades taking it in turns to hold the earthworks on the north bank, close to the destroyed railroad bridge.

Meade responded by sending the Union infantry carefully forward on October 20, seeking news of Lee's whereabouts. The First Corps moved from Haymarket to Thoroughfare Gap to protect the right flank of the army as it moved forward, and also to provide confirmation that Lee was not lurking with intent to surprise Meade with another flank attack. The Second Corps moved to Auburn where it was learned that Lee had retired behind the Rappahannock. The Third Corps moved to Catlett's Station, camping on the south side of the railroad tracks. The Sixth Corps had earlier moved forward along the pike to Warrenton, followed by the Fifth, which halted at New Baltimore. As the 77th passed beyond New Baltimore, where Judson Kilpatrick's division had been forced back by Stuart's troopers, they "passed the bodies of many of our cavalrymen, who had been killed in the constant skirmishes which had been going on since our advance . . . the bodies of . . . men lay scattered along the roadside, nearly all of them stripped of their clothing by the rebels." At Warrenton, the Sixth Corps halted and the 77th's camp occupied a pleasant ridge just in front of the town. [27]

At Warrenton, the 77th busied themselves as best they could in camp, but due to the cold and wet weather, remained close to their fires and tents. The weather made it a miserable time, with heavy rains combined with a sharp drop in temperature and windy conditions, to make everyone uncomfortable. October 24, Captain Martin Lennon's diary read, "Cold enough to freeze the devil." October 25, Lennon noted, "So cold that the chaplain preached with gloves on, and a short sermon at that." Surgeon Stevens wrote, "The cold northwest winds swept through our camps, carrying chilly discomfort everywhere. The men shivered over their log fires; but while the fitful wind drove the smoke and fire into their faces, it froze their backs." Hoping that their camp would become winter quarters, the New Yorkers set their attention upon building comfortable quarters. Alonzo Bump wrote to Ell, his sister, "i have sean some hard times since i come down hear . . . i have Bin to worke all Day and Built me a chimey in my tent. i built it with Sods and now while i ame wrighting you i have Got a fier that makes me sweat." [28]

While Meade was able to quickly move the Army of the Potomac to Warrenton and establish headquarters at Bristoe Station, his primary supply line - the Orange and Alexandria Railroad - was in shambles. Lee had torn it up while falling back from Centreville. Because of the railroad's destruction, Meade did not believe he could safely move any further until the railroad was repaired, for it was not possible for 90,000 men to subsist off an area two armies had occupied and fought over for more than a year. George Stevens wrote after the war, "To attempt to advance in a desert country without first either providing a supply for many days, or opening ready communications with our base of supplies, would have been suicidal . . . The newspapers at the north that condemned the delay at Brandy Station, and sneered at the idea that the army needed a base of supplies, simply exhibited their profound ignorance of the first principles of campaigning." [29]

As Meade awaited the completion of repair work on the Orange and Alexandria Railroad, he contemplated his next move against Lee. After a disturbing tug of war with Lincoln and Halleck, Meade formulated his plan of operation to get at Lee behind the Rappahannock. The Federal commander set his sights on the Confederate pontoon bridge at the town of Rappahannock Station, the only connection Lee retained with the northern bank of the river. The bridge was protected by a bridgehead on the north bank consisting of two redoubts and connecting trenches manned by Jubal Early's division in addition to four pieces of artillery in the redoubt on the north bank and eight others in similar works on the south side. Plus there were sunken batteries for two guns and rifle pits arranged to command the Orange and Alexandria Railroad embankment. The bridgehead was an integral part of Lee's strategy to defend the Rappahannock River line. As he later disclosed, by holding the bridgehead he could "threaten any flank movement the enemy might make above or below, and thus compel him to divide his forces, when it was hoped that an opportunity would be presented to concentrate on one or the other part." [30]

On November 6, Meade issued orders for John Sedgwick to attack the Confederate bridgehead at Rappahannock Station with the Fifth and Sixth Corps and Major General William French to attack Kelly's Ford five miles downstream with the Third, Second, and First Corps. Once both Sedgwick and French were safely across the Rappahannock, the reunited Army of the Potomac would march to Brandy Station. Ten o'clock that evening in the 77th's camp came the order: "Reveille at half-past four; move at daylight." [31]

The New Yorkers, with the Sixth Corps, broke camp at 8 a.m. on the morning of November 7, rapidly marching twelve miles along the direct road to Rappahannock Station, and halting about 2 p.m., one mile before the Confederate bridgehead, well within sight of the Rebel entrenchments. One 77th soldier, identified only as *Yours Truly*, wrote home to the *Daily Saratogian*, "At the Station the river makes a sharp bend, running between two high knolls, on the top of which were the earthworks of the enemy, in which were placed their artillery, extending from a point on the river above the bridge in a half circle, say half a mile, to a point below, covering a deep ford on which were rifle pits of a formidable character. From these works their cannon and muskets were able to reach the whole open country for nearly a mile over which we obliged to march to the attack." In a low line of hills before the regiment, George Stevens saw that "within pistol shot of us, were rebel cavalry pickets, sitting upon their horses and facing us with the coolest impudence; but not a shot was fired at them." Sergeant James E. Barnes (Co. A) noted, wishfully, that while the New Yorkers carried three days of rations and forty cartridges each, they "hardly dreamed of a fight that day, although we knew the rebels were strongly fortified, and had quite a heavy force on our side of the river." [32]

In a matter of minutes, one half mile from the Confederate works, the Sixth Corps was drawn up into line of battle. Albion Howe's division held the right; Brigadier General Horatio Wright's First Division was positioned on the left, with one brigade from Brigadier General Henry Terry's Third Division in the center. Sedgwick ordered Howe's men to take the Rebel advanced line, in the low rolling hills next to the river that screened the main defenses at the bridge. Howe formed his two brigades in column, the 77th's Third Brigade in the front and the Vermont brigade is close support. The 43rd New York was thrown forward as skirmishers and began to drive the Confederate skirmishers back to and across the Rappahannock.

Soon, Sergeant Barnes recalled, "the cannonading commenced to our left, and we knew by this time that the first division were engaged with the enemy." At 3 p.m., Howe ordered his column to the attack. As soon as the 77th set off on the double quick, Confederate "shells commenced flying around, and bursting on all sides of us." The ground was uneven with occasional hollows and knolls affording some protection against Rebel shells. "By going at a double quick over the knolls, and slower in the hollows," one 77th soldier wrote, "we were enabled to keep a good alignment." The New Yorkers crashed "threw brush," charged "over ditches . . . all the while the Rebs doing there prettiest to hit some of us with their shells as they had a good range on us; but we gained the cover of the hill, no one hurt." The Confederate skirmishers were easily brushed aside, and as the 77th came within musket range, they were "swung around to the river and . . . ordered to halt and not to advance without orders." [33]

After gaining the cover of a hill, Sergeant Barnes remembered that the 77th "lay there for an hour, under a heavy fire all the time, their shells bursting all around us, but luckily they did no damage of any account; they wounded a few horses, but none of our men were hurt." Howe placed artillery batteries on this and nearby hills that pounded the Confederate earthworks with a "rapid and vigorous" fire. At dusk, from their position, the 77th watched as Wright's First Division assaulted the enemy works on their left on their way to occupying the pontoon bridge over the Rappahannock. Confederate resistance dissolved as hundreds of soldiers threw down their arms and surrendered. Others sought escape by swimming across the icy river, many drowning in the attempt, or by running the gauntlet of Federal rifle fire at the bridge. Southern troops south of the Rappahannock looked on helplessly as Northern soldiers herded their comrades to the rear as prisoners of war. In all, 1,670 Rebel soldiers were killed, wounded, or captured in the brief struggle, more than eighty percent of those engaged. *Your Truly* wrote, "The rebels ... seemed as happy to surrender as we to conquer. They only fought for their colors, and not very ardently for those." [34]

Major General French was equally successful in crossing the Rappahannock at Kelly's Ford. Meade then determined to follow up his victories by pushing both wings of the Army of the Potomac forward to Brandy Station in hope of catching Lee and forcing him to fight in the open field. However, on November 8 thick fog thwarted Federal efforts to get across the Rappahannock in force and discover what the Rebels were doing. Once the weather cleared, assuming Lee would make a stand at Brandy Station, Meade ordered his troops forward, but they did not come upon Lee's army until they reached the Rapidan River. Much to Meade's chagrin, Lee had slipped away to the high ground on the river's south bank.

As soon as Meade determined Lee's position south of the Rapidan, he began working on plans to attack it, even though the weather had turned bitterly cold and the mountains just west of Culpeper were already covered with snow. Once repairs of the Orange and Alexandria Railroad were complete and sufficient stockpiles of supplies were established, Meade planned to rapidly march his army forward to turn the Confederate right. Having received intelligence that Lee's army was stretched over a thirty-mile front with Clark's Mountain separating its two corps, Meade planned to move quickly across Jacobs, Germanna, and Culpeper Mine Fords. Once over the Rapidan, Union troops would advance to the Orange Plank Road and then crush Richard Ewell's Second Corps before driving west to destroy A. P. Hill's Third Corps. As the plan was predicated on speed and surprise, Meade issued his soldiers with eight days' worth of rations to eliminate the need for a large baggage train.

The 77th went into camp on the right of the army, two miles from Brandy Station "in a nice piece of hard-wood timber, the property of John M.[Minor] Botts." George Stevens wrote, "Mr. Botts boasted that he owned six hundred miles of fence when we came upon is possessions. He could not say that when we had been there a week!" *Yours Truly* reported, "We . . . have drawn a quantity of new axes and it would make your farmers cry to see the noble oaks, venerable maples, beautiful spoke timber, and hickory for axe helves, and flail swingles, all heaped on the fire and mercilessly consigned to ashes." Nearby were the remains of Confederate camps. One 77th soldier was impressed that the Rebels "had some very nice cantonments, leech tubs, to enable them to make soap, and bread troughs in which to make their own bread, and nice shingled log-houses, showing that they intended to remain the winter – They are very economical indeed, not a bone can be picked up in their tracks." [35]

Sergeant James Barnes spoke for the 77th when he wrote home, "As regards future operations this fall, of course we soldiers don't know anything, but from indications going on around us, I don't think we will remain here any longer than until the Railroad is repaired up to the river; then I think Gen. Meade will push ahead." Whether sooner than later, the spirits of the New Yorkers remained high. *Yours Truly* proclaimed "all [were] anxiously waiting for the command to go forward. It matters not when. We are an army of Veterans and can fight in any situation. Let the word be given and 60,000 muskets are ready to open on the foe." Another soldier proudly asserted "the 77th can stand anything, except shell and balls." Private Alonzo Bump, however, wrote to his wife and expressed more personal thoughts about future battles with these somber words: "well Dear if we have Got to fight it out I hope that they will Go in to it and have it Don with and if it is my Lot to fall upon the Battle Field then so Bee it But I hope that God will wach over me and Protect me from all Dainger." [36]

On November 24, George Meade intended to send the First, Fifth, and Second Corps to cross the Rapidan River at Culpeper Mine and Germanna Ford, and the Third and Sixth Corps at Jacob's Mill. All five corps would then converge at Robertson's Tavern on the Orange Turnpike leading to Orange Court House, and turn Lee's right flank. However, luck did not travel with the Federal army, for heavy rains descended upon the region, forcing Meade to push his operation back by two days.

At sunrise on the morning of November 26, the national day of Thanksgiving declared by President Lincoln, the Army of the Potomac was on the move. The 77th, with the Sixth Corps, was to follow the Third Corps to Jacob's Mill. However, the head of the column unexpectedly halted in the middle of the undisturbed camps of the Third Corps. Surgeon Stevens complained that "the Third Corps . . . should have been out of camp before we arrived, but as yet not a tent was struck nor a wagon loaded, and most of the men were asleep in their quarters." Consequently, the Empire State veterans were forced to halt and stand in the Virginia mud for a number of hours waiting for the delinquent corps to break camp and get out of the way. [1]

By 11 a.m., the Third Corps vacated their camps and the 77th moved again toward the Rapidan. The march was torturous for the soldiers. For miles the road was little more than a narrow passage cut through the forest; "a dense growth of stunted pines and tangled bushes, filling up the space between the trees of larger growth." The Sixth Corps moved along at a snail's pace and the narrow road created a bottleneck, the men halting for a time then advancing a few yards, then standing still again for several minutes, and again moving forward for a few steps. George Stevens recalled, "The men were faint and weary, and withal discouraged. They were neither advancing nor resting." [38]

The Third Corps did not reach Jacob's Mill until long after dark, causing yet another delay as the Union engineers did not have enough boats to complete the pontoon bridge. Once the engineers with poles cut from nearby trees improvised and completed the bridge, it took several more hours for the Third Corps to cross the Rapidan. Strung out for miles along the wood-lined road waiting for the Third Corps to cross the river, the woods echoed with the same cry: "coffee! coffee! passed from one regiment to another, until there could be heard but the vociferous demand for coffee." Finally, Sergeant George Bolton (Co. B) wrote, "after ten o'clock . . . we got permission to make for ourselves a little coffee." The sergeant mused, "We was all on the go some on one road some on another but anyway we got our coffee at last which is the greatest luxury we ever have when on the march, or for any other time I guess." The roadside was quickly dotted with thousands of little fires over which the soldiers of the Sixth Corps were cooking their favorite beverage. The pause for coffee was brief and a little after 11 p.m., the 77th crossed the Rapidan at Jacob's Mill and halted seven miles before their appointed destination at Robertson's Tavern. The men were exhausted and threw themselves upon the ground without waiting to erect shelter tents. George Bolton remembered, "we . . . was in our beds in a very few minutes, it was freezing pretty hard but we managed to keep midling warm." [39]

At 5 a.m. the next morning, November 27, the 77th arose from the cold ground and enjoyed a leisurely hearty breakfast in a large field filled with the soldiers of the Sixth Corps. The Third Brigade's band played familiar tunes as the men ate and drank their coffee around morning fires. Sergeant Bolton remembered, "We had lots of music I tell you, the first two tunes that our Brigade Band played I could not help but notice – When This Cruel War is Over and Rally Round the Flag Boys and I guess they didn't forget Home Sweet Home. I know I didn't." [40]

While the 77th enjoyed breakfast and martial music, Major General Gouvernor K. Warren's Second Corps was on a collision course with elements of the Confederate army. As Meade's soldiers the day before struggled through the thick Virginia mud, a Rebel scout reported the movement to Lee. The Southern commander responded by shifting his army east in an effort to block the Union flanking maneuver. At 11 a.m., skirmishing began near Robertson's Tavern between the van of the Second Corps and the Confederate divisions of Major Generals Jubal Early and Robert Rodes. The fighting continued throughout the day as both sides awaited the arrival of reinforcements.

Three miles to the south Union cavalry, under Brigadier General David Gregg, clashed with their Confederate counterparts led by J. E. B. Stuart, near New Hope Church. Holding the ground, Stuart's troopers were relieved around 2:30 p.m. when Major General Henry Heth's division occupied a hill to the west. This success proved short-lived as elements of George Syke's Fifth Corps arrived and swiftly drove Heth's troops from the heights. Although he had the upper hand, Sykes received orders from Meade to hold his position until the entire army was ready to attack. However, Major General William French's Third Corps was seriously delayed and far from being able to provide support to Sykes.

Throughout the morning, the 77th could hear the distant booming of cannon echoing the fighting at Robertson's Tavern. Earlier, French's Third Corps advanced slowly from Jacob's Mill to the crossroads at the Widow Morris farm in an effort to unite with Warren's corps engaged with the enemy. The right fork led directly to the tavern after merging with Raccoon Ford Road, which was picketed by Confederate cavalry. It also led to the exposed flank of Rodes' left flank. The left fork too led to the tavern, but by a much longer route. French lost valuable time pondering which road to follow, compounding his delay by choosing the longer route.

While French deliberated about which road to take, Confederate Major General Edward "Alleghany" Johnson led his division down the Raccoon Ford Road to connect with Rode's left. About 4 p.m., he collided with French's soldiers at the Payne farm. Unaware that he faced an entire Federal corps, the aggressive Johnson attacked with his 5,300 veterans. Heavy fighting quickly developed as the opposing troops charged and countercharged one another across the Payne farm fields and through the adjacent woods. Johnson's Southerners effectively halted the Northerners and thereby protected the left of Rode's division at Robertson's Tavern.

When the fighting noticeably intensified at Payne's farm, the 77th, with the Sixth Corps, marched from their camps to come to the support of the Third Corps. The New Yorkers "went off on the double quick" along a narrow and winding path toward Payne's. As they neared the battle scene, George Stevens wrote, "The sulphurous smoke filled the woods, and the roar of musketry became so general, and the forest echoed and reechoed the sound, so that it lost the rattling usually heard, and became a smooth, uniform roll." As Sedgwick's Sixth Corps arrived on the field, it was posted on the right of the Second Corps. Alonzo Bump wrote, "we Got so clost to the Rebals that we could see the flash from their Canons . . . the Rebs Began to Shell the woods whare we Ley and they maid some Good shots at us for the Shell Birst al around us." But, Sergeant Bolton wrote, "thank god the 77th was fortunate once again. We had only a few wounded." One of the least fortunate, however, was Private Isaac Boyce (Co. B). George Bolton wrote in a letter to his wife, "Poor Isaac Boyce had another very near escape. He had been wounded twice, once in front of Richmond, and at Fredericksburg, this time a piece of shell just grazed his head. He would never had known what hit him if his head had been an inch or two higher from the ground." The unlucky private would receive yet another wound six months later in the Wilderness. [41]

Surgeon Stevens after the war ended told of a humorous, yet macabre, event in the midst of the terror of battle:

> While the fight was in progress, General Sedgwick and his staff dismounted and were reclining about a large tree, when the attention of all was directed to two soldiers who were approaching, bearing between them a stretcher on which lay a wounded man. As the men approached within a few rods of the place where the general and his staff were, a solid canon shot came shrieking along, striking both the stretcher bearers. Both fell to the ground – the one behind fatally wounded, the other dead. But the man upon the stretcher leaped up and ran away as fast as his legs would carry him, never stopping to look behind at his unfortunate companions. Shocking as was the occurrence, neither the general nor the members of his staff could suppress a laugh at the speedy restoration of the man who was being borne disabled from the field. [42]

By evening, except for the occasional picket fire, the fighting ceased. Meade realized that his plan to steal a march and place his army on Lee's left flank had failed. During the night he concentrated the Federal army on a line perpendicular to the Orange Turnpike, west of Robertson's Tavern. Warren's Second Corps advanced some distance beyond Robertson's Tavern. The First Corps moved up to the support of the Second. The Fifth Corps, which had supported Gregg's cavalry division in an engagement at Parker Store on the Orange Plank Road, was also brought up in support of Warren, and early the next morning, November 28, the Third and Sixth Corps came up on the right of the Second.

In the midst of heavy rains and muddy roads, Meade sent the Union army forward. It was a difficult march for the 77th. George Bolton wrote, "today we had very bad weather, rained all day which made very bad for us to get through all kinds of places, rough road, crossings through woods, swamps, bushes, creeks, it beat all, but no matter we kept up just as close as was becoming for us with any kind of safety." The 77th had not gone far when Sixth Corps skirmishers began driving back their counterparts. Bolton observed, "The Rebs kept falling back until they got into their rifle pits and across their swamps and a creek." The night before Lee had withdrawn his army back to a new position on the high ground west of Mine Run and constructed earthworks. A correspondent for the *The New York Times* described in detail the Confederate defenses behind Mine Run:

> The line was of the most formidable character. It extended along a prominent range or series of hills for a distance of six or eight miles. This series of hills formed all the angles of a complete fortification, and comprised the essential elements of a fortress. The centre of the line presented four or five well-defined facings of unequal length, occupying a space of more than 3,000 yards, with

such angles of defence that the fire of the enemy was able to enfilade every avenue of approach, while his right and left flanks were not less strongly protected. Stretched immediately in the rear and on the flanks of his position was a dense forest of heavy timber. About 1,200 yards in front of his lines was Mine Run – a stream of no great width, but difficult for infantry to cross, from the marshy ground and dense undergrowth of stunted timber with which was frequently flanked on either side, as well as from the abrupt character of its banks. In addition to these natural defenses, the enemy had felled in front of a large extent of his position a thick growth of pine, as an abattis, while he had also thrown up earthworks of great strength along his entire line. Thus the position was much stronger than ours at Gettysburg, and more formidable than the enemy's at Fredericksburg.

That evening, the opposing armies held their position in close proximity as Meade considered his next move. [43]

The next day, November 29, with heavy rain again falling, Meade worked to gain the initiative. He ordered Warren and Sedgwick's Sixth Corps to swing south with the goal of getting around the Confederate right. Although it took all day, Warren's Second Corps was in position to roll up the Confederate right flank at 5 p.m. but could not advance due to darkness. Albion Howe's division constituted the extreme right of the line with the Third Brigade the right of the division, and the 77th the right of the brigade. George Stevens recalled, "The dense thicket and a gentle eminence concealed the corps from the view of the rebels, who were but a few yards distant; and in order to insure secrecy, orders were issued that the men should avoid all noise, and refrain from lighting fires." The lack of fires made for a miserable night. Sergeant George Bolton complained,

"Here we had the privilege of lying down, but oh dear, talk about sleeping, it was easier to freeze. We had no fire and didn't have coffee before we started which made it a great deal more tedious, one man died with the cold but I think it was through being without overcoat, all that we could do was to keep walking to be the least comfortable . . ." [44]

That evening, Warren was confident that the Second Corps could overwhelm the Confederate force in his front the next morning, and he convinced Meade that the plan would work. The Federal commander strengthened Warren, directing two Third Corps divisions to operate under Warren's orders. With his command numbering about 26,000 men, it was expected that would crush the Confederate right. Meanwhile some of Sedgwick's division commanders had discovered weak points on Lee's left, no works being thrown up. Sedgwick assured Meade the Sixth Corps could successfully attack the Confederate force in his front. Accordingly, Meade ordered an attack for the morning on November 30th, the right and center to open with artillery at 8 a.m., at which time Warren was to make the main attack. At 9 a.m. Sedgwick was to assault Lee's left with five divisions of the Fifth and sixth Corps

Also that evening, as reflected the increasing effectiveness of the medical service, Sixth Corps surgeons prepared for the influx of the expected wounded in the next day's battle. George Stevens wrote, "At the hospitals everything was in perfect readiness. Hospital tents were all up, beds for the wounded prepared, operating tables were in readiness, basins and pails stood filled with water, lint and dressings were laid out upon the tables, and surgical instruments spread out ready for the grasp of the surgeon." [45]

At daylight, the 77th took their place in line of battle with "orders to load and prime." Union artillery was posted along the entire front.

At the appointed time, Sixth Corps batteries opened up, followed by artillery on the left and center. Utilizing lyrical metaphor, Sergeant Bolton wrote, "Our folks commenced their best music all along the lines with a number of their big tunes . . . Awful as it is nonetheless it is Grand sublime in the extreme . . . It is nice to hear it. But better to be a long ways off." Suddenly the cannonading ceased, but no sound came from Warren's direction. George Bolton and the rest of the regiment "wondered what was the matter." During the night, Lee strengthened the defenses behind Mine Run. Warren retired the night before confident of victory, but in the morning he saw on the heights before him a line of strong works thrown up overnight, well-filled with infantry, and heavy batteries covering the slope which it was necessary to charge. Therefore a successful attack was deemed impossible. He immediately reported to Meade the reasons for his failure to attack, that he misjudged the strength of the enemy's position, and that he was unwilling to sacrifice his command. Meade immediately postponed the assault. After personally reconnoitering the Confederate positions, the Northern commander agreed with Warren and called off the attack. [46]

The 77th maintained its position through the rest of the day in freezing temperatures. Surgeon Stevens wrote, "It was a day of discomfort and suffering long to be remembered." Sergeant Bolton complained the regiment had "been without anything warm to eat for 26 hours and 18 hours without a spark of coffee." The New Yorkers had to settle for the hardtack issued to their division, which was often the case, old and riddled with worms. Stevens wrote it was "difficult for a man to know whether his diet was to be considered principally animal or vegetable." Thomas Neill sat with his staff when he was handed some hardtack that seemed to be moving. The general broke the cracker, and handing it back to the servant, said, "Jim, give us one that hasn't so many worms in it." [47]

One December 1, frustrated by Lee's countermove, low on provisions, and faced with worsening bad weather, Meade decided to withdraw the Army of the Potomac back across the Rapidan. The pickets were ordered to build fires and keep up a show of force. The 77th that night was on the picket line and formed the tail of the rear guard of the army on its retreat. After a rapid march, the regiment crossed the pontoon bridge at Germanna Ford. The next evening, the New Yorkers were back in their old camp near Welford's Ford at Brandy Station. Although grateful to be back in their camp, Alonzo Bump spoke for the regiment when he wrote "we are all tiard out for we ware up night and Day for 8 days." [48]

With the return to Brandy Station, the Army of the Potomac was finished campaigning for the year. The decision not to attack Lee at Mine Run was applauded not only by the 77th, but also by the rest of the army. For all who saw the enemy's position agreed, in the words of one member of the Iron Brigade, "To have charged those heights . . . would have been sheer murder." One officer of the Fifth Corps wrote: "I can truly say there was not an officer or man in the division but that felt it now simply impossible to carry such entrenchments. It could not be done. It were madness to attempt it, worse than at Fredericksburg to allow it." A Pennsylvania colonel concluded, "The army, perhaps the Union cause, was saved, due to the clear judgment and military skill of those grand officers, Meade and Warren." [49]

Although the 77th was thankful to be back in comfortable winter quarters, 1863 closed out with a most somber scene. The New Yorkers were called out to "witness one of those sad scenes, a military execution." One member of the regiment identified only as *X* was haunted by the scene:

Two men of the Second Vermont Brigade of our division were shot for desertion. The regiment was called out for parade and marching to a field not far from our camp we formed with the rest of the Division on three sides of a square. On the remaining side their being a wide grave. The occasion of course sobered the minds of the men somewhat, but in the half hour we stood shivering in the cold and waiting, there was displayed much of the exuberance of spirit which always characterizes a body of soldiers. After a while the solemn cortege made its appearance – two ambulances, each containing one of the prisoners and his coffin – the Provost Guard of the Division marching on each side, and behind were the two religious attendants, Chaplain Mack of the 3d Vermont, and Chaplain Hale of the 5th. Arriving at the grave the coffins were placed on the ground. The proceedings of the Court Martial were read and the prisoners asked if they had anything to say. The followed the solemn scene, the saying of the service for the burial of the dead over forms still throbbing with life and health, and throughout the vast multitude, the uncovered head witnessed the power of the solemnity of the moment. This being over, the prisoners kneeled on their coffins, and the Provost Guard formed in front. A white paper was placed over the heart of each to guide the fire. The fatal word was given, and the muskets rang sharply out on the cold air. One fell dead as a stone. The other gave a wild shriek, and exclaiming 'Oh! Dear me,' fell forward on his face; then raising himself on his hands, sank again and expired. The whole Division then marched past them as they lay upon the ground, and thus concluded the sad and harrowing scene. [50]

11

"BOYS, DON'T RUN"

During the winter of 1863-1864, the Army of the Potomac, with its cavalry, was tightly packed in the V of land between the Rappahannock and Rapidan Rivers. Gouverneur Warren's Fifth Corps was headquartered at Culpeper, with divisions north and south of the town. Six miles east, Major General Winfield Scott Hancock's Second Corps blanketed Cole's Hill, a low, round elevation extending from Stevensburg north toward Brandy Station. Uncle John Sedgwick's Sixth Corps spread from Brandy Station to the Rappahannock, with the 77th's Third Brigade near Welford's Ford. Ambrose Burnside's Ninth Corps, joining Meade's army from Annapolis, was stationed along the Orange and Alexandria Railroad to Bull Run to protect the vital rail link with the North.

Supplies by the trainload flowed into Brandy Station, and virtual nineteenth-century shopping mall sprang up there. "Persons of almost any trade are improving the time by making money from the soldiers," wrote one New Yorker. "There you will see a sign over the door of a little board shanty, 'Oysters,' 'Fresh Fish,' 'Condensed Milk,' 'Beer,' and numberless other signs which tempt the pocketbook of the soldier." Private Alonzo Bump wrote his wife, "i ame as fat as a hog. i have Got about 2 inches of fat on my ribs now. We Live first rate. We have Pork and Beeans and all the soft Bread we Can eat and that is enough to make a man fat who don't have eny more then we Do." The daily arrival of newspapers at 3 p.m. added an air of normality to the burgeoning military encampment, as newsboys spread throughout the camps yelling the papers' names. Library books, concert bands, and an influx of women brightened the winter days. "One agreeable feature of this encamp," Surgeon Stevens reminisced, "was the great number of ladies . . . On every fine day great numbers of ladies might be seen riding about the camps and over the desolate fields, and their presence added greatly to the brilliancy of frequent reviews." More than one officer of the 77th enjoyed visits from their wives. Stevens noted, "Great taste was displayed by many officers in fitting up their tents and quarters for the reception of their wives. The tents were usually inclosed by high walls of evergreens, woven with much skill, and fine arches and exquisite designs beautified the entrances to these happy retreats." [1]

During the winter, one tangible source of pleasure for the men of the 77th, and a vivid demonstration of support from home, was the work in camp of the Christian Commission that looked to the spiritual needs of the soldiers. The Christian Commission "made arrangements by which it loaned to nearly every brigade in the army, a large canvass, to be used as a roof for a brigade chapel." The Third Brigade's chapel, *Sweet Briar*, was "built of logs and covered with the canvass . . . and was large enough to hold three hundred people." At *Sweet Briar*, religious services were held not only on Sundays, but also on week day evenings. The efforts of the Commission spurred something of a revival in the 77th. Members of the regiment gathered on the bank of the Hazel River one morning and Chaplain Norman Fox baptized Corporal Hiram Burt (Co. A) and eleven others of their brethren. Private David McNeal, Jr. (Co. E), who would be killed in action at the Wilderness, wrote to a friend in Saratoga Springs, "our chaplain drew up a league for a Christian Society, to which about thirty put their names – pledging their faith that they would live before their fellow soldiers as becomes christians. I have always believed that for a soldier to be able to discharge his duty to his Country, he needs the guidance of an unerring God. There is nothing that will enable a man to go so soberly and boldly into battle as the assurance in his own heart that, whether he stands or falls, his eternal good is secure." Owing to the energy of the devoted chaplain, the chapel also served as a reading room where "all the principal papers, secular and religious, literary, military, pictorial, agricultural, and scientific were furnished." Alonzo Bump told his wife, Mary, that *Sweet Briar* held a spelling school. However, he didn't seem to benefit much from the instruction as revealed when he wrote, "we have meetings 3 times a weeak and we have spelling Schools some nights and the Boys Goe thair and sit and read all day." [2]

Sweet Briar was also the scene for the first president's birthday. One 77th soldier wrote home describing the day of celebration:

> On Washington's Birthday the weather was fine and the day was passed in preparing the chapel for an evening of celebration. Our 'Storm Flag' was beautifully festooned in the rear of the speaker's stand, wooden chandeliers were made, and everything put in trim for a quiet, soldierly celebration of the birthday of the Father of his Country. Precisely at six o'clock P. M., the Brigade Band struck up 'Hail Columbia' in front of the Colonel's quarters, and in an instant every tent in the camp was depopulated and the band surrounded by a noiseless multitude, each one eager to catch every note of the soul-stirring air. Soon officers began to arrive from all over the Division, and our Chapel was filled to overflowing. While the space outside

was thronged by the men of our own and the Vermont Brigades... The exercises lasted until 'taps' when the band once more favored the crowd with some of their excellent music, and the party adjourned with the hope that the next 22d February might be celebrated throughout a restored and happy Union. [3]

With abundant fresh food, warm beds, the social and religious community at *Sweet Briar,* and the welcome addition of women in camp at Brandy Station, the morale of the 77th was high. George Stevens wrote, "Many pleasant recollections cluster around the old camp . . . which will never be effaced from the memory of the soldiers of the Army of the Potomac." None of this, however, diminished the New Yorkers longing for home. Private Alonzo Bump wrote to his wife,

> Dear i hope that it wont Bee long Before i shall Bee at home . . . O dear if i was a Bird i would Bee thair with you Before to morrow night . . . Dear i think of you more than 20 times every day that i Live and i wish i was thair with you to night. i Should Bee the happest man on Earth . . . After you Git thiss . . . wright, wright, Wright, wright, wright, wright. [4]

The regiment quickly settled in the camp routine of drill and picket duty. However, on the evening of February 26th, orders were received at the 77th's headquarters to be ready to march the next morning at 7 a.m. Brigadier General George Custer's cavalry brigade was to make a reconnaissance toward Charlottesville, and the Sixth Corps was ordered to move in that direction to support Custer. One soldier identified only as *W* wrote, "A guard was to be left in camp, and some few men, who were unable to stand the fatigues of the march, were also allowed to remain behind." At 8 a.m., on the morning of the 27th, the 77th moved forward in the direction of Culpeper. At that point they passed about 11 a.m., and at night camped near James City Courthouse - a distance of nearly seventeen miles. Early the next morning, the march was resumed, and shortly after noon the New Yorkers halted near Madison Court House. *W* reported, "It being understood that they were going no further, the men went to work with all the zeal and energy natural to a soldier, and soon a little village of brush houses were erected, (the tents being left in camp) where they made themselves quite comfortable, as the weather was mild and dry. In short time the brigade butchers killed and prepared fresh meat for the troops, and the hides of the cattle were taken by some for the roofing to their shanties, in case of rain." *W* recounted that, "It was soon ascertained that some very nice poultry was in the vicinity, and the soldiers, learning it might not be properly cared for, owing to the destitution of the country, kindly gathered it in, and, by so doing, were enabled their masticators quite a surprise. – Luckily the change of diet did them no harm, though some hinted at 'fowl' play being connected with the affair." [5]

At Madison Court House, the artillery accompanying Custer's troopers could be heard in the distance. The firing lasted throughout the day even though the Union cavalry was at least twenty five miles away. In no danger of battle, the New Yorkers "were all in the most uproarious good humor." One anonymous soldier wrote:

> 'Duck-stone,' 'leap frog,' and other games were called in to vary the monotony. And now some incautious wight would be surprised by finding himself astride a rail and elevated on the shoulders of a yelling crowd. One fellow came riding through the line as an old 'crowbait,' and first he knew he and his horse also were in like manner were lifted off their feet and treated to a ride. And tossing in a blanket was a favorite sport. A dozen stout men taking hold around the

edge with one on the blanket, all at once it is drawn tight with a 'one two three' and the unlucky individual is sent ten or fifteen feet into the air, coming down with a somersault perhaps, head-first or inverted order, only to be caught upon the blanket and sent flying again.

That night a heavy rain set in. By morning the rain had turned to "snow, and the few deserted houses in the neighborhood were soon leased on very liberal terms, and became dance houses and minstrel halls for the entertainment of the 'Yanks.'" [6]

On the evening of March 1, Custer's cavalry returned to Madison Court House, looking the worse for wear, and muddied from their reconnaissance. Reveille sounded in the 77th's camp at 5 a.m. on the morning of May 2, and at 7 a.m. the 77th and the Sixth Corps headed back to their camp at Brandy Station. *W* reported to the *Saratogian* that the Union force "started on the return trip, bringing in horses, mules, and innumerable contrabands." The march was difficult "as the recent storms had caused an abundance of Virginia's great staple, and consequently the soldiers shoes weighed a great many more ounces to the pound than ordinarily." Twenty-three miles later the same day, the New Yorkers arrived at their camp near Welford's Ford. [7]

One evening back at camp the 77th at dress parade was read a nonsensical order from Major Nathan Babcock, in temporary command of the regiment while Winsor French was back in Saratoga recuperating from an illness. The order was that no soldier could go outside camp without a pass from regimental headquarters. As the 'outhouse' was outside the camp limits it was "decidedly inconvenient to have to go to the major for a pass thereto, particularly if one was in a hurry. So the 'boys' concluded to 'boom' the officer in command during the temporary absence of the colonel, who the boys wanted back to lead them." Private John Y. Foster (Co. I) aptly recorded the event:

> Empty cans were filled with combustibles and discharged near regimental headquarters; the noise whereof disturbed the sleep on many in the brigade; on this particular night, which was somewhat darker than usual, a rifle barrel was loaded to the brim and put into a length of stove pipe and then carried carefully and placed as near the major's tent as practible and then the short fuse lit. The whole camp was quiet when suddenly oh! What a report . . . The major and a squad of soldiers were quickly on the scene, supposing that the camp was attacked. Nowhere could be seen the enemy who in their hasty retreat left their gun, which was captured and taken to regimental headquarters . . . This brought the wrath of the brigade commander [Thomas Neill] on us in an order to the temporary commander of the regiment that if there is any more noise in the camp of the Seventy-seventh he would place the whole regiment under arrest. [8]

Possibilities for the spring campaign were limited only by George Gordon Meade's imagination. That, however, was precisely what concerned President Lincoln. As the war's third year opened in Virginia, it was painfully clear that simply doing as well as Lee would not be enough. The result had been stalemate, and if 1864 brought more of the same, the war-weary North might lose its resolve. Victories, not textbook marches and drawn battles, were imperative. A new catalyst was needed, someone who played by different rules that capitalized on the Federal advantage in numbers, someone whom Lincoln could trust. Major General Ulysses S. Grant was the president's answer to the impasse in Virginia.

On March 1, 1864, Congress passed a bill reviving the rank of lieutenant general, and two days later, Grant was appointed to that rank and accepted the office of General-in-Chief of all Union armies. Grant arrived in Washington on the afternoon of March 8 and, after a quick meal, headed over to the Executive Mansion to meet the president. After a whirlwind round of receptions and meetings, the lieutenant general decided to pay a visit to the Army of the Potomac. Grant arrived at Brandy Station the afternoon of March 10 and headed to Meade's headquarters. The commanding general was well aware that Meade was in low favor in Washington. Secretary of War Edwin Stanton told Grant before he headed down to Brandy Station "you are going to the Army of the Potomac and you will find a very weak irresolute man there and my advice to you is to make a change at once." But after meeting with Meade, Grant was impressed and decided to retain him as commander of the Union army. [9]

Ulysses S. Grant was well-received with hopeful expectation by the 77th. "He is a very plain looking personage indeed," yet, "The men express the utmost confidence in Lieut. Gen. Grant, and expect to take Richmond the coming season." Although the New Yorkers were optimistic, they were grimly aware that, "Some very hard fighting will of course be necessary, but none harder than the army of the Potomac has done and stand ready, willing and anxious to do again, if the subjection of the rebel army of Virginia is to be the fruit of their efforts." [10]

On March 23, the War Department issued orders consolidating the Army of the Potomac's five infantry corps into three. The Second, Fifth, and Sixth Corps were left intact. Dismantled and redistributed among those corps were the First and Third Corps. The orders allowed the soldiers in the abolished corps to retain their old corps badges – an attempt to minimize the painful disruption. The 77th's division commander, Albion Howe, was put in command of the Artillery depot and in charge of the Office of the Inspector of Artillery in Washington. Taking his place was Brigadier General George W. Getty. Well respected, Getty was appointed to West Point at the age of sixteen and for the next forty eight years he made his career in the army. Getty was brevetted for gallantry in the Mexican War and fought during the Seminoles Wars. At the beginning of the Civil War he was captain of the 4th Artillery and became acting chief of artillery of Ambrose Burnside's Ninth Corps during the Maryland Campaign. He was promoted to brigadier general of volunteers and at Fredericksburg commanded the Third Division of the Ninth Corps. Before assigned command of the Second Division, Getty served as acting inspector general of the Army of the Potomac.

After his initial meeting with Meade, Grant decided against remaining in the west and now thought he should make his headquarters with the Army of the Potomac. There he developed a grand strategy to suppress the Confederacy. Grant aimed at a simultaneous movement all along the line, from one end of the Confederacy to the other, bringing the entire Federal strength to bear. While Union armies east of the Alleghenies were crushing Lee, those west of the mountains were to meet out similar treatment to Joseph E. Johnston, who was commanding the Confederate Army of Virginia that Grant had seriously wounded at Chattanooga. Convinced that the rebellion would collapse only when its military power was broken, Grant aimed "first to use the greatest number of troops practicable against the armed force of the enemy," and second, "to hammer continuously against the armed force of the enemy and his resources, until by mere attrition, if in no other way, there should be nothing left to him" but surrender. [11]

The General-in-Chief intended to go at Lee from all sides. Given the primary role, the Army of the Potomac would be increased to maximum strength and hurled across the Rapidan. At the same time, Benjamin Butler's Army of the James was to advance up the James River's south bank toward Richmond. His assignment was to sever Lee's supply lines, threaten the Rebel capital, and possibly combine with Meade, depending on how things fared at the Rapidan. The third offensive would come by way of the Shenandoah Valley, where Major General Franz Sigel was slated to threaten Lee's left flank. Hemmed in and isolated from his supplies and reinforcements, Grant hoped Lee would finally be cornered and vanquished.

Lee was Grant's target, but it was not immediately clear how best to get at the Confederate general. After considering his options, Grant decided that the Rapidan was the best place to launch his war of attrition. His subordinates all agreed that a frontal assault would be madness, incurring unsustainable casualties. Maneuvering Lee from behind his earthworks onto ground where the Federal army's overwhelming number in infantry, cavalry, and artillery would make a decided difference offered the best strategy and track. Swinging around the Confederate downriver flank seemed to be the most advantageous route. However, once across the Rapidan, the Yankees would become enmeshed in the Wilderness, a broad stretch of impenetrable thickets and dense second growth of low-limbed and scraggly pines, chinquapins, scrub oaks, and hazel that had replaced forests cut down to fuel local iron and gold furnaces. Old mining pits were everywhere, and winding streams added to the difficult terrain. More so, the tangled vegetation nullified the very advantages that Grant sought to exploit. The second growth forest had few negotiable roads, clearings were scarce, and visibility rarely exceeded a few hundred feet. The cavalry was next to useless, gun crews had no fields of fire, and complex infantry maneuvers were impossible.

Once beyond the Wilderness, however, the Army of the Potomac would enter open country suitable for fighting. The key to maneuvering past Lee's downriver flank was getting through the Wilderness as quickly as possible. Grant accepted Meade's chief of staff Andrew A. Humphreys' proposal that Burnside's Ninth Corps would guard the rail line until otherwise ordered. The combat units, accompanied by their first-line transport, would march in two parallel columns. The right column, composed of Brigadier General James Wilson's Third Cavalry Division, Warren's Fifth Corps, and the 77th's Sixth Corps was to cross the Rapidan at Germanna Ford and march to Wilderness Tavern, a ramshackle two-story stagehouse of stones and hewn logs at a weedy clearing where the Germanna Plank Road intersected with the Orange Turnpike. Moving in tandem with the right, the left column, composed of Brigadier General David Gregg's Second Cavalry Division, Hancock's Second Corps, and the Artillery Reserve, would pass over the Rapidan at Ely's Ford and proceed to Chancellorsville. By Humphrey's calculations, if the Federal army started at midnight, hard marching could bring it through the Wilderness and nearly to Mine Run before sunset the same day. That would get the army out of the heavily wooded terrain and catch Lee by surprise.

In preparing for a battle on or near the south bank of the Rapidan, Meade directed the issuance of sixteen days' marching rations, 14,000,000 rounds of small arms ammunition (fifty rounds to be carried by each soldier), ten days' full allowance of grain for 56,000 horses and mules, and, in case of the Medical Department, all necessary field hospital supplies on the basis of 12,000 wounded. The supply train would number 4,300 wagons, 835 ambulances, and a herd of cattle to slaughter as needed. *The New York Herald* correspondent, Sylvanus Cadwallader, estimated that lined up end to end, Meade's supply train would reach from the Rapidan to below Richmond. [12]

The official order for the advance against Lee's Army of Northern Virginia was issued May 2. On the 3rd, Federal cavalry would set out to ensure that the routes from Culpeper to the Rapidan fords were secure. The Union infantry was not scheduled to move out until almost midnight May 3. The 77th's Sixth Corps was to march at 4 a.m. on the 4th by way of Stevensburg and the Germanna Plank Road to Germanna Ford, following the Fifth Corps, and after crossing the Rapidan, bivouac on the heights beyond.

Sylvanus Cadwallader arrived at Brandy Station on the evening of May 2, and the following morning witnessed what he described as "probably the busiest period I witnessed during the war." Commissaries scrambled as the North's largest and most extravagantly provisioned army made ready to move: "Cartridge boxes, haversacks and caissons were all filled, fires were burning day and night for many miles in all directions, troops and trains were taking their assigned positions, staff officers and orderlies were galloping in hot haste carrying orders, whilst the rumble of artillery wheels, the rattling and clanking of mule teams, the shouting, song, and laughter of thousands of men" merged in a deafening din. Locomotives chugged in, belching smoke and steam, disgorged supplies and new troops then puffed back to Alexandria crammed with everything not essential for the march. Mule drivers swore a multiplicity of oaths as they cracked their whips and jockeyed their teams by the railroad tracks. "An army is as bad as a woman starting on a journey," was Colonel Charles S. Wainwright's explanation for the pandemonium, "so much to be done at the last moment." [13]

Soon after dark, Hancock began assembling his Second Corps under a clear, starry sky. Between 11 p.m. and midnight, Hancock's infantry began the march from Stevensburg towards Ely's Ford in two columns. Warren's Fifth Corps was roused out at 1 a.m. The corps struck their tents and within an hour and a half Warren's soldiers headed toward Stevensburg by way of Culpeper Courthouse. Reveille sounded at 2:30 a.m. in the 77th's camp. Simultaneously, bugles blared throughout the Sixth Corps bivouacs. The New Yorkers bid adieu to their comfortable winter quarters, and by 4:30 a.m., the 77th, with their Second division, started toward the Rapidan, with Wright's and Rickett's following. George Stevens remembered, "It was a lovely day, and all nature seemed rejoicing the advent of spring. Flowers strewed the wayside, and the warble of the blue bird, and the lively song of the sparrow were heard in the groves and bushes." Nevertheless, after months of inaction, the men of the army had become soft, and the sides of the road were littered with thousands of overcoats, blankets, knapsacks, and articles of clothing. Some of the regiment's soldiers eagerly exchanged their old equipment for new items when they found them. [14]

The Fifth Corps infantry came within sight of the dual 220 foot-long pontoon bridges spanning the Rapidan at Germanna Ford at 6 a.m. Within an hour, they were passing over the pontoons and by noon Warren's foot soldiers were entirely over the Rapidan. There they halted for an hour waiting for the Sixth Corps to catch up with it. Getty's Second Division soon came into view and Brigadier General Henry I. Eustis' Fourth Brigade thundered across the bridges, followed by the Third Brigade. When the 77th approached the river, the New Yorkers erupted in loud cheers as they saluted Grant astride his bay horse, Cincinnati, calmly smoking a cigar while observing the progress of the Federal army. After crossing the river, the regiment marched another three miles and bivouacked near Flat Run and the plantation of Mrs. J. R. Spottswood.

South of the Sixth Corps, Warren's troops settled in their camps within easy reach of the intersection of the Germanna Plank Road and the Orange Turnpike, with Charles Griffin's forming the extreme right flank of the Army of the Potomac covering the Orange Turnpike west of Wilderness Tavern and toward Lee. Earlier, Hancock's Second Corps crossed the Rapidan at Ely's Ford and bivouacked at Chancellorsville. Federal supply trains rolled across the river at Culpeper Mine Ford late that afternoon and were closing in on Chancellorsville. Grant was satisfied that by night, May 4, the Union infantry were safely in their designated positions and the supply wagons were arriving into place on schedule.

The Confederate signal station on Clark's Mountain discovered Federal troop movements as early as midnight, May 4, and immediately alerted Lee's headquarters. The direction of the enemy's march was clarified at daybreak. At 9:30 a.m., the Clark's Mountain observation post signaled the magnitude of Grant's advance and that the blue-clad columns were moving to Gemanna and Ely's Fords. By 10 a.m., Lee had settled on a course of action; he would march east to meet Grant. The Southern general directed Ewell to start the Second Corps east on the Orange Turnpike. At the same time, Lee ordered Hill's Third Corps to advance through Orange Court House and continue east on Orange Plank Road. The two Confederate corps would be within easy supporting distance of each other and would have a short march the next morning before encountering Grant's soldiers. Longstreet was directed to march north to Orange Courthouse, then to take up position behind Hill on the Orange Plank Road.

That evening, after sending a dispatch to Burnside to cross his corps at Germanna Ford, Grant and Meade huddled around their crackling campfire to discuss the Army of the Potomac's projected infantry movements. Instead of sending Meade's soldiers below Mine Run as originally had been planned, the generals decided to establish a static line within the Wilderness. Accordingly, Meade's general order for May 5 was to position the Federal army toward Lee on a convex line from the Rapidan to Shady Grove Church. Hancock was to march out the Catharpin Road and extend north. Warren was to stop at Parker's Store and connect with Hancock's right. And

Sedgwick was to follow Warren and take up the Fifth Corps old position, posting a division at Germanna Ford until Burnside came up with the Ninth Corps. The decision to position the army into line and to keep it there until Burnside arrived stemmed from growing conviction that Lee would fight as he did the previous November behind Mine Run. Though wrongly, it was believed that Lee's evident digging in along Mine Run afforded the Federals the opportunity to put the finishing touches on their own troop dispositions. The established line within the woods would serve as a jumping off point.

May 5, the Fifth Corps was on the move by 5 a.m. Guarding the rear of Warren's column was Brigadier General Charles Griffin's First Division which remained on the Orange Turnpike. About an hour later, as Warren rode to join the marching column, a courier galloped with the message that Confederate infantry were on the turnpike. They were forming a line of battle, and ominous clouds of dust pointed to a large movement of soldiers from Lee's direction. Warren was shocked as Lee was supposed to be miles away fortified behind Mine Run. He hurriedly dispatched an aide to inform Meade of this unexpected development. At 7:15 a.m., Warren's messenger caught up with Meade and announced Lee's infantry was on the turnpike, less than two miles from Wilderness Tavern. Canceling the day's plan, he ordered Warren to halt his column and attack the enemy with his full force. Meade immediately forwarded news of Lee's movement to Grant, and an hour later received his reply: "If any opportunity presents itself of pitching into a part of Lee's army, do so without giving time for disposition." [15]

Shortly after the Fifth Corps began positioning itself for battle, Sedgwick advanced the 77th's Second Division down the Germanna Plank Road and massed Getty's men in the fields around Wilderness Tavern. Nearly two miles behind, Brigadier General Horatio G. Wright halted his division at the intersection of the Germanna Plank

Road and the Culpeper Mine Road. Having left a brigade north of the Rapidan with the division's wagon train, Wright asked for reinforcements from Getty's division. Around 10:30 a.m., while Wright's division was still maneuvering onto the field, a messenger arrived at Getty's headquarters at Wilderness Tavern with the request for additional troops. Getty not being yet engaged, sent the 77th, with its sister regiments to assist Wright. The regiment retraced its steps along the Germanna Plank Road to Spottswood, forming the tail of Wright's column.

The Confederate infantry spotted by Fifth Corps pickets were of Edward "Allegheny" Johnson's division leading Ewell's Second Corps column. Upon reaching Saunders Field and seeing Yankees ahead, Johnson's Confederates began spreading on either site of the Orange Turnpike and constructing a strong defensive line along the field's western boundary. To support Johnson, Ewell placed Major General Robert E. Rodes' division in a second line several hundred yards behind, its left wing anchored on the turnpike. By noon, nearly 10,000 Rebel soldiers were dug in across from Warren. Jubal Early's division, another 4,500 men, waited behind in reserve.

Shortly after receiving news of Confederates on the Orange Turnpike, Grant left the gabled farmhouse at the Rapidan that served as his headquarters and arrived at the Lacy house. There, Meade greeted him with the latest intelligence. Another Rebel column, A. P. Hill's corps was advancing up the Orange Plank Road, threatening Warren's left flank. Measures were immediately taken to block Hill's column before it reached the Brock Road. It appeared Hancock was best situated to cover the endangered roadway, but there was considerable doubt whether his soldiers could reach the critical intersection of Brock and Orange Plank roads in time. Accordingly, at 10:30 a.m., Grant ordered George Getty's remaining three brigades down the Brock Road to fight a holding action until Hancock could arrive. Once united, Getty and Hancock were to push west toward Hill's seasoned veterans.

Hill's vanguard, slowed only by Lieutenant Colonel John Hammond's weakened 5th New York Cavalry, was less than a mile from the junction of Brock and Orange Plank roads. Getty, on the other hand, had over two miles to cover his objective. His men set off at a rapid pace, and as the Federal soldiers neared the crossroads, a Union cavalry detachment galloped up the roadway in their direction announcing that Rebel infantry were advancing up the Orange Plank Road. Getty ordered his men on the double-quick, reaching the crossroads as gray forms could be distinguished advancing toward them. For now, the Northerners' timely arrival stemmed Hill's advance.

At the same time Getty was dispatched down the Brock Road, Warren and Sedgwick received strongly worded orders to press ahead in the turnpike sector. By 11 a.m., Horatio Wright's division, followed by the 77th's Third Brigade, began slanting along Culpeper Mine Road toward Warren's right flank. Impossible terrain, however, brought Wright's advance to a harrowing crawl. Jungle-like undergrowth snatched at the arms and legs of the Saratoga regiment, and the intertwining briars snagged at their clothing. George Stevens wrote, "The wood through which our line was now moving was a thick growth of oak and walnut, densely filled with a smaller growth of pines and other brushwood; and in many places so thickly was this undergrowth interwoven among large trees that one could not see five yards in front." Forced to press on Indian style in columns rather than sweeping lines, the Federal soldiers were especially vulnerable to Confederate skirmishers. "As our line advanced," Stevens later recounted, "it would suddenly come upon a line of gray-coated rebels, lying upon the ground, covered with dry leaves, and concealed by the chapparal, when the rebels would rise, deliver a murderous fire, and retire." While the Federal troops had about a mile and a half to reach Warren's right flank, it would take nearly four hours to arrive at the scene of battle now echoing through the woods in Warren's front.[16]

Despite receiving peremptory orders at 10:30 a.m. to "attack the enemy at once and push him," Warren's division commanders seemed curiously resistant to doing anything quickly. On the Fifth Corps left, Brigadier General Samuel Crawford remained snuggled in behind earthworks at the heights at Chewning farm, sending only four regiments under the command of Colonel William McCandells northward to link up with the left of Brigadier General James Wadsworth's division. It was late morning before Wadsworth had managed to maneuver his division's three brigades into a line extending from Saunders Field southward. Brigadier General Charles Griffin's division was immediately north above the Orange Turnpike. Yet, Griffin vehemently objected to attacking the entrenched Confederates until Warren's entire line was in place and until Sedgwick had advanced to cover his exposed flank. Frustrated by the delay, Meade ordered Warren to attack before Sedgwick could arrive.[17]

Sometime around noon, Griffin's division moved out from its earthworks and pressed across the tangle of thick underbrush. To Griffin's left, Wadsworth's soldiers hacked through the forest, trying to stay at pace. Instantly alignments broke apart. Regiments lost sight of one another amidst dwarf pines and prickly underbrush, emerging in tangled confusion with other detachments or veering off on tangents of their own. Companies snaked single file through slashing patches of thornbush interwoven with briers and stumbled into fetid swamps and gullies where vision was limited to a few yards. Whole regiments were swallowed up.

MCKEAN'S SUNDAY SCHOOL BOYS GO TO WAR

Shortly before 1 p.m., Griffin reached Saunders' Field and Wadsworth was in position. On the right of the turnpike was Brigadier General Romeyn Ayers brigade, on the left Joseph Bartlett's men with Colonel Jacob Sweitzer's brigade in support. Connecting to the left was Wadsworth's division, the brigades of Lysander Cutler, Roy Stone, and James Rice spreading southward in that order. Brigadier General John Robinson's division waited near Wilderness Tavern. Sedgwick was nowhere in sight, and McCandless was still struggling to connect with Wadsworth's left from the Chewning farm.

The assault up the turnpike would be made not by two corps, as Meade had planned, but by two divisions forming a fluctuating line across two miles of woodland, both flanks wide open to the enemy. Six hours after Meade's first order to attack, Warren was at last poised to attack. Confronting him was Ewell's entire Second Corps, firmly entrenched with an unobstructed field of fire spanning much of his front. The Federal troops, on the other hand, were hobbled by disadvantages that handicapped an attacking force, particularly in the dense terrain of second forest growth.

At 1 p.m., Union bugles sounded the attack. Griffin's division, two lines deep, rose from the woods and determinedly stepped into the sunlit Saunders Field. Presented with ideal targets, Ewell's riflemen fired as fast as they could load. Frightening gaps almost immediately appeared in Griffin's formation. In some places, Union soldiers made minor inroads. In others, they were struck down almost as soon as they left the cover of their earthworks. Ayer's brigade was forced to take cover in a gully traversing Saunders' Field to avoid enfilading fire. The brigade of Joseph Bartlett surged beyond Ayer's left and overran the position of Brigadier General John M. Jones' Virginians, killing the Confederate commander. However, Bartlett's right flank was now exposed to attack and his brigade was forced to beat a hasty retreat back across the clearing. Bartlett's horse was shot out from underneath him, and he barely escaped capture.

Wadsworth's three brigades, extending south from Saunders Field had started forward at the same time as Griffin's division. To Bartlett's left, Lysander Cutler's Iron Brigade advanced through woods, thorns tearing at their clothes, south of the field and smashed into a brigade of Alabamians commanded by Brigadier General Cullen A. Battle. Although initially forced back, the Confederates counterattacked with the brigade of Brigadier General John B. Gordon, routing the Iron Brigade for the first time in its history. Further to the left, at Higgerson farm, the brigades of Colonel Roy Stone and Brigadier James C. Rice smashed into George P. Doles' Georgians and Junius Daniel's North Carolinians. Their attacks failed under heavy fire and Wadsworth ordered his men to pull back. Meanwhile, Warren ordered a section of artillery into Saunders Field to support his assault, but it was captured by Rebel soldiers who subsequently were pinned down and prevented by Federal musket fire from moving the guns until darkness. In the midst of hand-to-hand fighting at the guns, the field caught fire and men from both sides were forever haunted by the screams of their wounded comrades burning to death.

Meade's futile turnpike offensive was over by 2:30 p.m., an hour and a half after it began. At 3 p.m., Horatio Wright's Sixth Corps division, with the addition of the 77th's Third Brigade, finally emerged above Saunders Field. Colonel Emory Upton's brigade led the charge and hooked up with Robinson's two Fifth Corps brigades, and the long-anticipated Federal right flank connection had been achieved. Consideration was given to immediately attack across the clearing, but in Upton's opinion to do so was madness, and no assault was made. The remainder of Wright's force struggled to form in the woods to the north. Colonel Henry Brown's New Jersey Brigade took position to the right of Upton; the 77th's Third Brigade moved next to Brown, forming the extreme right, and Brigadier General David Russell's regiments fell in behind to form a reserve.

Whether Wright could make a difference however remained to be seen. The segment of Ewell's line responsible for repulsing Wright was held by Allegheny Johnson's division. Maryland Steuart's brigade was behind formidable earthworks on the western edge of Saunders' Field. To Steuart's left was the famed Stonewall brigade now led by James Walker, affectionately named Stonewall Jim. To Walker's left, anchoring the far Confederate northern flank, was Leroy Stafford's hardnosed outfit. Originally disparaged as wharf rats, hotheads, and ne'er-do-wells, the motley Louisiana Brigade earned a solid reputation for drinking, pillaging, and most importantly, hard fighting.

Companies D and G of the 49th New York, detailed as Third Brigade skirmishers, fanned out into the woods to develop the enemy and to provide cover fire while the five Third Brigade regiments were maneuvering into three lines. The 49th New York, with the 7th Maine on the right, formed the first line. The 61st Pennsylvania covered the rear of the 49th New York. The 43rd New York, with the 77th to its left, fell in behind the Pennsylvanians. The 49th New York and the 7th Maine tentatively advanced up to a wooded ridge which ran south into the swale between the Fifth Corps and Ewell's Confederates. The swale was, as Surgeon Stevens remembered, little more than "a strip of level marshy ground, densely wooded like the rest of the wilderness." [18]

Suddenly the woods in front exploded with rifle fire. Brigadier General Leroy Stafford's Louisianans crested the top of the ridge no more than a minute or two after the Third Brigade's Mainers and New Yorkers had gone into position. The Yankee soldiers poured a searing volley into the front of his brigade. Stafford immediately ordered his troops to halt and return fire. The volleys became a continuous roar as Stafford's Louisianans slugged it out with the Third Brigade. A musket ball took Major John H. Crosby of the 61st Pennsylvania out of the fight seriously wounded. Crosby was struck on the right side of the face, ripping away part of his scalp and bruising his skull. Yet Stafford's soldiers could not move forward as their commander deemed it foolish and suicidal to cross the marshy swale.

Around 3:30 p.m., Sedgwick arrived on the field to supervise Wright's efforts. By then, shot and shell from two Confederate 12-pounders posted on the western side of the swale under the command of Lieutenant Michael Garber were pounding the Third Brigade's front line. With tremendous force, a solid shot "crashed through the woods and struck Sergeant Joseph Seville of Company F [61st Pennsylvania] in the face, taking his head off." His comrades looked on in horror as Seville's headless body remained "upright for a perceptible time after the head was gone." Corporal Edward Jennings (Co. H) looked to his left at Company D when "a shell from the enemy instantly killed five of our boys." Other shells screamed over the 77th and burst amidst Sedgwick's staff. In the ensuing pandemonium, the New Jersey Brigade was double-quicking toward Sedgwick's aide, Thomas Hyde, on their way to reinforce the Third Brigade. Hyde remembered:

> I had dismounted to fix my horse's bit, when a canon-ball took off the head of a of a Jerseyman; the head struck me, and I was knocked down, covered with brains and blood. Even my mouth, probably gaping in wonder where the ball would strike, was filled, and everybody thought it was over with me. I looked up and saw the general [Sedgwick] give me a sorrowful glance, two or three friends dismounted to

pick me up, when I found I could get up myself, but I was not much use as a staff officer for fully fifteen minutes. [19]

Realizing that he could not maintain his position much longer, Stafford ordered his men to the rear to the right. Moving by files, the Louisiana regiments slipped back through the underbrush toward the ridge. The thickets being nearly impassable, Stafford's soldiers degenerated into a panic stricken mob. The Confederate general had no choice but to order a further retreat to his original line. As the 1st Louisiana worked their way by him, Stafford turned his back to the bluecoats when a minie ball whizzed through the green foliage and passed through his body, armpit to shoulder blade, severing his spine. Paralyzed and in bone-crushing pain, Stafford was carried to the Southern entrenchments. Despite the searing pain, Stafford nevertheless spurred on fresh Rebel troops hurrying to the front to break the 77th's brigade. The reinforcements were more Louisiana soldiers under Harry Hays; they had been held in reserve for just such a moment as this. Sweeping around Ewell's line, Hays' brigade moved into position on the far Confederate left.

Hays' five Louisiana regiments dashed into the woods, passing the mortally wounded and Stafford urging them on, and hit the skirmishers of the 7th Maine on the north end of the Third Brigade. Literally fighting from tree to tree, the Rebel soldiers wove their way through the woods, steadily driving back the skirmishers of the 7th Maine until they came to the edge of the small clearing where Stafford's earlier attack sputtered to a standstill. Having shot all their ammunition on Stafford, the 7th Maine retired to the Third Brigade's second line to the rear of the 49th New York. The New Yorkers pulled back their right wing to cover the position vacated by the New Englanders. The 7th Maine faced by the rear rank and refilled their cartridge boxes. To the south, the 43rd New York and the New Jersey Brigade (in two lines) rested in formation facing west. Directly behind the 43rd New York, the 77th nervously stood in line of battle listening to the fast approaching sound of rifle fire. [20]

The steady popping from the skirmish line suddenly increased and the resounding echo of rifle fire echoed through the woods to the rear of the 7th Maine. Their skirmishers bounded back toward the main line of the Third Brigade, alerting the troops of the new Confederate drive. The 4th New Jersey, which stood in the woods south of the brigade fixed bayonets and brought their muskets to "charge bayonets." Colonel Edwin Mason brought the Maine regiment to its feet just as the 6th Louisiana charged to take the New Englanders from the rear.

Mason quickly pivoted the 7th Maine to face west, which exposed the New Jersey Brigade to enfilade fire. The oncoming Confederates unleashed a destructive volley into the Jerseymen. The brigade unleashed a rolling fire by the right oblique straight into the backs of the New Englanders who were to their right front. In danger from Confederate riflery from the front and Yankee bullets from the rear, Colonel Mason ordered the 7th Maine to change front. The veteran soldiers about faced and by companies from the right began to swivel back to their former position. With the 49th New York to their south, the 7th Maine stood their ground and hammered the Confederates with well-placed volleys. Harry Hays' Louisianans stubbornly tried to slug it out with the Third Brigade. Twenty minutes later, unwilling to sustain more losses, Hays ordered his soldiers to retreat. Hays' brigade entered the fray with just little less than 500 effectives and sustained 250 casualties left in the clearing and woods. Hit the hardest by Confederate bullets, the 7th Maine lost 81 of its men, and the 49th New York, to its left, lost under one third of that number. The 77th anxiously endured the strain of standing in line while the battle raged just beyond their sight and came out of the fight unscathed, yet George Stevens vividly described the intense tempo of the afternoon's fighting on the Federal right:

> ... the battle had raged furiously all along the line. The rattle of musketry would swell into a continuous roar as the simultaneous discharge of ten thousand guns mingled in one grand concert, and then after a few minutes, became more interrupted, resembling the crash of some huge king of the forest when felled by the stroke of a woodman's axe. Then would be heard the wild yells which always told of a rebel charge, and again the volleys would become more terrible and the broken, crashing tones would swell into one continuous roll of sound, which presently would be interrupted by the vigorous manly cheers of the northern soldiers, so different from the shrill yell of the rebels, and which indicated a repulse of their enemies. Now and then the monotony of the muskets was broken by a few discharges of artillery, which seemed to come in as a double bass in this concert of death, but so impenetrable was the forest that little was made of artillery, and the work of destruction was carried on with the rifles. [21]

When Hays' Rebels scampered back to their staging position, they left behind many of their dead and wounded, along with those from Stafford's brigade, upon the ground. The Confederates immediately dug in bracing themselves for a Federal counterattack. Stevens later explained, "The confederates now commenced to strengthen the position on their side of the ravine, felling timber and covering it with earth. The woods resounded with the strokes of their axes, as the busy workmen plied their labor within three hundred yards, and in some places less than one hundred yards of our line, yet so dense was the thicket that they were entirely concealed from our view." [22]

As Stafford's and Hays' Louisiana brigades were being repulsed by the 77th's Third Brigade, their Second Division commander, George Washington Getty, launched an attack with his three remaining brigades westward down the Orange Plank Road from the intersection at the Brock Road. Almost immediately, things began to go wrong. As Warren and Sedgwick discovered, it was impossible to maintain formation in the dense second-growth forest and underbrush. Men standing next to each other on the Brock Road moved forward into the woods. Some had a clear path, others had to detour around thickets, and still others got hung up in the underbrush. Getty's soldiers could not move through such ground without signaling their advance to waiting Confederate infantrymen. The brush was so thick that the Rebels lay in wait until the Federal bluecoats were almost on top of them, and then Confederates got in the first volley at point blank range. South of the Orange Plank Road, Rebel fire was so heavy that the men had to crawl into position. Colonel Lewis Grant soon realized his Vermont Brigade was heavily outnumbered, and he pulled his New Englanders into a semicircle for their own protection.

Frank Wheaton's First Brigade soldiers advanced through marshy ground, listening to the roar of musketry on both flanks as their sister brigades came up against A. P. Hill's Confederates. Wheaton's first line received a volley from barely fifty yards away. Pinned in place, the Pennsylvanians and New Yorkers could only fire away at the puffs of musket smoke to their front signaling the presence of the enemy. To their right, Henry Eustis' Fourth Brigade fared little better as they were staggered by an uncontested Confederate volley. The 2nd Rhode Island was flanked and broke before rallying. On its left the 10th Massachusetts was pounded on both front and right flank, but held its line until depleting its ammunition, when the 7th Massachusetts moved up from the second line to replace the 10th. The 37th Massachusetts never got into the fight.

The attack quickly degenerated into a large-scale bushwack, with neither side able to advance. Volleys of musketry continued until about 6:30 p.m., when the firing died out and Hancock's Second Corps soldiers moved up to relieve the Second division. Getty's troops rose and fired off their last remaining rounds, about faced, and marched back to their second line in reserve.

While combat in Getty's sector of the Orange Plank Road rapidly accelerated, and after the failure of Warren's and Sedgwick's attacks, the woods around the turnpike had shifted into an uneasy quiet. Despite the stalemate on his northern front, Meade was determined to assemble a coordinated assault against Ewell. Another charge, he believed, would wreak destruction on the Confederate line. With the arrival of Brigadier General James B. Rickett's Sixth Corps division, William H. Morris' First Brigade was sent to Warren and posted on the turnpike. The other brigade – a mixed unit of men from Ohio, Pennsylvania, and Maryland under Brigadier General Truman Seymour – was assigned to Sedgwick.

At about the same time Rickett's arrived, one of Warren's signal stations reported Confederate troops marching from Ewell's southern flank in the direction of the Orange Plank Road, most likely to assist A. P. Hill. When this intelligence was forwarded to Grant, he mistakenly concluded that Ewell must have weakened his line, when indeed the gray-clad soldiers did not belong to Ewell but to Cadmus Wilcox's men moving to reinforce A. P. Hill on the Orange Plank Road. Based on this faulty intelligence, Grant concluded that now was the time to renew the turnpike offensive. The Union general resolved to slam Ewell with every available man. Accordingly, at 6 p.m., Meade ordered an all-out assault.

Just after sunset, the 77th's Third Brigade, with David Russell's New Jersey regiments and Truman Seymour's brigade, made a combined attack in the woods north of Saunders Field where Brigadier General John Pegram's Virginians and Hays' Louisiana Brigade lay solidly behind their entrenchments. The 119th Pennsylvania, a battalion of the 5th Wisconsin, the 49th New York, 4th New Jersey, 6th Maryland, add 110th Ohio straddled the Culpeper Mine Road and formed the first line from north to south, respectively. The 49th, south of the road, 61st Pennsylvania, 77th, and 43rd New York to the north comprised the second line. (The 7th Maine, having been relieved by Seymour's two regiments, had moved to the rear.) The rest of the New Jersey Brigade stood behind in three lines. As the infantry moved forward, Sedgwick directed the 15th New Jersey away from the column to fill a gap in his line. [23]

On the right of the line, Seymour dispatched skirmishers forward to find the Rebel line. They immediately came in sight of Pegram's brigade sharpshooters. At the first sounds of musketry, the 4th New Jersey, 6th Maryland, and 110th Ohio fixed bayonets and stepped off. Pegram's Virginians silently waited while the skirmishers scampered back through the woods and bounded over the entrenchments. Halting not more than one-hundred yards away, the Federals unleashed a volley then the three Northern regiments charged. The Virginians stayed down behind their earthworks until Seymour's soldiers were barely forty yards away. Rising en masse, the Confederates fired point blank into the blue ranks. The Union soldiers recoiled under the blast, but rallied, loaded, and returned the volley. Unable to see the Confederates in the dark, Seymour's three Federal regiments aimed at the muzzle flashes from the impenetrable woods to their front. The Virginians and Hay's Louisianans repeatedly raked the Federals with alternating volleys by files from the right and then the left oblique, mowing them down like a scythe going through high grass. The 4th New Jersey, 6th Maryland, and the 110th Ohio melted away and streamed to the rear.

Sergeant Samuel S. Craig (NYSDMNA)

To the south, the 119th Pennsylvania, 5th Wisconsin, and 49th New York struggled through the underbrush and scrub oaks from the 6th Maryland's left rear, but disintegrated under intense firing. The Third Brigade supports, the 61st Pennsylvania, 77th, and 43rd New York quickly replaced them. The dreadful Rebel musketry knocked down large numbers of men. Private Michael Lama (Co. F), who had triumphantly captured the 18th Mississippi's battle flag at Marye's Heights was shot dead. Private Hermanus Bower's (Co. C) clutched his stomach and fell to the ground mortally wounded. A Confederate minie ball passed through Private William Watson's (Co. C) shoulder and he staggered to the rear. Corporal Thomas Beisty (43rd New York) caught a bullet in the upper side of his head. Colonel George F. Smith (61st Pennsylvania) dismounted from his horse and steadied his men. He wanted his men to see him that day to refute regiment gossip about his bravery under fire. Unable to withstand the severe pressure, the Third Brigade stubbornly withdrew back to their works, but not before the men of the 77th had fired off all their ammunition, their Enfield rifles getting too hot to hold where the hand came in contact with the barrel.

Safely ensconced behind earthworks south of the Orange Turnpike, Warren's Fifth Corps never attempted to advance. The Fifth Corps general refused to enter the deadly thickets. Confederate artillery dampened Warren's resolve. Ewell's artillery crews concentrated a killing fire along the turnpike. The 10th Vermont of Rickett's division, was especially hard hit. The Vermonter's chaplain remembered "a perfect tornado of shell, that burst above and in the midst of the men." One shell exploded near Ricketts, killing three horses. Another Green Mountain soldier, Lemuel A. Abbott, wrote in his diary that "the air was full of solid shot and exploding shells as far each side of the pike as could be seen. A shell burst inside one soldier, "completely disemboweling and throwing him high in the air in a rapid wheeling motion above our heads with arms and legs extended until his body fell heavily to the ground with a sickening thud." Nearby troops were "covered with blood, fine pieces of flesh, entrails, etc., which makes me cringe and shutter whenever I think about it." Charging into the hellfire of Confederate gunnery was unthinkable. [24]

Throughout the day, the Army of the Potomac's surgeons feverishly worked to care for the constant stream of human wreckage flooding the field hospitals. "Thousands of wounded men," George Stevens remembered, "were stretched in and about the several field hospitals, and long trains of ambulances, loaded with more bleeding victims, were constantly bringing new subjects to care." The 77th's Second Division field hospital was set up in the rear of the 61st Pennsylvania on the banks of Wilderness Run, near an abandoned gold mine, and within a few yards of Meade's headquarters. Steven's wrote later, "All the hospital tents belonging to the division were filled to overflowing with the unfortunate victims of the battle. There, all the space between the rows of tents, and for many yards in front and rear, was covered with others, from whom there was no room under the canvass, and, finally, long rows of them were laid upon the ground at a little distance from the hospitals as close as they could lie, covering many rods of ground." [25]

To the surgeon, the groans and cries of the wounded left between the lines were heart-rending, but it was at the field hospital where the resulting carnage was seen in all its horrors:

> There, wounded men by the thousands are brought together, filling the tents and stretched upon every available spot of ground for many rods around. Surgeons, with never tiring energy, are ministering to their wants, giving them food, dressing their wounds or standing at the operating table removing shattered fragments of limbs. Men wounded in every conceivable way, men with mutilated bodies, with shattered limbs and broken heads, men enduring their injuries with heroic patience, and men giving way to violent grief, men stoically indifferent, and men bravely rejoicing that it is *only a leg*. To these the surgeons are to give such relief as lies in their power, a task the very thoughts of which would overcome physicians at home, but upon which the army surgeon enters with as much coolness and confidence as though he could do it at once. [26]

Darkness brought an end to the organized battle of the day, but there was little rest for the exhausted 77th. With Pegram's Virginians behind their stout earthworks on a ridge not more than one hundred yards away and across the marshy ravine, no one dared spread their blanket upon the ground to catch some much needed sleep. Rather, "Each man sat with musket in hand during the wearisome hours of the night, prepared for the onset of the enemy." George Stevens explained, "Skirmishing was kept up during the night, and at times the musketry would break out in full volleys, which rolled along the opposing lines until they seemed vast sheets of flame." [27]

Chaplain Norman J. Fox, Jr. (L. Tom Perry Special Collections)

The plight of wounded soldiers left between the lines could not be ignored as their pleas for help echoed in the night's darkness. During the day, ambulance corpsmen struggled through the woods and thickets to drag the wounded away from the battle. Difficult enough in daylight to penetrate the thickets and carry injured men to safety, in the moonless night it was practically impossible. Bodies were imperceptible in the dark forest, and holding a lantern aloft spelled certain death before skittish skirmishers from both sides. The slightest light or sound between battle lines was guaranteed to spark an avalanche of musketry. The dangerous mission to succor the wounded, however, did not deter Chaplain Norman Fox. With a canteen of warm medicinal whiskey in each hand, the chaplain carefully crawled through the underbrush and soon came upon Captain Albert Nickerson of the 7th Maine who had been shot through both legs just above the knees. Barely conscious, Fox poured some whiskey into Nickerson's mouth and splashed some warm water on his face. The burning liquor revived him, and seconds later, the Maine captain was hoisted upon a stretcher and brought to a waiting ambulance. Placed in the ambulance, Nickerson was surprised to share it with his own lieutenant, Eli H. Webber.[28]

In the evening, Grant and Meade sat around a campfire at headquarters. Talk turned to the day's conflict, which Grant understood as a prelude to the real fighting that was to occur the following morning. The Federal General-in-Chief planned to send in all four Union corps – Hancock's, Sedgwick's, Warren's, and Burnside's – in unison against Lee's army. Sedgwick and Warren were to renew their attack against Ewell as a diversion to occupy the Rebel Second Corps. In the meantime, the real assault would occur on Hancock's front. The Pennsylvanian was to attack down the Orange Plank Road with Getty's troops and his own corps. To ensure success, Burnside's two divisions were to insert themselves between the Rebel wings, then shift southward and savage A. P. Hill's flank. Though planned for 4:30 a.m., Meade sought a delay until 6 a.m. to ensure Burnside would be in place. Grant feared that if the assault was delayed until 6 a.m., Lee would then seize the initiative. Even so, he authorized an extra thirty minutes to prepare. The Army of the Potomac would launch a coordinated assault to destroy the Army of Northern Virginia at 5 a.m, May 6.

Robert E. Lee also prepared to launch an assault the next morning. Longstreet's First Corps and Richard H. Anderson's division of the Third Corps were to arrive before dawn and relieve Hill's fought-out soldiers, enabling Hill to shift northward and fill the troublesome gap between the two Confederate wings. Ewell would advance out the turnpike at morning's first light. Ideally, Ewell would rout Sedgwick and break Grant's supply line. Accordingly, the eccentric commander arranged his brigades to deliver a crippling blow. John B. Gordon was shifted to the far north of Ewell's line, by Flat Run, and was aligned with the rest of Early's men. Artillery was stationed in Gordon's support. Rode's division remained below the turnpike, while Johnson's and Early's extended above it. Throughout the night, Ewell's soldiers chopped trees to strengthen their earthworks.

The 61st Pennsylvania spent a horrible night on the picket line one-hundred yards west of the Third Brigade's line in the swampy bottom land which separated the two armies. They ducked from sporadic sniping from Confederate sharpshooters as search parties struggled through the tangled undergrowth looking for the wounded. All night they anxiously listened to the enemy cutting down trees and constructing log earthworks. Brush fires flared and crackled all along the line, stinging their eyes.

At 4:30 a.m., as the morning sun's rays began to filter through the woods on May 6th, a section of Colonel Thomas Carter's Virginia artillery began shelling the lines of Seymour's brigade and the Third Brigade. A 12-pounder case shot sailed over the 61st Pennsylvania and hit Company B of the 49th New York which was lying down on the crest of the ridge to the east. While his men buried their faces in the dirt, Captain John F. E. Plogstead sat down with his back against a huge oak to the right front of the line. Private Christopher C. Funke heard the shell burst a second before a case ball struck Private Christopher Wilken, the man next to him, in the head. The cast iron ball, without losing momentum, bore through Wilken's skull and kept going. Paralyzed by the sight, Funke stared at the puddle of bone and brains of his comrade. Seconds later a 10-pounder bolt whirled through the woods, crashing through the oak tree at the right front of the company, leaving Captain Plogstead's body a mutilated heap. It then plowed under to the right of Funke. The impact threw men into the air like dried autumn leaves in the breeze. To the left of Second Lieutenant Julius C. Borcherdt, the bolt struck Private John Weissmantel in the chest and sent his body flying six feet into the air. [28]

The 77th hugged the ground just below the crest of the ridge to the right rear of the 49th New York. Though somewhat protected by the crest, Confederate shells screamed also into their line. Private Issac Boice (Co. B) received his third wound of the war when a shell fragment hit him. Another shell exploded next to Corporal Charles Burnham (Co. C) splattering his comrades with torn pieces of flesh and bits of bone. Still another dropped in between Privates Walter Dwyer (Co. D) and George Deal (Co. B) and Sergeant William Saxton, sending their bodies in grotesque flying cartwheels of death. [29]

Shortly after Carter's Virginia artillery opened up, the men of Pegram's brigade, now commanded by Colonel John S. Hoffman, and that of Hays swarmed out of their earthworks and advanced in line of battle across the marshy ground toward the Third Brigade and Seymour's Maryland, Ohio, and Pennsylvania regiments. Launched without warning and pushed forward with furious intensity, Hoffman's Virginians swept over Federal skirmishers north of the Culpeper Mine Road, driving them back to Seymour's line. To the south, straddling the road, Hays' Confederates drove back the 61st Pennsylvania to the ridgeline held by the Third Brigade.

While the Confederate advance initially met only slight resistance, the force of the attack nevertheless was quickly blunted by the marsh's heavy undergrowth between the enemies. Crouched for the forward movement ordered at 5 a.m. the previous evening, the regiments of Seymour and the 77th's Third Brigade sprang into action. The assault almost immediately dissolved into uncoordinated regimental charges into the tangled thorns and the marshy bottomland. The ferocious shock of attack and counterattack - at times volleys fired at point-blank range - swayed back and forth. Surgeon Stevens was awed by the intensity of the battle: "The volleys of musketry echoed and reechoed through the forests like peals of thunder, and the battle surged to and fro, now one party charging, and now the other, the interval between two armies being fought over in many places as many as five times, leaving the ground covered with dead and wounded. Those of the wounded able to crawl, reached one or the other line, but the groans of others, who could not move, lent an additional horror to the terrible scene whenever there was a lull in the battle." [30]

The full force of Seymour's and the 77th's brigades were thrown into the counterattack. But if Ewell failed to press an overwhelming assault, he was well prepared to offer a stout defense behind sturdy breastworks. According to Colonel D. Bidwell, commanding the Third Brigade when Thomas Neill replaced the wounded division commander, Getty, the pursuing blue infantry ran up against an impenetrable line of log and dirt earthworks. He later reported:

> . . . at the appointed hour we made a vigorous assault, but the enemy having during the night strengthened their position, combined with the natural obstacles in our front of a marsh covered by a heavy growth of thorn bushes, caused us to retire with a heavy loss to the line occupied during the night. About two hours later we were again ordered to advance with the whole line, but could not gain any ground, when an order came to entrench where we were.

By 8 a.m., the 77th and its sister brigades and Seymour's soldiers settled down to skirmishing. [31]

Shortly after 5 a.m., near the intersection of the Brock and Orange Plank roads, a signal gun sounded and Hancock attacked with Getty's Sixth Corps depleted ranks in support. Hancock's infantrymen in front of Getty's Second division broke through A. P. Hill's troops on the south side of the Orange Plank Road, driving them back on James Longstreet's approaching corps, which stalled the Union advance. Getty's division followed in support, occupying a portion of the front line in time to receive part of Longstreet's fierce counterattack. In the ensuing chaos, Getty's three brigades were badly intermingled with Hancock's corps. The Second division re-formed behind some captured Rebel earthworks, drew ammunition, and became Hancock's main reserve. At about 11 a.m., Longstreet shattered another Federal assault, counterattacked, and drove Hancock's soldiers back through Getty's division toward the vital Brock-Orange Plank intersection. The Sixth Corps troops were also driven back after both flanks were turned and entrenched at the Brock Road. Here, Private William Armstrong (Co. K) reunited with the Army of the Potomac. Decades later, he reminisced:

> Early in the morning . . . I started to return to the regiment from Washington, D. C. The battle of the Wilderness was in full blast. Having no gun or equipments, I removed the equipments from the body of a dead comrade when I go on the battlefield and put them on, and taking his rifle, I was ready for action. Seeing a detachment of our division – the Second, known by the white cross – moving to the left and thinking that my regiment was amongst them, I followed them and took part in the action that ensued late in the afternoon.[32]

Private Armstrong quickly placed himself behind the hastily built log and dirt entrenchments protecting Getty's division as thick smoke from fires caused by muzzle blasts and cannon fire blew across the Union front from the south. Just then, the Rebel yell echoed through the tangled woods as Lee had ordered another assault on Hancock's line. Under the smoke, the Confederates charged right up to the breastworks on the Brock Road. They broke through one of Hancock's divisions, but Getty's soldiers stubbornly plugged the breach, firing point-blank into the Rebels spilling out of the smoke.

The breach was shut, and the Confederate attackers scrambled back into the woods.

After this final assault on this portion of the battlefield, William Armstrong set out to find the 77th. Told that his regiment was with the Third Brigade on the right, Armstrong found himself in a dangerous position between the lines and did not make it back to the 77th that night:

> Marching to where I thought was the right for my regiment, over ground upon which there were many Union dead, their bodies sheltered from the fierce rays of the sun by the dense thicket of scrub oak and pine, I began to get apprehensive, and pausing on a low hill to get a better view, a shot close to my ear disclosed that I was unconsciously near the picket lines of the enemy. My legs thereupon making good racing time, I was soon back in our lines. After passing the night under guard, as a straggler, the next morning I was allowed to go to my regiment. [33]

While brisk skirmishing continued in the woods north of Saunders Field late in the morning, the 77th, along with the rest of Wright's division, began the work of fortifying their position with logs, decayed wood, and brush and at some points rifle pits dug by regimental pioneers. Confederate sharpshooters made the task difficult. Yet the pioneers, with axes and shovels, were able to also clear and level some spaces for Union artillery along the Sixth Corps lines, where batteries were planted and used with great effect when Confederates attempted to advance from their fortifications on the ridge opposite the swampy ravine. By then the underbrush in a section of the woods in front of the 77th's Third Brigade were sheathed in flames. Attempts to rescue the wounded from both armies were abandoned, consigning their bodies to the fires. The stench of bloated and bursting bodies, coupled with the nauseating smell of burning flesh, made the New Yorker's position nearly untenable.

While Ewell's northern flank was strengthened by Brigadier General Robert D. Johnston's North Carolina brigade, Sedgwick's was weakened. The Sixth Corps was stretched thin. The intense fighting of May 5 had taken a fearful toll, the futile attacks of the following morning had depleted Sedgwick's force even more, and the continuous Confederate sniper and artillery fire continued to reduce the Federal's ranks. Seymour, whose brigade held the flank reported heavy losses, including his best officers. The problem was compounded when the Third Brigade, posted to the left of Seymour, shifted south to help fill in the gaps in the Sixth Corps' lines. Stretching to occupy a longer line, Seymour's brigade was dangerously thinned.

To shore up the Union flank, Sedgwick ordered Brigadier General Alexander Shaler's brigade of three New York regiments to the Federal right wing and placed the New Yorkers under Seymour's command. At first, Shaler was posted in a line perpendicular to the Federal front, facing north and closing the Union flank. However, as the 77th's Third Brigade edged southward, Shaler was forced to deploy one regiment as skirmishers and to detach another to assist Bidwell. By this time, Seymour's brigade was so thinly stretched that Shaler's last regiment was called into the front ranks. No protecting force remained and the Federal flank was wide open to attack. Seymour's and Shaler's brigades were now virtually in a single line. Only two Union regiments that had been bled dry the previous evening formed any kind of rear guard.

A little after midnight on May 5, after the firing had died out, John B. Gordon's Georgia Brigade swung around to Ewell's far left flank, next to Hoffman's brigade. Gordon forwarded scouts eastward to feel out the Federal line. In the light of early dawn, his scouts returned and reported back. The Union line ended in a thick patch of Woods across from Hoffman. Gordon's Georgians were unopposed and extended well beyond the end of Sedgwick's formation. The Confederates were handsomely poised to enfilade the Union infantry with minimal resistance. This news was almost too good to be true, prompting Gordon to personally reconnoiter Sedgwick's right. He soon returned ebullient. His scouts' reports were correct. In addition, the terrain provided the Rebels an ideal place to form for the attack. A few hundred yards above the Union flank was a small field, concealed from the Federals by some woods. Gordon could use the clearing to form his soldiers before sending them forward. As far as the Southern general could see, the Federal soldiers were seated on the margin of rifle pits, taking their breakfast, while their muskets leaned against earthworks in their immediate front.

Gordon was satisfied and saw an unprecedented opportunity for victory. As he concluded, his own soldiers were to descend on the unsuspecting Yankees while the rest of Ewell's corps launched a simultaneous attack against the Union front. As each of Sedgwick's brigades gave way, planned Gordon, "the corresponding Confederate brigade, whose front was thus cleared on the general line, was to swing in column of attack on the flank, thus swelling at each step of advance the numbers, power, and momentum of the Confederate forces as they swept down the line of works and extended another brigade's length to the unprotected Union rear." As Gordon envisioned the results, the Army of the Potomac would be rolled up and its very existence would be in jeopardy. [34]

Though Gordon reported to Ewell and Early of the Union's exposed right flank, it took nearly the entire day, and Lee's intervention, to convince the Confederate generals that Gordon's proposed flanking movement would succeed. Once given the go ahead, Confederate preparations for the attack were speedily completed. Just beyond the end of the Federal line was an open field, cut by a deep ravine that formed a T across the Union flank. Gordon's brigade moved into the clearing and deployed over a 2,100-foot front. On Gordon's left, positioned to slice behind the Federals, was Robert Johnston's 1,300-man North Carolina Brigade. Hoffman's Virginians faced opposite against the Federal front on Gordon's right. The three Confederate brigades were to advance simultaneously, crushing the Union flank and precipitating Sedgwick's collapse.

At dusk as the woods began to darken, near the extreme end of the Federal line, the 1st battalion of the 4th New York Artillery Regiment finished erecting shallow fortifications for artillery and retired behind its works. Two men at a time went to a nearby stream to fill canteens. Shaler's soldiers on the front stacked their rifles boiled coffee and fried pork on small campfires. Suddenly, their repast was interrupted by the unearthly screeching and yelling of Gordon's men as they swept along the front and around the rear of the 4th New York. Blue-clad soldiers stampeded rearward, leaving the pork in the pan and their arms. Shaler's brigade disintegrated in a matter of moments under the unexpected attack. Plowing into the shattered Federal flank, Gordon's soldiers began tearing through Seymour's brigade. Portions of Seymour's brigade held briefly, but the Confederate onslaught was unstoppable and his troops retreated in wild confusion and joined the fleeing panic.

Captain Charles E. Stevens (L. Tom Perry Special Collections)

When Gordon launched the Rebel attack, Shaler and Seymour were at Sedgwick's headquarters on Spotswood Road. At the sound of gunfire, the three generals mounted their horses and rushed toward the threatened front to rally the panicked troops. Sedgwick arrived just as the last of Seymour's breastwork gave way. Rebels leaped over the head logs, led by an officer mounted on a black horse. The rider pointed his pistol at Sedgwick and shouted, "Surrender, you Yankee S. O. B." Before the southern horseman could fire, a New Yorker shot him down. Sedgwick spurred his horse for a nearby wagon track where the 77th's Third Brigade had formed. Ewell's cannoneers, however, had the road clearly in range. Shells smashed into the Union ranks. One shell burst, tearing off the legs of Private William Gregory (Co. A), mortally wounding him, and a fragment from another ploughed a two-inch gash in Captain Edward Winnie's (Co. F) scalp revealing his skull awash in blood. Sedgwick struggled to organize Shaler's and Seymour's fugitives. Private Milton Sweet's (Go. G) courage was bolstered as he watched Sedgwick hatless and swinging his sword, shouting, "Boy's don't run. I will stay here with you and get you out." [35]

Shaler desperately tried to re-form his brigade along the wagon track, but was quickly surrounded by a dozen or more Confederate soldiers, each pointing his gun in his direction. One jerked away Shaler's sword. Another took his horse, and he was led to the rear and turned over to one of his subordinates. Seymour was also captured riding toward the enemy to ascertain their position. He and Shaler were later reunited at Robertson's Tavern, behind Ewell's lines.

The veterans of the 77th, along with the rest of the Third Brigade, listened apprehensively as the sound of fighting rolled toward them. The 7th Maine, on the right of the 43rd New York, turned front to rear on the tenth company and wheeled left until it formed a right angle with the rest of the brigade along the Culpeper Mine Road. The 43rd New York with the 77th on its left anchored the Third Brigade line, facing west. Private Sweet remembered that the Confederate "firing was in front, from our right and behind," simultaneously demanding that the Federals surrender. The 7th Maine's Major James P. Jones defiantly yelled back, "All others may go back, but the 7th Maine never!" [36]

One-hundred yards to the east of the Third Brigade's line, the 49th New York and the 61st Pennsylvania (25 paces to the rear) steadied themselves for the inevitable. Private Christopher Funke (49th New York) crouched down behind a head log and laid a handful of cartridges on the flat side of another log so he could load more quickly. As the firing drew closer from the west, he fired off a round over the heads of the line in front and an officer scolded him for firing without orders.

To the northwest, the 122nd Ohio, having come under fire from the front, flank, and rear, bolted toward the southeast across the 77th's front, heading for the Third Brigade's right flank. Alarmed by the stampede of blue-clad soldiers around his regiment, Colonel George F. Smith promptly ordered the 61st Pennsylvania by the right flank file right which placed the regiment squarely across the front of the fleeing troops. "Shoot them, bayonet them, stop them any way you can," he shouted, to no avail. The tidal surge of Union soldiers carried away over two-thirds of the 61st Pennsylvania, including Colonel Smith. Major William Ellis (49th New York) raced into the shaken ranks of the 250 Pennsylvanians still in the field with their regimental and state colors and ushered them into a southeasterly running line, diagonal to the 49th New York's right flank. By then, the Pennsylvanians saw Gordon's Georgians, who appeared as a solid mass of black floating through the woods, coming at them at the double quick. The regiment stepped forward, halted and fired a well-aimed volley at close range.[37]

Under fire from three directions, the 49th New York's colonel, Daniel D. Bidwell, ordered his men to leap to the reverse side of their breastworks and return fire. Within a few moments, Sedgwick galloped into their ranks and ordered Bidwell to clear a way through the woods toward the Germanna Plank Road and the Sixth Corps right flank. With a huzzah, Major Ellis took companies B and D over the works and into the woods, followed closely by the rest of the regiment.

The 77th remained on the crest of a ridge behind their breastworks facing west, when skirmishers skittered back from the woods and joined their line. Colonel John Hoffman's Virginians had split apart as soon as it left the woods, with its right wing straying right to the south of the Third Brigade. Hoffman's two remaining regiments, 31st and 58th Virginia, stumbled up the hill toward the 77th

and the 43rd New York. Suddenly, the Virginians heard a voice ring out, "Boys, here we are," and the New Yorkers stood up behind their works and volleyed. Hoffman's men returned fire, but could not advance. In the ensuing maelstrom of bullets, color bearer Corporal Michael McWilliams (Co. B) was shot dead. Receiving particularly intense fire on their compacted front, Company E's Sergeant Samuel S. Craig, Corporal David McNeal, and Private Lewis Smith were killed and Private Charles Ruggles mortally wounded. Lieutenant Charles E. Steven's (Co. A) orderly sergeant was seriously wounded and staggered back a short distance where he saw Sedgwick holding his hat and standing in the Culpeper Mine Road with an aide. The bleeding sergeant said, "General, I am wounded. Where is the rear?" Sedgwick replied, "I haven't any rear, but will soon have one." [38]

The 31st Virginia could not withstand the withering Federal fire, its men steaming down the ridge and back across the ravine, leaving behind many dead and wounded. The 58th Virginia broke seconds later and headed back to its works, and by around 9 p.m. the force of the Confederate flank attack died out with the Third Brigade stubbornly holding their position. Sedgwick began consolidating the Sixth Corps line. The 61st Pennsylvania occupied the trenches previously held by the 77th and 43rd New York. The 43rd New York stood across the Culpeper Mine Road, facing north. The 7th Maine, the 77th and the 49th New York finished the formation to the east. Henry Eustis' and Frank Wheaton's brigades were moving north from the Brock Road toward Wilderness Tavern.

Hoffman's remaining regiments floundered through the woods. The 49th Virginia was in front followed by the 52nd Virginia, then the 13th Virginia. None of the regiments maintained an organized formation as they fragmented into squads. The Virginians passed through the swamp in the bottom of the ravine and quietly started up the hill in their front. Barely above the sound of their feet on the forest floor, Surgeon Stevens remembered "the low tones of command of the rebel officers as they urged their men against our rear and flank." Colonel Smith of the 61st Pennsylvania ordered his men to lie down as they had no earthworks, and to reserve their fire. Near and nearer the dark gray line deftly approached the Pennsylvanians. At a distance of ten feet, Colonel Smith's voice rang out, "Fire!" The 61st Pennsylvania rose in unison and volleyed point-blank into the faces of the Confederates. The withering fire raked the Rebel ranks and sent them reeling back into the darkness "but a line of prostate forms where the fire from our line had met the advancing column, told of its terrible execution." Twenty minutes later, the 13th Virginia, Stevens recounted, "advanced silently but in stronger force, directly in front of our breastworks. They advanced slowly and in silence until within a few feet of the Union line, when with wild yells they leaped forward, some even mounting the breastworks. But a sheet of flames instantly flashed along the whole of our works; the astonished rebels wavered for a moment and then beat a hasty retreat." [39]

Hoffman's repulse marked the end of fighting that evening between the men Lee's and Grant's armies. John Brown Gordon's two-brigade flank attack had torn a tremendous hole nearly half a mile wide and half a mile deep in the Federal right flank. The Confederates scattered and demoralized 17 regiments, forced Meade to send two battle fatigued brigades on a four-mile countermarch to reinforce the Sixth Corps, captured 600 men, two generals, and inflicted numerous casualties. The Third Brigade entered the wilderness with 2,467 men. Of that number, 105 were killed, 397 wounded, and 117 missing in action. With 453 muskets, the 77th's casualty list included 11 killed, 44 wounded, and 9 missing. Hardest hit was the 43rd New York with 198 casualties. Surgeon Stevens openly mourned that, "Our regiments which a few hours before were filled, were now but fragments of regiments; and our hearts were weighed down with heavy grief when we thought of the many grand spirits who had left us forever." Even so, the Third Brigade did not break, and the Union right flank was stabilized. Neither side gained any decided advantage in the Wilderness. [41]

"Scarcely a man of the Union force was injured" by Hoffman's last charge, George Stevens noted, "but the dead and wounded from the rebel ranks literally covered the ground. There was no help for them." Stevens lamented that, "Our men were unable even to take care of their own wounded which lay scattered through the woods in the rear." Consequently "the rebel wounded lay between the two armies, making the night hideous with their groans." [42]

After Gordon's flanking movement was repulsed, the 77th lay tensely behind their breastworks, waiting for another Confederate assault. Behind them, army engineers were reconnoitering and marking out a new line to be occupied by the Sixth Corps on the right flank of the Army of the Potomac. Shortly after midnight, the word was passed, and the tired soldiers moved to the rear. The 77th crossed the Germanna Plank Road in the vicinity of Spotswood near an old gold mine mill where the Sixth Corps field hospitals had been located. The New Yorkers immediately set to work entrenching their new position in preparation for continued fighting in the morning.

Grant's field hospitals were also busy that night. Ambulance trains returned from Chancellorsville to bear the more than 10,000 Federal wounded from the hospitals behind Wilderness Run and around the old gold mine to larger hospitals there. Surgeon Stevens remembered later "we loaded ambulances and army wagons to their utmost capacity, making a train of many miles in extent." Three-hundred-twenty-five wagons and 488 ambulances moved down the Germanna Plank Road. The trains traveled east along the Orange Turnpike, arriving at Chancellorsville near morning. New tents were erected, and piles of severed arms and legs rose at the new site. The next day, ambulance wagons began heading for Fredericksburg, where wounded men hoped receive more consistent treatment. [42]

Transportation of the wounded to Chancellorsville, and then on to Fredericksburg, was nothing short of absolute misery for the hapless travelers. George Stevens wrote, "Over a rough road . . . these unfortunate men, with shattered or amputated limbs, with shots through the lungs or head or abdomen, suffering the most excruciating pain from every jar or jolt of the ambulance or wagon, crowded as closely as they could be packed, were to be transported . . . They were worn out with fatigue and suffering . . . Slowly the immense train labored over rough road, now corduroy, now the remains of a worn out plank road, and anon a series of ruts and mud holes, until, at three o'clock on the morning of the 9th of May, the head of the column arrived at Fredericksburgh." [43]

The process of unloading the thousands upon thousands of wounded from the trains was slow due to the lack of healthy manpower. Local slaves in Fredericksburg were pressed into service carrying the desperate wounded soldiers to shelter. All the churches and public buildings were seized and filled, "The churches were filled first, then warehouses and stores, and then private houses, until the town was literally one immense hospital." Even then, the wounded continued to flood Fredericksburg and were laid out on the sidewalks, covering them, as long trains of ambulances filled the streets with more. [44]

Many private citizens, while not sympathetic with the Union cause, nevertheless willingly opened their homes for the care of the wounded, but not all were so welcoming. After the war, Stevens recounted one surgeon's experience in commandeering a private home to house some wounded Federal officers:

At one fine mansion a surgeon rang the door bell, and in a moment saw the door open just enough to show the nose and a pair of small twinkling eyes of what was evidently a portly woman. 'What do you want?' snarled out the female defender of the premises. 'We want to come and see if we can place a few wounded officers in this house.' 'You can't come in here!' shouted the woman slamming the door together. A few knocks induced her again to open the door two or three inches. 'Madam, we must come in here; we shall do you no harm.' 'You can't come in here; I am a lone widow.' 'But I assure you no harm is intended you.' Again the door was closed, and again at the summons was opened. 'Madam, it will be much better for you to allow us to enter than for me to direct these men to force the door; but we must enter.' The woman now threw the door wide open and rushing into the yard with as much alacrity as her enormous proportions would admit, threw her arms out and whirled about like a reversed spinning top shouting for help. She was again assured that no harm was intended her, but that unless she chose to show us the house we should be obliged to go alone. Concluding that wisdom was the better part of valor, she proceeded to show us the rooms. [45]

To address the wants of the wounded were initially no more than forty surgeons detailed from the field. Wounds were left undressed as the surgeons transferred the soldiers from the ambulances and wagons to hospitals set up in the churches, public buildings, and private homes. Many unfortunate soldiers became victims of gangrene as amputated arms and legs had not been dressed since the first day of fighting in the Wilderness. George Stevens remembered. "It was one grand funeral; men dropping away on every side." Local slaves and a large number of nurses were detailed as burial parties, and very little rest was afforded them as men died by the hundreds in a matter of days. [46]

Desperate family members from the north spread out through Fredericksburg seeking information regarding a son who had been wounded, or as they feared, killed. Twenty-one-year-old Private Hermanus Bowers (Co. C) was severely wounded when he was shot through the chest on the first day of fighting in the Wilderness, and was brought to the southern city. Residing in Albany, New York, Hermanus' father rushed to Fredericksburg upon learning his son was dangerously wounded. Upon arrival, the elder Bowers inquired about his son, but learned only that the private was transported to the city from the 2nd Division field hospital in the Wilderness. Bowers sought out Quartermaster Jacob F. Hayward who agreed to help find his son. They immediately approached Surgeon Stevens for information about Private Bowers' location. Stevens did not know the whereabouts of the young private as the surgeons were so overwhelmed by attending to the urgent needs of thousands of wounded, that no records were made by which a particular wounded soldier could be found. However, the 77th's surgeon instructed some nurses to assist the anxious father in finding his son. After two trying days spent in the fruitless search, word was sent to the elder Bowers that his son was in a particular church. Buoyed with the news that his son was alive, the father rushed to his son. Upon arriving at the church, he broke into tears of anguish to find that his son had died just a half hour earlier. [47]

By dawn, May 7, the new lines marked out by Federal engineers were manned. Entrenched along its entire front, Grant's army was formed right to left in the order - Sixth Corps-Fifth Corps-IX Corps-II Corps - with Sheridan's cavalry on the left rear. Lee also completed the entrenchment of his front. His field works ran from Ewell's right in two parallel lines over Chewning's plateau to the Plank Road and thence by a single line across the unfinished railroad. From left to right in order were Ewell's corps, A. P. Hill's corps, and Longstreet's corps, with cavalry on the extreme right facing Sheridan.

That morning, U. S. Grant was faced with the prospect of attacking strengthened Confederate earthworks. Instead, he chose to maneuver. By moving south down the Brock Road, Grant hoped to reach the crossroads at Spotsylvania Court House, which would place the Army of the Potomac between Lee and Richmond, forcing Lee out of his entrenchments to fight on ground more favorable to the Union army's advantage in numbers. He ordered preparations for a night march that evening, determined to reach Spotsylvania ten miles to the southeast by the morning of May 8.

12

"ATTENTION, BATTALIONS! FORWARD, DOUBLE-QUICK! CHARGE!"

Early on May 7, at 6:30 a.m., Grant issued orders for the battered corps of the Army of the Potomac to move from their entrenched positions toward Spotsylvania. By 3 p.m., Meade issued specific instructions for the advance toward Spotsylvania. The slow moving wagon trains were to head for Chancellorsville at 4 p.m. to clear the way for the troops. The Reserve Artillery would move as well to Chancellorsville at 7 p.m. and were then to move further to the rear to clear the way for the Sixth Corps. Leading the way, Warren's Fifth Corps was ordered to move south at 8:30 p.m. down the Brock Road via Todd's Tavern for Spotsylvania, passing behind the Ninth and Second Corps. Next, the 77th's Sixth Corps would move along the Orange Turnpike and Orange Plank Road for Chancellorsville and head south for the intersection of the Piney Branch Church and Spotsylvania Road with a route leading from Alsop's to Old Courthouse. The Second Corps would hold its position to screen the movements of the rest of the army and then follow the Fifth Corps route south. Burnside's Ninth Corps would follow the Sixth Corps route to Chancellorsville taking the Germanna Plank road to the Orange Plank Road and then south to Piney Branch Church.

The Fifth Corps movement began a little after sundown, while the Sixth Corps got under way at 9:30 p.m., heading southward. The veterans of the 77th were heartened that the army was continuing its advance, instead of retreating as had been done with previous commanders, thus rendering their hardships and sacrifices and deaths of comrades meaningless. William B. Lapham of the Third Brigade's 7th Maine was jubilant over moving forward. "I only judge others by myself, and I was truly happy we were advancing, which indicated that we had not been beaten. The rank and file of the army wanted no more retreating, and from the moment when we passed the roads that led to the Rappahannock fords and continued straight on towards Spotsylvania, I never had a doubt that General Grant would lead us to final victory." As Grant passed by the snaking blue columns, soldiers erupted in cheer after cheer for their aggressive commander. Rather than being elated by their adulation, the general was concerned only of the success of the advance and remarked to his aides, "This is most unfortunate. The sound will reach the ears of the enemy, and I fear it may reveal our movement." [1]

Prior to the Sixth Corps march out of the Wilderness, its Second Division field hospital had under its care about 2,000 wounded, covering a four acre field. The evening of May 6-7, ambulances and wagons carried off as many as possible to Chancellorsville, leaving behind 400 upon the ground to the enemy. Leaving behind defenseless comrades for Surgeon Stevens was especially difficult:

It was, indeed, a sickening thought that these noble fellows, who had nobly fallen in their country's cause, must be abandoned to the enemy, many of them, perhaps the majority of them, to die in their hands. All communication with their friends at home hopelessly cut off, and with no expectation of any but the roughest treatment from their enemies, it was a sad prospect for the unfortunate ones. [2]

The 77th's Assistant Surgeon Justin G. Thompson, Dr. Edwin Phillips, surgeon of the 6th Vermont, and several nurses were detailed to stay behind to tend to the remaining wounded of the Second Division. The next day was occupied in operating upon those requiring immediate attention, and concentrating the wounded spread over four acres into less space for convenience in caring for them. Many Union stragglers came into the field hospital and were detained to serve as nurses and burial parties to dispose of the great number of corpses rotting under the sun. Surgeon Thompson, at a regimental reunion many years later remembered, "The weather being quite warm this could not be postponed without great discomfort to the living. A long trench was dug. And wrapped in their army blankets they were laid side by side without ceremony. The location of those who could be identified in any way was marked by pieces of cracker boxes with the names of company and regiment marked with a lead pencil, many could not be identified." [3]

On the morning of May 9, a company of Confederate provost guards came through the hospital camp and without ceremony began pillaging, taking from the wounded anything that they considered of value to them. The lieutenant in command entered the headquarter tent where Thompson was tending to four wounded men, one a Rebel sergeant whose leg the surgeon had amputated the day before due to critical hemorrhaging. Without saying a word, the

Confederate officer grabbed Thompson's coat, threw it over his shoulder and headed out of the tent. The wounded Rebel sergeant loudly objected, causing the Southern officer to drop the coat, but not before taking Thompson's prize meerschaum pipe from the coat pocket and claiming it for himself. A few minutes later a Confederate lieutenant colonel entered the tent demanding to know where Thompson had hidden his horses. "I informed him," Thompson recalled, "that my horses were safe in charge of an orderly and with Grant's army and that he was welcome to them if he could get them." After roundly cursing the surgeon, the lieutenant colonel walked to the other side of the field to demand the same of Surgeon Phillips "but before doing so," Thompson told his listeners, "he stopped near my tent and drawing a knapsack from under the head of a wounded man who died one hour later, he examined the contents and finding nothing which he considered worth taking except a small zinc backed pocket looking glass, which I could see was broken, but in which he could see himself, perhaps not as others saw him – he quietly put in his pocket." [4]

Assistant Surgeon Justin G. Thompson (L. Tom Perry Special Collections)

The next day, a brigade of Rebel cavalry filed through the hospital camp and rested for an hour on a plateau nearby. A number of the horsemen told Thompson they had been guarding the Rappahannock fords expecting the Army of the Potomac to make an attempt to re-cross the river in retreat, but were puzzled why it moved south instead, and "wanted to know what kind of man Old Grant was?" After the Confederate cavalry brigade moved on Confederate commissaries appeared and brought much needed supplies, furnishing the wounded soldiers coffee and hardtack. [5]

After nearly a week in the field hospital, Assistant Surgeon Thompson was greatly relieved when a train of Union army ambulances and wagons with a cavalry escort entered the hospital camp with orders to evacuate the wounded to Fredericksburg. Relief soon turned to discomfort when Thompson discovered he was not to go with them, but was sent across the battlefield to a hospital established by the Ewell's corps during the battle. The scene crossing Saunders Field haunted the doctor for the rest of his life. "On our way across this battlefield we had the opportunity to witness something of the carnage of war; in one small field traversed by a deep ditch the unburied were numbered by the hundreds and the ditch literally filled with dead bodies; the bloated and discolored appearance of the bodies together with the terrible stench, hurried us across the field at a double quick." [6]

After a short trek of four miles, Thompson and surgeon Phillips came to the Confederate field hospital under the care of Rebel surgeons, Drs. Moffit and Galespi, who in turn detailed them to care for their wounded soldiers. Surgeon Thompson possessed a good supply of the anesthetic, chloroform, but no morphine or other medical supplies, and quickly exhausted the store bandages, dressings, and silk for sutures and ligatures. To compensate for the lack of supplies, Thompson recalled, "Our assistants visited the battlefield and from knapsacks abandoned or belonging to the dead secured a quantity of shirts and other material which did good service as dressings; again in these knapsacks they found many of those little conveniences which soldiers call housewives; these contained some silk but mostly linen thread, which they were obliged to unite wounds and ligate arteries and we were surprised to find that wounds did fairly well with these crude appliances." [7]

Thompson's time at the Confederate field hospital was also touched by the temporary insanity sometimes resulting from the excruciating pain and hunger of the untended wounded soldier:

> Soon after our arrival at this hospital a strong well built man perfectly nude was seen skulking around the quarters: he would dart out from behind a tree and seize and devour ravenously refuse from the cook's tent. One of the cooks succeeded in tempting him with food and finally bringing him to our headquarters, where after judicious, feeding his reason returned so he could give us his name and the fact that he belonged to the Sixth Maryland cavalry: a ball had shattered the shoulder and he had been left on the battlefield; crazed with hunger and with fever he had divested himself of all clothing and wandered aimlessly: fortunately he came near the cook tent and instinctively sought food and drink; we amputated his arm at the shoulder joint and he made a good recovery. [8]

After a little more than a month of service at the Rebel hospital, surgeons Thompson and Phillips learned that they were to be sent south to the infamous prisoner of war camp at Andersonville. Having no desire to spend the remainder of the war as prisoners, the doctors decided to make their way to Washington and safety.

Thompson regaled veterans of the 77th with a striking account of their escape and journey north as he continued his reminisces:

> ... at nightfall after visiting all our patients and seeing that they were comfortable for the night, we left camp accompanied by a private who had served us well as an attendant. The night was dark and rainy and after traveling all night in the wilderness we were unable to find a ford in the Rapidan and camped on the south side for the day ... at night we found a small leaky scow boat at the mouth of a stream; with the private in the bow and by aid of a board for a paddle I tried to propel the craft across the Rapidan at this point about 200 yards wide; the boat soon began to fill with water and when about two-thirds across, down it went; the private made for the shore leaving me in mid stream with the boat and contents to bring to shore; I succeeded in saving the paddle, my overcoat and haversack of hardtack while a canteen of confederate rye floated majestically down the stream; after emptying the boat I returned for my brother physician, the boat by this time being well soaked and seaworthy I had no trouble carrying him safely over. We had not traveled far when a sight greeted us which gave good promise; two horses, saddled and bridled, and hitched at the entrance of a lawn leading to a house several rods from the road. We cautiously approached the coveted prizes, but when within a few feet of them, a pack of hounds set up a terrific howling, and lost no time in covering the distance to the horses. We concluded then and there that we did not want the horses, and made a rapid detour through the fields, striking the road half a mile ahead ... Our plan was to strike the Orange and Alexandria railroad at Kelly's Ford; but in the multiplicity of roads, traveling through the woods at night, we came

out at Brandy Station instead, and from there we followed the railroad to Alexandria, sleeping concealed in the woods hot days with an army of mosquitos to fight, with no provision for three days – our hard tack becoming sour from the soaking it got in the Rapidan, and no water except such as we could get from muddy streams . . . We were obliged to ford the Rappahannock, and all the streams (six in number), the R. R. bridges all being destroyed. On the morning of the fourth day we camped near Warrenton Junction and our companion generously made a break for provision; he called at a farmer's house, told him he was deserting the union army, was tired of war and wanted to go to his home in Pennsylvania; the confederate citizen gave him a good breakfast, a dozen boiled eggs, a dozen biscuits and a canteen of coffee and gave him instructions how to avoid Union pickets: our companion brought us a savory breakfast and you can guess whether we did justice to it. After traveling five nights a distance of nearly 100 miles with blistered feet and tired limbs we arrived at the picket post 10 miles west of Alexandria when we were served with a sumptuous breakfast; the commandant telegraphed to Alexandria and a special car was sent to take us to that place; this being Sunday we reported to the surgeon general Monday morning and after half an hour's interview with him, received orders to join our commands then on the peninsula. The next morning found us on board a steamer en route to our respective regiments.[9]

The 77th's march toward Spotsylvania was perfectly exhausting. The New York veterans, weary from two days of hard fighting, stumbled on a sultry night through thick choking clouds of smoke from lingering forest fires caused by the Wilderness battle. Their discomfort was compounded by the addition of fine flour-like dust kicked up by their own marching. As was always the case with large numbers of marching soldiers, the column was beset with an endless series of starts and stops which aggravated their weariness. No doubt the tired regiment's soldiers looked with envy upon the long line of soldiers of the Second Corps sleeping behind low breastworks lining the roadside. When the New Yorkers finally halted, Private Andrew Jackson Sprung (Co. K) thought back to the two days of battle in the Wilderness remarked, "I was happy when we went into camp after a hard day's march and hard fighting and thought how lucky I was in not getting wounded or killed, and to look back . . . and see how many of our old comrades had given their lives for "Old Glory" and one of the best old Unions and the best country that the sun ever shone upon." [10]

Warren's corps, Grant's leading column, arrived at Todd's Tavern around 1 a.m. on May 8 to find Grant and Meade's headquarters and escort blocking the road and halted. Once the road was cleared, the column resumed the march, only to halt again for Merritt's cavalry division, still making preparations for moving out, now blocked their way. While Warren waited for the cavalry troopers to get on their way, his soldiers started arriving in bone-tired masses and dropping to sleep almost as soon as they halted. The Fifth Corps general decided not to press matters and let his tired troops rest while Merritt got out of his way. His corps would not be on the move again until 6 a.m.

Robert E. Lee received numerous reports on May 7 that Grant was preparing to move his army, but what his destination might be was unclear. If Grant had given up the fight, he might be attempting to retreat to Fredericksburg. However, he might also be continuing his advance by moving for some point further south toward Richmond. Lee decided to move to a new line south of his current position to the vicinity of Spotsylvania Court House. There, he would have the opportunity to get on the flank of the Federals if they intended to retreat or get in their way if they were advancing. In preparation for operations toward Spotsylvania, Lee sent Stuart to scout out the roads south leading to the court house.

Lee also desired to send a substantial infantry force to Spotsylvania which required cutting a route through the Wilderness forest from the Orange Plank road to White Hall Mill. Richard Anderson's First Corps, on the right and closest to Spotsylvania, was detailed to make the eleven mile march starting no later than 3 a.m. on May 8. Anderson, ahead of schedule, set out at 2:30 a.m. after being notified that the new military road was open. Brigadier General Joseph B. Kershaw's division was the first to leave the Rebel breastworks, followed by Major General Charles Field's men. Stumps and trees not fully removed from the path made the march tough going for Anderson's tired soldiers. As the forest all around them was still on fire, there was no suitable place for the men to fall out to rest; instead the weary infantrymen trudged on. Anderson's corps finally halted a little before dawn just west of the Block House Bridge over the Po River only three miles west of Spotsylvania Court House. Ominously, while the Army of the Potomac was making its way to Spotsylvania Court house, a significant portion of the Army of Northern Virginia was also on the move there as well, unknowingly paralleling the march of their armies. As the Army of the Potomac and the Army of Northern Virginia left one gruesome and bloody battlefield, another one just as appalling lay only a few miles farther down the road. [9]

On May 8, the battles around Spotsylvania Court House commenced as both armies headed down the maze of northern Virginia roads for that small, but militarily vital crossroads town. A running fight began in the early morning hours as Phil Sheridan's cavalry pushed Confederate troopers south. Around 3:30 a.m., Merritt's horsemen butted up against Fitzhugh Lee's cavalry blocking their path on the Brock Road. The Confederates stubbornly resisted but were slowly pushed back. In pursuit, the Federal troopers were hampered by cut trees laid across the road. Nearby Rebel troops fired upon any one who ventured forward to move them. Just before dawn, Wilson's Union cavalry had set out from Alrich's and on to the Fredericksburg Road before getting into a fight with Thomas Rosser's cavalry brigade near Spotsylvania Court House.

Fitzhugh Lee's tenacious troopers slowed Merritt's progress, compelling him to request infantry support from Warren's Fifth Corps at 6 a.m. Exhausted from the previous night's march, Robison's division led the way. By 8 a.m., Federal infantry were only three miles away from Spotsylvania at a clearing near Alsop's farm near the intersection of the Brock Road and the Old Court House Road. Across 400 yards of open ground was a low rise called Laurel Hill where Fitzhugh Lee's Confederate troopers, reinforced by a four-gun battery, were hastily entrenching in preparation for making a stand. But Lee's men would not be alone fighting Warren's infantry. Anderson's First Corps Confederates were near at Old Court House after a hard early morning march. When a courier from Fitzhugh Lee rode up with news that he was hard pressed, Anderson ordered Kershaw to send two of his brigades to help the troopers fighting on the Brock Road. The South Carolina Brigade of Colonel John W. Henagan and Brigadier General Benjamin G. Humphreys' Mississippians rushed for the breastworks of rails on a hill near the Old Court House Road and Brock Road intersection. Major John C. Haskell's artillery brigade had arrived earlier, and was directing their fire towards the oncoming Union infantry.

Fitzhugh Lee was also hard pressed by Federal horsemen of Wilson's cavalry division moving toward Spotsylvania down the Fredericksburg Road from the northeast. All that stood before

Wilson was one Confederate cavalry regiment. Two brigades under William T. Wofford and Goode Bryan hurried there to help. Wilson drove the Rebel troopers from Spotsylvania and were engaged in preparing to hold it against the approaching Confederate infantry. However, by a strange twist of fate, Wilson received an order from Sheridan to withdraw his troops from this vital Federal strategic point.

Meanwhile around 8:30 a.m., the Fifth Corps infantry was gathering for the attack on Laurel Hill. Though Robinson's division was not yet fully up, Warren impatiently ordered him to attack with the forces he had. Robinson reluctantly sent in Colonel Peter Lyle's brigade to advance 400 yards across a succession of ridges, dotted with clumps of pines and oaks. Disorganized from the difficult terrain they were attempting to cross, most of Lyle's brigade broke and melted to the rear while a few hung tough, reaching the base of the hill where they found cover and dug in.

The rest of Robinson's division, Colonel Richard Coulter's Second Brigade and Colonel Andrew W. Denison's Maryland Brigade, was then added to the fray. Robinson determined to press his soldiers by leading the assault himself. He encouraged his men forward as they advanced to within fifty yards of the Confederate line where a Rebel bullet mangled his left knee. The wound caused Robinson to be removed from the field and the attack was roundly beaten back. The only Federals to keep a toehold on Laurel Hill were some soldiers from Lyle's brigade at the base of the rise, and even these were driven to the rear by the arrival of Humphrey's Mississippi regiments.

As the divisions of Charles Griffin and Lysander Cutler came up, Warren sent them also into battle. These tired troops advanced in good order for some 250 yards before the Confederates unleashed a brisk fire that brought the attack to a halt. Then Rebels appeared on Cutler's right, driving Union soldiers back in confusion.

Just as Warren's troops had been arriving on the field, so were the rest of Anderson's Confederate First Corps units. Major General George Field's division extended the growing Confederate line to the Po River, and around 8 a.m., Lee ordered Ewell's Second Corps - Robert E. Rode's division in the lead - to march south to Shady Grove Church. The rest of the Army of the Potomac was converging on the scene as well. Eager for the opportunity to crush the Confederate force at Laurel Hill before the rest of the Rebel army moved to join it, Grant ordered the 77th's Sixth Corps to Warren's position in the hope that a combined attack of both corps might yield a victory. The Second and Ninth Corps also were instructed to march in the direction of the fighting to support Warren.

George Stevens remembered that the Sixth Corps arrived on the field at 2 p.m. "The day," he wrote, "had been the most sultry of the season, and many of the men, overcome by the intensity of the heat, and exhausted by the constant fighting and marching since the morning of the 4th, had fallen by the wayside." Sedgwick's troops rested for about two hours, and were then ordered to the front to the assistance of Warren's corps. Again Stevens wrote, "We pressed forward along a narrow road leading through a thick growth of timber, until we came where the Fifth Corps was contending the ground." There the Sixth Corps was drawn up in line of battle awaiting orders to advance. [11]

Surgeon Stevens recalled, "Before us the ground was rolling and partially wooded, admirably adapted for defensive warfare. A wooded ravine, at a little distance from our front, concealed a rebel line of battle, and in our rear, were dense woods extending to the road along which our line was formed. These woods were on fire, and the hot blasts of air which swept over us, together with the burning heat of the sun, rendered our position a very uncomfortable one." The Sixth Corps, however, was soon ordered to take position in the woods on Warren's left flank. The 77th was relieved to move away from the suffocating heat from the burning woods. [12]

With Brigadier General Samuel Crawford's Fifth Corps Pennsylvania Reserve Division to their right, the 77th's Second Division was formed in three lines for the last assault of the day. The Federal combined attack got underway at 6 p.m., but was not a vigorous one. Warren's troops were too tired from marching and battle and the Sixth Corps Second Division was too unfamiliar with the situation there for any coordinated effort to take place. Less than half the men designated for the attack actually stepped forward. Crawford's division, the 77th's Third Brigade and Brigadier General Henry L. Eustis' Fourth Brigade of the Second Division stumbled upon Rode's Confederate division going into position. The Northerners were driven back by forceful attacks by Brigadier General Cullen A. Battle's and Brigadier General Stephen D. Ramseur's brigades that devolved at points into hand-to-hand fighting. Darkness brought an end to the fighting, causing Rode's Confederates to suspend their counterattack and return to their line.

May 9, both armies were converging their remaining forces on the fields, farms, and woods north of Spotsylvania Court house. Lee's troops spent the next two days entrenching a formidable set of fortifications while Grant consolidated his forces and searched for any weakness in the Confederate position to exploit. Hancock's Second Corps crossed the Po River at Warren's right, halting at the Shady Grove Church Road and before Block House Bridge. Ambrose Burnside's moved southwest down the Fredericksburg Road, crossing the Ny River and halting near the Beverly house. At the same time, the Fifth and Sixth Corps dug in, strengthening their earthworks.

During the day, the 77th, along with its Third Brigade regiments, were entrenched in a clearing on the side of a hill which descended toward the Confederate lines into a swamp. Sixth Corps artillery was planted behind the brigade and throughout the day sent shells into the enemy's breastworks which lay beyond a strip of woods. Rebel guns in turn sent their iron messengers of death which exploded in and around the Third Brigade. One shell struck near the 77th, striking the rear rank of Company D of the 61st Pennsylvania. Lieutenant O. A. Parsons (Co. D) related:

> The shell first struck Thomas R. Connor's knapsack; the missile then took the heads off of Thomas E. Ellis and William H. Ward, not injuring Wm. Coon, who seemed to be in line, but killing John L. Fairchild, J. L. Hays and Crandel A. Wilcox, taking parts of their heads and shoulders and slightly wounding the next man. Connor, whose knapsack was hit, received a severe shock which disabled him for several weeks. [13]

The Confederates constructed a seven mile line laid out by Lee's chief engineer Martin Smith utilizing the defensive aspects of the local terrain to full advantage, following an arcing ridge and passing through scrubby and dense woods. The Southerner's position bulged out with a salient, later dubbed the "Mule Shoe," nearly three quarters of a mile long and almost 1,200 yards at its widest point, a huge spearhead pointing almost directly north. Confederate soldiers grimly fortified their line, knowing full well the battle destined to come. Strong defenses were constructed with abatis thrown out in front and mounds of fence rails covered with dirt protecting the trenches. With troops well sheltered from enemy fire behind these works and their musketry bolstered with cannon strategically placed about their position, the Rebel line at Spotsylvania would be virtually impregnable against infantry attacks.

A no-man's-land separating the armies, in places only a few hundred yards wide, continually echoed with musketry. Sharpshooters sent forth death on the wings of a sniper's bullet, forcing soldiers to dig in for their lives, throwing up earthworks for protection against the incessant rain of lead. Before the day ended, the Sixth Corps would lose their beloved commander, Uncle John Sedgwick, to a sharpshooter's keen eye.

That morning, Sedgwick went to the angle formed where Brock Road's two branches joined on the northern border of the Spindle farm. Battery H of the 1st New York Artillery was positioned there, and the place was a favorite target of Confederate sharpshooter's. General William H. Morris had been shot from his horse while tending to his brigade that morning, and the 15th New Jersey's color sergeant had been shot through the breast. A lone Rebel sharpshooter posted in a tree appeared to be inflicting the most damage.

"General, do you see that section of artillery?" Sedgwick's chief of staff, Martin T. McMahon, asked in a jesting tone. "Well, you are not to go near it today." Sedgwick jokingly answered, "McMahon, I would like to know who commands this corps, you or I?" The aide playfully responded, "Well General, sometimes I am in doubt myself." McMahon continued in a more serious way: "Seriously, General, I beg of you not to go to that angle; every officer who has shown himself there has been hit, both yesterday and today." Sedgwick answered, "Well, I don't know there is any reason for going there." [14]

Later that morning, the New York artillery withdrew and was replaced by a section of Captain William H. McCartney's battery. Sedgwick was disturbed that soldiers had moved in front of the guns, obstructing their fire. "That is wrong," he muttered and walked over with McMahon to correct the alignment. McMahon ordered the soldiers to move, which gained the notice of Rebel sharpshooters.

Bullets whizzed and spattered into the dirt. Some of the men dodged, making Sedgwick laugh: "What! What! Men dodging this way for single bullets! What will you do when they open fire along the whole line? I am ashamed at you. They couldn't hit an elephant at this distance." At the same moment a sharpshooter's bullet passed with a long shrill whistle, and a soldier just in front of Sedgwick dodged to the ground. The general touched him gently with his boot, and said, "Why, my man, I am ashamed of you, dodging that way," and repeated the remark, "They couldn't hit an elephant at this distance." The man rose off the ground and good-naturedly told the general, "General, I dodged a shell once, and if I hadn't, it would have taken my head off. I believe in dodging." [15]

For a third time, the same shrill whistle of a bullet ended with the heavy dull thud of lead smashing into flesh and bone. Suddenly, McMahon remembered, "the general's face turned slowly to me, the blood spurting from his left cheek under the eye in a steady stream. He fell in my direction; I was so close to him that my effort to support him failed, and I fell with him." With McMahon, brigade surgeon Ohlenschlager, Major Charles A. Whittier, Major Thomas Hyde, and Lieutenant Colonel Kent, who had been grouped nearby, surrounded the fallen Sedgwick. "A smile remained upon his lips," McMahon wrote, "but he did not speak. The doctor poured water from a canteen over the general's face," but, "The blood still poured upward in a little fountain." The men in the line of rifle pits kneeled and looked toward the group of officers, and the news of Sedgwick's death quickly traveled down the line. An ambulance, followed by his staff, brought the general's body to Meade's headquarters, and placed on a bower of evergreen's where it was mourned over by officers and enlisted men. Profoundly aggrieved, George Stevens wrote, "Never had such a gloom rested upon the whole army on account of the death of one man as came over it when the heavy tidings passed along the lines that General Sedgwick was killed." [16]

With Sedgwick dead, Brigadier General James B. Ricketts was now the ranking officer of the Sixth Corps, but he declined to assume command because Sedgwick had wanted Brigadier General Horatio G. Wright to succeed him. Hailing from Connecticut, Wright graduated second in his class at West Point in 1841 and was posted to the Corps of Engineers. He was made brigadier general of volunteers in September 1861, and proved to be a competent combat leader, rising to commander of Sixth Corps First Division prior to the Gettysburg Campaign. The order from army headquarters promoting Wright to the command of the Sixth Corps was sent at 10 a.m.

By the morning of May 10, U. S. Grant was fully aware that the Army of Northern Virginia was now on the scene in his front, well entrenched and waiting for an attack. The strength of Lee's earthworks spoke volumes of the folly that would result from a frontal infantry attack. However, frustrations throughout the day influenced Grant to launch unwise assaults up and down the Confederate line on May 10 which had stood no chance of success. For all the senseless fighting and casualties that the Federal army suffered for his aggressiveness that day, Grant did find a possible opening that might gain victory if properly executed.

Early in the afternoon Lieutenant Ronald S. McKenzie of the U. S. Corps of Engineers had been scouting the open fields around the Shelton house. He had followed an old wagon track to the southeast which entered a pine woods and came to the edge of a field across which, at a distance of two hundred yards, McKenzie saw Brigadier General George Dole's line occupied by three Georgia regiments. He had been accompanied by Brigadier General David Russell, and they examined the Confederate position from the edge of the trees. Russell had determined that, if an attack force could be massed there unseen, it should be able to reach the Rebel works without taking to many casualties, even though the works appeared quite formidable, with abatis in front containing head logs on top and traverses to the rear. Several well-placed artillery pieces would multiply the destructive fire power that could come from those defenses. And, even more ominous, about one hundred yards behind these works, another line of fortifications was being constructed.

Russell reported the position to Wright who approved the proposed site of attack. The generals decided to assault with twelve infantry regiments drawn from the 77th's and Russell's divisions. The selected regiments were the 5th Maine, 96th Pennsylvania, and 121st New York from Colonel Emory Upton's brigade; 5th Wisconsin, 6th Maine, 49th and 119th Pennsylvania from Brigadier Henry Eustis' brigade; 43rd and 77th New York from Colonel Daniel D. Bidwell's brigade (Bidwell replaced Thomas Neill who took command of the Second Division when Getty was wounded in the Wilderness); and the 2nd, 5th, and 6th Vermont from Colonel Lewis Grant's brigade. Combined, these regiments would total approximately 5,000 infantrymen. Command of the flying assault column was entrusted to Upton, whose convincing handling of his brigade in the successful assault at Rappahannock Station the previous November had marked him as a steady fighter. Upton was to attack at 5 p.m., preceded by a ten minute artillery bombardment to soften the Confederate line held by Dole's Georgians. [15]

Major Nathan Babcock and the other regimental commanders went with Upton to the observation point to study both the intended route and the Rebel works on the opposite side. Upton then informed them of the details of the attack. The formation would consist of four lines of three regiments each. The first line from right to left was to include the 121st New York, 96th Pennsylvania, and 5th Maine; the second line the 49th Pennsylvania, 6th Maine, and 5th Wisconsin; the third line the 43rd New York, 77th New York, and 119th Pennsylvania; and the fourth line 2nd Vermont, 5th Vermont, and 6th

Vermont. The four regiments on the right flank were to line up to the right of the path, and the remaining eight regiments to the left. The first line was to load and cap its muskets, while the remaining three lines would just load them. They were to fix bayonets. The intervals between the four separate lines were supposed to be only ten feet. [16]

Upton instructed the commanders of the 121st New York and 96th Pennsylvania to turn by their right flank after crossing the first line of works and to charge a Confederate battery stationed one hundred yards down the line. The 5th Maine on the left of the first Federal line was to turn in the opposite direction and to open an enfilading fire. The second line was to halt at the works and to fire to the front as necessary. The third line in which the 77th was to be positioned was to lie down behind the second line and to await orders. The fourth line was to advance only to the edge of the trees, lie down, watch, and be ready for any assignment. Upton alerted the commander of the this final line, Colonel Thomas O. Seaver of the 3rd Vermont, that he might have to form his three regiments obliquely to the left to cover the flank of the assault column. All officers were instructed to repeat the command, "Forward!" constantly from the beginning of the advance until the works were carried. [17]

Brigadier General Gershom Mott's Second Corps division was supposed to support Upton's column assault from its position on the left and rear of the Sixth Corps. Conflicting orders, however, diluted the potential strength of Mott's planned attack. Hundreds of his men were detached as skirmishers to maintain a link with the Ninth Corps. At most, Mott was left with a weak attack force of up to 1,500 men in all. Despite his protest, Wright ordered Mott to do the best he could do by attacking at 5 p.m. with what forces he had and to use his artillery to demoralize the enemy.

Upon return to camp, Babcock called his captains together, informing them of the planned attack. Originally designated for 5 p.m., the time was pushed forward one hour. The 77th's officers returned to their companies to ready them for the assault. The sudden stir of activity caught the attention of Corporal Cyrille Fountain (Co. A), and he wondered what it meant. Fountain's question was soon answered when his captain, George S. Orr, barked orders for the company to "Strip every thing . . . except there guns & Straps & canteens [and] get ready for the use of the bayonet." [17]

After forming west of the Shelton house the 77th joined the attack force and moved silently down the wagon trail in column of fours. The front rank halted in the woods fifty yards or so from the edge of the field. There "they threw themselves upon the ground, and all orders were given in suppressed tones . . . and the minies of their [Confederate] skirmishers were whistling among the trees and brushwood." Suddenly, the booming of cannon and musketry to their left could be heard. Not being informed of the one hour delay, Mott launched his attack at 5 p.m. When his men emerged into the field 600 yards from the Confederate breastworks, the enemy's twenty two artillery pieces were ready for them. The Rebel gunners waited until the Yankees reached the slight crest that Landrum lane ran along before opening fire with canister. In a matter of minutes, Mott's soldiers broke and fled to the rear in confusion back to the safety of the trees, with most of the men returning all the way to their starting point. Mott's troops would be of no help to Upton's attack should it successfully piece the Confederate trenches. [18]

George Stevens recorded that, "At six o'clock all things were ready, and the artillery from the eminences in our rear opened a terrific fire, sending the shells over the heads of the charging column, and plunging into the works of the enemy." The barrage lasted for ten minutes, and then the Sixth Corps batteries ceased firing. Then there was a moment of silence. An officer rode along the right side of the waiting troops. Word was whispered down the line: "Fall in. Forward!" and the Federal infantrymen moved quietly to the edge of the trees. Then Colonel Emory Upton's voice rang out, "Attention, battalion's! Forward, double-quick! Charge!" "And in an instant," Stevens wrote, "every man was on his feet, and, with tremendous cheers, which were answered by the wild yells of the rebels, the column rushed from the cover of the woods. Quick as lightening, a sheet of flame burst from the rebel line, and the leaden hail swept over which the column was advancing, while the canister from the artillery came crashing through our ranks at every step, and scores and hundreds of our brave fellows fell, literally covering the ground." [19]

It probably took the three first line regiments no longer than 60 to 90 seconds to reach Dole's works. Union soldiers broke through the abatis and climbed the work's parapet, where a deadly hand-to-hand combat ensued. The Georgians, driven down into their pits, sat with their loaded rifles held upright and bayonets fixed' killing a number of Yankees. After several soldiers of the 121st New York dropped with bullets through their heads, the rest of the New Yorkers began holding their muskets at arm's length, pointing them over the parapet, and firing straight down. Others took their barrels of their muskets and used the stocks as clubs. Some even pitched their bayoneted weapons over the parapet like spears. [21]

Captain William B. Carpenter (L. Tom Perry Special Collections)

Lieutenant William F. Lyon (L. Tom Perry Special Collections)

The impact of the attacking Yankees was exceptionally violent, but brief. Upton's numbers soon prevailed, and his soldiers began jumping over the topmost logs and into the Rebel trenches. As the first line turned to the right and left, some men continued straight ahead to the second line of Confederate works. They were soon joined by comrades of the second line. The 77th's third line also rushed over the works headlong to the second line of entrenchments. Bullets filled the air like a thick swarm of bees, killing and wounding officers and enlisted men of the 77th. Respected Captain William B. Carpenter (Co. E) fell to the ground dead. So too Lieutenant William Lyon (Co. A). Private Albert Snyder "fired a number of times, while putting on a cap after reloading my rifle, a ball entered my left arm near my shoulder which caused me to be sent to the rear." Corporal Edward Jennings (Co. H) received a severe leg wound and later told his comrades, "I had a presentiment about five minutes before I got it, about halfway between two rebel rifle pits. Just before we started, as I was standing methought 'have been lucky so long in escaping without a scratch, but I will get it now." Private Benjamin Frank Stillwell (Co I) fell in the Confederate breastworks, both legs mangled by enemy bullets. Determined not to die in their works, Stillwell crawled 20 feet to the rear before he was noticed by drummer Private John E. Evans. The 16-year-old drummer remembered, "I then crawled on my hands and knees, amid the heavy firing; and lying on my stomach pulled poor Frank on my back and brought him into our lines. Laid him on his back, and put my blouse under his head. I said to my comrades as I lay me down to go to sleep, 'Wake me up before they take Frank away.' When I awoke, Frank was gone. Also my blouse, pipe and tobacco. But as everything is fair in LOVE AND WAR I went over to the 'Bloody Angle' where off the dead got another one." Private William Armstrong (Co. K) reminisced years later that when the attack column pierced the Rebel line, "I was among those who jumped over the second line of works. The front had now become a mere skirmish line. I got demoralized and suddenly sought safety in flight to the first line of works where many of the charging column was so exposed by a flank fire from the left that I proposed to continue my flight, when a mounted officer showed which direction duty was, emphasizing it with his sword." [20]

Upton's attack completely pierced the Confederate line and forced an opening through which at least a division could have moved unmolested. However, while success was at hand, the Union assaulting column had lost its organization and reinforcements were desperately needed if the surprise attained was to be maintained. Upton rode back across the field to the trees to call his fourth line into the battle, but caught up in the excitement of fighting, the Vermont regiments had charged the works almost as soon as the column moved forward. No reinforcements were anywhere to be seen. Mott's planned supporting attack prematurely had begun a little over an hour earlier and had been an utter failure.

While the 77th and Upton's other regiments failed to receive any reinforcements, the Confederate command skillfully maneuvered troops to seal and patch up the breach the Northerners had made. Brigadier General James Walker's Stonewall Brigade, on the right of the breakthrough, rallied his men and got them firing against the Yankees while Colonel William Witcher leading Jones' brigade came up on their left. George H. Steuart also came up on Upton's left preventing the Federals from further advancing. Ewell also rode up and ordered some of Brigadier General Junius Daniel's North Carolinians to retake a captured battery. Soldiers from John B. Gordon's division along with Cullen A. Battle's brigade double quicked from the Army of Northern Virginia's reserve to join in the effort, sweeping back the Federals. Once the guns were recaptured, gunners sent by Lee to replace those that were captured earlier in the fight worked the pieces against the Yankees.

With darkness swooping over the field, all Upton could do was to hold on until he could extricate his men in the night or hope reinforcements arrived to help. At 7:30 p.m., General Russell decided upon the latter course and ordered a rapid retreat. Surgeon Stevens bemoaned, "It was but a shattered remnant of that noble column that rushed from the woods against the hostile works" that retired across the field back into the trees. Retreating across the open field presented its own horrors. Blue-clad forms sprawled everywhere. Exhausted men from the 77th dragged wounded comrades with them, bending low to avoid bullets. Many of the injured soldiers had to be abandoned. "The woods were full of these unfortunate creatures, and sounded all night with their cries and groan," one Union officer remembered. A Confederate band assembled near the woods and played "Nearer God to Thee." A Federal band countered with the "Dead March," and the Confederates answered with "The Bonnie Blue Flag," followed by ringing rebel yells. The "The Star Spangled Banner" drifted from the Union lines, accompanied by Yankee cheers, and the Southerners replied with "Home Sweet Home" to wit a united yell went up in concert from the soldiers on both sides. [21]

Private William Armstrong (Co. K) reminisced years later providing his audience a personal account of Upton's failed charge:

> We were ordered to carry rifles, equipments, canteen and haversack and marched out of the breastworks, where General Sedgwick was killed the day before, across low swampy ground into woods where we formed in line of battle. 'Forward, double quick, charge,' and we were running across an open field that separated the woods, we formed in from the woods . . . the rebels were strongly intrenched in behind two lines of breastworks, with flank rifle pits.

Many brave soldiers fell in that famous Upton charge. Among those killed were Sergeant Wells and [private] Harrison Davenport (Co. A). The rebel line was pierced and completely broken. I was among those who jumped over the second line of works. The front had now become a mere skirmish line. I got demoralized and suddenly sought safety in flight to the first line of works where many of the charging column was so exposed by a flank fire from the left that I proposed to continue my flight, when a mounted officer showed which direction duty was, emphasizing it with his sword. Not being properly supported we had to abandon the works we had taken and returned to our own lines, which were reformed in proper order. About nine o'clock p. m., feeling hungry, I put my hand back for a hard tack, but alas! No hard tack was with me, as a fact my haversack, containing five days rations, had been shot off; my bayonet sheath hung by a mere thread and the left side of my coat was riddled by shot. [22]

Colonel Upton's brief success came with a severe cost. Of 5,000 men, more than 1,000 were killed, wounded, or missing. The 5th Maine lost all but one of its captains and nearly half of the 49th Pennsylvania was left on the field, including its colonel and lieutenant colonel. The deaths of Captain Carpenter and Lieutenant Lyon, and the war-ending wound of Captain Deyoe – all revered officers – were a severe blow to the 77th. The regiment incurred 75 casualties in the intense fight. George Stevens lamented, "The regiment crossed the Rapidan six days before with over 500 men, and now, after this charge, less than ninety were left." Perhaps only one hundred Confederate soldiers were killed, but a huge number were captured, around 1,000 – 1,200 Rebel troops were brought into Union lines. [23]

Lieutenant Carlos Rowe (Co. I) and some others reached the second line of Confederate works and stubbornly held their ground, unaware of the Federal retreat. Suddenly Rebel soldiers were swarming in their front, flank, and rear, and Rowe and his comrades were taken prisoner. They were taken a short distance to the rear when the unhappy lieutenant heard,

> ... my name called and saw some men of our regiment who were wounded and prisoners. 'Lieutenant, are you wounded?' one asked, and learning that I was not, they begged me to stay with them and take care of them. One whose arm was broken at the elbow, the bone protruding in an ugly manner, the sleeve of his coat torn and bloody, asked me to cut it off, which I did as carefully as I could, when to my surprise he said that he meant his arm, the poor fellow supposing that it would relieve the pain. Could he have had proper attendance no doubt he would have lived, for he died afterward from the effect of the wound. [24]

Lieutenant Rowe was taken two miles further to the rear to a camp holding about 1,200 prisoners and a small number of officers. There, he soon determined to escape when the opportunity presented itself. "I had a pocket compass with me and had obtained from a fellow prisoner a map of the part of the country we were in," Rowe told an attentive audience many years later. The lieutenant did not have to wait long for his chance to escape his captors. [25]

M^CKEAN'S SUNDAY SCHOOL BOYS GO TO WAR

Lieutenant Carlos Rowe (Saratoga Springs Public Library)

A day or so later, Rowe and a number of fellow prisoners were marching southward under guard toward a railroad station where a train would take them to Andersonville prison, when they came to a creek swollen to waist deep by recent rains.

> The guards tried to make us march through it, but the men ran off, right and left, gathered rails and spanned the creek in narrow places and so got over dry shod. This scattered the guards . . . Something said to me this is your time . . . Most of the guards were at the creek trying to get the men together. After crossing the creek I had kept on up the hill and into the bushes, among the thickest of which I lay me down; though I knew it was a dangerous move, for if discovered I might be prodded with a bayonet, if not shot; but if not seen, I might, with my compass and borrowed map, get back to my regiment . . . Consulting my map I saw by crossing the Orange and Alexandria railroad and keeping on the opposite side I could get around the rebel army and get into our lines at Fredericksburg,

or keep on to Washington . . . For ten days I had been on very short rations, and I was hungry as a bear which had been fasting . . . I heard children shouting, so I knew there was a house near. As Moseby's guerillas were about in this country, I reconnoitered enforce, then walked straight up to the house. Of the woman who came to the door I asked for something to eat. After hesitating she got me something and I was allowed to stay all night, though I knew it was risky to do so, but as the woman had trusted me I concluded to trust her, and I was not deceived. She gave me some rations to carry with me and I gave her two dollars and started in the morning greatly relieved. [26]

Two days later, Lieutenant Rowe was rather carelessly walking along the road to Brandy Station when he suddenly "came face to face with a couple of rebel scouts . . . There was no chance to dodge and fighting was out of the question, as they were armed and I was not. So I put on a brave face and walked straight up to them and stopped to talk." The Confederate scouts concluded that the bold lieutenant was a deserter and allowed him to pass. Rowe then came to the Rappahannock; he first thought of swimming across, but decided to make a raft. "After an hour's work getting rails, poles, and pieces of boards together I had something that would float me, and starting out I paddled across." Once on the other side Rowe came to a stack of straw and rested for the remainder of the night and the next day, hidden from the occasional Rebel horseman riding by. Following the river two days later, the city of Fredericksburg loomed in front of the tired lieutenant. There he found some friends from the 77th recovering from their wounds and later received a pass to Washington. Several days after, Rowe returned to the 77th, now diminished from additional fighting at Spotsylvania and Cold Harbor. [27]

MCKEAN'S SUNDAY SCHOOL BOYS GO TO WAR

Grant rose early morning, May 11, and after a Spartan breakfast of a cup of coffee and some badly charred beef, he entered his tent and wrote to Henry Halleck. With an ever present cigar firmly clenched between his teeth, the northern general expressed satisfaction in the conduct of the campaign, and the results thus far attained. Grant requested reinforcements, noting that an infusion of fresh soldiers would encourage the depleted ranks of the troops involved in the offensive. Never before seen in previous commanders of the Army of the Potomac, Grant made clear his bulldog determination, "I propose to fight it out on this line if it takes all summer." [28]

Afterwards, Grant, impressed with Upton's attack, looked to launch a similar attack, but on a much larger scale. He spent much of the day reconnoitering the Confederate position in order to discern the most suitable point for such an assault. Grant became convinced that the Mule Shoe salient was the most opportune place for an attack and orders for that purpose were issued at 3 p.m. His plan to launch a sledgehammer-like blow on the tip of the salient required a complicate set of movements of the Army of the Potomac. Hancock was to send David B. Birney's and Francis C. Barlow's Second Corps divisions all the way around Warren's Fifth Corps and Wright's Sixth Corps under cover of darkness, finally taking position on the left of the 77th's Sixth Corps and directly a half mile north of the apex of the salient on the fields of the Brown house. Gibbon's division would remain in place until just before daylight at which time it would pull back and rejoin the rest of the Second Corps. At 4 a.m. on the 12th, Birney's and Barlow's soldiers along with Mott would attack in concert with Burnside's Ninth Corps. Warren and Wright were instructed to keep their men as close to the enemy as possible in order to take advantage of any opportunities the assault might present. Russell's and the 77th's Second Division were to stand ready to move wherever they were most needed.

In the early evening, the Union army began implementing the necessary moves for the next day's offensive. Clouds that had been gathering all that day let loose a hard, driving rain, making the movement cumbersome. Hancock's troops slowly groped their way through the perfect darkness of the wet night, stumbling through woods in mud that was ankle deep. Nevertheless, the Second Corps arrived at its launch point well before dawn and began setting up for their charge which would bring to bear 15,000 men against the apex of the Mule Shoe. Burnside, after an embarrassing misstep, was also in position. Captain Martin Lennon – unaware of the significance of the army's movements and the bloodshed to come – wrote from the 77th's trenches in his diary only, "Heavy cannonading the whole length of the line at intervals during the day . . . sharp skirmishing all day." [29]

As the Second Corps awaited the appointed hour for it to sweep down on the Mule Shoe, Lee himself committed an error in judgment that would seriously weaken his line at the very spot the Federals planned to attack. Misleading intelligence he received during the day indicated a possible Union retreat. In the evening, Lee told Henry Heth and later Ewell that the Yankees would retreat to Fredericksburg and he planned to strike a blow when they moved. Believing that the Federals were not present near the Second Corps, Lee ordered Ewell to withdraw his troops. Ewell asked that his men should be permitted to rest out the rainy night in their trenches. Lee granted his request though he ordered the corps artillery withdrawn. Most of the artillery pieces located near the point of the Mule Shoe were limbered up and taken away, though four batteries remained.

Hancock's assault was scheduled to commence at 4 a.m.., but a heavy fog hugged the ground, its thickness obscuring the ground over which the assaulting columns would march, thus causing Hancock to delay the attack. At 4:35 a.m., Hancock finally gave the order to attack and the powerful mass of thousands of blue-clad soldiers stepped off toward the Confederate earthworks. From one hundred to one hundred fifty yards away from the enemy's main line, the Yankees encountered a depression containing abatis. Pioneers with axes hacked away while others clawed with their bare hands to clear the obstruction. Still others crawled through the obstacle.

The attack shattered the Rebel works, virtually annihilating Colonel William Witcher's Virginia Brigade. As Barlow's division swung around to the eastern tip of the Mule Shoe, it speedily overran the brigade commanded by Brigadier General George "Maryland" Steuart, capturing Steuart and his division commander, Alleghany Johnson, along with nearly 3,000 prisoners. On Barlow's right, Birney's division ran into stiff resistance from Colonel William Monaghan's consolidated Louisiana Brigade and Brigadier General James A. Walker's Stonewall Brigade, with fierce hand-to-hand fighting. Still, the Union troops continued to spread south along the western edge of the Mule Shoe.

The Federal assault opened a gaping hole in the Confederate line, but the formidable attacking column by now was a completely disorganized mass of men crowded into a narrow front about a half mile wild. Officers valiantly made attempts at reorganization, but the surging blue column confounded their efforts. Despite the confusion, however, the Second Corps continued to press forward into the woods in the center of the salient toward Spotsylvania. Soon, they were encountering an increasing volume of musketry from the enemy forcing them to halt. All of a sudden the attacking Second Corps soldiers found themselves the target of a surprise assault by counterattacking Confederate brigades that had been drawn from up and down Lee's entrenchments.

Following the initial shock, the Confederate command began to react with professional precision to the Federal onslaught. John

B. Gordon sent Brigadier Robert D. Johnston's brigade of North Carolinians charging toward the gap where Steurart's men had been routed. Although Johnston was wounded, his brigade successfully stemmed the breakthrough in that sector. Gordon then sent forward Colonel John S. Hoffman's Virginians and three regiments from Colonel Clement A. Evan's brigade. Robert E. Lee was at the scene to witness these men moving forward and attempted to lead them to the fight, only to be stopped by Gordon and the chants from the soldiers, "Lee to the rear!" These brigades were able to secure most of the eastern leg of the Mule Shoe after about 30 minutes of fierce fighting. On the western leg, Major General Robert E. Rodes coordinated the defense and the brigade of Stephen D. Ramseur suffered heavy casualties as they fought their way to regain the earthworks lost by the Stonewall Brigade.[32]

By 6 a.m., Grant's grand offensive had sputtered to a standstill. On the eastern side of the salient, Burnside's troops were pinned under a fierce Confederate artillery cannonade. Hancock's line had shrunk to a few hundred yards of earthworks between the east and west angles. While Lee successfully blunted Grant's momentum, the Federals still held two important cards. The Fifth and Sixth Corps – fully half the Union infantry force – stood poised to enter the contest. It appeared to Grant that the Confederate army had to be near its breaking point. One more hard push, the Union commander reasoned, and the Rebel defenses would surely crumble.

Meantime, the 77th's Second division formed in a field to the northwest of the Brown house to await assignment. Shortly after 6 a.m., Wright was ordered to move the Second Division forward to Hancock's right. Colonel Oliver Edwards' Fourth Brigade, closest to Hancock, was first to be ordered forward. Edward's New Englander's entered the woods southwest of the Brown house. Emerging from the cover of the trees, they crossed the Landrum Lane Ridge and arrived at an area along the captured Confederate works forever after known as the Bloody Angle. This portion of the line contained two slight bends which were approximately 50 yards apart. The east bend was a little more than 300 yards west of the apex of the salient. Immediately behind the works there stood a large oak tree, measuring about 20 inches in diameter. North of the works was a swale in the Landrum field. Opposite the oak tree, this little valley was about 30 yards from the works, but it angled northeast to about 100 yards from the works. From there the swale curved southward nearly to the works about 70 yards up the line from the oak. The edge of the valley opposite the Confederate works is referred to as the crest. Fighting in this area began shortly after Edwards three regiments at 6:30 a.m. The fighting would last for more than 20 hours.

Captain Orrin P. Rugg (NYSDMNA)

The 77th's Third Brigade, under Colonel Bidwell's command followed closely behind Edwards' New Englanders. Bidwell halted the brigade at the edge of the woods approximately one hundred yards to the rear Edwards' brigade, and deployed his regiments from right to left: 77th, 49th New York, 61st Pennsylvania, 43rd New York, 7th

Maine. The 77th and the 49th New York charged across the swale in Landrum field and quickly took possession of the crest commanding the works at the Bloody Angle. The left of the 49th New York continued Edwards' right, and the 77th fell to the right of the 49th New York. The New Yorkers were immediately met with a blinding sheet of musketry from Ramseur's North Carolinians, killing and wounding a number of the 77th, including newly married Captain Orrin Rugg who died while being carried off the field from a shot to the breast. Private Cyrille Fountain wrote in his diary, "I had my hair cut from my head by a Shell, it knocked me down but did not hurt me much. My frying pan Saved my life." Private William Armstrong was again in the thick of the fight and recalled,

> After firing eight rounds, I was struck by a rebel bullet in the left side of my head, and fell unconscious. When I regained consciousness I found I was covered with blood, the wing of my left ear split, the bone immediately behind it fractured. Thinking myself dangerously wounded I went to the division hospital tent. An operating surgeon asked my 'what ails you?' 'A bullet in my neck,' said I. 'There is not,' said the surgeon, as he examined the wound. 'There is; cannot I feel,' said I. 'Not another word, or I shall put you under arrest,' said he as he washed off the blood and put on a piece of sticking plaster. 'Go back to your regiment,' said he. I waited a few days, however, before obeying the surgeon's order. [30]

At the Bloody Angle, the 77th's veterans had the unusual experience of manning the front side of a defensive work. The New Yorkers rested against the wall of excavated dirt in front and peered under the head logs. The rain, which commenced during the previous night, continued to fall intermittently throughout the morning, and at times was heavy, so that by now the soldiers were covered with mud from head to toe presenting a most bedraggled and unmilitary appearance.

Around 7:30 a.m., Ramseur's brigade was about to break from Yankee fire. Coming to Ramseur's assistance were Alabama troops under Brigadier General Abner Monroe Perrin. Met with intense musketry, Perrin's men piled into fortifications next to Ramseur, closer to critical high ground and vulnerable to a deadly plunging fire. Mississippians under Brigadier General Nathaniel H. Harris followed Perrin's troops. A swarm of Union bullets forced them to seek cover in entrenchments to the right of the Alabamians. More Confederate reinforcements swarmed to the right of Harris. Brigadier General Samuel McGowan's South Carolina Brigade arrived around 9 a.m. and was bloodied by Federal flank fire. Though suffering from severe losses, McGowan's men drove the Federal bluecoats from their commanding position and secured a toe-hold on critical high ground.

Sometime just before 9:30 a.m., Wright's Sixth Corps First Division under Brigadier General David A. Russell arrived to do battle. The lead brigade was headed by newly promoted Brigadier General Emory Upton, and his soldiers occupied a crest overlooking the works on the right of Edwards' brigade just as its right was breaking up. The first of Upton's regiments to reach the field was the 95th Pennsylvania. Its front line was nearly decimated by a maelstrom of Rebel bullets. Despite the terrific hail of lead, Upton urged the men on calling them to hold their ground. The rest of Upton's brigade took up position, getting into a heavy firefight with the Confederate troops only 300 yards away.

Deciding to bring some artillery to bear on the Rebel troops, Upton sent a staff officer to have a nearby battery, Battery C of the U. S. Artillery send a section for his use. The commander of the guns,

First Lieutenant James Gillis initially refused Upton's lieutenant, only to have the man return with an officer of higher rank who ordered Gillis to obey. No longer able to refuse the order, Gillis sent Second Lieutenant Richard Metcalf's two guns into the white heat of combat. The guns unlimbered near Upton and immediately attracted the attention of Harris' Mississippians who surged forward in an attempt to take them. Just to the left rear of Metcalf's guns, stood the 61st Pennsylvania of the Third Brigade. The guns exploded with canister, mowing down a number of attackers, and the 61st Pennsylvania faced right and drove the Confederates back almost to their works before being forced back to their position near Metcalf's cannon.

Metcalf's guns were then pushed forward even closer to the enemy line. In a few moments, most of the artillerists were lying on the ground dead or wounded. A. T. Brewer of the 61st Pennsylvania described what happened next.

> At this time an artillery officer ran along the line of the 61st calling for volunteers to man the guns. He did not call in vain, for men dropped their muskets and followed him and soon the cannons roared again, sending showers of canister into the rebels only a hundred feet away. In Company A one sergeant and four men volunteered, but the new gunners were soon disabled by the rebel fire, and the canon were once more silent. The rebels made another rush for the battery, but were again beaten back, some being killed among the guns . . . The rebels could not take the battery nor could it be used by the Union troops. It stood all day a noiseless menace and temptation to the rebels and to the Union men, a silent witness of destruction of artillerists whose dead bodies were strewn among the guns with the infantry volunteers.

Metcalf's section had gone in with 23 men and one officer. His engagement had left all of the horses of his section killed, seven of his men dead and sixteen wounded. Brewer remembered that toward the evening "the guns sunk down, the rebel fire having cut off the spokes of the gun carriage wheels. A sponge bucket hanging under one of the guns had 27 bullet holes in it." [31]

After a little more than three hours of firing their muskets at the enemy from the front side of the Confederate breastworks, the 77th and 49th New York were fast running out of ammunition, and were relieved by elements of Brigadier General Frank Wheaton's brigade. The New Yorkers fell back 100 yards to just behind the crest overlooking the Bloody Angle. Wheaton's troops could not hold their position and were driven back to the crest where the New Yorkers had been resupplied with a full complement of cartridges. Both the 77th and the 49th New York and a number of soldiers from Lewis A. Grant's Vermont Brigade formed and retook the vacated point in the Federal line.

As the morning faded into afternoon, a hard rain continued to fall and water reddened by the blood of the wounded and dead pooled at the bottom of the trenches. From late morning to afternoon, the fighting at the salient remained so intense, particularly at the Bloody Angle where the 77th furiously fought to maintain its position, the opposing forces were literally firing into each other's faces. Private Milton Sweet claimed to have loaded and fired his Enfield 270 times. "After firing two-hundred eighty-five rounds," Private Frederick Keeholts (Co. B) "got up on the breastworks to have guns handed him to fire; but his temerity cost him his life." According to Surgeon George Stevens,

> ... the battle became a hand to hand combat. A breastwork of logs separated the combatants. Our men would reach

over this partition and discharge their muskets in the face of the enemy, and in return would receive the fire of the rebels at the same close range. Finally, the men began to use their muskets as clubs and then rails were used. The men were willing thus to fight from behind the breastworks, but to rise up and attempt to charge in the face of an enemy so near at hand and so strong in numbers required unusual bravery. Yet they did charge and they drove the rebels back and held the angle themselves. It was in one of these charges that the gallant Major Ellis of the Forty-ninth New York, was shot with a ramrod through the arm and in the side, from the effects of which he afterwards died. The trees in front of the position held by the Sixth Corps during this remarkable struggle, were literally cut to pieces by bullets. Even trees more than a foot in diameter, were cut off by the constant action of bullets.

Captain Charles E. Stevens (Co. A) remembered, "Over the works I counted 12 rebels who lay dead under a large limb of a tree that had been cut down by a shell from our guns." [32]

Unfortunately for Grant, neither Burnside's Ninth Corps nor Warren's Fifth Corps pursued their participation in the battle with much force. Both probed and skirmished, but the major attacks that might have broken the enemy line or at least diverted Confederate troops from joining the fight going on at the salient never came.

During the afternoon, Lee decided that, even despite his reluctance to allow his line to be broken, he would not be able to drive the Federals entirely away from the salient. As a result, the position would have to be abandoned in favor of a new line 1,200 yards to the rear where a new line had already begun. Survivors of Allegheny Johnson's division, artillerymen, and stragglers rounded up by the provost marshal's troops built the new line throughout the day. Unfortunately, the Confederate soldiers battling away at the salient wouldn't be able to fall back to this new position until cover of darkness and thus would have to remain in combat for the time being. Warren's inaction during the afternoon provided Lee the opportunity to send reinforcements to areas of need as Benjamin G. Humphreys' and John Bratton's brigades were drawn from the First Corps lines and sent into position at the reserve entrenchments.

While Lee's soldiers were digging a new line of breastworks, Federal commanders were benumbed by anxiety and readjusted their lines in fear of a Confederate counterattack. The 77th and the rest of the Third Brigade were withdrawn about three hundred yards and went into bivouac for the night. The battle which began at 4:30 a.m. continued with diminishing intensity as darkness cloaked the field. Still, while "there was a lull in musketry . . . the artillery continued its work of destruction." The wounded that fell in the darkness had the misfortune of ending up on the missing lists and in unmarked graves. By the time it finally ended, the raging carnage had gone on for nearly twenty four hours, a full day of fighting. Dawn would reveal to both sides the full consequence of their deadly work. Standing at the Bloody Angle, Surgeon Stevens wrote, "Behind the works the rebel dead were lying literally piled one upon another, and wounded men were groaning under the weight of bodies of their dead companions." Walking over the site of battle, Cyrille Fountain noted in his diary, "O O Such horrible sights. it rained all day the wounded Still layed out on the field. the dead rebles were piled 3 deep." [33]

The evening fears of a Confederate counterattack did not prevent Grant from sending Henry Halleck a triumphant dispatch, claiming 3,000-4,000 enemy soldiers as prisoners, including two general officers and thirty pieces of artillery as special prizes. He went on to claim, "The enemy are obstinate and seems to have found the last ditch. We have lost no organization, not even that of a company, while we have destroyed and captured one division (Johnson's), one brigade (Dole's), and one regiment entire of the enemy." [34]

Lee's soldiers began retreating from the Mule Shoe salient in the early morning of May 13. Confederates, brigade by brigade, retreated from the ground they fought and bled so heavily to regain the day before. Their destination was the new entrenchments prepared at the base of the salient, on a slight rise paralleling the Brock Road. It was not long before their Federal adversaries discovered this readjustment.

Just after dawn, the Yankee army began probing the enemy position only to find the enemy had disappeared. Sixth Corps commander Wright reported at 5:30 a.m. that the West Angle was empty of the enemy and his troops were occupying the bloodied ground. In response to his report, Wright was ordered to continue advancing in a reconnaissance and his forces complied by advancing down the west side of the salient. Probing to the left of the Sixth Corps, Hancock's soldiers had marched a half mile into the salient also without meeting any opposition. By 7:30 a.m., however, the advancing Federals were beginning to make strong contact with the enemy. Scattered skirmish fire intensified as Sixth and Second Corps soldiers began to close in on the new Confederate breastworks. By late morning the new Southern line at the base of the salient was fully uncovered by Federal troops, but no plans were made for an attack against it that day. Instead, the Union forces retreated to the old Confederate works which were refitted to face south against their old occupants.

The decision not to resume the fighting of May 12 was a wise decision as an accounting of the unimaginably fierce fighting the day before revealed a terrible toll. Grant's army suffered a huge loss of

7,000 Federal casualties. Combined the Federal losses on May 12th with all the fighting from the Wilderness totaled 36,872 men with almost a third of these missing. In eight straight days of fighting, the 77th incurred 173 casualties. Nearly 6,000 Southern soldiers – men that could not be replaced – may have been lost in the May 12 fighting, with almost half being captured from Johnson's division during Hancock's morning attack.

During the respite from combat, attention was paid to burying the dead. The Union dead were treated with little ceremony, an unfortunate fact a soldier of the 49th New York witnessed. "They were laid side by side in blankets. Enclosed in the blanket was the full name and rank of each one and at the head of each grave was placed a cracker box board with their names in large letters, so their friends could easily identify them." No doubt the family of Captain Orrin Rugg was grateful for this courtesy, for six month later they traveled south from Saratoga Springs to retrieve his body for reburial back home. Dead Confederates received even fewer niceties from Yankee hands. Many of the Southern dead lay at the bottom of their trenches. They were left there just as they fell. Burial squads covered the dead bodies with dirt from the top of the trenches. [35]

On May 14, the 1st Vermont Heavy Artillery, 1,500 men in all, arrived from the Washington defenses and was assigned to Lewis Grant's Vermont Brigade. In line of battle in the nearby woods, the 77th's and its brigade comrades watched the heavies' in crisp new uniforms and carrying fresh accoutrements as they formed and stacked their arms. Hungry and thirsty, the rookies scattered in search of water and wood to make fires. The Third Brigade veterans dashed out of the woods and proceeded to appropriate new gum blankets and exchanged their old rusty guns for bright new ones. A half hour later Confederate artillery fired on their position, sending shot and shell crashing through the trees. The new soldiers, responding to the bugle call, promptly fell into line, ready for action. In a few minutes the artillery fire ceased and the heavies again broke ranks. By now, they discovered what had happened. As the 77th watched the new regiment's Colonel Warner approach Brigadier General Thomas Neill and after saluting him said, "General, many of your men have taken our guns, blankets, and other equipment." Neill, feigning offense, replied in deep, grave tones. "Impossible, colonel; my men have no use for your guns or other property." "But," said Warner, "they have actually taken many of our guns," and pointing to various weather-beaten men in dirty garments nearby, the agitated colonel said, "there is a man with one of our guns, and there is another, and beyond I can see some of our new blankets." Neill replied, "Oh, no, you are mistaken; it is impossible; when you stacked arms, you put a guard over them; you are too good a soldier to leave your property unguarded. Besides, if you need any guns you can pick up on this battlefield ten for every one you have lost." Colonel Warner realized that he had made a great mistake in not putting a guard over his equipment, and said nothing more. [36]

On the 15 of May, the 77th and other troops were in line of battle behind fortifications made chiefly of logs not far from the Fredericksburg Road. While in that position, a verbal order repeated by field and line officers came along from in these woods: "Don't cheer." The New Yorkers understood someone important was coming whose life might be endangered by cheering, as the noise would reveal the Union position to the enemy. In a few minutes, inspecting the Federal line, U. S. Grant atop his bay horse, Cincinnati, came from the right, proceeding toward the left, riding slowly through the brush, keeping his eye on the breastwork. When he came within two hundred feet, the veteran soldiers began to throw up their hats and make a noise like cheering, but almost inaudible. The noise grew louder, and before Grant passed the 77th, the men broke into a tremendous cheer, which extended back along the line until it died away in the distance and kept a hundred feet ahead of the general as he proceeded. At the same moment, Confederate batteries opened up firing shells, one of which burst over Grant's head, sending a shower of debris upon him. His horse crouched and shivered as he proceeded, but did not rear or plunge like the other horses of his aides and orderlies. Unperturbed, Grant gave no notice that he heard the cheering or cannon firing, but proceeded quietly out of sight and the incident ended, "the men liking the general better for not making a fuss out of nothing." [37]

After several days of reconnoitering the Confederate position for potential weaknesses to exploit, at 4 a.m. on May 18, Grant settled upon a plan for the Second Corps and Sixth Corps to attack the new Southern entrenchments at the base of the Mule Shoe. This meant the Federals would have to advance from and over the very ground which had been fought over during the raging inferno of combat on May 12, now known as "Hell's Half-Acre." This required Hancock to march his troops by night to the vicinity of the Landrum house where his charge against the Confederate position would be launched. The 77th with the Sixth Corps was to march from its position below Massaponax Church Road around the entire Federal army to the Second Corps right where it would jump off for its attack. By 3 a.m. May 18, Hancock reported that Barlow's and Gibbon's divisions were readying for their drive in the Landrum fields and that the Sixth Corps was taking position on his right. But not all went accordingly. The Sixth Corps experienced difficulty getting into attack position and Robert O. Tyler's rookie division of converted heavy artillery was late. Nevertheless, Hancock sent Barlow and Gibbon forward at 4:30 a.m. Hancock's soldiers advanced in two battle lines while the rest of the corps remained in reserve. Shortly after, the 77th with Wright's Second Division stepped off in four brigade lines, Wheaton's brigade leading followed by Edwards', then the 77th's Third Brigade, and finally by Lewis Grant's six Vermont regiments – the veteran Green Mountain regiments in front and the large green 1st Vermont Heavy Artillery behind.

The Rebel position that the Hancock's and Wright's troops would attack was formidable. The enemy's defensive works lay along a rise that descended north toward the attackers. The works had traverses every 15 or 20 feet and in some cases were enclosed across the rear as well. Extensive abatis had been constructed out in front to distances of more than 100 yards, especially along the eastern half of the line, which was in the woods. Perhaps even more demoralizing was the ground over which they would have to advance, littered with the carnage of the previous fighting made worse by exposure to the rain and sun. Blackened and bloated corpses were strewn about everywhere, some partially concealed in shallow graves with a leg or arm sticking out while others, who had been shot while climbing through the abatis, hung on the cut branches and looked from afar like they were standing. The stench from the rotting flesh was so sickening and terrible and many of the men became deathly sick from it. Some soldiers stuffed leaves into their nostrils to dampen the smell. The appearance of the dead who had been exposed to the sun so long was horrible in the extreme. [41]

Barlow's and Gibbon's men advanced taking heavy fire from musketry and cannon fire, and their forward movement stalled at the extensive abatis arrayed before the Confederate line. As the Second Division advanced down the western face of the salient with its left in the McCoull field, Wheaton and Edwards' obliqued to the left bringing the 77th's Third Brigade to the front line. Almost immediately, the 77th stumbled into corpses that had been lined together several days before for burial. Their ranks nevertheless trampled on the bloated corpses causing some to burst. The New Yorkers were immediately pounded on the flank and the front by deadly artillery fire. The Third Brigade climbed over the Confederate reserve works and clamored into the ravine to join Edwards' soldiers already huddled against the slope. Colonel Bidwell commanding the Third Brigade reported they could do nothing than cower close to the ground under a "heavy fire of all sorts of missiles." The 7th Maine's Captain John Chauncy spied a brass cannon that was shooting down the length of the ravine filled with the Yankee soldiers. He could see the piece and when it was about to fire alerted his companions to duck by hollering, "Look out boys, here it comes." Failing to heed his own advice, an exploding shell sliced a deep furrow above his right eye. Blood streamed over his face, and the Maine captain shook his fist at the rebel gunners. "I have fought you a good many times and I'll fight you again," he shouted in defiance. "Here it comes," he yelled once again as the cannon fired. Then he turned and hobbled to the rear. Informed of the failure of the attacks, Grant brought a halt to the operation. The Second Corps withdrew, while the Sixth Corps returned to its position on the Fifth Corps right. [38]

Satisfied that the opportunity to defeat Lee could not be had at Spotsylvania Court House, Grant wanted to move the Army of the Potomac on to a more fruitful open ground battlefield somewhere closer to Richmond. He planned another turning movement around the Confederate right and to get between Lee and Richmond. Pursuant to this plan, Grant sent one hundred artillery pieces back to Washington so his marches would not be slowed by large artillery trains. He also informed Halleck of his intention to change his supply base from Fredericksburg to Port Royal so he could draw sustenance for his army up the Rappahannock River. The 77th's veterans would be glad to leave the blood soaked battleground, but before they did, the New Yorkers would incur one last fatality when the popular Private Aaron B. Quivey (Co. C) was shot through the breast by a Rebel sharpshooter, dying a few minutes later. George Stevens recalled, "His faithful Christian character, his undoubted bravery, and his ardent patriotism, had endeared him to all." [39]

13

"WE ARE LICKING THE REBS EVERY TIME WE MEET THEM"

After the heavy fighting and subsequent stalemate at Spotsylvania, Grant decided once again to sidle around Robert E. Lee's right flank. The Northern general's objective was the North Anna River, about 25 miles south, and the important intersection of the Richmond, Fredericksburg & Potomac and Virginia Central Railroads at Hanover Junction. By seizing both, Grant could not only sever Lee's supply lines, but deny the Army of Northern Virginia its next strategic defensive line, forcing the Confederate army to attack Grant in the open under more favorable terms. To lure Lee out in the open, he directed Winfield Scott Hancock to march his Second Corps southeastward through the town of Bowling Green and on to the hamlet of Milford Station. If Lee took the bait and left his entrenchments to attack as Grant hoped, the remainder of the Army of the Potomac was to pounce on the Rebels and crush them. In the event that Lee stayed put behind his fortifications, Hancock would simply continue on to the North Anna River, clearing the way for the rest of the Federal army to follow.

During the night of May 20, Hancock initiated his diversionary march. When Lee learned of the Union movement, he concluded that Hancock was spearheading an advance to Richmond and positioned Ewell's corps across the Telegraph Road, closing the main highway south to the Federals and cutting off Hancock from the rest of the Federal force. Lee also notified Major General John C. Breckinridge, who had just defeated Major Franz Sigel's small Union army in the Shenandoah Valley and was enroute to join Lee, to halt at Hanover Junction and defend the North Anna River line until Lee could join him. Growing increasingly anxious about Hancock's safety, Grant directed Meade to evacuate his entrenchments at Spotsylvania Court House and march to Hancock's assistance. As Warren's Fifth Corps began marching to Massaponax Church, Grant received intelligence about Ewell's Second Corps blocking the Telegraph Road and changed Warren's orders to proceed instead to Guinea Station and follow Hancock's troops. Burnside's Ninth Corps came upon Ewell's men on the Telegraph Road, and Burnside ordered them to turn around and proceed to Guinea Station. Massed around the Gayle House, Wright's Sixth Corps followed the track of the Ninth corps. The 77th marched rapidly all night, halting for a few moments for breath once or twice, and then pressing forward again. The New Yorkers arrived at Guinea Station, the site of Stonewall Jackson's death one year earlier, at 11 a.m. the next morning and halted for several hours. A number of the regiment's officers and enlisted men took the time to visit the outbuilding of the Chandler Plantation where the famous southern warrior died.

The evening of May 21, Warren's Fifth Corps bivouacked a mile east of the Telegraph Road. That night, Lee's soldiers completed their withdrawal from Spotsylvania Court House and marched south toward the North Anna River; at times passing Meade's sleeping pickets by less than a mile. Sheridan's cavalry was absent on a raid, leaving Grant without intelligence of Lee's proximity, and the Union general's opportunity to bag Lee's army outside of its entrenchments went unexploited. The Army of Northern Virginia's tired troops crossed the North Anna the morning of May 22 and went into camp a few miles south of the river at Hanover Junction. Anxious to protect this critical rail link a mere 25 miles north of Richmond, Lee chose Hanover Junction as the next place to make a stand.

Grant followed south in the wake of Lee's army on May 22, fanning the Army of the Potomac across a wide swath of countryside. Uncertain whether Grant meant to continue across the North Anna or swing further to the east, Lee looked for signs of his adversary's intentions. The answer came the next day as the Federal army's scattered elements converged at Mount Carmel Church, several miles above the North Anna. From the church, Hancock marched toward the main river crossing at Chesterfield Bridge while Gouverneur Warren took his Fifth Corps west along a side road, intending to cross a few miles upstream at Jericho Mills. With the Sixth Corps, the 77th followed behind the Fifth Corps, and Burnside's Ninth Corps took another side road to Ox Ford, midway between Warren and Hancock.

Nearing the North Anna, Hancock's troops came under fire from Colonel John Henagan's South Carolina Brigade tucked into a three-sided redoubt next to Chesterfield Bridge. Charging the isolated Confederate outpost, Hancock's soldiers easily overwhelmed the defenders, capturing many of the enemy and driving the rest back across the river. In short order, Henagan's redoubt and Chesterfield Bridge were in Union hands.

Five miles upstream, Warren swatted away a handful of mounted Rebels at Jericho Mills. Federal engineers constructed a pontoon bridge, and by 5 p.m., the Union Fifth Corps was treading across the river and deploying in neighboring fields. Confederate scouts discovered the blue-coated interlopers but gravely underestimated their numbers, reporting to A. P. Hill that only two Union brigades had crossed. Misled about the strength of the Federal force, Hill sent a single division commanded by Major General Cadmus Wilcox to repel the enemy. Warren easily repulsed the attack but surprisingly elected not to press his advantage, later stating he was uncertain how many Confederates he faced.

As the Sixth Corps left their camp at Harris' Store, the 77th veterans could hear Colonel Charles S. Wainwright's Fifth Corps artillery lined along a ridge overlooking the north side North Anna subjecting Wilcox's troops with plunging fire. As the New Yorkers approached Jericho Mills, the roar of the Union guns was astounding due to the conformation of the ground and the reverberations seemed louder than the original discharges. The 61st Pennsylvania's A. T. Brewer wrote that the men "found it necessary to walk on tiptoe and use other precautions to avoid ear ruptures. The air seemed highly charged with electricity and the shocks were startling, but when the column reached a point where the high bluff was only on the south side, the peculiar effect ceased." By the time the Sixth Corps was in position to support Warren's corps, Wilcox had been repulsed and the corps rested the remainder of the day. Many of the 77th took this time to wash their clothes and get rid of part of the Virginia mud accumulated in the preceding weeks. [1]

With a formidable part of Grant's army now poised on the south side of the North Anna, Lee recognized that he was in serious trouble. That evening, Lee and his chief engineer, Major General Martin L. Smith, surveyed a new defensive line. The Army of Northern Virginia was spread out into a wedge-shaped formation, its apex touching the North Anna River at Ox Ford and each leg reaching back and anchoring on strong natural positions. The tip of the wedge was unassailable, and with the Virginia Central Railroad connecting the wedge's two feet, Lee could shift troops from one side to the other as needed. When Grant advanced, the wedge would split the Federal army in half, allowing Lee to hold one leg with a small force while concentrating his army on the other leg. Favoring interior lines to the North Anna's topography, Lee had given the smaller Confederate army an advantage over his opponent.

On the morning of May 24, the 77th with the Sixth Corps crossed the North Anna at Jericho Mills, and by 11 a.m. both Warren and Wright had advanced to the Virginia Central Railroad. At 8 a.m., Hancock's Second Corps crossed the Chesterfield Bridge. Downriver, the Confederates had burned the railway trestle, but soldiers from the 8th Ohio cut down a large tree and the men crossed on it single file. This was soon supplemented by a pontoon bridge and Major General John Gibbon's division quickly crossed. Witnessing the ease of crossing the river, Grant assumed the Rebels were retreating. "The enemy has fallen back from North Anna. We are in pursuit." he wrote Washington in jubilation, unaware that he was marching into Lee's trap. [2]

The only visible opposition to the Federal crossing was the apex of the wedge at Ox Ford, which Grant believed to be a rear guard action. The Union commander ordered Burnside's Ninth Corps to take the enemy position. Brigadier General James H. Ledlie crossed the North Anna at Quarles Mill with orders to dislodge the Rebels holding the bluffs at Ox Ford. To Ledlie's surprise, the heights were topped by earthworks still occupied by a veteran Confederate division under Brigadier William Mahone. His judgment clouded by alcohol, Ledlie led his brigade in two orderly lines. Musketry exploded from the Rebel earthworks, and Ledlie's formation dissolved into a confused blue-clad mob. Artillery raked the field as a thunderstorm broke overhead drenching the men in a burst of rain with the flicker of lightening arcing across the sky. Completely drunk, Ledlie abandoned all pretense of command, abandoning his soldiers to their fate. Incredibly, Ledlie escaped court martial and a few weeks later received command of a division, where he would cause even greater mischief at the battle of the Crater in July. [3]

During Ledlie's ill-advised attack, Hancock tried again to probe south but was stopped by Major General Richard H. Anderson's strongly entrenched position on the wedge's eastern leg. Other of Hancock's troops followed the Richmond, Fredericksburg & Potomac Railroad south but were stymied by Ewell's corps. Lee's moment had come. His plan to split the Union army had worked, isolating Hancock east of the Confederate position. But the Army of Northern Virginia could not strike a blow. Taken ill with dysentery the day before, Lee lay confined to his tent. Physically unable to command, and lacking a capable subordinate to direct the army in his place, Lee saw no choice but to forfeit his hard-won opportunity.

While Lee lay on his cot with dysentery, Hancock made one last effort to advance. Pressing across the Doswell farm, Federal soldiers came under even stiffer fire than before and bivouacked on the rain-soaked battlefield. Warren's Fifth Corps and the 77th's Sixth Corps, massed between Jericho Mills and the Virginia Central Railroad, also advanced but ran against A. P. Hill's entrenchments and began constructing their own earthworks across from the Rebels. Nowhere during the day did the Federals seriously threaten the Confederate line.

May 25 saw the 77th's veterans perfecting their entrenchments south of the North Anna, near Noel's Station. Confederate earthworks loomed only a few hundred yards away, clearly visible across open fields. Confederate soldiers had mastered the art of field fortifications, and the North Anna position was their most impressive effort yet. The Rebel line manifested itself as a mound of red dirt atop commanding ground that looked across killing fields cleared of brush and trees. Heaped along the face of the fortifications, abatis of sharpened branches faced outward. Dirt and wood ramparts rose several feet, surmounted by head logs that protected the defenders while firing. Carefully placed artillery lunettes rendered the position impregnable. The New Yorkers were well acquainted with Lee's fortifications at the Bloody Angle at Spotsylvania Court House, and had no stomach for testing them here on the North Anna.

Later in the day, the 77th cautiously advanced to Little River during a heavy, soaking rain but did not cross the swollen waterway, instead trading pot shots with Confederates on the opposite bank. Private Cyrille Fountain noted in his diary that some of the New Yorkers spent the day with other elements of the Sixth Corps doing their best to destroy the Virginia Central Railroad, a key Confederate supply line from the South's breadbasket, the Shenandoah Valley, to Richmond. The veterans built bonfires to heat the rails and wrapped them around trees making decorative loops. By the evening, they had happily wrecked the railway ten miles west to Beaver Dam Station. [4]

That evening, Grant and Meade met with their corps commanders to discuss ways to break the stalemate with Lee. Some argued that a maneuver west of Lee would catch the Confederates off guard.

Grant vetoed that move, insisting that the Union army needed to stay east of Lee to protect its supply routes back to the Chesapeake Bay. Virginia's topography indicated a shift around Lee's left flank. Below the North Anna, the Federals would face three sizeable streams – Little River, New Found River, and the South Anna River – each flowing west to east and only a few miles apart. With high banks and swollen from recent rains, these rivers would present the retreating Rebels ideal defensive positions. A few miles southeast of Lee's position, the rivers joined to form the Pamunkey River. By sidling downstream along the Pamunkey east of Lee, Grant would put the waterways behind him at one stroke. Further, White House, the highest navigable point on the Pamunkey, was well-suited as Grant's next supply depot. Too, as the Yankees followed the Pamunkey's eastward course, they would vector progressively closer to Richmond. Grants most likely crossings – Nelson's Bridge, Dabney Ferry, and New Castle Ferry – near Hanovertown, thirty miles southeast of Ox Ford, were only eighteen miles from Richmond. Once the Army of the Potomac was over the Pamunkey, only the Chickahominy River would stand between them and the Confederate capital.

Grant decided to begin his flanking maneuver at night to increase the chances for success. To speed his march, he determined to advance in two columns, one crossing at Dabney Ferry and the other downriver at New Castle Ferry. The most difficult part of the operation would be disengaging unnoticed by Lee. Grant's solution to this dilemma was a deception, followed by a phased withdrawal. On the morning of May 26, Brigadier General James H. Wilson's cavalry division would ride to Little River, west of Lee, to create the impression that he was preparing the way for the entire Army of the Potomac. At the same time, portions of Brigadier Generals Alfred T. A. Torbert's and David Mcm. Gregg's cavalry divisions were to drive east to Littlepage Bridge and Taylor's Ford on the Pamunkey. Their charge was to further confuse Lee about Grant's intentions by making it appear the Federals were considering crossing there as well.

While Union cavalry orchestrated its diversions, Brigadier General David A. Russell's Sixth Corps division, along with two four-gun batteries, was to withdraw from its earthworks, cross to the north side of the North Anna River, and bivouac at Chesterfield Station. At dark, Russell, accompanied by cavalry and engineers with pontoons, was to march along the Pamunkey toward Dabney Ferry. While cavalry screened their movement, Russell and the engineers were expected to reach Dabney Ferry at Hanovertown shortly after daylight on May 27 and secure the Pamunkey crossing. The rest of the Yankee army was to withdraw from its entrenchments the night of May 26. Screened by a heavy posting of pickets, Wright was to withdraw the rest of his corps, cross to the north side of the North Anna, and follow Russell's route to Dabney Ferry. Warren was to take a route several miles to the left of Wright that would bring him to New Castle Ferry. Burnside and Hancock were to cross the North Anna, screen Wright's and Warren's departure, and follow behind them. If all went according to plan, the Army of the Potomac would be marching across the Pamunkey late on May 27 or early on May 28.

May 26 brought another storm of heavy rain, and the 77th spent a miserable morning on the North Anna line. Torrential rain pelted down unabated, flooding the New Yorker's trenches. The water-soaked veterans hunkered low behind earthworks slippery with mud and knee-deep in water to avoid exposure to enemy snipers. Southern sharpshooters plied their trade with unusual malice, adding to their discomfort. One Yankee officer counted a dozen rounds whizzing by each minute. Some of the regiment's more industrious veterans piled logs in front of their shelter tents to stop Rebel bullets. Others dismally huddled under rubber blankets and shivered in the rain. Over the popping off of rounds by Confederate snipers, Captain Martin Lennon listened intently to sharp skirmishing along the front of the Fifth and Sixth Corps, no doubt hoping it did not signal an imminent full-scale battle. [5]

Shortly after dark, Wright threw out a heavy curtain of pickets to conceal the Sixth Corps disengagement from its entrenchments and retrograde movement to the North Anna River. He also instructed his soldiers to imitate the appearance of routine camp life. The 77th's regimental band joined others of the Sixth Corps and played patriotic music and Rebel bands responded with "Dixie," "My Maryland," and other southern favorites. Brigadier General James B. Rickett's division was first to leave its works, followed by Sixth Corps artillery, with the New Yorker's Second Division closing up behind. The 77th gladly withdrew from their flooded trenches near Noel's Station on the Virginia Central Railroad and headed to the pontoon bridges spanning the North Anna at Jericho Mills.

After crossing the river at Jericho Mills, the 77th filed along the narrow road with the Sixth Corps to Mount Carmel Church. "Several days of rain," Surgeon Stevens wrote, "rendered the roads, proverbial for their mud, almost impassable." For several miles, the mud was knee-deep, and the horses, weak from hard service and lack of forage, were constantly stumbling and falling and required the assistance of already fatigued soldiers to get them up. Here and their soldiers amused themselves waiting beside holes in the road and watching unsuspecting men fall in, sometimes up to their waists in the muddy soup. Many soldiers trudged on barefoot after losing their shoes in the mire. [6]

Before long, infantry and wagons mixed on the narrow, muddy roads into a horrific traffic jam, forcing and tired and wet soldiers to stand in the mud only to advance several yards before halting again for an indeterminate time. Midmorning, the 77th halted at the smoldering ruins of Chesterfield Station, the buildings having been set ablaze by Russell's division the night before. Bone tired after their all night march from the North Anna, the New Yorkers settled beside the road, eating what rations they could. Grant rode by on a small black pony named Jeff Davis with his entourage, and soldiers gathered along the roadside, standing in silence and lifting their kepis as he passed. Taking the ever-present cigar from his mouth, Grant acknowledged the salutes with a smile.

By sunup on May 27, Lee was informed that the Federals had left their earthworks below the North Anna. Shortly after 6 a.m., a report that Torbert's cavalry and Russell's infantry were streaming across the Pamunkey River at Dabney Ferry made Grant's intention clear. Wilson's cavalry demonstration at Little River had been a ruse. Grant was continuing his pattern of maneuvering past the right side of the Confederate line. Lee decided to abandon the North Anna line and shift fifteen miles southeast to a point near Atlee's Station on the Virginia Central Railroad, a mere nine miles north of Richmond. This would position the Confederate army southwest of Grant's growing concentration at Hanovertown, in place to block the likely avenues of Union advance. Grant, by his move to the Pamunkey, had turned Lee out of his North Anna entrenchments in much the same manner that he maneuvered Lee from his strongholds in the Wilderness and at Spotsylvania Court House. However, Lee's response was equally shrewd, as it would enable him to confront Grant head-on along a new line of his choice behind the Totopotomy Creek.

The Army of Northern Virginia was on the march by 10 a.m., traveling south along parallel routes. Ewell's soldiers followed Telegraph Road to Taylorsville, crossed Little River, then cut across on another road to the Virginia Central Railroad. From there they crossed the

South Anna River on a trestle and wound along a patchwork of narrow country lanes, reaching Hughes' Crossroads, halfway between Ashland and Atlee's Station, near dark. Breckinridge, followed by Anderson's First Corps, headed due south along the Richmond, Fredericksburg & Potomac Railroad. The Rebel column advanced across Little River and the South Anna on railroad bridges, passed through Ashland, then turned east toward Hughes' Crossroads. Breckinridge at the Crossroads near Ewell, and Anderson bivouacked a few miles away between Hughes' Crossroads and Half Sink. The army's wagon and artillery trains rolled along Telegraph Road. A. P. Hill and Picket's division of Anderson's corps remained at the North Anna until everyone had left, then brought up the rear, following behind Anderson and camping near Ashland.

Around 7 a.m., the 77th left the burning embers of Chesterfield Station and marched a few miles behind Grant's headquarters entourage. A little after noon, the Sixth Corps tramped past Concord Church. The late spring sun burned off the morning mist and the day grew excessively hot. The thirsty veterans clothed in heavy wool uniforms of blue suffered along the way. Bathed in sweat, the heat and dust kicked up from the drying mud taxed them almost to their limit. Private Cyrille Fountain commented on the growing foul mood of the New Yorkers who "seemed as good natured as a wasp." [7]

In order to pass well clear of Lee, Grant had planned to cross Wright and Hancock at Dabney Ferry, and Warren and Burnside at New Castle Ferry. But Torbert's subsequent move from Hanovertown to Crump's Creek gave the Federals possession of Nelson's Bridge. By crossing there and at Dabney Ferry, Grant could jettison the longer march to New Castle Ferry and move the Army of the Potomac more quickly. At 4:15 a.m., Meade issued new orders. The Sixth Corps was to turn south at Calno, a short distance west of Mangohick Church, march partway to Nelson's Bridge, and camp for the night.

The next morning Wright and Hancock were to cross the Pamunkey at Nelson's Bridge, and Warren and Burnside were to go over at Dabney Ferry. In the evening, the 77th with the Sixth Corps went into camp, halting a few miles short of Nelson's Bridge in flatland along Hornquarter Creek. By afternoon on May 28, if all went according to plan, the Yankee army would be below the Pamunkey and readying for its next – and possibly final – battle against Lee.

At 4 a.m. on May 28, Private Cryrille Fountain awoke sore from the previous day's march as the 77th pried itself from its camp near Hornquarter Creek, and with the Sixth Corps, marched past McDowell's Millpond and headed southeast toward Nelson's Bridge. A few miles to the New Yorkers' rear, Hancock's troops followed Wright. Warren's men were also on the move, covering the mile from their Dorrell Creek bivouacs to Mangohick Church, then taking the road through Enfield and on to Dabney Ferry. In the Federal army's rear came Burnside's soldiers. The bluecoats moved in three parallel columns giving the appearance of three rivers of blue flowing toward their destination. [8]

Marching men soon bottlenecked on the road to Nelson's Bridge, bringing the Sixth Corps column to a halt. Many of the regiment's veterans took advantage of the stop to light a roadside fire to boil coffee. Once on the move again, the 77th continued with the Sixth Corps, winding through a labyrinth of farm roads, and passing by Wyoming Plantation, a large, wooden, tumble-down house with a considerable garden owned by the widow Henrietta Nelson. From there, the New Yorkers descended a sharp bluff to the broad flatland by the Pamunkey.

As the Sixth Corps approached the river, Captain William Folwell's engineers were busy assembling a serviceable pontoon bridge. Folwell reached the crossing at 6 a.m. Short on decking, the engineers improvised by spacing canvass pontoons farther apart than usual, making an unsteady but functional bridge. The 77th reached the Pamunkey around 7 a.m. and halted, intently watching the engineers finish their work. Within an hour, a 146-foot bridge spanned the river and the Sixth Corps was tramping across the shaky bridge. Officers ordered soldiers to march out-of-step to keep the bridge from swaying. A second and sturdier wooden pontoon bridge was erected later in the day.

All morning, Federal infantry streamed across the Pamunkey River. In the Sixth Corps column, the 77th crossed the pontoon bridge and cut across Mrs. Hundley's fields where corpses, dead horses, and discarded accoutrements were scattered about, the results of a cavalry fight the previous day between Brigadier General George Custer and Colonel John Baker. Turning west on the Hanover River Road, Wright formed a defensive line along Crump's Creek, anchoring his corps northern flank on the Pamunkey and bending its southern end back to Dr. Pollard's. The New Yorkers' Second division held the upper portion of the line across the Hanover River Road. Two of the division's brigades and three batteries were positioned on high ground west of the creek, and two brigades east of the stream. Russell's division came up from its camp at Hanovertown and formed on the Second Division's left, blocking the road to the Sledd farm. Rickett's division camped on Dr. Pollard's farm.

As Private Fountain crossed the pontoon bridge over the Pamunkey, he remarked, "we could hear fireing at a great distance to our left." Only a few miles southeast, the bloodiest cavalry battle since Brandy Station in 1863 was raging in fields surrounding Haw's Shop, a substantial blacksmith's shop owned by John Haw. On Atlee Station Road half a mile west of Haw's Shop, the prosperous blacksmith and his family lived in a well-appointed two-story house called Oak Grove, honoring the stately trees on the property. Both Grant and Lee lacked adequate intelligence as to where their enemy's main army lay. In an attempt to find out, both generals threw out strong cavalry forces to uncover each other's line. Federal and Confederate troopers slammed into each other at Haw's Shop and fought it out for seven hours before withdrawing from each other. In the end, nearly 800 soldiers were counted as killed, wounded, or missing. One dead soldier was Private John Huff who earlier mortally wounded J. E. B. Stuart at Yellow Tavern. During the conflict, Oak Grove was converted to a field hospital. After the fight, John Haw counted forty four dead horses at or near his home. [9]

By midmorning, Warren's corps filed across the Pamunkey at Dabney Ferry and deployed in double lines of earthworks on high ground, spreading from Mrs. Newton's property by the river two miles south to a branch of the Totopotomoy Creek. Griffin anchored the fifth Corps' right, Cutler the middle, and Crawford the left. After inspecting his line, Warren set up headquarters at Mrs. Newton's house.

A little after noon, Hancock's Second Corps began treading the twin pontoon bridges at the Nelson's Bridge site. Turning onto the road to Dr. Pollard's farm, Hancock's men marched behind the Sixth Corps trenches and took up a line on Wright's left. Gibbon's division occupied Dr. Pollard's farm, sharing the fields with Ricketts men. Union engineers planned earthworks to run through the Pollard family cemetery. The doctor's wife was buried there, and Pollard asked the engineers to avoid disturbing her grave. When they ignored his pleas, Dr. Pollard appealed to Hancock, who had set up headquarters in his yard. Taking pity upon the aggrieved doctor, Hancock directed the engineers to curve the breastworks around the cemetery.

On the south side of the Totopotomoy Creek, Lee was rearranging his troops. At 10:30 a.m., Early had reached Hundley's Corner, at the intersection of Shady Grove Road and the road running north to Totopotomoy Creek and Polly Hundley Corner. Lee was becoming ever more concerned that Grant might be massing his army behind the Union cavalry screen at Haw's Shop. If that were the case, Federal soldiers would be poised to march south from Haw's Shop, cross the Totopotomoy Creek well east of Early, and swing southwest toward Richmond along roads leading through Mechanicsville. To prevent such a move, Lee ordered Early to extend his corps south across Old Church Road, a major road paralleling Shady Grove Road about a mile to the south.

The day before a flotilla of twenty ships and barges assembled at Bermuda Hundred Landing and City Point. Disappointed with Major General Benjamin butler's army bottled up at Bermuda Hundred, a triangle of land formed by the confluence of the James and Appomattox Rivers, Grant summoned Major General William "Baldy" Smith's Eighteenth Corps, supplemented by a Tenth Corps division, and an artillery brigade to join the Army of the Potomac now south of the Pamunkey River. The plan was for Smith's 17,000 soldiers to float down the James River, round the point at Fortress Monroe, where they would disembark and march the rest of the way to join Grant. "Am now embarking," Smith wrote Grant at 10:30 p.m. on May 28. "I will proceed as rapidly as possible to West Point or White House, according as I find it best to land." [10]

On Sunday, May 29, the weather had turned refreshingly cool, raising the spirits of the 77th's veterans who had enjoyed a peaceful night's rest. Chaplain Fox gathered the regiment's faithful, offering a morning sermon. Private Alonzo Bump was upbeat as he wrote to his wife back home in Victory, "we are all in Good spirits and hope that thiss will Be the Last Battle that we shall have . . . we are Licking the Rebs every time we meat them. they are a Putting for Richmond as fast as they can and we are right tight on thair heeals. i think that

Old Grant will Beat them in to Richmond yet." Nevertheless, there was room for complaint. The main gripe among the soldiers involved food. Supply wagons had still not caught up with the army, and rations were exhausted. "All day nothing to eat," Private Fountain grumbled. "This was a lonesome Sabbath." [11]

At daybreak, the New Yorkers observed a steady stream of slaves coming into Union lines from surrounding plantations. War correspondent Charles C. Coffin had compassion for their plight. "Old men with venerable beards, horny hands, crippled with hard work and harder usage," he noted in describing the seemingly endless procession, "aged women, toothless, almost blind, steadying their steps with sticks; little Negro boys, driving a team of skeleton steers, mere bones and tendons covered with hide, or wall-eyed horses, spavined, foundered, and lame, attached to rickety carts and wagons piled with beds, tables, chairs, pots and kettles, hens, turkeys, ducks; women came with infants in their arms, and a sable cloud of children trotting by their side." Not able to supply its own men, the Federal army was in no condition to care for the contrabands. Provost Marshal Patrick developed a temporary solution by sending them on to White House with a large number of Confederate prisoners. By a quick count, Patrick estimated 600 blacks of all ages traveled in the caravan. [12]

Though May 29 saw the 77th and the Union army safely across the Pamunkey River, Grant was undecided about what to do next. The sharp battle at Haw's Shop revealed that Rebel cavalry was up in force, and Lee's infantry was surely close behind. Confederate horsemen, however, were successfully screening troop dispositions, leaving Grant to speculate about Lee's actual location. Suspecting that the enemy was nearby south of Totopotomoy Creek, the Federal commander was unwilling to commit to a course of action until he solved the mystery of Lee's whereabouts.

Typically, it was the cavalry's role in finding the enemy, but after fighting at Haw's Shop had ended, Sheridan took his mounted men east to rest, effectively removing them from the immediate operations. The cavalry commander left Grant little choice but to send infantry to find Lee. Late in the morning, Meade developed a plan to advance large bodies of foot soldiers along three routes radiating from his position. Wright was to send Russell's Sixth Corps division northwest along Hanover River Road, aiming for Hanover Court House; Hancock was to forward Barlow's division west along Atlee Station Road, making for Totopotomoy Creek; and Warren was to drive Griffin's division south across Totopotomoy Creek, hit Shady Grove Road, and reconnoiter west toward Pole Green Church and Hundley's Corner. Finally, Burnside was to keep his soldiers ready to support Hancock or Warren and to probe the roads between their two corps if need arose.

Lee was well prepared for Grant's searching maneuver. He had lined the Army of Northern Virginia along Totopotomoy Creek's south bank, covering Grant's possible approaches. Early's Second Corps stood across Shady Grove Road, its left close to Pole Green Church and its right continuing south toward Beaver Dam Creek and Old Church Road. Breckinridge remained entrenched across Atlee Station Road at Totopotomoy Creek, and A. P. Hill's Third Corps had shifted into line on Breckinrigde's left, facing north to cover the Virginia Central Railroad and the road from Hanover Court House . Anderson's First Corps, positioned on Shady Grove Road in the rear of Early, could support Hill, Breckinridge, or Early as needed. Lee's formation along Totopotomoy Creek was masterful. For Grant to attack, the Yankees would have to cross the creek and its swampy lowlands and charge uphill across cleared land and abatis into the heart of Rebel earthworks. Each portion of the Confederate line was built to support the others, and enough troops stood in reserve.

The three Federal divisions set out on their assigned routes at noon. As the 77th continued work improving their entrenchments, on their right Russell's men headed northeast along Hanover River Road. Around 3 p.m. they approached Mechump's Creek. Confederate horsemen on the opposite bank were easily swept aside, driving the Rebel troopers from Hanover Court House. Russell bivouacked south of the town along Mechump's Creek. Nearby, Union soldiers ripped up rails on the Virginia Central Railroad, heated and bent them, set fire to the Court House train station, and destroyed two railway bridges.

Russell was less than comfortable with his position. He was isolated several miles from the army, and his rations were exhausted. Wright was equally concerned about Russell's hazardous situation, and decided at 6 p.m. to send Brigadier General Frank Wheaton's predominantly Pennsylvania brigade and Colonel Oliver Edwards' mixed Massachusetts and Rhode Island brigade, both of the 77th's Second Division, to Hanover Court House. They were directed to take the more southerly road past the Sledd farm. The blue coats reached Hanover Court House after dark and formed two lines on Russell's left, facing south across Richmond Pike. The 77th's Third Brigade and the Vermont Brigade remained in their entrenchments along Crump's Creek.

Barlow marched west along Atlee Station Road from Haw's Shop. His men passed Enon church, site of the previous day's cavalry battle, and saw intermingled the dead bodies of men and horses. At Polly Hundley Corner, where Atlee Station Road crossed the road running south from Hanover Court House to Pole Green Church, Barlow's column scattered a handful of Rebel troopers disputing the way. A local woman informed Barlow that Confederates (Breckingridge's soldiers) were behind earthworks at Totopotomoy

Creek. Barlow threw out a heavy screen of skirmishers and the rest of the column continued on. Musketry became lively at 3 p.m. as Union skirmishers approached the brick mansion of sixty six year old Colonel Shelton. From Shelton's, a wide field descended a half mile to Totopotomoy Creek. The stream made a short cut to the south where Atlee Station Road crossed, and Breckinridge's men held both banks. Barlow's skirmishers were met with a hail of bullets and rounds of cannon fire, convincing him that his division could go no further. Forming his division across the Shelton fields perpendicular to the road, Barlow sent a dispatch to Hancock that he had met substantial Confederate infantry and needed support.

The third prong of the Union probe, Griffin moved south toward Totopotomoy Creek. Around 3 p.m., Griffin's lead elements dropped down into marshes around the creek. After wading across, they climbed the far bank into the fields of the Via family. Mrs. Via's house stood in a fifteen acre clearing surrounded by woods. Confederate horsemen were there and sounded the alarm. Skirmishers from Early's Second Corps immediately began peppering the intruders with bullets. Bartlett's and Sweitzer's brigades dug entrenchments on the Via farm facing south. Ayres' brigade continued across the Via farm and followed a cow path south three quarters of a mile, and its lead elements broke onto Shady Grove Road. Early rushed troops to meet the enemy and pushed Ayres back to the Via farm. Griffin then arranged his brigades across the grounds.

Grant and Meade had no intention of initiating battle at this juncture. The day's reconnaissances had given the Union commanders a practical picture of Lee's location. The Army of Northern Virginia held the far side of Totopotomoy Creek on a line from Atlee Station through Pole Green Church. The next step was to press the Confederate line. In the morning, Hancock was to advance the rest of his corps to the Shelton home and pin Breckinridge in place, locking down the center of the Rebel position on Atlee Station Road. At the same time, Wright was to shift the entire Sixth Corps south, moving athwart the Confederate army's left flank and linking with Hancock's right. Warren was to continue Griffin's advance with his entire corps, testing the Southern right flank on Shady Grove Road. Burnside was to move forward as well and bridge the gap between the Second and Fifth Corps. The plan was for the Federal Fifth and Sixth Corps to strike Lee's flanks while the Second and Ninth Corps advanced frontally, preventing Lee from reinforcing his embattled flanks.

In the early morning hours of May 30, the Army of the Potomac began a general advance. Meade's order for the day directed Hancock's Second Corps, holding the Union center along Atlee Station Road, to probe Breckinridge. Hancock's skirmishers pressed to Totopotomoy Creek and discovered Confederates strongly posted on the south bank. Sharp firefights erupted and flared in the dense thickets on either side of the stream between snipers hiding behind trees and logs and swiftly constructed rifle pits. Around 11 a.m., two New York regiments waded across the Totopotomoy and overran some Rebels on a small ridge immediately beyond. Breckinridge's main line was in sight on the next ridge, and the New Yorkers were instantly pinned down by severe fire from the enemy of musketry and some artillery.

The previous evening, Hancock had directed his artillery chief, Colonel John C. Tidball to post the Second Corps cannons along the crest behind the Shelton house. Shortly after noon, an artillery duel broke out between Confederate guns along Breckinridge's line and Tidball's batteries. Signal officers on the Shelton house roof aided in directing Tidball's fire. To drive them away, Rebel guns focused on the house. Artillery caissons stood parked near a row of slave cabins by the main house. At the height of the cannonading, an elderly black woman came out of a cabin and dumped a pan of hot coals near a limber chest filled with ammunition. The coals ignited and the limber chest exploded, killing several soldiers and burning the eyes out of others. The side of a barn also blew out, setting loose panicked geese and hens. "It was not supposed that the negress had any intention of doing mischief," Hancock's aide reported. "She was so crazy that none believed she knew what she had done." [13]

After an hour of trading shells, Confederate and Federal artillery fire slackened. The artillery duel destroyed the Shelton house, and left a number of Union and Rebel soldiers dead or wounded. In accomplished nothing, however, to advance either side's prospects. Soldiers in blue and gray spent much of the day facing each other across the creek girding for subsequent developments.

Wright's Sixth Corps assignment was to connect with Hancock's right flank at Overton farm and to place himself on the Confederate left flank. At 5 a.m., Russell's soldiers started south along the Virginia Central Railroad to Peake's Station, where the railway crossed a major east-west road three miles south of Hanover Court House. Russell reached Peake's Station at 9 a.m. and deployed his division across the railroad. Famished soldiers were jubilant when they found a bounty of pigs, chicken, and corn. One bluecoat scrounged up some cornmeal and baked it into bread that he later pronounced "as nutritious and palatable as from a cup full of white straw dust." Here, commissary wagons finally caught up with the infantrymen and the soldiers rested and ate. With bellies full, some of the men "burnt two new buildings and a boarding car belonging to the railroad, a small barn and a deserted negro shanty." More organized parties tore up the railway's tracks in the vicinity. [14]

While Russell's men filled themselves with the newly brought rations at Peake's Station, his scouts roamed east. Halfway between the railroad station and Cash Corner they came upon Mechanicsville Road, a major road that did not appear on any of their maps. Mechanicsville Road descended south through McKenzie's Corner, crossed Totopotomoy Creek, and continued on to Mechanicsville, paralleling the Virginia Central Railroad. Russell sent Brigadier General Emory Upton to reconnoiter south along the newly discovered route. As they neared McKenzie's Corner, skirmishing became brisk with Fitzhugh Lee's cavalry patrolling the approaches to Totopotomoy Creek. Hill's Third Corps was entrenched along the far side of the creek to guard against the flank attack that right was contemplating. Emory's force was too small to engage Hill and retired.

The 77th left their trenches along Crump's Creek with Rickett's division around 5 a.m., marched three miles toward Hanover Court house, and turned south to Cash Corner. This placed the New Yorker's a mile east of Russell at Peake's Station. The road forked at Cash Corner – the right prong led west to Peake's Station, and the left fork, locally known as the Richmond Pike, continued south to the Overton farm. Wright caught up with Russell and Ricketts around 10 a.m. and was advised of the Mechanicsville Road that Russell's scouts had discovered. Intrigued, Rickett's started some of his men towards it, expecting to follow Upton's probe. Intelligence came back, however, that Upton had run into A. P. Hill's skirmishers. Happily for Cyrille Fountain, supply wagons brought up rations while Wright considered his options. The New York veterans wolfed down their food, and Wright dispatched scouts down Richmond Pike to find Hancock's right flank and to advise him how best to get there. [15]

Rickett's portion of the Sixth Corps moved south from Cash Corner around 2 p.m. The 77th and its sister regiments had earlier advanced toward Peake's Station and had to backtrack. To make up for lost time, Wright allowed them to cut cross country. Numerous streams and rivulets forming the headwaters of Crump's Creek flowed through the region, creating "a swamp and tangle of the worst character." Shortcuts devolved into marshy detours. At 5 p.m., nearly twelve hours after the Sixth Corps had set out from its camps that morning, Rickett's lead elements, followed by the 77th marched into the Overton fields and linked up with the right of Hancock's line. [16]

Russell remained at Peake's Station until 3 p.m., shifted over to Mechanicsville Road, and marched south. Colonel Oliver Edwards' brigade acted as rear guard. As soon as Russell's main column was under way, Edwards' men crossed to Richmond Pike and provided cover for Rickett's rear. Edward's camped at Phillip's Mill and protected Rickett's rear from harassment by roaming Confederate cavalry men.

The Sixth Corps was in position shortly after 5 p.m. The 77th with Neill's Second Division formed the right, near McKenzie's Corner; Russell held the middle; and Ricketts deployed on the left, at Overton farm. Two artillery batteries went into position near the Overton house, facing Swift Run. The bluecoats hoped for rest, but headquarters had other plans. A little after 5 p.m., Meade ordered Wright to throw out skirmishers, develop the Confederate position in his front, "and, if practicable, attack the enemy in the case he appears weak." [17]

Meade wanted Warren and Burnside to move onto Hancock's left flank to extend the Union line south. Griffin's division of Warren's Fifth Corps was already established below Totopotomoy Creek at Mrs. Via's farm. Warren intended to start Griffin west along Shady Grove Road early in the morning, then the rest of the Fifth Corps across the creek to follow behind him. Burnside was to advance across Totopotomoy Creek and hook his left onto Warren's right, protecting the Fifth Corps flank, while attaching his own right onto Hancock's left somewhere north of the creek. Before Burnside readied his corps to march, Warren moved the rest of his Fifth Corps across the creek and deployed on Shady Grove Road. Warren's divisions began probing west along the road, Griffin leading, followed by Major General Samuel W. Crawford and Brigadier General Lysander Cutler.

Lee interpreted these movements as a continuation of Grant's campaign strategy to slip around Lee's flank and toward the southeast bringing the Union army closer to Richmond. He ordered Jubal Early's Second Corps, which was entrenched across Warren's path, to attack the Fifth Corps with the assistance of Anderson's First Corps. Early planned to send the division of Major General Robert E. Rodes on a flanking march along Old Church Road, turning north at Bethesda Church, and follow paths that Fitzhugh Lee's horsemen had precut through the underbrush to smash into Warren's rear.

As the Fifth Corps slowly moved forward, Warren became increasingly anxious about the safety of his left flank. He sent Crawford's division south along a farm track to Old Church Road, where they erected simple earthworks. Crawford ordered forward Colonel Martin D. Hardin's brigade, men of the Pennsylvania Reserves whose enlistment was due to expire that same day. Rodes' troops marched directly into Hardin's brigade around noon and routed them, causing the Pennsylvanians to retire behind Beaver Dam Creek. With the route of Hardin's soldiers, Crawford's entire division collapsed, exposing the Fifth Corps left flank. Their blood up, Rodes lost control of his men who ran past their objectives in a confused mass. The Confederate general hesitated to continue with Early's plan, which called him to push north into the rear of Warren's corps. Much of Early's force was still marching in column.

Also, Anderson's corps, which was supposed to support Early, was late in arriving. Warren feverishly began shifting his corps to face south toward Early and Crawford reformed at the farm lane. Griffin moved in to support Crawford and the Fifth Corps artillery, under Colonel Charles S. Wainwright, arrived and set up batteries north of Shady Grove Road on Crawford's left. Griffin's division dug in on Crawford's right.

Major General Stephen Dodson Ramseur, of Early's corps, newly promoted to division command, recklessly charged the Federal artillery at 6:30 p.m. with only Pegram's brigade, commanded by Colonel Edward Willis. They advanced heroically through a killing crossfire of musketry and cannon. Though they were able to advance to within fifty yards of the Union position, Willis was mortally wounded and the Confederate brigade fell back to its starting point. The attack was a costly repulse, but the Southern soldiers' heroism earned the admiration of the Yankee infantrymen who witnessed it. The historian of the 13th Pennsylvania Reserves recorded the event: "The slaughter was so sickening that Major Hartshorne leaped to his feet and called upon his assailants to surrender. Some hundreds did so. Rebels or no rebels, their behavior and bearing during the charge had won the admiration of their captors, who did not hesitate to express it." A surviving Virginian recalled, "Our line melted away as if by magic. Every brigade, staff, and field officer was cut down, in an incredibly short time." [18]

Nightfall found the opposing armies in close proximity of each other, pickets in places barely a stone's throw apart. The Sixth Corps held the Union right along Totopotomoy Creek. The 77th's Second Division anchored the flank at McKenzie's Corner followed by Russell and Ricketts' division at the Overton house, facing A. P. Hill. Hancock continued the line east on Wright's left, bent south along Swift Run, and wound east along Totopotomoy Creek, facing

Breckinridge and Anderson. Burnside extended south from his junction with Hancock at the Whitlock place across Totopotomoy Creek to Shady Grove Road, facing Anderson. Jubal Early withdrew west of Bethesda Church, positioning Rodes across Old Church Road at the Dickenson and Johnson farms, Gordon on the right, and Ramseur in reserve. Warren advanced to fill the ground left by Early, holding his right on Burnside's left at Shady Grove Road and anchoring his own left a short distance south of Bethesda Church on a millpond at the head of Matadequin Creek.

Grant's plans for the next day focused on Baldy Smith's reinforcements. The break of dawn, May 30, witnessed Smith's transports rounding the point at Fort Monroe and steaming up the York River. Sailing by Yorktown and Williamsburg, the boats floated to West Point, where the York split into the Mattaponi and Pamunkey. They continued slowly into the Pamunkey. Broad marshland, giving way to distant wooded bluffs, lined both sides of the river. The lead transports in Smith's flotilla reached White House around noon. All day, soldiers were loaded into boats and brought to dry land, grateful to be on firm land once again.

By afternoon, White House Landing was the face of a bustling port city. Squads of soldiers repaired the Richmond and York River Railroad trestle across the Pamunkey and bivouacked on surrounding fields. A number of officers gathered under a broad-limbed tree near the ruins of the Custis mansion. Many were respectful of the plantations history. Here, George Washington had courted the Widow Martha Custis. More recently, it had been the home of Robert E. Lee's son, Rooney, and was burned to the ground by Federal soldiers during McClellan's occupation in 1862. Sheridan's horseman added to the destruction when they passed through on his Richmond raid. A New Hampshire soldier met an ancient black man who claimed to be 113 years old and to have served as George

Washington's body servant when the general visited White House many years before. [19]

Grant desired Smith to finish unloading during the night and to join the Army of the Potomac the next day. At 7:30 p.m., he directed Smith to "march up the south bank of the Pamunkey to New Castle, there to await further orders." Confederates, he warned, might attempt to interject between the Eighteenth Corps and the Army of the Potomac. But Grant was not overly concerned, as he was prepared to attack the Confederates if they tried to move past his left flank and strike in the direction of Old Church. "They will be so closely watched that nothing would suit me better than such a move," he assured Smith. [20]

During the afternoon, Lee received distressing intelligence of the arrival of Smith's reinforcements. Lee telegraphed Richmond warning that the consequences could be catastrophic, as Grant could send Smith to Cold Harbor without weakening his line along Totopotomy Creek. Lacking sufficient troops to block Smith and hold the Federal army at bay, Lee would have to forfeit the critical road junction, enabling Grant to turn his right flank. Reinforcements were Lee's only hope. He telegraphed Beauregard who had effectively taken Butler out of Grant's calculations at Bermuda Hundred, but he refused to send troops on his own initiative. At 7:30 p.m., Lee telegraphed President Davis and bluntly decreed that any delay in sending reinforcements would result in disaster, and called for the immediate transfer of Major General Robert F. Hoke's 6,800 man division from Beauregard's command. Davis consented and Hoke's division began marching at 2 a.m. on May 31.

On the same day, Grant and Meade did not want a major engagement. They merely wanted to maintain pressure against the Rebels to prevent Lee from slipping away unnoticed. At 7:30 a.m., Meade directed his corps commanders to "press forward their skirmishers up against the enemy to ascertain whether any change has taken place in their front, and report the result." [21]

On the Union right, Horatio Wright ordered skirmishers into the lowland around Totopotomy Creek. A densely wooded marshy bog three hundred feet wide traversed the Sixth Corps' front. The 77th could see Hill's sharpshooters on the far side alert to any movement, and behind the rifle pits rose a high ridge, in many places cliff-like and impossible to ascend. Slashed timber covered the slope of the ridge and abatis ran along the top. Skirmishers from the 77th advanced a little distance, passing by the graves of soldiers of the 44th New York who had died in previous fighting, and halted. Captain Martin Lennon reported a sharp skirmish to the left flared when Brigadier General Gershom R. Mott's Second Corps brigade charged across Totopotomoy Creek near the Overton plantation and drove Hill's skirmishers from their rifle pits. Mott's men, however, were soon pinned down by enemy snipers and shell fire, and could advance no farther. Lying prone to the ground, the desperate bluecoats dug breastworks with bayonets and tin cups to shield themselves Confederate bullets and shells. Correctly assessing the situation, Wright reported to Meade, "It is impracticable to attack along my front." [22]

By evening, opposing infantry lines remained largely unchanged. Elements from the Sixth Corps had dug in on the Confederate side of Totopotomoy Creek, so too some of the Second Corps and all of the Ninth Corps. However, there was no chance of a Union breakthrough anywhere along the Rebel line. Sharp skirmishing resulted in a remarkably high number of casualties. 732 men were wounded in the Second Corps alone. Meade's chief-of-staff accurately recorded the day's affair: "The infantry corps were pressed up against the enemy as close as practicable without assaulting, but the position was so strong naturally, and so well entrenched, and the entrenchments so strongly held that an assault was not attempted." [23]

Federal infantry probes did not much concern Lee during the day. The Totopotomoy line of entrenchments overlooking the creek was impregnable. Lee was concerned, however, about the possibility a strong Union force slashing through Cold Harbor, turning his right flank, and advancing to Mechanicsville or across the Chickahominy River into Richmond. News of Baldy Smith's corps approaching from White House heightened his concern, for the only Confederates holding the strategic crossroads were Brigadier General Matthew C. Butler's South Carolina cavalrymen who had been bloodied earlier at Matadequin Creek. Unwilling to drain troops from Totopotomoy Creek and to send them to Cold Harbor, Lee turned to Hoke, whose division at 2 a.m. had started from Bermuda Hundred. Hoke had been ordered to advance up the Virginia Central Railroad to Atlee's Station. Countermanding the order, the Confederate general ordered the Southern reinforcements to Cold Harbor.

Lee also sent Fitzhugh Lee's cavalry division to reinforce Butler's fought-out troopers and secure the crossroads at Cold Harbor. Union cavalry commander Alfred Torbert was equally determined to take Cold Harbor, and launched a series of attacks against Lee's troopers who were reinforced by Hoke's lead brigade of North Carolinians commanded by Brigadier General Thomas L. Clingman. Federal horsemen gained the upper hand late in the afternoon, driving Lee and Clingman from the vital crossroads. The Confederates rallied to high ground about a mile west from Cold Harbor, and began fortifying a line running north to south across Cold Harbor Road. To their relief, more of Hoke's division arrived from Mechanicsville to extend Rebel line.

By 4 p.m., it seemed to General Lee that Grant was aiming to take Cold Harbor. Lee had already dispatched Hoke and Fitzhugh Lee to guard the crossroads, but reports of Baldy Smith's troops being not far off prompted him to send more infantry to Cold Harbor. At this point, the day's spate of Federal probes seemed spent, and Lee felt safe pulling troops from his main line and forwarding them to vital intersection. He sent orders for Anderson to withdraw from Totopotomoy Creek, shift behind Early, and march southeast to join Hoke. Shortly after, Anderson started pulling his troops out of line.

As the evening of May 31 progressed, Warren's pickets detected Anderson's soldiers marching behind Early's breastworks. After dark, Sheridan sent word that he held Cold Harbor and Confederate infantry were present, actively extending south to cover the bridges over the Chickahominy. Jarred by the news, Grant and Meade sprang into action. Sheridan was directed to defend Cold Harbor at all costs. Wright was instructed to take the Sixth Corps to Cold Harbor, but the night march would be long and difficult. The troops had to follow narrow roads from the Overton plantation to Polly Hundley Corner, through Haw's Shop to Linney's Corner and Old Church, then down Bottom's Bridge Road and back along Cold Harbor Road, a distance of fifteen miles.

Grant also realized that Baldy Smith might play an important role. When Wright reached Cold Harbor, nearly three miles would separate him from Warren's left flank near Bethesda Church. This critical gap would provide Lee an opportune moment to slice between Warren and Wright and turn the flanks of both Federal corps. Marching to Cold Harbor, Smith could form on Wright's right flank and reach north to Warren.

The 77th and Wright's soldiers were not at all happy with their assignment. They had torn up the Virginia Central Railroad near the North Anna River on May 26, marched without sleep all that night and the next day, continued to Crump's Creek on May 28th, pushed out to Hanover Court house on May 29, marched twelve hours on May 30 to Totopotomoy Creek, and skirmished all day on the 31st. Now the tired veterans were being asked to make a 15-mile, all-night march to Cold Harbor. "Our night and day marching, when not on a fixed fight," one Sixth Corps soldier complained, "had completely worn us out and [we] were so reduced in strength and mental perception that it was a matter of disputed whether we were living or dead." [24]

June 1, Hoke arranged his division along a slight ridge perpendicular to Cold Harbor Road. Brigadier General Thomas L. Clingman's Tar Heels, on Hoke's left, strung north to a small stream flowing west into Gaines' Mill Pond. Alfred Colquitt's Georgians continued Hoke's line south from Clingman's left to Cold Harbor Road. During the night, Brigadier General James G. Martin's North Carolina brigade arrived furthering the line south of the road, immediately began digging in throwing up earthworks. Johnson Hagood's South Carolinians appeared around 3 a.m., and formed slightly in rear of Hoke in reserve.

Brigadier General Joseph B. Kershaw's division, the vanguard of Anderson's corps, reached Mrs. Allison's farm road shortly before daybreak. After a momentary rest, the southerners started northeast along the farm road to initiate the First Corps phase of reconnaissance. Anderson anticipated that Hoke would advance in tandem on Cold Harbor road, Hoke and Kershaw supporting each other. However, while Kershaw edged eastward, Hoke's soldiers remained behind their earthworks.

Leading Kershaw's division toward Beulah Church and the Woody house was a brigade of South Carolina troops under the command of the ardent secessionist and champion of slavery, and ex-congressman, Colonel Lawrence M. Keitt. As Keitt's column reached Beulah Church, his skirmishers uncovered Torbert's pickets and began exchanging perfunctory fire. Riding at the head of his command, Keitt called a halt along Allison's Road and formed his troops in a compact mass, company front. As the Confederates angled toward Beulah Church Road, Torbert's cavalrymen patiently waited. When Keitt's soldiers came within point blank range, there was a crash of musketry and a sheet of flame burst from the cavalry line. Keitt, riding bravely at the head of his men, was shot from his horse, mortally wounded. Union bands provided an eerie backdrop to the carnage playing "Yankee Doodle," and "Hail Columbia." [25]

While Keitt's men scrambled for safety, the rest of Kershaw's division, stringing back toward Mr. Allison's house, instinctively hurriedly began erecting breastworks. After a few adjustments, Kershaw's soldiers stood behind fortifications facing east. A densely wooded ravine cut by a small stream, later called "Bloody Run," that ran back to Gaines' Mill Pond separated Kershaw from Hoke's division. Hoke filled the gap by shifting Hagood's brigade about 150 yards in front of the ravine.

Withdrawing the Sixth Corps from the Army of the Potomac's right flank took considerably longer than Meade had calculated. Expecting Wright to reach Cold Harbor near dawn, Rickett's leading division was not on the road until after midnight. Russell's division followed soon afterward. Captain Martin Lennon recorded in his diary that the 77th left its trenches at 4 a.m., but the rear elements of Beau Neill's division could not get off until 4:30. The New Yorkers, exhausted from nearly two months of marching and combat, labored along Virginia's notoriously dusty roads in oppressive heat. "The day was sultry," George Stevens reminisced, "and the dust, ankle deep, raised in clouds by the column, was almost suffocating. It filled the air and hung upon the leaves of the trees like snow. Seldom had our men experienced such a march." Dehydrated by the intense heat, horses, mules, and men were dying of thirst, yet good drinking water was scarce, and no time was given to halt at streams were the water was pure. [26]

Close to 9 a.m., Wright's aide and previous major of the 7th Maine, Thomas Hyde, rode into Cold Harbor to alert Sheridan that the Sixth Corps was approaching. Hyde remembered, "I had seen him [Sheridan] before, but not to speak to him, and I found him the most nervy, wiry incarnation of business, and business only, I had yet met." Except for their short jackets and carbines, the aide thought the dismounted cavalrymen looked like infantry. Hyde borrowed a carbine from a wounded trooper and joined the firing line. "We had a belief in the infantry that those carbines would not hit anything, and I confirmed the belief so far as I was concerned," Hyde reminisced, "To be sure there was nothing but smoke to fire at as a general thing, and though in dead earnest, I am happy in the conviction that I did not hurt anybody." [27]

Rickett's soldiers, at the van of the Sixth Corps, soon marched into Cold Harbor. Brigadier General George Custer's brigade band greeted the tired infantrymen with "Hail Columbia" as they filed into the trenches formerly held by Torbert. "Never were reinforcements more cordially welcomed," Major James H. Kidd exclaimed. "In a solid array with the quick step [the Sixth Corps] marched out of the woods in rear of the line, and took our place. The tension was relaxed and for the first time since midnight the cavalrymen drew a long breath." [28]

Meanwhile, due to an unforced error, Smith's Eighteenth Corps was ordered to New Castle Ferry. At sunrise, Smith's corps camped at Mr. Bassett's place, received a dispatch to place his soldiers on the right of the Sixth Corps from Grant's aide, Orville Babcock. The aide really intended Smith to go to Cold Harbor and had inadvertently substituted "New Castle" for the proper destination. Learning that Smith was at New Castle, headquarters corrected Babcock's mistake. Smith retraced his steps and pushed on to Old Church, where Wright's Sixth Corps blocked the way. As they passed Smith's command, Surgeon Stevens recorded, "It was a relief to the old soldiers of the Army of the Potomac to see these full regiments, and they felt that with such large reinforcements our success must now be insured." For the New Yorkers, "It was also a source of much gratification to the old Second division to meet again our friends Generals Smith and Brooks, whose names were so intimately connected with the division, and who still held a large place in the affections of the men." Through the long and hot morning, Smith's troops marked time while Wright's soldiers passed by. By noon, the Sixth Corps had passed, and Smith's command started for Cold Harbor. [29]

Ricketts' division of the Sixth Corps advance had reached Cold Harbor around 10 a.m. after a grueling march of eleven hours. From Cold Harbor, Ricketts ushered his soldiers north along Beulah Church Road. Colonel Benjamin F. Smith's brigade stopped halfway to Mr. Woody's house and took position in the woods west of the road. Colonel William S. Truex's brigade deployed on Smith's left, extending the line south toward the Cold Harbor intersection. The dust-covered men were grateful for shade but were disturbed to find they shared the ground with the corpses from Keitt's and Torbert's fight earlier that morning. The woods had burned in places, and charred bodies lay strewn about in patches of smoldering ashes where fires had raged.

Around noon, Russell's division arrived at Cold Harbor and moved into position straddling Cold Harbor Road, two brigades north of the roadway and two south. A fine grove of mulberry trees bursting with ripe fruit was nearby, and eager soldiers quickly denuded the trees and feasted on the berries. The Federals dug rudimentary rifle pits, and sent out details to bury dead rebels from the morning fight.

In the afternoon, the 77th took to the side of the road to make way for ambulances returning with wounded cavalrymen, and learned from them that Torbert had been engaged with Rebel cavalry and infantry at Cold Harbor. Though exhausted, the veterans pushed on rapidly with their division, arriving Cold Harbor about 2:30 p.m. Neill's lead elements marched into fields west of Dispatch Station Road and drove back pickets from Fitzhugh Lee's cavalry. Leaving Wheaton's brigade east of Cold Harbor to guard the division's wagons, Neill arranged the rest of his division into a compact formation facing west. In front was Colonel Lewis A. Grant's hardened Vermont brigade. Colonel Oliver Edwards' Massachusetts and Rhode Island brigade stood behind Grant and was supported by 77th's brigade of Maine, New York and Pennsylvania troops.

As the Sixth Corps massed at Cold Harbor, Wright received the order from Meade to attack as soon as possible. Earlier, Grant and Meade had considered the concentration at Cold Harbor as a defensive move. By midmorning, however, they began to view the movement in a different light. Two infantry corps would soon be massed at the strategic crossroads. Opposing them were Hoke's division and some of Anderson's First Corps. The majority of these Confederates had only arrived recently and had not time to entrench. If Wright and Smith attacked now, they might be able plow through the Confederate right flank and get into Lee's rear.

The troops of Baldy Smith's Eighteenth Corps came up close to 3 p.m. Smith was under orders to both join Wright in the afternoon's assault and to stretch north to Bethesda church and link up with Warren. On arriving at Cold Harbor, he realized he could not do both. To fill the gap between the First and Sixth Corps would leave him without enough troops to aid in the attack. Rather than spread his force thin, Smith determined to deploy in strength north of Wright, extending the Union line to Woody's farm. In this compact mass, he hoped to throw the Eighteenth Corps entire weight into the assault. Smith's foremost division, commanded by Charles Devens, appeared first at Cold Harbor. Marching north along Beulah Church Road, Devens' tired infantrymen massed on Ricketts' right in a patch of woods. The division commander placed soldiers too fatigued to fight in rear of his division.

At about 4 p.m., Wright's artillery opened to soften the distant rebel line for the impending attack. George Stevens remembered, "The artillery of the Sixth corps was at once run out, and a brisk fire opened upon the rebels." Smith's guns rolled into place along Beulah Church Road and joined the cannonade. Stevens noted that the Confederates replied with their guns, but with little vigor. Nevertheless, Rebel shells still hit their mark. A projectile ripped through the orchard south of Cold Harbor, and struck William Oliver of the 15th New Jersey on the head, killing him and tossing his body into the air. One Federal shell exploded early, blowing off the arm of the 96th Pennsylvania's adjutant and shattering another man's foot. [30]

At 5 p.m. Smith's First Division, under William Brooks, arrived and marched into place north of Devens, extending the Union line past the smoldering ruins of Beulah Church. John Martindale's division arrived around 5:30 p.m. Baldy Smith was apprehensive about the two-mile gap between the northern end of his line and Warren's southern flank. Instead of adding Martindale to his battle line, he positioned Martindale perpendicular to the rest of his troops, facing north toward the gap to prevent Confederates from turning his northern flank.

While the 77th's division marched up and extended the Federal line south of Cold Harbor, Hoke became concerned. Brigadier General James G. Martins three Tar Hill regiments already held works south of the road, but Neill's appearance lengthened the Union line beyond Martin's southern flank. To keep his earthworks abreast of Neill, Hoke directed Hagood's South Carolina brigade to extend the lower end of his line. Hagood was guarding the ravine between Clingman and Kershaw, but as Hoke saw it, Neill's division's threat to the Confederate southern flank took priority. He ordered Hagood to take up a new position on Martin's right, facing the 77th's division. Hagood's South Carolinians double-quicked south in column of fours behind the Rebel entrenchments and lengthened Hoke's line to the steep-banked Boatswain Creek, a firm natural barrier for the southern end of the Confederate line.

As Hagood's soldiers dug in, he immediately sent Captain James F. Izlar of the Edisto Rifles, 25th South Carolina to reconnoiter the lower end of Neill's line. Supporting him was a battery of horse artillery attached to Fitzhugh Lee which began enfilading the Federals. Itzlar's appearance and the sudden cannon fire from the south put a scare into Beau Neill, who had no idea of the size of the enemy force materializing below him. To refuse his lower flank, he bent the lower end of the Second Division's line east to Dispatch Station Road. When he had completed his dispositions, Edward's brigade, the 77th's Third Brigade, and most of Lewis Grant's brigade faced south. Only Pingree's 2nd Vermont and Charles K. Fleming's battalion of the 1st Vermont Heavy Artillery faced west and remained position to participate in the anticipated assault.

Neill sent the 3rd Vermont to drive off Izlar and his artillery support. The Green Mountain soldiers advanced under intense fire from Confederate artillery and musketry to within 500 yards of the enemy's works and finding it impossible took to the ground and began to dig pits with their bayonets. Neill also ordered Edwards and the 77th's brigade to press south. They set off on the double quick and Rebel skirmishers broke for the cover of the defenses in a skirt of woods. Rather than pursue, Edwards' and Bidwell's veterans went to work with bayonets, tin plates, tin cups, and bare hands scooping up Virginia sand to provide shelter from Confederate bullets.

By 6 p.m., Federal battle lines were complete. Eight hours had passed since midmorning, when Wright's lead division had reached Cold Harbor. Barely two hours of daylight remained. Wright and Smith had to attack now or wait until morning. Aware that this was the last opportunity to attack before the Rebels were fully dug in, Wright ordered the assault. Union batteries quieted their fire, and soldiers slipped off their knapsacks and made ready with a sense of doom as the veterans knew full well the bloody futility of charging entrenchments.

Dotted by small farms, the gently undulating ground between the armies was marked by a checkerboard of fields, forest, and ravines to favor the defense. George Stevens remembered that in "In front of our line was an open space two-thirds of a mile in width, beyond which was a strip of pine woods. In these woods the enemy had intrenched." A little west of the Union line, Confederate skirmishers patiently waited in rifle pits large enough to hold two or three men. Dirt piled up in front for added protection, the "gopher holes" looked like animal burrows. Half a mile further west was an advanced line of entrenchments, then a cleared field of fire, then abatis, and finally the main Confederate line, arrayed on commanding ground brimming with infantry and artillery. [31]

At 6:30 p.m., the attack Grant and Meade had ordered finally began. Surgeon Stevens recalled, "The storm of battle seemed suddenly to have broken without the usual warning... Volleys rang out upon the evening air, crashing louder and still louder... The whole line thundered with incessant volleys of musketry, and the shot and shell of the artillery shrieked and howled like spirits of evil. The sun was sinking, red, in the west, and the clouds of dust and smoke almost obscured the terrible scene." Field hospitals came alive as "Hundreds of our brave fellows were falling on every side, and stretcher bearers were actively engaged in removing the wounded from the field." [32]

Wright's soldiers made little progress south of the Mechanicsville Road, which connected New and Old Cold Harbor, recoiling from heavy Confederate fire. North of the road, Emory Upton's brigade encountered heavy fire from Thomas Clingman's brigade. "A sheet of flame, sudden as lightning, red as blood, and so near it seemed to singe the men's faces," one Federal soldier recalled. Although Upton gallantly tried to rally his men forward, his brigade fell back to its starting point. [33]

To Upton's right, the brigade of Colonel William S. Truex of Ricketts' division found the gap in the Confederate line between the brigades of Clingman and Brigadier General William T. Wofford created when Haggod's South Carolinians were ordered to strengthen the Rebel southern flank. The gap, a swampy wooded ravine cut by Bloody Run, was full of charging Federals. As Truex's men advanced through the ravine Clingman swung two regiments around to face them, and Anderson sent in Brigadier General Eppa

Hunton's Virginia regiments from his corps reserve. Truex became surrounded on three sides and was forced to withdraw, although his men brought back hundreds of Georgians from William T. Wofford's brigade as prisoners with them.

Eighteenth Corps division commander, Brigadier General Charles Devens, had deployed his troops north of Ricketts and parallel to Beulah Church Road. The brigades of Colonels William Barton and Jeremiah Drake charged toward Wofford's main line. Together with Ricketts savaging his flank, the frontal assault was wildly successful. Wofford's entire brigade fled their earthworks. Triumphant men in blue ordered captured Rebels to the rear in a steady stream. The captives made for the rear running as fast as they could to avoid the storm of Confederate bullets seeking a target.

Brooks' brigades under Colonel Guy V. Henry and Brigadier General Hiram Burnham stepped off simultaneously with Devens' division. Many of the soldiers looked forward to proving themselves in the fight, which would be their first. Henry's men advanced from its wooded cover along Beulah Church Road into an open plane. They were momentarily shaken by severe enfilading artillery fire. Some of Henry's troops reached the first line of Rebel rifle pits but could go no further, for ensconced behind multiple lines of pits and entrenchments, making their position invincible' was Benjamin Humphreys' Mississippi brigade. Burnham's attack north of Henry was bloody but brief, lasting perhaps five minutes. His soldiers charged three hundred yards across open ground to a little ridge where they took cover.

While fighting raged on the southern end of the battlefield around Cold Harbor, the three corps of Hancock, Warren, and Burnside were occupying a five-mile line that stretched southeast to Bethesda Church, facing the Confederate commands of A. P.

Hill, John Breckinridge, and Jubal Early. At the southern flank of the Ninth Corps was the division of Major General Thomas L. Cittenden, recently transferred from the west following his poor performance at Chickamauga. Crittenden held a doglegged position with an angle that was parallel to the Shady Grove Road, separated from the Fifth Corps by a quagmire known as Mongolia Swamp. Two divisions from Early's corps – Major General Robert E. Rodes on the left, Major General John B. Gordon on the right – charged across the swampland for an attack that began at 7 p.m. Warren later described this attack as a "feeler," and despite some initial successes, aided by the poor battle management of Crittenden, both Confederate probes were repulsed.

"As darkness came on," Surgeon Stevens wrote, "the conflict still raged, and sheets of flame rolled from one end of the line to the other, as the discomfited rebels strove desperately to regain their lost ground." But as the sound of battle died away, wounded men lay stranded between the lines, some cursing, some praying, some calling for water, while others cried for help, all mingled together in one haunting continual howl. The ambulatory Federal wounded made their way to field hospitals in the rear. The Sixth Corps hospital, near the orchard south of Cold Harbor Road, was well supplied. The Eighteenth Corps, however, had arrived without medical provisions, and its wounded gathered on a hillside near the Kelly house, half a mile east on Cold Harbor Road, drawing on the Sixth Corps medical supplies. Stevens counted 960 wounded from the Sixth Corps and 650 from the Eighteenth Corps. A final tally off casualties totaled 2,200, made up of 1,200 for the Sixth Corps, and 1,000 in the Eighteenth Corps. Confederate losses amounted to 1,800 men. [34]

Sharp skirmish fire periodically erupted up and down the line throughout the night. Despite the occasional Rebel bullet whizzing by, Union soldiers followed what now had become second nature.

Cyrille Fountain recorded in his diary, "we worked all night at Brest works." By morning, using whatever material and tools available, entrenchments were dug using bayonets, tin plates, and tin cups. Head logs were placed atop the trenches and dirt piled up against them. [35]

Although the June 1 attacks had been unsuccessful, Grant believed that an attack on June 2 could succeed if he was able to amass sufficient forces against a favorable location. The Union commander decided to attack Lee's right flank. Anderson's Confederates had been hotly engaged there on June 1, and it seemed unlikely that they had found the time to build substantial defenses. If the attack was successful, Lee's right would be driven back into the Chickahominy River. Grant ordered Hancock's Second Corps to shift southeast from Totopotomoy Creek and take up position to the left of the Sixth Corps. Once Hancock was in position, Grant would attack from Old Cold Harbor with three corps in line numbering 31,000 soldiers: Hancock's Second Corps, Wright's Sixth Corps, and Baldy Smith's Eighteenth Corps. Warren and Burnside were directed to attack Lee's left flank, for Grant was convinced that Lee was shifting troops from his left to fortify his right.

Hancock's troops left the Totopotomoy defenses after dark and marched through the night and were too fatigued for an immediate attack that morning. Reluctantly, Grant agreed to let the men rest and postponed the attack until 5 p.m., and then again at 5:30 p.m. on June 3. But Grant and Meade did not give specific orders for the attack, leaving it up to each corps commander where they would charge the Confederate lines and how they would coordinate with each other. No senior commander had reconnoitered the enemy position. Baldy Smith wrote that he was "aghast at the reception of such an order, which proved conclusively the utter absence of any military plan." He gravely remarked to his staff that the whole attack was "simply an order to slaughter my best troops. [36]

The ground the 77th' Six Corps and Smith's had fought on June 1 remained fairly quiet on June 2. Private Fountain remembered skirmishing throughout the day, but no attempts to escalate to general battle. In front of the New Yorkers lay a number of dead and wounded covering the fields between Cold Harbor and the road from Mr. Allison's to the Woody place. One Union soldier wrote corpses lay "in every conceivable position. Many bodies bent backwards, as if the spine were trying to touch ends that way. One body is thus arched up, and is resting upon the shoulders and heels. The coat capes are turned up over many faces, other faces are bare, others hidden, the bodies lying face down; but the most lie as they fell, and are badly torn – it is a walk of sickening and unutterable horrors." [37]

Lee took good advantage of the Federal delays to bolster his defenses. When Hancock withdrew from Totopotomoy Creek, the southern commander was free to shift Breckinridge's division to his far right flank, where he would once again face Hancock. Breckenridge drove Union troops off strategic Turkey Hill, which dominated the southern part of the battlefield. Lee also drew troops from A. P. Hill's Third Corps, the divisions of Brigadier General William Mahone and Cadmus M. Wilcox, to buttress Beckinridge, and stationed Fitzhugh Lee's cavalry to guard the army's right flank.

The result was a curving line on low ridges, seven miles long, with the Rebel left flank anchored on Totopotomoy Creek, the right on the Chickahominy River, preventing Grant from making a flank attack. Barricades of earth and logs were erected. Artillery was posted with converging fields of fire on every avenue of approach, and stakes were driven into the ground to aid artillerists setting fuses for shells. A war correspondent described the works for readers: "Intricate, zig-zagged lines within lines, lines protecting flanks of lines, lines built to enfilade an opposing line . . . [It was] a maze and labyrinth of works within works." [38]

MCKEAN'S SUNDAY SCHOOL BOYS GO TO WAR

On the northern end of the battlefield, Warren's Fifth Corps linked up with Burnside's Eighteenth Corps near Bethesda Church. Early's Confederates on Lee's flank probed Warren's front and captured some skirmishers. Early's reconnaissance had no effect on the main battle to come. Burnside was encouraged to attack Early's unprotected flank on Shady Grove Road, but he balked at the suggestion.

Nightfall found the two armies locked closely together in a sprawling formation resembling an upside-down L. Hancock's corps dug in on the Federal army's left flank south of Cold Harbor and largely along Dispatch Station Road. Wright's Sixth Corps divisions shifted north to support the Eighteenth Corps. Russell's division deployed west of Old Cold Harbor and straddling Cold Harbor Road. Rickett's entrenched just north of Cold Harbor, followed by Neill. Smith's corps continued the Union line north, followed by Warren's Fifth Corps. The northern flank was anchored by Burnside's Ninth Corps.

June 2 saw scattered showers throughout much of the day. Rain picked up after dark. "Then," Surgeon Stevens remembered "a most violent thunder shower set in." Even so, trenches and earthworks had to be built. Private Fountain and his comrades were relieved that sharp skirmishing during the day was abated, but exhausted for they "threw up Brest works . . . [and] . . . worked all night like beevers." Continuing rain during the night filled trenches and doused cooking fires. Wet clothes only made the night more uncomfortable. [39]

Just before daybreak, June 3, rain began to fall. A heavy mist settled close to the ground, cloaking objects little more than a few yards ahead. Dew dripped from trees and fog was unusually dense. The atmosphere was eerily familiar to the 77th and their fellow soldiers. Three weeks prior, on a rain-soaked, foggy morning much like this one, they had lined up for a 4:30 a.m. charge against Lee's Mule Shoe salient at Spotsylvania Court House. Now their commanders wanted them to repeat that bloody and ultimately futile assault. A signal gun was to announce the attack, sending Hancock's, Wright's, and Smith's corps, racing toward the Rebel entrenchments. Warren and Burnside were to strike the enemy as well, pinning down Confederate troops there and swinging south, if possible, rolling up the enemy line and taking pressure off of Smith's northern flank.

Tension was high among the New Yorkers as "the skirmishers, leaving the cover of the rifle pits, were advancing." George Stevens remembered, "Presently they fell in with the skirmishers of the enemy, and the sharp cracking of rifles betokened the storm of the battle." As opposing skirmishers were trading a brisk fire, Union artillery opened up on the Confederate works, signaling the attack. In Richmond, twelve miles away, its citizens were jarred out of bed as their windows rattled. Three corps numbering near 50,000 soldiers stepped from their trenches and started toward the enemy. Massive fire from the Confederate works caused heavy casualties, and the survivors were pinned down. Stevens wrote of the deadly work: "Amid the deafening volleys of musketry, the thunders of the artillery, and the wild yells of battle, our brave fellows pressed rapidly across the space between the hostile lines of work, and the whole Union force was thrown against the rebel breastworks almost simultaneously. But the works were too strong, the abatis too troublesome, and the rebel forces too numerous. Their line could not be taken." [40]

Only Francis Barlow's division of the Second Corps on the Union left flank pierced the Confederate works. His soldiers were able to break through a portion of Breckinridge's front line and drive the enemy out of their entrenchments in hand to hand fighting. Several hundred prisoners and four guns were captured. However Confederate batteries were brought to bear on the entrenchments, turning them into a death trap for the Federals. Breckinridge's reserves counterattacked Barlow's troops and drove them off. Hancock's other division, under Brigadier General John Gibbon, was bedeviled at once. About two hundred yards from their starting point, his men hit a deep swamp that was not marked on any map. The swamp, like a wedge, broke Gibbon's line into two bodies that flowed along either side and were forced further apart as the swamp widened toward the Confederate line. Heavy enemy fire pinned down Gibbon's men, killing Colonels H. Boyd McKeen and Peter A. Porter. One soldier in Gibbon's command complained bitterly of a lack of reconnaissance, wrote, "We felt it was murder, not war . . ." [41]

On the 77th's Sixth Corps front, the attack by Russell's and Rickett's divisions, advancing in one great line, was stopped almost immediately as a torrent of musketry and artillery broke across the front and flanks of that line. Not all of Russell's men advanced. Emory Upton was not willing to sacrifice his men in a futile gesture. He later wrote, "June 3, another assault was ordered, but, being deemed impracticable along our front was not made." Captain Lemuel Abbott of the 10th Vermont of Ricketts' division remembered, "We never even reached the enemy's works . . . We advanced under a murderous fire in our front from the enemy's artillery, sharpshooters and when in range of its main line of battle . . . were simply slaughtered." [42]

The 77th's Second Division and the rest of Beau Neill's troops had shifted onto the Sixth Corps right flank on June 2, relieving Deven's division of the Eighteenth Corps. The position the New Yorkers had left was unpleasant, but the new front seemed even worse. Jammed between Ricketts on his left and Brooks' Eighteenth Corps division on his right, Neill shoehorned his troops into a narrow column, brigades stacked one behind another. In front came Wheaton's fresh brigade. Behind Wheaton were the brigades of Grant, the 77th's

Third Brigade, and Edwards, the latter containing many troops whose terms of service were almost finished.

On Wright's Sixth Corps front, with Ricketts' and Russell's divisions bogged down between enemy lines by overwhelming gunfire, Brigadier General Thomas Neill's reserve division was ordered in on the right. The 77th and the Second Division moved forward in column, like a great battering ram. Wheaton's soldiers carried the first line of rifle pits in a skirt of woods. Passing through the woods, Wheaton's troops reached the edge of a clearing and saw the main Confederate line 200 yards away. Marching into the field the Federals were hit from the front and both flanks as alert Georgians and Arkansans hustled into flanking trenches and shot down the length of Wheaton's line. Raked by converging musketry and artillery fire, Wheaton's shattered brigade fell back to the first line of works it had crossed during its advance.

Lewis Grant's Green Mountain Brigade had lined up close behind Wheaton and prepared to attack. The 3rd and 5th Vermont now held Neill's front line. Leaving the protection of the captured entrenchments and moving up to the tree line, they came under fierce fire from the main Confederate works. The Vermonters had no protection except the trees at the edge of the woods. Colonel Grant later wrote, "I asked for authority to withdraw these regiments, leaving only a skirmish line to hold the edge of the woods. This authority was refused. Being, however, satisfied that men were needlessly exposed, and that a skirmish line would hold the position as well as a line of battle with less loss of life, and having obtained the direction of the assistant adjutant general of the division in the matter, I withdrew those regiments, leaving a skirmish line from each." [43]

The repulse of the Vermont Brigade marked the end of Neill's advance. Skirmishers from the 3rd and 5th Vermont continued a brisk fire with the enemy, lying on the ground at the edge of the trees. The 77th stood ready to advance and witnessed the shattering of Wheaton's brigade and the repulse of Grant's soldiers, but was not engaged. The Vermont Brigade lost about 100 men, most of them from the 3rd and 5th Vermont. The 1st Vermont Heavy Artillery, in the brigade's rear, lost one man. Wheaton's losses amounted to about 180 men.

On the Union right, Smith's soldiers advanced through terrain that channeled into two ravines. When they emerged in front of the Confederate line, rifle and artillery fire mowed them down. Double canister cut wide swaths through Smith's lines, sending heads, arms, legs, and muskets flying high in the air at every discharge. Sergeant Enoch C. Piper of the 12th New Hampshire remembered, "Men bent down as they went forward, as if trying, as they were to breast a tempest." Confederate general Evander McIver Law thought, "I had seen the dreadful carnage in front of Marye's Hill at Fredericksburg, and on the 'old railway cut' which Jackson's men held at Second Manassas; but I had seen nothing to exceed this. It was not war; it was murder." Smith realized the futility of his attack and terminated the assault and wrote Meade, "My troops are very much cut up, and I have no hopes of being able to carry the works in my front unless a movement of the Sixth Corps on my left may relieve at least one of my flanks from this galling fire." [44]

The only movement on the northern end of the battlefield was by Burnside's corps, facing Jubal Early. The side-whiskered Burnside launched a belated, but powerful, assault that overran Confederate skirmishers but mistakenly believed he had pierced the Rebel main line, and halted his corps to regroup before moving on.

The grand assault by three Union corps lasted less than an hour. Grant had in mind a coordinated offensive by the entire army, but only the Second, Sixth, and Eighteenth Corps had participated. Even that attack was piecemeal, and more than half the troops available for the attack were never seriously engaged. Union casualty estimates have ranged from 3,500 to 7,500 men. Meade's chief of staff, Andrew Humphreys, tallied 4,517 wounded and at least 1,100 killed. The 77th's Sixth Corps lost approximately 219 soldiers.

Over the years, Union soldiers who participated in the Cold Harbor assault to a man condemned the cluster of disconnected charges on June 3. Tactical problems that come with coordinating as assault across a seven-mile front doomed the effort from the outset. The operation, Wright's aide Thomas Hyde declared, "would have shamed a cadet at his first year at West Point." Grant in his memoir agreed that the offense had been botched. "I have always regretted that the last assault at Cold Harbor was ever made." Grant clearly stated, "No advantage whatever was gained to compensate for the heavy loss we sustained." Captain Martin Lennon bitterly remarked, "At night we held nothing but the enemy's first line." [45]

Around sunset, Brigadier General James G. Martin launched his three North Carolina regiments in an ill-conceived counterattack against the left of the Sixth Corps and the right of the Second Corps. George Stevens wrote later, "Suddenly, at eight o'clock, the rebels . . . leaped over their works and rushed with a yell toward our lines. At the same time their artillery opened upon us. The course of their shells was marked by long curves of fire upon the dark sky, while the flashes of the guns and bursting missiles made a sublime display of pyrotechnics." The Federals were almost joyful to see their enemies come out from their entrenchments to fight. Stevens continued, "It had, during all these long days of battles, been ours to charge well defended earthworks almost invariably; and whenever the rebels chose to assume the offensive, our men were glad to show them the difference between being assailants and the assailed." [46]

Martin's counterattack was brief and his North Carolinians were easily driven back. Stevens wrote:

> Now the rebels came on with determination, but their attack was met by volley after volley of musketry aimed for effect; and our well directed fire of artillery made great gaps in the advancing lines. The attack was nobly repulsed, and many grey-coated soldiers who advanced to the charge, were left by their retreating comrades, dead between the two lines, while others were ordered in as prisoners. The rebels returned to their place, and again all was still." [47]

At night, the 77th moved to the front line and threw up heavy earthworks. Surgeon Stevens noted:

> The battle was over, and again the occupants of the opposing lines of defenses watched each other, the quiet being only disturbed by the occasional shots of sharpshooters. Darkness closed over the plains of Cold Harbor, and even the sharpshooters desisted from their work. The stars shed a mild light upon the two armies which had so lately been engaged in fierce conflict, each now securely resting behind its line of earthworks, and the plain which lay between them, which the hurricane of battle had so lately swept, was still as though the noises of war had never been heard before. [48]

Martin's assault closed active fighting at Cold Harbor. For the next nine days, the opposing armies faced off, sometimes a mere seventy five yards apart. Private Alonzo Bump wrote to his wife, "we are in the edg of woods and the Rebs are Just acrost the open field in the Edg of another Peace of woods. our Pits are in the edg of woods and thairs in the other. they dare not come acrost the fieald nor we dare

Goe their . . . there is one Peace of artillary that they can not worke for as soon as they try and Load it our Boys will Set the Rifal Balls fly at them and they haft to Keeap down and while i am a wrighting the miney Balls are a flying over my head and striking in the treeas." [49]

The lines were so close that any visible object became an instant target. George Stevens wrote, "we daily lost many men by the shots of the sharpshooters who were perched in trees, and who kept up a fire at every moving thing which showed itself within our lives." The evening of June 4th, Sergeant George Bolton was stationed at the front with the rest of 77th. He left the trench to light his pipe from one of the camp fires. As he approached the camp fire to where his form could be seen from a distance, a Confederate sniper fired a single shot, hitting Bolton and killing him instantly. [50]

"Never before had our army been in a position where there was constant danger as at Cold Harbor," Surgeon Stevens remembered. "High breastworks were thrown up at all angles with the main line, and deep trenches were dug, in which men might pass to and from the front without being observed. Even with all these extraordinary precautions, no man was safe in venturing to go to the rear by daylight. If a soldier collected canteens of his companions and started to the rear for water, he was obliged to crawl along the trenches with the utmost secrecy, and even then he was liable to be shot." General officers had their tents erected in deep excavations surrounded by embankments of earth and "special duty men had each prepared for themselves burrows in the ground, many of which were credible specimens of engineering." The scene brought to Steven's mind "the colonies of prairie dogs with their burrows and mounds." [51]

The trenches were hot, dusty, and miserable. Thousands of wounded men caught between the lines suffered horribly without food, water, or medical assistance. The unburied dead compounded the misery of soldiers under a harsh sun without shade. Many of the bodies had been rotting since June 1. "The air was laden with insufferable putrescence," said one Union soldier, "We breathed it in every breath, tasted it in the food we ate and water we drank." Grant was reluctant to ask for a formal truce that would allow him to recover his wounded and to bury the dead. He and Lee traded requests across the lines from June 5 to June 7 without coming to an agreement. When Grant formally requested a two-hour cessations of hostilities, it was too late for most of the unfortunate wounded, who were now swollen, blackened corpses. [52]

While the stench of death lingered among the living, Grant pondered his options. "I now find, after more than thirty days of trial, that the enemy deems it of the first importance to run no risks with the armies they now have," he wrote Halleck. "They act purely on the defensive, behind breastworks." Continuing the offensive at Cold Harbor required a greater sacrifice of human life than Grant was willing to make. The Federal commander contemplated sending Sheridan west to Charlottesville to destroy the Virginia Central Railroad, then shifting the Army of the Potomac south and west, cutting off the rest of Lee's supplies and isolating Richmond. If Grant could steal yet another march on Lee, and rapidly follow it up, the campaign would become a siege that Grant and Lee both understood spelled the Confederacy's doom. Fifteen miles south, the James River followed a winding course east. Here, Grant knew, was the key to his next move. [53]

14

THE THREE JIMS

During the stalemate at Cold Harbor, just eight miles east of the Confederate capital, Ulysses S. Grant made the decision to cross the James River. His new target would be the South's commercial and transportation hub at Petersburg, the Cockade City, twenty miles south of Richmond along the Appomattox River. By taking Petersburg, Grant could effectively starve the Confederates out of their defenses around Richmond, which would allow him to defeat them on open ground of his own choosing. To do so, Grant would have to steal a march of nearly fifty miles from Lee across swampy, ravine-rippled ground and cross the half-mile wide tidal river undetected, and capture Petersburg before Robert E. Lee could react.

Meade's chief of staff Andrew A. Humphreys was directed to draft the operation order. The Army of the Potomac would withdraw from Cold Harbor in four coordinated columns. The move was to begin with the Fifth and Second Corps crossing the Chickahominy River at Long Bridge. Once over, the Fifth Corps was to turn west to the 1862 battlefield of Glendale to provide a screening force, and to create the impression that Grant planned to launch an offensive north of the James toward Richmond. Once in place, the Fifth Corps would occupy a five-mile long defensive position from White Oak Swamp to Malvern Hill. Simultaneously, the Sixth and Ninth Corps were to follow separate routes to Jones' Bridge on the Chickahominy and continue to Charles City Court House. A third column made up of the army trains, accompanied by Brigadier General Edward Ferrero's division of United States Colored Troops was to cross the Chickahominy west of Jones' Bridge. Baldy Smith's Eighteenth Corps was to march to White House Landing and embark for Bermuda Hundred. If all went according to plan, two days of maneuver should see Smith arriving at Bermuda Hundred and the Army of the Potomac crossing the James on a combination of ferry and pontoon bridge, and marching on Petersburg unopposed. The march to the James would begin June 12.

The morning of June 11, the veterans of the 77th were relieved to get word that there were to be no more attempts to break Lee's lines at Cold Harbor. Their curiosity about Grant's next move intensified as troops began moving to the rear. It became clear that the army was to move when the wounded boarded ambulances and headed for White House, and long trains of forage, ammunition and commissary supplies began to pass to the rear. Though the New Yorkers could only guess where Grant was taking them, they were glad to leave behind their fetid trenches and the lingering stench of rotting corpses still not buried in the no-mans-land between enemy lines.

At 3 p.m., June 12, the long hospital train of the Sixth Corps moved out toward the left a few miles and halted to await the passage of the infantry. Three hours later, the 77th's band joined Federal brass bands which resounded along the ten-mile Union line while Warren's Fifth Corps began their march southward. Warren's troops reached the Chickahominy after frequent delays, where they waited for two hours until the pontoon bridge across the river was completed. Once over, Brigadier General Samuel Crawford's division turned west, skirting the southern edge of White Oak Swamp. Near the intersection of the road from White Oak Bridge, Crawford's soldiers formed a line of battle and threw up breastworks.

Screened by the Fifth Corps, the rest of the Army of the Potomac went into motion. Smith's Eighteenth Corps moved east to White House Landing, where his men would board river transports to Bermuda Hundred. Around 11 a.m., Hancock's Second Corps abandoned its position and followed Warren toward the Chickahominy to Long Bridge. A short time later, the 77th and the Sixth Corps moved out. Their destination was Jones' Bridge four miles downstream from Long Bridge. Jones' Bridge had to be rebuilt for the crossing. Federal engineers began construction on the afternoon of June 13, and were finished a little more than an hour later. Once Baldy Smith had cleared the roads, Ambrose Burnside's Ninth Corps left its trenches.

The 77th marched hard this day. "The march," George Stevens declared, "was kept up all night, a short halt only being allowed in the morning at Dispatch Station." Then the New York veterans pressed on; "the men almost suffocated with the dust, which hung over the column like a huge cloud; no halt was made at noon, and the men, deprived of their coffee, choked with dust, and burned with heat, marched wearily toward night." The 77th approached Jones' Bridge when "the sun was sinking in the west, tingeing clouds with purple, and crowning the distant hills gold." The veterans then joined the rest of the Sixth Corps and crossed the Chickahominy, followed by Burnside's corps, where they bivouacked on high ground a mile from the river. The crossing was completed by 10 a.m. on June 14, and Federal engineers dismantled the army's bridge. [1]

The Sixth Corps line of march took the 77th through a countryside dotted with comfortable farm houses and fine mansions that presented a striking contrast with the devastation of northern Virginia that the New Yorkers had been accustomed. As the regiment descended from piedmont to tidewater toward a little cluster of homes called Charles City, the James River and all its beauty came into view. Ever the botanist, Surgeon Stevens vividly described the panorama before him:

> The river in the distance bordered by green fields, on undulating slope four or five miles wide, and twice as long, presented a scene of surpassing beauty. There were large fields of grain already yellow and nearly ripe for harvest, green meadows lay in beautiful valleys, the gentle breeze dallied with the tassels of the long rows of corn, which gave rich promise of an abundant harvest; fine groves upon the hillside, in the valleys and on the plain, gave a charming diversity to the scene, and the old mansions, embosomed in vines and trees, and surrounded by colonies of outhouses, reminded us of the ease and comfort which had reigned here before the ravages of war had desolated Virginia. [2]

The 77th halted near the once prosperous Charles City, now nearly deserted. Hancock's soldiers had already reached the James at Wilcox Landing, and were preparing to cross. The New Yorkers "were delighted with the opportunity of once more spreading their tents over clean grassy turf, and each quickly pitched his shelter tent preparatory to a refreshing rest." Some of the more enterprising veterans enjoyed a special treat that evening. Private Cyrille Fountain recorded, "here we cut down a bee tree had all the honey that we could ask for. great times getting it out." Captain Martin Lennon and the regiment's officers passed the time drinking Assistant Surgeon William DeLong's cache of whiskey. [3]

Within two miles of the 77th's camp was the residence of the ex-president John Tyler and Confederate House representative, who died in 1862. Except for the grounds immediately surrounding the house, the property had become overgrown with scrub vegetation. The house was desecrated, stripped of almost everything. Tyler's large library had been looted and piles of letters lay strewn about the floor. Furniture was broken and curtains torn down. Stevens wrote "such a sad scene of destruction was rare, even in the track of a great army." [4]

During the night of June 14-15, boats ferried Hancock's corps across the James from Wilcox's Landing to Windmill Point, followed by the Fifth Corps, and the First and Third Divisions of the Sixth Corps. The 77th's Second Division occupied a defensive pocket covering several miles from the mouth of Queen's Creek to Tyler's Mill. Three miles downstream, near the tip of Wyanoke Neck, work on a pontoon bridge across the James began at 4 p.m. on June 14. Army engineers working from both banks built the floating structure on successive rafts toward mid-river. The James was between 85-90 feet deep at this point, and the swift river rose and receded three to four feet with the tide. A number of large schooners were anchored upriver and lashed to the bridge to serve as a boom against the river current. Five ships loaded with stone were scuttled well upstream to prevent Confederate gunboats from blocking the crossing. The bridge, 2,100 feet long with 101 wooden pontoons, was finished about 11 p.m., though the work on the approaches took another four hours.

As soon as the approaches to the pontoon bridge were constructed, the Ninth Corps and artillery began crossing, followed by the trains and artillery of the Fifth and Sixth Corps. The 77th with its Second Division then marched down to the river while drums and brass bands filled the air with martial music. As the New Yorkers tread across the bridge, George Stevens noted that the "river was full of shipping, the forest of masts making strange contrast with the native forests on the riverbanks." Near the crossing was a magnificent old mansion, the home of a Confederate general, surrounded by a row of slave quarters. Stevens and a number of Sixth Corps officers walked the grounds and admired the grand old magnolia trees in full bloom and the elegant gardens festooned with beautiful flowers. One of the slaves on the premises "was a white-haired negro, who was one hundred and eight years old." He told the surgeon that his wife, who lived on a neighboring plantation, was 104 years of age. "The old fellow," Stevens recounted, "manifested no sympathy for the cause of his master, and even he sighed for freedom." When Stevens asked of what value freedom could be for him at such an advanced age, he impatiently answered, "Well, massa, isn't a hundred and eight years long enough to be a slave?" [5]

The crossing greatly uplifted the morale and spirits of the 77th's veterans who were out of the horrific trenches at Cold Harbor. As the 7th Rhode Island reached the James, its brigade band serenaded them with "Ain't I glad to Get Out of the Wilderness." Grant stood watching the grand spectacle of the Army of the Potomac on the move, hands clasped at his back. "The great bridge was the scene of a continuous movement of infantry columns, batteries of artillery, and wagon trains," remarked the aide Horace Porter. The approaches to the river on both banks were covered with masses of troops moving briskly to their positions or waiting patiently their turn to cross. The scene thought Porter, "was a matchless pageant that could not fail to inspire beholders with the grandeur of achievement and the majesty of military power." Grant was satisfied. One of Meade's aides saw the general break into a smile. "I think it is pretty well to get across a great river, and come up here and attack Lee before he is ready for us," he said out loud to himself. [6]

Grant's crossing the James brought an end to the brutal Overland Campaign. Forty days of fighting and maneuvering had cost the Federals 55,000 soldiers, almost as many casualties as Lee had men in his entire army at the start of the campaign. The Army of northern Virginia's losses totaled 32,000 men who could not be replaced. Stated another way, Grant lost 45 percent of his original force and Lee almost 50 percent. Never had the country witnessed bloodletting on such a massive scale. The period from May 22 through June 5 – from the North Anna to the crossing of the James – contributed substantially to the campaign's gruesome tally. Grant sustained losses of nearly 18,000 men killed, and captured. Lee's casualties during that period were slightly over 7,000.

Once across the James, George Stevens reflected:

> Our army had, during the period of a little over a month, fought the most extraordinary series of battles, and executed some of the most remarkable movements on record. Never was heroic valor exhibited on a grander scale than had been manifested by the Army of the Potomac throughout this long struggle, in which everyman's life seemed doomed . . . Day after day they had been called upon to assault earthworks or formidable character, defended by veteran troops; and it was usually the case that they had seen, as the only fruits of their daring, almost reckless, charges, the ground in front of the host strewed with the lifeless bodies of their comrades, while the enemy still held the coveted line of works . . . The men had for more than a month engaged the enemy in mortal combat only to find themselves again face to face with the enemy in the morning.

Nevertheless, Stevens and the Empire State veterans remained determined:

> From the crossing of the Rapidan to the halt at Cold Harbor, in all our battles and all our flank movements, we had not swerved from the direct line to Richmond; and now, with unimpaired vigor and still restless determination, the Army of the Potomac, and the imperturbable leader of the Union armies, were ready to undertake the capture of Richmond, by way of Petersburg, fully assured that their illustrious valor and never failing courage must sooner or later meet their award. [7]

Grant's plan had enabled Baldy Smith to reach Petersburg June 15 with an overwhelming advantage in numbers. His 14,000 soldiers faced a mere 2,200 Confederates who were supported by 2,000 militiamen composed of recovering wounded soldiers, elderly men, and boys in the Dimmock line, an earthen shield for Petersburg built in 1862 under the direction of Captain Charles H. Dimmock. After crossing the Appomattox River from Bermuda Hundred on a pontoon bridge at Point of Rocks, Smith concentrated his force at City Point and then approached Petersburg, receiving artillery fire from the Dimmock Line midafternoon. After a prolonged personal reconnaissance by Smith, he attacked at 7 p.m., and broke open a mile of the Confederate defenses with startling ease. At least eight Southern batteries fell in the federal assault. Almost inexplicably, Old Baldy halted while Petersburg lay wide open. Winfield Hancock's Second Corps had crossed the James by ferry the previous day. He had been ordered to support Smith, but was delayed by confusing orders and the need to draw rations. By then darkness had fallen and the arrival of Robert F. Hoke's division of 5,000 men, released from the Army of Northern Virginia to Beauregard's command by Lee, sealed the breach. Instead of sealing the doom of the Confederacy by capturing Petersburg, the subsequent trench warfare would continue for another 292 days. [8]

June 16, the 77th and the rest of Neill's Second Division marched all night toward Petersburg, from which direction the New York veterans heard cannonading all day. At Petersburg, the Second Corps divisions of Gibbon and David Birney sent out reconnaissances in force at daybreak. Gibbon's Third Brigade on the right made minimal headway. On the left, Colonel Thomas Eagan's brigade of Birney's division captured Battery 12 after a sharp fight with ex-Virginia governor Henry A. Wise's brigade. This briefly broke open a gaping hole in the Confederate line, but Hancock did not exploit the Union advantage.

At 6 p.m., Grant attacked the Confederates at Petersburg. Two brigades from Smith's corps supported Hancock's right and two brigades of Burnside's corps supported Hancock's left. Battery 4 fell, together with their connecting lines. Heavy firing stopped at dark.

During the aborted Federal attacks, the 77th's march was once again taxing for the veterans. The column moved rapidly, George Stevens recalled, "leaving scores of stragglers, who quietly rolled themselves in their blankets and lay down behind the hedges to sleep till morning." The day's heat sapped the New Yorkers strength, "and the dust was very annoying. The men were weary from want of sleep." Late that evening, Neill's division reached Petersburg, and relieved Smith's corps division commanded by Brigadier General William T. H. Brooks. There the 77th took possession of a strong redoubt in support of a battery; its sister regiments took position in nearby trenches. The Green Mountain Brigade and the First Brigade filed into advanced rifle pits. [9]

The redoubt occupied by the 77th was on a high bluff and commanded the surrounding ground whereby the men could trace the line of Rebel trenches which had already been captured, and those yet in enemy hands. Stevens described what the New Yorkers saw stretched out before them.

> The defenses of Petersburg consisted of a line of strong earthworks, in the form of a semicircle. Immense redoubts, like the one we now occupied, were placed at frequent intervals, upon commanding positions, and these were connected by a line of rifle pits and high breastworks. At all advantageous point, also, were well constructed rifle pits, in front . . . of the main works. Smith's corps had captured eleven of these forts and the strong works which were intended for the defense of the town now bristled with cannon pointing toward it . . . The line of powerful forts and breastworks commenced about two and a half miles below Petersburg, on the Appomattox, and circling the city, terminated two or three miles above . . . Before us stretched the valley of the Appomattox in all its beauty, the level plain between us and the river clothed in the verdure of summer, the green fields of corn yet untrodden by the troops of either side. Below the heights, stretching far to the right and left, was the line of rifle pits now occupied by our men, and beyond these could be traced the outline of the new works the rebels were throwing up. [10]

Two years earlier during McClellan's Peninsula Campaign, the Army of the Potomac laid in sight of Richmond, close enough to hear the church bells ringing. Now the Federals under Grant's command lay equally close to Petersburg. Writing to his wife with a sense of confidence in the outcome, Private Alonzo Bump exclaimed, "we now Ly on the Battal Fieald a supporting a Battery. we are in Plain sight of the citty of Petersburg so near that our Batterys Can throw shot and shell in to the city and i think it wont Bee Long Before we Shall have the citty Probably Before night at Least i hope we shall. i ame willing for one to help take it. it is a splendid Place. I can sit hear and count 3 church steapels. our frunt line of Battal is so near the Plaice that they can shoot musket Balls in to it. [11]

After midnight, June 18, Beauregard withdrew his soldiers before Hancock's corps. His men immediately began entrenching in their new position. While they labored, Lee realized that Grant's entire army had crossed the James. Leaving Pickett's division to hold the Bermuda Hundred works, Lee immediately sent Joseph B. Kershaw's division to Petersburg. Major General Charles Field's division closely followed Kershaw. A. P. Hill's corps began marching to Petersburg, taking the pontoon bridge at Drewey's Bluff before daybreak. The head of Hill's column started from Malvern Hill, 26 miles from the Cockade City.

The night of June 20, the Third Brigade was ordered some two miles out from the redoubt held by the 77th and nearby rifle pits. There, the brigade formed in line of battle along the Jerusalem Plank Road. The 77th formed the right flank of the brigade with Company A on the right of the regiment. During the night, the New Yorkers threw up earthen works in front and transverse pits between each company. The next day proved to be oppressively hot. After spending most of the morning expecting to be called into action, Sergeant James E. Barnes and Corporal James A. Lawrence, both of Company A, stretched their shelter tents over the rifle pit they occupied. Barnes and Lawrence refreshed themselves with hardtack and coffee about 1 p.m. and then lighted their pipes, spread their blankets in the pit, and lay down beside Private James G. Allen (Co. A) and Corporal Chauncey A. Ballou (Co. A), amusing each other with jokes. James Barnes remembered, "It was not long before firing commenced from

Petersburg on our right and occasionally a shell would explode in the air in our rear." A big 32-pounder shell came shrieking overhead, causing consternation among Company A, for it appeared it would land in their midst. Sergeant Barnes saw it and yelled, "Boys that means us." The shell came down and burrowed under their feet and exploded. The "three Jims" were hurled ten feet in the air in different directions. Barnes was thrown to the left, Lawrence to the right, and Allen on top of the breastworks. When picked up, Allen's teeth had closed with a death grip on the pipe stem in his mouth. Corporal Ballou was also seriously wounded. Quick thinking Sergeant Albert Reed (Co. B) jumped over the transverse and buckled his knapsack strap above the knee of Barnes' torn leg. [12]

Sergeant James E. Barnes (L. Tom Perry Special Collections)

Corporal Lawrence years later at a regimental reunion recalled, "When I came to – for all had been rendered unconscious – I heard groans from Barnes as he pitifully cried, 'Oh! My God! My leg is torn from me.' Allen, reviving, joined in with a sad cry, 'Oh! My leg is torn to pieces.' I grieved for my two unfortunate Comrades as I thought,

'I've escaped unharmed.' I started to rise; to my horror the effort disclosed that my left leg was nearly off up to my knee. I called to Barnes and Allen, 'My leg is torn off, too.' Comrades gathered around. One remarked, 'It has taken every Jim out of Company A.' Lieutenant Colonel French came up, ordered stretchers, brought on which we were tenderly placed and carried back to the field hospital." [13]

George Stevens reminisced, "The poor fellows were taken to the field hospital completely prostrated from the shock, cold sweat stood upon their pallid brows, and life seemed but to flicker before going out." The Second Division surgeons were making haste to load the wounded and sick into ambulances to send to City Point, for the division had received orders to march at a moment's notice. "You can do nothing for those men," said the wide awake, enterprising Doctor Hall, who was superintending the loading of ambulances, as he saw Stevens prepare to amputate the three Jims' mangled legs. "Better to put them into ambulances and let them have a chance for their lives! There is no time for operations." The 77th's doctor asked, "How long will it take you to load your ambulances, doctor?" Hall answered, "Twenty minutes, at least." To which Stevens responded firmly, "Then I will have the men ready for you." [14]

Surgeon Stevens, assisted by William DeLong, gave each Jim a glass of brandy, then administered chloroform, and in less than 30 minutes amputated the limbs, dressed the stumps, placed the men in ambulances, and they started for City Point. Chaplain Norman Fox saddled his horse, and accompanied the three Jims. Upon arriving at their destination, Chaplain Fox succeeded in placing them in one of the large hospital tents before sundown. Sergeant Barnes wrote, "We lay there until the afternoon of 3d of July, and Oh! How those poles did ache while we lay there." That afternoon the wounded Jims were put aboard the steamer *Connecticut*, and arrived at Washington about 8 p.m. the evening of July 4th. They were taken to

Stanton Hospital, and by Barnes' request, Surgeon Lidell placed the three Jims side by side in Ward 7. The sergeant told veterans of the 77th seventeen years later:

> Then talk about comfort with legs off! We were stripped of our bloody and dirty clothes, washed all over very nicely, clean shirts and drawers to put on, and placed in one of those little beds, and – well, its no use talking, you may well believe we appreciated it after laying in those holes [at Petersburg] for two weeks. With good care and nursing, we got along very nicely. In four weeks from the day my leg was amputated, I was on crutches, and on the 26th of August I got my sixty day's furlough and went home, came back before my furlough expired and took my discharge. Lawrence and Allen, in the meantime, had taken their discharges and gone home. [15]

One June 23, the 77th and the Sixth Corps advanced toward the Weldon Railroad. Within two miles of their destination, they halted and entrenched with Lewis Grant's Green Mountain boys at the farthest point westward. Sharpshooters were sent forward to secure the railroad, and working parties reached it and began tearing up the rails, while other soldiers of the brigade were posted in scattered and isolated positions to provide protection from any Rebel interference. Suddenly musket fire erupted in the woods ahead of the 77th, making Private Cyrille Fountain apprehensive about "awful firing heard on the right of us." William Mahone's Confederates were sweeping over the railroad throwing the Vermonters in complete disarray, forcing them back to an entrenched position in the woods. Colonel David A. Wesiger's Virginians struck the 4th Vermont picket line, splitting the regiment in two and fanned out in its rear. [16]

Captain William C. Tracy gathered the left wing of the 4th Vermont and rallied his men for a brief stand. He soon fell dead, shot through the neck, and after a number of more men were killed or wounded, the rest surrendered. Major Pratt and the right wing of the regiment hurriedly edged north to link with Major Fleming's battalion at his breastworks in the woods. Brigadier General Joseph Finnegan's Florida Brigade pushed north and met Harris' Mississippians moving south behind Fleming's earthworks in the woods. The New Englanders were trapped, and at dusk when their ammunition ran out, Majors Pratt and Fleming surrendered their commands totaling 344 officers and enlisted men. During the hot firing, a stray bullet struck Private John R. Hall (Co. A) in the shoulder. He would recover and be discharged from the 77th at the defenses of Washington.

The next several days the 77th remained in their trenches and were made miserable by the heat and the ever present Virginia dust. Private Alonzo Bump wrote home that the New Yorkers "Dug Pits and now we Ly in them with our Littal shelter tents for a shelter. it is the hottest weather hear now that i ever saw. the men will sweat Lying in the shade. we have Got to stop fighting for it is Getting so hot . . ." George Stevens complained, "The light sandy soil soon became reduced to powder, and the continual passing of mules and army wagons raised huge clouds of dust, which completely enveloped the army. At sunset this cloud would settle down and become so dense so that one could not see objects twenty yards from him." Nevertheless, the army's surgeons "had their hospitals neatly fitted up, and nurses and attendants took great pride in adorning the hospital tents with boughs of the magnolia and other beautiful shrubs and flowers." Quarter masters and the Sanitary Commission provided a generous supply of lemons and vegetables to the sick and wounded "so notwithstanding the intense heat . . . there was comparatively little illness." [17]

In the morning, June 29, the 77th busied itself with laying abatis in front of their lines. In the afternoon, the Sixth Corps was ordered to Ream's Station on the Weldon Railroad. At 4 p.m., the regiment set out from its camp and marched the remainder of the day and into the night. Upon arrival at the station, the New York veterans saw the bodies of Federal cavalry that were roughly handled by Confederate infantry earlier in the day. Cyrille Fountain recorded in his diary, "our Pioneers baryed the dead Cavelry that had been killed the day before." The 77th "worked all day tareing up the Rail Road & burning the tyes & heating & bending the rails." Then a breastwork was cut into the railroad grade adding to the destruction. Some of the "boys plundered Every thing they could get hold of." Later in the day the Sixth Corps retraced their steps, and arrived at night within a couple of miles of the position previously held, where, Fountain remembered, "we lay down in a gandy [dandy] Corn field for the night." In the morning the 77th and the Sixth Corps rejoined the Army of the Potomac, and resumed their previous position at Petersburg. [18]

From the trenches of Cold Harbor to the works at Petersburg, the soldiers in the Federal army daily experienced the sharpshooter's bullets, cannon fire, skirmish and picket fire to the point that it became a normal part of the day not to be noticed any more than sitting back and enjoying a pipe. George Stevens wrote to Hattie, his wife,

> The Sixth Corps holds the left of the army line and there is very little fighting here. A little way to the right there is constant firing of artillery and musketry accompanied by the booming of mortars and heavy guns. This keeps up all night. During the day this firing is not so active but never ceases. We have become so accustomed to this constant pounding that it does not attract the slightest attention. We go on about our employments without thought of what others are about. [19]

While the Army of the Potomac moved out from its Cold Harbor position, Lee ordered Jubal Early to withdraw his troops from the Confederate front line. June 12, Early prepared to march to the defense of the Shenandoah Valley – the Confederacy's bread basket – against Major General David Hunter's Federal army. At 3 a.m. the next morning, Early's soldiers set out for the Valley by way of Louisa Court House and Charlottesville. Lee ordered Early to unite with Major General John C. Breckinridge's force and destroy Hunter's command. But the Southern commander had in mind an even larger objective. Lee also desired his lieutenant to march up the Shenandoah Valley, cross the Potomac River and threaten Washington. Such a move, Lee hoped, might disrupt Grant's campaign by forcing him to withdraw a considerable number of men from the Union army to meet Early's threat to Washington.

Hunter had replaced ineffective Major General Franz Sigel in command of the Army of the Shenandoah, who had earlier been ordered to move into the Shenandoah Valley to destroy the railroads and the agricultural economy there. Grant instructed Hunter to employ scorched earth tactics similar to those used later in the year during Sherman's March to the Sea. He was to advance through Staunton to Charlottesville and Lynchburg, living off the country and destroying the Virginia Central Railroad beyond possibility of quick repair.

On June 5, Hunter defeated Major General William E. "Grumble" Jones at the Battle of Piedmont. Following orders, Hunter moved up the Valley through Staunton and Lexington, destroying military targets such as blacksmiths and stables that could be used to support the Confederacy. After reaching Lexington, Hunter's troops burned down Virginia Military Institute (VMI). Hunter ordered the home of Governor John Lector burned in retaliation for its absent owner's having issued a proclamation calling the Valley's citizens to rise and wage guerilla warfare against the invading Yankees.

From Lexington, Hunter advanced against Confederate supply and canal depots, and the large hospital complex at Lynchburg. Reaching the outskirts of town on June 17, his first probing attacks were thwarted by the timely arrival by rail of Jubal Early's vanguard from Charlottesville. Hunter withdrew the next day after sporadic fighting because of a critical shortage of ammunition and supplies. His line of retreat through West Virginia effectively took his army out of the war for nearly a month, and opened the Shenandoah Valley for Early's men to advance into Maryland.

Reacting to Old Jube's presence in the Shenandoah Valley, Grant dispatched two brigades of the Sixth Corps, about 5,000 men, under Brigadier General James B. Rickets on July 6, the same day the Rebel force crossed the Potomac River. Until those troops arrived, however, the only Federal force between Early and Washington was a command of 6,300 men (mostly untested Hundred Days Men) commanded by Major General Lew Wallace. At that time Wallace was the commander of the Union's Middle Atlantic Department, headquartered at Baltimore. Very few of Wallace's soldiers had ever seen battle.

At Frederick, following skirmishing of July 7 and 8, Confederate cavalry drove Union troops from the town. Early demanded, and received, $200,000 ransom to forestall his sacking of the city. Wallace saw Monocacy Junction, three miles southeast of Frederick, as the most logical point of defense for both Baltimore and Washington. The Georgetown Pike to Washington and the National Road to Baltimore both crossed the Monocacy River there as did the Baltimore & Ohio Railroad. If Wallace could stretch his force over six miles of the river to protect both turnpikes, the railroad bridge, and several fords, he could make Early disclose the strength and objective of the Confederate force and delay him as long as possible.

At first Wallace's command along the Monocacy consisted only of Brigadier General Erastus B. Tyler's First Separate Brigade and a cavalry force commanded by Lieutenant Colonel David Clendenin. His prospects improved with word that the first contingent of Sixth Corps troops commanded by Ricketts had reached Baltimore, and were rushing by the Baltimore & Ohio Railroad to join Wallace at Monocacy. On July 9, the combined forces of Wallace and Ricketts, numbering around 5,800 soldiers, were positioned at the bridges and fords of the river. Tyler's brigade occupied two blockhouses and trenches the soldiers had dug with a few available tools near the bridges. Rickett's division held the Thomas and Worthington farms on the Union left, tearing down fences to erect breastworks.

Confederate Major General Stephen Dodson Ramseur's division encountered Wallace's men on the Georgetown Pike near the Best Farm; Major General Robert E. Rode's division skirmished with the Federals on the National Road. Believing that a frontal attack across the Monocacy was suicidal, Early sent John McClausand's cavalry down the Buckeystown Road to find a ford and outflank the Yankee line. McClausand forded the Monocacy below the McKinney-Worthington Ford and attacked Wallace's left flank. Wrongly believing they had outflanked the Federal positions, and due to rolling terrain, they did not notice Rickett's men behind a fence separating the Worthington and Thomas farms. The blue line exploded with musketry that panicked the mounted Confederate troopers. MClausand rallied his brigade and launched another attack, but could not break the Sixth corps veterans.

When it became apparent that confederate cavalry alone would not be able to break the Federal flank, Old Jube sent Major General

John B. Gordon's division across the ford to assist in the attack. Gordon initiated a three-prong attack against Rickett's center and both flanks. Federal regiments on the right flank were pushed back, allowing the Confederates to enfilade the rest of the Union line. Due to the pressure from Ramseur's attack on the Federal center, Wallace could not reinforce Ricketts, rendering the entire Yankee line untenable, and he ordered a retreat toward Baltimore, with Tyler's brigade and the cavalry serving as rearguard. By late afternoon, Wallace's defeated men hurried toward Baltimore, leaving behind over 1,294 dead, wounded, and captured.

Jubal Early moved his headquarters across the Monocacy near the railroad bridge as firing died away in the east. Stiff resistance and reports from wounded Federals confirmed that part of Rickett's Third Division, Sixth Corps had been in support of Wallace's cobbled command. This was critical intelligence. As Lee had hoped, Early's expedition caused Grant to detach some of his army, and the rumor was that the rest of the Sixth Corps had also embarked for Washington. The stoop-shouldered Southern general knew of the heavy fortifications which surrounded the Yankee capital. He also knew that he could march into Washington only if there were few defenders in the forts. If the entire Sixth Corps came up from Petersburg, then the Confederates risked a bloody repulse. Time became the all-important factor.

While Early realized he could still escape south of the Potomac, he never seriously considered the possibility. His natural aggressiveness made it easy for him to decide the opportunity far exceeded the risk. However, it was certain that Wallace had successfully bought a day's time for the beleaguered Federal capital. It was too late in the afternoon of July 9 to resume the advance. Further, the Rebel invaders were tired and needed the rest from combat. Accordingly, Old Jube planned to advance early in the morning on July 10.

By the afternoon of the 10th, news came that Early's men had turned toward Washington sparked fear in the streets. It turned to panic as refugees straggled in with hyped stories of outrage and destruction. So many of them entered the city that there was a shortage of shelter and food almost immediately. Journalist Noah Brooks aptly described the panic in the nation's capital:

> The city is in a ferment; men are marching to and fro; able-bodied citizens are gobbled up and put in the district's militia; refugees come flying in from the country, bringing their household goods with them; nobody is permitted to go out on the Maryland roads without a pass, and every turn an inquiring newspaper correspondent is met by some valiant in soldier straps, pompous and big with importance, in the rear of all danger, with 'By what authority are your hear sir?' Last night, while passing by the War Department, I saw an awkward squad of Quartermasters' clerks drilling in the park. Some were short and some were tall; there were three slab-sided clergymen who had forsaken the pulpit for the clerky desk, first young men in for a frolic; grim, saturnine men buckled into armor and looking destitute of all friends; men in linen coats and men in half-uniform; these all were being put through the manual by an impromptu captain, who, not being very well-informed in such matters, was prompted by his orderly sergeant, a messenger in the War Department. [20]

Early's convincing defeat of Wallace at Monocacy Junction prompted Grant to dispatch the remainder of the Sixth Corps and a contingent of the Nineteenth Corps (then arriving in Virginia from New Orleans) to Washington by water. 9 p. m., July 9, the 77th received orders to march to City Point at once where they would board waiting transports. Within two hours the New York veterans left their camp. Although the men were happy "that they were not forced to endure the misery of a long march under a burning sun," the roads were composed of dry beds of dust "6 inches deep" in which the veterans sunk at every step. Surgeon Stevens remembered "the cloud which rose as the column moved along filled their throats and eyes and nostrils." [21]

The 77th reached the James River at City Point at 6 a.m., and quickly boarded steamers ready to float them to Washington. A small contingent with Captain Martin Lennon boarded the *Alla Night*, while the rest of the 77th, the staff of Daniel Bidwell's Third Brigade, part of the 49th New York, the brigade band, and one-hundred horses climbed aboard the *Escort*. The transport steamer could barely accommodate its load, with the enlisted men closely crowded together, but George Stevens, Lieutenant Colonel Winsor French, and Major Nathan Babcock secured "a fine state room to ourselves and are very comfortable." As they cast off for Washington, the brigade band serenaded the soldiers with patriotic tunes. Stevens reminisced: "Great satisfaction was felt be all at the prospect of leaving the region whose natural desolation was heightened by the devastation of war, and going to a country of plenty, which so many pleasant remembrances were associated. Each man breathed more freely as the steamer swung upon the river." [22]

Steaming down the James, the 77th sailed by many landmarks, most of which were intimately connected to their 1862 participation in McClellan's failed Peninsula Campaign. Surgeon Stevens offered his audience a brief travelogue of their journey:

> There at our left, almost as soon as we were under way was Harrison Landing, the camping ground of two years before and the last one on the Peninsula up which our army had marched so proudly, an army at last crowded here for

protection before marching back in retreat. Cruising up and down the fine river or resting anchor were the Union gunboats, some of which had not long since changed both names and flags. As we watched them we thought of the Gunboat Teaser, which treated us to our first knowledge of real live hundred pound shells, as we bivouacked at New Port News in the early spring of 1862. The further down the river was Hampton, the scene of the earliest Peninsular experiences, the bay at New Port News made famous by the Monitor and the Merrimac, and I strained my eyes to get a glimpse of the little hospital at the river bank where I had been accustomed to see the men who were wounded on the sunken Congress and Cumberland, and to hear from them their story of the marvelous fight... There, pointing above the waters of the bay the masts of the Cumberland still told of the most memorable sea fight that had ever occurred in western waters or in fact any waters. [23]

As the 77th passed Old Point Comfort and around into Chesapeake Bay, Private Cyrille Fountain complained "the wind blew awful in the night." The violent rocking and rolling of the steamers caused a number of the veterans crowded together to become nauseous. Stevens remembered, "a goodly part of our number commenced with the determination and bravery of old soldiers, to try to conceal that the qualms of disgust at water transportation had fastened their sticky grip on them." He continued, "Sea sickness is bad enough under favorable circumstances, but when one has scant standing room, to say nothing of room for repose the malady of a chopping sea is at its worse." Soon, however, the transports were in the quieter waters of the Potomac River, raising still more recollections for the New Yorkers. Aquia Creek was passed, bringing to mind the encampment at White Oak Church. Just as they did two years earlier when the 77th sailed in the opposite direction to the Peninsula,

"The bells of our transport ships," the doctor recalled, "tolled as we passed the resting place of Washington at Mount Vernon." At 3 p.m., July 11, the regiment's steamers, *Alla Night* and *Escort*, touched the wharf at the foot of Sixth Street, Washington. [24]

After sweeping aside Wallace's small army, and while the 77th was ensconced aboard their steamers, Jubal Early resumed his march on Washington. Time was of the essence, but heat and humidity quickly sapped the strength of his soldiers. Northern Virginia had been suffering one of the longest hot spells in its history, experiencing 47 days without a drop of rain, and daily temperatures in the mid-90s. Early watched as the column of gray uniforms trudged through Rockville. No doubt the general viewed with rising concern the fatigue which etched so many faces and the sore-footed gait of hardened soldiers. The march was "an endless treadmill in a brown, gritty cloud, where the dust clotted bloody wounds and the throat hawked up goblets of dark spittle and each crease of skin was sanded raw." At times Early could scarcely make out his soldiers through the dust billowing among the lines. Countless exhausted stragglers dropped down by the roadside, but Old Jube still urged officers to push the column. That night, Early's exhausted men made their camps around Rockville and Gaithersburg to catch much needed rest. [25]

Little rest, however, was had by the Confederates. Early noted that the "heat during the night was oppressive and but little sleep had been obtained." At dawn, July 11, the air was already sultry, and the thermometer would hover in the mid-nineties for the next several days. Though unrested, the Southern soldiers broke camp around Gaithersburg and Rockville, knowing that the day's march might bring them to Washington and victory. [26]

It was a 20-mile march from their camps to Fort Stevens, but as the hours and miles dragged by, it became obvious that the Rebel column, gasping in the mid-90s heat and dust of the march, was reaching a state of collapse. Men by the scores fell out from the march, lying down by the roadside. Early described the day: "[It was] an exceedingly hot one and no air stirring. When marching, the men were enveloped in a suffocating cloud of dust and many of them fell by the way . . . I pushed on as rapidly as possible . . . [but] it became necessary to slacken our pace." Ramseur later wrote to his wife that "the heat and the dust were so great that our men could not possibly march much further." One soldier, whose regiment was with Gordon's division, claimed the entire division was stretched out so thin from stragglers that it looked like a line of skirmishers. [27]

The whole Confederate army (infantry, artillery, wagons, prisoners, plunder) turned eastward on an old well-maintained roadway known as the Washington and Brookville Turnpike, while in the District of Columbia it bore the name Seventh Street Road. The gray column turned onto the turnpike leading southward past Sligo Post Office (now Silver Spring) toward the District. Rodes' division took the lead, followed by Ramseur, Gordon, the army train, with Brigadier General John Echol's battalions in the rear, and Armistead Long's artillery batteries interspersed between the infantry divisions. The thermometer hit 94 degrees at W. H. Farquar's farm near Sandy Spring, and more dust and extreme fatigue bedeviled the marching Confederates. Due to its crushed flintstone base, the turnpike was mud-less in the winter, but it was hard on sore feet and lungs in the dry summer, as the Rebels discovered that day.

As Early approached Washington, Federals manning the northern part of the fortifications protecting the city spotted the huge dust cloud kicked up by marching Confederates. The fortifications encircling Washington marked thirty miles of forts, batteries, trenches, military roads, barracks, and other structures. Over 60 forts and 93 additional field gun battery positions were placed along the complex. Army camps and storage facilities, hospitals, and ordnance depots clustered around each fort. On paper, strength figures on July 10 showed 31,231 officers and men with a compliment of 944 heavy and 35 light artillery pieces deployed to defend the capital. The true number available to man the battlements against Early, Major General John G. Barnard warned his superiors, totaled barely 9,600 men. Unfortunately, many of these men were marginal soldiers – convalescents, militia, and provost martial units. Their heavy guns were difficult to maneuver, and the city lacked both the hardened veterans needed to repulse an attacker or the trained artillerists required to service the heavy fortress guns. Fort Stevens, which would be central to Early's advance down the Seventh Street Road, had merely 209 defenders manning its 375-perimeter yards boasting four 24-pounder seacoast cannon in a barbette, six 24-pounder siege guns in an embrasure, two 8-inch siege howitzers (in an embrasure), five 30-pounder Parrotts firing through an embrasure, and a 10-inch siege and a 24-pounder coehorn. [28]

With too many generals and too few veteran soldiers, Federal high command had been confused, overlapped, and almost useless. July 10, stragglers and refugees continued to stream into the capital, along with several herds of frightened cattle driven before Early's soldiers. Confederates at Washington's door set off alarms among the citizenry; the capital had virtually succumbed to terror. Now that the enemy was close at hand, the only voice of calm to be heard in the hysteria of panic was the President's. To a terrified group of Baltimore citizens who blatantly wondered aloud if they could count on Lincoln for full protection, the President calmly replied, "Let us be vigilant, but keep cool. I hope neither Baltimore nor Washington will be taken." [29]

At about 1 p.m. on July 11, the Confederate advance had come within the siege guns stationed on the Washington fortification.

Early was eager to ride ahead and supervise the field, but it was more important to close his column so that he would at maximum strength to attack the capital's ramparts. Old Jube rode along the tired troops, urging, cajoling, and threatening them in order to close up the column. But, the exhausted soldiers could do just so much. Those who clung to the march barely moved at a snail's pace. At times Early galloped up and down the line assuring his men he would have them in the Federal capital by nightfall, yet even that news failed to quicken their step. As the Southern general looked at his men, an unpleasant awareness arose in Jubal's mind: if time still worked for him, nature worked against him. If he won the race of time, he might lose the match to sultry summer heat.

Finally Early galloped ahead of his infantry to observe the field. As far as he could see, things looked favorable. Atop his horse, he examined the enemy work through his field glasses. In his front about 1,100 yards away rose a large earthen work, curtained, scarped, and embrasured. Early scrolled open a map of Washington's defenses, located Seventh Street Road, and saw that he was looking at Fort Stevens. Designed to protect the vital highway leading to the heart of Washington, the fort stood to the right of the road and was slightly elevated. Between Old Jube's vantage point and the fort were clumps of trees, occasional farmhouses, and cleared fields. Prominent on the ground before him were the homes of Francis Preston Blair and that of his son Postmaster General Montgomery Blair. Neither of the owners or their families were present, having left Washington earlier in the week.

Early clearly saw that there were few defenders occupying Fort Stevens. If the fort had few defenders, he believed, there were few defenders for all of Washington. Jubal had beaten the clock. All he had to do was assemble a line and occupy the works. However, organizing a battle line proved impossible. Little more than 10,000 exhausted

Rebels were still with his army, and of those not more than a third were fit for immediate battle. Early found Rodes leading his division down the turnpike from Silver Spring. He ordered Rodes to send out skirmishers and deploy a line of battle, and see if the works could be taken. Rodes' soldiers were strewn out and all he could do for some time was spread his skirmishers into the fields in front of the Yankees. Suddenly, around 1:30 p.m., Early noticed a shroud of dust rising over the capital. Taking up his field glasses once more, he saw a column of blue swinging into view. These were no untrained militia or convalescents, for these men wore the faded blues of seasoned campaigners. These men were surely some of Grant's veterans, but Jubal had no way of knowing how many there were.

The men in faded blue uniforms that Early spied through his glasses were indeed Grant's battle hardened veterans from Horatio Wright's remaining two divisions of the Sixth Corps. Federal reinforcements from the Army of the Potomac had begun arriving at Washington's Sixth Street wharves earlier that day. When the 77th disembarked from their transports, they could see "some immense sea steamers, crowded with troops of the Nineteenth Corps just arrived from New Orleans (Only around 600 men from the 114th and 153rd New York would actually land from this corps). President Lincoln "stood on the wharf, as we left our ships, and watched the process of disembarking with deep interest, chatting now with this soldier and now with that one," teasing them from time to time about hurrying if they wanted to catch Jubal Early. "And," George Stevens remembered, "to show that he was in sympathy with the men in all sorts of ways he nibbled at pieces of hard tack as he chatted." [30]

Once on dry ground the Empire State veterans took up the line of march with their Sixth Corps comrades through the city up Seventh Street Road. The 77th marched past the Smithsonian Institute, the Patent Office, and the Post Office. The New Yorkers would never forget their afternoon march through the capital. "Thousands of people," Stevens remarked in an address he gave in 1901, "were gathered along the route of march, for Washington was in a state of panic and the advent of veteran troops was a matter of no small interest . . . As we marched between the crowds of eager spectators, many of whom were some women holding children in their arms, the veterans with brown faces and with uniforms worn and grimed by a campaign lasting from the Wilderness through Cold Harbor and Petersburg were the objects of intense interest and curiosity." As they marched by the excited crowds, over and over again they heard what blended into one continuous chorus: "Thank god! We are safe now! It's the old Sixth Corps. Those are the men who took Marye's Heights! They say they are regular devils! Them's no clerks. Them's fighters." [31]

Marching through the city, the 77th could hear the sound of siege guns in their front above the din of the crowds, and quickened their step. The veterans marveled at the bedraggled refugees they encountered on the march: "Families, with a few of their choicest articles of household furniture loaded in wagons, were hastening to the city, reporting that their houses were burned, or that they had made their escape leaving the greater part of their goods to the mercy of the rebels." The New Yorkers continued north, making their bivouac for the night in a shaded grove of trees in the rear of Fort DeRussy. The good doctor Stevens, and other surgeons organized a Second Division field hospital in the barracks just in the rear of Fort Stevens. [32]

Wright learned to his surprise that his veteran soldiers would be held in reserve while the ramparts and rifle pits continued to be manned by a motley crew of reservists. The strategy was to have his combat hardened corps ready to maneuver to any point where a Confederate breakthrough seemed eminent, and be ready to counterattack and annihilate Early's entire army if possible. Wright reported to Major General Alexander McCook at Fort Stevens about 3 p.m. Despite Halleck's orders, McCook directed Wright to send out 900 of his veterans for picket duty during the night.

Wright turned to Brigadier Frank Wheaton, commanding First Brigade, Second Division, Sixth Corps (and the entire division during the temporary absence of Brigadier General George W. Getty who was recovering from a wound received in May at the Wilderness). Three of his Pennsylvania regiments, the 98th, 102nd, and 138th, with the 93rd and 62nd New York in support, moved up to the works, formed in lines of battle, and set out down the slope toward a creek running through a swale before the fort. The firing intensified as the lines closed on Robert Rodes' skirmishers, who grudgingly began to fall back. As soon as Wheaton felt comfortable with his defensive position, about 1,000 yards out from Fort Stevens, he halted his troops and his soldiers dug in. It was now 7 p.m., and the sun had already set below the wooded hills to his left and front. Old Jube's last chance to mount an attack was rapidly ticking away. He would council with his generals that night and assess the situation the next morning.

As soon as there was light on the eastern horizon the morning of July 12, Jubal Early was in the saddle and rode to the front. From a small hill, he carefully scanned the Federal forts and rifle pits. Early at once saw that the rifle pits were well-manned with soldiers in faded blue uniforms. The gunnery ports in the forts too teamed with gun crews, and the ramparts were occupied by Wright's veterans. The Sixth Corps flag of the Greek Cross sealed any doubt Early might have had about the identity of the Yankee force before him. The odds for a successful attack were all against him. Early determined his only viable option was to withdraw from the Federal works. The Southern commander ordered his soldiers to hold the front while he planned the Rebels retreat. Yet Old Jube was equally determined to stay put for a day to emphasize the threat to Washington. Consequently, Gordon and Rodes formed battle lines, not to launch an attack on the works, but to cover the retreat that was planned for that night.

As the morning sun rose, the 30-pounder Parrot rifled cannon at Fort Stevens belched shells toward the Carberry house, marking the beginning of a steady barrage from DeRussy's eleven guns, Stevens' twenty-three guns, and Slocum's twenty-five that would drop over 225 shells on the Confederate positions. The gunners fired upon every target from 1,000 yards outward, bodies of troops moving against distant woods, houses from which Rebel sharpshooters fired from windows, even the Blair houses, well over 3,000 yards up the turnpike.

All morning the whizzing of bullets and the demonic shriek of descending shells and the crackle of musketry rang out in the vale before Fort Stevens. By the afternoon, Rebel skirmishers were creeping closer to the Yankee positions. Their work was made easier for them by the fact that Confederate sharpshooters occupied two houses across the ravine. These snipers were picking off numbers of blue-clad soldiers as they disputed the skirmishers advance. Wright and McCook came to the conclusion that the houses needed to be eliminated, and in addition, two small hills commanding a section of rifle pits must be captured.

Throughout the morning, and into the afternoon, curious sightseers clogged the road to the front and Fort Stevens. Sixth Corps veteran James Bowan remarked, "In the fort were gathered . . . officers and citizens of both sexes who had come out from the city to see the VI Corps whip Early . . ." Among the visitors were Secretary of the Navy Gideon Welles and William Henry Seward and his son, William Henry, Jr., the commander of the 9th New York Heavy Artillery, who had been wounded on the Monocacy and escaped by riding a mule back to his regiment. So too were Edwin Stanton and Postmaster Montgomery Blair. Lucius Chittenden, who worked in the treasury, made his way to the fort with other civilians, and was heckled by whiskey-fueled soldiers shouting, "Skedaddle white livers! Comin' out here to get another Bull Run, aren't ye!" [33]

At 4 p. m., Abraham Lincoln and his wife, Mary Todd, drove up to Fort Stevens' barracks unattended, except by their coachman and footman, and halted at the door of the Second Division hospital. George Stevens clearly remembered President and Mrs. Lincoln's arrival:

> I was standing there at the moment and the President and his affable wife entered at once into conversation, inviting me to take a seat in the carriage as it would be more sociable. They flattered me by showing that they knew well the record of our men and they assured me that the people of the country knew and appreciated the wearers of the Greek Cross . . . For nearly an hour we chatted on various topics, mostly relating to army life until General Wright and his staff arrived. Then we all went to the fort. [34]

Upon Horatio Wright's arrival, his staff, Lincoln, and Surgeon Stevens went to the fort, leaving behind Wright's wife and Mary Todd Lincoln at the barracks. The party walked through the fort's open interior and up a ramp to a parapet where Lincoln looked out at the battlefield. Before the President was a seemingly calm countryside dotted with puffs of white smoke along a line where men in gray crouched, stood briefly, fired their muskets, and again crouched to reload. Confederate sharpshooters fired from the windows of houses in the fields below the fort, keeping the Union soldiers pinned down in the rifle pits. At six-foot-four-inches tall and wearing a black stovepipe hat, Lincoln was a conspicuous target, which profoundly worried Stevens. Bullets whizzed over the ramparts. Standing between the President and Wright's aide Thomas Hyde, Surgeon C. V. A. Crawford of the 102nd Pennsylvania suddenly keeled over, seriously wounded when struck by a sniper's bullet that ricocheted after striking the wheel of a siege gun. Soldiers and civilians alike urged Lincoln to step down out of danger, but he remained at the rampart engrossed by the skirmishing before him. Stevens remembered that "General Wright suggested to the President that he should descend, but when the latter did not heed the warning, the General said, 'Mr. President it is my duty to insist that you descend from this place of danger.' To which the President replied, 'General Wright, I always obey orders of my superior officers!' and he got down." A chair was brought for him to sit close to the parapet, but he did not sit long before he popped back up again. One of his cabinet pointed toward the field of battle and said, "Mr. President, if you will look over in that direction, you can see just where the rebels are." Lincoln replied, "My impression is that if I am where I can see the rebels, they are where they cans see me." With that, Lincoln once again descended the parapet and sat down in his chair. [35]

After the close call with Lincoln and the presence of a number of people of importance gathered in the vicinity of Fort Stevens, something had to be done to ensure their safety. McCook looked to Wright and asked that a full brigade be readied for the attack, with the object of clearing out the Confederate skirmish line, and putting an end to sharpshooter's bullets from nearby homes. Wright decided that Frank Wheaton should be given the assignment of clearing the front of the Rebels. The 77th's Third Brigade would be the principle attack force, with Wheaton's own First Brigade as immediate backup, while Edwards' Third Brigade of Russell's First Division would take a reserve position directly in front of Fort Stevens, and help if necessary.

According to plan, Colonel Bidwell would signify the Third Brigade's readiness to begin the attack by waving the new national flag of the 77th recently presided to Lieutenant Colonel Winsor French by the citizens of Saratoga Springs while he was recuperating from illness. The batteries of Fort Stevens and Fort Slocum would bombard the houses providing cover from the troublesome Confederate marksmen. Three salvos would be fired, and after the thirty-sixth shot, equaling the number of stars on the national flag at this time, the brigade would charge the Rebels.

At 5 p.m., Bidwell led the Third Brigade out of the fort for deployment. As Private Edward Fuller reached the parapet, he passed by President Lincoln, who "doffed his hat" in salute to the determined veterans of the regiment. The Third Brigade's colonel deployed his regiments with the 77th at the right flank position on the first line with the 7th Maine, and Bidwell's own 49th New York under Lieutenant Colonel G. M. Johnson. The 43rd New York, 61st Pennsylvania, and the 122nd New York, which had joined the brigade only two days earlier, formed the second line.

As soon as the 77th and the Third Brigade entered the field in front of the fort, they came under severe fire from the Rebel line of snipers in the houses. Bidwell ordered his soldiers to hit the ground. From Fort Stevens and nearby DeRussy, heavy artillery roared to life, "and sent volley after volley of 32 pound shells howling over the heads of our men and through the Carberry house where so many of them had found shelter." The 61st Pennsylvania's Daniel Bee, while awaiting orders to charge, counted 25 shells that hit the Carberry house, setting it on fired. Five Confederates jumped from the upstairs windows as the house became enveloped by flames. The heavy guns then concentrated their fire upon the survivors in the road and fields surrounding the burning buildings.[36]

Charge of the Third Brigade at Fort Stevens (Saratoga Springs Historical Society)

Around 6 p.m., his brigade was ready for the attack, and Bidwell ordered the 77th's color bearer to wave the regiment's new flag, and the guns at Fort Stevens erupted, sending shells into the Confederate line. As soon as the shells exploded in the Rebel line, Bidwell ordered "Forward! Double Quick, March!" Private Fuller told listeners many years later that the 77th "Soon ran past the skirmish line, our Colonel French, commanding in the lead. The fire of the men's rifles cracking oftener and more general as they advanced." The brigade carried a ridge which bisected the Seventh Street Road, and pressed on past the Carberry and Rives properties. Abruptly, a ripping staccato came from the Confederates in a line of trees, and a solid sheet of flame burst in front of the 77th, staggering the New Yorkers. Fuller remembered, "There goes a man down; it is [Private William] Lattimore of Company G, through whose breast a rifle ball has passed. Soon another falls; it is [Private Andrew J.] Dowen of H Company, not to rise again. And there goes [Private Alvarah] Morey of old K Company, to be followed by [Private Ambrose] Mattot of G Company, neither of the three to rise again until the day when we are taught all will rise." [37]

Bidwell called for supporting regiments. His men had surprised the Rebels, but had in turn been surprised. Instead of hitting a thin line of Confederate pickets, they had blundered upon a line of battle organized by Major General Robert Rodes. The major general fired upon the advancing Federals with his own artillery and sent one or two of his own brigades to bolster the flagging skirmish line. A sharp firefight developed a little beyond the Rives place. The high ground north of the Rives property was hotly contested as Edwards' brigade and Wheaton's own brigade had to be sent to help out.

Company C of the 122nd New York, to their consternation, found themselves isolated forward of the Third Brigade. Private William Eugene Ruggles described his company's predicament: ". . . we got shelter behind the fence and stumps, halted and looked around to see the condition of things, and it was there we found we were far in advance of the rest of the line . . . We remained there some time, until we feared they had a cross fire on both flanks, then the First Sergeant ordered us to fall back to the house . . . We did go, and found they had a cross fire on us still, but we laid low and held our ground." Edward Fuller recorded that "the enemy stood the attack for a while, and then wavered. Stubbornly fighting they yielded, and then gave way to the vigorous charge of the Sixth Corpsers. Over a mile they were driven, and until darkness stopped the fray, leaving the Third Brigade in possession of the field." [38]

Though brief, the fight in front of Fort Stevens killed or wounded every regimental officer of the Third Brigade. Surgeon Stevens lamented, "Lieutenant Colonel Johnson, commanding the Forty-ninth, a brave man, who never shrunk from danger, and who had shared in all the varied fortunes of the brigade since its organization, fell mortally wounded. Colonel Vissher, of the Forty-third, who had but lately succeeded the beloved Wilson, was killed. Major Jones, commanding the Seventh Main, was also among the slain; and Major

Crosby, commanding the Sixty-first Pennsylvania, who had but just recovered from the bad wound he received in the Wilderness, was taken to the hospital where the surgeon removed his left arm from the shoulder." Lieutenant Colonel Winsor French caught a ball in the groin, but remained on the field urging his men forward. [39]

Of the 1,000-man brigade, 280 certain, and perhaps 375 had been killed or wounded. The 49th New York entered the battle with 85 men and could count only 59 men when the combat ended. The 77th fared slightly better. Privates Andrew J. Dowen (Co. H), Matthew Love (Co. H) Andrew Manning (Co. H), Alvarado Morey (Co. K), and Corporal Ambrose Mattot (Co. G) were killed. Private Hubbard M. Moss, who joined the regiment eight days earlier, was seriously wounded and died of his wounds August 5 in Mount Pleasant Hospital in Washington. Eleven others were wounded, but recovered and served out their terms of enlistment. As S. A. McDonald of the 122nd New York declared years later, "That the percentage of killed was unusually large" was sown in comparison to Antietam, Chancellorsville, and Gettysburg, where, taken as a whole, Union losses in killed alone were "16 per cent of the aggregate killed and wounded." The figure at Fort Stevens in the Third Brigade stood at 35.8 per cent. Victory, however, had been gained and the Confederate raiders driven back about a mile, and pressure relieved on the Federal defenses. Lincoln and the number curious civilian dignitaries delighted in seeing the pitched battle. But as Private Ruggles observed, "I suppose they think it was a splendid sight, but we poor fellows could not see much fun in it." [40]

"The fight," George Stevens remarked, "had lasted but a few minutes when the stream of bleeding mangled ones began to come to the rear. Men leaning upon the shoulders of comrades borne painfully on stretchers, the pallor of their countenances rendered more ghastly by the thick dust upon them, were brought into the hospitals by scores where medical officers were hard at work binding up the wounds, administering stimulants, coffee, food, or resorting to the hard necessity of amputation." Stevens would be on his feet for forty-eight hours straight, amputating arms and legs and dressing wounds. The surgeon vividly recalled one of the 77th with a life threatening wound:

> How well do I remember some of those wounded men and how satisfied they seemed to be that they had given themselves for their country in sight of the President of theta country. Even now I seem to see the pale face of Private [William] Lattimore of Company G through whose chest a Minie ball had passed, ploughing a great hole through the lung, as he lay upon the table while I stripped away his bloody garments, drew from his wound shreds and masses of clothing and dressed his wound. There was no flinching, no repining; he said that he meant to get well, and the boy whose body was shot through in July, shouldered his musket in September and in the great battle of Cedar Creek in October, Corporal Lattimore stood shoulder to shoulder with his comrades of Company G of the 77th. [41]

That evening, the pale moonlight added to the orange glow of burning houses, and curious citizens toured the battlefield. Lucius Chittenden made his way onto the contested ground and approached a house in flames. "On all the floors, on the roofs, in the yards, within reach of the heat, were many bodies of the dead or dying, who could not move, and had been left behind by their comrades. The odor of burning flesh filled the air; it was a sickening spectacle!" Later the treasury employee came upon a fallen sharpshooter who still clutched an Enfield rifle and cartridge box and wore body armor, "the only things about him which did not indicate extreme destitution." Here was the gruesome face of war up close: A sprawled, bony body that had marched more than three hundred

M^CKEAN'S SUNDAY SCHOOL BOYS GO TO WAR

miles in six weeks and fought on many fields, his haversack containing "a jack-knife, a plug of twisted tobacco, a tin cup and about two quarts cracked corn, with, perhaps, an ounce of salt, tied in a rag."[42]

In the morning, Federal burial squads fanned out over the battleground. The dignitaries and privileged citizens that had come out to watch the battle were nowhere to be found. For them, the excitement was over. George Stevens had bitter scorn for the spectators who delighted in the battle:

> We gathered our dead comrades from the field where they had fallen, and gave them the rude burial of soldiers on the common near Fort Stevens. None of those high in authority, who had come out to see them give up their lives for their country, were present to pay the last honors to the dead heroes. No officer or state, no lady of wealth, no citizen of Washington was here; but we laid them in their graves within sight of the capital; without coffins, with only their gory garments and their blankets around them. With the rude tenderness of soldiers, we covered them in the earth; we marked their names with our pencils on the little head-boards of pine, and turned sadly away. [43]

Sometime after dark, Early was planning the orderly withdrawal of his army from the Washington fortifications. By 11 p.m. on the 12th, his soldiers were fully on the move toward Rockville. The gray tide was ebbing north and west. By morning, the lines before Fort Stevens were empty of Southern soldiers. But, the 77th would soon again clash with Early's men in the Shenandoah Valley. Left behind were the Confederate wounded and prisoners. "The prisoners," Stevens wrote, "declared that they did not expect to meet veteran soldiers and inquired, referring to the creek crosses worn by our men, 'How the devil did you Catholic fellows get here?'" [44]

15

"WE HAVE GOT EVERYTHING, GOD DAMN THEM!"

No more than a few minutes after midnight of July 13, the last of Jubal Early's soldiers abandoned their trenches west of the capital. The stillness of daybreak was broken only by the occasional bark of a nervous picket's rifle and the bray of a mule and the low of a cow. Federal cavalry were sent out to scout the enemy's lines and soon reported back that they were empty of Rebels.

The key to bagging Jubal's army lay with concentrating Federal forces in the region and cutting off his line of retreat. President Lincoln anxiously called for pursuit of the Confederates on the River Road. Once Grant was certain that Lee had not sent reinforcements to Early, he made plans to chase the Rebel army. Horatio Wright's Sixth Corps was to pursue the Confederates as long as there was "any prospect of punishing" them, and then return with the Nineteenth

Corps to Petersburg for other operations. Grant concluded that by aggressively pushing the enemy that Early could be driven from Maryland, and his army destroyed.

At 1 p.m. on July 13, the 77th left its camp behind Fort Stevens with the column of Wright's Sixth Corps, beginning the active pursuit of Jubal Early's army. However, Wright was unnecessarily cautious, contending that he had only 10,500 soldiers facing three or four times that number in Early's command. The Virginia heat, ever-present choking dust, and untrained wagon masters and their balky mules slowed the Federals down. The 77th reached Offutt's Crossroads, also known as Potomac Crossroads, by nightfall and bivouacked to get some sleep, but the Sixth Corps stretched all the way back to the defensive line in the vicinity of Fort Stevens, and the 77th and their corps comrades were seriously played out by the fifteen mile march. A Vermont captain in the Green Mountain Brigade wrote his father that they had left Fort Stevens at 3 p.m. on the 13th and had marched all night past "new mules and green drivers with nary a mouthful to eat." [1]

Early's army had a whole day on his pursuers. His triumphant soldiers waded back across the Potomac at White's Ford near Poolesville on the morning of July 14, and spread out over the Virginia hillsides to get much needed rest before moving on to Leesburg, while Early's trains, prisoners captured at Monocacy, a large number of beef cattle, and artillery also crossed the river. Major General Robert Ransom's cavalry and several cannons covered the crossing as rear guard. Federal cavalry caught up to the Confederate rear guard causing a noisy skirmish until evening when Ransom's troopers also re-crossed the Potomac. During the afternoon, the two antagonists traded artillery and musket fired across the river. Jubal's men we glad to be back in Dixie again.

The 77th and the Sixth Corps resumed their pursuit of the Rebel army at 4:30 a.m. The same morning the corps was crossing the Potomac, and reached Poolesville late afternoon July 14. But Wright's dust-shrouded column continued to stretch back to the Washington fortifications. Many of the regiment's men grumbled about the lack of water on the march. At least, Surgeon Stevens remarked they marched "through pleasant country" unspoiled by war. The New Yorkers bivouacked for the night while the rest of their comrades closed up the column. [2]

Both armies were given a two day break from marching, and the Federal soldiers fanned out to forage the fertile fields and well-stocked farms around Poolesville. Except for the execution of a deserter-turned-spy from the 67th New York witnessed by Private Cyrille and a large crowd, the days were uneventful. Captain Martin Lennon recorded in his diary, "A rebel spy was hung at noon on July 15. He was captured near Petersburg. He first deserted from the rebels and joined our army, and, after getting a bounty several times, at last became a rebel spy." [3]

At 6 a.m. July 16, the 77th resumed the march, moving with the Sixth Corps to White's Ford on the Potomac. For George Stevens, the spectacle at the ford was novel and exciting, and he painted a detailed picture of an army crossing a river:

> The stream was wide, but no more than two or three feet deep. The bottom was rough and stony, and the current was strong. For nearly a mile up and down the river the brigades were crossing; the stream filled with infantry wading with difficult steps over the uneven bottom, mounted officers carefully guiding their horses lest they should stumble, trains of artillery and wagons slowly toiling through,

and groups of pack animals scarcely able to keep their footing under their huge burdens. The laugh of hundreds sounded up and down the river, as some unfortunate footman, slipping from a smooth stone, would for a moment, disappear beneath the surface of the river, or as some overloaded mule or pack horse, losing his footing, would precipitate his load, and peradventure the small negro boy, who, in order to secure a dry passage across the ford, had perched himself on the top of the bags and bundles, into the rushing waters. [4]

Once across the Potomac, the refreshed soldiers emptied the water in their boots and shoes, and wrung the water from their stockings. But then the march resumed, and once again their uniforms were wet from sweat. John B. Southard of the 49th New York wrote his sister in Rexford Flats, Saratoga County, that after crossing the Potomac they were soon once again dust covered. He thought the soldiers looked like mud statues marching. The 77th marched through Leesburg and marched three more miles before halting at 8 a.m. at Clark's Gap for the day. The New Yorkers camped "in a ploughed field" and were more than "dissatisfied at the idea of sleeping on ploughed ground while fresh meadows were on every side of us." Being that it was Sunday, Chaplain Norman Fox held a well-attended worship service. [5]

When Early was approaching the Washington fortifications, Major General David Hunter's Army of West Virginia was slowly reappearing in the theater of operations. His forward elements reached Martinsburg, West Virginia, as Early's soldiers battled before Fort Stevens. Hunter spent two days resupplying his army at Martinsburg while awaiting the arrival of the rest of his troops from Cumberland, Maryland. By July 14, a portion of Hunter's army reached Harpers Ferry. While there he received a dispatch from

Wright at Poolesville, urging him to join his forces at Leesburg, Virginia, across the Potomac. Hunter sent forward Brigadier General Jeremiah Sullivan with 7,000 infantry and 2,000 cavalry under the Frenchman Brigadier Alfred Duffie. Using the towpath of the Chesapeake & Ohio Canal, Federals crossed at Knoxville and Berlin, Maryland, and headed south. However, instead of passing on directly to Leesburg, Sullivan turned right through Hillsborough and Purcellville. Unknowingly, they were within striking distance of Early's force as they marched through Lovettsville. Here, the Little River Turnpike divided into the Ashby's Gap Turnpike to the west and the Snicker's Gap Turnpike to the northwest. Sullivan's column would have bisected Early's line of retreat from Leesburg through Snicker's Gap, had he not bivouacked at Hillsborough on the night of July 15.

On July 16, Hunter's other division commander, Brigadier General Gorge Crook, rode up to Hillsborough, took over command from Sullivan whom he considered incompetent, and sent off Duffie's troopers to find Early's Rebels. At Waterford, Duffie uncovered the whole Confederate army slowly moving westward on the road to Snicker's Gap. The Yankees attacked the Rebel column on the outskirts of Purcellville shortly after noon. The cavalry slashed through the Confederate wagon train and cut out over one hundred horses and mules, about eighty wagons and ambulances. Rodes' infantrymen came up and easily drove off the Yankee horseman.

That same night, Early bivouacked both in and beyond Snicker's Gap on the Blue Ridge mountains. The next day, his soldiers crossed the Shenandoah River and encamped in strong positions near Berryville. Here, Early was prepared to dispute the river crossings of the Shenandoah. Gordon and Ramseur took positions controlling Castleman's Ferry. Two miles downstream, Rodes guarded Rock's Ford.

At the same time Early halted for the night on the Blue Ridge, Crook's command bivouacked around Purcellville, half a dozen miles from Wright at Clark's Gap near Leesburg, and reported to him for orders. Wright instructed Crook to move a force to Snicker's Gap. Crook dispatched Duffie's and Colonel James Mulligan's cavalry for this purpose, but Early, who had crossed the Shenandoah at Snicker's Ferry opposite the gap, placed two guns there, and checked a farther Federal approach.

On the afternoon of July 18, from the summit of the Blue Ridge, Crook's soldiers could see Confederates on the heights beyond the Shenandoah. Early's command was around Berryville, and John C. Breckinridge guarded the fords of the river. At about 2 p.m., Crook ordered Colonel Joseph Thoburn to cross his division and the Third Brigade of the Second Division to dislodge the Rebels there. Thoburn's men moved to Island Ford a mile or so below Snicker's Ferry. A small contingent of Confederate pickets contested Thoburn. Colonel George D. Well's brigade carried the ford, capturing a number of enemy skirmishers. From these, Thoburn learned that Early's main force was only a couple of miles away. Thoburn relayed this intelligence to Crook, and was instructed not to move up to Snicker's Ferry, but to await a division of the Sixth Corps which would cross for his support. Not more than a half hour later, Breckinridge advanced against Thoburn's left and center, while Early sent Rodes to assail the Federal right. The Confederate attack drove Thoburn's men back across the Shenandoah. Federal dead and wounded were left on the field. The next day, Confederate squads buried their dead and removed their wounded.

At 6 a.m. on July 18, the 77th fell in with the Sixth Corps as it resumed the march to join Crook's command. Unlike so many previous grueling marches, it was an easy one for the New Yorkers. George Stevens noted "our little army" passed "through the delightful scenery of Loudon County, and through the diminutive villages of Hamilton and Purcellville." Private Cyrille Fountain thought otherwise as he grumbled, "we see the Stars & Bars to enly one house." In the afternoon, the Third Brigade deployed as flankers on opposite sides of the road. Soon thereafter, the 77th found "ourselves toiling up the ascent of the Blue Ridge, pleasant farm houses and fine orchards greeting our sight on either side of the road." At nightfall, the Sixth Corps passed through Snicker's Gap, following a winding, rough, unkempt road. By moonlight, the 77th encamped at the foot of the Blue Ridge, and spread their blankets for a night's rest. [6]

The next morning, the 77th received orders to be ready to move at a moment's notice. Private Fountain "was quite Sick," and "was Sent to the Ambulance train." While the sick private sought medical help, the Sixth Corps First Division, with Crook's troops, moved down to the river, but made no attempt to cross. Later in the day, the 77th and the Sixth Corps were ordered to be ready to march to Washington at night. Not long after, the order was countermanded, and the New Yorkers bedded down in a hard rain. Rather than return to the regiment, Cyrille Fountain "Stade at the Division Hospital," happy to be out of the rain. [7]

July 20, the 77th with the Sixth Corps moved down to the Shenandoah and crossed at noon to the site of Thoburn's battle of the 18th where there "were visible many Union dead, heads, arms and legs protruding from the slight heaps of earth hastily shoveled over them, while many Confederate graves also marked the field." Wright and Crook discovered Early was gone from their front and marched to Berryville. Unexpectedly, Wright decided that Early was no longer a threat to the Valley, about-faced and ordered his men to return to Washington where they would board transports to reunite with Grant at Petersburg. [8]

The 77th was once again on the march. Still too sick to march, Private Fountain climbed into a wagon in the supply train. Wright expected it would be an easy two-day march. Instead, it turned out to be a grueling race to get back to the steamboats to join Grant before Early could return to Lee's army. At dark, the 77th were again passing through Snicker's Gap and, as George Stevens recorded, "the infantry and teams crowded together in the narrow defile to the great inconvenience of the footmen and annoyance of the artillerymen and teamsters." The Federal soldiers marched rapidly all night and the next day, halting once only briefly for coffee. 9 a.m. they reached Leesburg, and rested for a couple of hours, and then followed the turnpike toward Chain Bridge. Passing Drainsville, the New Yorkers crossed Goose Creek and spent the night marked by heavy rainstorms at Fire Creek. The march left behind many stragglers, one of whom was Private Walter Freeman (Co. A). He was scooped up by Mosby's Raiders four times before finally escaping. Feeling better, Cyrille Fountain left the wagons and returned to the regiment, but lamented that "Some of the wounded died on the way." July 23, the regiment at 7 a.m. left camp taking the Alexandria Turnpike, crossed the Potomac on the Chain Bridge halting five miles from Washington behind Fort Gaines where they bivouacked. During the night, Privates James Myers (Co. A) and Orris P. Thompson (Co. A) and many other stragglers caught up to their regiment. How much rest they would get was unknown. In his diary, Captain Martin Lennon wrote, "Orders to be ready to move at a moment's – supposed that we are to return to the Potomac." [9]

Learning of Wright's return to Washington, Jubal Early decided to enact further Lee's original instructions in June. Crops were ripening and remained to be gathered for the Confederacy; the rebuilt Baltimore & Ohio Railroad awaited renewed destruction; and, northern Maryland and southern Pennsylvania remained ripe for further raids. Early also needed something to inspire his men. July

23, then, began the second phase of his summer campaign. His first objective was to hit George Crook's force that had taken an exposed position just south of Winchester at Kernstown, and drive it out of the Valley.

Early attacked Crook's 12,000-man army at Kernstown in the morning on July 24. By noon the battle became a bloody slugfest. Things seemed favorable for the Union side until Old Jube's men simultaneously flanked Crook both right and left. The beaten Federal army fled back past the old Opequon Meeting House and the graveyard through Winchester. Fleeing blueclad soldiers retreated through open fields and crowded the macadamized valley turnpike. Confederate cavalry struck Crook's column on the pike, stampeding the teamsters and causing seventy two wagons and twelve caissons to be abandoned and burned. Federal losses totaled 1,185 with nearly 500 captured. The outnumbered Confederate force came out nearly unscathed with 150 killed, wounded, and missing.

Crook's demoralized army re-crossed the Potomac on July 26 and regrouped in the vicinity of Sharpsburg, Maryland Heights, and Pleasant Valley. Early and his soldiers were again loose unopposed in the lower valley. First order of business was to interrupt the Baltimore & Ohio Railroad. The Rebels once more ripped up fifteen miles of newly re-laid railroad from Martinsburg to Harpers Ferry on July 26 and 27. Two days later, Early's horsemen crossed the Potomac headed for southern Pennsylvania and western Maryland. Confederate infantry waded across the river once more and moved on to Hagerstown.

July 24 and 25, the 77th enjoyed the rest from nearly continuous marching. On the 24th, the New Yorkers fell in for a regiment inspection and received their pay. Flush with cash, Private Cyrille Fountain sent home $75 before he laid down in his shelter tent during "an awful Shower in the night." It continued to rain hard the next morning, and before long and to his consternation, Fountain learned "our Indian did not Send eny [money] home he went down Town & got drunk & Some one Robed him of all his money & a nice 40 dollar watch." July 25th, heavy rains continued. Captain Martin Lennon and a good number from the regiment received passes and went into Washington seeking a break from hardtack and salt pork, and comfortable lodging for the night. Lennon noted, "The city was full of the Sixth Corps, who were wandering about without passes." A good many of the New Yorkers had more than their share of whiskey in the capital. Private Fountain's diary recorded a "good meny Stade there. Officers as well as men got drunk as owels." [10]

On receiving news of Crook's defeat at Kernstown, the Sixth Corps was ordered to march back to the Shenandoah Valley. The 77th left their camp behind Fort Gaines on July 27 at 7 a.m. and marched through Rockville, stopping 20 miles later for the night at dark. Fountain and "Some of the boys ware pretty tyard & sore feet." The day had been hot, and, as George Stevens remembered, "many of the men, weary from long marches, had been forced to fall out, but, most of all, bad whiskey from Washington had demoralized great numbers, and these, with the sick and weary, made up a great crowd of stragglers. The New York regiment was assigned the task of rear guard "urging these inebriated and discouraged ones toward their commands, [it] was not an easy or agreeable" duty. [11]

July 28, the 77th took up the line of march at 5 a.m., passing through Clarksburg, Hyattsburg, and Mourbanna, to within one mile of Frederick. The New York veterans forded Seneca Creek just before going into camp. At daylight, the regiment shook off the urge to sleep and marched through Jefferson, Petersville, Sandy Hook, and Warrenton to Harpers Ferry. The men crossed the river and marched another three miles to Halltown. The Sixth Corps had covered seventy five miles in two days and twenty hours.

In the meantime, Early was determined to ransom northern towns to reimburse the local Jefferson County, West Virginia families who had lost homes and property to "Black Dave" Hunter's men. One such settlement Early chose was Chambersburg, Pennsylvania, in the agricultural-rich Cumberland Valley. Old Jube also burned for revenge of Hunter burning the Virginia Military Institute to the ground in June. By 5 a.m., July 30, McCausland's cavalrymen appeared on the western outskirt of Chambersburg. Several hours later, the southern troopers occupied the town, and McCausland demanded a ransom of $100,000 in gold or 500,000 in U. S. greenbacks. Otherwise, Chambersburg would be set to the torch. The townspeople did not believe the threat and did not raise the money. Around noon Rebel horsemen procured kerosene from one of the stores and started fires which quickly spread through town. Hundreds of buildings were destroyed with nearly one-third of the 6,000 residents rendered homeless and one dead in the flames.

In response to the Confederate raid and the burning of Chambersburg, the Sixth Corps was ordered to re-cross the river at Harpers Ferry. At 2 p.m., while flames spread through the Pennsylvania town, the 77th joined the corps and crowded into the deep valley at Harpers Ferry. George Stevens complained "the day was sultry even for that locality, not a breath of air seemed to be stirring, and the high mountains on either side reflected the heat and kept off the breeze. Into this hot, dusty inclosure among the hills, the whole army poured, and as there was only a single pontoon bridge to serve as an outlet, there was of course great delay. Horses stood harnessed to the cannon or under the saddle, the sweat literally pouring off their sides like rain, while men panted for breath and seemed almost on the point of suffocation." It was late in the night when the 77th crossed over the bridge. [12]

The New Yorkers marched with little rest in the scorching sun and oppressive humidity. Captain Martin Lennon's diary recorded the 77th, "took the road to Frederick – reached Petersville at 4 a.m. – left Petersville at 9 a.m. – the weather terrible hot and roads dusty. There must have been about 100 men lost by sunstroke. We marched through the middle of the day and until 6 p.m., when we reached a small grove, about two miles from Frederick." Private Cyrille Fountain remembered "men fell like Sheep [from] Sun Stroke. Our Company had only 3 guns to stack when we got into Camp. The rest of the Regt was about as bad." Surgeon Stevens observed during the march that, "horses would drop down by the dozens along the road, unable to rise again. Their riders would strip them of their saddles, and leave the worn out steeds to their fate. If, by chance, one of these deserted horses, after a few hours of rest, could muster strength to rise to its feet, he was doomed to be seized by some drummer boy, or other wight of the 'bummer' tribe, mounted and rode till his strength again failed. Then the dismounted bummer would remove his hempen bridle, shoulder his drum, and seek another steed." The exhausted veterans awoke in the morning of August 1 and were relieved that they were not to march that day. Stevens took time out to write a letter to his wife: "We have had a very hard time since we left Washington. We are all very tired from our previous campaign and this one has been one of constant marching day and night. We are completely worn out... In fact our corps is 'played out,' as the army saying is. I have not seen so hard a campaign so far as marching is concerned. We hardly get in camp at night before the bugles call us to go again." [13]

August 2 was a relatively quiet day for the 77th. In the early morning hours, the veterans were ordered to be ready for inspection at

MCKEAN'S SUNDAY SCHOOL BOYS GO TO WAR

10 a.m. Just as the New Yorkers were falling in for inspection, the men received the wholly unwelcome orders to be prepared for yet another march. Before falling out of line, an officer read an order to the regiment prohibiting straggling. After grimly packing up their camp, the New York veterans were relieved that the order to march was countermanded, only to have renewed orders at 7 p.m. to march at 4:20 a.m. in the morning.

At dawn on August 3, the 77th and the Sixth Corps broke camp and marched via Lime-Kiln Switch to Buckeystown, arriving there by 10 a.m. They then crossed the Monocacy River, camping on the south side. The regiment spent a better part of two days there, something almost unheard of after nearly a month of constant marching in the heat and humidity in the Virginia countryside. George Stevens reflected, "The different brigades of the corps were scattered about on the hillsides which bounded the pleasant valley of the Monocacy, where pure fresh air was in abundance, and the men gladly availed themselves of the privilege of bathing in the delightfully clear waters of the river. For a distance of nearly two miles the river was filled with bathers at all hours, except in the hottest part of the day and in the night, and even then some might be seen enjoying the luxury of the bath." Writing to his wife, Stevens asserted that "soldiers take to water as naturally as young ducks." [14]

By an act of Congress, August 4 was designated a day of fasting and prayer. In observance of the proclamation, the 77th participated in a dress parade and a religious service in the morning. In the afternoon, the entire First Division and the 77th's Third Brigade gathered for the funeral honoring Major Ellis of the 49th New York. Known as energetic and brave, he had been wounded at Spotsylvania May 12 during the hellish fighting at the Bloody Angle. A ramrod bore through his left arm and impaled his chest near his heart. After recuperating at home, the beloved major returned to active duty, and was assigned to Brigadier General David Russell's First Division staff. However, ever since his wound "he had complained of severe neuralgic pains in the region of his heart." In the morning, Ellis sent his servant from the tent for a moment, and when the man returned, he had slumped out of his chair dead. Surgeon Stevens, with twenty other surgeons observing, performed an autopsy, which revealed that a sharp splinter of bone from one of Ellis' ribs had pierced his heart. [15]

"The funeral display was the most imposing ever witnessed in any corps of the Army of the Potomac," Stevens recalled. The surgeon described in detail the solemn sublimity of the military honors for Major Ellis:

> The remains were laid in state in a large tent near General Russell's head-quarters, wrapped in a silken flag, and the tent itself was draped in the Stars and Stripes . . . the Forty-ninth New York came as mourners, unarmed, and formed two ranks facing each other near the tent. Then the chaplain of the Forty-Ninth, led in a short religious service . . . while the whole of the First Division was being formed in two parallel lines facing each other, and about eighty paces apart. The service over, a regiment of heavy artillery [2nd Connecticut Heavy Artillery] came to act as escort. The remains, inclosed in a rude coffin . . . were placed in an ambulance, and the funeral cortege began its slow march through the long lines of sunbrowned veterans who stood on either side. First in the procession was the escort, the muskets of the men reversed, preceded by a band playing a solemn dirge. Then the ambulance with the remains, the major's hat, coat and sword laying upon the coffin; then his riderless horse, saddled and bridled, and led by a servant; then the regiment as mourners; and finally General

Russell and the staff of the First division with the division flag, and the staffs of the three brigades of the division, and our Third brigade, Second division, each with its flag, with a concourse of officers, personal friends of him whose remains were thus honored . . . As the cortege proceeded with slow steps between the lines of soldiers, they stood with arms presented, and the colors of the regiments drooped as the procession passed. Thus attended the remains were conveyed to the railroad station . . . where they were placed on board of a train for Washington. [16]

When Grant realized that Jubal Early's presence in the Shenandoah Valley was a permanent menace to the North, he resolved to assemble an overwhelming force against the Confederate raider. The first task, however, was to consolidate under a single leader several geographic commands: Department of West Virginia, Department of the Susquehanna, Department of Washington, and Middle Department. From these various commands, the Middle Military Division was formed. August 4, Grant left City Point and traveled to Monocacy Station to meet with Hunter. Upon his arrival, the Northern commander found Federal troops covering the fields around the railroad stop and Frederick. Grant ordered a general advance of the entire force at Frederick to Halltown, West Virginia, four miles southwest of Harpers Ferry. Hunter was to push up the Valley and to make sure that nothing would be left to invite Early to return. He was to "Take all provisions, forage, and stock wanted for the use of your command; such as cannot be consumed, destroy. It is not desirable that buildings should be destroyed – they should rather be protected; but the people should be informed that so long as the army can subsist among them, recurrences of these raids must be expected, and we are determined to stop them at all hazards." Grant emphasized to Hunter "the object is to drive the enemy south; and to do this you want to keep him always in sight. Be guided in your course by the course he takes." [17]

On August 5, the 77th quietly relaxed in camp, glad not to have orders to march. However, Private Cyrille Fountain complained "just as we layed down at night the orders came to march." After packing up, the veterans of the Sixth Corps proceeded to Monocacy Junction to board trains to Harpers Ferry. Arriving at 1 a.m. at the railroad station, the First and Second Brigades of the Second Division boarded the cars and departed for the Ferry. The 77th's brigade spread their blankets on the ground and laid down until morning. In the meantime, the quartermasters and hospital trains followed rapidly by the wagon roads. [18]

At daylight, the New Yorkers boarded open cars in the rain to Harpers Ferry. The railroad cars groaned under the weight of the soldiers who crowded within and blanketed the roofs. The ride on the rickety train harshly jostled those within. A goodly number jabbed their bayonets in the roofs to steady themselves. But for those on top, this only made the journey more hazardous. Upon arrival of their destination, the veterans gladly put their feet to the ground and marched to Bolivar Heights, where they went into camp. Writing home to Hattie, George Stevens exclaimed, "We have traveled the same [route] from the Monocacy to Harpers Ferry & back so often we have become quite familiar with every part of the road." [19]

The same day, Major General Philip Sheridan, just commissioned commander of all Union forces in the Valley newly minted the Army of the Shenandoah, arrived at Harper's Ferry. The rise of Philip Henry Sheridan during the war was meteoric. The son of Irish immigrants, born March 6, 1831 in Albany, New York, Sheridan grew up in Ohio before entering West Point, where he graduated in the bottom third of the class of 1853. At the outbreak of war, he initially served as chief quartermaster and commissary of the Army of Southwest Missouri. By March 1863, Sheridan was a major general.

What people first noticed when they met Sheridan, was his size. One cavalry officer, in the spring of 1864, estimated that Sheridan stood about five feet, three inches and weighed between 115 and 120 pounds. Colonel Charles S. Wainwright claimed, "He is short, thickset and common Irish-looking. Met in the Bowery, one would certainly set him down as a 'b'boy'; and his dress is in perfect keeping with that character." Sheridan was broad-shouldered, with a large chest, but he possessed unusually short legs. To his men, he was "Little Phil." [20]

Few generals of the war had a head which drew so much attention as did Sheridan. Those who met him inevitably commented that he had a peculiarly shaped head. It appeared somewhat like a flattened minie ball. Dr. A. D. Rockwell, surgeon of the 6th Ohio cavalry, remarked it "was not a common head." Sheridan's soldiers speculated that he had a hard time wearing a hat which explained why in battle he generally held it in his hand. [21]

Sheridan's arrival as commander of the Army of the Shenandoah's 48,000 soldiers boosted morale in the ranks. George Stevens wrote years later, "One thing pleased us at the start. Our new general was visible to the soldiers of his command; wherever we went he was with the column, inhaling the dust, leaving the road for the teams, never a day or two days behind the rest of the army, but always riding by the side of the men. His watchful care of details of the march, his interest in the progress of the trains, and the ready faculty with which he brought order out of confusion when the roads became blockaded, reminded us of our lamented Sedgwick." A. T. Brewer of the 61st Pennsylvania remembered, "He possessed a nervous, sanguine temperament, and when riding over battlefields had a habit in times of excitement of extending his legs to a position nearly at right angles with his body; this was an exhibition of physical energy properly belonging to a person of great mental activity... He had the power possessed only by great generals, of inspiring those under him with limitless confidence in his ability, thus securing devotion of men and hearty cooperation on the part of officers." [22]

August 9 was "an awful warm day." Private Fountain recorded, "we had Dressporade & we had orders read about the Sentence of fellows that had been Court-martialed for Straglin on the march," after which the veterans lounged in camp happy for another day of rest. After weeks of marching, Surgeon Stevens told his wife, "For a wonder I have remained two whole days in the same camp and there seems a fair prospect that we may remain still another day. I can assure you that we appreciate this grand opportunity to rest. I really enjoy this respite very much." The doctor spent the day "in making calls upon my friends. Among others I called upon Genl. Getty & spent an hour with him very pleasantly. The general told me a new name for our Corps. He calls it 'Harpers Weekly' referring to our weekly visits to this place." [23]

The 77th's rest was curtailed by orders received late in the day to prepare for yet another march. Sheridan ordered a general forward movement on the morning of the 10th. The Yankee's objective was Berryville, fourteen miles south of Halltown and a dozen miles east of Winchester. With Early's army at Bunker Hill, Sheridan, by moving to Berryville, positioned his force beyond Early's right and rear with a direct path to Winchester. To protect his supply to the upper Valley and to prevent being caught between the Army of the Shenandoah and the Potomac River, Early would have to withdraw, most likely beyond Winchester. In one day's march, then, Sheridan could rid the lower Valley, north of Winchester, of the Southerners.

McKEAN'S SUNDAY SCHOOL BOYS GO TO WAR

Revelry sounded at 4 a.m. and within an hour the 77th left their camp and marched with the Six Corps column. As the sun rose over the Blue Ridge, beads of sweat trickled down the New Yorkers' faces. Cyrille Fountain complained "it was a horrible warm day" and "men fell like flyes" from sunstroke. Captain Martin Lennon recorded, "One man of the Seventh Minnesota Volunteers was buried on the march – he having died on the march." Countless others lay prostrate along the roadside. Adding to their hardship was the want of water. George Stevens wrote, "The turnpike along which we marched was parallel with a fine stream of water on either side, but the water was so far distant as to be useless to the soldiers" At some point, the column came upon a large spring that was underneath a huge willow tree. The crystal clear water poured out from a fissure in the rock and formed a large brook. Stevens took note that "Soldiers . . . covered the great rocks, crowded the grove, and for many yards around a dense mass of men pressed to get near the tempting fountain . . . No one can know with what delight the soldiers quaffed the sparkling fluid from their sooty coffee pots, who has not suffered the torture of extreme thirst." [24]

At length, the New York veterans passed through Charlestown where John Brown was executed, and marched by the courthouse where he was convicted of treason, and the jail from which he was led to execution. "How had all things changed!" Stevens exclaimed. "The people who stood about the gallows of John Brown, and gnashed their teeth in bitter hatred, were now themselves guilty of treason." The courthouse and the jail were now in ruins. As Sheridan's army marched through the streets, every band and every drum corps played "John Brown's body lies mouldering in the grave." The surgeon stated "that whenever our army or any part of it had occasion to pass through this town, the bands always struck up this air, as if to taunt the inhabitants with the memory of their victim, and played it from one limit of the town to the other." In Stevens' mind, "John Brown was revenged!" [25]

The 77th halted miles later at the Clifton farm. The soldiers gathered firewood, and soon flickering flames were boiling their coffee. Private Fountain, and others "went forigeing and got lot of Sheeps & honey." After the feast of mutton and the sweetness of honey, the New Yorkers spent another night under the "beautiful canopy of heaven with its mottled clouds and twinkling stars and flying meteors, for our tent." [26]

The Union advance continued throughout August 11 and 12, taking the Winchester Turnpike on the 11th to within five miles of Winchester when they turned west, and marching through Middletown and Newton, halting at Cedar Creek. Both days, Private Fountain recorded, were "awful warm" and "quite a lot of men fell dead in the road by being Sunstroke." Overheated, Private John T. Mosher (Co. H) early fell behind and by evening could not go on. Mosher obtained permission to ride in an ambulance of the First Division. During the night, the sun struck private was found to be dying. Dr. Crehore of the First Division, and one of his assistants, tended to him, but Mosher died before morning. A grave was dug, "and a few of his comrades stood around it while he was lowered to his bed of earth, wrapped in his blanket." Chaplain Norman Fox "offered a brief prayer; his fellows in arms fired a parting salute, and we left him to sleep in the valley." [27]

With Sheridan threatening the Confederate flank and rear, Early fell back to Fisher's Hill, a steep bluff which shadowed the village of Strasburg, a "dingy, dilapidated village," one Yankee thought. By nightfall of August 12, the two enemies camped only four miles apart, with the Federals bivouacked along Cedar Creek south of Middletown, and the Confederates bedded down on Fisher's Hill. Picket outposts punctuated the ground between the two armies within gunshot range of each other. [28]

While Sheridan's army was settled on the north bank of Cedar Creek, Little Phil received conflicting reports that the Confederate First Corps had reached the valley. If these Rebels had entered the Shenandoah, particularly if they had come in by Front Royal beyond the Union left flank, Sheridan's troops were in a precarious position with their extended supply line. The evening of August 14, the Union commander received confirmation from Grant that "it is now certain two divisions of infantry have gone to Early, and some cavalry and twenty pieces of artillery." In fact, a strong Confederate force dispatched by Lee from Petersburg under Lieutenant General Richard H. Anderson was arriving at Front Royal at the northern end of the Luray Valley. Sheridan immediately decided to retreat to Halltown where he could form a defensive line where a smaller number of troops could hold a greater number. The next day, the Army of the Shenandoah received orders to march. August 15, Emory's Nineteenth Corps set out for Winchester at 11 p.m. Crook's command and the Sixth Corps were ordered to march at 8 p.m. on the 16th. [29]

The 77th received their orders to march at dark, and fell into line with the Sixth Corps in the direction of Winchester at 10 p.m. Fully accustomed to long, grueling marches, the veterans forged ahead through the night, and reached Winchester at 7 a.m. Surgeon Stevens looked on as "the rebel women came out by the hundreds to rejoice at our retreat." Private Fountain recorded that the rejoicing women were met with "Bands playing & Collars flying" as the blue column picked up their step passing through the Southern town. Foreshadowing the destruction to come to the Valley, The New Yorkers then "Stopt by a griss mill & burned the mill" before arriving at Clifton farm for the night. [30]

A hard rain blew into the Valley during the night of August 17-18, and continued intermittently through the 20th. The 77th left Clifton at 5 a.m. along with the Sixth Corps. The rain-soaked veterans glumly marched sixteen miles in the deluge. At Berryville, Captain Martin Lennon and his comrades saw the charred remains from John Mosby's Raiders lightning strike a day earlier on the Union supply train "where one hundred and forty wagons were burned to the ground when the army was at Strasburg." The regiment's soldiers were sorely offended with word that "Old men, women and children, joined in the work of destruction, setting fire to the wagons, and carrying off whatever articles they could easily remove from them." By nightfall, the New Yorkers made their beds one mile from Charlestown. With their rations nearly depleted, Cyrille Fountain and a number of his comrades in arms promptly set out to "forige Sheeps honey and corn." [31]

August 21, the Sixth Corps remained in the vicinity of Charlestown, with the 77th's Second Division south of the Harpers Ferry – Winchester Turnpike. Without warning at 9 a.m., during morning inspection, "we found shells pitching into our camp among the standing tents, and bullets whistling among the trees that afforded us shelter from the sun." Swarms of Confederate skirmishers came into view over a nearby ridge, sending Union pickets fleeing back into camp ahead of them. [32]

In the midst of the chaos of officers shouting orders and the staccato of enemy musketry, Colonel Lewis Grant formed his Vermont Brigade into line as George Getty rode up and ordered the division's picket line reestablished. The Green Mountain Boys advanced through some woods and deployed in the open, with the 3rd, 4th, and 6th Vermont in loose skirmish formation, and the 2nd, 5th, and 11th Vermont behind them in line of battle. Charging the enemy, the Vermonters pushed the butternuts back over the ridge, and over another ridge after that. Companies and regiments drifted from each other during the assault to the point where the New England soldiers now formed a mile long skirmish line. They took cover behind trees, rocks, and every rise available, firing at will at the Confederates. At darkness, the Rebels withdrew. The Vermonters expended 56,000 rounds that day and lost 24 killed and 100 wounded. The 77th was then detailed to the skirmish line and busied themselves building breastworks. The unlucky Private Benjamin Wood (Co. A) strayed too far beyond the pickets and was captured, and seven months later paroled at East Bridge, North Carolina. [33]

August 22, the 77th and the Army of the Shenandoah filed into their old entrenchments. Early's soldiers trailed the retreating Federals and occupied Charlestown that same day. Sheridan's withdrawal from Cedar Creek to Halltown planted in Old Jube's mind the dangerous notion that his opponent "possessed excessive caution which amounted to timidity." His mission continued to be posing as a threat Maryland and Pennsylvania, and preventing the use of the Baltimore & Ohio Railroad, and the Chesapeake and Ohio Canal, as well as keeping a large a force as possible from Grant's army to defend the nation's capital. However, to accomplish these goals, threatened Early's lines of communication up the Valley and required his men to harvest and grind their subsistence in an area already suffering from the Yankee's destruction. [34]

On August 25 and 26, while Anderson's troops held the works at Charlestown, Early took his soldiers up the Potomac River to feign another invasion of Maryland and Pennsylvania was imminent. Early hoped Sheridan would take the bait and send part of the Army of the Shenandoah across the Potomac. But Sheridan was unclear about conflicting intelligence reports of Rebel reinforcements, and held his troops in the Federal lines. On the 27th, Early gave up the ruse of an invasion and reconcentrated his force at Bunker Hill. Sheridan would follow the next day, reoccupying Charlestown.

The evening of August 27, the 77th received orders at 10 p.m. to march at daylight. Private Fountain recorded in his diary, "We got up this morning at 3 o clock, got our breakfast & packed up everything. we marched at 8. we marched a few miles & haulted for dinner. we Started again & marched to Charles Town & Stopt for the night." As the 77th settled in its bivouac, Captain Martin Lennon perhaps spoke for the New Yorkers, "Don't know where the enemy are, and don't want to." [35]

Captain Frederick Smith (L. Tom Perry Special Collections)

August 29 – September 2, the 77th finally had a respite from nearly two months of continual marches. Relaxing in camp, Captain Lennon reflected, "I like this better than either marching or fighting." The regiment welcomed eight new recruits from New York City, formed for inspection, received mail and their pay was doled out. On the 2nd, the court martial sentence against an officer of the 77th took place. Sixty one year old Captain Frederick Smith (Co. B) "was found guilty of leaving the regiment & going to Harpers Ferry, getting drunk with a private soldier, forging passes for himself & the soldier & insulting people. The when he was arrested he refused to tell his regiment or division, but his [Greek] Cross betrayed him." Major General Getty ordered the guilty captain drummed out of the service. As the entire Third Brigade was forming to witness the execution of the sentence, Surgeon Stevens finished a letter to his wife and observed, "It is the most severe sentence ever executed in this division." [36]

On September 3, Sheridan marched his force toward Berryville. Reveille sounded at 4 a.m. in the 77th's camp. The veteran New Yorkers fell in and stacked arms at daylight. The regiment moved out toward Clifton at 8 a.m., halting after marching some two miles, where Captain Martin Lennon's Company I and five other companies were sent out as flankers. Twelve hours later, the 77th reached Clifton and made camp. Throughout the 4th, the Yankees erected field works which extended from Berryville to Summit Point, a distance of eight miles. Early probed Sheridan's new lines on the 4th and 5th, before retiring to the vicinity of Winchester. Torrential rain began pelting the veteran soldiers the night of the 5th and continued for several days. Moribund, Captain Lennon wrote in his diary, "Heavy rain storms, which nearly flooded our tents, and running in streams through some of them . . . Awoke this morning and found myself laying in water about an inch deep . . . Rain continues all day. If it don't give a man a fit of the blues to sit humped up in a dog tent, what does I should like to know?" The rains halted movement, and from the 6th until the 18th, the two armies remained stationary, divided by the Opequon Creek. [37]

September 14, with Sheridan remaining on the defensive, Early and Anderson decided to return the First Corps troops to Petersburg. Most likely, the two commanders concluded that Lee had more need of Kershaw and the artillery battalion than Early. Anderson wasted no time to set out for Petersburg. At sunrise, September 15, the First Corps departed Winchester, and marched south up the Pike. Nightfall they bivouacked on the North Fork of the Shenandoah River opposite Buckton. For the next three days, the Confederates moved at sunrise, through Front royal, up the Luray Valley and out of the Shenandoah at Thornton's Gap. They halted on the 18th two miles east of Woodville in the Virginia Piedmont.

September 16, Grant traveled from the stalemate at Petersburg to Charlestown to meet with Sheridan. For the General-in-Chief, the time had come for Sheridan to drive the Confederates out of the Valley and burn the crops. The two soldiers from the West met alone under a large oak tree. Little Phil did most of the talking, Grant most of the listening. Sheridan told his superior that he could "whip them." Grant only asked if he could advance within four days hence. "Oh, yes," Sheridan exclaimed. That was enough for Grant, and he simply said, "Go in." [38]

Intelligence of Anderson's troops leaving the Valley, coupled with a dispatch from William Averell that a Confederate cavalry brigade and the infantry divisions of Rodes and Gordon were enroute to Martinsburg, fired Sheridan. Early had committed a serious blunder by dividing his army. Little Phil decided to crush Ramseur's and Gabriel Wharton's divisions before the Southerners could regroup. The Federal commander planned to hit Early's two divisions at Winchester, the scene of two previous Civil War battles. The Army of the Shenandoah would move at 2 a.m. on the 19th.

With William Jackson's horsemen in the lead, Rodes and Gordon left Bunker Hill at daybreak, arriving at Martinsburg about 9 p.m. Early, who accompanied the column, learned that Grant met with Sheridan September 16th. Old Jube knew for the Union commander to come to the Valley from City Point, some movement from

Sheridan was imminent. The Southern general ordered a forced return march back up the Valley Pike. By nightfall, Rode's soldiers encamped at Stephenson's Depot, Gordon's at Bunker Hill, with orders to march at dawn for Stephenson's. Early had quickly reconcentrated his army; Gordon lay fourteen miles north of Ramseur, whose three brigades bivouacked east of Winchester across the road to Berryville.

September 18, a supply train arrived from Harpers Ferry, and quartermasters dispersed ammunition and rations to the Yankee regiments. Orders traveled down the chain of command to send all baggage to the rear and to be ready to march at 2 a.m. The shelter tents were taken down, knapsacks were filled; rifles and ammunition boxes received a final inspection. In the midst of the feverish activity, Cyrille Fountain took time to note in his diary, "the boys mistrust that Some thing is going on wrong. things look like a fight." [39]

The general call to arms resounded from brigades to regiments at 1 a.m., September 19. The 77th stirred from their bivouac, with the New Yorkers stretching their limbs, striking their tents, and boiling coffee. One hour later, in compliance with Sheridan's orders, James H. Wilson's horsemen mounted and headed westward on the Berryville Pike toward Openquon Creek. Wesley Merritt's troopers, under the personal direction of A. T. A. Torbert, shortly followed slanting northwestward toward the Opequon's lower fords. At 2 a.m., the Sixth Corps, with the 77th's Third Brigade in the vanguard, led the infantry of the Army of the Shenandoah toward the creek. The veterans trod along each side of the pike while the wagon train and artillery units rolled upon the road.

Wilson's cavalrymen arrived opposite Spout Spring or the Berryville crossing of the Opequon before 4 a.m. Across the ford loomed the entrance to Berryville Canyon through which the pike passed. Wilson's orders instructed that his division clear the canyon and seize a foothold on the open ground beyond the narrow ravine. Accordingly, Brigadier General John B. McIntosh deployed his leading regiments, the 2nd and 5th New York Cavalry, for the attack with the 18th Pennsylvania Cavalry formed in their rear as support. Captain Charles H. Pierce's Batteries B and L, 2nd United States Horse Artillery, readied to follow the charging troopers. McIntosh's remaining three regiments and Brigadier General George H. Chapman's brigade waited in the rear.

Captain Walter C. Hull's 2nd New York Cavalry dove into the two-mile long canyon. The front of the assault column, narrowed by the wooded slopes of the steep ravine, struck Confederate pickets at the western entrance. The surprised butternuts, the 23rd North Carolina under Colonel Charles C. Blackmall, instantly fled to the rear before the Northerners. The North Carolinians, however, regrouped a formed a slow fighting withdrawal against Hull's troopers, now strengthened by Major Abram H. Krom's 5th. In the feint light of dawn, the blue-clad Yankees forged ahead out of the canyon.

The North Carolinians fell back upon their brigade, which was several hundred yards from the mouth of canyon. Commanding the brigade, Brigadier General Robert A. Johnston sent a courier to inform division commander, Dodson Ramseur, of the attack, and deployed his command of five North Carolina regiments. Ramseur responded immediately to Johnston's report and to the increasing rattle of musketry. He dispatched Brigadier General John Pegram's Virginians forward to shore up Johnston's left flank and front. Pegram led his soldiers out from his position in a large tract of woods which extended to Red Run north of the Berryville Pike, and began to align his brigade on Johnston's left rear. Meanwhile, Johnston's Tar Heels skirmished with Wilson's dismounted troopers. It was now nearly 6 a.m.

Silhouetted by the rising sun, the New York cavalry advanced. Johnston's men blunted the charge with a well-aimed volley. Behind Johnston, a battery supported the Confederate infantry with shell fire. The New Yorkers retreated toward the canyon, where McIntosh had deployed the 18th Pennsylvania Cavalry and Pierce's two unlimbered batteries. The battered 2nd and 5th New York Cavalry regrouped while the Pennsylvanians advanced in a mounted charge. Southern fire twice staggered the cavalrymen, seriously wounding McIntosh. The Pennsylvanians regrouped and, supported by the New Yorkers and Pierce's guns, charged the enemy nearly routing Pegram's and Johnston's men. Ramseur ordered the 57th North Carolina from Brigadier General Archibald C. Godwin's brigade forward to stabilize the shaken line. Ramseur was able to rally his broken brigades in some woods bordering the pike only 500 feet behind their lines. The mingled Confederate commands repulsed the pursuing Northerners, who withdrew to the ground near the gorge.

Sometime before 7 a.m., the action was waning when Sheridan and his staff rode on to the field. He halted upon a steep elevation on J. A. Eversole's farm, near the mouth of the canyon, and established his headquarters. About the same time, riding ahead of the regiment, George Stevens "galloped up to the brow of the hill," where Sheridan stood and "looked over the roughly uneven country where shortly was to be fought a most notable battle." Little Phil took no notice of Stevens as he scanned the terrain. The broad-chested commander carefully examined the ground and selected positions for his infantry, who were then entering into the deep ravine. But, there would be an unforeseen delay of more than two hours before the van of his infantry debouched from the west side of the canyon.[40]

Back at Spout Spring, Sheridan's plan for a prompt advance lay foiled by the entanglement of wagons and artillery. While Wilson combated Ramseur, Horatio Wright funneled his infantry into the canyon. The 77th with its Third Brigade entered the gorge about the same time Little Phil established his headquarters. James Rickett's Third division followed Getty's three brigades, and splashed across the Openquon about 7 a.m. Behind them on the pike came Wright's artillery and wagons followed by his First Division under David Russell. Two miles from the ford, William Emory's two Nineteenth Corps divisions lounged in the fields, watching the wagons and Russell's soldiers pass.

As instructed by Sheridan, Emory was to report to Wright upon his corps arrival at the crossing. Emory met Wright at Spout Spring and learned that his men had to wait until the Sixth Corps passed. But as the long line of wagons and cannon slowly rumbled by, Emory exploded and demanded that Wright clear the road and the ford for the Nineteenth Corps. Wright refused, infuriating the exasperated Emory who ordered his infantry to advance, bypassing the wagons. It was nearly 9 a.m. when Russell's division was entering the canyon.

As the 77th approached the western mouth of the canyon along the Berryville Pike, Surgeon Stevens remarked, "we were warned of the active work we might expect in front, as we saw cavalrymen coming to the rear, some leading their wounded horses, others with their heads bound in bloody handkerchiefs, some with arms hanging in slings, others borne on litters." Beneath the shadow of a large tree just off the pike "was gathered a little group of boys in blue, performing the last acts of kindness to a comrade in whom the vital spark was almost extinguished, and a surgeon bending over the dying soldier striving to render less painful the few lingering moments of life." [41]

From Eversole's hill, Sheridan impatiently watched the plodding Federal deployment. When Getty's leading brigade, Bidwell's Third Brigade, exited the deep ravine, he ordered it southward to form his left flank where they were immediately targeted by Rebel cannon and snipers. Bidwell deployed his men in a cornfield on his right regiment, the 122nd New York. To the left of the 122nd, were the 43rd New York, 49th New York, and the 7th Maine. The brigadier ordered the 61st Pennsylvania across Abraham's Creek to guard his left, while the 77th served as support. Lieutenant Colonel Winsor French reported, we "advanced through a cornfield and took position in an old road on the crest of a hill . . . somewhat protected from the enemy's fire, which was quite severe, by temporary breastworks taken from the enemy by Wilson's cavalrymen, which we relieved. I at once detailed twenty good shots to go a little in advance, with orders to fire upon the enemy's pieces of artillery, and which were annoying to us, and also to act as sharpshooters to keep down those of the enemy who were constantly picking off my officers and men, [and they], together . . . in a measure kept the two pieces silent." However, "There were two other pieces of the enemy's artillery in a ravine running between the First and Third Brigades, and so far in front as to be out of rifle reach, which gave us trouble." Here "it was Lieuts. Ross, Gillis, VanDerwerker and Worden, were wounded, all slightly, or at least not dangerously." Hunkered down in the cornfield, French, "dreaded to advance, for our front was a wide-open field, with no protection whatever, and across the skirt of a wood, the enemy were in line, and their artillery fire was very severe." [42]

As the blue infantry continued to pass through the canyon and deploy west of the gorge, Jubal Early responded swiftly to Wilson's cavalry attack. He received a message of Wilson's assault around daybreak at the Stephenson's Depot, five miles north of Winchester where he had his headquarters the night of September 18, and where Robert E. Rodes's division was bivouacked. Old Jube ordered Rodes' men to advance and then rode for Ramseur's line. The Southerner recognized that this Federal movement imperiled his army. When the stoop-shouldered Early found Ramseur, he quickly recognized that Sheridan's movement threatened his communications, and the defeat of his army. Accordingly, he ordered a re-concentration of his forces.

Rodes' four brigades (commanded by brigadiers Bryan Grimes, William R. Cox, Philip Cook, and Cullen A. Battle) were already set to march when Early's orders arrived. Between 9 a.m. and 10 a.m., as Sixth Corps soldiers filed out of the canyon, Grimes' brigade passed Winchester on the east and deployed. Rodes aligned his three remaining brigades in open fields and a patch of woods 300 to 400 yards north and west from Ramseur's left. Cook anchored the division's left; behind a stone wall, Cox held the center, and Grimes manned the right. Battle's Alabamians acted as a reserve. The division was book-cased on the left and right by Lieutenant Braxton's artillery battalion. Rodes' sharpshooters stepped forward to harass Yankees coming on to the field.

When Rodes completed his deployment, the van of Early's second division, commanded by Major General John B. Gordon, approached the field. Gordon hastened his men to the sound of cannon and musketry. Gordon soon left the Valley Pike and marched across the fields. Before 10 a.m., Gordon arrived, his soldiers and Rodes' bringing slightly over 5,000 muskets to Old Jube's line.

Gordon's lines extended over the Hackwood farm, built in 1777 by Revolutionary War General John Smith and owned in 1864 by Lewis P. Hartman. William Terry's Virginians formed the division's right front. Zebulon York's Louisianans held Gordon's center on Terry's left. Edmund Atkinson's Georgians stretched the line through the trees to the country lane which crossed the Hackwood farm. North of the lane, seven guns of Braxton's battalion guarded Gordon's left and covered the ground to Red Bud Run. Early's re-concentration of his forces was completed well over an hour before the coordinated Union attack.

Early consolidated his line by pulling back Ramseur when Rodes and Gordon came on the field. Ramseur's lines now overlapped the Berryville Pike around a barn and farmhouse owned by Enos Dinkle, Sr. The Confederate front stretched along a largely wooded plateau between Abraham's Creek and Red Bud Run. On Jubal's northern flank, across Red Bud Run, six cannon of Major Breathed's Battalion of Stuart's Horse Artillery were posted. From their position, the gunners could sweep the fronts of Rodes and Gordon with an oblique fire.

Early's soldiers in their line watched across the intervening ground the Yankee columns maneuver into position. Separating the two enemies was eleven hundred yards of undulating ground, consisting of pasture and ripened corn, belts of timber overgrown with underbrush traversed by deep ravines almost stripped of timber. For the Union soldiers the ascent would be gradual until they neared the plateau where the Rebels waited. Only Ramseur's brigades and their sharpshooters and skirmishers were visible from the Yankee lines.

Shortly after 10 a.m., Wright's Sixth Corps were in their appointed position. Getty's Second Division line extended from Abraham's Creek to the Berryville Pike. Bidwell's brigade formed in a cornfield with its left across the creek, where it eventually connected with Wilson's troopers. Brigadier General Wheaton's First Brigade aligned itself on Bidwell's right. Colonel James M. Warner's Green Mountain Brigade, forming on Wheaton's right, completed the division front to the Pike. Rickett's two brigades extended the front. Colonel William Emerson's command formed under the crest of a hill and deployed next to the Pike, and Colonel J. Warren Keifer's brigade manned the division's right. Wright's remaining division, under Russell, filed into position as support for Getty and Rickett's. Covering the expanse from Abraham's Creek and the Berryvillle Pike, Getty's division was formed a single line

Emory's Nineteenth Corps soon appeared and began filing into line. Cuvier Grover's leading division slanted to the right beyond Ricketts and entered a large stand of trees (hereafter designated as the First Woods). Grover aligned his four brigades into two lines. William Dwight's two brigades followed Grover's infantrymen into the woods. The First Division general sent a strong line of skirmishers along Red Bud Run. Sheltered by the trees and not under Confederate artillery fire, Grover's and Dwight's soldiers relaxed and cooked their midday meal.

With his infantry finally in position, Sheridan dispatched orders for a coordinated attack by the Sixth and Nineteenth Corps. Up and down the Federal line the instructions called for the assault to commence with the firing of a single cannon, brigades to charge, guiding on the Berryville Pike. The veterans of the 77th steeled themselves for the bloody carnage certain to come with the charge across open ground. "Awaiting orders!" as one Union soldier described this moment. "That is the time that tries the courage of the bravest . . . to stand at a safe distance, though within easy sight and hearing of the conflict, ready, expectant, every nerve sprung, awaiting the word of command to march into a hailstorm of death, that is the crucial test. It is at such a time that all the mental struggle involved in a soldier's death is undergone." [43]

At 11:40 a.m., a single Federal cannon sounded. By nightfall, nearly 8,700 Yankees and Rebels would be numbered as dead, wounded, and missing.

Both Getty and Ricketts advanced at the firing of the signal gun. From his vantage at Eversole's hill, George Stevens thought, "It was an imposing spectacle to watch that line of battle . . . as it moved toward the rebel lines, the men as composed as though on parade, the line straight and compact, the various division, brigade, and regimental flags floating gaily in the sunlight . . . Onward, through the cornfields and over the grassy knolls, now descending into a ravine and now rising upon the open plain, where the rebel artillery swept with terrible effect, the long line pressed forward, regardless of the destructive fire that constantly thinned our ranks." Stevens' attention was further directed the human wreckage that followed: "At every step forward, men were dropping, dropping; some dead, some mortally hurt, and some with slight wounds. Now on this side, now on that they fell; still the line swept forward, leaving the ground behind it covered with the victims." [44]

Not long before Wright and Emory advanced, Lieutenant Colonel Winsor French "was ordered to throw out skirmishers, connecting with the First Brigade [Wheaton's] on the right, which rested in a deep ravine . . . and extending left to the road in which we were lying." French deployed four companies "under the charge of Major Babcock, and the six remaining companies moved so as to give them support." Keeping in connection with Wheaton's brigade, the 77th's "skirmishers moved forward and in good style, closely followed by the six companies in line." The lieutenant colonel reported, "The enemy's [Ramseur's division] fire of artillery and musketry were very severe, their infantry holding a strong position on the crest of a hill and behind a fence directly in front." Soon, however, "their infantry broke and ran, leaving the open field clear for 500 yards to a piece of woods, to which we quickly advanced, keeping good connection with the First Brigade." In advancing, Wheaton's mixed brigade changed direction to the left, compelling French to do the same. When the 77th reached the woods, Wheaton's Pennsylvanians and New Yorkers slowly fell back, but owing to the conformation of the line the lieutenant colonel was able to keep the 77th's position and line intact. In the meantime, Bidwell summoned McKnight's Battery M, 5th United States Artillery forward for artillery support. [45]

Warner's Green Mountain Boys, on Wheaton's right, faced much stiffer resistance. Outdistancing Wheaton's soldiers initially, the Vermonters reached a ravine, on whose opposite crest lie butternut sharpshooters. The brigade dropped to the ground as the Rebels opened fire. At this point, the pike veered to the left, and under orders to guide on the road, the Vermonters plunged into the ravine. The miry hollow, with steep slopes covered with hedge high evergreens, provided a small element of protection. But a number of Confederates swung around Getty's right flank and enfiladed Warner's brigade. Unable to retreat, the Green Mountain soldiers took to the clusters of evergreens, opened fire for the first time that day and waited for Ricketts' attack to close up on their right.

Close to 12:30 p.m., acrid smoke hung low to the ground and obscured a large portion of the field, choking the wounded lying on the ground in cornfields and hollows. The two brigades of Ricketts' division encountered trouble immediately. Assigned the critical task of guiding the Federal assault and maintaining an unbroken front with Getty on the left and the Nineteenth Corps on the right, Ricketts' soldiers struggled against a perfect storm of shot and shell from Confederate gunners. Colonel Emerson, on the left, adjoining the Berryville Pike, barely reached his skirmish line before the exploding shells halted the advance. Nevertheless, the brigade formed in two battle lines, veered left and into the ravine east of Warner's Vermonters.

Keifer's brigade on Emerson's right advanced into the broken ground of Ash Hollow. The scarred terrain provided an element of protection for Keifer's men as they fumbled forward. The Union colonel conformed his line to Emerson's leftward shift, but lost connection with Emory's Nineteenth Corps, creating a dangerous gap in Sheridan's front. Little Phil's orders to advance along the Berryville Pike were seriously flawed, for 600 yards beyond the main Federal line, the pike angled sharply to the south, veering toward Enos Dinkle's farm.

When Keifer's first line of battle came abreast Emerson's brigade, the division charged up the hill which rose ninety feet above the Yankees. Warner, then Wheaton, then the 77th's brigade pressed forward. Ramseur's North Carolinians and Virginians let go with a staggering volley, but the Union veterans leaned forward into the storm of bullets and continued to advance. Emerson's soldiers punctured the Confederate center at the Dinkle farm. Squads of Rebels fought from behind Dinkle's barn before being driven off by Emerson's and Keifer's men. Ramseur's division spilled back westward toward Winchester. Planted 1,000 yards west of Dinkle's barn in a stand of oaks around Josiah Baker's home, Major Kirkpatrick's Amherst Battery threw shells into the Northerners with their newly forged cannon from Tredegar Iron Works.

"Thus far," George Stevens thought, "all had gone well," as Getty's and Ricketts' divisions rimmed the Dinkle farm. But the crescendo of musketry rolling from the north bespoke disaster. "Now our hearts were sick as we looked far to the right and saw the Nineteenth corps and our Third Division falling back, back, back the grape and canister of the hostile cannon crashing through the now disordered ranks, and the exalting rebels following with wild yells of victory." [46]

The divisions of Brigadier Generals Curvier Grover and William Dwight launched their attack at the same time the Sixth Corps stepped off after the signal gun fired. John Brown Gordon's three-brigade division of Georgians, Virginians, and Louisianans seemed demon possessed as they counterattacked and wrecked the Nineteenth Corps divisions scattering them rearward. About the same time, Robert E. Rodes sent his soldiers into the gaping hole between the Sixth and Nineteenth Corps. Cullen Battle's Alabama brigade came out of the woods like a whirlwind sweeping Keifer's regiments to the rear. The Alabamans pressed their advantage, disintegrating Ricketts' entire line. Keifer and Emerson's troops scrambled off the plateau in a confused mass. The 77th's division also abandoned the ridge, but the veterans maintained a loosely organized withdrawal.

Phil Sheridan and Horatio Wright witnessed the Confederate counterattack from Eversole's hill, the collapse of the Union line and the resultant rout. The Army of the Shenandoah faced certain defeat, if not destruction, and Little Phil reacted immediately. He ordered Wright's remaining division under Brigadier General David A. Russell into the breach. As Wright later reported, "the fate of the day depended on the employment of this force." [47]

In the Federal center, Battery E, 5th Maine Artillery and the 1st New York Independent Battery stubbornly maintained their position, firing over the heads of the routed blue-uniformed fugitives. Already two of Russell's brigades were double-quicking toward the guns. The West Pointer had his command on the move before Sheridan's orders, through Wright, reached him. Lieutenant Colonel Edward L. Campbell placed his three New Jersey regiments across the Berryville Pike. To his right, Colonel Oliver Edwards deployed his four regiments and two battalions. While personally overseeing the maneuver, Russell caught a minie ball in the left breast, but refused to leave the field. His two brigades stepped into the ravine and scrambled up the opposite hill. Unseen before them, was Rodes' entire division, Brigadier General Bryan Grimes in command after a shell exploded above Rodes, killing him instantly, his skull shattered.

While Cullen Battle's Alabamians tore into Ricketts' men, the other three Confederate brigades advanced. Grimes deployed his

MCKEAN'S SUNDAY SCHOOL BOYS GO TO WAR

North Carolinians beyond Battle's right. Brigadier General William R. Cox and his Tar Heels extended Battle's left, and Brigadier General Philip Cook's Georgians completed the line of battle. For 30 minutes a torrid, stand up musketry raged between the two enemies. In the first few minutes of the desperate struggle, the beloved Russell, like Rodes earlier in the day, died instantly from an exploding shell which ripped into his heart.

Along the threatened Federal front, amid the dying and wounded, the Confederate division nevertheless pushed forward. Still, Campbell's and Edward's bedeviled veterans blunted their thrust. Suddenly, beyond the Union right, advancing obliquely across their front, Russell's third brigade, under Brigadier General Emory Upton, charged.

When Russell ordered his division forward, he sent Upton's brigade into the woods at the edge of Ash Hollow, where Emory's routed command was regrouping. His regiments extended beyond the left of Grimes' division at an oblique angle. Upton ordered bayonets fixed and not to fire until the he commanded. When the charging Rebels closed to within 200 yards, he shouted, "Ready, aim, fire!" A volley of musketry sliced into Cook's stunned Georgians. Upon then commanded, "Forward, charge!" and his men stormed from the hidden position. Grimes' division's left crumbled, sending Confederates scurrying to the rear. Campbell and Edward added their brigades to the attack. The graybacks withdrew to their original position, regrouped and, once again fended off the Federals. Ricketts' division disengaged and, with Gordon's and Emory's fighting drawing down to an end, the action subsided to desultory firing between skirmishers. Both armies for now had had enough. [48]

Back on Eversole's hill, Sheridan turned to his West Point roommate and close friend, Brevet Major General George Crook, and told him to advance his two divisions of the Army of West Virginia. Crook sent his aides at a gallop eastward through the Berryville Canyon. The time had passed noon. Russell's division was locked in a dance of death with Rodes when Crook's couriers entered the gorge, riding toward Opequon Creek.

The aides found Isaac Duval's and Joseph Thoburn's soldiers, nearly 6,000, and Captain Henry A. DuPont's Artillery Brigade, resting on the eastern bank of the creek. Veterans of many forced marches, the men soon shifted into marching ranks. With Duval's men in the lead, the Army of West Virginia crossed the Opequon. Entering the narrow canyon, Crook's infantrymen encountered the human wreckage and material debris which had hampered Emory's march and had by the early minutes of the afternoon increased in volume. Besides numerous wounded and cowardly skulkers covering the banks, ambulances and ammunition wagons were hopelessly tangled into one log jam on the road. Like the Nineteenth Corps, Crook's veterans made their way along the ravine's sides.

At approximately 12:30 p.m., Early ordered Breckinridge, with Gabriel Wharton's 1,800 infantrymen and Floyd King's artillery battalion, to Winchester. While the battle in full force raged at Winchester, Jubal Early decided he needed Breckinridge's command to bolster the Second Corps. He had drawn upon every reserve he possessed into the counterattack against the Federal infantry. Victory or defeat would be decided on the plateau east of Winchester, and Old Jube needed every musket and cannon he could gather.

A little less than two hours had passed since Russell's division hammered the counterattack of Rodes' division to a halt and Sheridan instructed Crook to bring his two divisions on to the field. In the interim, the two bloodied enemies clung to the same position they held when the fighting subsided and then died.

Emory's shaken Nineteenth Corps, its two divisions badly mixed, had reassembled a battle line at the edge of the First Woods. To the south, Wright had managed to regroup his three divisions along the base and crest of Ash Hollow to Abraham's Creek, the 77th's Third Brigade forming on the left of the Sixth Corps. Across the cornfields and pastures carpeted by the wounded and dying, Early's Confederates, except for Ramseur's division, maintained their original position. Gordon's division held the Second Woods; Rodes' veterans, Grimes now commanding, remained in the trees from which they had launched their counterattack; and Ramseur's soldiers, driven from the Dinkle farm, were aligned on Grime's right flank.

As Crook's men cleared the canyon, Sheridan conferred with the general and directed the Ohioan to extend Emory's flank along Red Bud Run. The passage through the gorge had taken over an hour, and it was nearly 2 p.m. when the two divisions and DuPont's batteries angled northward. Crook detached Thoburn's two brigades, which entered the First Woods behind the Nineteenth Corps. As Thoburn was forming his troops into two battle lines, Emory reigned up before the colonel. Emory informed Thoburn that his center remained weak, and asked him to move deeper in the woods, relieving Duval's division on the corps' right. Thoburn did so and Emory in turn readjusted his lines in the woods.

Meanwhile Crook led Duval's soldiers and artillery on a lane which crossed Red Bud Run at an ancient manufacturing establishment called "The Factory." At this point, across the stream, the Federal column turned to the west, moving behind open level tableland mostly void of trees. The blue stream of marching men passed the houses of George Keller, Eveline Moore and Charles Wood before halting near A. Huntsberry's farmhouse. The Hackwood house could be seen about 800 yards to the southwest. Crook's soldiers had passed beyond Early's left flank, Gordon's division lying in the Second Woods.

At precisely 3 p.m. the 77th "heard rapid firing away on the right of the forest." Moments earlier, Crook after surveying the terrain and his fortuitous position, formed Duval's brigades into two lines. Future president Rutherford B. Hayes' four Ohio and West Virginia regiments formed the left, and Daniel D. Johnson's four regiments from the same states the right. Just west of the Huntsberry house, Captain DuPont unlimbered his three batteries of eighteen cannon. Crook then sent another future president, William B. McKinley to order Thoburn forward when the division commander heard Duval's attack. The musketry the New Yorkers heard was the result of Duval's soldiers who "with a tremendous shout which resounded along the lines of the Nineteenth Corps . . . rushed forward to the charge." [49]

DuPont's guns thundered as the cheering Federals charged down the slope of the ridge toward Red Bud Run. The bluecoats came in opposite Hackwood's farm, behind Gordon's lines in the Second Woods. The Rebel commander, however, had refused his left flank westward, and his soldiers lying behind the ruined stone Hackwood house responded with a shower of minie balls. Farther south, the left regiments of Rodes'/Grimes' added their muskets against this new Union attack. Behind Grimes' flank, and running perpendicular to it, Gabriel Wharton's brigades of Augustus Forsberg and Thomas Smith were deployed. They had just filed into position west of Grimes when Crook launched his assault.

The men of these three Confederate divisions caught Duval's Yankees in a cornfield and a meadow. Rebel bullets whizzed over the exposed ground as the Northerners went down the slope. Almost instantly, Duval caught a minie ball in the thigh, but refused to leave the field. Nevertheless, the battle-hardened Ohioans and West

Virginians kept coming. At the bottom of the ridge coursed Red Bud Run, a deep stream thirty to forty yards wide, with a bottom of soft mud and a thick bed of moss for a surface. Into this quagmire, the Yankee regiments plunged. All of the Federals floundered immediately. The soft mud sucked at the shoes and legs of the Yankees as they struggled to reach the opposite bank. Rutherford Hayes soon found himself mired in the mud. The colonel managed to pull his horse's front legs loose from the suction, but the animal fell on its side, throwing Hays into the morass. He then crawled to the opposite bank, one of the first to cross.

Duval's Northerners finally reached the opposite bank of Red Bud Run, regiment and brigade organization had disappeared. But the mud-soaked Federals, much like a huge swarm of hornets, drove through the grounds of the Hackwood farm. The Confederate ranks exploded open like the doors of a blast furnace. Russell Hastings, one of Hayes' aides, recalled, "I never saw the killed and wounded lying thicker on the ground than here." [50]

Thoburn's two brigades, under Colonels George Wells and Thomas Harris, broke out of the First Woods minutes after the rousing cheer from across the Red Bud run signaled the charge of Duval. With Wells on the left and Harris on the right, these Yankees charged across the six hundred yards of open field separating the two stands of trees. Gordon's men unleashed a volley when Thoburn's soldiers reached the midpoint, but the bluecoats responded in kind and kept going. The Confederates abandoned the Second Woods as the Yankees entered. The tangled underbrush in the woodlands disrupted the Union ranks, and the two brigades cleared the tree line as a "victorious throng."

Crook's two divisions, with both their ranks sorely disrupted by the penetration through the Second Woods and the crossing of Red Bud Run finally linked up. Duval and Thoburn launched their attacks at nearly the same time, but the latter arrived before the Confederates ahead of Duval, whose men floundered in the mire. Between these two commands, Gordon's soldiers could no longer stay in the Second Woods and began an orderly retrograde movement. The Southerners refusal to panic, the terrain's slowing of the converging Yankee wings and the fire power of Grimes and Wharton on the plateau east of Winchester saved Gordon's veterans from destruction. While the Federal divisions joined ranks, Gordon reformed his command between Grimes and Wharton, with his front paralleling Wharton and perpendicular to Grimes.

Duval's and Thoburn's men, not bothering to reform, rushed on heedless of the destructive fire of Rebel musketry, shot, shell, and canister. The Yankees, however, had about 800 yards of open ground to cross to reach the Rebels lying behind stone walls and haphazard fieldworks on a plateau. An occasional dip in the ground, some rock outcroppings and a few intervening stone walls offered the only protections for the bluecoats. It would not be enough, for the five brigades of Gordon and Wharton and the artillery crews blistered the charging Northerners with a deadly hail of lead and iron, while part of Grimes' division riddled the Federals left flank. Up and down the line of the two divisions, Confederate firepower brought their attack to a standstill.

As Crook's veterans pressed the Confederate left flank and center, James Wilson's cavalry division had crossed Senseney Road on Early's right flank and was hard pressing the Confederate cavalry brigades of Bradley T. Johnson and Wiliam L. Jackson. Torbert's cavalry divisions of William W. Averell and Wesley Merritt had pushed back Fitzhugh Lee's troopers from Stephenson's Depot to a point just north of Winchester. Averell's brigades were aligned west of the Valley Pike, and Merritt's on the east. No organized body of Southerners lay between Thorton's horsemen and Old Jube's works on the plateau. The blue-jacketed troopers were headed straight for the divisions of Wharton and Gordon.

Meanwhile, the Sixth Corps received orders to prepare for an advance. Wright's three divisions, eight brigades in total with over 10,000 soldiers still in the ranks, stretched across the center of the battlefield from the eastern fringe of Ash Hollow to Abraham's Creek where the 77th's Third Brigade lay. Colonel Charles H. Tompkin's six batteries were at the ready behind the infantry. It had been three hours since their slugging match with Ramseur's and Rodes'/Grimes' divisions. George Stevens remembered that as every man stood to his arms ready to advance, "Sheridan came to our part of the line, his face all aglow with excitement, the perspiration rolling down his forehead, his famous black steed spotted with foam, a single orderly in the back." Sheridan galloped straight to Major General George Getty, and bellowed, "General, I have put Torbert on the right, and told him to give 'em h—l, and he is doing it. Crook, too, is on the right and giving it to them. Press them, General, they'll run! . . . Press them, General, I know they'll run!" The Yankee veterans erupted into a cheer which momentarily drowned out the noise of battle and then stepped out, moving across terrain they had held briefly earlier in the day. It was now 4 p.m. [51]

The front of the Sixth Corps extended for nearly 1,500 yards, with Russell's division, now under Emory Upton, on the right, Ricketts' in the center, and Getty's on the left. Approximately 1,000 yards ahead to the west, the divisions of Ramseur and Grimes, with skirmishers in front and supported by William Nelson's gunners and some pieces from Carter M. Braxton, gripped their muskets and waited. Confederate artillery had been sending shot and shell into the Union ranks even before the battle line got underway. Few were struck by shells sending their deadly fragments of iron into the standing Yankees but, when they were, it served to remind the Northerners of grisly work ahead.

Despite the shower of shells, Wright's battle-tested soldiers steadily closed the gap between them and the gray infantry. On the right, it became a resumption of the fierce stand-up fight between the soldiers of Russell and Rodes now commanded by Upton and Grimes, respectively. South of Upton the divisions of Ricketts and Getty were now fully engaged, applying pressure to Grimes' right and Ramseur's entire front. Ricketts' two brigades under Colonels William Emerson and J. Warren Keifer, crossing open fields, suffered murderous artillery fire but never wavered as they drove forward.

Getty's Second division on the left of the corps came head-to-head with Dodson Ramseur's Rebels. Extending Grimes' right flank, Ramseur's men held a ridge east of the Josiah Baker house and about 800 yards west of the Dinkle farm. When the 77th went forward with their division, they initially passed through the Dinkle ground, the area they had taken and then lost in the 11:40 a.m. attack. The veterans first struck Ramseur's skirmish line just beyond Dinkle's. The sharpshooters fell back before the oncoming battle line as the distance between the enemies lessened.

The Confederate divisions began ebbing westward before the mounting Federal pressure. Ramseur, Grimes, Gordon, and Wharton abandoned their positions and shortened their lines. Surgeon Stevens recounted that "The rebels would run, then reaching a commanding position, they would turn their artillery upon us and sweep our line with iron hail." To his left, Stevens saw Brigadier James H. Wilson, "with the cavalry charging through the growing corn, the sabres gleaming in the sunlight, the iron scabbards clanging against iron spurs, the horses dashing madly forward in seeming disorder, but all rushing, like an avalanche, against the right wing of the enemy." [52]

Soon after the Sixth Corps stepped off to attack the Confederates, Sheridan abandoned Eversole's hill to be with the troops, offering them encouragement. Little Phil, mounted on his huge black horse, Rienzi, galloped back and forth several times among his fighting ranks before the Rebel held works. His location was marked by the loud cheers of his soldiers. Private Alonzo Bump told his wife, "we ware on the Left of the line and we Got relieved and ware Goin up on the Right of the Line to join our Brigaid and we met him in the woods and hee ses Boys Goe in and do your Best. we have Drove them and we have Got every thing God dame them. give to them and we will have the hole army. then the boys cheeared him and on we went." 53

Charging south on the east side of the Valley Pike, Merrit's cavalrymen surged into the works held by Wharton's gray infantry. The divisions of Wharton and Gordon promptly disintegrated, heading rearward before the Union horsemen. Soon after, Grimes' and Ramseur's men hemorrhaged also to the rear. Lieutenant Colonel Winsor French wrote to "Messrs. Potter & Judson," editors of the *Saratogian*, "the enemy ran in the wildest disorder, horses were riderless, pack horses galloping, strewing the ground with officers' mess stuff, tents, kettles, baggage, & c. Men threw away their arms, artillerists cut their horses loose, and rode them off at the wildest speed; in short, it was a complete rout." 54

Jubal Early's army streamed south of Winchester, where the Confederates organized a final rear guard position, which saved the wagon trains and some artillery crews. Parts of Gordon's, Wharton's, and Grimes' commands plus some cavalry joined the line, but Ramseur's division composed the main part of the rear guard. The brave Rebels repulsed a few feeble thrusts from the cavalry and the Sixth Corps. Sheridan's men most likely were as nearly spent as the Confederates and nightfall was fast approaching.

Darkness mercifully ended the combat. Strung along the Valley Pike, Early's Confederates stumbled through the dark, most not halting until they passed Newtown. In the fields surrounding Winchester, the victorious Union veterans built campfires, cooked suppers, and rejoiced in their victory, while regimental bands played patriotic songs and some that reminded the soldiers of home. The 77th settled for the night in Winchester's cemetery. Lieutenant Colonel French stood looking at a row of grave stones, and was deeply moved when he realized he was standing before the grave of one of the heroes of the 1777 Battle of Saratoga: "upon one of the tomb stones . . . was inscribed the name of Major General Daniel Morgan, died 1802, & c. I could not help but think of Saratoga, the Bemis Heights battle ground, when the then Colonel did such noble service for his country, and how his sharpshooters made the red coats run. And I wondered if his spirit did not hover over this battle field, fighting to uphold the cause he fought to establish, and to continue the Government he fought to inaugurate. Surely the God of battles must aid our just cause." [55]

Lieutenant George M. Ross (L. Tom Perry Special Collections)

If the day had been one of action on the battle field, it had been no less so in the Union field hospitals. Soon after the fighting commenced, ambulances loaded with the wounded trundled to the rear where they were received by the surgeons. Every building of the historic village was crowded with the maimed and dying. Surgeons worked all day and all night amputating limbs and dressing wounds. Of the 77th, Lieutenant George M. Ross (Co. G) had his shattered shoulder dressed. Private James O. Fairchilds (Co. K) had his left leg amputated. Private Andrew Leonard (Co. K), shot through the chest, had the bullet cut out of his back. Corporal Francis Cooney (Co. K) and Private Edward Connors (Co. K) both were hit in the feet with grape shot. Thirty five others in the regiment were brought to the Second Division field hospital to have their wounds treated.

16

"MY GOD, GENERAL! SEE 'EM RUN!"

The night of September 19 was miserable for Early's Army of the Valley. Defeated, hungry, and exhausted, the embittered gray uniforms stumbled up the Valley Pike for hours. Most of the Confederates stole a couple of hours of sleep, spreading over the fields from Kernstown to south of Newtown. They slept unmolested, with the retreat resuming long before sunup.

Old Jube arrived at Fisher's Hill around daybreak. The final contingent of his troops filtered on to the heights of Fisher's Hill. Officers directed the butternuts to their positions on the eminence. The men then started little camp fires and cooked what rations they had and those that could, curled up and slept. Much had been taken out of them in the past twenty four hours, but they were resilient. John B. Gordon overheard a soldier say: "Cheer up boys; don't be worried. We'll lick them Yankees the first fair chance, and get more grub and guns and things than our poor old quartermaster mules can pull." [1]

The Southern commander chose to make a stand at Fisher's Hill. If Early were to bar the entrance to the upper Shenandoah, then, it had to be here. In the undulating, fertile valley Fisher's Hill appeared as a geologic aberration. Nestled against the Massanutten on the east and Little North Mountain on the west, the elevation extended for nearly four miles. It was a steep, rock-strewn bluff, crisscrossed by ravines, and dotted with woodlots. Along its base, Tumbling Run flowed into the North Fork of the Shenandoah River. The Southerners boasted of it as "their Gibraltar;" When Winsor French saw the bluff he considered it "one of the ugliest positions I ever saw, strongly fortified with batteries, bearing upon every avenue of approach." If properly manned, Fisher's Hill was nearly impregnable. [2]

Early placed Gabriel Wharton's infantrymen on his right where the face of the bluff was at its steepest and a bend in the North Fork confined to area of attack, making it virtually unassailable. Aligned on Wharton's left, across the Valley Pike, Gordon's veterans held the works. Next in line came Dodson Ramseur's three brigades, now under the command of Brigadier General John Pegram. General Pegram assumed command because Jubal transferred Ramseur to the division of Rodes. Ramseur's four brigades continued the infantry front to the Middle Road, where the bluff sloped into a small valley before butting against Little North Mountain. The artillery battalions of William Nelson and Carter Braxton were intermingled with the infantry. To the west of Ramseur's soldiers, the dismounted brigades of Lunsford Lomax's cavalry division were deployed in the low ground and on a ridge which paralleled Fisher's Hill. This ridge was also wooded, restricting the view of the defenders.

At 6 a.m. September 20, the 77th left its camp and joined Sheridan's infantry in giving chase to the defeated butternuts. The 82nd Pennsylvania of Oliver Edwards' Sixth Corps brigade and the medical personal were left behind for the grisly duty of gathering and burying the corpses and the neglected wounded. The casualties covered miles of ground. Lines of ambulances congregated to unload the wounded at the field hospitals along Opequon Creek or in the converted buildings in Winchester. Union surgeons finally filled twenty buildings in town with the wounded, established a tent hospital near Shawnee Spring and enlarged a 300-bed hospital at Sandy Hook, Maryland to accommodate 1,300 patients. Six days after the battle, Surgeon John H. Brinton reported 4,201 wounded still in the hospitals.

The infantry marched on either side of the Valley Pike, while the artillery and wagons rumbled down the macadamized road. Despite miles of corpses and wounded soldiers, the spirits of the New Yorkers improved with the warming day. They were filled with determination with the sense that they would not, like a month earlier, be racing back to Winchester. Adding to the Northerners satisfaction, while passing through the town, the 77th viewed hundreds of Confederate prisoners in the public square before the court house.

The 18-mile march to Strasburg consumed most of the day. The 77th arrived north of the town, a "dingy, dilapidated village" at 3 p.m. About 5 p.m., the rest of Wright's and Emory's foot soldiers replaced Union cavalry that had held the position earlier in the day. The three divisions of the Sixth Corps filed into position west of the turnpike. To the east of the road, the Nineteenth Corps anchored their front on the North Fork of the Shenandoah River. The wagon train and Crook's two divisions bivouacked north of Cedar Creek, the infantry staying out of the view of Confederate signal stations. Lieutenant Colonel French was detailed Corps officer of the day, and established the Sixth Corps picket line.[3]

Little Phil reconnoitered the works on the heights and called for a council of war for that night. Sheridan, Wright, Emory, and Crook met at army headquarters, and the four officers quickly dismissed the notion of a frontal assault. Crook, who also had inspected the terrain, suggested a turning movement against Early's left flank at Little North Mountain. Wright and Emory voted against this proposal, but Sheridan thought Crook's suggestion had a good chance of success. He then brought Joseph Thoburn and Rutherford Hayes, Crook's division commanders, to the council. The Federal commander wanted their opinion on the feasibility of the plan. Although never officially recorded, one version of the council stated that Thoburn and Hayes seconded Crook's proposal.

The remainder of the meeting focused on the details of the operation. Success depended on the element of surprise, the ability to march Crook's "Mountain Creepers" to Little North Mountain without detection. It was decided to move his command forward into concealed positions only at night. When the council broke up, Crook returned to his headquarters and shifted his troops into a stand of woods north of Cedar Creek.

It was a relatively quiet day at Fisher's Hill on September 21. With Wright's and Emory's infantry, the 77th rose at dawn, cooked breakfast, drank coffee, and relaxed for several hours. Private Cyrille Fountain "went into the Village & got all the peaches & plums I wanted" and was disgusted with "awful rank Sechesh womans" there. Crook's soldiers remained hidden in the trees north of Cedar Creek. On the bluff, the Southerners strengthened their entrenchments. A gun crew occasionally sent a shell toward the Union camps. Fountain recorded "Skirmishing going on quite Sharp all day." [4]

A little before noon, the 77th with the Sixth Corps and Nineteenth corps formed into marching columns. Before the New York veterans started, an officer read telegrams from Abraham Lincoln, Edwin Stanton, and U. S. Grant, congratulating them on their victory at

Winchester. "Have just heard of your great victory," said the grateful president, "God bless you all, officers and men." They learned also that one hundred cannon had been fired at the capital and by the Army of the Potomac at Petersburg in honor of their triumph. Stanton's wire also reported the promotion of Little Phil to brigadier general in the Regular Army. The 77th and their comrades in the Army of the Shenandoah responded with three cheers.[5]

Moments later, Wright's divisions began Sheridan's swing around Strasburg. Emory's veterans followed the Sixth Corps. Horatio Wright halted his command about 4 p.m. west of where the broken up Manassas Gap Railroad bent south toward Fisher's Hill. The Sixth Corps front overlapped the ruined roadbed. The 77th along with Wright's veterans piled fence rails along the line for breastworks. Ricketts' two brigades held the right, and the three brigades of George Getty extended the Third division's left to the railroad. Russell's two brigades, now under Brigadier General Frank Wheaton, connected with Emory's corps deploying astride the Valley Pike.

While Federal skirmishers from each division drew fire from their counterparts, Sheridan and Wright surveyed the ground. To the right front of the Sixth Corps, Gray-clad skirmishers held a knoll, which, according to Little Phil, would give him an unobstructed view of the Rebel lines on the bluff. He ordered Wright to seize the rise, known locally a Flint Hill.

The 126th Ohio from Ricketts' division and the 139th Pennsylvania from Getty's rushed the hill but Confederate defenders unleashed a galling fire into the ranks, repulsing the sortie in less than ten minutes. Getty then summoned Colonel James Warner's veteran Pennsylvanians and New Yorkers into line 150 yards from Flint Hill. Reforming ranks and fixing bayonets, the mixed regiments charged across the field and up the hillside, wresting the crest from the outnumbered Rebels. Warner's soldiers at once dug rifle pits and Sheridan had his unobstructed view of Early's position.

It was now past nightfall. The Federal front stretched from Strasburg westward to near the Amos Stickley farm, a distance of nearly two miles. Emory's corps blanketed the ground between the North Fork and the railroad. William Dwight's brigade's right connected with Wheaton east of the tracks. The 77th's Second division closed on Wheaton's right and Ricketts completed the line, forming the Sixth Corps' right flank.

The capture of Flint Hill by Ricketts demanded a westward shift by Getty and Wheaton and Emory's Nineteenth Corps during the night of September 21-22. The final portion of Sheridan's infantry, Crook's two divisions, crossed Cedar Creek that evening. Reinvigorated after spending the 21st hidden in the woods, the veteran soldiers advanced soon after dark into another stretch of trees located north of Hupp's Hill, a rise a mile from Strasburg. Crook's troops then lay down for several hours of rest, ready for a fight in the morning. After two days of peace, the Nineteenth Corps general's seasoned fighters were scheduled to bear the brunt of the day's operation.

Sheridan ordered pressure applied while Crook's soldiers marched to Little North Mountain. He was anxious that Confederate signalmen not discover Crook's movement and doom the Federal plan. It was imperative that Early believed that the Yankees might attempt a frontal assault. Accordingly, at 12:15 a.m., Emory advanced upon a string of Confederate "bull pens" (three sided enclosures made of fence rails, manned by two or three men) on Quarry Hill about 400 yards in front of Dwight's and Grover's lines. His infantry easily overran the "bull pens," giving Emory a continuous line of fieldworks approximately 500 yards short of the base of Fisher's Hill.

At the right of the Union line, Horatio Wright instructed Ricketts to shift farther to the west, opposite the left front of the Rebel infantry works held by Dodson Ramseur's division on School House Ridge. Between 1 and 2 p.m., Ricketts attacked with two brigades. Before this force, the Confederates fled to their main line on Fisher's Hill. The 77th with their division and Wheaton's remained stationary, but the Sixth Corps was where Little Phil wanted them.

From Fisher's Hill, Old Jube observed with increasing concern the Federal sorties. Ricketts' attack convinced him that Sheridan was preparing for an assault on the Confederate works. Knowing he was vastly outnumbered, Early issued orders down the chain of command for a withdrawal after dark. The Southern commander instructed caissons and ammunition chests to the front to expedite the retreat, and then waited for darkness.

At the same time Early issued orders for a nighttime withdrawal, Crook's "Mountain Creepers" were approaching the foot of Little North Mountain, north of the Rebel left flank. Rutherford Hayes' and Joseph Thoburn's soldiers had been on the move since early morning. They had marched slowly, circuitously through ravines and woodlands. At Saint Stephen's Church, Crook halted his column, where he brought Thoburn's trailing division up beside Hayes' to form two parallel columns. The blue-clad men dropped their knapsacks and arranged tin canteens and bayonet scabbards so that no clinking metal could reveal their presence. The march up the mountainside then resumed a difficult ascent because of steep slopes crisscrossed by many ravines. Rocks, huge boulders, and thick underbrush also slowed their progress. The veterans grabbed onto the rocks, brush, vines, and tree trunks to pull themselves up the slope.

Crooked halted his columns 200 yards beyond the Rebel picket post, faced the infantrymen to the east and brought Thoburn up on the left of Hayes. The divisions deployed into two battle lines, one brigade behind another, separated by fifteen to twenty yards. The four brigades of 5,500 men, formed under sporadic Confederate artillery fire. Crook passed instructions along the lines not to yell until he gave the signal, but the Northerners' blood was up and they nevertheless emitted a tremendous shout. Crook later boasted, "And unless you heard my fellows yell once, you can form no conception of it. It beggars all descriptions." [6]

The Yankees charged down the slope of Little North Mountain like an oncoming storm. The steep decline, almost impenetrable cedar thickets, and boulders immediately disrupted the Crook's battle lines. The Federal infantry sensed the surprise they had accomplished, and scrambled individually toward the bottom. "The men rushed on," Hayes reported, "no line, no order, yelling like madmen." [7]

Blue uniforms charged into Lunsford L. Lomax's cavalrymen like an avalanche of boulders. The troopers of Bradley Johnson, William "Mudwall" Jackson, and George Smith were no match for the emotion-charged Federals. The stunned defenders were thunderstruck and scattered on impact. Most raced for their horses or fled into the woods to the south. The 1st Maryland Battalion launched a counterattack to save their comrades and horses, but the Yankees easily swept them beside, with their captain falling with a serious wound.

To Lomax's right, Ramseur reacted quickly to the unexpected onslaught. He shifted Cullen Battle's Alabama brigade from their earthworks to a prominent ridge paralleling the Federal advance. The Alabamians crouched behind stone walls and their muskets sent forth a storm of lead. At the end of Battle's line at the main works, Thomas Kilpatrick's Virginia gunners hand-wheeled their cannon to the left, with the pieces bursting with double canister. The momentum of the Yankees briefly slowed, especially Thoburn's division which followed the Confederate works. Some of the Federal soldiers turned back toward the wooded mountain only to be met by Crook who pelted them with rocks. Given the choice between a hopping mad Crook and his supply of rocks or the butternuts, most of the skulkers chose the Rebels.

Battle's brigade gave way to the charging Federals, relinquishing their grip on the stone walls. Ramseur, meanwhile, brought William R. Cox's brigade out of the main works and sent it toward Battle's left. However, Cox was guilty of making a serious blunder. Responding to the urgent command from Ramseur, the North Carolinian became confused and ultimately lost in the wooden terrain, while marching his six regiments to the sound of battle. He marched his command to the southwest, passed unseen by Hayes' charging soldiers and finally stumbled upon Lomax and some of his men. Lomax's troopers guided Cox's troops to the turnpike. His command reached the Valley Pike by nightfall in time to participate in Early's rear guard.

Cox's mistake paved the way for Hayes' division to penetrate far beyond Battle's left and the enfilade the ranks of the Alabamians. The Southerners had enough and scattered in a frightened mass across the countryside. Crook's men rushed on crossing a series of timbered ridges in their advance. Three North Carolina regiments were posted upon one of these slight prominences. The Tar Heels unleashed a staggering volley, but the "Mountain Creepers" returned the fire which leveled a good many North Carolinians. But the three regiments stubbornly held their ground. To their right, in their works on Fisher's Hill, their comrades were abandoning the crest before another wave of Yankees – the 77th's Sixth Corps was storming the heights.

The three divisions of the Sixth Corps attacked en echelon from the right to the left, with Ricketts' division initiating the assault. He launched his attack minutes after he heard the sounds of Crook's assault. Federal skirmishers preceded Colonels William Emerson's and J. Warren Keifer's brigades with orders to concentrate on Confederate gunners. The crest of the bluff exploded with musketry and battery fire. The Yankee brigades obliqued to the west under what Emerson described as "heavy artillery fire." Colonel James H. Tompkins countered by rolling four of his batteries into line, carpeting the crest of the heights with shell fire. Ricketts' eleven regiments, momentarily sheltered by wood lots, reached the base of the bluff and then scrambled up the steep face. [8]

When Ricketts' men reached the heights, they converged with those of Crook. Only the North Carolinians of Brigadier General Bryan Grimes were left of Ramseur's division to clash with the wave of Yankees. The Tar Heels now found themselves the target of Federal musketry from three sides. Dodson Ramseur galloped up to Grimes and ordered the general to save his command, for Crook's fighters were only 100 yards away. But the order came after the North Carolinians had taken all the fighting they could and were flooding eastward toward John Pegram' division. Ramseur now commanded three bloodied brigades and a lost one.

From Flint Hill, George Stevens was standing near Sheridan and George W. Getty when they "heard shots to the right" heralding Crook's flank attack. Stevens watched as "the right wing [Ricketts division] of our forces began to move forward down into the valley and up the steep slope toward the enemy." The surgeon "stood upon a rock overlooking the valley," while Little Phil and Getty "were conversing earnestly, and as they talked they looked up the valley toward the right. Suddenly Sheridan threw his arms around Getty and leaping and whirling about like a lunatic shouted, 'My God, General! See 'em run! See 'em run!' Then the jubilant Sheridan mounted his warhorse, Rienzi, and galloped toward Fisher's Hill to urge his soldiers forward. [9]

The 77th's Second Division advanced a few minutes after Ricketts' men launched their assault and smashed into John Pegram's division. Lieutenant Colonel Winsor French remembered the 77th "dashing through the woods, over hills, into hollows, across gulleys, over walls, fences, and every conceivable obstruction, and the enemy at the same time pouring upon us all his fiery vengeance, in the shape of shot and shell. Soon as the line was sufficiently swung around a Division of the 19th Corps charged, and then the roar of artillery and musketry was terrific; but amid it all the cheers of our advancing column rang out into the troubled air." Little Phil "came along the lines almost unattended, seeming to appear at every place where there was the least wavering – and such enthusiasm I never saw." French told readers of the *Saratogian* back home, "The men rushed almost wildly forward, regardless of lines of battle, each striving to outdo the other in noble daring. – Oh, if there is anything that will stir the deepest feelings of man's nature, making ready and willing to die for our country, it is battle. Its horrors and awful grandeur no one who has not seen one can imagine." [10]

"On, on, went this blue mass of living men," French recalled, "and back rolled the Rebel horde, shattered, frightened and demoralized, too cowardly to make a good fight even behind earthworks." The men of the 77th and their Second Division comrades poured over the Confederate works in a confused and delirious mass. A mad scramble followed with triumphant blue uniforms fired their guns wildly into the air. Sergeant Sylvester D. Rhodes of the 61st Pennsylvania was among the first to enter the breast works, capturing one of the guns, and with the help of some soldiers from the 43rd New York turned it upon the fleeing enemy. Rhodes received a

Medal of Honor for his valor. Another member of the 43rd New York, Private James Connors, grabbed a Rebel flag, earning him also a Medal of Honor. [11]

To the east of the 77th, Frank Wheaton's two brigades dislodged Gordon's troops from their earthworks, bagging scores of his men and Carter M. Braxton's Artillery Battalion. Wheaton's soldiers scaled the bluff minutes after Getty's men swept over the crest, leaving the entire line west of the Valley Pike broken to pieces. Several Rebel units maintained their organizations, but most of the Second Corps fled the battlefield. Gabriel Wharton's graycoats and Floyd King's Artillery Battalion got caught in this flood of Early's broken army and were swept south with it. Grover's division of the Nineteenth Corps stormed over Wharton's, captured one of King's guns, and turned it on this part of Early's up the pike.

The scene in the fields and wood lots was marked by pandemonium. French remarked, "The enemy fell back in disorder, without the least formation – just one mass of gray backs scattered over the plain, moving back like a vast mob, all running for dear life, and our men chasing them with but little better formation." The 77th's lieutenant colonel proclaimed, "Truly it was a soldier's fight, and the charge being underway, the heights would have been taken without an officer save our noble chief." French triumphed "So the battle of Strasburg was fought and won, with this valley, one of the finest in the world, reclaimed from rebel rule." [12]

The routed Early's army, stampeded south down the Pike toward Woodstock, and continued throughout most of the night. The main part of the Southern army bedded down for a brief rest south of Woodstock at the Narrow Passage. The wagon train halted beyond Mount Jackson, another twelve miles south of Woodstock.

Casualties were unusually low considering the number of soldiers in each army. The Confederate loss totaled merely 30 killed and 210 wounded. Old Jube reported an additional 995 missing, estimating that only half were captured by Sheridan's men. Fourteen Rebel cannon were captured by the Federals. Though routed, the Southerners had been spared by the advent of darkness, the cloud-burst of a tremendous thunderstorm near the end of the battle, and confusion in the Union ranks. Early's Army of the Valley lived to fight again, but for now it needed time to heal, so the graycoats marched most of the night, putting good distance between them and their pursuers, heading for toward safety in the Blue Ridge.

The Union army was also nearly unscathed at Fisher's Hill. The human cost was 36 killed, 414 wounded, and 6 missing. In his report, Wright was ebullient: "the annals of the war present, perhaps, no more glorious victory than this." Several weeks later, Lieutenant Colonel French still reveled in the nearly bloodless victory and exuded confidence in the army:

> "I am led to inquire what Rebel soldiery will fight, if Early's army will not. They are certainly the finest body of men I ever saw bearing arms, strong, healthy, intelligent fellows – the very best troops in the Confederate service. The old Brigade, Division and Corps of Stonewall Jackson – of which we have so long stood in terror – is almost, and I trust will be quite, annihilated... Our army is in the highest spirits, and finest state of discipline. The result of this last fight is so much more glorious from the fact that our loss was comparatively nothing. How is it possible to accomplish so much with so little loss I cannot conceive. God be praised for this glorious victory." [13]

Less than a month before the victories at Winchester and Fisher's Hill, the Democratic National Convention met in Chicago, Illinois, setting forth a peace platform, later coined the "Chicago Platform" by political cartoonist, Thomas Nast, and nominating George B. McClellan for president. Like so many of his comrades in the Union army, suing for peace now, after so many years of bloodletting, Winsor French saw this as a betrayal of their sacrifice:

> We are continuing saying, what an effect this will have upon our people at home. Will they clamor for "Peace at any price," and a "cessation of hostilities?" Is it possible that after so much blood, that our people will be deceived into a delusive hope? Tell the citizen population of your town and county that we who are fighting to sustain our country's honor and republican institutions will look back with sorrow upon any compromise with traitors. Rebels with swords must be conquered by the sword . . . Have we not taken the planks out of the Chicago Platform? – Let them all be taken out, they are rotten and deceptive. McClellan can not have the suffrage of true soldiers. He has many personal friends in the army – those who knew him in the army before the war, and on the Peninsula. His friends have killed him, politically speaking. 'God bless our noble President and our country,' I heard a private say last night, after he exhausted all his eulogies on Phil. Sheridan. [14]

Back home at Saratoga Springs, the 77th's veteran, Captain Seth DeYoe, discharged from the army due to his wound at Spotsylvania, underscored the thinking of French and the Union army. Asked to give his estimate of McClellan and his prospects DeYoe strongly replied:

I have always been a Democrat, and am a Democrat still, but now I must vote with the party which is for crushing this rebellion, instead of the party which is for cringing and yielding to the rebellion. As to McClellan, we all had confidence in him until our reverses before Richmond. During the battles we fought he was not on the field. We knew not where he was, and we lost confidence in him. We came reluctantly to regard him as a failure. At Antietam, where he did himself the most credit, he failed to make his success a complete triumph; failed to crush Lee's army, as he might have done, by giving a long truce, during which Lee recrossed the Potomac and saved his army. The feeling then spread through the whole army that with McClellan at the head, all our movements would be ineffective, and if victorious, the fruits of victory would be lost. If the election is decided by the soldier's vote, there is no more danger of his success than his being struck by lightning in the month of January.

The Saratogian, strongly Republican, referring to this exchange offered a brief editorial: "The Copperheads may impose upon a few honest men who have remained at home; but a Democrat like Capt. Deyoe, who has lost an eye in the war, can yet see clearly who are true to the country, and who are playing into the hands of the rebels." 15

Organized pursuit of Early's butternuts took some time to form amid the celebrations, disordered units, rain and darkness. When the officers managed to untangle regiments and companies, Emory's corps, with Grover's division in the forefront, led the pursuit. The 77th's Sixth Corps followed while Crook's Army of West Virginia guarded prisoners and bivouacked on the battlefield. The march was numbing, and the ranks thinned with each successive mile. Exhausted veterans dropped out of the ranks all along the turnpike to rest or sleep. Many of the Yankees, falling to the ground near another soldier, discovered in the morning that they had slept beside a Rebel.

The leading elements of the pursuit force entered Woodstock about 3:30 a.m. on September 23. The 77th passed through the village where a number of Confederate prisoners were held, and camped at Edinburg just outside of Woodstock. The next morning the 77th departed from Edinburg with Sheridan's army. The infantry of Wright and Emory strode along the sides of the Valley Pike as the artillery and wagons rumbled on it. About 10 a.m., the New York veterans passed "through Mount Jackson, where were large hospitals, occupied by wounded confederates, and attended by confederate surgeons; then pressing on to New Market," halting before the Confederates on Rude's Hill. [16]

Perched on the hill, the Southerners had a clear view of the Federal movement. Early ordered a withdrawal of the infantry and artillery, for the wagon train had already departed. The odd-numbered brigades in each division went first, retiring a mile up the turnpike, and redeploying. Bugles then summoned the even-numbered brigades to relinquish their position on Rude's Hill, passing through the newly formed line to establish their own two miles farther south. This movement was repeated as the graycoats retreated through New Market to Tenth Legion church, where a full battle line was formed.

Little Phil halted his troops south of New Market about 5 p.m. The 77th broke rank and built campfires and the Northerners settled in for a meal and sleep. But Early's infantry and artillery were marching. The Confederates halted at midnight, slept until daybreak and then continued via Port Republic. By sunset, September

25, the Rebel foot soldiers were camped in Brown's Gap of the Blue Ridge. Joseph Kershaw's division, ordered back to the Valley, came through Swift Run Gap, joining Early later in the morning, adding much needed soldiers to the Army of the Valley.

The Federal army did not continue pursuit of the Confederates, marching instead to Harrisonburg. By late in the afternoon, September 25th, the commands of Wright and Emory covered the fields surrounding the town, which was ten miles due west from Port Republic. Crook's corps halted for the day at the intersection of the Pike and Keezletown Road. One Union soldier wrote in his diary: "The Rebels are scarce in the Shenandoah Valley just now." [17]

Unlike the grueling marches of the previous month chasing Early, the march to Harrisonburg was that of a victorious army. George Stevens took time to reflect on the movement from Fisher's Hill to Harrisonburg:

> Our march had been a grand triumphal pursuit of a routed enemy. Never had we marched with such light hearts; and, though each day had found us pursuing rapidly from dawn till dark, the men seemed to endure the fatigue with wonderful patience. Our column, as it swept up the valley, was a spectacle of rare beauty. Never had we, in all our campaigns, seen anything to compare with the appearance of this victorious little army. The smooth, wide turnpike was occupied by the artillery, ambulances and baggage wagons moving in double file. The infantry marched in several parallel columns on either side of the pike, and a line of cavalry, followed by skirmish line of infantry, led the way. Cavalry, too, hung on either flank, and scouted the country. It was intensely exciting to watch the steady progress of the advancing skirmishers. Now, as

they reached the base of some sloping eminence, the rebel skirmishers would confront them; then, as they advanced, never halting nor slackening their pace, the confederates would surrender the ground, to appear in front on the next commanding ground. So we marched up the valley – a grand excursion – skirmishing only enough to maintain a constant state of pleasant excitement. [18]

Though a Pennsylvania sergeant wrote at Harrisonburg, "The Rebels are scarce in the Shenandoah Valley just now," Jubal Early was not finished in the Valley. Before the 77th would leave the Shenandoah, the New Yorkers' mettle would be sorely tested. The "state of pleasant excitement" chasing Early would soon become the terror and bloody carnage of a desperate battle. [19]

17

"GIVE TO THEM, DAMN THEM; THEY ARE COWARDS, AND I KNOW IT!"

Except for an easy march to and back from Mount Crawford, the 77th quietly spent the next eight days resting in their camp. The days included inspection, and a battalion drill, something the veterans had not done for six months. The mail train came up, and the men greedily read their mail and wrote letters home to their loved ones. Perhaps the highlight of their stay at Harrisonburg was the bountiful crops in the surrounding fields and a seemingly never ending supply of cattle, sheep, hogs, and fowl in pastures and barnyard pens. Cyrille Fountain foraged each day, bringing back "honey, honey butter & apple butter . . . a lot of Sheeps . . . bacon & Chickens." The private's excursions for food were not met with protest, for "the citizens ware awful scart to see the blue Jackets." [1]

Tuesday, October 4, Fountain recorded in his diary: "Today all the houses & barns ware burned 5 miles Square for retaliation of killing [an] officer last night." During the previous night, October 3, Lieutenant John R. Meigs, Sheridan's engineer officer, and two assistants, while conducting a military survey, encountered three Rebel scouts outside of Dayton. What then happened in the growing dark is not clear. Meigs either did or did not draw his pistol, and was shot in the head by either F. M. Campbell, B. Frank Shavers or George Martin, Virginia cavalrymen. One of Meig's assistants managed to escape, spurring his horse on a gallop back to headquarters where he reported the young officer's killing to Sheridan. [2]

Little Phil listened to the shocking account with a full rage. Meigs, the first son of Union Quartermaster Montgomery C. Meigs and an 1863 graduate of West Point, who ranked first in his class, had been a favorite of Sheridan. The young officer had been a favorite of the commander's headquarter staff. Sheridan blamed the "murder" and "atrocious act" on Confederate guerillas and the civilians who harbored them. Little Phil wanted revenge and issued orders that all houses in Dayton and in a five-mile area surrounding the village be burned. Sheridan was determined "to teach a lesson to these abettors of the foul deed – a lesson they would never forget." [3]

The avenging began at night with the burning of Noah Wenger's barn. The body of Meigs had been found there where it had fallen – in the road adjoining Wenger's farm. With the break of dawn, George Custer's troopers arrived. Though they found their charge distasteful, the troopers burned 17 houses and five barns, plus some outbuildings. A few residents were allowed time to remove furnishings from their homes, but they were the exception. One of the victims described it as a "holocaust of fire," and the area became known as the "Burnt District." Before Custer's horsemen readied to torch Dayton, Sheridan countermanded his orders. Colonel Thomas F. Wildes, commander of the 116th Ohio, which occupied the town, had successfully interceded with Sheridan, convincing the general that the inhabitants were loyal Unionists. Little Phil's rage had subsided, and he agreed to the request. When the Ohioan departed, the grateful residents gave them many provisions and delicacies. [4]

Ulysses S. Grant was an uncompromising "hard-war man" who suffered few illusions about the art of making war. His Overland Campaign of 1864 brought unremitting pressure against the South, a war of attrition the Confederacy could ill afford. It also became a conflict heretofore unimaginable human and material cost, but the fall of Atlanta and the victories at Third Winchester and Fisher's Hill, justified the bloody sacrifices. The Rebel nation teetered toward destruction under these critical blows in Georgia and the Shenandoah Valley, and Grant was determined that the Confederacy never recovered.

For the General-in-Chief, Sheridan's campaign in the valley had two purposes: the defeat of the Southern defenders and the destruction of the lush region. Grant's order to Sheridan instructed that officer that "in pushing up the Shenandoah Valley . . . it is desirable that nothing should be left to invite the enemy to return." He then admonished Little Phil: "Take all provisions, forage, and stock wanted for the use of your command; such as cannot be consumed, destroy." No longer would the Valley's fertile limestone soil feed the Confederates; nor would its tanneries give them leather shoes and harnesses; no longer would it supply them with horses and mules. [5]

Sheridan, believing Early's army was no longer a threat to the Valley, issued orders for a full-scale retrograde movement down the Valley. From October 6-8th, Federal horsemen systematically burned, slaughtered, and devastated nearly everything which could supply Early's men between the Alleghenies and the Blue Ridge.

The mounted soldiers ravaged the entire area from Harrisonburg to Strasburg. George Stevens wrote:

> We fell back from Mount Crawford to Harrisonburg, burning barns, mills and granaries, driving before us cattle and sheep . . . From Harrisonburg we again fell back, retracing our steps through New Market, Mount Jackson and Woodstock, and encamped on the evening of the 8th of October on the north bank of Cedar Creek. Each day as we marched, dark columns of smoke rose from numberless conflagrations in our rear and on either flank, where the cavalry was at work carrying out of the edict of destruction of the valley. A certain number of mills with the grain contained, a specified number of wheat-stacks and granaries, and cattle and sheep sufficient for the wants of the people of the valley were saved; all other mills, barns, stacks and granaries were burned, and all other cattle and sheep driven away. Seventy mills, with the flour and grain, and over two thousand barns filled with wheat, hay and farm implements were thus committed to the flames, and seven thousand cattle and sheep were either driven off or killed and issued to the men.

Wesley Merritt estimated the amount of damages by his cavalry division alone totaled $3,304,672. Americans had never before seen such destruction, conducted with skill and thoroughness. Yet the Yankee soldiers, as did Stevens, felt, "This destruction, cruel as it seemed, was fully justified as a matter of military necessity." [6]

Thousands of Valley residents chose to abandon their land. From the vicinity of Harrisonburg over 400 wagons loaded with people and possessions, joined the blue column. Most of the refugees were slaves seeking their freedom. One party of slave refugees joined the Sixth Corps hospital train. Surgeon Stevens remembered, "The party rode in one of the huge Virginia wagons, so familiar to those who have spent much time in those parts, and consisted of an aged colored woman, probably more than ninety years old, one or two younger women, a black man of fifty, who was cripple, a boy of twelve or fifteen years, and a very large number of small children varying in hue from jet black to dark brunette. The load was drawn by four broken down, spavined animals, the cripple man riding one of the horses of the rear span, the boy on one of the leaders." Curious soldiers freely divided their hardtack and coffee with the refugees. The doctor reigned his horse to the side of the wagon and asked the elderly woman, "Well, aunty, are all those your children?" "Lor, no massa, dey's only eighteen ob 'em" Startled by her answer, Stevens rode on ahead. [7]

On October 10, Sheridan's infantry and artillery left their bivouacs at Strasburg and continued down the Valley. William Emory and George Crook halted their commands north of Cedar Creek between the stream and Middletown. The 77th's Sixth Corps, however, continued on through Middleton and eastward on the road to Front Royal, pausing for the night on the north bank of the Shenandoah River. The next morning at 6 a.m., the corps moved down to Front Royal, where the 77th was detailed for provost duty. Captain Martin Lennon thought "Front Royal is the meanest secesh town I have ever seen." The New Yorkers "fixed up nice tents, using the lumber of an old hospital in town" and made themselves comfortable. "In the afternoon," Captain Lennon "went with a detail to gather grapes in a vineyard of Mrs. Marcus Buck." Private Cyrille Fountain "went out forigeing and got a lot of honey, chickens, grapes & potatoes." Later in the evening, the New York private "went into the village . . . with Some of the boys & we had a grand consert with the Secesh Girls. They gave us an invitation to take dinner with them the Next day." To his lament, however, orders to march at 4 a.m. the next morning precluded Fountain's enjoyment of the "Secesh Girls" of Front Royal. [8]

Though Sheridan firmly believed the campaign had concluded following the burning of the Valley, Old Jube was not cowed into submission. On the contrary, Early's Rebels were on the move. At sunrise, October 12, the Army of the Valley vacated their camps at New Market to the cheers of Valley residents who had witnessed the burning of their granaries, crops, and barns, and the rustling of their livestock. The bulk of the army bivouacked for the night around Woodstock.

At 6 a.m., on the 13th, the Southern foot soldiers and artillery again marched down the Valley Pike. Leading the gray column, John Gordon's division halted at 10 a.m. at Hupp's Hill, a mile and a half distant from the Union camps beyond Cedar Creek. Gordon positioned his troops in a stand of trees, while the divisions of Stephen Ramseur, Gabriel Wharton, John Pegram, and Joseph Kershaw formed a line beneath the brow of the hill.

Rebel gun crews wheeled their cannon forward, rammed in the charges and sent shells whistling toward the Federals. The missiles exploded in the camps of the Nineteenth Corps, sending the startled Yankees scrambling for cover. William Emory ordered counterfire from his own batteries. George Crook soon joined Emory, and the two ordered Joseph Thoburn's division of Crook's corps forward in a reconnaissance. As the Federals crossed Cedar Creek and advanced across the Abraham Stickley farm 1,000 yards south of the stream, Brigadier General James Conner's brigade of Kershaw's division charged. The two battle lines roared with musketry at contact. The combatants hammered at each other for more than an hour before Conner's South Carolinians, supported by additional troops, broke the Union line, routing the Yankees. The Rebels pursued to the Stickley farmhouse, where they came under fire from Union artillery across Cedar Creek. This ended the action, and later in the afternoon, the butternuts withdrew through Strasburg and settled into their old works on Fisher's Hill.

The Confederates' arrival at Hupp's Hill and this engagement at Stickley's farm, prompted Sheridan to recall the 77th's corps back from Front Royal. Martin Lennon recorded in his diary on October 14, "At 3 a.m. were ordered to pack up and fall in. Started at 4 a.m., and marched rear guard, by way of Newtown, to Middletown, where we encamped for the night." Sheridan stated in his memoirs that he planned an offensive when the Sixth Corps returned, but Early's withdrawal to Fisher's Hill cancelled the undertaking. [9]

October 14, Secretary of War Edwin Stanton telegraphed Sheridan, calling Sheridan to Washington for a consultation. Still convinced Old Jube could no longer launch an offensive movement, Little Phil left for Washington the next day. He arrived at the capital early the next morning, breakfasted at Willard's Hotel before going to the War Department. In meeting with Stanton and "Old Brains" Halleck, it was agreed that the bulk of Sheridan's army would rejoin Grant while engineers laid out a defensive position east of the Blue Ridge in the vicinity of Manassas Gap. With his aides and two engineers, Little Phil boarded a west bound Baltimore & Ohio train shortly after noon chugging toward Martinsburg, where they spent the night. Escorted by 300 cavalrymen, Sheridan rode the next morning, October 18, to Winchester, and decided to stay for the night. Nothing indicated the need for the general to rejoin the army. All was quiet in the camps at Cedar Creek Colonel Oliver Edwards, Provost Marshal at Winchester, reported.

The camps and works of the Federal army stretched across a series of ridges between Cedar Creek and Middleton. The uneven terrain, with wooded crests, steep-banked ravines, and the oxbow curves of the stream, determined the dispositions. The blue-clad infantry and artillery batteries occupied the successive ridges en echelon running from east to west. Torbert's two cavalry divisions guarded the more level ground extending toward the Back Road. The Northern line spread five miles from flank to flank.

The 77th's Sixth Corps held the infantry's right on a mass of hillocks and hollows between the cavalry and Meadow Brook, a significant tributary of Cedar Creek whose course paralleled the Valley Pike emptying into the larger stream about three quarters of a mile west of the turnpike bridge. Sheridan positioned Wright's three divisions along this portion of the line, supposing that if the Confederates attacked it would be against the right flank. If Early assaulted the opposite end, then Wright would have difficulty shifting his hardened veterans across the eroded and deep ravine chiseled by Meadow Brook.

Emory's two divisions of the Nineteenth Corps, across the gorge, to the southeast, occupied a crest 150 feet above Cedar Creek. The line extended from above the mouth of Meadow Brook to the pike bridge. Emory's foot soldiers had dug a trench along the hilltop, piling the ground to a height of three feet. The corps' artillery batteries commanded the bridge, two fords, and the approaches south of the stream. The camp sites blanketed the plain behind their works which sloped downward toward the ravine of Meadow Brook. Emory was confident that his command could smash any frontal assault which had to cross the creek and scale the precipitous slope.

George Crook's Army of West Virginia and Colonel J. Howard Kitching's Provisional Division held the ground east of the Pike. Kitching's command, a combined force of regiments from the Sixth, Eighth, and Nineteenth Corps, totaling 6,000 men in three brigades, had just joined Little Phil's army as reinforcements. Sheridan placed Kitching's with Rutherford Hayes' fighters on a barren ridge around 400 yards from the Valley Pike and due east of Emory's camps. Because the Northerners thought it unlikely an attack would come from the Federal left, the soldiers of the two divisions did not build earthworks. Tents dotting the position indicated more a campsite than a battle line. The tents paralleled the Valley Pike, with Kitching lying north of Hayes. Between these two commands on level ground, the Yankees parked most of their ambulances and ammunition wagons.

Joseph Thoburn's First Division of Crook's command manned a knoll over one half of a miles south of Hayes and approximately a mile southeast of Emory's corps. Thoburn's command was the eastern and southern end of the main Union line. His troops had erected a heavy abatis of timber and Captain Frank Gibb's Battery L, 1st Ohio Light Artillery buttressed the infantry firepower. Henry Dupont's remaining two batteries were unlimbered on a ridge between two ravines. This artillery reserve lay several hundred yards to the right and rear of Thoburn. Woods and underbrush covered the ground between Dupont and Thoburn. If a Rebel attack overran Thoburn's works and dislodged Dupont's cannon before infantry reserves arrived, the flanks of both Emory and Hayes would be exposed to an enfilade attack. The First Division's isolated position was the weak point in the Union line.

October 18, the 77th and their comrades stirred before daylight and lay at arms for two hours before cooking their breakfast and boiling their coffee. Most of Sheridan's regiments spent the day washing, mending, and writing letters. More than a few, like Private Cyrille Fountain, "Sent my Vote home for honest old Abe, the right man in the right place." The day before, Captain Isaac D. Clapp (Co. C) commanded 140 veterans of the regiment detailed for picket duty. "The

17th and 18th," Clapp reminisced, "demanding only routine was sort of a picnic for those off duty, for they visited farm houses adjacent, returning with honey, chickens, etc., whereby we were enabled to enjoy the delicacies of the season." Back at the regiment's camp on the evening of the 18th, George Stevens and the New Yorkers "threw ourselves upon the ground, wrapt in our blankets, as free from anticipation of impending danger as though we had retired to our chambers at home. It is true that there had been some picket firing in different parts of the line for a day or two past, but we felt quite sure that it had no very serious meaning." [10]

For the 77th and Sheridan's soldiers, the 18th was marked by the routine and the pleasurable with thoughts of home. For the Southerners, it was a day of decisions and war making. Not wanting a costly frontal attack on the Federal line, Jubal Early the day previous instructed Gordon, Brigadier General Clement A. Evans, and Jedediah Hotchkiss, Old Jube's topographical engineer, to conduct a thorough examination of Sheridan's works from the summit of Massanutten's "Three Sisters." The trio of officers climbed the steep slope of the "Three Sisters" during the afternoon. From the peak they could see miles of the Valley colored by the leaves of autumn. With their field glasses the officers examined every part of Sheridan's line, counting cannon and observing the distinctive flags of infantry, artillery, and cavalry. Hotchkiss mapped out the Union line for use at their meeting with Early. Gordon and the engineer collaborated on a plan, discussing the details as they descended the mountain.

Returning after dark, Hotchkiss met with Early and John Pegram briefly outlined Gordon's plan, pointing to the map he had sketched earlier. The Southern general then summoned his senior officers to headquarters. Soon Gordon, Ramseur, Kershaw, Wharton, Rosser, Tom Carter and William Payne joined Early, Pegram, and Hotchkiss.

Gordon proposed a night march by his Second Corps around the exposed Federal left flank. Pegram objected and questioned Gordon on how he could march an entire corps between the sheer northern face of Massanutten and the North Fork of the Shenandoah River coursing along its base. Gordon firmly rebutted Pegram, saying a way would be found, and he would accept full responsibility for failure.

Early's generals unanimously endorsed Gordon's plan – a daring gamble unparalleled in the war. The remaining commands were then given their roles. While the Georgian commander led the Second Corps over the river and along the mountain, Kershaw would move to the Bowman's Mill, a ford of Cedar Creek downstream from the Bowman family's Mount Pleasant home, and assault Thoburn at the specified hour. Wharton, with the artillery, was instructed to follow the Pike to Hupp's Hill, crossing the creek after Gordon and Kershaw attacked, pressing his advance down the Pike toward Middleton. Tom Rosser, crossing at Minebank Ford, would begin the offensive by engaging the Federal cavalry. In the meantime, Payne would precede Gordon, round up any Union pickets and then dash toward Belle Plain, an impressive limestone house which served as Federal headquarters, and then try to capture Sheridan. All attacking units were to be in position by 5 a.m.

At 8 p.m. on October 18, the Second Corps filed down Fisher's Hill, marching eastward. The Confederate column forded the North Fork at George Hupp's, two miles south of Strasburg. Once over, the foot soldiers passed through some fields before arriving at the base of Massanutten. Turning north, they followed Gordon's route, a "pig's path," marching single file. Couriers from the corps were stationed at every fork along the path preventing Gordon's soldiers from turning in the wrong direction. A bright moon dimly lit the narrow path.

The Southerners came to the end of the mountain opposite the house of Andrew Pitman, turned eastward and continued to the lane running down to Bowman's Ford. The head of the column lay down waiting for the attacking elements to close up. A thick blanket of fog hugged the river and banks, but the Confederates could see mounted videttes from Colonel Alpheus S. Moore's brigade of Powell's division guarding the shallows. When all his infantry arrived, Gordon ordered Payne forward, and the Virginian troopers plunged down the bank into the water. Gunfire broke the stillness, and the stunned cavalry pickets were overrun. Payne's horsemen then continued on toward their assigned mission.

Behind Payne's troopers, Gordon's infantry silently slipped into the cold chest-deep river. The graycoats struggled up the slippery bank in their clinging wet clothes. Officers hurried the regiments forward as the men "trotted up" the country road. At the J. Cooley house, a mile and a half due north of the ford, Gordon deployed his battle line and wheeled it to the left. A dense fog shrouded the field, limiting vision to a matter of feet. The silence ahead in the mists indicated that they had arrived undetected beyond the Union flank. It would be another half an hour before they charged, so these seasoned veterans quietly waited, alone with their private thoughts.

On a knoll less than a mile away overlooking Bowman's Mill on Cedar Creek, Jubal Early atop his horse was also waiting. Around him, Joseph Kershaw's men were poised for their charge over the creek. Rosser, Wharton, and Carter's gunners were also ready at their assigned positions. The bearded, gray-haired general hoped the assault would mark a time of redemption and revenge for Winchester and Fisher's Hill.

The foremost picket post of Joseph Thoburn's division of George Crook's Army of West Virginia was manned by the Second

Battalion, 5th New York Heavy Artillery during the early morning hours of October 19th. Since midnight, the battalion had become increasingly wary while listening to disturbing sounds to the east, toward the base of Massanutten. Convinced that danger approached, Captain Frederick C. Wilkie reported this to brigade headquarters of Lieutenant Colonel Thomas F. Wildes. Then about 4 a.m., the Empire State volunteers distinctly heard the sharp exchange of carbine and rifle fire at Bowman's Ford when William Payne's Virginia horsemen overran the mounted videttes of Colonel Alpheus S. Moore. The 77th's pickets under Captain Isaac D. Clapp too heard the reports rifle and carbine. The New York captain reported, "We were startled by sharp firing on our right." Clapp at once started up the picket line to learn the cause when he "met a mounted orderly who told me that the rebel cavalry had attacked our pickets and that the division officer of the day had been killed." The alarmed captain hurriedly returned to his command and "got the reserve in line and waited" for further developments, "but the firing . . . ceased near daylight." [11]

About 5:40 a.m., and the arrival of daybreak, Isaac Clapp and the 77th pickets nervously peered into the thick fog when "heavy musketry firing began far away on our left, which after a while was augmented by cannon." The captain later stated "We knew then that a general engagement was on, and though we could tell by the receding reports, that our lines were going back, having no orders to the contrary, we stayed in our position." Little did they know that the sound of musketry and cannon signaled the charge of Jubal Early's infantry, initiated by Joseph Kershaw's four Confederate brigades, numbering 3,000 veterans from South Carolina, Georgia, and Mississippi. [12]

The Georgia brigade of Colonel James P. Simms led the advance of Kershaw's division. Behind Simm's soldiers came the brigades of

Brigadier General William Wofford and Benjamin G. Humphreys and Major James M. Goggin. Simms moved his Georgians a short distance eastward, faced them left and brought them into battle formation. While Simms' soldiers stepped forward into a clump of trees, the other three brigades started deploying. Wofford swung his command to the right flank of the division. Humphreys led his Mississippians into the gap between Simms and Wofford, while Goggin formed his men on the divisions left flank. Each soldier carried sixty rounds of ammunition, but Kershaw ordered no firing until the brigades reached the works of Thoburn's division.

As the morning son sent slivers of light in the eastern sky, Simms' Georgians steadily marched toward the isolated works of Thoburn's two brigades. The Rebel battle line closed to within paces of the Union line and then burst in a roar of musketry. The volley loudly reverberated from one end of the valley to the other. Screeching like uncaged wildcats, the butternuts poured over entrenchments, flowing into a gap between the brigades of Thomas F. Wildes and Colonel Thomas M. Harris. The Georgians swung left and right, raking the trenches with enfilading fire. Harris' regiments were outflanked and rolled up one by one, and fled rearward in a confused rout. Humphrey's arriving Mississippians, likewise, wrecked Wildes' brigade. Thoburn's bloodied division streamed westward toward the Valley Pike and the position of the Nineteenth Corps. The rout of the Federal infantry of the division commander was swift, taking only about fifteen minutes to complete, sweeping them several hundred yards to the rear. Of Thoburn's nine regiments, all but two had been broken beyond temporary repair.

Kershaw's advance briefly stalled because of the ground-hugging fog as the attacking brigades were having difficulty maintaining cohesion. A number of gray-uniformed men left the ranks and plundered the Union camps. The kettles of hot coffee, the stacks of rations and clothing were too inviting targets for the Rebels to pass up. Captain H. H. Stevens, 17th Mississippi, complained that members of his brigade were "eating, drinking, and feeling big and brave." The plundering clearly began at the outset of the Confederate attack, and would strip away strength from Rebel regiments which needed every man in the ranks. Even so, the southeast anchor of the Union line had been effectively erased, uncovering the left flank of the Nineteenth Corps located nearly a mile away to the north and west. [13]

To Kershaw's north and east, the Second Corps under Gordon launched its assault on the divisions of Rutherford Hayes and J. Howard Kitching within minutes of his advance on Thoburn. Gordon had positioned his three divisions in the woods and fields west of the J. Cooley farm, about one half of a mile from the Federal camps. The division of Clement A. Evans held the left front of the corps. Behind Evans' three brigades, John Pegram formed his two brigades of North Carolinians and one of Virginians. Adjoining Evans' right, extending the battle line northward, Stephen Dodson Ramseur aligned the corps largest division of four brigades of Alabamians, Georgians, and North Carolinians.

As the battle line – seven brigades wide – neared the Northern camps on a ridge, the soldiers broke into a run and howled the hellish Rebel yell. The three brigades of Evans, erupting from the fog, stormed into the Union position occupied by Rutherford Hayes' soldiers. Hayes, who was joined by Horatio Wright and George Crook, immediately ordered his two brigades into line. Because of previous attachments, the division counted only 1,445 men. Only Hayes' left brigade, commanded by Colonel Hiram F. Devol, were under arms and in some sort of combat formation when the Confederates hit. Lieutenant Benjamin F. Choates' brigade, minus the detachments of the 14th West Virginia and forty men of the 34th Ohio, were still in their tents. Adding to Hayes' deployment problems were the broken ranks of Thoburn which poured past and through the right of his line.

The shocked Federal division rapidly disintegrated before the ferocity of gray and butternut uniforms sweeping in from the east. Devol's troops fired off a volley of musketry, but the Virginians of Brigadier General William Terry and the Louisianans led by Colonel Edmund Pendleton lambasted the brigade with frontal and flank fire. Devol's Ohioans and West Virginians cracked under the onslaught and streamed toward the rear.

On the left of Terry's Virginians and Pendleton's Louisianans, John H. Lowe's Georgia brigade smothered Coates' understrength brigade. The Northerners stampeded to the rear while some sought shelter in a tree-covered ravine. The Georgians entered the ravine on the heels of the Yankees loading and shooting as fast as they could. Coates' men finally scrambled up the opposite bank, their knapsacks providing targets for the Georgians.

In the middle of the wreckage on his division, the future president, galloping the rear, had his horse shot from beneath him. The sudden fall briefly knocked Hayes unconscious and injured his right ankle. Some of his troops passing by his still body spread the word that their commander had been killed. But Hayes regained his senses as the Rebels were closing and hobbled toward the turnpike. The Rebels ordered him to stop, but the colonel fortunately found an aide, who relinquished his horse, and Hayes escaped.

Farther north on the ridge, Dodson Ramseur's veteran division was routing the untested 6,000-man command of Kitching. Cullen Battle's Alabamians, on the division's right, spearheaded Ramseur's assault, tore into and around the Federal left flank. Close behind battle came the Georgians of Philip Cook and then the North Carolina Tar Heels of William Cox and Bryan Grimes. The men in gray caught many of the Yankees half-dressed and still in their tents. A number of Rebels grabbed new rifles and ammunition left behind by panicked Northerners running to the rear. Ramseur's casualties were few, but they included the capable Cullen Battle, who was brought down with a crippling wound which invalided him for the remainder of the war.

The low-lying mists concealed the magnitude of the Union defeat and rout which took place in the span of less than thirty minutes. On the plain west of the Valley Pike, from Middleton to the Nineteenth Corps position overlooking Cedar Creek, crumpled remnants of three Union divisions, more than 9,000 soldiers, were flooding westward toward Meadow Brook. Some officers rallied pockets of fleeing soldiers, which turned around and offered battle. Private Albert Snyder (Co. F), recently recovered from a wound received during Upton's column assault at Spotsylvania, found himself caught up in the westward blue tide:

> In the midst of the confusion in the sudden early morning attack I was detailed with others to help load the officers' baggage. When I got through I went back to my tent and finding that the regiment had been ordered to the left, where the fighting was, and it being dark and foggy I was thinking what to do, as I had not had breakfast, when an officer rode up and in an excited manner ordered all to leave as quick as they could, for the enemy would be on that ground in ten minutes. So I went back with the crowd. We halted, faced about, formed into a line of battle and stood for a while. Then faced to the rear and went farther back, halted and faced to the front. Again were we about faced and marched further back. We finally made a last stop and

helped to turn the backward movement. This line of battle was composed of men of the different corps, commanded by officers of the different corps, until we were ordered to rejoin our respective regiment. [14]

Though Surgeon George Stevens from within his tent heard brisk firing in front of "the Eighth (Crook) and Nineteenth Corps, [he] imagined that there was a picket skirmish." Stevens soon learned of his mistake. At a 1901 reunion of 77th veterans, the doctor recalled his experience as the Rebels were driving three shattered Union divisions:

> My tent-mate, always an early riser, after going outside pulled open the flies and called to me. 'Get up quickly, there is trouble brewing.' I did not start till he called again; this time in urgent tones. I arose and looking out upon the field saw a sight such as I never witnessed before. Amusement and consternation, if such a combination can be imagined, took possession of us. Hundreds of men were going with hasty steps and lengthy strides to the rear. Stragglers in all stages of dishabille filled the space in the concavity of the horse-shoe and far to the rear. They went each man by himself; some without hats, others without coats or boots, some with suspenders dangling behind, a few with guns, many wearing the shoulder straps of officers, but all, whether in full dress or most scantily clad, all were bent upon one object, namely to get the greatest distance toward Winchester in the shortest space of time . . . Riderless horses were galloping here and there, cows, with which the army was well supplied, were bellowing, mules were braying . . . By the time I had taken a glance at this extraordinary scene, turning toward the left, I saw the Confederates pouring toward the Winchester turnpike and presently heard the whistle of many bullets about

my head. Gathering my company of assistants and attendants, we made as dignified a retreat as possible toward our own Corps, but we had not gone far before that Corps was advancing rapidly toward us, so that we were sandwiched between our own men and the advancing line of the enemy. [15]

Crook, Thoburn, Hayes, and Kitching, and subordinate officers formed fragments of the three divisions around army headquarters at Belle Grove mansion, which lay about one half of a mile west of the original Hayes-Kitching position. George Crook was astonished to see his "Mountain Creepers" fleeing before the Confederates. He had ridden from headquarters at the initial volley, but he, too, could not prevent the break up of Hayes' and Kitching's ranks. Swept back with his soldiers, Crook and the others rallied approximately 1,500 fugitives, forming them between Belle Grove and the turnpike. A stand here was crucial, or the army's wagon train would fall into Confederate hands.

The park of wagons extended from Middleton, along the plain by Belle Grove, to the camps of the Nineteenth Corps. At the outburst of musketry, the teamsters and their escorts started the teams northward. As the Federal lines broke, spilling infantrymen across the pike onto the plain, a number of wagons overturned in ditches and were abandoned. Sections of the train parked near Middleton escaped with little difficulty, but scores of wagons and ambulances remained. Some of the battles first stand-up combat now followed as the patchwork Yankee line bought time for the safe passage of the vehicles. For the next thirty minutes the enemies bloodied each other in the fog. Many Union officers grabbed muskets and stood in the ranks with the enlisted men. The slugfest took its toll among officers of both sides, but the most grievous loss was that of Colonel Joseph Thoburn. A physician prior to the war, Thoburn had fought in twenty four battles, rising from regimental to divisional command. A few days earlier, he told surgeon Alexander Neil that "he only wanted to fight one more great battle and then he would be satisfied." Though he got his wish on this day, Thoburn was mortally wounded, dying an hour and a half later. [16]

Cook's and Cox's hardened Confederates relentlessly pressed ahead, finally shattering the Federal line, which ran back through the fields, down and across the Meadow Brook ravine. The Southerners captured a number of ambulances and wagons, but the gallant defense saved most. The wagoneers escaped by driving their teams into the ravine and over the small stream.

While this desperate combat raged from Middleton to Belle Grove, the rising tide of the Confederate divisions of Evans and Kershaw charged the only Union command still remaining east of Meadow Brook, Major General William "Old Brick Top" Emory's Nineteenth Corps. Holding the bluffs overlooking Cedar Creek, from Meadow Brook to the Valley Pike, Emory's men had been under arms in their works before daybreak. Coatless, hatless, and uncombed, Emory was saddling his horse when the Southerners attacked. He immediately sent his aide, Captain John DeForest to inform Wright of the attack on Crook and then galloped toward his troops.

Emory, like many others of rank, rode in those early minutes unaware of the scale of the Confederate offensive because of heavy fog. But he was anxiously aware that if Thoburn and Hayes and Kitching broke under the attacks, his flank and rear were exposed to the Rebels. Further, neither of his two divisions were under the command of experienced officers. Grover was absent from his post because of wounds suffered at Winchester. As a result of a bitter quarrel between Grover and Dwight, Emory several days previous, relieved Dwight of command. Brigadier General James W. McMillan now commanded Dwight's three brigades; Brigadier General Henry W. Birge, Grover's four.

"Old Brick Top" found his troops motionless and expectant behind their breastworks. The fog cloaked the storm on their left flank, but the sounds ebbing ever closer, indicated that Early's butternuts were fast approaching. After ordering James Ricketts to send two Sixth Corps divisions to the front, Horatio Wright, the acting army commander in Sheridan's absence, joined Emory, staunching blood with a handkerchief after being clipped between his lower lip and chin by a minie ball.

Emory redeployed all five of his brigades before the approaching gray battle lines crashed into his position. The Nineteenth Corps dispositions were completed under artillery fired from Southern batteries located south of Cedar Creek and from the captured cannon of Battery D, 1st Pennsylvania Light to the east. For the first time in the battle, the artillerymen of William Nelson, Carter Braxton, William McLaughlin and Wilfred Cutshaw joined the action, throwing solid shot and shells into the camps of the Federals.

The battle was a little short of an hour when the Rebel infantry closed on Emory's corps. From the south and east came the brigades of Goggin, Simms, and Humphreys of Kershaw's division. From the east came the brigades of Lowe, Pendleton and Terry of Evan's division. Kershaw's troops were moving toward a head-on collision with the base of Emory's line, while Evan's were kniving in on an angle just north and east of Kershaw.

Colonel Daniel Macauley's soldiers and Lieutenant Frederick Chase's Battery D. 1st Rhode Island Light's gunners first viewed the enemy through the fog and gun smoke at a distance of 150 yards. The Union line erupted with musketry and cannon blasts. The graycoats replied with a withering fire, engulfed the Federal position, and were met by musket-clubbing, bayoneting Yankees. Fierce hand-to-hand slaughter ensued, with Rebel numbers prevailing. Macauley's embattle troops broke for the rear. Exhorting his men to stand and fight, Macauley tumbled from his horse with a severe chest wound.

As Kershaw's butternuts routed Maccauley's regiments, Evans veterans hammered Colonel David Shunk's command, wrecking it, also. The Rebel general's division, like Kershaw's, broke like a tidal wave on the Union brigade with sheer numbers. The combat was fierce for a brief few moments as Shunk's Hoosiers and Ohioans held while Chase's Rhode Island gunners brought off their pieces. His artillerists rode off with all but one cannon as Shunk's line collapsed. The battery lost another piece as it retreated across Meadow Brook with Shunk's brigade.

The destruction of Macauley's and Shunk's brigades placed Emory's three remaining brigades in an untenable position. One by one the commands abandoned the earthworks, moving into the direct path of the Confederates; one by one they were swept of the field by the two Southern divisions.

The scene at this point, barely lent itself to concise description. The flotsam of Emory's corps poured across the thigh deep Meadow Brook. The command's disorganization ranged from individual soldiers escaping on their own to regiments still formed around their colors. Meanwhile, Captain Isaac Clapp and the 77th pickets had anxiously held their position for more than an hour while the battle raged to their right. Losing connection with his left, Clapp ordered his men to fall back toward camp. He instructed Lieutenant David A. Thompson (Co. F), who would later be wounded this day, to take care of the reserve and fall back, keeping in supporting distance of the picket line which would also fall back to camp. The New York captain wrote in a letter:

> No sooner had our picket line began their backward movement then the rebel(s) began to press us. We had gone some distance when the discharge of cannon was plainly heard. Looking through the woods I saw the reserve on the double quick. Running to the left and looking around again, I espied a rebel battery on a rise of ground where our regimental pioneer corps was encamped where we left our camp two days before. Again looking to the left . . . I saw our line of battle of blue nearly a mile away, when I 'double quick' ordered. The reserve was not losing any time in getting back, our retrograde movement was considerably accelerated by the music of that rebel battery, the shot and shell from which plowing up the ground throwing some of it upon us; but we did not stop to brush it off . . . After we had come to a walk and within a short distance of our line of battle, I saw an orderly, who was dressed in our uniform, wheel his horse and ride for the rebel lines, and one of our men staggering. I ran to him and seeing he was splitting blood I asked him if he was seriously hurt. He replied, 'I don't know, but I don't allow any rebel to call me a Yankee son of a gun and get away if I can prevent it.' I looked to where I had seen the rebel last, just as he reeled off his horse and fell to the ground. We then marched inside our lines, and finding a good place to make coffee, halted, and as we had no breakfast, prepared one. [17]

Emory, who had his horse killed beneath him, formed a line around the batteries of Chase and Captain Elijah Taft on Red Hill in the vicinity of the home of Dr. Shipley, about 1,200 yards west of

Belle Grove. Still weak from his Winchester wound, Grover, atop an old mule, brought his skeleton brigades in on the left of the artillery while McMillan formed on the right. The time neared 7:30 a.m.

Captain Isaac D. Clapp (NYSDMNA)

Across Meadow Brook, the Yankee camps and fieldworks swarmed with gray uniforms. In less than two hours, Early's Southerners had driven five Federal divisions from the plain between Middleton and Cedar Creek and captured over 1,300 prisoners, including Private Alonzo Bump who quickly escaped into the fog, and eighteen cannon. A number of men fell out of their ranks to pillage supplies from the Union camps, causing partial disarray in some of the victorious regiments. Yet there was more work before them.

With Horatio Wright temporarily in command of the army, James B. Ricketts directed the Sixth Corps, and he had the 77th and his veterans, numbering over 9,000, stirring before daylight. The

New Yorkers and their comrades were boiling coffee and grumbling over the morning chill when the Confederates attacked George Crook's command. Unaware of the seriousness of the early morning attack, the Union soldiers expected an easy repulse of the enemy. Suddenly bullets were whizzing above their heads from three different directions. The long roll of drums sounded through the camps, and officers ordered their men under arms and into the ranks. The war-hardened veterans instantly struck tents and packed their knapsacks. Columns were formed, and, within twenty minutes of the initiation of the Southern offensive, the Sixth Corps, marching by the left flank, headed east toward the sound of battle. Visibly reluctant to enter the anticipated combat, three-year veteran Corporal John Horrigan (Co. G) protested, "My time is out November 23d. I am old soldier enough to keep out of battle for thirty-five days." But, "while John was proposing there was ONE disposing. John was among those killed at Cedar Creek, October 19th, 1864." [18]

Ricketts hurried his soldiers on the double quick as Wright had called for two divisions at once. The corps advanced en echelon by the left flank: The 77th's division under George Getty in the van, then Frank Wheaton's, and finally Ricketts', now commanded by J. Warren Keifer. The ghostly fog seemingly rained bullets, the result of overshooting by the Rebels. As the divisions approached the Meadow Brook ravine, the regiment encountered the first signs of the rout unfolding across the gorge. Following the 77th, the Vermont Brigade's Major Aldace F. Walker grumbled,

> I am utterly unable to describe the universal confusion and dismay that we encountered. Wagons and ambulances lumbering hither and thither in disorder; pack horses led by frightened bummers, or wandering at their own free will; crowds of officers and men, some shod and some barefoot, many of them coatless and hatless, few without their rifles;

but all rushing wildly to the rear; oaths and blows alike powerless to halt them; a cavalry regiment stretched across the field, unable to stem the torrent; and added to the confusion and consternation the sight of blood, ambulances, wagons, men, stained and dripping, with here and there a corpse; while the whistling bullets and the shrieking shell told that the enemy knew their advantage and ground. It was a sight that might have demoralized the Old guard of the First Napoleon. [19]

Getty's troops reached the western edge of Meadow Brook ravine first and came under fire from butternut skirmishers in a piece of woods on the opposite plain. The 5th and 6th Vermont, and Major Walker's battalion of the 11th Vermont, were ordered forward to clear the woodlot. The Green Mountain boys quickly dislodged the enemy. Getty brought his three brigades across the stream behind the Vermonters, and formed a line approximately 1,000 yards north of Belle Grove and 500 yards south of Middleton. But Wright, realizing that no part of the original line could be held, countermanded his orders to Ricketts, and ordered the Sixth Corps to form a defensive position west of Meadow Brook. Wright's command, however, took time filtering down through the chain of command, for Ricketts was severely wounded in the chest and right shoulder. Accordingly, the divisions withdrew incrementally.

Keifer began his retreat toward the hills behind the command's original campsite as the fleeing units of William Emory's Nineteenth Corps poured across Meadow Brook before the divisions of Kershaw and Evans. So great were the number of broken troops that for a time the lines had to be opened at intervals to allow them to pass to the rear. Wheaton brought his two brigades into position approximately 250 yards east and slightly north of Keifer's left flank only minutes before Kershaw's Georgians, Mississippians, and North Carolinians struck hard Keifer's division. Evan's soldiers followed closely and moments later crashed into Wheaton's division. The hard-pressed bluecoats fought back, but they were driven backwards by the flood of Confederates flushed with victory.

The time was now nearly 8 a.m. Two divisions of the Sixth Corps – Kefier's and Wheaton's – and the organized remnant of the Nineteenth Corps were flowing northward over the farmlands west of Meadow Brook. These commands regrouped about three-fourths of a mile from the hills and ridge from which they had been driven. The only Federal infantry command still remaining on the field south of Middleton was the 77th's Second Division commanded by George Washington Getty. The retreat of the latter two divisions placed Getty in an untenable position with Kershaw and Evans beyond his right flank. He directed his three brigades back about 300 yards to "a strong crest, semi-circular in form and partially wooded." The Union commander chose wisely as it was the best defensive position on this sector of the field. As the 77th joined the ranks on the hill, the New Yorkers noticed that it was the site of Middleton Cemetery. [20]

James M. Warner's brigade of one New York and three Pennsylvania regiments held the division's right, facing nearly south. On Warner's left, in the center Getty deployed Grant's Vermonters. The 77th's brigade, Daniel D. Bidwell commanding, covered the left front line that was parallel to and bordering Meadow Brook. From left to right were the 61st Pennsylvania, 77th, 49th New York, 1st Maine (battalion of veterans of the 7th Maine who reenlisted after their term of enlistment ended), 122nd New York, and 43rd New York. Skirmishers from the 1st Maine and 43rd New York completed the alignment by connecting with videttes of Thomas Devin's cavalry brigade. Captain Charles E. Stevens (Co A) and a contingent of the regiment were thrown to the front "for the purpose of observing the movements of the enemy." Captain James McKnight's Battery M, 5th United States Artillery unlimbered in the cemetery between Grant's left and Bidwell's right. Getty's line resembled a horse-shoe. Along with their comrade regiments, and Warner's division, the 77th was sheltered by a grove of oak trees. Grant's division occupied open ground. The New York regiment's veterans hastily threw up temporary breastworks of rails and dirt, while others lay down behind the top of the hill, and waited for the shock to come. [21]

The anxious Yankee veterans did not have long to wait. As Getty deployed his division, John Pegram's 1,600-man division of Virginians and North Carolinians and Lieutenant Colonel Edwin L. Hobson's five Alabama regiments marched across the plain below Middleton. The Confederates crossed Meadow Brook ravine, and emerged from the fog, ascending toward the waiting Federals in two lines of battle. Pegram's three brigades, commanded by Brigadier General Robert Johnston, Colonel John S. Hoffman and Lieutenant Colonel William S. Davis, passed on both sides of the Samuel Sperry house on a path to Warner's and Grant's brigades. Hobson's Alabamians, marching almost due west, headed for a collision with the 77th's Third Brigade. Captain Stevens and his skirmishers fired a few shots announcing the advancing Rebels approach, and quickly withdrew to Getty's main line. Along with the rest of Getty's division, numbering 4,000, the 77th rose to a kneeling position. The division general issued orders prohibiting firing until the Rebels closed to within thirty yards. It was 8:30 a.m., and the fog was beginning to lift. [22]

The New York veterans tightened their grip on their muskets and aimed. Surgeon Stevens recorded the Confederates "rushed upon our lines with those wild, exultant yells, the terror of which can never be conceived by those who had not heard them on the field." When the butternuts were within thirty paces, the kneeling defenders, protected by trees and some breastworks of rails and stones, slammed the attackers with terrible effect. For Stevens, "It was like the clash of steel to steel." Staggered by the hail of bullets, the

Southerners fired a round of musketry before receding down the slope. Warner counterattacked Pegram with the 93rd and 102nd Pennsylvania, while Bidwell ordered his brigade to charge Hobson's Alabamians. "Rising from their places in the little graveyard and the grove," the 77th's brigade rushed forward, "the rebels, breaking and running in confusion down the declivity which they had but just ascended with such confidence, and crossed the little stream" Corporal John Horrigan (Co. G) became the first color bearer to be shot down this day. Captain Martin Lennon was mortally wounded in his upper left chest, dying two weeks later. Lieutenant William J. Tabor (Co. K) was shot through the bowels, dying within minutes on the field. Captain George S. Orr (Co. A) lost his left arm nearly to his shoulder when a shell exploded beside him. Lieutenant John W. Belding (Co. I) also fell mortally wounded. An unnamed young soldier from Private Alonzo Bump's hometown, Victory, "was Kild. After he was shot he run about 10 rods and then fell down Ded." Warner's men and Bidwell's soldiers returned to their positions on the crest. Captain Stevens once again descended the hill with his pickets. 23

Lieutenant William J. Taber (L. Tom Perry Special Collections)

Captain George S. Orr (L. Tom Perry Special Collections)

As the four Confederate brigades retreated across the plain, Warner's Pennsylvanians and the 77th's brigade retired to their original line, and Confederate batteries "concentrated a terrible fire of artillery upon our position, and shells from thirty guns flew, screaming devilishly, over and among us." The New Yorkers hugged the ground just behind the crest, but few were hurt as the shells overshot their position. During the half an hour cannonade, Getty learned of Ricketts' wounds and assumed command of the Sixth Corps. He turned over the division to Brigadier General Lewis Addison Grant and then rode northward in search of Keifer's and Wheaton's command. [24]

As Rebel battery fire diminished, Charles Stevens and 77th pickets again melted back to the main line announcing another charge by gray infantry. The oncoming Confederates belonged to Bryan Grimes' North Carolina Brigade. The Empire State volunteers, with the rest of Bidwell's brigade and the Vermonters, now under Lieutenant Colonel Amasa S. Tracy, again kneeled with their muskets primed to fire on the enemy. As the North Carolinians ascended the hill, they again screamed their blood curdling yell. When the single battle line of the enemy were within twenty paces of Bidwell and Tracy, the crest once more flashed with the fire from hundreds of rifles. Grimes' soldiers kept coming and, in the words of Vermonter Aldace Walker, "pressed us harder and harder, the lines being but a few yards apart." The 61st Pennsylvania and the 77th on Bidwell's right began to give way, gradually retreating step by step almost to the western foot of the crest, of which the Rebels now held the summit, while the left regiments of Tracy also swung back to maintain the continuity of the line. The 5th and 11th Vermont nearly panicked. [25]

Daniel Bidwell galloped toward the breach, urging his men to hold their ground. General Bidwell "sat erect upon his horse a few paces behind his prostrate brigade, as cool as tho the storm of fire and death was not playing around him." Sitting atop his horse beside Bidwell was Colonel Selkirk of his staff. "A shell had dropped and exploded among the men a little distance down the line, and they both were intently looking to see what fatal work it had done." At that instance, Bidwell was struck down. "A shell had torn his left shoulder away" and "pierced his lung" and hurled him, unconscious, to the ground. The lightning could not have been swifter or more noiseless in its stroke." Colonel Selkirk "heard nothing but one moan, and turned to find the General stretched upon the earth. His riderless horse stood still, as tho it had not felt the emptying of his saddle." [26]

Nearly insensible from the loss of blood, Bidwell was placed in an ambulance and brought to back to a field hospital in the rear. Surgeon Stevens had been amputating limbs and dressing wounds when an aid "rode to me saying that General Bidwell . . . was calling for me." The 77th's doctor "left my table in charge of others and mounting, rode at once to where the General was. An ambulance had already arrived and the General, who was a very large man, had been placed in it." Stevens recalled, "As I mounted the step of the ambulance, I saw that the whole of the left shoulder had been torn away by a shell. The wounded man said, 'Doctor, I suppose that there is no hope of recovery?' When I replied that I feared that there was no hope, he exclaimed, 'Oh, my poor wife!' And then, after a moment, 'Doctor, won't you see that my record is right at home; tell them I died at my post, that I did my duty." Bidwell then asked that a young contraband boy who had been his servant for some time be sent to Buffalo, and committed to the care of his family and friends." Lingering in and out of consciousness, the 45- year-old brigadier from western New York died that night. [27]

As Bidwell was carried off the battlefield, command devolved to Lieutenant Colonel Winsor B. French. Trusted by the soldiers of the Third Brigade, French rallied his men and the Pennsylvanians; the Vermonters steadied. French shouted, "Don't run till the Vermonters do!" and with loud huzzah, the 77th and 61st Pennsylvania sprang forward reaching their previous position on the crest. The astonished Rebels "formed in rows behind the trees for protection" The Yankees raked the Tar Heels from three sides, blasting them off the hill. Many surrendered themselves as prisoners. The Green Mountain soldier, Aldace Walker, recorded that two of the Rebel prisoners were later "killed together, far behind our line, by the same rebel shell." Grimes reformed his regiments east of Meadow Brook. [28]

At this point in the battle, Jubal Early rode down the Valley Pike and found Ramseur and Pegram who informed the Southern commander that they opposed part of the Sixth Corps. Old Jube ordered Gabriel Wharton forward without support. Wharton's three brigades of 1,100 effectives went in gamely. Behind the infantry, Captain Thomas A. Bryan's Lewisburg Battery unlimbered 300 yards from the Union position and opened fire. Following the attack path of Pegram, Wharton's Virginians drove toward the Federal right center. Stubbornly holding fast, Warner's and Tracy's men ripped apart the Confederate ranks, repulsing them handsomely. Bryan pulled back his cannon while Wharton reported the outcome to Early and his men reformed near the turnpike. The fog now had sufficiently lifted for Early to view the 77th's division's position, and concluded that a fourth assault from the pike could not succeed.

Lewis Grant received orders from Getty to withdraw at 9:30 a.m., and within minutes the 77th and the Second Division abandoned the embattled hilltop and cemetery. For over an hour they had stood fast, repelling three assaults, and slowing the momentum of the Confederate offensive. The bluecoats withdrew to a position behind a long fence made of stone and rails on a wooded ridge about a mile and a half north of Middleton, near the farm of David Dinges. No Northern troops rendered greater service on this day than these soldiers from New York, Pennsylvania, Vermont and Maine. Their defense gave the Union army a breathing spell and time to reorganize its troops.

Unlike the defeated troops of Crook's and Emory's commands, Getty's withdrawal from the crest was not one marked by panic and desperation. John Gordon reported the Sixth Corps retreat was "sullen, slow and orderly." One Yankee soldier said the command "went leisurely." George Stevens presented a more detailed account of the unbowed division: "We went back quietly and in good order, a single regiment, the Second Vermont, holding without any difficulty the position we abandoned. We carried with us all our wounded, all our shelter tents and all our personal property of every description, and the rebels did not dare to attack." [29]

Cavalry Corps commander Alfred Torbert, when he heard the roar of the Rebel offensive, immediately reacted. He ordered tents struck, horsemen to their saddles and wagons sent rearward. Within minutes his headquarters campsite was cleared. Sometime after 9 a.m., Wright ordered Torbert to move his entire corps to the left. Halting north and east of Middleton, Merrit deployed his brigades between the Valley Pike and the right of Moore. Devin held the ground adjacent to the turnpike. On his left, Kidd brought in his Michigan Wolverines, and Charles R. Lowell, Jr.'s Reserve Brigade linked with Moore. Five batteries of horse artillery anchored the position, which lay east of the road. The Union cavalry completed the dispositions by 10 a.m. shortly after Getty withdrew his soldiers. Torbert's numbered 7,500 troopers in the ranks.

Mere minutes later, the soldiers of Gabriel Wharton and William Wofford, clearing the village, encountered Merritt's troopers. Wharton's men charged Lowell's men who had taken position behind some stone walls, but were quickly repulsed. Many of the Union horsemen carried Spencer repeaters, giving them a decided edge in firepower. The contest continued as a brisk skirmish. Opposing artillery batteries added weight to the carbine and rifle fire. Pegram's division soon joined the fight, but the Confederates, outnumbered and overlapped on their right, could advance no further.

This was the situation when Old Jube rode into Middleton after 10 a.m. After examining the Federal position, he became concerned that the blue-jacketed cavalry might roll up his right flank. He determined that his army needed help on that flank before it could initiate another assault. Early sent instructions to Lunsford Lomax's division of 1,700 troopers, miles away beyond Fort Royal to move to Middleton as quickly as his men could ride. The courier never reached the cavalry commander, and Lomax kept riding farther away from the field.

By 10:30 a.m., the Confederate offensive had lost its steam. The divisions of Pegram, Wharton, and the brigade of Wofford were fought to a standstill before the Federal cavalry. Ramseur, sent by Early to occupy the crest left vacant by Getty's withdrawal, was moving forward to his subsequent position alongside Pegram. Kershaw was most likely enroute but behind Ramseur, while Evans was even further back. Early simply did not have the troops present to launch another coordinated frontal assault.

Not only were the Rebel infantry divisions not in place, but Early's ranks had been seriously depleted because of those absent plundering the Union camps. Private John Worsham, 21st Virginia, offered a reason for the breakdown in discipline:

> The world will never know the extreme poverty of the Confederate soldier at this time. Hundreds of men who were in the charge and who captured the enemy's works were barefooted. Every one of them was ragged. Many had on everything they had, and *none* had eaten a square meal for weeks. As they passed through Sheridan's camp, a great temptation was thrown their way. Many of the tents were open, and in plain sight were rations,shoes, overcoats, and blankets. The fighting continued farther and farther, yet some of the men stopped. They secured well-filled haversacks, and, as they investigated the contents, the temptation to stop and eat was too great. Since most of them had had nothing to eat since the evening before, they yielded. While some tried on shoes, others put on warm pants in place of tattered ones. Still others got overcoats and blankets – articles so much need for the coming cold. They had already experienced several biting frosts to remind them of the winter at hand. [30]

After tending to the mortally wounded Bidwell, the 77th's surgeon "returned to my extemporized field hospital, consisting of an operating table and surgical appliances." Stevens remembered, "I had just finished the amputation of the arm at the shoulder joint of brave Captain Orr and was applying bandages when looking down the turnpike, I saw Sheridan riding to the front. There was a line of ambulances along the pike, filled with wounded men. As Sheridan came on, every man in those ambulances who was able to rise joined in the shout of welcome and some even leaped out of ambulances." Philip Sheridan was now on the field. His very presence and fiery confidence now tipped the balance in favor the Federals. [31]

From Winchester, pickets from Colonel Oliver Edwards' Sixth Corps listened to the ominous distant rumble at daylight, October 19th. An officer with the pickets rode to post headquarters, a large brick home owned by tobacco merchant Lloyd Logan. Arriving before 6 a.m., he was escorted upstairs to Sheridan's room, where he informed the major general of the firing south on the pike. Believing the fire was only the sound of a scheduled reconnaissance by Curvier Grover's division, Sheridan was largely unconcerned. Little Phil dressed, walked downstairs, and requested breakfast and his horse saddled.

Phil Sheridan left the Logan home sometime before 9 a.m. and mounted Rienzi, an animal of tremendous strength and endurance. At Mill Creek, barely one half of a mile out of town, he was joined by his escort, the 17th Pennsylvania Cavalry. Minutes later, south of Mill Creek, the horseman encountered the first evidence of the disaster taking place at Cedar Creek – a stalled tangle of wagons. The brigade of Colonel William Curtis of George Crook's command guarded the train, which had been creaking toward the army when fugitives bearing "terrible tales of rout and ruin" caused a temporary panic. Curtis' troops were untangling the mess and moving the wagons off the highway when Sheridan approached. A quartermaster officer informed the commander that the Union army had been defeated. Moments later, another officer who had been on the field, confirmed the news, claiming that the army headquarters had been captured and the troops scattered. The staggering intelligence told of the entire Federal campaign in jeopardy. [32]

Sheridan instantly spurred Rienzi toward Cedar Creek, accompanied by a small escort of perhaps twenty men and two aides. As Little Phil passed the wagons and stragglers, he shouted, "Boys if you don't want to fight yourselves, come back and look at others fighting. We will whip them out of their boots before 4 o'clock." Each successive mile brought further signs of a defeated army. The Valley Pike teemed with wagons and fleeing soldiers. The major general paused along the way beside these fugitives, telling them that they should return to the battlefield. To one group: "Boys turn back' face the other way. I am going to sleep in that camp to-night or in hell." More than a few were inspired by his bravado: "The cheers and the huzzas were of the wildest, and stragglers turned back, and even some of the slightly wounded turned about to get a whack at those who served them so badly," George Stevens asserted. [33]

Approximately at 10:30 a.m., Sheridan bridled up behind the line of Lewis Grant's division, lying on the pastures of David Dinges. "What troops are those," shouted Sheridan. "The Sixth Corps," was the response from a hundred voices. "We are all right," said Sheridan. "Never mind, boys, we'll whip them yet; we'll whip them yet! We shall sleep in our old quarters tonight!" Little Phil then proceeded to a hillside between Crook's and Grant's men and found Horatio Wright, Crook, William Emory, Alfred Torbert and others. Wright, looking "tired and a little dispirited," greeted his commander, saying, "Well, we've done the best we could." "That's all right; that's all right," replied Sheridan. Emory then reported that his soldiers were reorganized and could cover the retreat to Winchester. "Retreat-Hell!" bellowed Little Phil, "we'll be back in our camps tonight." [34]

Sheridan asked his corps commanders for the status and dispositions of the Yankee units. The army, he learned, was dispersed but in reasonable order. Frank Wheaton's and J. Warren Keifer's divisions and Emory's command had regrouped and lay to the right and rear of the 77th's Second Division, stretching out for a distance of two miles. Torbert's troopers, skirmishing with the southerners, held the army's left flank, east of the pike. As the diminutive Federal commander listened, he instantly decided to attack the left flank of the Confederate army. Little Phil informed Wright that the army would fight on Grant's line and that the soldiers of Wheaton, Keifer, and Emory should be deployed on this front. He further directed Custer to shift from the left flank to the right flank. Quick deployment of these troops was crucial, for Sheridan expected to be attacked soon by Early's butternuts.

The Rebels, however, did not attack, and the redeployment was completed, except for Emory's men, between 11 a.m. and noon. During that time, Sheridan formally retook command of the army, with Wright taking direction of his corps and George Getty supplanting Grant at the helm of the division. He still expected a Confederate attack at any moment but, except for some skirmishing, nothing developed. About noon, Sheridan's chief of staff, Lieutenant Colonel James W. Forsyth, suggested to the general that he ride along the entire line so the infantrymen could actually see for themselves that he had returned to the army. William McKinley, who was present, offered that Sheridan remove his overcoat and hat that he might be more easily identified – no other general in the army possessed his unmistakable, bullet-shaped head.

What happened next perhaps has no equal in the chronicles of the Civil War. A renewed spirit, a palpable sense that all would be righted in a flash rapidly spread through the length of the Army of the Shenandoah. This small statured commander, overflowing with energy and confidence, possessed a charismatic presence that could not be denied. Where others before him failed, Philip Sheridan brought victory. Winchester and Fisher's Hill cemented them as an army. The Union soldiers attributed it to him, and now they reciprocated.

As he rode along the front of each successive regiment, holding his hat in hand, speaking to them, the men exploded with their approval. Passing by the 77th and their companion regiments, "the men threw their hats high in the air, leaped and danced and cheered in the wildest joy." It was this bond between Little Phil and the soldiers in the ranks which caused their jubilant response to his appearance. He could inspire men in battle like no other Yankee commander at this time in the war. He had a battlefield presence of undeniable worth. Writing the day after the battle to his wife in his inventive spelling and grammar, Private Alonzo Bump verbalized the confidence and affection of hardened Federal soldiers toward Phil Sheridan:

> All i have Got to say they Got a Good Licking one that they will long Remember i think but if it had not bin for Geniral Sheridan coming Back Just as hee did i think they would whipt us But as soon as hee come the tide of Battle turned. you could hear men cheearing all along the Line as they found out that hee had come Back. Eaven the wonded men and Dying would cheear him when hee Past them. the hole army farly worship him for in time of Battel hee is right up in the frunt with us. hee haint Back in the Rear two or 3 miles But right up front whare hee can see the Rebal movements. O he is a Brick to fight. hee will ride along the Lines and say Boys Give it to them Dame them they are cowards and I know it. Yesterday while we ware a fighting some of our men in the Rear that could not Keeap up. thair was a officer rode up to one man and was Goin to cut him down

and Just then Geniral Sheridan was a riding along and hee ses sur none of that. i cant Git my men in to Battel without that Boy and then hee spoke to the man Boy Goe up and Help the Boys. We can whip them and i know it and then they all Give him a cheear and went to the frunt like men. that is the kind of man hee is. Hee always speaks Kindly to the men. for that reason they all Like him. [35]

To the south, across cow pastures and trampled grain fields, divided by stone walls, were the morning's victors. The Southerners' main line stretched through the fields for three miles, from Abram Stickley's farm on the west to beyond the angle of the Cedarville and Buckton roads on the east. William Payne's troopers guarded the army's right flank beyond the Cedarville-Buckton roads. From there to the Valley Pike, the ground was held by Gabriel Wharton's three brigades and William Wofford's brigade of Joseph Kershaw's division. These soldiers occupied a sunken road perpendicular to the Pike, with a number of sharpshooters using some of the houses as vantage points. John Pegram's division connected with Wharton's left brigade at the highway and extended the front to the eastern edge of Meadow Brook. Across the brook, in succession from right to left were the divisions of Stephen Dodson Ramseur, the remaining three brigades of Kershaw and the division of Clement Evans, whose flank that abutted Middle Marsh Creek at the Stickley household. Thomas Carter's twelve artillery batteries were posted among the infantry units.

It was this line where the Rebel offensive stopped. The Confederates could go no further in the view of Jubal Early, until the threat posed by the Yankee cavalry had been removed and the plunderers returned to the ranks. Except for a tentative reconnaissance-in-force by Evans, Kershaw, and Ramseur at 1 p.m., the Southerners remained quiet. Jubal Early believed a brilliant Confederate victory was won, and dismissed the notion of a possible Federal

MCKEAN'S SUNDAY SCHOOL BOYS GO TO WAR

counterstroke. He issued orders sending the 1,300 prisoners, the captured stores, and cannon southward.

Earlier in the morning, Captain Isaac Clap and the detail of 77th pickets found their way to the rear, and after having breakfast and some rest, "We hunted for our regiment about 2 o'clock in the afternoon. Clapp remembered "Our comrades joyfully welcomed us, as they supposed we had been captured, and then told us of the morning's fight." Someone called out to the young officer, "Captain, see where Gil (Adjutant Gilbert Thomas, Co. C) was hit." The adjutant "held up his sword scabbard and showed me where a bullet had hit it in the center, denting it so that he could not put in his sword." Thomas smiled as he held up his scabbard for Clapp's inspection. Little did Adjutant Thomas or his comrades know that the brave officer had but a few hours left to live. [36]

John Gordon was anxious that his left flank was dangerously weak, unsupported and with a lengthy gap between his westernmost brigade on the mainline. Clement's division occupying some wooded knolls held this section. Gordon extended his flank with the intention of linking his skirmishers with those of Thomas Rosser. This put Colonel John Lowe's Georgia Brigade about a fourth of a mile from Colonel Edmund Pendleton's Louisianans. Trying to establish contact with Rosser's horsemen, Lowe sent three companies of the 31st Georgia farther to the left. The Georgians never found the mounted troopers, so the Confederate companies established their own line, with about thirty steps between each man. Gordon personally rode to Early's headquarters in Middleton to urge Old Jube to reinforce the left and fill in the gap. Unfazed, the Southern commander instructed Gordon to stretch out the already weak lines and take a battery of guns to the left. Gordon galloped furiously to execute the movements, but it was too late for the Confederates.

The next few hours were spent organizing and planning for the Federal counteroffensive. With Sheridan's return to the army, Horatio Wright resumed command of the Sixth Corps, and George Getty went back to the Second Division. Light skirmishing continued, ammunition was drawn, and orders for the advance were issued. Little Phil's plan called for the Nineteenth Corps to turn the left flank of Gordon's position while the Sixth Corps, supported by Crook's soldiers, stormed the front. The plan was simple and powerful. In essence, the Army of the Shenandoah would break the enemy left and then swinging like a door to the left bagging Early's entire army. The 77th's Second Division faced the Confederate right and would act as the door's hinge, assaulting slowly on purpose, pinning Jubal's soldiers in place in the hope the flanking attack would catch them from behind.

Moments before 4 p.m., buglers announced the charge of the Union army, and what artillery remained belched forth its missiles. The entire line stepped out from the trees and soon became locked into fierce fighting all across the line. At the western end of the Federal line, reinstated to command by Sheridan earlier that day, William Dwight's division of two brigades spearheaded the attack. The Yankees drove straight into the gap between Lowe's Georgians and Pendleton's Louisianans, occupying two timbered crests. Confederate batteries, positioned behind the hills opened fire. As the Northerners approached the bottoms of the knolls, Lowe's Georgians, concealed from sight, suddenly blasted the flank of Dwight's right brigade commanded by Brigadier General James McMillan. The Union attack was brought to a halt by a murderous enfilading enemy fire. McMillan wheeled his brigade to the right, and Colonel Edwin Davis on McMillan's left swung two of his regiments in that direction.

McMillan's brigade, plus Davis' two regiments, then climbed up the hillside, covered in cedar trees and thick undergrowth. The

Georgians fought doggedly, but the Yankees weathered the storm of bullets and kept going. Lowe's line subsequently collapsed before the blue storm, and spilled down the opposite slope. When the Northerners reached the top, they hollered "Hurrah!" threw their hats in the air and literally jumped up and down in triumph.

Atop his sweat-speckled horse, Phil Sheridan joined the celebrating men on the crest. While Dwight's attack had not gone as desired, Sheridan was satisfied that one Rebel brigade had been broken and the Nineteenth Corps division now overlapped the left flank of Gordon's main line. He instructed McMillan to close with Davis and wait until George Custer's cavalry division advanced on their right. When the blue-jacketed troopers appeared, the infantry should charge. Little Phil then rode toward the Federal center and left of his advancing lines.

The division of Cuvier Grover, who reassumed command during the lull in fighting, advanced with reckless disregard on the left of Dwight. Grover's four brigades swept aside Rebel skirmishers from a stone wall, around 400 yards in advance of the main Confederate line, but then came under a fierce fire from Pendleton's Louisianans and William Terry's Virginians of Evans' and Kershaw's left brigade. Grover, as did every regimental commander in Colonel David Shunk's brigade, went down with a wound as the attack stalled. Mounted on an old mule, Colonel Henry Birge took over command of the division. However, before the hail of bullets and exploding shells, Birge could not advance and his troops remained behind the stone walls.

On Birge's left, Frank Wheaton's Sixth Corps division fare little better. Opposing mostly Kershaw's veterans, these Northerners also dislodged the Rebels from stone walls and then went no further. They were particularly tormented by a battery behind the gray infantry. A shell fragment struck Colonel Ranald MacKenzie on the shoulder, forcing the regiment's competent officer to leave the field. This Federal Division, too, had been stopped.

The situation for J. Warren Keifer's division, aligned on Wheaton's left, was probably even worse. Before his soldiers advanced at 4 p.m., Keifer issued instructions to his brigade commanders, Colonels William Ball and William Emerson to dress to the left in the advance and close up all intervals. Unfortunately, when the division stepped out, Emerson angled too quickly to the left, massing his brigade behind Ball's. This opened the right flank, and the Confederates on Kershaw's right and Ramseur's left, enfiladed the exposed flank. Keifer's lines wavered and then broke toward the woods, leaving a number of dead and wounded on the field. Officers stabilized the line, and within five minutes, the Yankees again charged. Rebel skirmishers fled from their position behind some rock fences, beat a hasty retreat and fell back to their main line. Keifer's soldiers halted at the walls and squeezed off a round of musketry. The firing resounded, but the blue infantrymen could not advance further.

This initial repulse of Keifer's division briefly disrupted the 77th's Second division as it advanced on Keifer's left. Getty's three brigades opposed Ramseur's hard-fighting Southerners, whose line centered around the house, brick mill, and outbuildings of D. J. Miller. Ramseur's front was thick with skirmishers and they, supported by batteries to the rear, blistered the Federals as they stepped from the trees. Each of George Getty's brigades fought separate battles for a while.

On the division's right flank, Colonel James Warner's brigade, instead of closing leftward, had to angle in the opposite direction when Keifer fell back. On the brigade's right, the 93rd Pennsylvania, breaking under a killing fire on its uncovered flank, caused the shift. Warner accordingly obliqued his other regiments rightward, and cleared out gray videttes from a stone wall. The Pennsylvanians quickly rallied, and as Keifer sealed the breach, Warner's men dueled with their Southern counterparts.

Brigadier General Lewis Grant's Green Mountain Brigade held the center of Getty's line. A low ridge separated Grant's regiments from Warner's, precluding coordination between the commands. The Vermont soldiers lost sight of Warren's troops when they obliqued over the rise. They went in bravely on a path leading directly toward Miller's property, and "halted behind a fortunate wall, low, and just long enough cover" the brigade, and opened a brisk fire. There, the New Englanders encountered a heavy fire from an unknown number of Ramseur's troops positioned in and among Miller's house, mill, and outbuildings. The Vermonter, Aldace Walker, remembered that the buildings were "swarming with the enemy, our only approach to which was along a narrow road by the side of a little mill-pond formed by a dam across our old annoyance, Meadow Brook." With this obstacle in front and with their left flank expectantly unprotected, the Vermonters stayed put. [37]

Covering the ground between the Green Mountain regiments' left and the Valley Pike, the 77th's veteran Third Brigade, now under Lieutenant Colonel Winsor French's command, "adjusted their equipments, pulled their hats tight on their head, rammed charges into their muskets, and got themselves ready for the fray." The 77th was not only the left flank of the brigade, but it was also the extreme left of the army's line of infantry. When the buglers announced the advance, the command was given to forward. "Steady men, steady," cautioned Captain David Caw (Co. H), now in command in lieu of French, "Steady, forward, guide left, march," and the whole line of the army pressed forward. [38]

Sheridan had hoped that as the Yankee divisions charged, the Nineteenth Corps, overlapping the Confederate left flank, would initiate a giant left wheel of the entire army which would roll up the Rebel line. Consequently, George Getty assigned French the dual role of guiding on the Valley Pike and acting as the pivot of the movement. This meant that the 77th's brigade had to march slowly across a long open field which sloped downward into a small declivity, where Mill's brick mill was located, and then upwards to a crest edged by another stone wall manned by Bryan Grimes' North Carolinians.

Adjutant Gilbert F. Thomas (L. Tom Perry Special Collections)

Accordingly, French's brigade of three regiments and three battalions marched deliberately across the open field. Casualties were few, until the brigade came near mill and a low stone wall. As they approached the swale "they entered a cauldron of musketry and canister." Tar Heel infantrymen behind the wall and sharpshooters posted in the mill and outbuildings and the ridgeline blasted the slow-marching Yankees while Confederate batteries, behind the North Carolinians and east of the turnpike, raked the

Third Brigade's ranks with sheets of the one-inch slugs. The 77th's color sergeant, Benjamin Briggs (Co. A), went down with a serious wound and was carried to the rear. Color corporal Henry Clayton (Co. E) picked up the flag and was immediately struck down, also with a serious wound. Adjutant Gilbert Thomas then, "grasping the flag, leaped over the fence in front of the line and with it in one hand and his sword in the other, he cried, 'Come on boys!' As he turned to advance a rebel ball pierced his brain. He fell forward at full length on his face dead, the flag falling, covering him." The brigade's line wavered and then cracked, with the men pouring back into the woods. Not willing to let the regiment's flag fall into enemy hands, Sergeant Albert J. Reed (Co. B) picked up the banner, and was lucky to make it back to the woods relatively unscathed dodging Rebel bullets and canister. He was hit seven times by minie balls and once by a piece of a gun barrel. One ball struck his belt buckle and glanced off. Another grazed his hip after passing through a tree trunk. A third passed through his pants below the knee. A piece of gun barrel hit his pocket diary on his left side, staggering him, but not wounding him. A fourth ball took off the corner of the heel of his left shoe. Still another ricocheted from a rock in the field and tore the strap on his knapsack near the left shoulder. Yet another ball hit his cartridge box and passed through his clothes. Finally a minie passed through the fleshy part of his left leg just below the knee and fell down into his shoe. [39]

French rallied his troops in the shelter of the trees and when he saw Getty, he cried, "I cannot take my brigade over that field slowly." "Then go quickly," responded Getty. It was the order French wanted, and he waved his soldiers forward again. This time the Third Brigade with a shout double-quicked across the field, rushing past the mill and up the ridge. On their right, the Green Mountain Boys circled the millpond, swarming among the Miller outbuildings, sending the Rebels scampering up the hill. Both Federal brigades then halted and traded fire with Ramseur's main line a few hundred yards to the south. The Vermont Major Walker claimed that for the next thirty minutes each of his comrades shot fifty rounds of ammunition. [40]

From the turnpike westward to where Cuvier Grover's soldiers fought, the Federal assault had been brought to a halt. The Northerners had driven back Rebel skirmishers but no part of the main Confederate line had been broken, and it blazed in defiance. Hardened by battle, the Southerners did not buckle against the frontal attack, showing the imperturbability that had exhibited at Winchester. But, the battle at Cedar Creek the contest turned with the entry of Union cavalry against the left flank of the Confederate line.

George Custer's cavalry division entered the field at approximately 4:30 p.m. The horsemen came in at a furious gallop. Confederate skirmishers were thinly spread across the path of the troopers, fired a round and then hastened toward Cedar Creek. Behind the gray skirmishers, their comrades from Lowe's brigade were right behind, retreating toward the stream after being routed by Dwight's bluecoats.

The arrival of Custer was the signal for Dwight's two brigades to charge eastward down the Confederate line. Dwight promptly advanced through the swale between the two hills tree-lined knolls and up the western face of the hill occupied by Edmond Pendleton's Louisianans. Hidden by the woods, the Yankees surprised Pendleton's infantrymen. The Southern brigade's line disintegrated in mere minutes, with the Rebel veterans ran headlong down the hillside in flight.

The rout of Pendleton's Louisiana Brigade sent the front toppling like a row of dominoes from left to right. William Terry's Virginians, on the Louisianan's right, within minutes broke next, followed closely by Joseph Kershaw's division and then Dodson Ramseur's. John Gordon later lamented, "Regiment after regiment, brigade after brigade, in rapid succession was crushed, and, like hard clods of clay under a pelting rain, the superb commands crumble to pieces." [41]

With the Confederate stampede to Cedar Creek, Bryan Grimes' North Carolinians holding off Winsor French's brigade left the stone wall and hurried to the rear. The Third Brigade rushed forward nipping at their heels. George Stevens narrated: "Our men, with wild enthusiasm, with shouts and cheers, regardless of order or formation, joined in the hot pursuit. There was our mortal enemy, who had but a few hours since driven us unceremoniously from our camps, now beaten, routed, broken, bent on nothing, but the most rapid flight. We had not forgotten our humiliation of the morning, and the thought of it gave fleetness to the feet of our pursuers." The surgeon continued, "From the point where we broke the rebel ranks to the crossing of Cedar Creek, was three miles, an open plain. Over this plain and down the pike the panic-stricken army was flying, while our soldiers, without ever stopping to load their pieces, were charging tardy batteries with empty muskets, seizing prisoners by the scores and hundreds, every Union soldier his own commander, bent on nothing but the destruction of the flying foe." [42]

The commands of Pegram, Wharton, and Wofford were the last to cross the creek. It was about 5:30 a.m. and the sun had set and dusk dimmed the field. No malediction could stem the flood of gray infantry coursing toward Fisher's Hill. It was virtually every man for himself; unit organization disintegrated. Rebels, by the thousands, carpeted the fields between Cedar Creek and Fisher's Hill. The supply train wagons, ambulances, and artillery obstructed the Valley Pike, halting movement to a near standstill. The magnificent warrior, John Gordon, standing in a wagon bed at the foot of Fisher's

Hill, pleaded with passersby to return and assist the teamsters, but only three soldiers responded to the warrior from Georgia. It was a dismal scene of disorder, worsened by the creeping darkness, and reminiscent of the rout at Fisher's Hill on September 22.

As the night deepened, Federal mounted troopers knived into the retreating gray column between Strasburg and Cedar Creek. Wielding sabers, the Federals cut among the teams, cutting down the horses. A bounty of wagons and ambulances, dozens of cannon, and hundreds of captives were soon gathered up by the cavalrymen. At one point along the pike a squad of troopers took possession of a cannon as well as the Rebels accompanying it. The Yankees had unknowingly gobbled up Tom Carter, Early's artillery chief, and his staff, but as the prisoners were led away, Carter and his staff slipped away in the darkness. Many Rebels had narrow escapes and were saved by the darkness, an echo of Federal soldiers' escapes into the dense morning fog.

Some of the troopers entered Strasburg and then retraced their steps. On Fisher's Hill, the Southern flight was ending, as the majority of soldiers hunted their old campsites and slept. Jubal Early was their too, trying to reform his bloodied ranks. The only organized body of troops he could find was the 1,300 Union prisoners and their provost guard. "Nothing saved us," Early groused in his report, "but the inability of the enemy to follow with his infantry and his expectation that we would make a stand there. The state of things was distressing and mortifying beyond measure." [43]

To the north, across Cedar Creek, the 77th and their comrades of the Sixth Corps, Nineteenth Corps, and Emory's Army of West Virginia, "returned to their camps, and as we took our old places, cheers made the welkin ring; and then as we heard constantly of new trophies, the wild huzzahs rang from one end of our army to the other.

Such wild joy has rarely been felt by an army. What cared the men of the Nineteenth corps that they were forced to lie upon the ground without tents or blankets? Our army was victorious and honor saved." Their redemption in the Shenandoah Valley was complete. [44]

That night, Surgeon Stevens reflected on the morbidity and debris of battle:

> The moon shining over the battle-field revealed the camps of the living revealed side by side with the resting places of the dead. All the way from Middleton to Cedar Creek the debris of battle was scattered over the fields. Here and there were seen the remains of our comrades of the morning . . . They lay like specters in the pale moonlight; here, still in death, under a cluster of bushes, was stretched a group; there, by the side of a wall, a row of inanimate bodies marked a spot where brave men had fallen at their posts; in the ravine where the little creek wound its way, and beneath the boughs of the chestnut trees of the grove, many slept their last sleep. Among our camps, the spades of the pioneers were heard as they hollowed out the shallow graves; and as we threw ourselves upon the ground to rest, we mourned for our comrades, and we rejoiced for our victory. [45]

The New Yorkers grieved also that evening over the deaths of several beloved officers. In particular, the death of Adjutant Gilbert Thomas was especially wrenching. Captain Isaac Clapp wrote, "Gil was a noble boy, brave and generous, a fair example of the boys who enlisted to save the Union. He died a noble death, and his memory will always be cherished by his immediate comrades." George Stevens offered a brief eulogy for the fallen adjutant: "Adjutant Thomas . . . had left us; our noble, beautiful boy. Could he have died a grander death had he been spared longer? Could his last words have been better chosen had he expired in the embrace of loved ones at home? 'Forward, men; forward!' Were they not grand dying words? Rest, brother; thy death was as grand as thy life was lovely." Captain Martin Lennon's impending death from a mortal wound also brought anguish to the 77th. Sadly, "Lennon's bright eye must soon close forever. We should never again hear his hearty laugh or listen to his sparkling wit. He had fallen as a hero falls, and his life had been the life of a hero and patriot." Lieutenant John W. Belding and Lieutenant William J. Tabor "too, brave captains of brave men, each had fallen in advance of his friends." All four bodies would be embalmed and sent back home to their grieving families and friends. [46]

The next day, Alonzo Bump sat down and wrote a letter to his wife Mary. "This morning I went out over the Battel fieald and I could see Ded a Lying around me and our Prisinars ware out a Picking them up and Bering them." Bump fumed "we had in our Core a Good meny wonden and they fell in to the Rebs hands when we fell Back and they took Every thing they had away from them, Eaven took their coats shues and Every thing they had in their Pockets" Private Cyrille Fountain's too went over the battlefield and was equally disturbed. His diary entry for October 20 read, "To day I went over the Battle field – awful Sight to See all our dead Stript from there clothes & left necked on the ground." [47]

The battle put a permanent nail in the coffin of the Confederacy. The South would never again have the capability to threaten the northern states through the Shenandoah Valley, nor protect the economic base in the Valley. Jubal Early became bitter about his defeat, putting the blame on his soldiers. He wrote to Robert E. Lee, "but for *their* bad conduct *I* should have defeated Sheridan's whole force." Three days after the battle, Old Jube addressed his army: Many of you, including some commissioned officers, yielded to a disgraceful propensity to plunder... Subsequently those who remained at their post, seeing their ranks thinned by the absence of the plunderer... yielded to a needless panic and fled the field in confusion." Cedar Creek effectively ended Early's military career. [48]

18

"MAKE THE FUR FLY!"

The 77th remained along Cedar Creek with Sheridan's army for several days before falling back to the vicinity of Winchester. Colonel Thomas Hyde, formerly major of the 7th Maine was appointed commander of the Third Brigade in Daniel Bidwell's place. The regiment's soldiers enjoyed easy duty. There was still picket duty and the occasional dress parade, but the men were finally in one place long enough to build comfortable quarters and there was plenty to eat. The weather was mild for that time of year, and the men hoped they would stay there and garrison the Shenandoah Valley. They were tired of war's carnage, but determined to see it to the end.

The political issue of the moment during the waning days of October, superseded military matters, for a presidential election on November 8, 1864 could well determine the final outcome of the war that hundreds of thousands of men had given their lives to, and countless others their arms and legs.

It is incomprehensible for modern day Americans to believe that Abraham Lincoln, one of history's most beloved Presidents, was nearly defeated in his reelection attempt in 1864. Yet by that summer, Lincoln himself feared he would lose. The country had not elected an incumbent President for a second term since Andrew Jackson in 1832 – nine successive Presidents in a row had served just one term. Lincoln's Emancipation Proclamation was still a problem for many Northern voters.

Despite Federal victories at Gettysburg and Vicksburg the previous year, the Confederate armies came roaring back with a vengeance. During the summer of 1864, over 65,000 Union soldiers were killed, wounded, or missing. In comparison, there had been 108,000 Federal casualties in the first three years. General Ulysses S. Grant was being labeled *The Butcher.* More so, the shock of Jubal Early's Rebel army coming within five miles from the White House rippled through the north already tired of war.

Opposing Lincoln were the Peace Democrats who hoped that the Union could be salvaged, but believed that the military suppression of the Confederacy was not justified. They asserted that the North was responsible for pushing the South into secession; that Republicans were committed to racial equality, a prospect opposed by many working class immigrants who wanted to protect their employment, and by racists; the war was a national tragedy that must be ended, even if that meant granting independence to the Confederacy. None other than George Brinton McClellan, the former commander of the Army of the Potomac affectionately called "Little Mac" became the nominee for President.

By fall, the tide for a negotiated peace began to ebb. September 6, 1864, Tecumseh Sherman seized Atlanta. Though knocking on the gates of Washington, Jubal Early was defeated at Fort Stevens. With successive victories at Winchester, Fisher's Hill, Cedar Creek, Grant laying siege to Richmond and Petersburg, the Peace Democrats began to lose their voice among the Northern electorate.

Many Federal soldiers would be voting for the first time, and their ballots would serve as a referendum on the Lincoln administration. The vote for Old Abe among the troops was far from assured. "McClellan was our first commander, and, as such, he was worshipped by his soldiers," noted Theodore Garrish, a Maine private. But Garrish and others were troubled by the Peace Democrats' assertion that the war was lost; they had given too much blood to save the Union to now negotiate an end to the War of Rebellion. [1]

That the 77th would vote for Lincoln November 8, 1864, was not in question; Abraham Lincoln was their man. George Stevens wrote from the Shenandoah Valley to Colonel James B. McKean, "*The army votes for Lincoln* – I know it. In conversation yesterday with a rebel surgeon, a very social gentlemanly man, he asked me how our army would vote. I told him, and asked him in return how *his* army would vote if it had a chance. 'Oh!,' the said he, 'of course we would vote for McClellan.' 'Why of course?' said I, 'Because in spite of his letter we believe him to be the peace candidate.'" [2]

November 8, 1864 Cyrille Fountain recorded in his diary, "Today I Sent my Vote home for honest old Abe, the right man in the right place." Three out of four Yankee soldiers voted as did Private Fountain. When the ballot was counted, Abraham Lincoln won the popular vote, with 2,203,831 to McClellan's 1,797,019. The disparity was greater in the electoral college which went to the incumbent by a margin of 212 to 21. "Lincoln's triumph was more complete than most of us expected," a Richmond official admitted. "The Yankee election was evidently a damper on the spirits of many of our people, and is said to have depressed the army a good deal." Writing to a friend about the election results, U. S. Grant concluded that the "overwhelming majority received by Mr. Lincoln and the quiet with which the election went off will prove a terrible damper to the Rebels. It will be worth more than a victory in the field both in its effect on the Rebels and its influence abroad." [3]

Many of the regiments of Sheridan's Army of the Shenandoah were mustered out while the Federal army camped around Winchester. The recruits and the men who reenlisted remained as battalions with the name of the original regiments. Among other regiments whose term of enlistment expired, was the 77th New York State Volunteer Infantry. The returning veterans left camp on November 19, leaving 250 men still to represent the organization.

The regiment's veterans returning home arrived at Albany, on the *Hendrick Hudson* at 8 a.m., November 23, after the freight train left for Saratoga. "On being apprised of the fact, and that it was very desirable that the regiment should proceed at once on its journey, S. M. Cramer, Esq., the gentlemanly Deputy Superintendent of the Northern road, immediately ordered out a special train to overtake the Troy freight at the Junction." The effort was successful and the 77th boarded the train. At Mechanicville, the regiment was joined by the Stillwater Band. At Ballston Spa, Rev. David E. Tully, the first chaplain of the 77th, and others climbed aboard to join in the reception of the regiment at Saratoga Springs. [4]

The train arrived at the Spa City shortly before 2 p.m. An immense crowd had assembled at the depot "to receive the war-worn veterans." The train "was received with three hearty cheers." On debarking, an elaborate procession was formed under the direction of Colonel George S. Batcheller, former commander of the 115th New York and Marshall, followed by the Stillwater Band, the Committee of Arrangements, the Clergy, the Firemen, led by Chief Engineer

Case, the Regiment with Lieutenant Colonel Winsor B. French at their head, and a multitude of cheering citizens. It then passed through Clinton and Church Streets to Broadway to St. Nicholas Hall, which would be packed to its utmost capacity during the grand reception for the returning New Yorkers. [5]

When the tables were cleared, C. S. Lester, Esq. remarked that it had been deemed appropriate to welcome the gallant officers and soldiers of the 77th regiment by public rejoicing, as a "testimonial of our gratitude for the deeds of the living, and the tender respect in which we hold the memory of the heroic dead . . . we look forward with hope and confidence to the greater rejoicing when the rebellion shall be extinguished – when 'the land shall have rest from war,' and the soldiers of a thousand regiments shall return to gladden a million homes." Lester continued: "The time will come when the soldiers of this war will enjoy the same reverence and regard bestowed on the soldiers of the revolution; like them, on each recurring 4th of July, the post of honor will be assigned them at national feasts and rejoicings." [6]

W. A. Sackett spoke of the reason for the terrible conflict, and likened the returning soldiers to the founding fathers that rebelled against tyranny:

> The rebellion grew out of a system of human bondage, which from small beginnings, had grown up until it had brought into existence a controlling influence inconsistent in its ruling Ideas with the principles upon which the Government was founded . . . Our fathers fought to secure liberty, equality, self-government, free institutions. They fought against arbitrary power. Our triumphant success as a nation is a glorious vindication of the objects for which they fought . . . It is against the purposes for which they struggled that this rebellion is waged. It is the freedom their triumphs secured

that this rebellion would destroy. On the issue of this contest hangs the question of liberty or despotism as the ruling power on this continent... To preserve the liberties our fathers established, and which we enjoy, these brave men whom we now honor, have periled their lives on many a well-fought field, and to them we bow with profound respect and reverence. Welcome to the brave! To perpetuate freedom they have nobly fought, and we welcome their return.

At the end of the festivities, the proud veterans paraded to Camp Schuyler, the rendezvous point that brought them together in 1861. Tuesday, December 13th, the soldiers of the 77th closed their military career, and were mustered out. "The men were called together, received their pay and bounty, and quietly betook themselves to their homes, apparently well pleased to be out from the military." Later, at an evening gathering at the Columbian Hotel, Chaplain Norman Fox noted "the number of our former comrades now lying beneath the soil of Virginia," and exhorted them "not to forget the brave dead." The chaplain ended by offering two resolutions that were unanimously passed:

> *Resolved*, That in returning to civil life we cherish with tendernest affections, and deepest reverence, the memory of our brave comrades who have fallen in battle, or who, after passing unharmed through perils of the field, have become victims of disease incident to the service; and while we ourselves can never forget these noble men with whom we have associated in the various scenes of joy and gloom which make up a soldier's life, we deem it proper that some fitting memorial should speak to the world of their heroic bravery and lofty self-sacrifice.
>
> *Resolved*, That a committee be appointed at this time to take suitable steps for the formation of a Seventy-Seventh Monument Association. [7]

Lieutenant Colonel David J. Caw (L. Tom Perry Special Collections)

On November 23rd, the remaining soldiers of the returned regiment were reorganized, becoming the 77th New York Battalion of five companies under the command of Lieutenant Colonel David J. Caw, former captain of Company D. December 9, the 77th and the Sixth Corps were ordered to return to the Petersburg lines. The New Yorkers boarded a freight train en route for City Point. The newly reenlisted veterans marched to Steven's Depot, and took another train for Washington, where they arrived on the night of the 10th. Embarking on the steamer *City of Albany*, the Empire State soldiers sailed to Petersburg, and reunited with Meade's Army of the Potomac the 14th of December. The battalion took up position on the Davis farm, two miles west of the Weldon Railroad. The Sixth Corps now faced the elaborate Confederate entrenchments in a sector southwest of Petersburg, running from the Weldon Railroad in the west, to within three miles of the Southside Railroad in the east.

Major General George Getty's men worked on their trenches, but they were occupying a part of the line vacated by Hancock's Second Corps where the balance of needed construction was already completed. The 77th Battalion's soldiers were far more concerned about organizing their camp and erecting comfortable quarters for the winter months. Commissary Sergeant Thomas M. White (Co. C) informed the *Saratogian*, "We are this winter blessed with more neat and comfortable quarters than ever before, all being logged up four feet high." Due to their surroundings being devoid of trees, "to procure the timber for which, we had the use of the brigade train." Proud of the results, White wrote, "The camp consists of five company streets well laid out and with sewers at the foot of each. Our water privileges could not be better as we have five good wells within the camp." [8]

By late 1864 and early 1865, desertion had reached crisis proportions within the Army of Northern Virginia. Within a one month period in 1865, nearly 3,000 of Robert E. Lee's soldiers risked being shot by friend or foe in order to run across the no-man's-land and into the Yankee works. Lee on January 27 sent a report to Richmond about the alarming frequency of desertions from his army. Lee identified the root causes of a critical lack of food and the nonpayment of the troops. Latter Lee added another cause that drove men to desert: "the representation of their friends at home who appear to have become very despondent as to our success." Lee concluded, "These desertions have a very bad effect upon the troops who remain and give rise to painful apprehension." [9]

Desertions in the opposite direction, while not at the same level, were not insignificant. In a one week period the previous October, 1,400 or so Union soldiers had deserted. Brigadier General Robert McAllister pointed his finger at bounty men who enlisted for the substantial cash payments and then deserted at the earliest opportunity. "The large bounties are demoralizing," McAllister grumble. "Also, they give us a class of worthless men." [10]

Deserters caught by the Provost Guard faced the extreme penalties of military justice. Most suffered some form of imprisonment and forfeiture of pay. Executions became a predictable part of the Union army schedule at Petersburg. Friday was the day most often set aside for the administration of sentences handed down by military courts. Friday hangings became a form of entertainment. The war-seasoned veterans, one New York soldier wrote after the war lost "all human feelings towards such dastards and traitors." In a letter to his wife, Private Alonzo Bump could watch three men hanged for desertion, and then nonchalantly go to dinner with a friend:

> Well Dear I have Got some news to tell you. I went Over Yestarday in to the 2nd Core and saw 3 men hung. they ware

hung for Disearting in to the Rebs Lines. we took them Prisinars while we ware in the Valley and sent them Back hear to Grant. 2 of them ware from a new hamspshear Regt. 1 was from a Mass Regt. they all went up on to the Scafold to once. To of them ware Irish. the Preast was thair with them & Praid with them. Dear I have hurd folks tell that they could not stand & see a man hung But I stood & saw them hung & I could seean forty more hung for the same Crime But after all I felt sorey for them to think that they would Bee so follish. One of them sed that hee intended to Go Over to the Rebs and then Diseart & take the Oath & Goe north but they Got caught at it. after I saw them hung I went Over & seean George Hoffman again & took Dinar with him. We had fresh Meat Potatoes coffee & hard tack & I made out Quite a Dinar. [11]

The winter lull in fighting allowed for visitors from Saratoga Springs to spend time with the battalion. January 8, 1865, one such group of citizens from the Spa arrived in the 77th's camp. The next morning, the visitors received a tour of the lines and the picket post of the 77th. Thomas M. White offered readers at home a description of the experience:

> Our faces were gladdened by the arrival among us of a brace of peaceful citizens from your village, and at about four o'clock in the morning of the 9th, as if for the amusement (?) of our guests, the Johnnies made an attack on our pickets, capturing three boys of this Battalion, namely: [Private] Henry Boyce, Co. "A," [Private] Samuel Phillips and [Private] William Jones, Co. D." . . . Our guests having visited the picket line, where the wild rebs were plainly visible, and being satisfied with their view of the elephant in his largest dimensions, started on their return trip last

evening, heavily freighted with news for friends and relatives of those here, and fully repaid of their trouble in visiting the 'Great Army.' [12]

The beginning of the end for the Rebels at Petersburg began during a concerted swipe at their supply lines. February 27, Sheridan rode out from Winchester with two cavalry divisions, with orders from Grant to tear up the Virginia Central Railroad at Staunton, continue down the Shenandoah Valley, cross the Blue Ridge and capture Lynchburg. There, Little Phil would wreck the South Side Railroad. Then, the cavalry commander would continue down into North Carolina, where he would join Tecumseh Sherman.

Sheridan's horsemen reached Staunton on the 28th. Discovering that Jubal Early's small Confederate command occupied Waynesborough, 14 miles east on the Virginia Central, Sheridan determined to deliver a fatal blow to Early's Rebels. On March 2, blue-jacketed troopers demolished the Confederate force at Waynesborough. Then the Federal cavalrymen began systematically ripping up the Virginia Central. When they advanced to Charlottesville, they began destroying the Orange & Alexandria Railroad in the direction of Lynchburg while continuing to wreck the Virginia Central toward Gordonsville. For good measure, Sheridan's riders also rendered the James River Canal unusable from New Market to Goochland Court House.

On March 13, Sheridan's troopers rode toward White House Landing, arriving at the Landing on the 19th. The same day, half of Sherman's army withstood the greatly diminished might of Joseph Johnston's entire army at the battle of Bentonville and bivouacked at Goldsboro on the 21st. There he rendezvoused with Major General John M. Schofield's Army of the Ohio, which had marched inland from Wilmington and New Berne.

Jefferson Davis and Robert E. Lee understood that the Army of Northern Virginia must abandon Petersburg and Richmond and retreat into the hinterland before Grant and Sherman united and surrounded or overwhelmed Lee's army. That day was not far off, because Johnston's shrinking army could not even be counted on to slow Sherman's advance any longer. However, Lee did not want to abandon Petersburg and Richmond before the roads dried. His starved horses and mules would need every advantage in order to escape Grant's forces and unite with Johnston in North Carolina.

Lee considered a number of possibilities for buying time before assenting to a plan suggested by John B. Gordon, who proposed an attack on Fort Stedman, about a mile south of the Appomattox River. The planned attacking force would include Pickett's division, two brigades of Major General Bushrod R. Johnson's, two brigades from Cadmus Wilcox's division, all of Gordon's corps except for a skirmish line left to hold its works southwest of Petersburg, and Rooney Lee's division of cavalry. This represented almost half of Lee's combined infantry. The assault would begin shortly before dawn on March 25. Southern infantry would storm Fort Stedman, then roll up the Yankee line to the right and left. Three selected combat teams would penetrate into the Union rear and seize Battery No. 4, Fort Friend and the Dunn House Battery in the second Federal line, which consisted of turned Confederate works. Rooney Lee's horse soldiers would ride through the breach to City Point. At the minimum, Lee hoped to force Grant to withdraw his left. This would expedite their retreat to North Carolina. If all went according to plan, the possibility existed to cut the Army of the Potomac off from the James River, destroy the massive depot at City Point, and even capture Grant.

Early in the morning on the 25th, the 77th Battalion was awakened by tremendous rattling volleys and cannonading off to the right. Not knowing the meaning of the firing, the New York veterans were kept ready to fall in at any moment. After a while, intelligence sifted down the ranks that John Gordon's Confederates had taken Fort Stedman at Hare's Hill and a number of batteries.

Gordon's planned offensive counted on the soldiers of Pickett's division and Rooney Lee's cavalry, but neither arrived in time to participate. After some delay, Gordon gave the order for his infantry massed at Colquitt's Salient to advance sometime after 4 a.m. The initial charge was successful. Gordon's and Bushrod Johnson's infantry burst through the Federal line on both sides of Fort Stedman and took the fort from behind. In a matter of minutes, the Confederates had overrun the Northern trenches from Battery X to Battery XII. Brevet Brigadier General Napoleon B. McLaughlen, who had overall responsibility for the Fort Stedman sector, sent his aides to spread the warning. He galloped into Fort Stedman and the arms of his Rebel captors.

Gordon's assault lost steam as his luck soon ran out. Battery IX on the breach's northern shoulder held, as did Fort Haskell on the southern shoulder. A good number of hungry Confederates fell out to plunder captured bombproofs and camps. Darkness, rolling terrain, and the presence of the reserves of Major General John G. Parke's Ninth Corps hindered further penetration by Gordon's special combat teams. The only special guides to approach their goal were pounded by the Federal artillery in Fort Friend. By daybreak, the assault had reached its high tide. Lee and Gordon realized they must withdraw. Knowing this, the Southern commanders did not commit the two brigades of Cadmus Wilcox's division.

Brigadier General John Hartranft, whose division of eight regiments was in reserve near the southern shoulder of the Rebel penetration, initiated the Federal counterattack. Ninth Corps artillery reserve unlimbered on the high ground between the breach and Meade's Station on the Military Railroad. Gun crews in Fort McGilvery, Battery IX, Battery No. 4, Fort Friend, and Fort Haskell laid down a devastating fire. Major General John G. Parke, Ninth Corps commander, ordered up reinforcements from Warren's and Horatio Wright's corps, but Hartranft had hurled back the last pockets of Confederate resistance by 8:30 a.m., before the reinforcements arrived. The provost guard marched 1,500 Rebel prisoners past Meade's headquarters to a nearby holding pen a little before President Lincoln arrived at army headquarters from City Point. Meade gleefully greeted Lincoln with the comment, "I have just now a dispatch from General Parke to show you." In reply, Lincoln gestured to the penned Southern prisoners. "Ah," he said, "*there* is the best dispatch you can show me from General Parke!" [13]

Supposing that Lee must have had to strip his lines to assemble Gordon's attack force, Federal corps commanders Horatio Wright and Andrew Humphreys initiated an attack on the Confederate line southwest of Petersburg. Colonel Thomas W. Hyde, former major in the 7th Maine and the Third Brigade's new commander, received orders for his brigade to fall in. New to brigade command, Hyde "felt the time had at last come, so often longed for, when it should be settled whether I could command six regiments in action to my own satisfaction. It was an unknown problem, a somewhat dreaded problem too." It was not a question of personal danger, Hyde thought. "What is to be dreaded is, not doing the right thing at the right time." [14]

In front of the Sixth Corps lines was the Union picket lines. However they did not meet in the center of no-man's-land, but were considerably closer to the Federal main line than the Confederate. Holding a wider swath of the open space between the enemy main lines offered some advantages to the Rebels, and corresponding problems for the Yankees. First, it was difficult for Federal officers to closely observe and study the Confederate works to discover weak spots for possible attacks. Nor was there enough room between the main Union trench line and the Union picket line in its present location to form up an attack force. If there was to be an attack in strength on the Southern trench works in the Sixth Corps front, the Rebel picket line would first have to be pushed back and their rifle pits captured.

Around noon, George Getty issued orders for Thomas Hyde to form the 77th's Third Brigade in close column of regiments behind the Vermont Brigade, on the right of Fort Fisher. Truman Seymour's Third Division went in at about 3 p.m., but was immediately stalled. Meanwhile, Colonel James M. Warner's First Brigade, Lewis Grant's Green Mountain regiments and the 77th's Third Brigade filed out through openings in the Union abatis and formed up in the open in front of Fort Fisher. Confederate shot and shell in increasing numbers rained down on the Yankees as the Union batteries in Forts Fisher and Welch roared back, trying to suppress the Rebel gun crews.

At 4 p.m., prompted by a signal flag waved from Fort Fisher's ramparts, Getty's division attacked. The Third Brigade had barely come into position when the Vermonters started forward at the double quick toward the enemy's picket line and forts. Behind them, the 77th advanced, bending low to conceal themselves as much as possible as Confederate bullets and shells found their mark. Thomas Hyde looked back over his brigade, and the picture was forever sealed in his mind: "More than two thousand bronzed, hardy, and well-known faces, and every eye was upon me." [15]

On the division left, Lewis Grant's Green Mountain soldiers captured the Rebel picket line near the Jones house on Church Road. The 2nd Vermont pressed all the way to the house itself, drove out the Confederate sharpshooters who had been firing from there, and burned the house so it could not be used for cover again. The 3rd Vermont Battery came up to the picket line in support, and began sending shells at the Rebel batteries.

The 77th's brigade surged past the right of the Vermonters toward the main Confederate trenches, when Colonel Hyde looked back and saw the Vermont regiments had halted at the picket line and were digging in. Hyde's regiments "were going in mad career" until they came to flooded "ground and the only access to the forts was a narrow milldam not wide enough for two men abreast." Recognizing his men could go no further, Hyde sounded the recall, and the brigade fell back to, and aligned with, the right of Grant's Vermonters. [16]

Lieutenant Stephen H. Pierce (USAMHI)

M^cKEAN'S SUNDAY SCHOOL BOYS GO TO WAR

Captain Sumner Oakley (NYSDMNA)

Hyde's right was in the air, "and from woods masking the rebel line to our right a strong force bore down on that flank." The colonel refused the 1st Main veterans and ordered the 122nd New York in with them. Just then the New York regiment's Colonel Augustus W. Dwight had his head torn off by a Rebel shell, and Hyde brought the 122nd in place beside the 1st Maine. The Third Brigade's fire was so effective that the Confederate attacking force sought shelter in a large ravine. But the position of the 1st Maine was desperate. There was an angle in the enemy's line off to the left, so that the Mainers were "taken in rear by cannon, enfiladed to their left by canon, besides a front fire." Hyde moved the 1st Maine several times within protecting distance of the right flank to lessen the effectiveness of Southern batteries. Not far from Hyde, Captain Sumner Oakley (Co. D), Lieutenant Stephen H. Pierce, and an unnamed officer were standing in a "little picket pit" when a shell screamed overhead and exploded, killing all three officers. Thomas Hyde remembered that "a foot, with boot and all, flew over my head. I recognized with pain a mangled lieutenant of the 77th New York to whom I was obliged a few days before to refuse a leave of absence." The only other death was that of Private Alfred Chase (Co. D). Four men were wounded: "Simeon Crosby, sergt. Co. D, in foot; John E. Stewart, private Co. D, both legs amputated; Nathan Eldredge, private, Co. B, in foot, severely; Edward Evans, private, Co. E, side, slight." [17]

As Hyde was standing between the 77th Battalion and the 122nd New York, a Vermont captain with his company approached the colonel, having been separated from his brigade, and asked for orders. At that moment a Rebel minie ball grazed Hyde's arm through his overcoat, and he saw the smoke of a musket from the roof of a large and comfortable-looking house between the lines. The colonel ordered the Vermonters forward to drive out the Rebels. In a matter of minutes the Vermont captain took his company forward an easily cleared them from the house. But soon after they returned, Confederate snipers in greater numbers once again occupied the house. Hyde ordered the Vermonters to take the house and burn it down, which was promptly done.

As the sun set, the 1st Maine rose to their feet and cheered. To the brigade's soldiers it was profound relief as Warner's First Brigade pushed through the brush to their right. As Warner's soldiers came abreast the 77th's brigade, Hyde ordered his men forward. They advanced through ravines for nearly half of a mile, taking several hundred prisoners. But with darkness falling, Hyde withdrew the Third Brigade and returned to the original Confederate picket line. The 77th's veterans joined their brigade comrades, and went to work with the spade, and soon the breastworks of the formerly Rebel rifle pits were reversed to face the Southern lines. The ground gained brought the Federals within 2,500 feet of the Rebel lines. An all-out Union assault from this close would leave the graycoats very little reaction time.

In the evening on April 1, the 77th and their brethren received the sensational news of Phil Sheridan's triumph at Five Forks, ten miles to the west of the Sixth Corps that afternoon, where Sheridan demolished George Pickett's division. That same evening, Grant issued orders for a general assault along the lines before dawn. Warned of this probability two days earlier, the Second Division and the rest of the Sixth Corps were already in motion preparing for an assault on Rebel lines.

After the Confederate picket line was captured on the 25th, Union officers searched for a weak point in the Rebel main trenches, and Lewis Grant believed he found one. In his Vermont Brigade front, Grant discovered a ravine running from just beyond the captured picket line all the way back to and through the main enemy works. This ravine had been heavily wooded, but the butternuts had cut the trees down during the winter for shelter and firewood, revealing the fact that the defensive works did not fully cross the ravine. The ravine was too narrow to permit more than a single regiment in column to pass through at one time. Lewis Grant informed Getty of his discovery, who in turn told Wright. George Meade came to Wright's headquarters, and the four officers examined the entire area and approach routes. Meade concluded that the Sixth Corps' assault would advance from between Fort Fisher and Fort Welch at 4 a.m. April 2. "The corps will go in solid, and I am sure will make the fur fly," Wright vowed to Meade. [18]

The 77th's Third Division was to lead the assault as the spearhead of the Sixth Corps attack formation that later became known as "The Wedge." Wright's remaining two divisions, Truman Seymour's Third and Frank Wheaton's First, would form on the left and right rear of Getty's soldiers, respectively. Getty's division was to mass by brigade, with narrow, regimental fronts, forming the tip of the wedge. Battalions would combine with one another. Lewis Grant's all Vermont Brigade would form to the left and rear of Thomas Hyde's

Third Brigade. To Hyde's right and rear, James Warner's would deploy his brigade.

Earlier in the day, some of the Third Brigade pickets called Colonel Hyde's attention to an opening in the abatis through which the Rebels used to come out to cut wood and go on picket. They also noticed there was always a large camp fire beyond the forts, that was directly in line with this opening, and that if the brigade advanced in a direct line to that fire, his men could easily pass through the abatis.

Colonel Hyde summoned his six regimental commanders and they went up a signal tower behind their camps. After surveying their front, Hyde issued orders to Lieutenant Colonel David Caw and the other regimental officers for the early morning attack, and directed them to repeat these instructions to their officers, and first and color sergeants. Years later, Hyde still had the envelope on which he had written the instructions:

1. Fall in at midnight.
2. Leave knapsacks and canteens in camp.
3. Load without capping.
4. File out to left of Fort Welch along ravine, and form as follows:
   43rd N. Y., Milliken; 77th N. Y., Caw; 350 men.
   1st Maine Vet., Fletcher, 350 men
   49th N. Y.; 122nd N. Y.; 400 men.
   61st Penn., Crosby, 500 men.
5. Forty sharpened axes in front rank.
6. Signal to start, -- a gun from Fort Fisher, one half hour before daybreak.
7. Guide on rebel camp-fire, over burnt ground and through openings in abbatis
8. When inside, keep right on and cut Southside R. R.

McKEAN'S SUNDAY SCHOOL BOYS GO TO WAR

In addition, George Getty issued other instructions. To avoid bunching, regiments were to remain fifty paces apart within the brigade column while forming up and during the assault itself. Once the Second Division had advanced to the assembly area in front of Fort Fisher under the cover of darkness, no lights or matches were permitted, and officers were not to shout orders. After receiving Hyde's orders, Lieutenant Colonel David Caw returned to the New York battalion to ready the veterans for what he hoped would be the final campaign of the war. The 77th's camp was broken up and tents and baggage were sent to the rear. [19]

Around midnight, the 77th and the rest of the Sixth Corps were marching from their camps behind Fort Fisher. Thomas Hyde remembered, "A heavy mist made the moonless night more dark and gloomy." Lewis Grant's Green Mountain regiments moved out in the chilly, damp, uncomfortable night. They marched out through an opening in the Union abatis to the right of Fort Fisher made for them by Yankee pioneers, and quietly moved to the left across the open space in front of the fort. At the edge of the ravine, they halted and formed in column formation for the assault, and then lay down and wait. By 1 a.m. the Vermont Brigade was in position. Hyde led the 77th's brigade in on the Vermont Brigade's right and lay down in formation, as did James Warner's First Brigade on Hyde's right. The colonel's "first thought after getting the brigade in position was to look for the camp-fire that was to be our bright beacon, and there it was shining peacefully through the mist." [20]

Lying on the cold, wet ground in silence, as yet unknown to the Confederates, the Second Division was now in position. The Rebel picket line was little more than 300 yards away from the 77th and 43rd New York at the point of the wedge. At the head of each brigade were the pioneers, men with axes to break up the Southern abattis. Alongside the axe-men, were artillery gun crew veterans with rammers and primers, with which to turn the enemy's guns. The ground between the blue and gray enemies was once covered with trees, which had long been cut down for lumber and firewood. It was now populated with numerous stumps, and there was a significant swamp just in front of the Confederate works through which Warner's soldiers would have to cross to reach the enemy line. The men lay in noiseless rows for several hours, waiting for the signal gun.

As Seymour's Third Division moved behind Getty's left, the Rebel pickets heard movement and fired upon Seymour's pickets, and "some idiot fired his piece" despite having been strictly ordered not to fire. The Confederates promptly sent mini balls whizzing through the Federal ranks, "and almost every shot they fired took effect in our column, as could be told by the thuds and stifled outcries." Lewis Grant was grazed in the head by a bullet, and he turned over command to Lieutenant Colonel Amasa Tracy of the 2nd Vermont. Even though every soldier hated to be fired on and unable to reply, the veterans of the Second Division did not return fire. The picket firing quickly died down, and a potential crisis was averted. Henry Heth's and Cadmus Wilcox's southern soldiers opposite Getty's men suspected nothing. [21]

At 4 a.m., Horatio Wright delayed the firing of the signal gun from Fort Fisher. The moonless night made the dark impenetrable, and the Sixth Corps general wanted his soldiers to have at least a glimmer of light with which to work. By 4:30 a.m., dawn approached and enough light appeared for a man to see where he stepped, and Wright gave the order to fire the signal gun. But the reverberating roar of heavy artillery firing from down the line in the Ninth Corps sector cancelled out the sound of the signal gun. Colonel Hyde started for the rear to find out if the gun had already signaled and came upon George Getty, who informed him it was time to go in. Hyde went over to notify Lewis Grant and was told Amasa Tracy was now in command of the Vermont Brigade. Finding Tracy, the colonel told him to push forward the brigade and hurried back to the Third Brigade. The Vermonters quickly rose and pressed forward, jumping over the old Confederate rifle pits as they did so. The 5th Vermont took the lead. When it had gone about a hundred yards, the 2nd Vermont moved out, followed by the 6th Vermont, until the entire brigade was in motion.

Returning to his regiments, Hyde stood "on the rifle pits in front of the brigade," and, "gave to each line of the column in as low a tone as possible the orders, 'Attention! Forward! Charge!' When the last line "of black forms in the blacker darkness were over the pits," Colonel Hyde "followed as fast as possible, greatly regretting I had been so foolish as to have left my horse." A scattered volley to the left of the 77th's brigade rang out, and the veterans heard the angry buzz of enemy minie balls as the Vermonters collided with the Confederate picket line. The graycoats fired a volley and careened back to their main line. With a shout, the Vermonters surged forward, and the charge was on. [22]

George Getty's soldiers broke into a flat run toward the Confederate lines. A Vermont veteran wrote later, "Officers and men vied with each other in the race for the works." Southern artillery thundered into action, and shells exploded and canister blasted the advancing Yankees. The Green Mountain soldiers entered the ravine, using it as a covered approach, and most of the Confederate fire sailed high. Surging down the ravine, they came upon the enemy abattis, with its rows of sharp branches and stakes. The Vermont pioneers hacked at it until some of the New Englanders grabbed on to the felled trees and pulled them aside. They then hit the

Confederate trenches at the ravine, and just to its right. In seconds they were up, over, and into the works, grappling with the Rebels. [23]

Sergeant William H. Wright (USAMHI)

To the right of Tracy, the 77th's Third Brigade also was undetected until it reached the picket line. "I remember ordering a lot of rebels to the rear as we crossed the picket pits," Colonel Hyde recalled, "for then the black darkness was becoming gray in the coming dawn, and the shot and shell from the enemy's forts were like so many rockets fired horizontally, and they were mostly a few feet over our heads." The seasoned veterans halted at the edge of the swamp near the main Southern line held by the Confederates of Cadmus Wilcox's division, while the pioneers set to work on the abattis. Captain Isaac Clapp was wounded while tearing away a portion of the abattis. The 77th and 49th New York reformed, and they then raced through the openings hacked out by the axe-men, their fellow regiments behind them following. Hyde followed and "they were soon over the works like so many cats, giving and receiving bayonet thrusts, and the canon were hardly silent before they were fired the other way" by Union artillery crews. First Sergeant William H. Wright (Co. E) was the first from the 77th to jump over the works into the Rebel trenches, and immediately went down with a wound in the leg. Catching up to his brigade, Hyde noticed the wounded soldier and said, "You should go to the rear." Wright would not budge and replied, "General, I promised my captain to stay with him as long as I can stand." Lieutenant Colonel David Caw was bayonetted in the breast as he stood on the works calling his men forward. A bullet bore into Private Henry Morgan's (Co. D) upper jaw, fracturing bone and breaking teeth before lodging in the maxillary sinus. Private John Kipp (Co. E) had the unfortunate distinction of being the last man in the 77th to be killed in action. [24]

Private Henry Morgan, the last casualty of the war (The Medical and Surgical History of the War of the Rebellion (181-65) Part 1, Vol. 2, 36)

On Colonel Hyde's right, Colonel James Warner's First Brigade swiftly drove in the Rebel pickets before them. Warner's soldiers had more difficult ground to advance over, and Confederate artillery threw canister at the leading 102nd Pennsylvania, temporarily causing disarray in the regiment. The following Pennsylvania regiments cleared the thin Confederate abatis, and quickly mounted the works. Some of Cadmus Wilcox's North Carolinians stood their ground, while many others surrendered without resistance. Warner's disordered regiments swarmed forward until he and his officers halted and reformed the men near the South Side Railroad.

The 77th with Thomas Hyde's regiments with wild disregard surged ahead with little to no resistance, crossing the Boydton Plank Road, the Cox Road, stopping only at the South Side Railroad already being torn up by other troops. Now riding his horse, Hyde "could see many of the brigade, each man for himself, pushing for the railroad; others dressed in Confederate officers' jackets were looting the camps; others were collecting prisoners; others were on the mules of a captured train, and others all about as happy a lot as could be imagined." [25]

After reaching the South Side Railroad, Warner's First Brigade and the 77th's Third Brigade both pulled back to the Boydton Plank Road, and reformed south of Cox Road and north of the Plank Road. Amasa Tracy, Thomas Hyde, and James Warner quickly conferred on how to exploit their success. With the rising morning sun, it was slowly becoming light, and the Yankee officers could pick out vital terrain features revealing how big a hole they had made in the sector of the Confederate line defended by Henry Heth's and Wilcox's soldiers. The bulk of the Rebel defenders retreated to Hatcher's Run, and the Second Division wheeled left into a line facing west, with Tracy's Green Mountain regiments on the left, the 77th's brigade in the center, and Warner's First on the right. The would sweep southwest, double quicking behind the Confederate trenches to the left of the breach, systematically outflanking and rolling up the Southern defenses, and forcing Lee's reserves in this area away from Petersburg.

MCKEAN'S SUNDAY SCHOOL BOYS GO TO WAR

Ambrose Powell Hill had anxiously fussed over his lines all day on April 1, and was trying without success to gain needed sleep this damp, misty night. Alarmed about the especially heavy picket and artillery fire, Hill rose from bed and hurriedly dressed, then left the house he shared with his wife and two children, and walked across Cox Road to his headquarters tent. His adjutant general, Colonel William H. Palmer, reported he had no intelligence to report. Hill decided to ride to Robert E. Lee's headquarters, and called for his horse. He instructed Palmer to "wake up the staff, get everything in readiness, and have the headquarters' wagons hitched up," and that "as soon as he would have an interview with General Lee, he would return." [26]

While A. P. Hill discussed the current situation with Lee and James Longstreet at his headquarters in the Turnball house, Colonel Charles Venable of Lee's staff burst into the room to warn that panicked teamsters were racing past headquarters, and that Federal troops had been spotted in the rear. The Southern generals went out to the porch and looked toward the southwest, and saw, as Longstreet remembered, "as far as the eye could cover the field, [was] a line of skirmishers in quiet march toward us." Before Lee could say a word, Hill, frantic with anxiety, mounted his horse and galloped toward the breach. [27]

Powell Hill did not know that his lines had already been overwhelmed. Indeed, the first wave of the Federal assault had pressed on toward the South Side Railroad. Hill, accompanied by his trusted courier, George Tucker, and at length the two soldiers emerged from a small stand of trees and looked to where the main line had been; squads of soldiers seemed to move aimlessly about the position. Hill took up his field glasses and saw that they were soldiers in blue uniforms from the Sixth Corps. Hill and Tucker spurred their horses to a group of trees a little north of the Boydton Plank Road.

Among the Sixth Corps troops that reached the South Side Railroad, were Private Daniel Wolford and Corporal John Mauk, both from the 138th Pennsylvania of Truman Seymour's division. After getting separated from their regiment, the two turned back to the Boydton Plank Road and joined a group of Yankee stragglers who were brewing coffee. At that moment Mauk and Wolford saw "two men on horseback coming from the direction of Petersburg, who had the appearance of officers." The Union soldiers ran behind a large oak tree and aimed their rifles at the approaching grayclad mounted figures. The Confederate riders traded demands to surrender with Mauk and Wolford, when the two Union men fired. Wolford missed, but Mauk's .58-caliber bullet knocked A. P. Hill from his saddle, shooting off his left thumb, piercing his heart, and blowing a bloody gaping exit hole in his back. [28]

The 77th's division moved rapidly two miles southwest towards Hatcher's Run against minimal resistance, brushing aside scattered pockets of disordered Confederates, and gobbling up prisoners. The New York battalion and the rest of Getty's soldiers again lost their cohesion in the excitement of their advance, pursuing the fleeing Rebels so closely that the fast moving butternuts hardly had time to stop and fire.

The 77th Battalion reached Hatcher's Run at about 9 a.m. Here Horatio Wright "learned from staff officers . . . that the Second and Fifth Corps and the cavalry were sweeping down in that direction, and that it was not necessary to proceed further." Wright about-faced the Second Division to the northwest and marched toward Petersburg, all three brigades advancing in columns abreast meeting no resistance, until they approached the point where they broke through the Rebel line. The Confederates still maintained a considerable presence from the right side of the breach, and could be seen preparing to offer an organized stand before Getty's Yankees. The Second Division deployed into line of battle, the 77th's brigade, Warner, and Tracy, left to right, with Tracy's right touching the Boydton Plank Road. Hyde, whose left flank was in the air, refused it, bending his left back so that the enemy attacking from that direction would face a solid line, rather than a vulnerable open flank ripe for enfilading fire. [29]

The 77th advanced with their division half a mile in a well-dressed line, all the while under brisk shelling from Rebel artillery. The division halted to wait for its artillery support to come up. Once the batteries unlimbered and occupied the Confederate guns, the Second Division stepped off again, pushing a Rebel skirmish line back into Petersburg's inner defense line studded with a formidable series of forts. Just north of the forts was the Turnball House, which had been Lee's headquarters until this morning. Unlimbered in its yard, a four-gun Confederate battery began sending canister and solid shot toward Getty's advancing line. Amasa Tracy's Green Mountain Boys, with Warner's men, charged the battery, shooting down the Southern artillery horses, preventing the withdrawal of the cannon, and capturing the battery.

It was now around 10 a.m., and the veterans of the 77th were just as utterly exhausted as were their comrades. The Second Division halted with its right at the Nottingham house, and its left resting on the Appomattox River. Colonel Thomas Hyde recorded, "Then we sink to the ground as we are; no supper, no blankets; nineteen hours of continuous marching and fighting has taken the energy well out of everybody. We are too tired to congratulate ourselves on our victory, and did not care if Petersburg was in sight or near, or grudge it to anyone who would make the capture." The Second Division's casualties were unexpectedly low for a frontal assault of an entrenched enemy: 4 officers and 36 men killed, 32 officers and 307 men wounded, and 16 men missing. In return, Getty's soldiers had captured 31 cannon, 9 battle flags, and 2,100 prisoners. [30]

The Confederate retreat from Petersburg began shortly after midnight April 3. The artillery and wagon trains led the way over the Appomattox River and headed westward. Longstreet and remnants of A. P. Hill's command followed next in line. Gordon covered the rear and set fire to the bridges. William Mahone abandoned the Howlett Line and marched toward Chesterfield Court House. The Rebel forces on the Peninsula, under Ewell's command, crossed the James River to Chesterfield County at and below Richmond and continued to the Genito Road. The rendezvous point for Lee's remaining commands was Amelia Court House. As the graycoats pulled out of Richmond and Petersburg, they burned the military stores in the railroad yards and warehouses. Looters and rioters, mixed in with frightened citizens, ran wild in the two cities.

Grant issued orders for an assault on the Petersburg and Richmond works early on the morning of April 3. However, before 3 a.m. Orlando Wilcox's soldiers discovered that Lee had withdrawn from Petersburg. They entered the city and quickly restored order there. Major General Godfrey Weitzel's Twenty Fifth Corps brought peace to Richmond at daybreak.

The 77th with its Second division joined in the pursuit of Lee to Appomattox, just missing the Battle at Saylor's Creek on the way. On Palm Sunday, April 9, Grant accepted the surrender of Lee's army that his soldiers had mortally wounded at Petersburg. The 77th's brigade commander, Colonel Thomas Hyde, recalled on that day, "Toward noon a sudden stillness came. The usual thunder around the horizon suddenly became strangely silent. It seemed to me as if we were marching in a vacuum." Hyde rode ahead of the Third

Brigade to discover what the silence meant. Within a mile, the colonel "came upon our revered division commander, General Getty, sitting under a tree, his face in his hands. 'What is it, general?' 'Lee has surrendered,' was the reply." Hyde thought, "I must tell the boys, and as I came back down the road at a pace only a Virginia running stallion can display, two thousand bright and eager faces were drawing near to meet me." "The war is over! Lee has surrendered!" Hyde cried out. The soldiers hijacked the colonel from his horse and carried him back and forth on their soldiers in celebration. They were no more soldiers for a while, but rejoicing American citizens. Union batteries fired blank cartridges, "and the most crazy joy" seized all alike. [31]

A large cavalcade soon trotted toward the 77th and nearby Sixth Corps troops. It was George Gordon Meade followed by his subordinate commanders and their staffs. "The men, 20 deep, line each side of his pathway and throw their caps and knapsacks under the feet of the horses." Hyde remembered it "as a saturnalia of joy," while also aware that, "not far away, happily unconscious of our ecstasies, the vanquished lion of the Confederacy and the remnant of his host are feeling:

>'All the griefs that brave men feel,
>When conquered, e'en by foeman worthy of their steel.' [32]

Early the next morning, Private Edward Fuller was walking to the War Department in Washington, where he had been detailed for clerical duty subsequent to receiving a serious wound while storming the heights behind Fredericksburg in 1863. "Every person I met cried out 'Lee has surrendered.' The private remembered. "Arriving in the office the fact was very potently reflected in the smiling faces of employees. Little work was done in the public offices that day; the employees kept busy going in and out in their enthusiasm to 'see a man.' In the afternoon and evening, Fuller continued, "prominent public men addressed the enthusiastic populace in front of the White House, War Department, Corcoran Art Building and Willard's hotel. All Washington city seemed to be joyous and rejoicing at the good fact; many became hilariously boisterous for the first and only time in their lives." Edward Fuller was in the crowd before the White House when President Lincoln spoke from the balcony. [33]

In the space of five days, the 77th went from the thrill of victory at Lee's surrender to the depths of despair and sorrow at Abraham Lincoln's assassination. But with Joseph Johnston's army still in the field in North Carolina, the New Yorkers with the Sixth Corps marched south to the railway hub of Danville, Virginia, in late April. The veteran soldiers marched from Burkesville Junction, covering one-hundred miles in a matter of four days. *The Sixth Corps News* later noted, "The first entry of Danville was made by the Third Brigade, Second Division, Sixth Army Corps, commanded by Col. Thomas W. Hyde . . . At the outskirts of the town they were met by the Mayor, Mr. Walker, who surrendered the place, and the stars and stripes once more assert their supremacy." Addressing the inhabitants of the city, the newspaper issued a warning and a note of hope:

> Of the people we only ask order – Keeping this their rights are guaranteed. To the unruly we can only give the warning, they tread on dangerous ground. But we know that all will see that union is far better than disunion; that without union they have no hope, and that the deluded people of the south starting anew, under one constitution, and one country will be, as heretofore, a prosperous people. [34]

Private Alonzo Bump wrote home that Danville, "is a very pretty city. it is about the size of union Village [Saratoga County, New York]. thair is 4 curches 4 hotels and Eny amount of stores and a

Large railroad Depot and Hospitals that the Rebals Had." The city was also the site of a prisoner of war camp consisting of six tobacco warehouses that held captive 7,000 Union soldiers. Small pox and dysentery killed 1,400 men. Bump told his wife "thair is a Bering Ground hear whare the Rebs Barid our prisinars. I should think that thair was about 4 thousand of them. they have All Got head Boards up to thair heads and I ame a goin down to see if I can find Eny one out of our Rigt Barid thair. probably I may come acrost Earl Greens [sergeant, Co. K, missing in action May 10, 1864 at Spotsylvania] Grave if hee was wonded and taken prisinar." [35]

May 16, the 77th with the Sixth Corps began moving north toward Washington. The New Yorkers boarded a train that moved barely ten miles an hour due to the poor condition of the railroad. Many in their brigade urged Colonel Hyde to burn the old Confederate prisons as they departed. The colonel demurred: "I should have winked at it, but the wind was toward the town, which forbade, as well as the attitude of the Danville people during our stay." [36]

At Richmond, the battalion debarked from the train, and marched through the city in ruins. Four years earlier with McClellan, they sat in their trenches where they could see the church spires and hear the bells tolling. The peaceful march to Washington over ground wetted by the blood of soldiers "seemed very queer," Hyde commented. "There was no firing on the picket line at night." Once in the capital, the 77th marched with their comrades in the review of the Sixth Corps on a blistering hot afternoon. Behind the banners of the Greek Cross, 12,000 hardy, and proud, veterans marched up Pennsylvania Avenue past President Andrew Johnson and Washington dignitaries. [37]

At their camp in the defenses of Washington, on a pleasant morning, June 16, the order was read and gleefully received: "FALL

IN! FOR MUSTER OUT." For Private Charles H. Benedict (Co. A), the order "was sure evidence that the war was over." A day after the muster out, the first contingent of veterans to go home marched to the railroad station in Washington. Later in the afternoon, the New Yorkers boarded a box car in the freight train that also carried veterans of the 43rd and 49th New York Regiments, all quite eager to get home. Benedict remembered, "The train started at sundown, moving very slowly, because the line to Philadelphia was greatly congested with other trains containing soldiers on the same errand as we. It was near midnight when we crossed at Harve de Grace on the ferry Boat that transported the cars without unloading. I was on top of a car on which I fastened myself with straps from my knapsack to prevent my rolling off should I go to sleep; which I did, so was quite refreshed when we got into Philadelphia at daylight." [38]

At Philadelphia, Private Benedict and his fellow mates marched to the *Cooper Shop*, where they washed up and had breakfast. Later in the afternoon, the battalion's veterans marched to the New York station and boarded a train for New York City. Arriving the same afternoon, Benedict marched, "and it was novel to us to do so without rifles, to the armory of the 9th New York Regiment – full of returning soldiers homeward bound as we are – our headquarters for the day". Soon after supper, the New York veterans marched once again, this time to the "west side wharf where we boarded the steamboat *Knickerbocker* for a trip on the Hudson River to Albany, where we were to go into 'camp' at the 'Fairgrounds' to wait until we received our discharges and pay." [39]

The *Knickerbocker* landed in Albany at 5 a.m. Charles Benedict and some others decided to bypass "camp" and find their own way home:

> We went to the Merchants Hotel . . . where we breakfasted. Soon after we got to the hotel Seymour Rice – a Saratogian – a

night operator at the Albany Telegraph office – State Street, corner Broadway – came in, inquiring for the Seventy-seventh boys. And soon found us. And such a glad time we had talking to him. A squad of the Seventy-seventh, Sergeant Gus Walker [Augustus Walker, Co. A], Privates C. H. Benedict. Obed M. Coleman [Co. A], Ed [Edward] and Bill [William] Thorn [Co. A] and one other, whose name has slipt from my memory, agreed we would not go to 'camp,' but go to Saratoga springs. Rice told us that a train left at 7 o'clock a. m. But, we had no money. Nor did Rice indicate that he was any better conditioned. He suggested that we go to the railroad ticket office, tell the agent our fix, to learn if he could help us. The squad got their traps together and funereally marched, enforce, to the ticket office. We convinced the ticket man we were not deserters, that the war was over, that we were stranded, volunteers returning, or trying to return, to our homes in Saratoga Springs, unwilling to be deterred by entering a camp to wait for our discharge and pay. Walker had the only valuable worth pawning – silver a watch. It was left in pledge; tickets were given. So soon as the train backed in we entered the car. As 'Bill' Thorn had a young bulldog pup in his arms, which he had picked up near Fredericksburg, as we marched to Washington from Richmond returning from the front, and our appearance not being in the up to date style, we were given a place in the baggage car. The train started promptly on time. We were really on our way to Saratoga Springs, which we had left as recruits in 1862, now returning seasoned soldiers... As our train entered the Saratoga Springs station our squad was on the car platform and steps, shouting and singing – like school boys when the term is ended – and hailing those we recognized. Getting off the car we were surrounded by a shouting pleased crowd. Getting without the depot each started their several ways home. The two Thorns, Coleman and Benedict started down Division Street. Somehow the news of the 'Returned Volunteers' traveled fast, for when we got to Matilda street our fathers met us with such a jubilee. Reaching Broadway we quickly became the center of a crowd. [40]

This scene of jubilant return to home and loved ones and friends was replayed in Ballston Spa, Schuylerville, Gloversville, Waterford, Stillwater, Elizabethtown, Keeseville, and in the smallest communities in Saratoga, Fulton, and Essex Counties. The country they had fought to save was now unified, slavery-free, and at peace. The 77th Bemis Heights Battalion's soldiers played as important role in winning the Civil War as any other unit in the Army of the Potomac. They would remember their experiences, both good and bad, for as long as they lived, and would gather annually as brothers in fifty reunions. Each man knew he had lived through one of the great moments in the country's history.

APPENDIX

Roll of Honor

Deaths, Effects of Gun Shots

William H. Boise, May 24, 1862
Clifford Weston, May 24, 1862
John T. Seeley, June 27, 1862
John W. Ham, June 28, 1862
James Todd, June 29, 1862
Lieut. Halsey Bowe, August 16, 1862
Henry Allen, September 17, 1862
Lieut. Ansel Denninson, September 17, 1862
Davis Green, September 17, 1862
Henry Haas, September 17, 1862
George Huntington, September 17, 1862
Benjamin F. Knapp, September 17, 1862
Joseph Muerer, September 17, 1862
Charles Munn, September 17, 1862
John A. Reuchler, September 17, 1862
Gideon M. Rowley, September 17, 1862

William H. Woolsey, September 17, 1862
Paul A. Brown, December 13, 1862
John W. Arnold, May 3, 1863
Benjamin H. Day, May 3, 1863
William H. Deyoe, May 3, 1863
Alonzo C. Hubbell, May 3, 1863
James Hendrick, May 3, 1863
Peter Knickerbacker, May 3, 1863
Dennis Sheran, May 3, 1863
Henry A. West, May 3, 1863
Capt. Luther M. Wheeler, May 3, 1863
Rex A. Havens, June 5, 1863
Michael Lama, May 5, 1864
William Van Saulsbury, May 5, 1864
Hermance Bowers, May 5, 1864
Charles K. Burnham, May 6, 1864
Samuel S. Craig, May 6, 1864
Walter Dwyer, May 6, 1864
George Deal, May 6, 1864
James Emperor, May 6, 1864
Michael McWilliams, May 6, 1864
David McNeil, Jr., May 6, 1864
Charles Ruggles, May 6, 1864
Alfred M. See, May 6, 1864
William H. Sexton, May 6, 1864
Louis Smith, May 6, 1864
Abraham Lapham, May 9, 1864
George G. Allen, May 10, 1864
Thomas Armer, May 10, 1864
John C. Barker, May 10, 1864
Capt. William B. Carpenter, May 10, 1864
Abram Coonradt, May 10, 1864
John B. Darrow, May 10, 1864
George R. DeYoe, May 10, 1864
William Divine, May 10, 1864
James Dawenson, May 10, 1864
Harrison Davenport, May 10, 1864
Herman H. Fowler, May 10, 1864
Patrick Gilroy, May 10, 1864
Earl Green, May 10, 1864
Leroy Hoyt, May 10, 1864
Charles M. Hart, May 10, 1864
Lieut. William F. Lyon, May 10, 1864
Martin V. Norton, May 10, 1864
Legare Strong, May 10, 1864
Oliver Shaw, May 10, 1864
Washington Sherman, May 10, 1864
Benjamin F. Stillwell, May 10, 1864
James C. Vandenberg, May 10, 1864
Lewis C. Ward, May 10, 1864
Charles Wheeler, May 10, 1864
William Walton, May 10, 1864
James Dorley, May 12, 1864
Henry Franc, May 12, 1864

McKEAN'S SUNDAY SCHOOL BOYS GO TO WAR

Frederick Keenholtz, May 12, 1864
Edmund A. Phillips, May 12, 1864
Capt. Orrin P. Rugg, May 12, 1864
Gustavus Tuck, May 12, 1864
John Allen, May 18, 1864
William H. Brown, May 18, 1864
Henry C. Darrow, May 18, 1864
William Hill, May 18, 1864
William Hill, May 18, 1864
Lewis Lakely, May 18, 1864
Aaron B. Quivey, May 21, 1864
Wliiam A. Cole, June 3, 1864
Charles VanKleek, June 3, 1864
Simon D. Russell, June 3, 1864
George Bolton, June 4, 1864
Francis Love, June 6, 1864
Michael S. Briggs, June 8, 1864
James Bortell, June 16, 1864
Andrew J. Dowen, July 12, 1864
Matthew Love, July 12, 1863
Andrew Manning, July 12, 1864
Alvarado Morey, July 12, 1864
Ambrose Mattot, July 12, 1864
Hubbard M. Moss, July 12, 1864
William Craig, September 19, 1864
John H. Briggs, September 19, 1864
Harlan A. Thomas, September 19, 1864
William Miller, September 19, 1864
Isaac Kipp, Jr., September 22, 1864
Hiram Burt, October 19, 1864
Lieut. John W. Belding, October 19, 1864
James Fairchild, October 19, 1864
Herbert Gallup, October 19, 1864
John Horrigan, October 19, 1864
Frank Hall, October 19, 1864
John G. Kitchner, October 19, 1864
Capt. Martin Lennon, October 19, 1864
Jacob Pung, October 19, 1864
John L. Root, October 19, 1864
Adjt. Gilbert Thomas, October 19, 1864
Lieut. William J. Tabor, October 19, 1864
Daniel Smith, December 29, 1864
Henry B. Shreeves, March 17, 1865
Alfred Chase, March 25, 1865
Capt. Sumner Oakley, March 25, 1865
Lieut. Stephen H. Pierce, March 25, 1865
John Stewart, March 25, 1865
John H. Kipp, April 2, 1865

DIED IN CONFEDERATE PRISONS

John L. Rector
James V. Fogg
William Arnold
Adna Abbs, Jr.
William C. Kimpton
Hiram Broughton
Benjamin H. Carr
Ira Tripp
Lewis W. VanDenberg
John Cady
Louis Sicard
Joseph Cormack
Stephen Welch

Hiram Tyrrell
Leonard Ingram

Died of Disease

One-hundred-Seventy-Six officers and enlisted men

PHOTOGRAPHIC GALLERY

Private Henry Allen & Daughter (Gloversville Public Library)

Captain Charles H. Davis (Saratoga Springs Public Library)

Adjutant Laurans VanDemark (NYSDMNA)

Captain Edward W. Winnie (NYSDMNA)

Lieutenant George H. Gillis (NYSDMNA)

Lieutenant Henry C. Rowland (NYSDMNA)

Sergeant Oscar F. Lockwood (L. Tom Perry Special Collections)

Captain Joseph H. Loveland (L. Tom Perry Special Collections)

Captain Jesse White (NYSDMNA)

Lieutenant Thomas W. Fowler (Saratoga Springs Public Library)

Sergeant Job S. Safford (L. Tom Perry Special Collections)

Lieutenant Alonzo Howland (L. Tom Perry Special Collections)

BIBLIOGRAPHY

Books

Boatner, Mark M. *The Civil War Dictionary.* Vintage Books 1988

Brands, H. W. *The Man Who Saved the Union: Ulysses Grant in War and Peace.* Doubleday 2012

Brown, Kent Masterson *Lee, Logistics & the Pennsylvania Campaign: Retreat from Gettysburg.* The University of North Carolina Press 2005

Bryant, James K. II *The Chancellorsville Campaign: The Nation's high Water Mark.* History Press 2009

Brewer, Abraham T. *History of the Sixty-first Regiment Pennsylvania, 1861-1965.* Regimental Association 1911

Bidwell, Frederick David *History of the Forty-Ninth New York Volunteers.* J. B. Lyon Publishers 1916.

Branch, Erskine B. *A Brig Sketch of the Experiences of A Union Soldier in the Late War.* Chronicle Print 1870

Cannan, John *The Antietam Campaign August-September 1862.* Combined Books 1990

The Spottsylvania Campaign May 7-21, 1864. Combined Books 1997

Catton, Bruce *The Army of the Potomac: Mr. Lincoln's Army.* Doubleday & Company, Inc. 1951

The Army of the Potomac: Glory Road. Doubleday & Company, Inc. 1952

Coco, Gregory A. *The Civil War Infantryman in Camp, on the March, and in Battle.* Thomas Publications 1996

Coddington, Edwin B. *The Gettysburg Campaign: A Study in Command.* Charles Scribner's Sons 1968

Cooling, Benjamin Franklin *Jubal Early's Raid on Washington.* The University of Alabama Press 1989

Symbol, Sword, and Shield: Defending Washington During the Civil War. The White Mane Publishing Company, Inc. 1975

Cotant, George *Path of Blood: The True Story of the 33rd New York Volunteers.* Seeco Printing Services 1996

Cullen, Joseph P. *The Peninsula Campaign of 1862: McClellan & Lee Struggle for Richmond.* Stackpole Books 1973

Dougherty, Kevin *The Peninsula Campaign of 1862: A Military Analysis.* University Press of Mississippi 2005

Dowdey, Clifford *The Seven Days: The Emergence of Lee.* University of Nebraska Press 1992

Field, Ron *Petersburg 1864-65: The Longest Siege.* Osprey Publishing Limited 2009

Foote, Shelby *The Civil War, A Narrative: Fort Sumter to Perryville.* Vintage Books 1958

The Civil War, A Narrative: Fredericksburg to Meridian. Vintage Books 1963

The Civil War, A Narrative: Red River to Appomattox. Vintage Books 1974

Ford, Christopher Lee, *Over the Wall: The Sixth Corps at Fredericksburg 1863.* Fredericksburg Press 1996

Fox, John J., III, *The Confederate Alamo: Bloodbath at Petersburg's Fort Gregg on April 2, 1865.* Angle Valley Press 2010

Fuller, Edward H. *Battles of the Seventy-Seventh New York State Foot Volunteers.* Survivor's Association Seventy-seventh Regiment New York Infantry Volunteers

Furgurson, Ernest B. *Chancellorsville 1863: The Souls of the Brave.* Vintage Books 1993

Not War But Murder: Cold Harbor 1864. Vintage Books 2000

Gallagher, Gary W. ed. *Antietam: Essays on the 1862 Maryland Campaign.* The Kent State University Press 1989

Chancellorsville: The Battle and Its Aftermath. The University of North Carolina Press 1996

The Wilderness Campaign. The University of North Carolina Press 1997

Grant, Ulysses S. *Personal Memoirs of U. S. Grant.* De Capo Press 1982

Grose, Edward F. and John C. Booth *Centennial History of the Village of Ballston Spa: Including the towns of Ballston and Milton.* Ballston Journal 1907

Haskell, Frank Lt. U. S. A., Col. William C. Oates C. S. A. *Gettysburg.* Bantam Books 1992

Heiss, Earl J. *The Union Soldier in Battle: Enduring the Ordeal of Combat.* University Press of Kansas 1997

Henderson, G. F. R. Col. *The Civil War: A Soldier's View.* The University of Chicago Press 1958

Hennessy, John J. *Return to Bull Run: The Campaign and Battle of Second Manassas.* Simon & Schuster 1993

History of Ballston, New York from Our County and Its People: A Descriptive & Biological Record of Saratoga County, New York. The Boston History Company 1899

History of Essex County, With Illustrations and Biographical Sketches of Some of Its Prominent Men and Pioneers. D. Mason 1885

Horn, John *The Petersburg Campaign June 1864-April 1865.* De Capo Press 1993

Hyde, Thomas W. *Following the Greek Cross or Memoirs of the Sixth Army Corps.* Houghton Mifflin 1894

Johnson, Curtis and Anderson, C. Jr. *Artillery Hell: The Employment of Artillery at Antietam.* Texas A & M University Press 1995

Judd, David *The Story of the Thirty-Third N. Y. S. Volunteers 1864.* Benton & Andrews 1864

Judge, Joseph *Season of Fire: The Confederate Strike on Washington.* Rockbridge Publishing Company 1994

Large, George R. & Joe A. Swisher *Battle of Antietam: The Official History by the Antietam Battlefield Board.* The Burd Street Press 1998

Leech, Margaret *Reveille in Washington.* Harper & Brothers 1941

Lewis, Thomas A. *The Guns of Cedar Creek.* Dell Publishing 1988

Linderman, Gerald H. *Embattled Courage: The Experience of Combat in the American Civil War.* Free Press 1987

Livermore, Thomas L. *Numbers & Losses in the Civil War in America: 1861-65.* Bloomington Press 1957

Lowry, Thomas P., M. D. *Tarnished Eagles: The Courts-Marshal of Fifty Union Colonel's and Lieutenant Colonels.* Stackpole Books 1997

Luvaas, Jay & Harold W. Nelson *The U. S. Army War College Guide to the Battle of Antietam: The Maryland Campaign of 1862.* Harper Collins Publishers 1987

Mackowski, Chris and Kristopher D. White *Chancellorsville's Forgotten Front: The Battles of Second Fredericksburg and Salem Church, May 3, 1863.* Saras Beatie, LLC 2013

Mahr, Theodore *Early's Valley Campaign, the Battle of Cedar Creek: Showdown in the Shenandoah October 1-30, 1864.* H. E. Howard 1992

Martin, David G. *The Second Bull Run Campaign July-August 1862.* Combined Books 1997

Matter, William D. *If It Takes All Summer: The Battle of Spotsylvania.* The University of North Carolina Press 1988

McPherson, James M. *Battle Cry of Freedom: The Civil War Era.* Oxford University Press 1988

For Cause & Comrades: Why Men fought in the Civil War. Oxford University Press 1997

Miller, Eugene C. and Forrest F. Steinlage *Der Turner Soldat: A Turner Soldier in the Civil War.* Calmar Publications

Mitchell, Reid *Civil War Soldiers: Their Expectations and Their Experiences.* Simon & Schuster 1988

Mudgett, Timothy B. *Make the Fur Fly: A History of a Union Volunteer Diviison in the American Civil War.* Burd Street Press 1997

O'Reilly, Francis Augustine *The Fredericksburg Campaign: Winter War on the Rappahannock.* Louisiana State University Press 2006

Parsons, Philip W. *The Union sixth Army Corps in the Chancellorsville Campaign: A Study of the Engagements of Second Fredericksburg, Salem church, and Banks Ford, May 3-4, 1863.* McFarland & Company 2006

Pfanz, Harry W. *Gettysburg— Culp's Hill & Cemetery Hill.* The University of North Carolina Press 1993

Pond, George E. *The Shenandoah Valley in 1864.* Charles Scribner's Sons 1881

Priest, John Michael *Antietam: The Soldier's Battle.* Oxford University Press 1989

Before Antietam: The Battle for South Mountain. Oxford University Press 1992

No Where to Run: The Wilderness, May 4th & May 5th, 1864. Vol. 1 The White Mane Publishing Company, Inc. 1995

Turn Them Out to Die Like A Mule. Gauly Mount Press 1995

Victory Without Triumph: The Wilderness, May 6th & 7th, 1864. Vol. 2 The White Mane Publishing Company, Inc. 1996

Putnam, George Haven *A Prisoner of War in Virginia 1864-5.* Address Presented to the N. Y.

Commandery of the U. S. Loyal Legion 1910

Rable, George C. *Fredericksburg! Fredericksburg!* The University of North Carolina Press 2002

Rafuse, Ethan S. *George Gordon Meade and the War in the East.* McWhiney Foundation Press 2003

Rhea, Gordon C. *Cold Harbor: Grant and Lee May 26-June 3, 1864.* Louisiana State University Press 1994

The Battle of the Wilderness May 5-6, 1864. Louisiana State University Press 1994

The Battle for Spotsylvania Court House and the Road to Yellow Tavern May 7-12, 1864. Louisiana State University Press 1997

To the North Anna River: Grant and Lee May 13-25, 1864. Louisiana State University Press 2000

Riggs, David E. *Embattled Shrine: Jamestown in the Civil War*. The White Mane Publishing Company, Inc. 1997

Robertson, James I. Jr. *Soldiers Blue & Gray*. Warner Books 1988

Schiller, Herbert A. ed. *Autobiography of Major General William F. Smith 1861-1864*. Morningside 1990

Schroeder, Rudolph J. III *Seven Days Before Richmond: McClellan's Peninsula Campaign of 1862 and Its Aftermath*. iUniverse 2009

Scott, Robert Garth *Into the Wilderness with the Army of the Potomac*. Indiana University Press 1985

Sears, Stephen W. *Chancellorsville*. Houghton Mifflin Company 1996

Gettysburg. First Mariner Books 2003

George B. McClellan: The Young Napoleon. Ticknor & Fields 1988

Landscape Turned Red: The Battle of Antietam. Book-of-the-Month Club 1983

To the Gates of Richmond: The Peninsula Campaign. Ticknor & fields 1992

Smith, Carl *Gettysburg 1863: High tide of the Confederacy*. Osprey Publishing Limited 1998

Starin, John H. *Personal Sketches, Grand Army of the Republic: Presented to Col Sammons Post No. 242.* Gloversville 1892

Steere, Edward *The Wilderness Campaign: The Meeting of Grant and Lee.* Stackpole Books 1960

Steiner, Paul E. *Disease in the Civil War: Natural Biological Warfare in 1861-1865.* Charles C. Thomas Publisher 1968

Stevens, George T. *Three Years in the Sixth Corps.* S. R. Gray 1866

Swinfen, David B. *Ruggles' Regiment: the 122nd New York Volunteers in the American Civil War.* University Press of New England 1982

Sylvester, Nathaniel Bartlett *History of Saratoga County, New York.* The Saratogian 1878

The War of Rebellion: A Compilation of the Official Records of the Union and Confederate Armies. 130 vols. Washington, D. C. 1880-1901

Tiche, Andrian G. *The Bristoe Campaign: General Lee's Last Strategic Offensive with the Army of Northern Virginia October 1863.* Xlibril Corporation 2011

Trudeau, Noah Andre *Bloody Roads South: The Wilderness to Cold Harbor, May-June 1864.* Fawcet Columbine 1989

The Last Citadel: Petersburg, Virginia June 1864-April 1865. Little, Brown and Company 1991

Vandiver, Frank E. *Jubal's Raid: General Early's Famous Attack on Washington in 1864.* McGraw-Hill 1960

Walker, Aldace F. *The Vermont Brigade in the Shenandoah Valley 1864.* The Free Press Association 1869

Warner, Ezra J. *Generals in Blue: Lives of the Union Commanders 1964.* Louisiana State University Press 1964

Watson, W. C. *Civil-Military history of the County of Essex, New York.* J. Munsell 1869

Wert, Jeffry *From Winchester to Cedar Creek: The Shenandoah Campaign of 1864.* Stackpole Books 1997

Wheeler, Richard *On Fields of Fury from the Wilderness to the Crater: An Eyewitness History.* Harper Collins Publishers 1991

Wiley, Bell I. *The Life of Johnny Reb.* Bobbs-Merrill Company 1943

The Life of Billy Yank. Bobbs-Merrill Company 1951

Winslow, Richard Elliot III *General John Sedgwick: the Story of a Union Corps Commander.* Presidio 1982

Worsham, John H. *One of Jackson's Foot Cavalry.* Edited by James I. Robertson, Jr. Mercer Press, Inc. 1964

Periodicals

Blumberg, Arnold. "War So Terrible." *Civil War Quarterly* (Summer 2012): 66-75.

Emerson, Jason. "Great Weapon or 'Fanciful Contraption'?" *Civil War Times* (December 2012): 32-39.

Fountain, Cyrille and David Chipman. "An Essex County Soldier in the Civil War: The Diary of Cyrille Fountain." *New York History 66:3* (July 1985): 280-317.

Fuller, Edward H. "Fort Stevens." *The National Tribune* (July 22, 1915)

Holzer, Harold. "War By the Numbers." *America's Civil War* (September 2012): 22-24.

Kreiser, Christine. "Fiasco at Fredericksburg." *America's Civil War* (November 2012): 54-57.

Seideman, Tony. "McClellan's Plantation." *Civil War times Illustrated* (January/February 1994): 20-21; 74.

Stevens, C. E. "Not a fighting Regiment." *The National Tribune* (October 8, 1908)

Walker, John. "Return to Manassas." *Civil War Quarterly* (Summer 2012): 66-75.

Newspapers

Albany Evening Journal
Ballston Spa Journal
Daily Saratogian
Elizabethtown Post
New York Herald
New York Times
New York Tribune
New York World
Saratogian
Nunda News

The Sixth Corps
Waterford Sentinel

Manuscripts

Eastern Washington University – Archives and Special Collections

William G. Watson diary

New York State Historical Society, Cooperstown

Stephen R. Frost Letters

New York State Library and Archives, Albany

Lt. Col. Winsor B. French Letter

Saratoga Springs Historical Society, Saratoga Springs, New York

Alonzo D. Bump Letters

Durkee's Reminiscences

Durkee's Scrapbook

Winsor B. French Letter

T. Scott Fuller Letters

Sylvanus Morse Letter

Orrin P. Rugg Letters

Charles E. Stevens Letters

William Tabor Letter

Shallum West Letters

Saratoga Springs Public Library

William H. DeYoe Letter

University of Rochester Libraries

Adam Clark Works Papers – Robert H. Skinner 1861-1863

William L. Clements Library, The University of Michigan

George T. Stevens Papers

Internet

George Bolton Letters *www.cwc.lsu.edu/other/ny77/george.txt*

Luther Wheeler Letters, Ruth Barton *mrgjb@sover.net*

MISCELLANEOUS

Report of the Annual Reunion of the Survivor's Association Seventy-seventh Regiment New York Infantry Volunteers. Published Annually 1893-1911, 1915, 1918.

Robert Philbrook, "Roscoe G. Philbrook and the 7th Maine at Antietam." *The Philbrook and Philbrook Family Association Newsletter* (February, 2001 Volume 3, Issue 2) 1-12

Erskine Branch, *Pension Certificate No. 36168*

NOTES

Chapter 1

1. J. David Hacker, "A Census-Based Count of the Civil War Dead," *Civil War History* Vol. LVII No. 4: 307
2. Jas. B. McKean, *Circular August 21, 1861*
3. Report of the Annual Reunion of the Survivor's Association Seventy-seventh Regiment New York Infantry Volunteers, *Fiftieth Anniversary*, Saratoga Springs, N.Y., June 26, 1915, 9
4. *Saratogian*, August 29, 1861
5. *Ibid*, August 31, 1861; October 31, 1861
6. *Ibid*, October 3, 1861
7. *Ibid*, October 31, 1861
8. *Ballton Spa Journal*, September 10, 1861
9. *Ibid*, September 17, 1861
10. *Ibid, September 24, 1861*
11. *Ibid*
12. *Ibid, October 1, 1861*
13. *Ibid*
14. *Saratogian*, September 12, 1861; September 19, 1861

15. *Ballston Spa Journal*, October 1, 1861
16. *Waterford Sentinel*, October 26, 1861
17. *Ballston Spa Journal*, October 8, 1861; October 27, 1861
18. *Elizabethtown Post*, September 26, 1861
19. *Saratogian*, October 3, 1861
20. *Robert H. Skinner Letters 1861-1863: Adam Clark Works Papers*, University of Rochester Libraries
21. *Saratogian*, October 24, 1861
22. Paul E. Steiner, *Disease in the Civil War: Natural Biological Warfare in 1861-1865* (Springfield, Ill.: Charles C. Thomas, 1968) 13
23. *Waterford Sentinel*, November 23, 1861; *Skinner*, November 12, 1861
24. *Skinner*, November 12, 1861
25. *Ibid*, November 8, 1861
26. *Saratogian*, November 7, 1861
27. *Skinner*, November 12, 1861
28. *Elizabethtown Post*, December 5, 1861
29. *Ballston Spa Journal*, October 1, 1861
30. *Ibid*
31. *Ibid*
32. *Ibid*
33. *Ibid*
34. *Ibid*
35. *Saratogian*, October 24, 1861
36. *Ballston Spa Journal*, October 1, 1861; *Skinner*, November 12, 1861; *Saratogian*, November 14, 1861
37. *Saratogian*, October 31, 1861; November 28, 1861
38. *Ibid*, November 24, 1861
39. *Ibid*, December 5, 1861
40. *Ibid*, November 14, 1861
41. *Ibid*, November 21, 1861
42. *Skinner*, November 21, 1861

Chapter 2

1. *Saratogian*, November 28, 1861
2. *Ibid*
3. *Ibid*
4. *Ibid*
5. *Ibid*, December 5, 1861; *Ballston Spa Journal*, December 3, 1861
6. *Saratogian*, December 5, 1861
7. *Ibid*
8. *Ibid*; *Luther Wheeler Letters*, November 25, 1861
9. *Saratogian*, December 5, 1861
10. *Ibid*
11. *Ibid*
12. *Ibid*
13. George T. Stevens, *Three Years in the Sixth Corps* (Albany, NY, 1866) 5-6
14. *Saratogian*, December 25, 1861; *Daily Saratogian*, February 28, 1881
15. *Saratogian*, December 5, 1861
16. *Skinner*, December 2, 1861
17. *Stevens*, 9; *Skinner*, December 2, 1861
18. *Ballston Spa Journal*, December 17, 1861
19. *Saratogian*, December 26, 1861
20. *Skinner*, December 23, 1861
21. *Ibid*, January 16, 1862
22. *Ibid*
23. *Saratogian*, February 13, 1862
24. *Skinner*, January 16, 1862
25. *Saratogian*, January 16, 1862; January 20, 1862; Report of the Annual Reunion of the Survivor's Association Seventy-seventh Regiment New York Infantry Volunteers, *Thirty-Ninth Annual Reunion*, Saratoga Springs, N.Y., 36

26. *Saratogian*, January 20, 1862
27. *Ibid*, January 16, 1862
28. *Ibid*
29. *Ibid*
30. Paul E. Steiner, *Disease in the Civil War: Natural Biological Warfare in 1861-1865* (Springfield, ILL., 1968) 25
31. *Shallum* West *Letter*; *Wheeler*, January 1, 1862; *Saratogian*, January 23, 1862
32. Report of the Annual Reunion of the Survivor's Association Seventy-seventh New York Infantry Volunteers, *Fiftieth Anniversary*, Saratoga Springs, N. Y., June 26, 1915, 53
33. *Saratogian*, January 30, 1862; *Skinner*, January 16, 1862
34. *Skinner*, January 16, 1862
35. *Saratogian*, January 23, 1862
36. *Ibid*, January 30, 1862
37. *Ibid*
38. *Skinner*, March 4, 1862; *Saratogian*, February 27, 1862
39. *Saratogian*, February 27, 1862
40. *Stevens*, 13-14
41. *Saratogian*, March 13, 1862
42. *Ibid*; March 11, 1862; *Skinner*, March 4, 1862
43. *Saratogian*, March 13, 1862
44. *Ibid*; *Stevens*, 16
45. *Stevens*, 17
46. Steven W. Sears, *To the Gates of Richmond: The Peninsula Campaign* (New York, N. Y., 1992) 3
47. *Saratogian*, March 13, 1862
48. *Stevens*, 18
49. *Skinner*, March 12, 1862
50. *Stevens*, 19
51. *Ibid*, 21; *Ballston Spa Journal*, April 1, 1862
52. *Ballston Spa Journal*, April 4, 1862
53. *Sears*, 21

54. *Skinner,* March 28, 1862
55. *Ingersoll's Century Annals of San Bernardino county 1769 to 1904* (Los Angeles, CA., 1904) 754; *Skinner,* March 28, 1862

Chapter 3

1. *Sears,* 28
2. *Ballston Spa Journal,* April 22, 1862
3. *Ibid; Skinner,* March 28, 1862
4. *Skinner,* March 28, 1862; *Stevens,* 27-28
5. *Ballston Spa Journal,* April 22, 1862
6. *Daily Saratogian,* February 28, 1881
7. *Cornelius Durkee Scrapbooks, 1862-1932*
8. *Stevens,* 28-29
9. *Ibid,* 30-31; *Ballston Spa Journal,* April 22, 1862
10. *Skinner,* March 28, 1862
11. *Daily Saratogian,* February 28, 1881; *Stevens,* 31
12. *Ballston Spa Journal,* April 22, 1862; Report of the Annual Reunion of the Survivor's Association Seventy-seventh New York Infantry Volunteers, *Fiftieth Anniversary,* Saratoga Springs, N. Y., June 26, 1915, 36
13. *Ibid*
14. *Saratogian,* April 24, 1862
15. *Orrin P. Rugg Letter,* April 9, 1862; *Stevens,* 34
16. *Rugg,* April 9, 1862
17. *Stevens,* 34-35
18. *Saratogian,* April 24, 1862
19. *Stevens,* 35; *Daily Saratogian,* February 28, 1881; *Ballston Spa Journal,* April 22, 1862
20. *Stevens,* 35; Report of the Annual Reunion of the Survivor's Association Seventy-seventh New York Infantry Volunteers, *Fiftieth Anniversary,* Saratoga Springs, N. Y., June 26, 1915, 37
21. Sears, *42*

22. *Daily Saratogian*, February 28, 1881
23. *Wheeler,* April 12, 1862; *Fifth Annual Report of the NYS Bureau of Military Statistics, Vol. 1* (Albany, N. Y., 1868, 715
24. *Stevens*, 38-39
25. *Durkee Scrapbooks*
26. *Ballston Spa Journal*, April 22, 1862; *Daily Saratogian*, February 28, 1881
27. Report of the Survivor's Association Seventy-seventh New York Infantry Volunteers, *Fiftieth Anniversary*, Saratoga Springs, N. Y., June 26, 1915, 37
28. *Stevens*, 38
29. *Ibid*, 40
30. *Ibid*, 43
31. *Saratogian*, April 24, 1862; *Stevens*, 42
32. *Ballston Spa Journal*, April 29, 1862
33. *Ibid*
34. *Stevens*, 45
35. Report of the Survivor's Association Seventy-seventh New York Infantry Volunteers, *Fiftieth Anniversary*, Saratoga Springs, N. Y., June 26, 1915, 38
36. *Durkee Scrapbooks*
37. *Skinner,* July 11, 1862
38. *Stevens*, 74-75; *Saratogian,* July 1, 1862
39. *Stevens*, 47
40. *Ballston Spa Journal*, May 27, 1862; *Durkee*
41. *Ibid*

Chapter 4

1. *Stevens*, 48; *Ballston Spa Journal*, May 5, 1862
2. *Stevens*, 48

3. *Durkee*; *Wheeler*, May 6, 1862; Report of the Survivor's Association Seventy-seventh New York Infantry Volunteers, Ballston Spa, N. Y., September 19, 1899
4. *Silvanus Morse Letters*, May 7, 1862; *Saratogian*, May 29, 1862
5. Earl C. Hastings, Jr. and David S. Hastings, *A Pitiless Rain: The Battle of Williamsburg, 1862* (Shippensburg, PA, 1997) 88
6. *Morse*, May 7, 1862
7. *Durkee*
8. *Saratogian*, May 29, 1862
9. *Daily Saratogian*, July 1, 1862
10. Report of the Survivor's Association Seventy-seventh New York Infantry Volunteers, Gloversville, N. Y., 1897
11. *Stevens*, 58
12. *Ibid*, 59
13. *Wheeler*, May 18, 1862; *Ballston Spa Journal*, May 24, 1862
14. *Daily Saratogian*, July 12, 1862; *The War of the Rebellion: A Compilation of the Official Records of the Federal and Confederate Armies*, XI, Pt. 1, 661
15. *Wheeler*, May 27, 1862
16. *Daily Saratogian*, July 12, 1862
17. *Ibid*
18. Skinner, July 11, 1862; Report of the Survivor's Association Seventy-seventh New York Infantry Volunteers, Ballston Spa, September 19, 1899
19. *O. R.*, XI, Pt. 1, 655, 657; *Durkee*
20. *Ibid*, 661; Report of the Survivor's Association Seventy-seventh New York Infantry Volunteers, *Fiftieth Anniversary*, Saratoga Springs, N. Y., November 23, 1911
21. *Daily Saratogian*, July 12, 1862; *Wheeler*, May 27, 1862; Report of the Survivor's Association Seventy-seventh New York Infantry Volunteers, *Fiftieth Anniversary*, Saratoga Springs, N. Y., June 26, 1915

22. *Daily Saratogian,* July 12, 1862
23. *Stevens,* 67
24. *Daily Saratogian,* July 1, 1862
25. Clifford Dowdy, *The Seven Days: The Emergence of Lee* (Boston, MA, 1992) 86; *Wheeler,* June 1, 1862
26. *Sears,* 134; *Stevens,* 82
27. *Sears,* 138
28. Joseph P. Cullen, *The Peninsula Campaign 1862: McClellan & Lee Struggle for Richmond* (Harrisburg, PA, 1973) 54
29. *Daily Saratogian,* July 1, 1862
30. *Ibid*
31. *Wheeler,* June 14, 1862
32. *Skinner,* July 11, 1862; *Wheeler,* June 20, 1862
33. Report of the Survivor's Association Seventy-seventh New York Infantry Volunteers, *Fiftieth Anniversary,* Saratoga Springs, N. Y., June 26, 1915, 38
34. *Skinner,* July 11, 1862
35. *Stevens,* 75; *Wheeler,* June 3, 1862
36. *Stevens,* 78
37. *Wheeler,* July 6, 1862; *Stevens,* 78
38. *Daily Saratogian,* July 23, 1862
39. *Ibid*
40. *Skinner,* July 11, 1862
41. *Wheeler,* July 6, 1862; *Daily Saratogian,* July 23, 1862
42. *Daily Saratogian,* July 23, 1862
43. Captain Martin Lennon, Letters and Diary, *Fifth Annual Report of the New York state Bureau of Military Statistics, Vol. 1* (Albany, N. Y. 1868) 716-720
44. *Daily Saratogian,* July 23, 1862; *Lennon,* 716-720
45. *Skinner,* undated letter, Camp at Harrison's Landing
46. *Daily Saratogian,* July 23, 1862
47. *Stevens,* 96-97
48. *Ibid,* 97-98

49. *Wheeler,* July 8, 1862
50. *New York World,* June 29, 1862
51. *Wheeler,* July 8, 1862
52. *Ibid*
53. *Daily Saratogian,* July 23, 1862
54. *Skinner,* July 11, 1862; *Wheeler,* July 6, 1862; *Daily Saratogian,* July 23, 1862
55. *Daily Saratogian,* July 23, 1862; Anders Henrikkson, "The Narrative of Friedrich Meyer: A Germin Freiwilliger (Volunteer) in the Army of the Potomac," *Civil War Regiments, Vol. 6* (El Dorado Hills, CA) 1-22
56. *Daily Saratogian,* July 23, 1862
57. National Park Service, U. S. Department of the Interior, *The Battles for Richmond, 1862*
58. *Daily Saratogian,* July 23, 1862
59. *Ibid*
60. *Ibid*

Chapter 5

1. *Wheeler,* August 2, 1862
2. *Daily Saratogian,* July 23, 1862; *Wheeler,* July 7, 1862
3. *Daily Saratogian,* July 23, 1862
4. *Ibid*
5. *Ibid*
6. *Stevens,* 112
7. *Daily Saratogian,* July 23, 1862
8. *Ibid*
9. *Ibid*
10. *Stevens,* 112; *Daily Saratogian,* July 23, 1862
11. *Skinner,* July 27, 1862
12. George Cotant, *Path of Blood: The True Story of the 33rd New York Volunteers* (Savannah, N. Y., 1996) 209

13. *Ibid*, 209-210
14. *Stevens*, 114
15. *Saratogian*, July 24, 1862
16. *Iibid*, July 31, 1862
17. *Rugg*, August 8, 1862
18. Stephen W. Sears, *George B. McClellan: The Young Napoleon* (New York, N. Y., 1988) 227-228
19. *Skinner*, July 11, 1862
20. *Wheeler*, July 21, 1862
21. *Ibid*
22. *Ibid*, August 2, 1862; *Stevens*, 115
23. *Stevens*, 121
24. *Sears*, GBM, 244
25. *Wheeler*, August 26, 1862
26. *Ibid*
27. *Wheeler*, August 26, 1862; *Lennon*, 716-720
28. *Stevens*, 123
29. *Ibid*, 123-124
30. *Lennon*, 716-720
31. *O. R. XII Pt. 3*, 473-474
32. *Stevens*, 129
33. *Ibid*, 129-130
34. *Durkee*
35. *Stevens, 131-132*
36. *Lennon*, 716-720

Chapter 6

1. *Stevens*, 134-135
2. *Ibid*, 135
3. David Wright Judd, *The Story of the Thirty-Third New York State Volunteers* (Rochester, N. Y., 1864) 180-181

4. John Michael Priest, *Before Antietam: The Battle for South Mountain* (Shippensburg, PA, 1989) 108-112
5. *Ibid*, 112; *GBM*, 282
6. *Stevens*, 137
7. *Ibid*, 138
8. *Ibid*, 140
9. Curt Johnson and Richard C. Anderson, Jr., *Artillery Hell: The Employment of Artillery at Antietam* (College Station, Tx, 1995) xix
10. *Cotant*, 232; *Nunda News*, October 4, 1862
11. Thomas W. Hyde, *Following the Greek Cross* (New York, N. Y., 1894) 94
12. *Priest*, 196
13. *Wheeler*, September 22, 1862
14. *Priest*, 197
15. WWW.HistoryNet.com/Antietam-eyewitness-accounts.html
16. *Priest*, 200
17. Reunion of the Survivor's Association Seventy-seventh New York Infantry Volunteers, Saratoga springs, N. Y., November 23, 1911, 25
18. Edward Fuller, *Batle of the Seventy-Seventh New York State Foot Volunteers*, 8
19. *O. R.*, XIX, Pt. 1, 415
20. *Skinner*, October 11, 1862
21. *Ibid*
22. *Ibid*
23. *Hyde*, 99-100
24. Thomas P. Lowry, *Tarnished Eagles* (Mechanicsburg, PA, 1997) 90-93
25. Reunion of the Survivor's Association Seventy-seventh New York Infantry Volunteers, Saratoga Springs, N. Y., September 18, 1912
26. *Wheeler*, September 22, 1862

27. *Stevens*, 153-154
28. *Ibid*, 155-156
29. Edward L. Grose, *Centennial History of Ballston Spa 1763-1907* (Ballston Spa, N. Y., 1907) 154-155
30. Reunion of the Survivor's Association of the Seventy-seventh New York Infantry Volunteers, Schulyerville, N. Y., September 17, 1902
31. *GBM*, 330
32. *Wheeler*, October 17, 1862
33. *Ibid*
34. *Alonzo D. Bump Letters*, Brookside, Ballston Spa, N. Y., October 1862
35. *Wheeler*, October 17, 1862
36. *Grose*, 155-156
37. *Stevens*, 162-163
38. *GBM*, 340
39. *Ibid*, 341
40. *Bump*, November 1862; *Wheeler*, November 13, 1862

Chapter 7

1. *Wheeler*, November, 1862
2. Francis Augustin O'Reilly, *The Fredericksburg Campaign: Winter War on the Rappahannock* (Baton Rouge, LA, 2006) 25
3. *Wheeler*, November 20, 1862
4. *Bump*, November, 1862
5. *Wheeler*, November 20, 1862
6. *Bump*, November, 1862
7. *Stevens*, 164; *Wheeler*, December 4, 1862
8. *Stevens*, 164
9. Arnold Blumberg, *"War So Terrible,"* Civil War Quarterly Summer 2012: 92
10. *Wheeler*, December 4, 1862

11. *Ibid*
12. *Lennon*, 716-721
13. *Lennon, 716-721;* Stevens, *167*
14. *Lennon*, 716-721
15. *Stevens*, 169
16. *Lennon*, 716-721
17. *Stevens*, 170
18. *Blumberg*, 94; *O'Reilly*, 145
19. *Lennon*, 716-720
20. *Wheeler*, December 18, 1862
21. *Lennon*, 716-721
22. *Wheeler*, December 18, 1862; *Lennon*, 716-720; *Durkee*
23. *Lennon*, 716-721
24. *Ibid*
25. *Stevens*, 171; *Cotant*, 275
26. George C. Rable, *Fredericksburg! Fredericksburg* (Chapel Hill, NC, 2002) 246
27. *Lennon*, 716-721
28. *Ibid*
29. *Stevens*, 173
30. *Lennon*, 716-721
31. *Ibid*
32. *Wheeler*, December 18, 1862
33. *Wheeler*, December 18, 1862; *Bump*, December, 1862
34. *Wheeler*, December 25, 1862
35. *Ibid*, January 6, 1863
36. *Ibid*
37. *William H. DeYoe Letter*, February 6, 1863
38. *Stevens*, 175-176
39. *Durkee*; *Stevens*, 177
40. Ernest B. Furgurson, *Chancellorsville 1863* (New York, N. Y., 1992) 19

Chapter 8

1. *Stevens*, 186-187
2. *Bump*, February 4, 1863
3. John Michael Priest, *Turn them Out to Die Like a Mule* (Leesburg, VA., 1995) 147
4. *George Bolton Letter,* January 9, 1863
5. *Bump*, April 12, 1863; *Wheeler,* January 6, 1863
6. *Stevens*, 180-182
7. *Ibid*, 182
8. *Ibid*, 185-186
9. *Ballston Spa Journal*, April 21, 1863
10. *Newspaper Clippings*, New York State Military Museum and Veteran Research Center, Saratoga Springs, New York
11. *DeYoe*, February 6, 1863; *Durkee*
12. *Newspaper Clippings*
13. *Ibid*
14. *Stevens*, 183
15. *Ibid*
16. *Ibid*, 184
17. *Ibid*
18. *Newspaper Clippings*
19. *Bump* April 12, 1863
20. *Stevens*, 188
21. *Ibid, Rugg*, May 11, 1863
22. *Rugg*, May 11, 1863; *Stevens*, 189
23. Philip W. Parsons, *The Union Sixth corps in the Chancellorsville Campaign: A Study of the Engagements of Second Fredericksburg, Salem church and Banks Ford, May 3-4, 1863* (Jefferson, NC, 2006) 35
24. *Rugg*, May 11, 1863; *O. R., XXV, Pt. 1, 171*
25. *Rugg*, May 11, 1863; *Newspaper Clippings*; *Furgurson*, 130
26. *Rugg*, May 11, 1863; *Stevens*, 190

27. *Rugg*, May 11, 1863; *Stevens*, 191
28. *Ibid*
29. *Henrikkson*, 1-22
30. *Newspaper Clippings*
31. *Parsons*, 48; *Newspaper Clippings*
32. *Stevens*, 193; *Judd*, 294
33. *Parsons*, 63
34. *Rugg*, May 11, 1863
35. *Rugg, Newspaper Clippings*
36. *Parsons*, 65
37. *Ibid*, 67-68
38. *Newspaper Clippings*
39. *Rugg*, May 11, 1863
40. *Ibid*
41. Erskine B. Branch, *A Brief Sketch of the Experience of A Union Soldier in the Late War* (Washington, D.C., 1870) 6
42. *Rugg*, May 11, 1863
43. *Erskine Branch Pension Certificate No. 36168; Branch*, 5
44. *Newspaper Clippings*; *Durkee*; *Lennon*, 726-730
45. *Newspaper Clippings*; *Lennon*, 726-730
46. *Durkee*
47. *Rugg*, May 11, 1863
48. *Hyde*, 128; *Stevens*, 200; *Branch Pension*
49. *Stevens*, 201
50. *Ibid*, 202
51. *Nunda News*, May 16, 1863
52. *Cotant*, 321
53. *Parsons*, 121
54. *Ibid*, 125
55. *Hyde*, 130
56. *Hyde*, 130-131; *Daily Saratogian*, May 14, 1863
57. *Parsons*, 129
58. *Newspaper Clippings*

59. *Newspaper Clippings*, Frederick David Bidwell, *History of the Forty-Ninth New York Volunteers* (Albany, N. Y., 1916) 31-32
60. *Hyde*, 133
61. *Daily Saratogian*, May 14, 1863
62. *Durkee*
63. *Ibid*
64. *Ibid*
65. *Ibid*
66. *Ibid*

Chapter 9

1. *Stevens*, 212
2. *Ibid*, 213
3. *Ibid*, 215-216
4. *Ibid*, 217
5. *Lennon*, 726-729
6. *Stevens*, 215
7. *Newspaper Clippings*
8. Rugg, May 11, 1863
9. *Bump*, May 10, 1863
10. *Stevens*, 221
11. *Ibid*
12. *Ibid*, 221-222
13. *Ibid*, 217
14. *Ibid*
15. *Ibid*, 217-218
16. *Ibid*, 219
17. *Ibid*
18. *Ibid*, 220
19. *Ibid*
20. Stephen W. Sears, *Gettysburg* (First Mariner Books, MA, 2004) 84

21. Reunion of the Survivor's Association of the Seventy-seventh New York Infantry Volunteers, *Forty-Sixth Anniversary*, Saratoga Springs, N. Y.; *Stevens*, 223
22. *Stevens*, 223-225
23. *Sears*, 79
24. *Stevens*, 225
25. *Stevens*, 226-27; *Bump*, June 19, 1863
26. Reunion of the Survivor's Association of the Seventy-seventh New York Infantry Volunteers, *Forty-Sixth Anniversary*, Saratoga Springs, N.Y.; *Stevens*, 227-229
27. *Stevens*, 230
28. *Sears*, 113
29. *Ibid*, 114
30. *Ibid*, 110-111
31. *Stevens*, 234-236
32. *Durkee*
33. *Sears*, 121-123
34. *Ibid*, 125; Ethan S. Rafuse, *Civil War Campaigns and Commanders: George Gordon Meade and the War in the East* (McWhiney Foundation Press, TX, 2003) 71
35. *Stevens*, 234-236
36. *Ibid*, 237-238
37. *Ibid*, 239
38. Carl Smith, *Gettysburg 1863: High Tide of the Confederacy* (Osprey Publishing, Great Britain, 1998) 42
39. *Sears*, 162
40. Reunion of the Survivor's Association of the Seventy-seventh New York Infantry Volunteers, *Forty-Sixth Anniversary*, Saratoga Springs, N.Y.
41. *Stevens*, 239-240
42. Abraham T. Brewer, *History of the Sixty-first Regiment Pennsylvania Volunteers, 1861-1865* (Art Engraving & Printing Co., PA, 1911) 62

43. *Stevens*, 240; *Sears*, 248
44. *Sears*, 248
45. *Durkee*, Reunion of the Survivor's Association of the Seventy-seventh New York Infantry Volunteers, *Forty-Sixth Anniversary*, Saratoga Springs, N.Y.
46. Harry W. Pfanz, *Gettysburg: Culp's Hill & Cemetery Hill* (The University of North Carolina Press, NC, 2003) 335
47. *Ibid*, 337
48. *Stevens*, 250
49. *Hyde*, 152-153
50. *Stevens*, 250; *Durkee*; *Sears*, 396
51. *Hyde*, 154
52. *Smith*, 96
53. *Ibid*, 97
54. *Newspaper Clippings*
55. *Stevens*, 251-252
56. *Sears*, 508

Chapter 10

1. *Brewer*, 68
2. *Stevens*, 253-254
3. *Ibid*, 254-255
4. *Ibid*, 256
5. *Ibid*, 257
6. Stephen R. Frost Letters, September 4, 1863
7. *Brewer*, 69
8. *Stevens*, 258
9. Reunion of the Survivor's Association of the Seventy-seventh New York Infantry Volunteers, Saratoga Springs, N.Y., October 5, 1888

10. Kent Masterson Brown, *Retreat from Gettysburg: Lee, Logistics, & the Pennsylvania Campaign* (The University of North Carolina Press, NC, 2005) 277-279
11. *Stevens*, 261
12. *Ibid*, 262
13. *Ibid*, 264
14. *Ibid*, 266
15. *Ibid*, 267
16. *Ibid*
17. *Ibid*, 274-275
18. *Durkee's Reminiscences*
19. *Grose*, 152
20. *Bump*, August 17, 1863
21. *Ibid*, September 7, 1863
22. *Durkee's Reminiscences*
23. *Rafuse*, 96-97
24. *Ibid*, 98
25. *Stevens*, 280
26. *Bump*, October 18, 1863
27. *Stevens*, 282
28. *Martin Lennon Diary*; *Stevens*, 282; *Bump*, November 3, 1863
29. *Newspaper Clippings*
30. *National Park Service Description Battle of Rappahannock station*
31. *Stevens*, 283
32. *Newspaper Clippings*; *Stevens* 283-284; *Durkee's Reminiscences*
33. *Newspaper Clippings*
34. *Ibid*
35. *Stevens*, 287; *Newspaper Clippings*
36. *Newspaper Clippings*; *Bump*, November 25, 1863
37. *Stevens*, 291
38. *Ibid*

39. *Stevens*, 291-292; *Bolton*, December 1863
40. *Bolton*, December 1863
41. *Stevens*, 293; *Bump*, November 25, 1863; *Bolton*, December 1863
42. *Stevens*, 293-295
43. *Bolton*, December 1863
44. *Stevens*, 295-296; *Bolton*, December 1863
45. *Stevens*, 297
46. *Bolton*, December 1863
47. *Stevens*, 297; *Bolton*, December 1863
48. *Bump*, December 15, 1863
49. *Rafuse*, 108
50. *Newspaper Clippings*

Chapter 11

1. *Rhea*, 32; *Bump*, January 24, 1864; *Stevens*, 300
2. *Stevens*, 301; *Durkee's Scrapbook*
3. *Newspaper Clippings*
4. *Stevens*, 302; *Bump*, February 19, 1864
5. *Newspaper Clippings*
6. Ibid
7. Ibid
8. *Durkee's Scrapbook*
9. *Rafuse*, 115
10. *Saratogian*, April 28, 1864
11. *Rhea*, 46
12. Noah Andre Trudeau, *Bloody Roads South: The Wilderness to Cold Harbor, May-June, 1864* (Fawcett Columbine, N.Y., 1989) 32
13. *Rhea*, 32
14. *Stevens*, 303
15. *Rhea*, 103
16. *Stevens*, 304-305
17. *Trudeau*, 45

18. *Stevens*, 306
19. *Brewer*, 82; *Durkee's Scrapbook*; *Hyde*, 184-185
20. John Michael Priest, *Nowhere to Run: The Wilderness, May 4th & 5th, 1864* (White Mane, PA, 1995) 120
21. *Stevens*, 306-307
22. *Ibid*, 306
23. *Priest*, 126
24. Lemuel A. Abbot, *Personal Recollections and a Civil War Diary* (Burlington, VT, 1908)
25. *Stevens*, 316-317
26. *Ibid*, 314
27. *Priest*, 213
28. John Michael Priest, *Victory Without Triumph: The Wilderness, May 6th & 7th, 1864* (White Mane, PA, 1996) 28-30
29. *Durkee's Scrapbook*
30. *Stevens*, 309
31. *O. R., XXXVI, Pt. 1, 187*
32. *Durkee's Scrapbook*
33. *Ibid*
34. *Rhea*, 407
35. Reunion Association of the Seventy-seventh New York Volunteers, Schenectady, N.Y., September 22, 1903
36. *Ibid, Priest*, 184
37. *Brewer*, 85
38. C. E. Stevens, *"Not A Fighting Regiment,"* The National Tribune, October 8, 1908
39. *Stevens*, 318; *Priest*, 187
40. Stevens, 319
41. *Ibid*
42. *Ibid*, 316
43. *Ibid*, 317
44. *Trudeau*, 214-219
45. *Stevens*, 342-343

46. *Ibid*, 340
47. *Ibid*, 345-346

Chapter 12

1. John Cannon, *Great Campaigns: The Spotsylvania Campaign May 7-21, 1864* (Combined Books, PA, 1997) 24-25
2. *Stevens*, 323
3. Reunion Association of the Seventy-seventh New York Volunteers, *Twenty-Second Anniversary*, Ballston Spa, N. Y., October 3, 1894
4. *Ibid*
5. *Ibid*
6. *Ibid*
7. *Ibid*
8. *Ibid*
9. *Ibid*
10. *Durkee's Scrapbook*
11. *Stevens*, 325
12. *Ibid*
13. *Brewer*, 90
14. Clarence C. Buel and Robert U. Johnson, eds., *Battles and Leaders of the Civil War, Vol. 4*, 1884-1888, 175
15. *Ibid*
16. *Hyde*, 193; *Stevens*, 327
17. Donald Chipman, *"An Essex County Soldier in the Civil War: The Diary of Cyrille Fountain,"* New York History, July, 1985
18. *Durkee's Scrapbook*
19. *Stevens, 331*
20. Reunion Association of the Seventy-seventh New York Volunteers, *Fiftieth Anniversary*, Saratoga Springs, N. Y., June 26, 1915

21. *Stevens*, 332; Gordon C. Rhea, *The Battles for Spotsylvania Court House and the road to Yellow Tavern May 7-12, 1864,* (Louisiana State University Press, LA, 1997) 174-175; *Trudeau*, 163-164
22. *Durkee's Scrapbook*
23. *Stevens*, 332
24. *Durkee's Scrapbook*
25. *Ibid*
26. *Ibid*
27. *Ibid*
28. *O. R., XXXVI, Pt. 2, 627*
29. *Lennon Diary*
30. *Chipman, Durkee's Scrapbook*
31. *Brewer*, 93-94
32. Reunion Association of the Seventy-seventh New York Volunteers, *Twenty-Second Anniversary,* Ballston Spa, N. Y., October 3, 1894
33. *Stevens*, 335, *Chipman*
34. *Cannan*, 156-157
35. *Bidwell*, 52
36. *Brewer*, 96-97
37. *Ibid*
38. *Cannan*, 182
39. *Stevens*, 337

Chapter 13

1. *Brewer*, 100
2. Gordon C. Rhea, *To the North Anna River: Grant and Lee May 13-25, 1864* (Louisiana University Press, LA, 2000) 330
3. *Ibid*, 337-342
4. *Chipman*
5. *Martin Lennon Diary*

6. *Stevens*, 338
7. *Chipman*
8. *Ibid*
9. *Ibid*
10. Gordon C. Rhea, *Cold Harbor: Grant and Lee May 26-June 3, 1864* (Louisiana University Press, LA, 2002) 110
11. *Bump,* May 29, 1864
12. *Rhea*, 93-94
13. *Ibid*, 127
14. *Ibid*, 121
15. *Chipman*
16. *Rhea*, 128
17. *Ibid*, 129
18. *Ibid*, 147
19. *Ibid*, 155
20. Ernest B. Furgurson, *Not War But Murder: Cold Harbor 1864* (Vintage Books, N. Y., 2000) 55-56
21. *Rhea*, 163
22. *Martin Lennon Diary*; *Rhea*, 165
23. *Rhea*, 173
24. *Ibid*, 197
25. *Ibid*, 200
26. *Martin Lennon Diary*; *Stevens*, 345
27. *Hyde*, 208-209
28. *Rhea*, 205
29. *Stevens*, 347-348
30. *Ibid*, 348
31. *Ibid*, 349
32. *Ibid*
33. *Rhea*, 241
34. *Stevens*, 349-350
35. *Chipman*
36. *Rhea*, 263

37. *Chipman*; *Rhea*, 295
38. *Newspaper Clippings*
39. *Stevens*, 351; *Chipman*
40. *Stevens*, 351-352
41. *Furgurson*, 149
42. *Rhea*, 343-355, 390
43. *O. R., XXXVI, Pt. 1, 708*
44. E. M. Law, *"From the Wilderness to Cold Harbor,"* Battles and Leaders, 139-141
45. *Hyde*, 211; U. S. Grant, *Personal Memoirs of U. S. Grant* (DeCapo Press, N. Y., 1952) 444-445; *Martin Lennon Diary*
46. *Stevens*, 353
47. *Ibid*, 353-354
48. *Ibid*
49. Bump, January 5, 1864
50. *Stevens*, 353-354
51. *Ibid*, 354
52. *Trudeau*, 303-304
53. *Grant*, 445

Chapter 14

1. *Stevens*, 355
2. *Ibid*, 316
3. *Ibid*, 317; *Chipman*; *Martin Lennon Diary*
4. *Stevens*, 357
5. *Ibid*, 358
6. H. W. Brands, *The Man Who Saved the Union: Ulysses Grand in War And Peace* (Doubleday, N. Y., 2012) 309-310; *Trudeau*, 48
7. *Stevens*, 359-360
8. John Horn, *The Petersburg Campaign June 1864 – Aril 1865* (DeCapo Press, 1993) 57-58
9. *Stevens*, 361

10. *Ibid*, 362-363,
11. *Bump,* June 19, 1864
12. *Daily Saratogian*, April 23, 1881
13. Reunion Association of the Seventy-seventh New York Volunteers, *Report of the Thirty-Seventh Annual Reunion*, Ballston Spa, N. Y., September 17, 1909
14. *Stevens*, 364-365
15. *Daily Saratogian*, April 23, 1881
16. *Chipman*
17. *Bump,* June 24, 1864; *Stevens*, 366-367
18. *Chipman*
19. *George T. Stevens Letters,* July 8, 1864
20. Benjamin Franklin Cooling, *Jubal Early's Raid on Washington* (The University of Alabama Press, Tuscaloosa, Al, 1989) 106
21. *Stevens*, 371
22. *Martin Lennon Diary, G. T. S.,* July 11, 1864
23. Report of the Survivor's Association Seventy-Seventh Regiment New York Infantry Volunteers, *Twenty-Ninth Annual Reunion*, Wilton, N. Y., September 23, 1901
24. *Chipman, Twenty-Ninth Annual Reunion*
25. Joseph Judge, *Season of Fire: The Confederate Strike on Washington* (Rockbridge Publishing Company, Berryville, VA, 1994) 214
26. *Ibid*, 226
27. *Ibid*, 231
28. *Cooling*, 92-93
29. *Cooling*, 134-135; *Judge*, 225
30. *Twenty-Ninth Annual Reunion*
31. *Ibid*
32. *Stevens*, 373
33. Frank E. Vandiver, *Jubal's Raid: General Early's Famous Attack on Washington in 1864* (University of Nebraska Press, Lincoln, NE, 1960) 166-167; *Judge*, 249
34. *Twenty-Ninth Annual Reunion*

35. *Twenty-Ninth Annual Reunion*; *Hyde*, 223; *Cooling*, 143; *Vandiver*, 167-168; Edward A. Fuller, "The Day Washington Was Saved," National Tribune, December 29, 1910
36. *Judge*, 253;
37. Report of the Survivor's Association of the Seventy-Seventh Regiment New York State Infantry Volunteers, *Report of the Forty-Second Annual Reunion*, Saratoga Springs, N. Y., July 11, 1914
38. David B. Swinfen, *Ruggle's Regiment: The One Hundred and Twenty-second New York Volunteers in the American Civil War* (University Press of New England, Hanover, MA, 1982) 150-151; *Fuller*
39. *Stevens*, 376-379
40. *Cooling*, 149-150
41. *Twenty-Ninth Reunion*; *Stevens*, 377
42. *Judge*, 151-154
43. *Stevens*, 378-379; *Twenty-Ninth Reunion*

Chapter 15

1. *Cooling*, 186
2. *Stevens*, 380
3. *Martin Lennon Diary*
4. *Stevens*, 380-381
5. John B. Southard Letter, July 16, 1864; *Stevens*, 381
6. *Chipman*; *Stevens*, 381
7. *Chipman*
8. George E. Pond, *The Shenandoah Valley in 1864* (Charles Scribner's Sons, N. Y., 1881) 84
9. *Stevens*, 382
10. *Chipman*; *Martin Lennon Diary*
11. *Chipman*; *Stevens*, 383
12. *G. T. S.*, August 1, 1864
13. *Martin Lennon Diary*; *Chipman*; *G. T. S.*, August 1, 1864
14. *G. T. S.*, August 3, 1864

15. *Stevens*, 385-386
16. *Ibid*, 386-387
17. *O. R., XLIII, Pt. 1*, 697-698
18. *Chipman*
19. *G. T. S.*, August 7, 1864
20. Jeffrey D. Wert, *From Winchester to Cedar Creek: The Shenandoah Campaign of 1864* (Stackpole Books, PA, 1997) 17
21. *Ibid*
22. *Stevens*, 388; *Brewer*, 111
23. *Chipman; G. T. S.*, August 9, 1864
24. *Chipman; Martin Lennon Diary; Stevens*, 389-390
25. *Twenty-Ninth Reunion*
26. *Chipman; Stevens*, 391
27. *Chipman; Stevens*, 391-392
28. *Martin Lennon Diary*
29. *Wert*, 32
30. *Stevens*, 393; *Chipman*
31. *Martin Lennon Diary; Chipman*
32. *Stevens*, 394
33. Timothy B. Mudgett, *Make the fur Fly: A History of a Union Volunteer Division in the American Civil War* (The Burd Street Press, PA, 1997) 95-96
34. *Wert*, 45
35. *Chipman; Martin Lennon Diary*
36. *Martin Lennon Diary; G. T. S.*, September 2, 1864
37. *Martin Lennon Diary*
38. *Wert*, 43
39. *Chipman*
40. *Twenty-Ninth Reunion*
41. *Stevens*, 397-398
42. *Newspaper Clippings; O. R., XLIII, Pt. 1, 219; Daily Saratogian*, October 3, 1864
43. *Wert*, 56

44. *Stevens*, 399
45. *O. R., XLIII, Pt. 1, 219*; *Daily Saratogian*, October 3, 1864
46. *Stevens*, 399
47. *Wert*, 67; *O. R., XLIII. Pt. 1, 325*
48. *Wert*, 69-70
49. *Martin Lennon Diary*; Scott C. Patchan, *The Last Battle of Winchester: Phil Sheridan, Jubal Early, and the Shenandoah Valley Campaign August 7-September 19, 1864* (Savas Beatie, CA, 2013) 346-347
50. *Wert*, 85
51. *Twenty-Ninth Reunion*
52. *Ibid*; *Stevens*, 401
53. *Bump*, September 23, 1864
54. *Daily Saratogian*, October 3, 1864
55. *Ibid*

Chapter 16

1. *Wert*, 109
2. *Daily Saratogian*, October 3, 1864
3. *Wert*, 108
4. *Chipman*
5. *Wert*, 113
6. *Ibid*, 121
7. *Ibid*
8. *Ibid*, 123
9. *Twenty-Ninth Reunion*
10. *Daily Saratogian*, October 3, 1864; *O. R., XLIII, Pt. 1, 220*
11. *Daily Saratogian*, October 3, 1864
12. *Ibid*
13. *Ibid, O. R., XLIII, Pt. 1, 153*
14. *Newspaper Clippings*
15. *Daily Saratogian*, September 29, 1864

16. *Twenty-Ninth Reunion*
17. *Wert*, 134
18. *Stevens*, 409-410
19. *Ibid*

Chapter 17

1. *Chipman*
2. *Ibid*
3. *Wert*, 145
4. *Ibid*
5. *Ibid*, 157
6. *Stevens*, 410-411
7. *Stevens*, 411-412; *Twenty-Ninth Reunion*
8. *Martin Lennon Diary*; *Chipman*
9. *Martin Lennon Diary*
10. *Chipman*; *Durkee's Scrapbook*; *Twenty-Ninth Reunion*
11. *Durkee's Scrapbook*
12. *Ibid*
13. *Wert*, 217-218; Thomas A. Lewis, *The Guns of Cedar Creek* (Dell Publishing, N.Y., 1988) 211
14. *Durkee's Scrapbook*
15. *Twenty-Ninth Reunion*
16. *Wert*, 188
17. *Durkee's Scrapbook*
18. *Ibid*
19. Aldace F. Walker, *The Vermont Brigade in the Shenandoah Valley 1864* (The Free Press Association, VT, 1869) 139-140
20. *Mudgett*, 107-108
21. *Durkee's Srcapbook*
22. *Ibid*
23. *Stevens*, 419; *Bump*, October 20, 1864

24. *Durkee's Scrapbook*
25. *Walker,* 142
26. *Bidwell,* 98
27. *Twenty-Ninth Reunion*
28. *Walker,* 143
29. *Twenty-Ninth Reunion*
30. John H. Worsham, *One of Jackson's Foot Cavalry.* Edited by James I. Robertson, Jr. (Mercer Press, Tenn, 1869)
31. *Twenty-Ninth Reunion*
32. *Wert,* 223
33. *Ibid;* 223; *Twenty-Ninth Reunion*
34. *Twenty-Ninth Reunion*
35. *Wert,* 224; *Bump,* October 10, 1864
36. *Durkee's Scrapbook*
37. *Walker,* 150
38. *Durkee's Scrapbook*
39. *Walker,* 150; *Durkee's Scrapbook; Newspaper Clippings*
40. *Stevens,* 425
41. *Wert,* 234
42. *Stevens,* 425
43. *Wert,* 236-237
44. *Stevens,* 426
45. *Ibid,* 426-427
46. *Twenty-Ninth Reunion; Stevens,* 427-428
47. *Bump,* October 20, 1864
48. *Wert,* 246

Chapter 18

1. *Trudeau,* 220
2. *Newspaper Clippings*
3. *Chipman; Trudeau,* 253

4. *Newspaper Clippings*
5. *Ibid*
6. *Ibid*
7. *Ibid*
8. *Ibid*
9. *Trudeau*, 294
10. *Ibid*, 295
11. *Bump*, December 17, 1864
12. *Saratogian*, January 19, 1865
13. *Trudeau*, 352
14. *Hyde*, 243
15. *Ibid*, 244
16. *Ibid*, 244-245
17. *Ibid*, 245-246; *Newspaper Clippings*
18. *Trudeau*, 376
19. *Hyde*, 250-251
20. *Ibid*, 251
21. *Ibid*, 251-252
22. *Ibid*, 252
23. *Trudeau*, 371
24. *Hyde*, 252-253
25. *Ibid*, 253
26. *Trudeau*, 369
27. *Ibid*, 372
28. *Ibid*, 373-374
29. *Ibid*, 376
30. *Hyde*, 259-260
31. *Ibid*, 263-264
32. *Ibid*, 264-265
33. *Durkee's Scrapbook*
34. *Sixth Corps News*, April 27, 1865

35. *Bump,* April 28, 1865
36. *Hyde,* 268
37. *Ibid,* 268-269
38. *Durkee's Scrapbook*
39. *Ibid*
40. *Ibid*

www.ingramcontent.com/pod-product-compliance
Lightning Source LLC
Chambersburg PA
CBHW070711160426
43192CB00009B/1151